International Database Engineering and Applications Symposium

IDEAS 2002

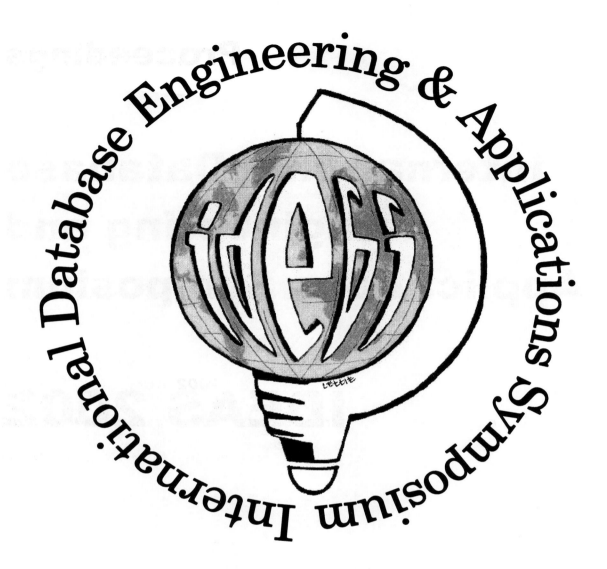

International Database Engineering & Applications Symposium

Concordia
UNIVERSITY

University of
Waterloo

IBM Toronto Laboratory

Proceedings

International Database Engineering and Applications Symposium

July 17-19, 2002 Edmonton, Canada

Editors: Mario A. Nascimento, M. Tamer Özsu, Osmar Zaïane

General Chair: Bipin C. Desai

IEEE
COMPUTER
SOCIETY

http://computer.org

Los Alamitos, California

Washington   •   Brussels   •   Tokyo

IEEE Computer Society Order Number PR01638
ISBN 0-7695-1638-6
ISBN 0-7695-1639-4 (case)
ISBN 0-7695-1640-8 (microfiche)
ISSN Number 1098-8068

Additional copies may be ordered from:

IEEE Computer Society
Customer Service Center
10662 Los Vaqueros Circle
P.O. Box 3014
Los Alamitos, CA 90720-1314
Tel: + 1-714-821-8380
Fax: + 1-714-821-4641
E-mail: cs.books@computer.org

IEEE Service Center
445 Hoes Lane
P.O. Box 1331
Piscataway, NJ 08855-1331
Tel: + 1-732-981-0060
Fax: + 1-732-981-9667
http://shop.ieee.org/store/
customer-service@ieee.org

IEEE Computer Society
Asia/Pacific Office
Watanabe Bldg., 1-4-2
Minami-Aoyama
Minato-ku, Tokyo 107-0062
JAPAN
Tel: + 81-3-3408-3118
Fax: + 81-3-3408-3553
tokyo.ofc@computer.org

Editorial production by Bob Werner
Cover art production by Alex Torres
Printed in the United States of America by The Printing House

Table of Contents

International Database Engineering and Applications Symposium (IDEAS 2002)

Invited Talk I

ToX: The Toronto XML Server
A. Mendelzon

Paper Session I (DBMS Implementation Issues)

Paper Session II (Mobile Data)

Paper Session III (XML & OO)

Invited Talk II

Paper Session IV (Applications I)

Paper Session V (Modelling)

Paper Session VI (DW/DM)

Invited Talk III

Stream Data Management: Research Directions and Opportunities
    N. Koudas

Paper Session VII (Applications II)

Foreword

IDEAS'02 is the sixth in a series of meetings to address the continuing need for engineering databases for complex applications requiring security, reliability and high availibility. Previous symposiums were held in Canada, France, Japan and the U.K. at Concordia University (Montreal, '97 and '98), Cardiff University (Cardiff, '98), Keio University (Yokohama, '00), and Grenoble University (Grenoble, '01).

I wish to express my gratitude to the many people in Edmonton and Waterloo, particularly Mario Nascimento and Tamer Özsu, the program co-chairs and Osmar Zaïane, the local organizing chair along with members of the local committee. They have all worked hard providing active support for IDEAS'02. In addition, Tamer and the local organizing committee were resourceful in arranging this meeting and providing excellent facilities for it. I would also like to take this opportunity to thank the people at Concordia including the departmental analyst pool, and Drew.

As in the previous years, the Program Committee and the external referees have ensured the quality of the symposium through meticulous referring of the submitted papers.

I would also like to thank IBM (CAS), University of Alberta, University of Waterloo, Concordia University, and the IEEE Computer Society for providing their support making IDEAS'02 possible.

Bipin C. Desai
IDEAS General Chair

Preface

As database technology matures, its application in new domains becomes increasingly important. The International Database Engineering and Applications Symposium (IDEAS) has, from the beginning, emphasized the engineering of database systems for new application domains and their deployment in them. It provides an international forum for discussion of the problems of engineering database systems involving not only database technology but the related areas of information retrieval, multimedia, human machine interface and communication.

This year the Symposium is hosted by the Computer Science Department of the University of Alberta and is co-located by a large number of other events, e.g., the 3rd Canadian Database Research Workshop (CanDB'2002), the 8th ACM SIGKDD Intl. Conf. on Knowledge Discovery and Data Mining (KDD'2002), and The 18th National Conf. on Artificial Intelligence (AAAI'2002). This, we hope, will give participants a chance to attend and enjoy a wide variety of technical sessions.

This IDEAS edition received 57 submissions out of which 28 were accepted. As usual, each paper was reviewed by three of the 45 people that made up the international Program Committee. They were also assisted in the review process by 22 external referees. In addition to the technical papers, we are fortunate to have three excellent invited talks by Prof. Alberto Mendelzon (University of Toronto), Dr. Surajit Chaudhuri (Microsoft Research) and Dr. Nick Koudas (AT&T Research).

We wish to extend our thanks to all members of the Program and Organizing Committees for their volunteer contributions of time and expertise. Their efforts ensured that we have an exciting technical program that touches upon many of the currently hot topics in database research.

Mario A. Nascimento
M. Tamer Özsu
IDEAS'02 PC Co-chairs
April 2002

Program Committee

Karl Aberer (EPFL, Switzerland)
Michel Adiba (Univ. of Grenoble, France)
Divy Agrawal (UCSB, USA)
Daniel Barbara (George Mason Univ., USA)
Roger Barga (Microsoft, USA)
Ken Barker (Univ. of Calgary, Canada)
Elisa Bertino (Univ. of Milano, Italy)
Michael Boehlen (Aalborg Univ., Denmark)
Klemens Boehm (ETH, Switzerland)
Luc Bouganim (Univ. of Versailles, France)
Alex Buchmann (Univ. of Darmstadt, Germany)
Fabio Casati (HP, USA)
Asuman Dogac (Middle East Technical Univ., Turkey)
Isabel Cruz (Univ. of Illinois at Chicago, USA)
Peter Fankhauser (GMD, Germany)
Ralf H. Gueting (Fern Univ. of Hagen, Germany)
Theo Haerder (Univ. of Kaiserlautern, Germany)
Jiawei Han (Simon Fraser Univ., Canada)
Ravikanth Kothuri (ORACLE Corp., USA)
Bettina Kemme (McGill Univ., Canada)
Brigitte Kerherve, (UQAM, Canada),
Martin Kersten (CWI, Netherlands)
Masaru Kitsuregawa (Univ. of Tokyo, Japan)
Nick Koudas (AT&T Labs, USA)
Gonzalo Navarro (Univ. of Chile, Chile)
Sergio Lifschitz (PUC-Rio, Brazil)
Paul Lu (Univ. of Alberta, Canada)
Sylvia Osborn (Univ. of Western Ontario, Canada)
Glen Paulley (Sybase, Canada)
Esther Pacitti (Univ Paris V, France)
Barbara Pernici (Politecnico di Milano, Italy)
Beng-Chin Ooi (NUS, Singapore)
Davood Rafiei (Univ. of Alberta, Canada)
Krithi Ramamritham (IIT Bombay, India)
Tore Risch (Uppsala Univ., Sweden)
Ron Sacks-Davis (RMIT, Australia)
Ken Salem (Univ. of Waterloo, Canada)
Joerg Sander (Univ. of Alberta, Canada)
Timos Sellis (NTUA, Greece)
Yannis Theodoridis (CTI Patras, Greece)
Agma Traina (USP at Sao Carlos, Brazil)
Jari Veijalainen (Univ. of Jyvaskyla, Finland)
Kyu-Young Whang (KAIST, Korea)
Grant Weddell (Univ. of Waterloo, Canada)
Osmar Zaïane (Univ. of Alberta, Canada)

External Reviewers

Aybar C. Acar

Masayoshi Aritsugi

Edgard Benitez

M. El-Hajj

Roberto Figueira Santos Filho

Edward Hermann Haeusler

Wook-Shin Han

Moon Jeung Joe

Caetano Traina Junior

Yildiray Kabak

N. Gokhan Kurt

Laks Lakshmanan

Gokce Banu Laleci

Suk Kyoon Lee

Yannis Manolopoulos

Miyuki Nakano

Gerbe Olivier

Apostolos Papadopoulos

Fabio Porto

Krishna Reddy

Panos Vassiliadis

Xifeng Yan

Organizing Committee

General Chair

Bipin C. Desai (Concordia Univ., Canada)

Program Co-chairs

M. Tamer Özsu (Univ. of Waterloo, Canada)

Mario A. Nascimento (Univ. of Alberta, Canada)

Local Organization (Univ. of Alberta, Canada))

Osmar Zaïane (Chair)

Davood Rafiei

Paul Lu

Joerg Sander

Alex Coman (Webmaster)

Paper Session I

(DBMS Implementation Issues)

On Implicate Discovery and Query Optimization

Kristofer Vorwerk*   G. N. Paulley

iAnywhere Solutions
415 Phillip Street
Waterloo, Ontario, Canada N2L 4V1
paulley@ianywhere.com

Abstract

Boolean expression simplification is a well-known problem in the history of Computer Science. The problem of determining prime implicates from an arbitrary Boolean expression has been mostly studied in the contexts of hardware design and automated reasoning. While many of the same principles can be applied to the simplification of search conditions in ANSI SQL queries, the richness of its language and SQL's three-valued logic present a number of challenges. We propose a modified version of a matrix-based normalization algorithm suitable for normalizing SQL search conditions in constrained-memory environments. In particular, we describe a set of tradeoffs that enable our algorithm to discover a useful set of implicates without requiring a complete conversion of the input condition to a normal form, preventing a combinatorial explosion in the number of terms.

1. Introduction and motivation

Query optimization in relational database systems, in particular the enumeration of join strategies, is largely based on the existence of conjunctive conditions in each query's Where clause. Conjunctive conditions, more formally termed *implicates* of a Boolean expression in *conjunctive normal form,* are useful because they must each evaluate to *true* for the query's Where clause to be satisfied. Hence conjunctive predicates can be naturally exploited for use in index processing; such a predicate is typically called a *matching* predicate [18]. Other semantic optimizations, such as predicate move-around [15] or exploiting materialized views [7], also rely on the existence of conjunctive conditions. Many of the algorithms involved in their analysis assume that the predicates in the Where clause are already in conjunctive normal form (e.g., [7]).

The problem of simplifying arbitrary Boolean expressions is a well-known problem in the history of computer science. Originally, the motivation for the study of this problem was its role in the minimization of Boolean functions and switching circuits [21, 22, 27]. Boolean state reduction has directly influenced power and material requirements by eliminating redundant gates and easing NAND implementation [4]. However, the difficulties of disjunctive to conjunctive normal form (DNF-to-CNF) conversion and redundant term elimination in SQL query optimization have been mostly overlooked. A logic minimizer focuses on reducing the *quantity* of gates, rather than preferring one gate over another based on the imperceptible speed differences between them. Conversely, a database query optimizer must focus on the discovery of *useful* implicates whose selectivity can be exploited to deduce a cheaper access strategy, *even though these conditions may be redundant or subsumed by the original expression.* Ideally, the most efficient SQL statement—in terms of the time required to rewrite the expression and the time required to execute it—could be determined by generating and costing all possible semantically equivalent forms. However, in a real-world setting, a database engine must generate useful implicates, along with other semantic transformations, without spending more time than is required to execute the unoptimized query [26]. In addition, the differing memory and execution costs for each SQL predicate must be considered. In the worst case, implicate generation requires resources that are exponential in the number of distinct propositional variables occurring in the formula [11]. In general, the number of prime implicants of a set of n arbitrary clauses is $O(3^n)$ [3]. Hence the conversion of complex SQL statements to CNF may exceed the storage capacity of low-memory handheld devices.

The Boolean simplification algorithms described in the literature [22, 27, 20, 5, 8, 28, 12, 11, 32] rely on *normal-*

---

* Author's current address: Department of Electrical and Computer Engineering, University of Waterloo, Waterloo, Ontario, Canada, N2L 3G2.

ized input—that is, the input expression is either in conjunctive or disjunctive normal form. The common approach used by these algorithms is to convert a CNF expression to DNF (or vice-versa), simplifying the output expression to minimize redundancy. The reverse transformation yields a simplified expression in the original form (CNF or DNF).

In relational database systems, however, the simplification of predicates in a Where clause presents particular challenges not addressed by existing algorithms. First, there is no guarantee that a query's Where clause is normalized. Some authors [32, 33, 7] have proposed normalizing the input as a preprocessing step prior to simplification and analysis. In practice, this would mean a complete expansion of the input into DNF, which could produce a combinatorial explosion in the number of terms. Second, ANSI SQL [9] requires the support of three-valued logic, meaning that several of the simplification techniques utilized by existing algorithms—in particular, the optimization of complementary predicates—no longer hold. Third, the simplification algorithm itself can be computationally expensive: Palopoli et al. [20] state that the generation of just one prime implicant from a normalized Boolean formula is NP-hard. Fourth, the goal of predicate simplification in a relational DBMS differs slightly from strict minimization of the number of terms. Though minimization is important—fewer predicates, in the main, reduces the size of the query's internal representation and reduces the number of operations required during query processing—the discovery of predicates that can be exploited by an optimizer is equally important.

EXAMPLE 1
Consider the simple DNF formula

$$(a \wedge b) \vee (c \wedge d) \qquad (1)$$

where each letter represents a literal (a distinct predicate). The equivalent formula in CNF is

$$(c \vee a) \wedge (c \vee b) \wedge (d \vee a) \wedge (d \vee b) \qquad (2)$$

which has double the number of individual predicates. If this latter expression, though now in CNF, fails to yield any improvements in the access strategy, it will likely be more expensive to evaluate, and will also require more RAM for its data structures within the server.

EXAMPLE 2
To further illustrate the difficulties of search condition simplification, consider Query 19 of the TPC-H Benchmark Specification [30], as shown in Figure 1. The Where clause in Query 19 is not strictly in DNF due to the presence of several In predicates. Optimization of Query 19 in its original form will likely yield a very inefficient access plan, since the query lacks a conjunctive join condition; the only alternative left to the optimizer is a (typically expensive) Carte-

sian product. However, a naïve transformation of the original Where clause's 24 predicates into CNF yields a Where clause now containing 378 predicates[1]. We would like to avoid the computational and memory overhead of generating this many terms. More importantly, we would also like to avoid the evaluation cost of each of these conditions during query execution.

In this paper, we present an efficient algorithm designed to perform simplification and normalization of search conditions in a relational database system. Our contributions are three-fold: we demonstrate how the algorithm can be implemented in any relational database system; (2) we show that our algorithm is practicable for complex queries, even in small-memory environments; and (3) we show that it is possible to adapt the algorithm to support the specific capabilities of a particular optimizer. We have implemented this algorithm in iAnywhere Solutions' Adaptive Server Anywhere[2] (ASA), an ANSI-compliant, small-footprint relational database system whose target market ranges from workgroup servers to small hand-held devices.

The rest of the paper is as follows. In Section 2 we define some necessary terminology, discuss various simplification algorithms described in the literature, and differentiate our approach from these existing techniques. In Section 3 we describe our algorithm in detail. We illustrate the utility of our algorithm in Section 4, and contrast our approach with other known algorithms in Section 5. We conclude the paper in Section 6.

2. Preliminaries

In the context of relational databases, a *predicate* is a truth-valued function, possibly negated, whose domain is a set of attributes and/or scalar values and whose range is {*true, false, unknown*}. A predicate corresponds to one of the many forms of conditional expressions, such as θ-comparisons, Like conditions, and Between conditions, that can appear in an ANSI SQL query's Where clause. The *two-valued complement* of a predicate[3] p, written $\bar{p}$, is defined only for predicates p that cannot evaluate to *unknown* and is simply the logical *not* of p.

---

1 In this example, we presume that the transformation does not detect subsumption, tautologies, or contradictions, and retains predicates in their original form (i.e., Between predicates remain intact and are not rewritten as a conjunction of inequalities).

2 The following are trademarks and/or servicemarks of their respective companies: Sybase, Adaptive Server, and SQL Anywhere are trademarks of Sybase Inc.; JAVA is a trademark of Sun Microsystems; TPC and TPC-H are trademarks of the Transaction Processing Performance Council.

3 In the literature related to the simplification of Boolean expressions (cf. references [21, 22, 23, 14, 27]), the basic unit of any expression is termed a *literal*. In this paper a 'predicate' corresponds to a 'literal' and 'search condition' to a 'formula'.

```
Select Sum( L-Extendedprice * ( 1 - L-Discount ) ) as Revenue
From  Lineitem, Part
Where( P-Partkey = L-Partkey and P-Brand = 'BRAND#12'
       and P-Container In('SM CASE','SM BOX','SM PACK','SM PKG')
       and L-Quantity ≥ 1 and L-Quantity ≤ 1+10
       and P-Size between 1 and 5
       and L-Shipmode In('AIR','AIR REG')
       and L-Shipinstruct = 'DELIVER IN PERSON' )
     or
     ( P-Partkey = L-Partkey and P-Brand = 'BRAND#23'
       and P-Container In('MED BAG','MED BOX','MED PKG','MED PACK')
       and L-Quantity ≥ 10 and L-Quantity ≤ 10+10
       and P-Size between 1 and 10
       and L-Shipmode In('AIR','AIR REG')
       and L-Shipinstruct = 'DELIVER IN PERSON' )
     or
     ( P-Partkey = L-Partkey and P-Brand = 'BRAND#34'
       and P-Container In('LG CASE','LG BOX','LG PACK','LG PKG')
       and L-Quantity ≥ 20 and L-Quantity ≤ 20+10
       and P-Size between 1 and 15
       and L-Shipmode In('AIR','AIR REG')
       and L-Shipinstruct = 'DELIVER IN PERSON' )
```

Figure 1. TPC-H Version 1.1 Query 19.

A *clause* is a conjunction of predicates (a *conjunctive clause*) or a disjunction of predicates (a *disjunctive clause*). A clause is *fundamental* if it does not contain (1) any redundant predicates, that is, a predicate p cannot appear more than once, and (2) any complementary pairs of predicates, that is, p and $\bar{p}$ cannot appear together in the same clause. A clause D is in *disjunctive normal form* (DNF) if it is a disjunction of conjunctive clauses $C_1, C_2, \ldots C_n$ such that $D = \bigvee_{i=1}^{n} C_i$. DNF is often termed *sum-of-products form*. A clause D is in *partial* DNF if it is a disjunction of clauses $C_1, C_2, \ldots C_n$ where at least one C_i is not a conjunctive clause. Conversely, a clause C is in *conjunctive normal form* (CNF) if it is a conjunction of disjunctive clauses $D_1, D_2, \ldots D_n$ such that $C = \bigwedge_{i=1}^{n} D_i$. CNF is often termed *product-of-sums form*. A clause C is in *partial* CNF if it is a conjunction of clauses $D_1, D_2, \ldots D_n$ where at least one D_i is not a disjunctive clause.

Finally, we use the term *search condition* to denote the conjunctive or disjunctive clause specified in a query's Where or Having condition, or an On condition in a table expression [9]. Note that, in ANSI SQL queries, a search condition is *interpreted* as *false* if it evaluates to *unknown*.

DEFINITION 1 (IMPLICANTS AND PRIME IMPLICANTS)
A conjunctive clause A is an *implicant* of a search condition E if $A \implies E$. Hence all conjunctive clauses of a fully normalized condition E in DNF are its implicants. A is termed a *prime implicant* of E if A is an implicant of E, A is fundamental, and there does not exist another implicant A' such that $A \implies A'$.

DEFINITION 2 (IMPLICATES AND PRIME IMPLICATES)
A disjunctive clause A is an *implicate* of a search condition E if $E \implies A$. Hence all disjunctive clauses of a fully normalized condition E in CNF are its implicates. A is termed a *prime implicate* of E if A is an implicate of E, A is funda-

mental, and there does not exist another implicate A' such that $A' \implies A$.

DEFINITION 3 (MINIMAL FORMULA)
A *minimal* CNF (DNF) search condition G equivalent to a CNF (DNF) formula F is a conjunction (disjunction) of prime implicates (implicants) of F such that if any clauses of G are removed $G \not\equiv F$.

DEFINITION 4 (EXPLOITABLE IMPLICATE)
An *exploitable implicate* is one which can be utilized during optimization and/or query execution to reduce the query's overall execution cost. Since the usefulness of any given predicate may depend on the physical query execution methods supported by the database server, any measure of an implicate's utility is somewhat system-dependent. In the case of TPC-H Query 19, it is clear that the derivation of the prime implicate P-Partkey = L-Partkey would be extremely useful to most if not all query optimizers, since it constitutes an equijoin predicate. On the other hand, the CNF form of Equation 2 in Example 1 would only be of benefit under specific circumstances. For example, if the predicates denoted by the letters a and c referred to the same indexed column, then an access strategy utilizing index union [16] may be worthwhile.

2.1. Classification of redundancy

A search condition may contain redundant predicates. This redundancy commonly occurs with application software that generates SQL queries. Wang [32, pp. 10–13] categorized various forms of such redundancies, and we restate them here. A PP-*redundancy* stems from the repetition of a literal (predicate), as $s \wedge r \wedge q \wedge r \iff s \wedge q \wedge r$ (idempotency). A PQ-QP-*redundancy* stems from commutative laws, as $srq \iff qrs$. An S-SP-*redundancy* follows from absorption laws, as $(p \wedge q \wedge s) \vee s \iff s$. All three categories of redundancy hold for both two- and three-valued logic.

A PP̄-*redundancy* results from the existence of non-fundamental clauses. In CNF, a non-fundamental clause C containing both a literal and its two-valued complement can be eliminated automatically since it always evaluates to *true* (C is a tautology). Similarly, a non-fundamental clause D in a DNF formula may be eliminated since it must evaluate to *false* (D is a contradiction). Note that identification of PP̄-redundancies in ANSI SQL is not trivial since search conditions utilize three-valued logic.

4

3. Algorithm

3.1. Overview

The goal of our normalization algorithm for SQL search conditions is to convert the original expression into CNF, subject to two constraints:

1. we must avoid situations requiring expansion of a clause into DNF that could lead to a combinatorial explosion in the number of terms, and

2. conversion to CNF does not result in an expression that is either more expensive to evaluate or represent.

Since our input is an arbitrary, non-normalized search condition, naïvely converting it to DNF as a starting point is unacceptable. Instead, our approach is to normalize the search condition piece-by-piece:

- if the top-level logical connective is And, then convert any disjunctive subtrees to CNF;

- otherwise, if the top-level logical connective is Or, then convert the entire expression into CNF.

In either case, complex clauses involving nested disjuncts (or conjuncts) in a subtree are treated as literals themselves, effectively treating complex subtrees as normalized expressions. In addition to converting the original expression piecewise, this avoids an explosion in the number of terms. The tradeoff, however, is that some opportunities for further simplification of the entire expression may be lost. Fortunately, in our experience, search conditions in SQL queries tend to be either in full- or partial-CNF or DNF; expression subtrees tend not to contain complex subtrees themselves. The following examples illustrate our approach:

EXAMPLE 3
Consider the disjunctive—but non-normalized—expression:

$$ab \lor c(e \lor fg) \tag{3}$$

For brevity we use multiplication to denote logical *and*. By treating the term $e \lor fg$ as a literal, DNF conversion can be applied to yield

$$(c \lor a)(c \lor b)(e \lor fg \lor a)(e \lor fg \lor b). \tag{4}$$

If both of the literals in $c \lor a$ (or $c \lor b$) reference an indexed base column, the query optimizer may be able to use the implicate to deduce a cheaper access strategy using index union [16]. Or, if one of the clauses refers to a subset of the tables in the query, it can be used as a local filtering condition prior to a more expensive algebraic operator, such as a join or a Group by. Retaining the original form of the expression may not enable these optimizations.

EXAMPLE 4
Consider the conjunctive—but, again, non-normalized—expression:

$$abc(d \lor ef). \tag{5}$$

Normalizing the whole (but treating $d \lor ef$ as a literal) would not discover any new, exploitable implicates. Rewriting the search condition in its fully-multiplied disjunctive form, $abcd \lor abcef$, prior to the conversion to CNF, is certainly possible, but may be a memory-intensive operation in the general case. On the other hand, we can disregard the conjunctive literals abc and simplify the DNF expression $d \lor ef$ alone to yield

$$abc(d \lor e)(d \lor f). \tag{6}$$

Like Example 3, the implicates $d \lor e$ and $d \lor f$ may allow new access plans to be discovered by the query optimizer, especially if either implicate can now serve as a local filtering condition.

EXAMPLE 5
The expression

$$a(d \lor e(f \lor gh))bc \tag{7}$$

is an extension of Example 4 in that the literal f has been replaced by the disjunct $f \lor gh$. Our algorithm treats $f \lor gh$ as a literal. This heuristic effectively imposes a limit on the depth to which sub-expressions are transformed. Depending on implementation requirements, sub-expressions, such as $f \lor gh$, could be normalized iteratively until a fully normalized expression is obtained; however, we chose to utilize this heuristic limitation to avoid a worst-case explosion of the number of terms. Thus, our implementation converts Equation 7 to

$$a(d \lor e)(d \lor f \lor gh)bc. \tag{8}$$

Two additional considerations differentiate our approach from prior art. The first concerns the discovery of exploitable implicates. During conversion, the algorithm monitors the size of the resulting CNF expression. By 'size' we simply mean the number of literals in the expression. If the normalized expression is larger than the original, full conversion to CNF is abandoned. Instead, the algorithm continues to generate implicates, though only 'useful' ones are retained. These redundant clauses are concatenated to the *original* expression, ensuring semantic equivalence. Some details of how this is done are outlined in Section 3.2.2; a complete description can be found in [31].

The second consideration is that not all expression branches are necessarily converted. Our algorithm does not attempt to normalize an expression containing expensive predicates, particularly those involving Like predicates, JAVA method invocations, user-defined functions, or subqueries. This heuristic prevents the duplication of these expensive predicates, even if the resulting expression would contain a smaller number of literals, in total, when fully normalized.

3.2. Detailed functionality

An SQL search condition is simplified and converted in two distinct phases. The first phase, termed *branch conversion,* takes an unnormalized search condition as input and evaluates the eligibility of the expression, or portions of the expression, for normalization. The second phase—called from within the first and termed CNF *conversion*—takes a portion of the condition, normalizes it, and returns a set of implicates that may either replace or be concatenated to the original.

In Adaptive Server Anywhere, search conditions are represented internally using an 'expression tree' commonly used by compilers [1] and SQL language parsers [6] to represent a conditional expression. Such a structure is not a requirement of the algorithm, though its use may support the simplification of the original condition through constant folding and predicate pushdown.

3.2.1. Branch conversion.
The branch conversion phase scans the operators and predicates of a search condition to assess their eligibility for transformation. The NORMALIZE function, whose pseudocode is shown in Figure 2, acts as the main dispatcher for the conversion routines. This function takes as input an expression tree representing the search condition to simplify. A linked list of pointers is used to track which branches in the expression tree should be converted. By iterating over this list and converting each branch contained therein, the prime implicants/implicates are generated. If the root node of the tree is an And, the tree is checked to see if it is in conjunctive normal form. If so, the entire tree can be converted from CNF to DNF, and back to CNF to eliminate redundancy. If the expression is conjunctive (at the top level) but contains disjunctive sub-expressions, the sub-expressions are treated as if they were in DNF, and their root nodes are added to the linked list of pointers. On the other hand, if the root node of the tree is an Or, the entire tree is treated as if it were in DNF, and any disjuncts nested within conjunctive terms are treated as individual literals to allow the conversion to take place. These steps allow partially-normalized search conditions to be simplified by considering whole branches as literals.

The function CHECKCONDITIONS, first referenced on line 10 of Figure 2 but omitted from this paper, accepts or disqualifies a branch of the expression tree from normalization. This function scans the predicates within a branch to assess two preconditions:

1. normalization is advantageous: that is, that there exists at least two predicates in the branch that refer to the same (base or derived) table, or, even better, the same (base or derived) column, whose normalization could result in a simplified expression or discovery of local implicates that could be further pushed down in the access plan; and

2. normalization is disadvantageous: the normalized form of the expression would consume too much memory or result in the duplication of expensive predicates, such as those containing large In lists, quantified subqueries, JAVA method invocations, and user-defined function calls (which invoke a stored procedure).

If the first condition is false, or the second is true, then normalization of this branch is avoided, and NORMALIZE considers the next branch in turn. The precise nature of these tests could be altered depending upon the database server's capabilities. In our implementation, we let the discovery of large In-lists or subqueries in a branch veto a decision to normalize, but other implementations may relax this condition if, for example, they support bit-mapped indexing schemes that can handle large In-lists efficiently [2].

3.2.2. CNF conversion.
Once the search condition has been scanned, the conversion routine INVERTNF is called to convert to CNF each branch of the tree in the linked list (see Figure 2, line 36). INVERTNF is an implementation of Socher's [28] minimization algorithm, which uses a *normal form matrix* as its basic data structure. The rows of the matrix represent unique literals, and the columns represent the particular conjunct (or disjunct) in which the literals appear. Prime implicants/implicates are discovered by generating all paths through the matrix and discarding subsumed paths. The primary advantage of Socher's algorithm is that it not only simplifies the original expression by eliminating PP and PQ-QP redundancies, but in doing so does not require naïve generation of redundant clauses, followed by a separate step to eliminate that redundancy. The clear advantage to this is significantly reduced memory requirements than with other algorithms.

The INVERTNF procedure uses our implementation of Socher's algorithm to remove redundancy by performing full CNF (or DNF) conversion on the original branch. Our implementation differs from Socher's in several ways. First, although our path generation function is similar to Wang's [32] implementation of Socher's algorithm (see Section 5), it differs in that we omit the detection and removal of PP̄-redundancies, avoiding the difficulties associated with identifying complementary SQL predicates.

Second, tautological and contradictory conditions are removed from the input expression prior to prime implicant generation. Pruning the conditions from the input data struc-

```
1    Procedure: NORMALIZE
2    Purpose: Discover implicates of expression E.
3    Input: A non-empty search condition E.
4    Local variables:
5      B, a list of pointers to expression branches.
6      s, a pointer to a branch in the expression tree.
7      satisfied, a Boolean variable.
8    begin
9      if the root node of E is an Or then
10       satisfied ← CHECKCONDITIONS( E )
11       if satisfied is false then
12         return
13       else
14         −−Consider E to be in DNF
15         Add its root node to B
16       fi
17     else if the root node of E is an And then
18       if E is in CNF then
19         Add the root node of E to B
20       else
21         for each sub-branch s ∈ E do
22           if the root node of s is an Or then
23             satisfied ← CHECKCONDITIONS( s )
24             if satisfied is false then
25               return
26             else
27               Add s to B
28             fi
29           fi
30         od
31       fi
32     else
33       return
34     fi
35     for each expression branch item s ∈ B do
36       call INVERTNF( s )
37     od
38   end
```

Figure 2. Pseudocode for the main normalization algorithm.

ture (such as an expression tree) is trivial and may be implemented in the SQL parser; however, its importance lies in the fact that memory consumption is reduced by decreasing the size of the input to the conversion routines.

Third, our INVERTNF procedure evaluates the utility of each generated implicate. If an expression is being converted from DNF to CNF, the implicates represented by each generated path are checked to ensure that they have the potential to be exploited in an access plan. Those implicates that are not exploitable by the query optimizer are tentatively marked for deletion. Implicates without sufficient utility are discarded if complete conversion is abandoned.

At the moment, implicate utility is judged heuristically and independently from the query optimizer proper. In our current implementation, only implicates that are either:

- an atomic equality comparison referencing at least one base table column, or
- a disjunctive clause involving only equality comparisons to columns from the same quantifier

are marked as 'useful'. A more sophisticated implementation might include an interface to the query optimizer, or an external costing mechanism, to evaluate the utility of an implicate in light of the original search condition and/or the implicates discovered by the algorithm thus far.

Fourth, and most importantly, INVERTNF continuously monitors the size of the converted expression being created. If the size of the resulting expression is smaller than the original, the original expression is discarded and the generated CNF expression is retained. However, if the number of literals generated during the conversion exceeds the number of literals *prior* to conversion *plus* the number of exploitable literals, then full CNF conversion is abandoned at that point. Instead, INVERTNF continues to generate implicates, but retains only those exploitable implicates that will later be concatenated to the original expression.

Once an implicate has been deleted, the resulting expression is no longer semantically equivalent to the original. However, since each implicate P is generated solely from the original expression E, we must have $E \implies P$. Therefore, we are free to concatenate ('And') those implicates that we consider worthwhile to the original clause, and can omit non-exploitable implicates from the result. Any non-exploitable implicates already generated are subsequently deleted.

Note that when full CNF conversion is abandoned, the resulting expression is correct, though no longer minimal. The insight to Socher's matrix conversion algorithm is that as the matrix gets smaller, the implicates have fewer literals. Typically, the last few implicates generated by INVERTNF are atomic conditions that are the easiest to exploit, since they often represent a join condition or a filtering predicate that can be pushed down. It is for this reason that INVERTNF continues to completion instead of halting immediately once the size of the converted expression exceeds that of the original. The characteristics of the newly-generated implicates, though not prime, can be customized to match the capabilities of the system's execution model and query optimizer.

EXAMPLE 6
Consider, once again, the expression in Example 3. When fully converted, Equation 3 yields $(c \vee a)(c \vee b)(e \vee fg \vee a)(e \vee fg \vee b)$. Assuming that the implicates $c \vee a$ and $c \vee b$ are exploitable by the optimizer (but that the implicates $e \vee fg \vee a$ and $e \vee fg \vee b$ are not), the fully converted

form would still require more literals than the original *plus* the number of exploitable literals (since $12 > 6 + 4$). Thus, to reduce both memory requirements and execution overhead but still retain exploitable implicates, the algorithm concatenates the terms $c \vee a$ and $c \vee b$ to the original, yielding the new conjunctive expression:

$$(ab \vee c(e \vee fg))(c \vee a)(c \vee b). \tag{9}$$

Even if a fully-converted CNF expression results, it may still contain various forms of redundancy. It may contain S-SP-redundancies due to the order in which Socher's algorithm generates paths through the normal form matrix [32]. Our algorithm includes a function to delete these S-SP-redundancies, though in practice they are relatively few in number [32]. In addition, $P\overline{P}$-redundancies may exist since we have avoided identifying fundamental clauses in a three-valued SQL expression. Finally, because INVERTNF considers disjunctive branches one at a time, some *global* redundancy is possible because the same implicate may be generated for more than one branch of the original search condition.

EXAMPLE 7
Consider the search condition represented by the formula

$$abc(d \vee e)(d \vee ef). \tag{10}$$

The NORMALIZE function will consider the conversion of only the conjunct $(d \vee ef)$, which will yield the formula

$$abc(d \vee e)(d \vee e)(d \vee f). \tag{11}$$

To eliminate global PP-redundancies, we implemented a separately-chained hash table to identify and remove redundant implicates from the final expression tree.

3.3. Remarks

Admittedly, a performance penalty is incurred for partial CNF expression trees with multiple DNF or partial DNF subbranches. However, we believe that this penalty is generally acceptable, for several reasons. Conversion of DNF or partial DNF branches within a conjunctive expression can yield useful results without incurring the exponential explosion in terms that would result from normalizing the query's search condition prior to conversion. Moreover, DNF-to-CNF conversion is not as resource-intensive as CNF-to-DNF-to-CNF conversion, and, in our experience, DNF or partial DNF subbranches are usually small. Hence the memory and time requirements for conversion tend to be within satisfactory limits.

```
and P-Partkey = L-Partkey
and L-Shipinstruct = 'DELIVER IN PERSON'
and L-Shipmode In('AIR','AIR REG')
and P-Container In('MED BAG','MED BOX','MED PKG','MED PACK',
                  'SM CASE','SM BOX','SM PACK','SM PKG',
                  'LG CASE','LG BOX','LG PACK','LG PKG')
and (P-Brand = 'BRAND#23' or P-Brand = 'BRAND#12' or
     P-Brand = 'BRAND#34')
```

Figure 3. Additional implicates added to the search condition of TPC-H Query 19.

4. Examples and analysis

EXAMPLE 8
Example 2 (see Figure 1) illustrated that TPC-H query 19 is difficult to evaluate efficiently since the query's search condition lacks a conjunctive join condition between the Lineitem and Part tables. However, our CNF conversion algorithm discovered the set of implicates shown in Figure 3, which are Anded to the original search condition.

Analysis. If we consider each In-list to be an atomic predicate, Query 19 is in DNF, containing 24 literals in total. However, our algorithm quickly discovers that converting the condition to CNF will yield a much larger formula; hence only useful implicates are generated, to be concatenated to the original condition. These implicates include the join predicate P-Partkey = L-Partkey and the disjunctive clause over P-Brand. In addition, the algorithm merges the individual In-list predicates referencing P-Container. Executing the modified query resulted in a 100-to-300-fold performance improvement, depending on the size of the database.

```
Create View Shipping ( Supp-Nation, Cust-Nation, Year ) As
    Select  N1.N-Name As Supp-Nation,
            N2.N-Name As Cust-Nation,
            Year( L-Shipdate ) As Year
    From    Supplier, Lineitem, Order, Customer, Nation N1, Nation N2
    Where   S-Suppkey = L-Suppkey
            and O-Orderkey = L-Orderkey
            and C-Custkey = O-Custkey
            and S-Nationkey = N1.N-Nationkey
            and C-Nationkey = N2.N-Nationkey
            and
            (
                ( N1.N-Name = 'Canada' and N2.N-Name = 'China' )
                or
                ( N1.N-Name = 'China' and N2.N-Name = 'Canada' )
            )
            and L-Shipdate between Date( '1995-01-01')
            and Date('1996-12-31');

Select Supp-Nation, Cust-Nation, Year
From  Shipping
Group By Supp-Nation, Cust-Nation, Year
Order By Supp-Nation, Cust-Nation, Year
```

Figure 4. TPC-H Version 1.1 Query 7.

EXAMPLE 9

TPC-H Query 7 (see Figure 4) also offers opportunities for exploiting additional implicates. Our algorithm analyzes the conditions on the `Nation` table to yield the two additional implicates illustrated in Figure 5.

Analysis. Unlike Query 19, the `Where` clause in the view 'Shipping' consists almost entirely of conjunctive terms. Consequently, CNF conversion is only performed on the disjunctive clauses on `N-Name`. Once again, fully converting this branch of the search condition to CNF yields an expression much larger than the original, so only the two useful implicates are retained to be concatenated with the original expression. Due to the discovery of these two implicates, the query optimizer altered its join strategy due to better estimation of the size of intermediate results, and performance was improved by 20%.

Query predicates in the remainder of the TPC-H queries are left untouched by our CNF conversion algorithm; none of the other queries contain redundant predicates or disjunctive clauses in their search conditions.

EXAMPLE 10

In Section 3.2.2 above we stated that a mechanism to evaluate the utility of any particular predicate would be beneficial. This would enable the normalization algorithm to discriminate useful implicates when the original expression is not amenable for complete CNF normalization.

Consider the query in Figure 6 over the TPC-H `Lineitem` table. This query is identical in form to query Q3B of O'Neil's *Set Query Benchmark* [19], except that the query in [19] contains `Between` predicates rather than inequalities. In Figure 6, the query's `Where` clause is in partial CNF, and the normalization algorithm quickly determines that full conversion to CNF is too expensive. Instead, the algorithm concentrates on the analysis of the disjunctive clause.

Analysis. Ordinarily, one would expect that comparisons between a literal constant and an indexed base column would be excellent candidates for concatenation to the original search condition. However, in this case, rewriting the original disjunctive clause results in eight disjunctive predicates containing only inequalities: the search condition in Figure 6 is equivalent to the formula

$$(ab \lor cd \lor ef)g \tag{12}$$

---

and (N1.N-Name = 'Canada' or N1.N-Name = 'China')
and (N2.N-Name = 'Canada' or N2.N-Name = 'China')

Figure 5. Additional prime implicates added to the search condition of TPC-H Query 7.

```
Select  Sum(L-Quantity)
From    Lineitem
Where (
        ( L-Partkey ≥ 400 and L-Partkey ≤ 800 ) or
        ( L-Partkey ≥ 10000 and L-Partkey ≤ 12000 ) or
        ( L-Partkey ≥ 30000 and L-Partkey ≤ 40000 )
        )
        and L-ReturnFlag = 'R'
```

Figure 6. Partial CNF query with inequalities.

---

and converting the disjunctive clause to CNF yields

$$(e \lor d \lor a)(e \lor d \lor b)(e \lor c \lor a)(e \lor c \lor b) \land$$
$$(f \lor d \lor a)(f \lor d \lor b)(f \lor c \lor a)(f \lor c \lor b)g. \tag{13}$$

This rewritten form will only add additional expense to its execution in ASA. Each resulting disjunction of inequalities is not selective enough to warrant an indexed access strategy, nor will it filter a sequential scan to any meaningful extent. On the other hand, to treat all inequalities as 'useless' implicates may result in lost optimization opportunities. But if the normalization algorithm is capable of detecting subsumptive clauses *after* normalization, then converting the search condition above to CNF may still yield a beneficial result. Hence the decision to generate a redundant clause should take into account the selectivity of that clause, in addition to its evaluation cost.

5. Related work

Several prime implicate-generating algorithms have been developed. Some perform the conversion and minimization in two steps, such as Quine's consensus method [21]:

1. The prime implicates are generated.

2. The minimal set of implicates is selected.

Quine's algorithm, like the Karnaugh map method [13] of similar vintage, requires a large number of basic operations and consumes a significant amount of memory for large expressions [27]. Tison's [29] method is also based on iterated consensus. On the other hand, the algorithm introduced by Slagle et al. [27] performs a depth-first search of a *semantic tree* to find prime implicants, although this algorithm can also find non-prime implicants. In [12], Jackson presented a matrix-based method which carries out a breadth-first search through a matrix of clauses; additionally, Jackson showed that this method outperforms the tree method in computing prime implicants. In [20], Palopoli et al. presented an algorithm for the selective enumeration of prime implicants using linear programming methods, and provided experimental results extolling its performance versus that of the matrix method for large Boolean expressions. Most of these algorithms are equally applicable to the problem of determining the prime implicates of a CNF formula.

9

Usually this is performed by first determining the prime implicants of an equivalent DNF expression, and then reconverting the DNF expression back to CNF.

Unfortunately, many of these algorithms are inadequate as solutions to the optimization problem for SQL queries. In some cases [29, 20, 11, 21, 14] the algorithms may require an expensive preprocessing step to normalize the input Boolean expression. Additionally, some algorithms, such as Tison's method, waste memory by generating more redundant clauses than the number of prime implicants (or implicates) in a minimal formula. Sometimes, they may even generate and delete the same clause repeatedly [32]. In other cases [21, 8, 10], the algorithm may rely on two-valued logic to exploit complementary literals, or the performance of the algorithm in the absence of complementary literals may be substantially reduced. Since ANSI SQL queries utilize three-valued logic, the ability to deduce whether one predicate is the two-valued complement of another requires detailed semantic analysis, increasing the cost of the algorithm. Moreover, in our experience, negated predicates in a search condition are relatively rare.

Wang [32] implemented a version of Socher's matrix method to convert Boolean expressions between normalized forms. Wang's implementation, intended for use in an SQL-to-IMS gateway, required normalized search conditions as input and assumed the use of two-valued logic. Our algorithm, on the other hand, features three advances that are key to allowing it to operate with reduced memory requirements on non-normalized, three-valued SQL search conditions.

Recently, Ramesh, Becker, and Murray [25, 24] introduced an algorithm PI that computes prime implicates from an expression in *negation normal form* (NNF), where negations are only attached to literals. PI generalizes the matrix algorithm of Jackson and Pais [12] which required normalized CNF expressions as input. While PI offers a significant advantage—it does not require an input expression to be in either CNF or DNF—it is not clear that PI represents the best choice for finding prime implicates of SQL search conditions. In addition to requiring a preprocessing phase, termed *dissolution* [17], to eliminate redundancy due to negations, PI requires rather exhaustive subsumption tests throughout the traversal of the semantic graph built to represent the dissolved input formula. Moreover, while Ramesh et al. offer three possible options for computing the prime implicates of an expression, two of them involve computing the negated expression, which, as described earlier, is problematic with SQL search conditions. With our modified version of Socher's algorithm, on the other hand, the generation of subsumed clauses is avoided through manipulating the matrix, albeit at the expense of normalizing the original expression. Moreover, we avoid the ill effects of diabolical cases (cf. [24, pp. 351–2]) by relaxing the requirement for fully-normalized formulas.

6. Concluding remarks

Our implementation of a modified version of Socher's matrix conversion algorithm seems a reasonable compromise between generating useful sets of prime implicates and being space efficient. It is particularly useful when optimizing SQL queries generated by third-party tools. In one customer example brought to our attention, a reporting query's unnormalized Where clause contained 98 disjunctive clauses with considerable numbers of redundant terms. Our algorithm converted the entire search condition to CNF, simplifying it to 18 predicates, two of which were conjunctive atomic conditions. Executing the rewritten query resulted in an enormous reduction in execution time.

At present, we are considering additional optimizations of the overall simplification process. First, we could augment the algorithm to detect and eliminate subsumed clauses, as mentioned in reference [33]. Subsumption checking could potentially reduce the size of the normal form matrix, immediately simplifying matrix processing. Additionally, determining subsumed clauses could reduce the size of the final expression. Second, we could similarly eliminate conjuncts due to empty ranges in DNF expressions. For example, $(x > 4) \wedge (x < 3)$ is *false*, so the entire conjunct can be eliminated from the original expression. Finally, we would like to investigate more efficient matrix implementations that can reduce the algorithm's CPU requirements.

References

[1] A. V. Aho, R. Sethi, and J. D. Ullman. *Compilers–Principles, Techniques and Tools*. Addison-Wesley, Reading, Massachusetts, 1986.

[2] C.-Y. Chan and Y. E. Ioannidis. An efficient bitmap encoding scheme for selection queries. In ACM SIGMOD *International Conference on Management of Data*, pages 215–226, Philadelphia, Pennsylvania, May 1999. Association for Computing Machinery.

[3] A. K. Chandra and G. Markowsky. On the number of prime implicants. *Discrete Mathematics*, 24(1):7–11, 1978.

[4] O. Coudert. On solving covering problems. In *Proceedings of the 33rd Annual Conference on Design Automation*, pages 197–202, Las Vegas, Nevada, June 1996. Association for Computing Machinery.

[5] O. Coudert and J. C. Madre. Implicit and incremental computation of primes and essential primes of Boolean functions. In *Proceedings of the 29th Annual Conference on Design Automation*, pages 36–39, Anaheim, California, June 1992. IEEE Computer Society Press.

[6] H. Garcia-Molina, J. D. Ullman, and J. Widom. *Database System Implementation*. Prentice-Hall, Upper Saddle River, New Jersey, 2000.

[7] J. Goldstein and P.-Å. Larson. Optimizing queries using materialized views: A practical, scalable solution. In ACM SIGMOD *International Conference on Management of Data*, pages 331–342, Santa Barbara, California, May 2001. Association for Computing Machinery.

[8] H. R. Hwa. A method for generating prime implicants of a Boolean expression. IEEE *Transactions on Computers*, 23:637–641, June 1974.

[9] International Standards Organization. (ANSI/ISO) *9075-2*, SQL *Foundation*, Sept. 1999.

[10] P. Jackson. Computing prime implicates. In *Proceedings of the* ACM *Conference on Computer Science*, pages 65–72, Kansas City, Missouri, Mar. 1992. Association for Computing Machinery.

[11] P. Jackson. Computing prime implicates incrementally. In *Proceedings, 11th International Conference on Automated Deduction*, pages 253–267, Sarasota Springs, New York, June 1992. Springer-Verlag. Available as Springer-Verlag's *Lecture Notes in Computer Science* Volume 607.

[12] P. Jackson and J. Pais. Computing prime implicants. In *Proceedings, 10th International Conference on Automated Deduction*, pages 543–557, Kaiserlautern, Germany, July 1990. Springer-Verlag Lecture Notes in Computer Science Volume 449.

[13] G. Karnaugh. The map method for synthesis of combinational logic circuits. *Transactions on Communications and Electronics, Part 1*, 72:593–599, Nov. 1953.

[14] A. Kean and G. K. Tsiknis. An incremental method for generating prime implicants/implicates. *Journal of Symbolic Computation*, 9(2):185–206, Feb. 1990.

[15] A. Y. Levy, I. S. Mumick, and Y. Sagiv. Query optimization by predicate move-around. In *Proceedings of the 20th International Conference on Very Large Data Bases*, pages 96–107, Santiago, Chile, Sept. 1994. Morgan Kaufmann.

[16] C. Mohan, D. Haderle, Y. Wang, and J. Cheng. Single table access using multiple indexes: Optimization, execution, and concurrency control techniques. In F. Bancilhon, C. Thanos, and D. Tsichritzis, editors, *Advances in Database Technology—EDBT'90 (Proceedings of the 2nd International Conference on Extending Database Technology)*, pages 29–43. Springer-Verlag, Venice, Italy, Mar. 1990.

[17] N. V. Murray and E. Rosenthal. Dissolution: Making paths vanish. *Journal of the* ACM, 40(3):504–535, 1993.

[18] P. O'Neil. *Database: Principles, Programming, Performance*. Morgan-Kaufmann, San Francisco, California, 1994.

[19] P. E. O'Neil. The set query benchmark. In J. Gray, editor, *The Benchmark Handbook for Database and Transaction Processing Systems*, pages 359–395. Morgan-Kaufmann, San Francisco, California, second edition, 1993.

[20] L. Palopoli, F. Pirri, and C. Pizzuti. Algorithms for selective enumeration of prime implicants. *Artificial Intelligence*, 111(1–2):41–72, July 1999.

[21] W. V. Quine. The problem of simplifying truth functions. *American Mathematics Monthly*, 59:521–531, 1952.

[22] W. V. Quine. A way to simplify truth functions. *American Mathematics Monthly*, 62:627–631, 1955.

[23] W. V. Quine. On cores and prime implicants of truth functions. *American Mathematics Monthly*, 66:755–760, 1959.

[24] A. Ramesh, G. Becker, and N. V. Murray. CNF and DNF considered harmful for computing prime implicants/implicates. *Journal of Automated Reasoning*, 18(3):337–356, 1997.

[25] A. Ramesh and N. V. Murray. Non-clausal deductive techniques for computing prime implicants and prime implicates. In *Proceedings, 4th International Conference on Logic Programming and Automated Reasoning*, pages 277–288, St. Petersburg, Russia, July 1993. Springer-Verlag Lecture Notes in Computer Science 698.

[26] S. Shekhar, J. Srivastava, and S. Dutta. A formal model of trade-off between optimization and execution costs in semantic query optimization. In *Proceedings of the 14th International Conference on Very Large Data Bases*, pages 457–467, New York, New York, Aug. 1988. Morgan Kaufmann.

[27] J. R. Slagle, C.-L. Chang, and R. C. T. Lee. A new algorithm for generating prime implicants. IEEE *Transactions on Computers*, 19(4):304–310, 1970.

[28] R. Socher. Optimizing the clausal normal form transformation. *Journal of Automated Reasoning*, 7(3):325–336, Sept. 1991.

[29] P. Tison. Generalized consensus theory and its application to the minimization of Boolean functions. IEEE *Transactions on Electronic Computers*, EC-16(4):446–456, 1967.

[30] Transaction Processing Performance Council, San Jose, California. TPC *Benchmark* H *(Decision Support) Standard Specification, Revision 1.1.0*, June 1999.

[31] K. Vorwerk and G. N. Paulley. Implicate discovery and query optimization in SQL Anywhere Studio. Technical report, iAnywhere Solutions, Waterloo, Ontario, Dec. 2000.

[32] Y. Wang. Transforming normalized Boolean expressions into minimal normal forms. Master's thesis, Department of Computer Science, University of Waterloo, Waterloo, Ontario, Canada, 1992.

[33] W. Zhang and P.-Å. Larson. SQL *Predicate Conversion in Multidatabase Systems*. University of Waterloo, Waterloo, Ontario, Canada, Jan. 1996. Unpublished manuscript, 20 pages.

11

Interval Processing with the UB-Tree

Robert Fenk* Volker Markl+ Rudolf Bayer*

*Bavarian Research Center for
Knowledge Based Systems
Orleansstrasse 34, 81667 Munich,
Germany
fenk@forwiss.de
bayer@in.tum.de

+IBM Almaden Research Center
K55/B1, 650 Harry Road
San Jose, CA 95120-6099,
USA
marklv@us.ibm.com

Abstract

Advanced data warehouses and web databases have set the demand for processing large sets of time ranges, quality classes, fuzzy data, personalized data and extended objects. Since, all of these data types can be mapped to intervals, interval indexing can dramatically speed up or even be an enabling technology for these new applications.

We introduce a method for managing intervals by indexing the dual space with the UB-Tree. We show that our method is an effective and efficient solution, benefitting from all good characteristics of the UB-Tree, i.e., concurrency control, worst case guarantees for insertion, deletion and update as well as efficient query processing. Our technique can easily be integrated into an RDBMS engine providing the UB-Tree as access method. We also show that our technique is superior and more flexible to previously suggested techniques.

Keywords: *interval management, parameter space, UB-Tree, intersection query*

1 Introduction

The management and processing of intervals is a special case of extended object handling with growing demand in various application areas.

Applications requiring interval matching and management include:

Temporal Databases [SOL94]; Quality Classes, Personalization and Fuzzy Logic/Matching where intervals can be utilized to describe the problem; Spatial Data where a spatial object can be approximated by a bounding box or set of intervals on a space filling curve. [FR89, BKK99, KMPS01]

For point data there are only a few well defined query types, e.g., *point query* and *range query*, but for intervals there are plenty different query types, e.g., the 13 Allen Relations [AH85] for temporal data.

Following [GG98] the basic query types we consider are: **Exact Match Query (EMQ):** Checks if the data base contains an interval which exactly matches the query interval; **Intersection Query (IQ):** Find all intervals which have at least one point in common with the query interval; **Point Query (PQ):** Find all intervals containing a certain query point; **Containment Query (CQ):** Find all intervals enclosed by the query interval; **Enclosure Query (EQ):** Find all intervals enclosing the query interval.

The IQ plays a crucial role in the calculation of most other relations as an efficient filter for a candidate set. But, depending on the application field additional query types might be necessary, e.g., the *Extent Match Query*, which finds all intervals with a given extent, *Adjacency Query* (meets, precedes), which finds all neighbours of a given interval, and the *Nearest Neighbour Query*, which finds the nearest object to a given object. While some of them (e.g., meets, precedes, before, etc.) can be mapped to intersection queries and post filtering, others (e.g., *Extent Match Query*) require different algorithms or indexing techniques in order to run efficiently.

Standard relational database management systems (RDBMS) so far do not support interval objects or spatial objects efficiently. Enhancing RDBMS by new indexing methods usually implies restrictions in concurrency control and recovery. Having a separate index structure which has not been integrated into the DBMS kernel results in applications which are more complex to develop and maintain. So the only economically reasonable solution to tackle interval indexing is to intelligently exploit the techniques provided by a DBMS. Recently new indexing techniques like the RI-Tree [KPS00, KMPS01] address this problem.

The contribution of our paper is to show the feasibility of the the parameter space approach when indexing it with the UB-Tree, allowing for a flexible and highly-performant interval access method. We show that the data distribution of the dual space is handled well by the UB-Tree, that the typical queries on intervals map to multidimensional range queries on the UB-Tree and compare the performance of our approach to prior art in interval indexing.

In order to implement and use interval indexing with a commercial RDBMS, we rely on existing indexing methods already provided by the DBMS. For that reason we compare the parameter space approach indexed by the UB-Tree, a multidimensional access method (MAM) provided by TransBase Hypercube DBSM, [TAS00] with the RI-Tree which also can be implemented on top of an existing B-Tree, e.g., the B-Tree provided by TransBase. We do not discuss the integration of the UB-Tree, since this has been already done in [RMF$^+$00].

The rest of the paper is organized as follows. Section 2 discusses the related work. Section 3 introduces the concepts and techniques of the parameter space and Section 4 describes how the UB-Tree can be used to index the parameter space. Section 5 describes the RI-Tree in more detail as this is the interval indexing technique we are comparing with. In Section 6 we present our performance analysis. Section 7 describes how to integrate our interval processing method into a DBMS featuring a B-Tree. Finally we conclude our paper with Section 8.

2   Related Work

A huge number of different techniques for interval management has been proposed. [KS91, TCG$^+$93, Boz98, MTT00] give surveys on them. We only consider secondary storage index structures, since main memory data structures usually can not be mapped directly to existing DBMS technology, e.g., the external Segment-Tree [BG94] is a nontrivial mapping of the Segment-Tree.

Further more we want to focus on indexing structures which can be used by exploiting the techniques of commercial RDBMSs, e.g., indexes like the B-Tree or UB-Tree. Therefore, we do not consider [SOL94, GLOT96, KS91] which require indexing techniques not available in any commercial DBMS.

[Ore90] utilizes an approach quite similar to ours, also featuring a Z-curve based access method and the parameter space transformation. However, he focuses on spatial objects and spatial joins, but not on intervals.

The use of regular B$^+$-Trees for indexing valid time intervals was suggested in [GLOT96]. Here, the intervals are mapped to two-dimensional points with the same mapping function used for the TP-index [SOL94]. These two-dimensional points are mapped back to one-dimensional points (not intervals) by defining a total order among them using either horizontal, vertical, or diagonal sweep lines. B$^+$-trees are used to index these points after the final transformation. Temporal queries also go through these transformations. In this scheme, some specific temporal queries transform into range search queries for the B$^+$-trees, and can be efficiently evaluated. However, because of the transformations, many queries require multiple range search operations, and cannot be handled efficiently.

The SR-tree (Segment R-tree) [KS91] is a variant of the R-tree to index segments. Unlike the R-tree, the SR-tree keeps data also in the internal nodes. Any segment that spans any of the children of a node is kept in that node and is checked every time that node is visited in a search query. The SR-tree is a dynamic index, i.e., it allows deletions and insertions at any time. However, insertion and deletion algorithms may cause a high degree of overlap between the nodes. One should also mention that, although insertion and deletion times are logarithmically bound, they are relatively more expensive compared to index structures such as the B$^+$-/UB-Tree. The same drawbacks hold also for the R-Tree and the R*-Tree. Moreover, no integrated R-Tree offers the excellent concurrency and maintenance properties of the B-/UB-Tree. Furthermore all the R-Tree variants integrated in commercial DBSMSs are secondary indexes and consequently they cannot perform as good as clustering indexes like the B-Tree or the UB-Tree.

The Relational Interval Tree (RI-Tree) [KPS00, KMS01, KMPS01] utilizes a virtual binary tree to partition the data space and group intervals to nodes of the binary tree. The node values are used as an additional attribute of the relation storing the intervals. Standard DBMS indexes (e.g., B-Trees) are used to index the relation. The intersection query maps to a SQL statement and can be processed efficiently by the DBMS. Due to its design, the integration into a DBMS or application is quite easy.

3   The Parameter Space

Simple geometric shapes can be considered as points in higher dimensional space called the *parameter space* [Ore90, GG98]. This doubles the number of dimensions and therefore it is also common to use the term *dual space* for this approach.

3.1   Data Transformation

The required transformation of an interval interprets the beginning and end of the interval as the coordinates of a point in two dimensional space. This transformation is called *endpoint transformation* and results in a parameter space with two dimensions of equal domain.

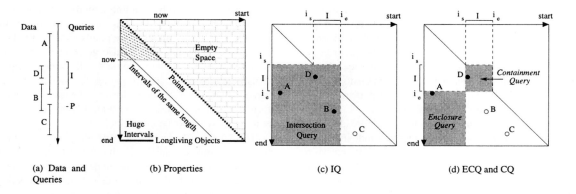

Data	Queries		
A			
D	I		
B	-P		
C			

(a) Data and Queries

(b) Properties

(c) IQ

(d) ECQ and CQ

Figure 1. Native Space and Mapping of Intervals and Queries to Parameter Space

$$[start, end] \xrightarrow[\text{Transformation}]{\text{End Point}} (start, end)$$

$$\text{1D Interval} \qquad\qquad\qquad \text{2D Point}$$

Fig. 1 shows the *endpoint transformation* of the intervals A, B, C and D. The horizontal axis denotes the start point of the intervals, the vertical axis denotes the end point.

This transformation results in the following properties of the parameter space, which are depicted in Fig. 1(b):

- the space above the main diagonal is empty, i.e., due to $s \le e$ no points are mapped to this space

- points are placed on the main diagonal, i.e., $s = e$

- intervals of the same length are mapped to a diagonal, i.e., $e = s + \text{length}$

- the bigger a interval gets the nearer it is to (min, max)

- intervals within a given range are mapped to a rectangular subspace, i.e., they can be clearly separated from the rest. e.g., when indexing time intervals we can get old data (before now) by the query box $[(min, min), (now, now)]$. See also CQ in the next section.

- temporal databases: long-living objects are mapped to $(start, max)$, e.g., time intervals where the end is not known

3.2 Query Transformation

We define the universe of intervals to be $U = \{[u_s, u_e] | min \le u_s \le u_e \le max\}$. Fig. 1(a) shows a set of intervals $\{A, B, C, D\}$, a query point P p and a query interval I $[i_s, i_e]$.

Mapping of the basic queries to parameter space results in 2d query boxes and can be formally defined as follows:

Exact Match Query: $\text{EMQ}([i_s, i_e]) = \{[r_s, r_e] | r_s = i_s \wedge r_e = i_e\}$ is a point query in parameter space; **Intersection Query:** $\text{IQ}([i_s, i_e]) = \{[r_s, r_e] | (r_s \le i_e) \wedge (i_s \le r_e)\}$ can be mapped to a query box $[(min, i_s), (i_e, max)]$ by adding the lower and upper bounds of the domain. Fig. 1(c); **Point Query:** $\text{PQ}(p) = \{[r_s, r_e] | r_s \le p \le r_e\}$ is actually a special case of IQ and results in the query box $[(min, p), (p, max)]$. **Containment Query:** $\text{CQ}([i_s, i_e])] = \{[r_s, r_e] | (i_s \le r_s \le i_e) \wedge (i_s \le r_e \le i_e)\}$ maps to the query box $[(i_s, i_s), (i_e, i_e)]$. Fig. 1(d); **Enclosure Query:** $\text{EQ}([i_s, i_e]) = \{[r_s, r_e] | (r_s \le i_s \le r_e) \wedge (r_s \le i_e \le r_e)\}$ can be simplified to $\{[r_s, r_e] | (r_s \le i_s) \wedge (i_e \le r_e)\}$ due to $r_s \le r_e$ and $i_s \le i_e$ and extended like IQ resulting in the query box $[(min, i_e), (i_s, max)]$. Fig. 1(d).

All the necessary transformations are simple and result in iso-oriented query boxes. This does not hold for all transformation methods proposed for parameter space, e.g., the *midpoint transformation* [GG98] has the problem that all typical interval queries result in query boxes, which are not iso-oriented and cannot be handled by standard MAMs. Therefore, we do not consider this transformation method.

Despite the conceptual elegance, the properties of the parameter space approach and especially the following ones have been regarded as problematic for indexing [GG98]:

1. The parameter space doubles the number of dimensions, i.e., instead of indexing one object of type interval, one has to index a two dimensional space

2. The data distribution in parameter space is highly skewed

Although the parameter space doubles the number of dimensions the curse of dimensionality, the problem of indexing high dimensional spaces, can be neglected in the case of intervals as two dimensions are handled well by all MAMs.

14

The data distribution in parameter space is highly skewed, i.e., start and end of intervals are highly correlated (i.e., $i_s \leq i_e$) and usually the length of the intervals in a data set is similar. Therefore, all data is below the main diagonal and usually distributed along some diagonals (intervals of similar length). Consequently the used MAM has to handle skewed data distributions well. For example, the the GRID-file cannot guarantee a good space utilization with this kind of data distribution and the R-tree and its variants cannot guarantee good query performance due to the overlap of bounding regions.

Due to these problems the parameter space approach has not been considered further in the past [GG98]. However, as we will show in the next section, the UB-Tree handles the skewed data distribution in the parameter space well, both with respect to storage utilization and query performance.

4 Interval Handling with the UB-Tree

In this section we shortly describe how the UB-Tree, a MAM for point data, can be combined with the parameter space approach to index intervals. We start with a short introduction to the UB-Tree and then focus on the indexing and querying of the parameter space.

4.1 The UB-Tree

The UB-Tree [Bay97, Mar99] is a clustering index for multidimensional point data, which inherits all good properties of the B-Tree [BM72]. Logarithmic performance guarantees are given for the basic operations of insertion, deletion and point query, and a page utilization of 50% is guaranteed. The UB-Tree clusters data according to a space filling curve, namely the Z-curve [OM84] and introduces the new idea of partitioning the data space into disjoint Z-regions, which map to disk pages. The Z-regions are then indexed by a B-Tree using last included Z-address as key, which is the ordinal of a point on the Z-curve.

These Z-regions in conjunction with a sophisticated algorithm for multidimensional range queries [BM97] and the Tetris algorithm [MZB99] for sorted reading of multidimensional ranges offer excellent properties [Mar99] for multidimensional applications like data warehousing, archiving systems, temporal data management, etc. Integrating the UB-Tree into a RDBMS providing a clustering B-Tree is simple [RMF+00].

The first commercial RDBMS with an integrated UB-Tree is TransBase HyperCube [TAS00], which has also been used for the measurements in this paper.

4.2 Indexing the Parameter Space

As described in section Section 3 we use the end point transformation to map an interval to a point in two dimensional space and then indexing the points by a UB-Tree. As previously mentioned the crucial question is, how well the UB-Tree can handle the highly skewed data distribution?

As the UB-Tree inherits the good properties of B-Trees it guarantees a 50% page utilization and usually it will be around 81% [Ks83, BY89]. Its Z-region partitioning adapts to the data distribution, i.e., densely populated areas are finer partitioned while the dead space above the main diagonal is covered by a few big Z-regions. Data structures like the GRID file would partition also the dead space, because of the fixed partitioning. Due to its disjoint Z-partitioning, point and range queries are always limited to just one path searches in the B-Tree index, which is not true for R-Trees due to the overlap problem of R-Trees.

The UB-Tree adapts well to the non-uniform data distribution in parameter space. The Z-regions of the UB-Tree narrowly adapt to the data distribution without degenerating. The empty part of the parameter space is covered by a few huge Z-Regions, but those are not empty as they occupy some populated part of the universe with a small spot. The Z-regions cluster the intervals according to their start and end. Therefore, it is likely that intervals within a Z-region have a similar position and length which is a benefit for query processing, since queries likely want to get these intervals together.

The correlation of the data, i.e., $start \leq end$, is no problem, since the query mapping fit to this. Also previous investigations [RMF+01] have shown that the UB-Tree handles skewed data distributions well.

Additionally the UB-Tree is a dynamic index structure and supports updates with logarithmic performance guarantees.

4.3 Query Handling

As we have seen in Section 3.2 all basic query types (EQ, IQ, CQ, ECQ) map to multidimensional range queries on the parameter space. The same holds for all the 13 Allen relations [AH85], they also map to range queries, since they apply only constant constraints to the attributes.

As the UB-Tree is designed to perform multidimensional range queries it is able to handle these query types efficiently. Further more we need just one algorithm to deal with all these query type and there is no further need for specialized algorithms dealing with a specific query type.

The Z-region partitioning, which tries to maintain rectangular Z-regions with just a few fringes, fits perfectly to the query profile created by the interval queries. Therefore, the UB-Tree mainly loads those data pages from disk which contribute to the result.

5 The RI-Tree

The conceptual structure of the RI-Tree is based on a virtual binary tree of height h which acts as a backbone over the range $[1, 2^h - 1]$ of potential interval bounds. Traversals are performed purely arithmetically by starting at the root value 2^{h-1} and proceeding in positive or negative steps of decreasing length 2^{h-i}, thus reaching any desired value of the data space in $O(h)$ time. This backbone structure is not materialized, and only the root value 2^h is stored persistently in a meta data tuple. For the relational storage of intervals, the nodes of the tree are used as artificial key values: Each interval is assigned to a *fork node*, i.e., the first intersected node when descending the tree from the root node down to the interval location.

An instance of the RI-Tree consists of two relational indexes which in an extensible indexing environment are at best managed as index-organized tables. These indexes then obey the relational schema *lowerIndex* $(node, start)$ and *upperIndex* $(node, end)$ and store the artificial *fork node* value, the *start* and *end* of the interval. Additionally, one can add an identifier or other attributes to the relation.

As any interval is represented by exactly one entry for each the lower and the upper bound, $O(n/b)$ disk blocks of size b suffice to store n intervals. For inserting or deleting intervals, the node values are determined arithmetically, and updating the indexes requires $O(\log bn)$ I/O operations per interval.

For processing intersection queries we collect the nodes of the binary tree which may contain intervals intersecting the query interval $[i_s, i_e]$. Theses nodes fall into three classes:

Those nodes which are left to i_s and where we have to test $i_s \leq r_e$ (*leftnodes*), those nodes which are to the right of i_e and where we have to test $r_s \leq i_e$ (*rightnodes*) and those nodes included by the query interval, i.e., $i_s \leq r_s \leq r_e \leq i_e$ (*contained*).

The *leftnodes* and *rightnode* are stored in transient tables and a SQL query is executed that joins these with the base table while checking the predicates.

The RI-tree can be implemented by (procedural) SQL or within the application and does not assume any lower level interfaces. In particular, the built-in index structures of a DBMS are used as they are, and no intrusive augmentations or modifications of the database kernel are required.

6 Performance Analysis

For our measurements we use generated data and queries. The data type of start and end is an integer with

the domain $[0, 2^2 0 - 1]$ and to each tuple we add an additional payload field of 200 bytes, resulting in a tuple size of 208 bytes. With a page size of 2kB this make 9 tuples per page. The page size is small compared to modern DBMSs, but it allows to measure results qualitatively similar those obtained by measuring with larger data sets.

We use a Sun Enterprise Server 450 with two Sparc-Ultra4 248 MHz CPUs and 512MB RAM. The secondary storage medium is an external 90 GB RAID system. The database system is TransBase HyperCube, which offers a product strength implementation of the UB-Tree.

In order to get an insight view and understanding of the measured indexing techniques we use four different data sets and two different query sets.

6.1 Data Sets

In order to reflect different applications scenarios we use four data distributions. The start position is always uniform distributed on the interval domain, while the length was varied. We used data set sizes of 1000, 10000, 100000 and 1 million tuples.

usul: uniformly distributed start and length

usul100k: uniformly distributed start and uniform distributed length within the range $[0, 100000]$

usel: uniformly distributed start and exponentially distributed length according to the exponential distribution function $\lambda e^{-\theta x}$ where $\lambda = 0.000476837$ and $\theta = 5.24288$

usel100k: uniformly distributed start and exponentially distributed length within the range $[0, 100000]$ according to the exponential distribution function $\lambda e^{-\theta x}$ where $\lambda = 0.002765655$ and $\theta = 367.0016$

The uniform distribution on start and end is used as it allows easier understanding of effects due to the availability of a cost model for UB-Trees. The exponential distribution of the length reflects most real world applications where short intervals are more likely to occur than long intervals. Further more, in real world applications there is usually a upper bound for the interval length[1] and therefore we use also variants of the data distributions that restrict the interval length to a given range.

6.2 Query Sets

We focus on intersection queries, since exact match queries are trivial, i.e., they are efficiently handled by a

---

[1] When storing transaction time intervals, they do not last forever since transactions will be aborted after a timeout period.

point query. The results for intersection queries also hold for the containment and enclosure query, as those are a subset of the intersection query.

We use two different query sets:

window scan: a set of 5000 queries sorted according to the start point and with a length of 300. This results in a query set covering the whole data space, while two consecutive query intervals have an overlap of 50%.

random: 1000 random query intervals, where the intervals have been taken from the **usel** data set.

The *window scan* query set is used to locate performance dependencies of the index structures which are based on the location of the query interval. On the other hand it gives the index structures/DBMS a chance to profit from caching and clustering, due to the overlap of query intervals.

The *random* query set is used to see how the index structures perform without caching. It shows how good the index structures handle ad-hoc queries, which deteriorate caching.

6.3 Index Structures

For our comparison we have used the composite key index (B-Tree) and UB-Tree provided by TransBase and variants of the RI-Tree [KPS00, KMPS01] as a reference candidate for indexing techniques designed for intervals. Multiple secondary indexes are neglected as they do not provide clustering and their performance degenerates with bigger result sets due to random accesses on the base table, which can been observed in test measurements.

COMP: one composite key index on $(start, end)$

RIS: RI-Tree with two secondary indexes, one on $(node, start)$ and the other on $(node, end)$

RIP: RI-Tree with primary composite key index on $(node, start)$ and a secondary index on $(node, end)$

UBPS: UB-Tree on $start, end$

The RI-Tree was chosen, since it provides the same practically important properties as our approach: it is easy to implement/integrate, uses standard DBMS methods and provides scalability, update-ability, concurrency control, space efficiency, etc. Further more it has been proven to be superior to the Window-List [Ram97], Tile Index (T-Index) [Ora00] and IST-technique [GLOT96] and so we can transfer our performance results to these indexing techniques.

Actually, we first implemented the RI-Tree as it was presented in [KPS00] with two secondary indexes and "transient" tables, but the performance was worse than that of multiple secondary indexes. So in order to cluster the data

we replaced the secondary index on $(node, start)$ by a clustering index on $(node, start)$ [KMS01]. Still the performance was not as good as expected. Actually, the problem was that TransBase does not support transient tables and the join of *leftnodes* and *rightnode* with the base table is not handled as efficiently as our solution, which was to embed the *leftnodes* and *rightnode* list as a IN clause in the SQL statement. The maximum length of the list is $\log_2 (max - min) - 1$ and for the data used in our measurements it was 19. However, the average length was just 8 and using an array search on such a short array is more CPU efficient than the operations caused by a join.

6.4 Qualitative Comparison of Index Structures

As we have seen before the UB-Tree handles all the discussed query types with its range query algorithm. This is superior compared to other techniques that support just a few or one query type, e.g., the RI-Tree as presented in [KPS00] handles just intersection queries. In order to handle other query types one has to use a combination of intersection query and possibly expensive post filtering or develop specific algorithms.

Furthermore, when indexing additional attributes one may just add them as additional dimensions to the UB-Tree. As UB-Tree clusters data symmetrically with respect to all indexed attributes range restriction on them will also be handled efficiently. When using the RI-Tree one has to add the attributes to its composite key index or use secondary indexes. However, most implementation of composite key indexes cannot handle multidimensional range queries efficiently, i.e., they only utilize the range restriction on the first indexed attribute, and secondary indexes do not perform well, since they do not cluster the data accordingly.

6.5 Results

When making performance measurements of index structures it is important to take all operations into account and not just the query performance. Theses are loading, space requirements, clustering, queries, updates, locking, archiving, etc.

We have concentrated on the following ones: Loading, space consumption, query performance and clustering, as updates, locking and archiving are handled well by the B-Tree underlying the tested indexing techniques.

6.5.1 Bulk Loading Time

Loading time scales linear for all index structures. The data was sorted according to start before loading it, since this can usually be assumed for real world data.

COMP loads fastest since it requires no further sorting of the input data. RIS follows as it only requires updates of its

count	COMP	UBPS	RIP	RIS
1000	148	150	146	171
10000	1450	1471	1402	1634
100000	14486	14681	13895	16189
1000000	143626	146788	146087	161489

Table 1. Space Requirements

indexes while just appending data to the base table. The RIP index requires even more time due to the clustering primary composite key index on $(node, start)$. UBPS is faster than RIP for small **usul** data sets and follows shortly after the RIP for all other data sets.

We have also performed bulk loading of unsorted data. The results of this were that UBPS was fastest, since it requires less sorting than COMP, which took 2.2 times longer in average. RIS and RIS followed with times longer by a factor of 2.32 and 2.35, due to their more expensive index maintainance and complex sorting.

6.5.2 Size of the Tables and Indexes

The overall size of the measured indexes is fairly the same and grows linearly with the data volume as shown in Table 1. The extra attribute *note* of the RI-Tree has only a minor influence, since four extra bytes do not contribute much to a tuple size of 208 bytes. However, it should be considered that tuples of the form $(start, end)$ would result in 50% higher space requirements, due to the extra *node* attribute.

In general COMP and RIP requires least pages, followed by UB-Tree and RIS. UBPS requires slightly more pages compared to COMP and RIP, because compression of UB-Tree data pages has not been implemented in TransBase HyperCube yet. However, the differences can be neglected as they are minimal. The page utilization of the different techniques is usually between 77% and 90% and varies with the scaling factor and no best indexing technique can be recognized.

At the maximum scaling factor of 1 million tuples the DB size was around 290 MB in average and UBPS requires 2% more pages than COMP while RIP/RIS require around 1% more pages than COMP in average.

6.5.3 Query Performance

We use a data base size of 10000 tuples for the measurements. Test measurements with bigger data sets have shown the similar qualitative results as those presented here. First we want to consider the **window scan** query set.

Fig. 2(a) shows the times for measuring the **usul100k** data set. All the measurements plots are sampled to fewer measurement points in order to be easier to distinguish.

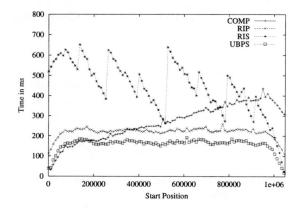

(a) Time **usul100k**

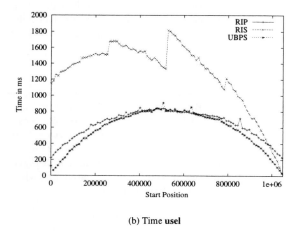

(b) Time **usel**

Figure 2. Measurement: homogen query

RIS is not a clustering index and we clearly see peaks which mark the nodes of the binary tree. When the scan window reaches a new node it causes random page accesses to disk pages containing tuples of that node. After that these pages remain in cache and therefore the performance gets better until the query window reaches the next node.

COMP reflects the fact that such an index is only able to exploit the range restriction on the first attribute *start*, but not the range restriction on the second attribute *end*. Due to the mapping of the IQ, an IQ at the beginning of the domain has a selective restriction on *start* and no restriction on *end*. As the query window shifts towards the end of the domain the restriction on *start* decreases while the restriction on *end* increases. Finally, only *end* will be restricted.

18

As we have seen in Fig. 2(a), the times for COMP and RIS are not only related to the result set size but they also show a high relationship between the position of the query window and the response time. We refer to this as *positional dependency*. RIP and UBPS show a better performance and the response time reflects no positional dependencies, but it is linear to the result set sizes (plot omitted). As there are less intervals at the beginning and end of the interval domain they are faster there.

The rations between COMP/UBPS, RIS/UBPS and RIP/UBPS. In average RIP requires 46% more time that UBPS and in the worst case RIP required nearly 8 times longer than UBPS. In general one can say, UB-Tree outperforms RIP for small result sets.

The measurements with the **usel100k** data set had similar results, due to this we omit them in this paper. In general the response times have been shorter as the result set sizes are smaller, because there are more shorter intervals in comparison to the data sets which do not restrict the length of the intervals. Due to this there are also more intervals assigned to lower nodes of the binary tree of RIS/RIP and RIS shows more peaks, but not so big ones. This holds also for RIP, while UBPS maintains its behavior.

Fig. 2(b) shows the measurement for RIP and UBPS with the **usel** data set. The results are similar as before, however the difference between RIP and UBPS becomes less. In this measurement RIP requires 30% more time in average and RIS was three times slower than UBPS. Again RIS shows the positional dependency. As before these results are also qualitatively observed fro the **usul** data set.

As the performance of COMP depends on the position of the query interval we do not consider it further, but we focus on RIP and UBPS which perform linear to the result set size. Further more we also show for completeness RIS.

The **random** query set has performed as follows. With small result set sizes UBPS is up to five times faster than RIP and 8 times faster than RIS. RIS shows again the unpredictable varying response times due to missing clustering. With growing result set size RIS and RIP become better and finally RIP is even 5% faster than UB-Tree, which comes from the better page utilization of the composite key index which is used for RIP. In average UBPS performs just 2% better than RIP.

6.6 Clustering

In order to get a better understanding on the differences between UBPS and RIP it is crucial to investigate their clustering and how it differs.

Fig. 3 shows the region partitioning (and also disk page clustering) for the UB-Tree and the RI-Tree with a clustering composite index on (node,start,end)[2]. The domain for

---

[2]Taking *end* not into account for the clustering of the RI-Tree would

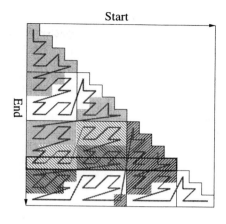

(a) UBPS

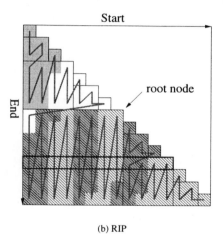

(b) RIP

Figure 3. Clustering and Page Partitioning

this picture is $[0, 14]$ and we assume a uniform distribution on *start* and length of the intervals. A *end-within* query (all intervals that end at a given range) is also depicted and the pages which have to be loaded are filled with a striped pattern. In this case the RI-Tree has to load twice the data pages (6) of the UB-Tree (3).

The UB-Tree clusters the data symmetrically, i.e., it treats *start* and *end* of an interval equally. This results in clustering intervals with respect to their position and length at the same time. The RI-Tree with a primary index on $(node, start, end)$ clusters according node and then to the composite key order resulting in a stripe like partitioning.

---

add random jumps to the space filling curve of the RI-Tree, since there would not be an order on *end*.

With growing data volume the UB-Tree would adapt its regions by making them smaller and more rectangular like. The RI-Tree will get even more strip like and a query like presented here will cut it like a puff-pasty, while the UB-Tree provides a good approximation for the query.

Therefore, the *meets*, *left-overlaps*, *left-covers* relations [AH85] are not handled well by a RI-Tree with the primary index on $(node, start)$ resp. *met by*, *right-overlaps*, *left-covered* are not handled well by a RI-Tree with the primary index on $(node, end)$. The reason for this is that those queries restrict just the *start* resp. *end* cannot be processed well by a clustering index on the not restricted attribute. Using the secondary index results in random page accesses and depending on the DBMS even multiple page accesses. Therefore, an index scan on the clustering index is usually more efficient, but it results in a complete scan of all affected nodes. Compared to this, the UB-Tree Z-region space partitioning allows for reading a good approximation of the subspace which contains intervals contributing to the result. With more data the UB-Tree will become even better compared to the RI-Tree.

However, a query restricting just start can be processed more efficiently by a RI-Tree on $(node, start)$, but also the UB-Tree can perform these queries and the RI-Tree is not able to outperform the UB-Tree by orders of magnitude.

6.6.1 Measurements

We use a **usul** data set with 100000 tuples for this measurement and move a restriction on *end* with length 10000 in steps of 10591 from the start of the domain to the end of it. Caching was enabled for this measurement. We also included the plots for multiple secondary indexes on a table without a specific sort order.

For the RI-Tree we used a modified version of the IQ query algorithm collecting just those nodes that might contribute tuples to the result, i.e., it works like the intersection query for intervals which are points, but is has to traverses only one path. This was done by traversing the virtual binary tree and collecting all those nodes with intervals which may contain the *start* resp. *end* point.

Fig. 4(a) shows the results for a query restricting just the end position. By shifting the restriction to the end of the domain the number of result tuples grows as shown in Fig. 4(a), since there are more longer intervals. UBPS times reflects the linear dependency to the result set sizes. RIP starts similar to UBPS, but the further the restriction moves the more nodes containing more tuples have to be scanned for results. Again we see the phenomenon of peaks we have only seen for RIS before. Whenever, the restriction shifts over a new node the data base has to fetch all the intervals corresponding to that node. The first two levels of the binary tree are clearly visible at 50% for the first level (root

node) and 25% and 75% for the second level. At 50% there is the highest peak, since suddenly the root node has to be processed, which was not cached so far. Additionally also pages from the nodes before the root node are affected by this query. COMP on $(start, end)$ has to perform an index scan since its implementation does not support a range restriction on end only. Its slightly increase comes from the growing amount of tuples which have to be transfered to the application. Fig. 4(a) depicts the linear relation between response times and number of loaded pages. MULT performs really bad. It loads fewer pages than COMP, but it has to fetch them by random accesses and therefore it is not able to exploit prefetching as COMP does, further more it has to load more pages than UBPS or RIP due to the lack of clustering. Speaking in averages, MULT is nearly 13 time slower than UBPS, COMP is 9 times slower than UBPS, where RIP is 4 times slower.

The results for a query restricting just *start* in the same way as *end* was restricted before are depicted in Fig. 4(b). As expected COMP performs best, since its clustering is perfect for this restriction. It performs linear to the result set size. RIP is only a bit slower, but again with peaks at the places where the query window covers new nodes. UBPS follows again performing linear to there result set size. MULT is again bad for the same reasons as before. Speaking in averages, MULT is nearly 12 time slower than UBPS, while COMP takes 67% and RIP 75% of the time UBPS required.

Finally speaking RIP requiring 400% of UBPSs time for *ends in* queries and 75% for *starts in* queries, therefore UBPS is better in the overall average.

7 DBMS integration

The parameter space technique can be implemented by embedding it into an application or building a middle ware using a underlying RDBMS with integrated UB-Tree. The UB-Tree adds efficient query processing by indexing the parameter space. It would also be possible to integrate it into a DBMS providing a procedural query language without modifying the database kernel. However, a DBMS integration is best, as this reduces programming overhead on the application side, allows for easy use and minimizes DBMS maintenance while maximizing the performance.

Both, the UB-Tree and the necessary parameter space transformations are straight forward approaches and they are easy to implement and robust to be used in large-scale applications. Additionally they can be integrated with minimum impact to existing parts of a RDBMS, as long as it supports a clustering B-Tree.

Only minor changes to the existing code of a RDBMS are necessary, i.e., there has to be a new data type for intervals in order to allow for the recognition of the required

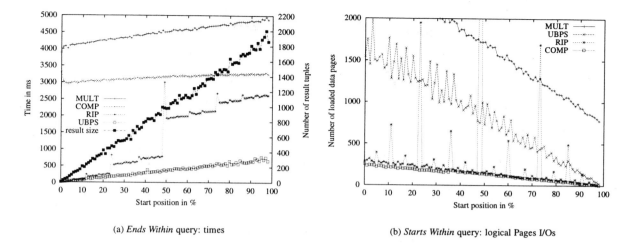

(a) *Ends Within* query: times   (b) *Starts Within* query: logical Pages I/Os

Figure 4. *Ends Within* **and** *Starts Within* **query**

parameter space transformations. With this we need just a new kernel module handling all the transformations of DDL statements, insert/update/delete statements and interval queries.

The DDL statement for creating a interval relation "CREATE TABLE t(i INTERVAL(INTEGER), ...)" is transformed to "CREATE TABLE t(istart INTEGER, iend INTEGER, ...)".

With this the query "SELCT * FROM t WHERE i INTERSECTS $[i_s, i_e]$" maps to the SQL statement "SELECT * FROM t WHERE istart BETWEEN $mininteger$ AND i_e AND iend BETWEEN i_s AND $maxinteger$".

8 Summary and Outlook

We have presented a hybrid method to manage and query intervals efficiently. It transforms intervals to a two dimensional space (parameter space) and indexes that space with a UB-Tree. Queries on intervals are transformed to query boxes in parameter space which are handled well by the UB-Tree range query algorithm. The required transformations of intervals and queries to parameter space are simple, efficient and independent of other DBMS functionality.

Further more, this technique is dynamic, i.e., it allows updates and deletes, it is superior compared to prior techniques with respect to query performance as well as the supported query types. Finally, it allows for indexing additional dimensions symmetrically and thus also provides efficient access to these.

In our further research we will investigate the usability

and performance of the described approach with real world data from data warehouses and spatial objects approximated by a space filling curve.

In addition, the parameter space technique can be generalized to index bounding boxes of higher dimensional objects, thus enabling indexing spatial objects (e.g., GIS data) in two/three dimensional space with the UB-Tree. For two/three dimensional objects we expect good performance, since earlier measurements [Mar99] have proven that the performance of the UB-Tree is also excellent for the number of dimensions (4 for 2d objects and 6 for 3d objects) required here.

References

[AH85]   J.F. Allen and P.J. Hayes. A common-sense theory of time. In *Proceedings of the 9th International Joint Conference on Artificial Intelligence*, volume 9., pages 528–531, 1985.

[Bay97]   Rudolf Bayer. The universal B-Tree for multidimensional Indexing: General Concepts. In *World-Wide Computing and its Applications '97 (WWCA '97), Lecture Notes on Computer Science*. Springer Verlag, 1997. Tsukuba, Japan.

[BG94]   Gabriele Blankenagel and Ralf Hartmut Gting. External segment trees. In *Algorithmica*, volume 12(6), pages 498–532, 1994.

[BKK99]   Christian Böhm, Gerald Klump, and Hans-Peter Kriegel. XZ-Ordering: A space-filling curve for objects with spatial extension. In *Proceedings of Advances in Spatial Databases, 6th International Symposium, SSD'99, Hong Kong, China, July 20-23,*

1999, volume 1651 of *Lecture Notes in Computer Science*, pages 75–90. Springer, 1999.

[BM72] Rudolf Bayer and E. McCreight. Organization and Maintainance of large ordered Indexes. In *Acta Informatica 1*, pages 173–189, 1972.

[BM97] Rudolf Bayer and Volker Markl. The UB-Tree: Performance of Multidimensional Range Queries. Technical Report TUM-I9814, Institut fr Informatik, TU Mnchen, 1997.

[Boz98] Toga Bozkaya. *Index Structures For Temporal And Multimedia Databases*. PhD thesis, Department of Computer Engineering and Science Case Western Reserve University, 1998.

[BY89] Ricardo A. Baeza-Yates. The Expected Behaviour of B^+-Trees. In *Acta Informatica 26(5)*, pages 439–471, 1989.

[FR89] Christos Faloutsos and Shari Roseman. Fractals for secondary key retrieval. In *Proceedings of the Eighth ACM SIGACT-SIGMOD-SIGART Symposium on Principles of Database Systems, March 29-31, 1989, Philadelphia, Pennsylvania*, pages 247–252. ACM Press, 1989.

[GG98] Volker Gaede and Oliver Gnther. Multidimensional Access Methods. In *Computing Surveys 30(2)*, pages 170–231. ACM Press, 1998.

[GLOT96] Cheng Hian Goh, Hongjun Lu, Beng Chin Ooi, and Kian-Lee Tan. Indexing temporal data using existing b+-trees. In *Data & Knowledge Engineering*, volume 18(2), pages 147–165, 1996.

[KMPS01] Hans-Peter Kriegel, Andreas Müller, Marco Pötke, and Thomas Seidl. Spatial data management for computer aided design. In *Proceedings of SIGMOD'01, Santa Barbara*. ACM Press, 2001.

[KMS01] H.-P. Kriegel, M. Ptke M., and T. Seidl. Interval Sequences: An Object-Relational Approach to Manage Spatial Data. In *Proc. 7th Int. Symp. on Spatial and Temporal Databases (SSTD'01), Redondo Beach, CA, 2001.*, 2001.

[KPS00] Hans-Peter Kriegel, Marco Pötke, and Thomas Seidl. Managing intervals efficiently in object-relational databases. In *Proceedings of 26th International Conference on Very Large Data Bases, September 10-14, 2000, Cairo, Egypt*, pages 407–418. Morgan Kaufmann, 2000.

[Ks83] Klaus Kspert. Storage Utilization in B^*-Trees with a Generalized Overflow Technique. In *Acta Informatica 19*, pages 35–55, 1983.

[KS91] Curtis P. Kolovson and Michael Stonebraker. Segment indexes: Dynamic indexing techniques for multi-dimensional interval data. In James Clifford and Roger King, editors, *Proceedings of the 1991 ACM SIGMOD International Conference on Management of Data, Denver, Colorado, May 29-31, 1991*, pages 138–147. ACM Press, 1991.

[Mar99] Volker Markl. *Processing Relational Queries using a Multidimensional Access Technique*. PhD thesis, DISDBIS, Band 59, Infix Verlag, 1999.

[MTT00] Y. Manolopoulos, Y. Theodoridis, and V.J. Tsotras. Chapter 4: Access methods for intervals. In *Advanced Database Indexing*, Boston, MA: Kluwer, 2000.

[MZB99] Volker Markl, Martin Zirkel, and Rudolf Bayer. Processing Operations with Restrictions in RDBMS without External Sorting: The Tetris Algorithm. In *Proceedings of the 15th International Conference on Data Engineering, 23-26 March 1999, Sydney, Austrialia*, pages 562–571. IEEE Computer Society, 1999.

[OM84] Jack A. Orenstein and T. H. Merrett. A Class of Data Structures for Associative Searching. In *Proceedings of the Third ACM SIGACT-SIGMOD Symposium on Principles of Database Systems, April 2-4, 1984, Waterloo, Ontario, Canada*, pages 181–190. ACM, 1984.

[Ora00] Oracle. *Oracle8i Data Cartridge Developers's Guide*. Oracle Corporation, Redwood City, CA, rel. 8.1.7 edition, 2000.

[Ore90] Jack A. Orenstein. A Comparison of Spatial Query Processing Techniques for Native and Parameter Spaces. In *Proceedings of the 1990 ACM SIGMOD International Conference on Management of Data, Atlantic City, NJ, May 23-25, 1990*, pages 343–352. ACM Press, 1990.

[Ram97] S. Ramaswamy. Efficient indexing for constraint and temporal databases. In *Proceedings of the 6th International Conference on Database Theory (ICDT)*, pages 419–431, 1997.

[RMF+00] Frank Ramsak, Volker Markl, Robert Fenk, Martin Zirkel, Klaus Elhard, and Rudolf Bayer. Integrating the UB-Tree into a Database System Kernel. In *Proceedings of International Conference on Very Large Data Bases, 2000, Cairo, Egypt*, 2000.

[RMF+01] F. Ramsak, V. Markl, R. Fenk, R. Bayer, and T. Ruf. Interactive ROLAP on Large Databases: A Case Study with UB-Trees. In *Proc. of IDEAS Conf. 2001, Grenoble, France*, 2001.

[SOL94] Han Shen, Beng Chin Ooi, and Hongjun Lu. The tp-index: A dynamic and efficient indexing mechanism for temporal databases. In *Proceedings of the Tenth International Conference on Data Engineering, February 14-18, 1994, Houston, Texas, USA*, pages 274–281. IEEE Computer Society, 1994.

[TAS00] TAS. *Transbase HyperCube*. TransAction Software, http://www.transaction.de, 2000.

[TCG+93] A.U. Tansel, J. Clifford, S. Gadia, S. Jajodia, A. Segev, and R. Sondgrass. *Temporal Databases: Theory, Design and Implementation*. Benjamin/Cummings, Redwood City, CA, 1993.

Graph Partition Based Multi-Way Spatial Joins

Xuemin Lin, Hai-Xin Lu, Qing Zhang
School of Computer Science & Engineering
University of New South Wales
Sydney, NSW 2052, Australia
lxue, cshlu, qzhang@cse.unsw.edu.au

Abstract

In this paper, we investigate the problem of efficiently computing a multi-way spatial join without spatial indexes. We propose a novel and effective filtering algorithm based on a two phase partitioning technique. To avoid missing hits due to an inherent difficulty in multi-way spatial joins, we propose to firstly partition a join graph into sub-graphs whenever necessary. In the second phase, we partition the spatial data sets; and then the sub-joins will be executed simultaneously in each partition to minimise the I/O costs. Finally, a multi-way relational join will be applied to merge together the sub-join results. Our experiment results demonstrated the effectiveness and efficiency of the proposed algorithm.

Keywords*: Spatial Databases, Spatial Joins, Query Processing.*

1. Introduction

Multi-way spatial join selects, from n sets of spatial objects in the 2-dimensional space, the tuples each of which consists of n objects respectively from the n data sets and satisfies some given spatial predicates. An example of a multi-way spatial join is "find all residential areas that intersect a lake that passes some golf courses". Spatial join is an important but expensive query form to process spatial information in GIS, satellite images, digital video, multimedia documents, etc. A multi-way spatial join can be modelled by a *join graph* whose vertices represent respectively different data sets and edges represent respectively spatial predicates between pairs of vertices. We will formally define a spatial multi-way join in the next section.

Due to high processing complexities and costs, a spatial join is usually executed in two steps [2, 14], *filtering* and *refinement*. In the filtering step, spatial objects are approximated by the isothetic *Minimal Bounding Rectangles*

(MBR); and then the MBRs are processed to produce a candidate result set. In the refinement step, each tuple from the candidate set is examined further, for the given spatial predicates, against the real objects instead of their MBRs. In this paper, we will concentrate on the filtering step. Therefore, the multi-way spatial joins discussed in this paper will be restricted to data sets where spatial objects are isothetic rectangles. A special predicate may be in various different forms; for instance, *direction* joins [22], *distance* joins [6], etc. In this paper, we will discuss only one of the most popular predicates - *overlapping*.

Spatial joins with the predicate of overlapping has received a great attention in the last twenty years. A number of different computation methods have been proposed for efficiently processing 2-way spatial joins, such as Z-order elements technique [13, 14], R-tree join [2, 5] and its variations, filter tree join [20], seeded tree join [9], partition based spatial merge join [15], spatial hash join [10], size separation spatial join [7], the scalable sweeping-based spatial join [1], and slot index spatial join [12]. However, there has been little research on the general multi-way (with more than 2 data sets) join until very recently. The papers [16, 17, 18] provided spatial join algorithms based on a synchronous traversal technique on R-trees, while the paper [12] proposed to apply a slot index spatial join method to handle a join of an intermediate join result and an indexed data set.

In this paper, we investigate the multi-way spatial join processing algorithms when no spatial data indexes exist. One way to process a multi-way join is by a sequence of 2-way joins; and then apply some non-index based spatial join algorithms [1, 10, 15, 7] to each two-way join. However, such an approach does not only have to involve extra I/O overheads to repartition every intermediate result set when it does not fit in the buffer but also has to involve some extra computation costs (e.g. if swapping-line algorithm is applied, data sets may have to be scanned more than once).

The experiment results in [1] suggest that a data partitioning based join approach [10, 15, 7] tends to have small

I/O overhead. Consequently, an alternative way to process a multi-way spatial join is firstly to partition the data space into a number of *buckets* [15]; and secondly to process data only in each bucket to produce the local multi-way join results; and thirdly merge the local sub-join results together by a union, like what was suggested in [10, 15] for 2-way joins. Unfortunately, such a data partitioning based method may miss some join result tuples; and we will illustrate them in the next section.

Motivated by the above facts, in this paper we will propose a novel multi-way spatial join algorithm based on a two-phase partitioning technique in the filtering step (that is, join sets of rectangles):

- Firstly, we partition (if necessary) a join graph into a set of subgraphs.

- Secondly, we partition the involved data sets into a number of buckets.

Once the two-phase partitioning is done, we simultaneously execute the joins, which correspond respectively to a subgraph, in each bucket by reading in spatial data only once. After the local joins have done for each data bucket, a relational join will be applied on the sub-join results to "merge" them together to produce the join results for the original query graph. This is the first and the principal contribution of the paper. The second contribution of the paper are the results we obtained for the optimal graph partitioning problem. The third contribution of the paper is that we completely characterise a class of join graphs where a graph partitioning is not necessarily required while applying our join algorithm. Finally, our experiment results confirm the efficiency of our algorithm.

The rest of the paper is organised as follows. In section 2, we present a precise definition of multi-way join, an overview of related work, and the difficulties to process a spatial multi-way join without indexes. Section 3 presents the framework of our two-phase partitioning technique, the fundamental, and the join algorithm. Section 4 reports our experiment results. This is followed by conclusions and remarks.

2 Background

A multi-way spatial join can be defined as follows. Assume that $\{R_i : 1 \leq i \leq n\}$ is a set of n spatial relations, and $\{C_{i,j} : (i,j) \in I \ \& \ I \subseteq [1,n] \times [1,n]\}$ is a set of binary spatial predicates. The multi-way join of $\{R_1, ..., R_n\}$ with respect to the given spatial predicates is to compute all n-tuples:

$$\{(r_{1,x_1}, ..., r_{i,x_i}, ... r_{n,x_n}) : \forall i, r_{i,x_i} \in R_i; \forall (i,j) \in I, C(r_{i,x_i}, r_{j,x_j})\}$$

As mentioned in the last section, in this paper we discuss only one predicate - overlapping. We also assume that each spatial data set consists of only isothetic rectangles.

Note that a multi-way spatial join of n spatial tables $\{R_i : 1 \leq i \leq n\}$ is represented by a join graph $G = \{V, E\}$ where $V = \{R_i, 1 \leq i \leq n\}$ and corresponding to each $C_{i,j}$, (R_i, R_j) is an edge. In a graph, a vertex is *adjacent* to another vertex if there is an edge connecting them. The number of the edges *incident* to a vertex is called *degree* of the vertex. Suppose that V' is a subset of V. The *induced* graph by V' from G is the subgraph of G whose vertex set is V' and whose edge set consists of the edges in G connecting only the vertices in V'.

2.1 Related Work

The study of 2-way join has gained much attention in the last two decades. Many techniques have been published for the case when spatial data sets are fully indexed; for instance, those in [2, 5, 14, 20]. Due to an equal importance of the applications where no spatial index exists, the papers [10, 15, 1, 7] studied spatial two-way joins without spatial indexes.

Consider that the number of data objects to be joined may be too large to fit in the main memory simultaneously. The Partition Based Spatial Merge Join (PBSM) [15] divides the data set into a number of different regions; and each region is called a bucket. To avoid missing hits, PBSM suggests to duplicate each object to the buckets which intersect the object. Then, the join algorithm is locally executed in each bucket to produce the local join results. Adding up the local join results from different buckets gives the join result.

Independently, the authors in [10] proposed another data partition based join algorithm - Spatial Hash Join (SHJ). In SHJ, the author proposed a data partition such that each object from one data set is assigned to only one bucket which contains it; this will avoid a post-process to eliminates duplicates among the local join results. However, unlike [15] buckets in SHJ may overlap with each other. Note in SHJ, the data objects from another data set still need to duplicate to the intersected bucket.

The Sized Separation Spatial Join (S^3J) [7] is a nontrivial variation of the data partition based join methods [10, 15]; and it has gone one step further to completely remove data replication in each bucket by applying a multiresolution idea. It involves a two-step data partitioning. The object space is firstly modelled into a multi-resolution space; and secondly the space for each resolution is partitioned by the Hilbert curve technique. Then the join is executed cross different levels of the multi-resolution space, such that 1) in the same level the join process needs to be carried out only within the same bucket, and 2) in the different levels the join process needs to be carried out only between a bucket from higher resolution level and the bucket in a lower level which contains the bucket in the higher level.

The Scalable Sweeping-based Spatial Join (SSSJ) [1] is mainly focused on improving the computation in the main memory by a novel application of *interval* tree technique from computational geometry [19].

In this paper, to efficiently do I/O we will develop a data partition based algorithm for processing a multi-way spatial join. Below we first show the difficulties/problems in such a paradigm.

2.2 Problems

A *partition based join paradigm* can be generally described below. Firstly, we partition the whole data space into a number of buckets (usually isothetic rectangles). Secondly we assign each object to some (at least one) buckets which intersect the object. Thirdly, bucket by bucket we process the data in each bucket to produce *local* join results. Finally, all the local join results are *merged* together to produce the results of the join. Note that in two-way spatial join, such a merge process is trivial [10, 15] - a union of all the local join results.

The following problems need to be resolved in a partition based join paradigm while processing a multi-way spatial join. As pointed out in [10, 15], an object may have to be duplicated into all the buckets which intersect the object, in order to avoid missing hits. For example in Figure 1, $b2$ has to be duplicated into the two buckets to get join tuples $(a2, b2)$ and $(a4, b2)$. Data replication will cause an extra computation in two ways. Firstly, some pairs may be repeatedly examined in different buckets. For instance in Figure 1, if the objects $a3$ and $b2$ are respectively duplicated into the two buckets then the pair $(a3, b2)$ will be examined twice respectively in each bucket to see if they intersect with each other. Secondly, some joint result pairs may be repeatedly obtained in different buckets; for instance, the pair $(a3, b2)$ is obtained in both buckets. Consequently, it requires an extra sorting process to remove all duplicates [15]. To resolve this, the authors in [10] proposed a non-uniform space partition such that each object from one data set chooses only one bucket, which contains the object, to assign; while the objects from another data set are replicated cross the buckets which intersect the objects respectively. We will apply this idea in our partition based join algorithm for multi-way joins. It will be shown in the next section that to ensure the algorithm correctness, we will have to apply this idea in multi-way spatial joins.

In multi-way spatial join, the "sparsity" of a join graph may cause missing hits in a data partition join paradigm **even if each object is duplicated to all the buckets that intersect with the object**. For example, regarding the join graph in Figure 2(b) we assume that data are partitioned into two buckets (as depicted in Figure 2(a)) where $a1$ is in

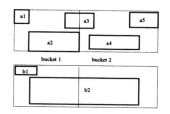

Figure 1. a3 and b2 are respectively replicated into two buckets

bucket 1, $c1$ is in bucket 2, and $b1$ and $d1$ are in both buckets. In this example, the joining tuple $(a1, b1, c1, d1)$ will be missed by applying the partition based join paradigm. This is because in both buckets we can only obtain a part of the tuple. In bucket 1, we obtain only $(a1, b1, d1)$, while in bucket 2 we obtain only $(b1, c1, d1)$. Therefore, we cannot obtain the joining tuple in either bucket.

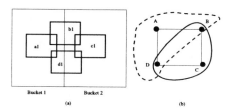

Figure 2. Sparsity missing hits problem

To resolve this *sparsity missing hits* problem, we may decompose the join graph in Figure 2(b) into two subgraphs: the one (depicted by a dotted curve) induced by vertices A, B, and D, and the one (depicted by a solid curve) induced by B, C, and D. Regarding the example in Figure 2(a), in each bucket we then execute simultaneously the local joins, which are respectively represented by the two subgraphs, by reading in the objects only once. Finally, we perform a relational join between two tables (A, B, D) and (B, D, C) with B and D being the join columns. In this example, the join tuple $(a1, b1, c1, d1)$ is obtained from the join of $(a1, b1, d1)$ and $(b1, c1, d1)$. This is the basic idea of our approach.

In the next section, we will present our join algorithm, its I/O management, and the correctness.

Note that that by similar examples, it can be shown that a trivial application of S^3J to multi-way spatial joins does not work either; that is, it is no longer correct in a multi-way spatial join that we only need to handle the join within one bucket in the same level. It is worth to point out that our graph partition based technique presented in this paper is also applicable to an application of S^3J to multi-way spatial joins, though it will not be presented in this paper.

3 Graph Partition Based Join Algorithm

In this section, we propose a new multi-way spatial join algorithm - Two-Phase Partitioning Join (TPPJ). TPPJ contains two partitioning phases, a graph partitioning and a data partitioning phase. To present our algorithm, the following notation is needed.

A graph $G = (V, E)$ is *star-like* if G has at least three vertices, and in G there is a *peak* vertex v_0 such that every other vertex is adjacent to v_0. For example, the three graphs in Figure 3 are respectively star-like. A graph consists of only two vertices is *2-graph*; that is, a graph has two vertices and one edge connecting the two vertices. A set of subgraphs $\{G_i = (V_i, E_i) : 1 \leq i \leq k\}$ of $G = (V, E)$ *covers* G if $E = \cup_{i=1}^{k} E_i$. Suppose that G is a star-like join graph and v_0 is a peak vertex of G, and P is a data partition for every vertex (data set) in G. We call P *compatible* with G and v_0 if:

- each object o from the data set v_0 chooses only one bucket to be assigned; and this bucket also contains o.

- each object o from other data sets (vertices) is duplicated to the buckets which intersect o.

A data partition P is *compatible* with a 2-graph G if each object from the data sets (vertices) in G is duplicated to the buckets which intersect the object.

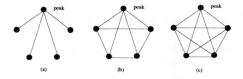

Figure 3. star-like graphs

Below is a framework of our spatial multi-way join algorithm TPPJ. It consists of four steps.

Algorithm TPPJ

Step 1: Decompose the join graph $G = (V, E)$ into a set $S = \{G_i = (V_i, E_i) : 1 \leq i \leq k\}$ of subgraphs of G such that:

- each G_i is either a star-like graph or a 2-graph, and
- S covers G, and
- for each star-like graph G_i, there is a *denoted* peak vertex $v_{i,0}$ with the property that for each pair of star-like graphs G_i and G_j, $v_{i,0}$ and $v_{j,0}$ are not adjacent, and

- any vertex in a 2-graph is not from those denoted peak vertices $\{v_{i,0} : G_i$ is star-like$\}$.

Step 2: Obtain a data partition P for all data sets (vertices) in G such that P is compatible with every star-like G_i and its denoted peak vertex $v_{i,0}$. P is also compatible with every 2-graph.

Step 3: For each bucket, do joins given by the subgraphs.

Step 4: Suppose that for each subgraph G_i, the join results obtained from step 3 over all buckets are maintained in a table denoted by T_i where each column of T_i corresponds to a vertex (data set) in G_i, and every tuple of T_i corresponds to a join result tuple for G_i but consists of only IDs for the corresponding objects. Do the multi-way equi-join on all T_i such that for each pair of T_i and T_j with some join columns, they have to perform an equi-join as part of the multi-way join. The relational multi-way join results will be the results of the spatial multi-way join.

For example, suppose that we have 4 data sets A, B , C, and D where each data set has only one object respectively $a1$, $b1$, $c1$, and $d1$. Assume that the join graph is the one as depicted in Figure 2(b). Below is an illustration of our algorithm.

- In step 1, we partition the join graph into two star-like graphs (A, B, D), and (B, C, D).

- In step two, we partition each data set into two buckets as depicted in Figure 2(a) such that in bucket 1 has $a1$, $d1$, and $b1$, and bucket 2 has $b1$, $c1$, and $d1$.

- In Step 3, we do the join for each bucket. In bucket one, we obtain a tuple $(a1, b1, c1)$ for the star-like graph induced by (A, B, C) and null for another star-like graph induced by (B, C, D). In bucket 2, we obtain a tuple $(b1, c1, d1)$ for (B, D, C) but null for (A, B, C).

- In step 4, we implement the relational equi-join between (A, B, C) and (B, C, D) where the join columns are B and C. The tuple $(a1, b1, c1, d1)$ is obtained; and it is also the result of spatial join as depicted in Figure 2(b).

Figure 4. an example

Note that in an ideal situation, we would prefer to decompose the graph into star-like graphs only with the properties required in Step 1; however, it is not always possible to do this. For example, the graph G as depicted in Figure 4 cannot be decomposed into a set of star-like subgraphs covering G such that the peak vertices are not *adjacent* to each other. This is the reason why we allow 2-graphs in Step 1.

Step 4 is about processing multi-way relational equijoins; and there are many existing techniques in the literature [11]. In our implementation, we apply a *left-deep* tree based hash join algorithm. Below we will detail every step except step 4. We start with the correctness of TPPJ and the theoretical reasons about why we put those constraints in TPPJ.

3.1 Fundamentals of TPPJ

Consider that our TPPJ is a special case of the partition based join paradigm. In this subsection, we will show that those constraints in TPPJ are sufficient and necessary. That is, we are going to show that the necessity of having the constraints, as well as the correctness of the algorithm. First, we show that if a join graph has at least 3 vertices then only a star-like join graph does not need to be partitioned into subgraphs.

Theorem 1 *Suppose that a spatial join of R_1, R_2, ..., R_n forms a star-like join graph G where R_1 is a peak vertex of the graph; and a data partition P is compatible with G and R_1. Then, the union of all local join results from all the buckets is equal to the join result for G.*

Proof: Suppose that there are m buckets, T_j denotes the local join result set for G in bucket j ($1 \leq j \leq m$), and T denotes the complete join result set for G. Clearly, $\cup_{j=1}^{m} T_j \subseteq T$. Below we prove $T \subseteq \cup_{j=1}^{n} T_j$.

Suppose that $\forall (r_{1,x_1}, r_{2,x_2}, ..., r_{n,x_n}) \in T$, B_l is the bucket containing the rectangle r_{1,x_1} from R_1. Then for $2 \leq i \leq n$, r_{i,x_i} must be in B_l as well; this is because that each r_{i,x_i} has to intersect r_{1,x_1} to qualify for a rectangle in the join result tuple. Consequently, this n-tuple $(r_{1,x_1}, r_{2,x_2}, ..., r_{n,x_n})$ is in T_l. $\square$

Theorem 1 means that if the algorithm TPPJ is applied to a star-like join graph then we do not need to implement the step 1 (graph decomposition) and the step 4 (relational multi-way join). On the other hand, we can show that only a star-like graph does not need a graph partition when implementing the partition based join paradigm.

Theorem 2 *Suppose that the join graph G of a spatial join is not star-like. Then, there is data partition P of the data sets (vertices) in G such that the union of all local join results from all buckets does not cover the join result for G.*

Proof: Since G is not star-like but connected, there must be 4 vertices, say, A, B, C, and D, such that A is adjacent to B and D. However, C is not adjacent to A and B is

not adjacent to D. Note that we are not interested in the relationship between C and B, nor that between C and D.

Suppose that a partition P restricted to A, B, C, and D is the one as illustrated in Figure 2(a). Further, suppose that $a1$, $b1$, $c1$, and $d1$ are respectively from A, B, C, and D, and their locations are illustrated as those in Figure 2(a). We assume that $a1$, $b1$, and $d1$ are in bucket 1, while $b1$, $c1$, and $d1$ are in bucket 2. We also assume that there is one object from each data set other than A, B, C, or D (if there are more than 4 data sets) in the join graph intersecting respectively $a1$, $b1$, $c1$, and $d1$; and also intersects each other. Consequently, $(a1, b1, c1, d1)$ must be one part of a tuple in the join result. However, according to a partition-based join algorithm any tuple containing $(a1, b1, c1, d1)$ cannot be in the result; this is because $(a1, b1, d1)$ has to be in bucket 1 while $(b1, c1, d1)$ has to be bucket 2. $\square$

In PBSM [15] and Theorem 1, it is already shown that that if a data partition is compatible with a join graph which is either a 2-graph or a star-like graph, then we can guarantee the correctness of an application of the partition based join paradigm. The examples below show that it is necessary to have a compatible data partition.

Example 1. A star-like join graph has three vertices, A, B and C. Suppose that a, b, and c are the objects respectively from A, B, and C. The whole space is divided into two buckets; the data partition and the locations of a, b, and c are shown in Figure 5(a), where a and b are assigned to bucket 1, and a and c are assigned to bucket 2. $\square$

Example 2. Suppose that A and B are two adjacent vertices in a join graph G. A and B respectively have only one object a and b. Assume that the whole space is partitioned into two buckets. The buckets and the locations of a and b are shown in Figure 5(b), where a is assigned to bucket 1 and b is assigned to bucket 2. We also assume that every vertex in G other than A or B has only one object which intersects a and b; and those objects from other vertices also intersect each other. $\square$

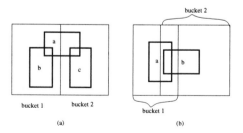

Figure 5. an illustration

Example 1 shows that even for a star-like graph G, if in a data partition P an object from the peak vertex is not contained by any bucket (therefore, P is not compatible with

G and the peak vertex) then the union of local join results may lead to some missing hits. In the example, the join result (a, b, c) cannot be obtained from a union of local join results in the two buckets even a has been duplicated into the two buckets.

Example 2 shows that even for a data partition which is compatible with the peak vertex may still lead to missing hits if an object from a non-peak vertex is not duplicated to all the buckets which intersect the object. In the example, there is actually only one tuple in the join result; however it will be missed in local joins in both buckets.

Now we show the correctness of the algorithm.

Theorem 3 *The algorithm TPPJ is correct; that is, TPPJ can produce the exact solution for any multi-way spatial join (G) where every data set is a set of isothetic rectangles.*

Proof: Suppose that G is a join graph, and G is decomposed into a set of subgraphs G_i $(1 \leq i \leq k)$ by the step 1 in TPPJ

From theorem 1, it follows that TPPJ can produce correct join results for every star-like G_i. The results in paper [15] also implies that our TPPJ can produce the correct join results for every 2-graph G_i.

Clearly, every tuple t in the join result for G can be decomposed into k sub-tuples which are respectively a tuple in a sub-join result (for G_i); and the tuple t can be recovered from those sub-tuples by the relational equi-join. On the other hand, it can be immediately verified that in step 4, any tuple in the result set of the multi-way relational join among all sub-join results also a tuple in the result set of spatial multi-way join (for G). □

Note that it can be immediately verified that the intersection of any pair of local join result sets from two different buckets is empty due to the fact that each object from a peak vertex is assigned to only one bucket.

In the next several subsections, we will show the details for steps 1, 2, and 3 in TPPJ.

3.2 Graph Partition

In this subsection, we investigate the step 1 in TPPJ - the graph partitioning problem. We will first formalise one optimisation problem in the graph partitioning. Then we will show the complexity of the problem, together with a heuristic.

Clearly, Step 1 in TPPJ is feasible. A naive way to do Step 1 is to decompose a join graph into a number of 2-graphs for each edge. However, such a decomposition may have many subgraphs. This not only means that we have to process too many intermediate results but also potentially increases the computational complexity in Step 4 (relational multi-way join) of TPPJ. Therefore, we propose to have a graph decomposition in Step 1 with the minimum number of subgraphs. The optimisation problem is thus described below.

Optimal Graph Decomposition Problem (OGDP)
INSTANCE: A connected graph $G = (V, E)$.
QUESTION: Decompose it into a set of subgraphs with the requirements specified in Step 1 of TPPJ such that the number of subgraphs is minimised.

Theorem 4 *OGDP is NP-hard.*

Proof: In this paper, we show only the basic idea of the proof. The interested readers may refer our full paper [8] for the detail.

We will transform the *vertex cover* [4] problem to a special case of OGDP. For each graph G in the vertex cover problem, we attach $2n^2$ adjacent vertices to each vertex of G to make an instance G' of OGDP; for instance, Figure 6 illustrates such a transformation (from (a) to (b)). Then, we can show that the optimal solution for G' has to consist of 1) the star-like graphs with the peak vertices which form a minimum vertex cover for G, and 2) the remaining uncovered 2-graphs in G'. □

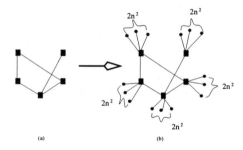

Figure 6. an transformation from vertex cover to OGDP

Now, we present a heuristic for solving OGDP. It applies a greedy heuristic to iteratively choose an available vertex with the maximum degree. Below is the algorithm.

Step 1 - Algorithm OGDP

Step 1.1: Iteratively do the following (till no such vertex to choose):

- choose a vertex v_0 from V with the maximum degree in G, which is at least 2, and then

- delete from V all vertices incident to v_0, as well as remove v_0, and then

- enter into the next iteration.

Step 1.2: For each chosen v_i, form the induced subgraph G_i of G with the vertex set which consists of v_i and all the adjacent vertices of v_i.

Step 1.3: For each edge left, form a 2-graph.

Step 1.4 Return the star-like graphs chosen in Step 1.2 and the 2-graphs in Step 1.3 (if any) to form a graph partition of G.

Note that each vertex v_i chosen in Step 1.1 is the denoted vertex which is not adjacent each other, and needs to be treated specially in the data partitioning phase.

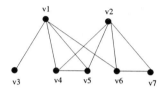

Figure 7. gdp algorithm illustration

For example, regarding the graph in Figure 7 the algorithm will output two star-like graphs respectively induced by $(v1, v3, v4, v5, v6)$ and $(v2, v4, v5, v6, v7)$, and one 2-graph $(v6, v7)$. Note that both star-like graphs include edge $v4$ and $v5$. In fact, we have the option of removing the edge (v_4, v_5) from one of these two star-like graphs. However, adding one more edge to a join graph will make the size of join result smaller. This was why we duplicate (v_4, v_5) in both subgraphs.

Note that the algorithm can run in $O(n \log n)$ time (n is the number of vertices) if we sort vertices in G first according to their degree values. Moreover, it may be immediately shown that the algorithm can guarantee a detection of whether or not a graph is star-like. If a graph is star-like, then the algorithm outputs only one subgraph - the G itself. However, due to NP-hardness of the problem OGDP, the algorithm OGDP cannot guarantee the minimality of the decomposition.

3.3 Data Partition

Suppose that a graph partition has been done in Step 1 of TPPJ. Assume that $S = \{G_i : 1 \leq i \leq k\} \cup \{G_j : k+1 \leq j \leq q\}$ is a set of subgraphs obtained in Step 1 where for $1 \leq i \leq k$, G_i is star-like, and for $k + 1 \leq j \leq q$, G_j is a 2-graph. Moreover, assume that for $1 \leq i \leq k$, $v_{i,0}$ is the denoted peak vertex in G_i; that is, every pair of $v_{i,0}$ and $v_{j,0}$ are not adjacent. In step 2 we need to partition the data sets. As mentioned before, a data partition P should be compatible with every G_i and $v_{i,0}$ for $1 \leq i \leq k$, and with every G_j for $k + 1 \leq j \leq q$. That is, find a data partition P such that:

- for $1 \leq i \leq k$, every object from $v_{i,0}$ should be contained by one bucket in P and is allocated to that bucket; and

- every object from other data sets (vertices) will be allocated to the buckets which intersect the object (possibly with some duplications).

We use a similar idea as that in [10] to partition the data sets. Our algorithm is described below.

Step 2 - Data Partitioning

Step 2.1: Obtain an initial partition with m rectangle buckets.

Step 2.2: Allocate each object r from every $v_{i,0}$ for $1 \leq i \leq n$ in the following way:

- In case if there is a bucket containing r, allocate r to this bucket.

- If there is no bucket containing r, then get all buckets which intersects r. Then choose the one from those buckets to expand to contain r such that the resultant area of the new bucket after an expansion is minimum. Assign r to this new bucket; and use the new bucket to replace the old bucket and remove any other buckets which are contained by the new bucket.

Step 2.3: Assign each object from the other vertices to the buckets intersecting the object.

In data partition, we manage I/O as follows. We allocate one page for each bucket. Once a page is full, we write it back to the hard disk. To distinguish objects from different data sets, we partition data sets one by one; and the denoted peak vertices $v_{i,0}$ start before the other vertices.

3.4 Join and Partitioning Skew

In Step 3, we execute local joins for the sub-join graphs bucket by bucket. To save I/O costs, in step 3 the data in each bucket will be read in once only into the main memory to simultaneously execute the sub-joins. In our algorithm TPPJ, we implemented a variation of dynamic interval tree based plane-sweeping line technique [3, 19] to do local joins in each bucket.

While partition data, we can roughly estimate the smallest number of buckets we should have in order to make the data in each bucket fit in memory. Suppose the data size of each data set R_i is denoted by $\|R_i\|$ where R_i is a set of rectangles and their IDs, k is the number of subgraphs, β is a page size, and M is the available memory size. Then, we compute the minimum number m of buckets by the following formula:

$$m = \lceil \frac{\sum_{i=1}^{n} ||R_i||}{M - k\beta} \rceil \qquad (1)$$

As data objects may be duplicated into several buckets, a conservative way is to double the figure calculated from (1). A *partition skew* may still occur; that is, one bucket may have extremely large number of buckets. Though our current implementation of the algorithm does not incorporate any of partition skew resolution techniques, we feel that the technique of "sampling the data sets to get a good initial partition" [10] will be a good choice. It is possible that the partition skew may still exist after using this resolution technique. Consequently, the data in one bucket may not entirely fit in the memory. If this occurs, then the technique of dynamically repartitioning the overflow bucket [15] will be our next choice.

4 Experiment Results

We implemented our algorithm TPPJ on a PENTIUM III/700 running Linux 2.4.7 with 256 main memory and 12GB local disk access. We examined the efficiency and scalability of our algorithm against different data densities, different data sizes, different graph sizes, different graph densities, and different bucket numbers.

In our initial experiment, we down-loaded the two group of data sets from TIGER/LINE file [21], as illustrated in Figures 8 and 9. The 10 data sets in Figure 8 are the road segment and hydrograph data of different counties from Washington state, while the 10 data sets in Figure 9 are the road segment from California State. The data sets from CA have more objects but less density. Note that to implement joins, the data sets from different counties are mapped to the same center by a translation.

County (WA)	#obj	density	County (WA)	#obj	density
A: Chelan	14701	0.13	F: Lewis	18440	0.24
B: Clark	11062	0.14	G: Skagit	12264	0.18
C: Cowlitz	16395	0.20	H: Stevens	20193	0.17
D: Grays Harbor	13811	0.20	I: Thurston	11099	0.10
E: Kittitas	15761	0.16	J: Whatcom	11131	0.15

Figure 8. 10 Counties from Washington

County (CA)	#obj	density	County (CA)	#obj	density
A: Alameda	53490	0.10	F: Orange	108919	0.10
B: Contra Costa	44774	0.10	G: Riverside	114186	0.08
C: Fresno	66637	0.04	H: Sacramento	53466	0.07
D: Kern	120878	0.11	I: San Diego	123093	0.10
E: Monterey	39150	0.08	J: Santa Barbara	32493	0.06

Figure 9. 10 Counties from California State

Our experiment was based on 4 groups of query graphs as depicted in Figure 10. The graphs in Group 1 are very sparse. The graphs in Group 2 have a medium density. The graphs in Group 3 are complete bipartite graphs - the graphs with a high density, while the graphs in Group 4 are the complete graphs - graphs with the highest density.

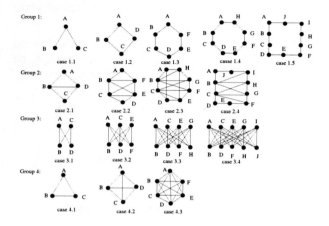

Figure 10. various query graphs

We also experimented the correlation between the number of buckets and the data sizes. As the number of buckets given in formula (1) provides only the basic requirement, there is a trade-off between the data partitioning overhead and local join costs. We implement the algorithm for 5 different bucket sizes, 256, 1024, 2304, 4096, and 5625. For each query graph, the average number of objects takes 15,000, 30,000, or more than 60,000. The average number of objects per set in the complete WA data in Figure 8 is about 15,000; and thus they are used in our experiment for the case of average 15,000 objects per data set. Figure 12 shows the experiment results. We then randomly choose 30,000 objects respectively from each CA data set; the experiment results are depicted in Figure 13 Finally, We use the first six complete CA data sets to implement TPPJ against the query graphs in group 4 where the average number of objects per data set is more than 60,000. For each query graph, the implementation of TPPJ has therefore done for each combination of an average data size and a bucket number.

From the experiment results, we can see a clear correlation between average data size and the number of buckets; that is, along with an increment of the data size, we should increase the number of buckets to achieve a fast response. The experiment results also suggest that our algorithm is quite scalable regarding the data size. An increment of query graph density does not seem to increase the join costs. Note that we did not provide experiment results against the situations when the number of buckets is 256 but the average number of data objects in each data set is at least 30,000; this is because the computation costs of using 256 buckets for large data volume are very high and we would like to concentrate on comparable costs.

5 Conclusion and Remarks

In this paper, we studied the problem of efficiently processing multi-way spatial join without presence of spatial index. We developed a novel graph partition based join algorithm TPPJ. The algorithm TPPJ involves a two-phase partitioning technique. Firstly, it divides the join graph into a set of subgraphs; and secondly it partitions the data space. Then in TPPJ, we run local joins in each bucket by reading data only once. Finally, the sub-join results against the subgraphs are joined together by a relational multi-way join.

In TPPJ, we also investigated a novel optimisation problem of graph partitioning. Our results include the complexity of the problem, as well as an approximate algorithm. Note that our graph partitioning paradigm may also be a necessary pre-process for applying S^3J to multi-way spatial joins. As one of our future work, we would like to implement this idea and compare it with TPPJ. Another future work is to investigate the situation where the data sets are partially indexed; that is, some data sets are indexed while the others are not.

References

[1] L. Arge, O. Procopiuc, S. Ramaswamy, T. Suel, J. S. Vitter, "Scalable Sweeping-Based Spatial Join", *VLDB'98*, 1998.

[2] T. Brinkhoff, H. Kriegel, B. Seeger, "Efficient Processing of Spatial Joins Using R-trees", *ACM SIGMOD'93*, 1993.

[3] T.H. Cormen, C.E. Leiserson, and R. L. Rivest, *Introduction to Algorithms*, MIT press, 1990.

[4] M.R. Garey and D.S. Johnson, *Computers and Intractability: a guide to the theory of the NP-Completeness*, Freeman, New York, 1979.

[5] A, Guttman. "R Trees: A Dynamic Index Structure For Spatial Searching", *ACM SIGMOD'84*, 1984.

[6] G. R. Hjaltason and H. Samet, "Incremental Distance Join Algorithms for Spatial Databases", *SIGMOD'98*, 237-248, 1998.

[7] N. Koudas, K. Sevcik, "Size Separation Spatial Join", *ACM SIGMOD'97*, 1997.

[8] X. Lin, H.X. Lu, and Q. Zhang, "Graph Partition Based Multi-Way Spatial Joins", *full paper*, 2001.

[9] M.L. Lo and C. V. Ravishankar, "Spatial Joins Using Seeded Trees", *ACM SIGMOD'94*, 1994.

[10] M.L. Lo and C.V. Ravishankar, "Spatial Hash Joins", *ACM SIGMOD'96*, 1996.

[11] P. Mishra and M.H. Eich. "Join processing in relational database", *ACM Computing Surveys*, 24(1):64-113, March 1992.

[12] N. Mamoulis, D. Papadias, "Integration of Spatial Join Algorithms for Processing Multiple Inputs", *ACM SIGMOD'99*, 1999.

[13] J. Orenstein, "Spatial Query Processing in an object-Oriented Database System", *ACM SIGMOD'86*, 326-336, 1986.

[14] J. Orenstein, "A comparison of spatial query processing techniques for native and parameter spaces", *ACM SIGMOD'90*, 343-352, 1990.

[15] J.M Patel, D.J. DeWitt, "Partition Based Spatial-Merge Join", *ACM SIGMOD'96*, 1996.

[16] D. Papadias, N. Mamoulis, and B. Delis, "Algorithms for Querying by Spatial Structure", *VLDB'98*, 1998.

[17] D. Papadias, N. Mamoulis, and Y. Theodoridis, "Processing and Optimisation of Multi-way Spatial Joins Using R-trees", *ACM PODS'99*, 1999.

[18] H. Park, G. Cha, and C. Chung, "Multi-way Spatial Joins Using R-Trees: Methodology and Performance Evaluation", *SSD'99*, LNCS 1651, Springer-Verlag, 229-250, 1999.

[19] F. Preparata and M. Shamos, *Computational Geometry*, Springer-Verlag, 1988.

[20] K. C. Sevcik and N. Koudas, "Filter Trees for Managing Spatial Over a Range of Size Granularities", *VLDB'96*, 16-27, 1996.

[21] "Tiger/Line files (Redestricting Census) (tm). 2000", Technical Report, U.S. Bureau of the Census, 2000.

[22] H. Zhu, J. Su, and O. Ibarra, "On Multi-Way Spatial Joins with Direction Predicates, *SSTD'01*, LLNCS 2121, Springer-Verlag, 217-235, 2001.

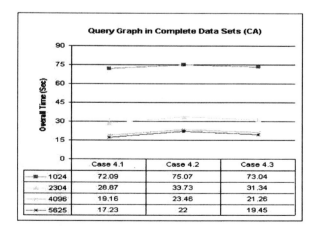

Figure 11. average more than 60,000 objects per data set

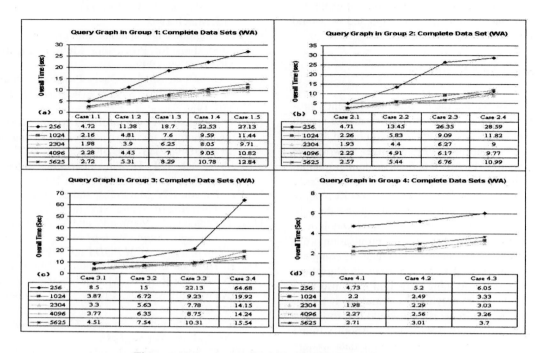

The following data tables appear within the figure:

Query Graph in Group 1: Complete Data Sets (WA)

	Case 1.1	Case 1.2	Case 1.3	Case 1.4	Case 1.5
256	4.72	11.38	18.7	22.53	27.13
1024	2.16	4.81	7.6	9.59	11.44
2304	1.98	3.9	6.25	8.05	9.71
4096	2.28	4.45	7	9.05	10.82
5625	2.72	5.31	8.29	10.78	12.84

Query Graph in Group 2: Complete Data Set (WA)

	Case 2.1	Case 2.2	Case 2.3	Case 2.4
256	4.71	13.45	26.35	28.59
1024	2.26	5.83	9.09	11.82
2304	1.93	4.4	6.27	9
4096	2.22	4.91	6.17	9.77
5625	2.57	5.44	6.76	10.99

Query Graph in Group 3: Complete Data Sets (WA)

	Case 3.1	Case 3.2	Case 3.3	Case 3.4
256	8.5	15	22.13	64.68
1024	3.87	6.72	9.23	19.92
2304	3.3	5.63	7.78	14.15
4096	3.77	6.35	8.75	14.24
5625	4.51	7.54	10.31	15.54

Query Graph in Group 4: Complete Data Sets (WA)

	Case 4.1	Case 4.2	Case 4.3
256	4.73	5.2	6.05
1024	2.2	2.49	3.33
2304	1.98	2.29	3.03
4096	2.27	2.56	3.26
5625	2.71	3.01	3.7

Figure 12. average 15,000 objects per data set

View Merging in the Context of View Selection

Changqing Chen
Computer Science Department
Huazhong University of Sci. & Tech.
Wuhan 430074, Hubei, China
ccqcl@263.net

Yucai Feng
Computer Science Department
Huazhong University of Sci. & Tech.
Wuhan 430074, Hubei, China
fyc@dm2.com.cn

Jianlin Feng
Computer Science Department
Huazhong University of Sci. & Tech.
Wuhan 430074, Hubei, China
jlfeng@public.wuhan.cngb.com

Abstract

Materialized views can provide massive improvements in query processing time, especially for aggregation queries over large tables. To achieve the potential of materialized views, we must determine what views to materialize. An important issue in view selection is view merging. View merging can take a set of candidate views generated by analyzing queries in a workload, and produce a set of merged views by exploiting commonality among those queries. View merging can efficiently reduce candidate views for view selection. In this paper we present a merging tree, as well as a fast and scalable algorithm for view merging based on such a tree. The merging tree can significantly reduce the search space of potential views to be merged. Our approach is more scalable than the alternative of sequentially merging all pairs of views every time.

1. Introduction

The presence of the right materialized views can significantly improve performance, particularly for decision support applications. To achieve the potential of materialized views, we must determine what views to materialize for a given set of queries. Many database systems contain hundreds, even thousands, of tables. Such databases may have hundreds of materialized views. A smart system might also cache and reuse results of previously computed queries. Cached results can be viewed as temporary materialized views, easily resulting in thousands of materialized views. In fact, materializing all queries is not always a possible solution because of the constraint of storage space.

Most previous papers on view selection focus only on the "exploration" problem of picking an interesting set of materialized views from a given set [7,9,10,11,14]. Thus, they implicitly assume that the given set is the set of all potentially interesting materialized views for the workload of queries. Due to this assumption, such an approach is not scalable in the context of large amounts of queries. We therefore need innovative techniques to deal with the large space of potentially interesting materialized views that are possible for a given set of queries.

We observed that if materialized views are selected without view merging, we may make sub-optimal choice for the workload. The following example 1 from the TPC-H benchmark illustrates such a case. This observation suggests that we need to consider those materialized views which although are not optimal for any individual query, but useful for multiple queries at the same time, and therefore may be optimal for the workload.

Example 1:

```
select   p_type, p_mfgr, count(*) as cnt,
         sum(p_retailprice) as sum_retail_price
from     part
where    p_size between <size1> and <size2>
group by p_type, p_mfgr
```

Assume we have 50 queries of such form, and each query has different constants for size1 and size2. We can merge these views to a single view as follows:

```
select   p_size, p_type, p_mfgr, count(*) as cnt,
         sum(p_retailprice) as sum_retail_price
from     part
group by p_size, p_type, p_mfgr
```

This can efficiently reduce the search space when using views to answer queries, and therefore the cost for the whole workload.

There are two important issues in view merging: one is to determine what kinds of views to merge and how to merge them, another is characterizing the space of views to be merged. Because views (unlike indexes) are multi-table structures that may contain selections, group-bys and aggregations, the algorithm for merging views is significantly different from that for merging indexes in [5]. There could be a large number of potential views to be merged, particularly for complex and large workloads, so an effective approach is needed to reduce the search space of potentially mergable views. Our approach addressed the above two issues in view merging and it is more scalable than the alternative of sequentially merging all pairs of views each time. We explore the search space using a merging tree. The merging tree is an index for view descriptions (not for actual view data). It is similar to the filter tree in [8], but they have different index conditions and the architecture of the two trees is also different.

The main contributions of this paper are as follows. First we present an efficient view merging algorithm. Second a merging tree is presented to quickly determine a small set of potential views on which view merging can be applied. View merging can be combined into a view selection algorithm, as part of view selection to efficiently improve selection quality. In fact it can also be used in the context of caching and reusing results of previously computed queries.

The rest of the paper is organized as follows. In section 2 we present the problem definition of view merging. Section 3 describes how to generate a set of merged views. Experiments are presented in section 4. Section 5 presents related work and section 6 gives conclusions.

2. Problem definition

In this paper we deal with the views that are defined by a single-block SQL statement containing selections, (inner) joins, and an optimal group-by. The views are based on bag semantics and subqueries are not allowed in a view. Views with selection-projection-join expressions are SPJ views and SPJG views involve aggregation functions and group by clauses as well. For simplicity, we only consider simple columns in the output list and the group by clause. For a SPJG view, its output list must contain a count(*) column so deletions can be handled incrementally. Other aggregation functions currently allowed are sum, min, max and avg. An aggregated column in the aggregation function is a simple column too. Because all simple columns in the output list of a SPJG view are used as a primary key, so they should be equal to the grouping columns, and this is necessary to guarantee that aggregation views can be updated incrementally.

We begin from a set of syntactically relevant materialized views V generated by analyzing a workload of queries Q. For a query q in Q, we propose: (1) a materialized view on a subset S of the tables of q containing join and selection conditions in q on S. (2) If q has grouping columns, then a materialized view similar to (1) but also containing grouping columns and aggregation expressions from q on S. It is also possible to propose additional materialized views that include a subset of the selection conditions or a superset of group by columns in q, since such views may also apply to other queries in the workload. However, in our approach, this aspect of exploiting commonality across queries in the workload is handled via view merging. We merge those initial views in V by exploiting commonality among them. The newly generated set of merged views, along with other views in V, are our candidate materialized views for further selection.

Given two views v_1 and v_2, referred to as the parent views, we now define what it means to merge two views. Our goal when merging v_1 and v_2 is to generate a new view v_{12}, called the *merged* view, which has the following two properties. First, all queries that can be answered using either of the parent views should be answerable only using the merged view. Second, the size of the merged view should not be larger than the sum of the size of v_1 and v_2. We use $|v|$ to represent the size of a view v. A view with disjunctive conditions is not considered in this paper.

Definition 1. *Merging a pair of views.* Two views v_1 and v_2 are said to be merged to form the view v_{12}, if (a) v_1 and v_2 have the same tables and the same equi-join conditions, (b) v_{12} contains all the output columns of v_1 and v_2, eliminating duplicate and (c) $|v_{12}|$ is not larger than the sum of $|v_1|$ and $|v_2|$.

By an iteration of the above merging, until no pair of views in the set can be merged, we will get the merged set of views. We now state the view merging problem:

Definition 2. *View merging problem.* Given a workload of queries Q = {q_1, q_2, ... q_P} and a corresponding initial set of syntactically relevant views V = {v_1, v_2, ...v_N}, V' is said to be a merged set with respect to the initial set V, if no views in V' can be merged by Definition 1.

3. Merging views

Considering the set of syntactically relevant materialized views V, we describe how to merge two views by Definition 1, and how to quickly and efficiently generate a set of merged views by a merging tree. A merging tree is an index for view descriptions which can be used to fast narrowing the search space of potential views to be merged. We present the merging algorithm for views, where the selection conditions are conjunctions of simple predicates. The algorithm can be extended to handle views with complex selection conditions. Section 3.1 deals with merging two views by range constraints. We describe a merging tree in section 3.2. Generating a set of merged views by the merging tree is presented in section 3.3.

3.1 Merging two views by range constraints

Obviously, if two views have an adjacent or overlapped range on one column and the same ranges on other columns, and the same output, they will be merged by Definition 1. We describe the tests applied to determine whether two views can be merged by such conditions, and if they can, how to merge them. This algorithm is called MVR (Merging two Views by Range constraints). We use these restricted conditions due to the space constraint of Definition 1. Using weaker conditions to merge two views is also discussed.

For simplicity, we assume that the WHERE clause has been converted into conjunctive normal form (CNF) and denoted by Conds(v). We divide the predicates in Conds(v) into two components *PE(v)* and *PR(v)*. *PE(v)* consists of all column equality predicates, and *PR(v)* contains all range predicates. A column equality predicate is any atomic predicate of the form $(R_i.C_p = R_j.C_r)$, where Cp and Cr are column references, and R_i and R_j are tables. A range predicate is any atomic predicate of the form $(R_j.C_r \ op \ c)$ where c is a constant and op is one of the operators "<", "≤", "=", "≥", ">".

A column equivalence class is a set of columns that are known to be equal. Based on the column equality predicates in PE, we can compute a set of equivalence classes using the same approach in [8]. A trivial equivalence class consists of a single column.

For two views v_1 and v_2, we first test if they reference the same tables and this test is direct. For other tests, we exploit column equivalences. We divide $Conds(v_1)$ into $PE(v_1)$ and $PR(v_1)$, and $Conds(v_2)$ into $PE(v_2)$ and $PR(v_2)$. Then we test if $PE(v_1)$ is equal to $PE(v_2)$, this is the equality predicate equivalence test. The range constraints of the two views should be the same except they are adjacent or overlapped on only one column, and this is the range test. To do this test, we further divide $PR(v_1)$ into $PR'(v_1)$ and $PR''(v_1)$, and $PR(v_2)$ into $PR'(v_2)$ and $PR''(v_2)$. $PR'(v_1)$ contains range predicates on only one column, which is adjacent or overlapped with $PR'(v_2)$ on the same column of v_2. $PR''(v_1)$ includes range predicates on other columns which is the same as that of $PR''(v_2)$. Formally we apply the following two tests:

Equality predicate equivalence test

$(PE(v_1) \Leftrightarrow PE(v_2))$

Range test

$(PE(v_1) \wedge PR''(v_1) \Leftrightarrow PE(v_2) \wedge PR''(v_2))$

$(PE(v_1) \wedge PR'(v_1) \ adj \ PE(v_2) \wedge PR'(v_2))$

Because of the column equality predicates, some columns are interchangeable in the PR predicates and the output columns. This ability will be useful to all tests later. After the equality predicate equivalence test has passed, $PR''(v_1)$ and $PR''(v_2)$ must be the same on the same equivalence class, in the meantime $PR'(v_1)$ and $PR'(v_2)$ are adjacent or overlapped on only one equivalence class. "adj" means two ranges are adjacent or overlapped. $(A \Leftrightarrow B)$ means A is equal to B and vice versa. The following tests are similar to that in [8], but the matching conditions are different.

Equality predicate equivalence test.

The equality predicate equivalence test amounts to requiring that all columns equal in the view v_1 must also be equal in the view v_2 (and vice versa). We implement this test by first computing column equivalence classes, both for v_1 and v_2, and then checking whether every nontrivial equivalence class of v_1 is equal to some equivalence class of v_2, and vice versa. Just checking that all column equality predicates in v_1 also exist in v_2 (and vice versa) is a much weaker test because of transitivity among columns. The effect of transitivity is correctly captured by using equivalence classes.

Range test.

We associate with equivalence classes, including trivial classes, in the view v_1 and v_2, a range that specifies a lower and upper bound on the columns in the equivalence class by the range predicates. The two views cannot be merged if their range constraints do not satisfy the following condition: their range constraints are adjacent or overlapped on only one equivalence class and on other equivalence classes are the same. This means the equivalence classes referenced by the range predicates of v_1 and v_2 must be the same at first. To check this condition, we consider each equivalence class in v_1 with range, find the matching equivalence class in v_2, and check whether their ranges are equivalent or adjacent or overlapped. So does to the equivalence classes in v_2. In this paper we only support the following data types to test adjacency or overlap: integer and date. If the above condition is not satisfied, the view v2 is rejected.

After the above two tests, we need to check whether all output columns of v_2 are the same as those of v_1 under column equivalence classes. This condition is to satisfy the storage constraint. If the output column of v_2 is a simple column reference, check whether it can be mapped (using equivalence classes) to an output column of v_1. For aggregation function columns of v_2, we check whether the output of v_1 contains exactly the same expression (taking into account column equivalences for an aggregated column in the function). We also need to check whether all output columns of v_1 are equivalent to those of v_2.

If all these tests passed, we will get the merged view satisfied Definition 1. The merged view is the same as the view v_1 except for the merged ranged predicates. The following example 2 illustrates how to merge two views by an adjacent or overlapped range constraint:

Example 2:

v_1:

Select   l_partkey, p_size
From   lineitem, part
Where   l_partkey = p_partkey
  and   l_partkey >= 150 and p_size = 1

v_2:

Select   p_partkey, p_size
From   lineitem, part
Where   l_partkey = p_partkey
  and   p_partkey >= 100 and p_partkey <= 160
  and   p_size = 1

Step 1: Compute equivalence classes.
Equivalence classes for view v_1: {l_partkey, p_partkey}
Equivalence classes for view v_2: {l_partkey, p_partkey}

Step 2: Check view equivalence classes equivalent.
The equivalence classes of v_1 are exactly equivalent to that of v_2, and vice versa.

Step 3: Compute ranges.
Ranges for v_1: {l_partkey, p_partkey} $\in$ (150, +∞),
          {p_size} $\in$ (1, 1).
Ranges for v_2: {l_partkey, p_partkey} $\in$ (100, 160).
          {p_size} $\in$ (1, 1).

Step 4: Check ranges.
The range (1,1) on {p_size} is equivalent. The range (100,

160) on {l_partkey, p_partkey} is overlapped with (150, +∞), so we merge the range to (100, +∞), and get the predicate ({l_partkey, p_partkey} >= 100).

Step 5: Check output columns.
The output columns of v_1 are exactly equivalent to that of v_2, and vice versa, under equivalence classes.

Because v_1 and v_2 passed all the tests, so we conclude that they can be merged. The merged predicates that must be applied to the merged view is {l_partkey, p_partkey} >= 100. The notation {l_partkey, p_partkey} means that we can choose either l_partkey or p_partkey. The merged view v_{12} below is just like v_1 except for the merged predicate.

v_{12}:

Select   l_partkey, p_size
From   lineitem, part
Where   l_partkey = p_partkey
  and   l_partkey >= 100 and p_size = 1

We note that if the lower and upper bound of a merged range constraint are the minimum and maximum value of the column domain separately, then we can delete this range constraint. If the column is not an output, we add it to the output list, and to the group clause for a SPJG view. Example 1 is such a case. In this case, the space of the merged view will increase by some percent but the number of views is reduced.

One extension of the algorithm MVR is that $PR(v_1)$ and $PR(v_2)$ can be adjacent or overlapped on more than one equivalence class, and the output columns of v_1 and v_2 need not to be equal. This means we construct a view v_{12} by taking the union of output columns of v_1 and v_2 and the union of grouping columns of v_1 and v_2 if they are SPJG views, eliminating the duplicate columns. If $|v_{12}|$ is larger than the sum of $|v1|$ and $|v_2|$, the merge fails. We note that this requires estimating the size of a materialized view. One way is to estimate by the query optimizer. Alternatively, less expensive heuristic techniques have been proposed in [15] for more restricted multidimensional scenarios. The following example 3 illustrates such an extension.

Example 3:

v_1:

Select   l_partkey, l_shipdate, count(*) as cnt,
           sum(l_quantity) as sum_qty
From   lineitem, part
Where   l_partkey = p_partkey
    and   l_partkey >= 150 and l_shipdate>'19970101'

v_2:

Select   p_partkey, l_shipdate, count(*) as cnt,
           sum(p_retailprice) as sum_retail_price
From   lineitem, part
Where   l_partkey = p_partkey
    and   p_partkey >= 100 and l_shipdate>'19980101'

v_{12}:

Select   l_partkey, l_shipdate, count(*) as cnt,
           sum(l_quantity) as sum_qty, sum(p_retailprice)
           as sum_retail_price
From   lineitem, part
Where   l_partkey = p_partkey
    and   l_partkey >= 100 and l_shipdate>'19970101'

3.2 A Merging Tree

To speed up view merging we maintain in memory a description of every materialized view. The view descriptions contain all information needed to apply the tests described in the above subsection. Even so, it is still slow to apply the tests to all pairs of views each time if the number of views is very large. Now we describe an in-memory index, called a *merging tree*, which allows us to quickly partition views that may be merged.

A merging tree is a multiway search tree where all the leaves are on the same level. A node in the tree contains a collection of (key, d-pointer, h-pointer). A key consists of a set of values, not just a single value. A d-pointer in an

internal node points to a node at the next level. An h-pointer points to a node in the same level, which has a different condition at this level but the same conditions at the former levels. A d-pointer in a leaf node points to a list of view descriptions. The following Figure 1 is an example of the merging tree.

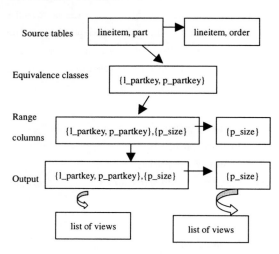

Figure1: A merging tree

A merging tree recursively subdivides the set of views into smaller and smaller non-overlapping partitions. At each level, a different partitioning condition is applied. The partition conditions used in our prototype are described as follows.

Source table condition: A view v_2 cannot be merged with a view v_1 unless the source tables of v_2 are the same as those of v_1.

Column equivalence class condition: A view v_2 cannot be merged with a view v_1 unless v_2's equivalence class list is equal to that of v_1.

We associate with each view a range constraint column list, where each entry references a column equivalence class. A column equivalence class is included in the list if it has a constrained range, that is, at least one of the bounds has been set. We now state the condition that must hold.

Range constraint column condition: A view v_2 cannot be merged with a view v_1 unless v_2's range constraint column list is equal to that of v_1 under equivalence classes.

As stated in section 2, the simple output columns are equal to the grouping columns for a SPJG view, so we do not consider grouping columns as a partition condition. SPJG views and SPJ views are differentiated by the following condition.

Aggregation function column condition: A view v_2 cannot be merged with a view v_1 by an adjacent or overlapped range constraint unless v_2's aggregation function list is equal to that of v_1.

We take into account column equivalences on the view and replace each column in the output list by a reference to the column equivalence class. We now state the condition that must hold.

Simple output column condition: A view v_2 cannot be merged with a view v_1 by an adjacent or overlapped range constraint unless the simple output list of v_2 is equal to that of v_1 under equivalence classes.

3.3 Algorithm for generating a set of merged views

Obviously, it is not scalable to compare each pair of views every time to generate a set of merged views. We use the merging tree to efficiently reduce the search space of potentially mergable views. When recursively going down the merging tree and arriving at each leaf node, the views reference the same conditions about source tables, equivalence class list, range constraint column list and simple output column list in a leaf node. For SPJG views, there is an additional aggregation function list. Along d_pointer in the leaf node, which points to a list of view descriptions, we compare one view by one view sequently,

calling MVR, to find if two views can be merged. This process needs a loop until no pair of view can be merged. When two views are merged, they need not to be merged with other views and are deleted at once. By the merging tree, we only consider merging each pair of views in the same leaf node, not between leaf nodes. If the lower and upper bound of a merged range constraint are the minimum and maximum value of the column domain separately, we can delete this range constraint, add the corresponding column to the output, and reinsert the view. If the leaf node has been tested, it needs to be tested again after a new view inserted.

1.	Construct a merging tree for a given set of views V
2.	Recursively go down the merging tree to each leaf node with a set of views N.
3.	While ($|N| > 1$)
4.	If no pair of views to be merged Break
5.	else let v_{12} is a merged view by calling MVR based on its parent views v_1 and v_2 Add v_{12} to N and remove v_1 and v_2 from N
6.	End If
7.	End While
8.	Adjust the merged views, deleting the range column on which the range constraints are merged and its lower and upper bound are the minimum and maximum of the column domain , then add the column to the output and reinsert the view.
9.	Return (all views in the leaf node of the merging tree).

Figure 2: Algorithm GMV for generating a set of merged views

Our algorithm GMV (Generating a set of Merged Views) is shown in Figure 2, exploiting a merging tree. We comment on several properties of the algorithm. First, note that it is possible for a merged view generated in Step 5 to be merged again in a subsequent iteration (Steps 3-7). This allows more than two views in V to be combined into one merged view even though the merge operates on only two views each time. Second, the search space of potential views to be merged is substantially reduced based on the merging tree. Third the output of this algorithm is relevant to the order of views. For example, if v_2 is adjacent with v_1 on one columns and adjacent with v_3 on another column, then the output is $\{v_{12}, v_3\}$ or $\{v_{23}, v_1\}$. An optimal output is our further work.

4. Experiments

We have implemented the view merging algorithm presented in this paper on Microsoft SQL Server 2000. Our goal was to keep the merging time low, even when the number of materialized views is high. We ran a series of experiments that measured the increase in merging time and the benefits of using the merging tree. We demonstrate that: (1) The time of merging views increases with the number of views but remains low even up to one thousand, for the merging tree substantially reducing the space that need to be tested. (2) The application of our view merging algorithm generates more compact recommendations.

We generated a set of SPJ and SPJG views syntactically relevant to a workload of queries over the TPC-H/R database, as stated in section 2. Queries used in our experiments have the following properties: 15% of the queries referenced one tables, 20% referenced two tables, 30% referenced three tables, 25% referenced four tables and 10% referenced five tables. The cardinality of the result is restricted to within 5-20% of the largest table used in the query. We generated a total of 1000 materialized views. The experiments were run on a machine with 550 Mhz CPU and 128 MB RAM. The database was TPC-H at scale factor 1 (1GB).

Figure 3 shows the total merging time for the varying number of materialized views up to 1000. The lower line was measured by the algorithm GMV using the merging tree. The merging time increases linearly with the number of views. The upper line shows the merging time by

sequentially merge without the merging tree. We observe that using the merging tree to merge views can significantly reduce the merging time. With 1000 views, the merging time increases by about 50% when the merging tree is disabled.

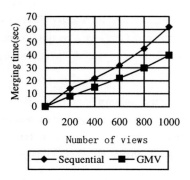

Figure 3: Merging time with the number of views

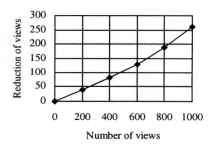

Figure 4: No of views reduced increasing linely

Figure 4 plots how many views are reduced by merging views. We carry out this comparison for different number of views. The views reduced increases linearly with the number of views. Our algorithm achieves the significant reduction of the space of views to recommend.

5. Related Work

The work reported in this paper is mainly inspired by view merging proposed in [1] and a filter tree proposed in

[8]. Rarely papers consider the issue of view merging in the view selection problem. Agrawal et al. [1] present an approach how to prepare candidate views for view selection and give an algorithm to merge a set of SPJG views to reduce recommended views. The merging algorithm in [1] is to sequentially merge all pairs of views every time. They prune syntactically relevant materialized views before merging. In this paper we concentrate on how to merge views and use a merging tree to efficiently narrow the search space of potentially mergable views. Furthermore, we use equivalence classes similar to [8] to match different conditions, not just syntactically match.

Goldstein and Larson [8] describe an algorithm for rewriting queries using views. The key novelty in this work is the filter-tree, an index structure that makes it possible to efficiently filter the set of views that are relevant to a particular SPJG expression. The index is composed of several sub-indexes in a hierarchical fashion. Each sub-index is built on a partition condition of the views (e.g., the set of tables in the view, the set of output columns), and further partitions the views according to another condition. A filter tree is used to test subsumption, however a merging tree is mainly used to test equivalence. So a merging tree is similar to the filter tree, but they have different partitioning conditions for each level and the architecture of them is also different.

Lehner et al. [12] gave an approach to generate common sub-expressions for a given set of related views, considering different predicates, grouping expressions, and sets of base tables. Their approach can only be used for a small set of views. The work by [4] selects materialized views by examining the query plans in the context of SQL workloads. However it is not scalable for large workloads.

Baralis et al. [2] considered materialized views that exactly match queries in the workload, as well as a set of additional views that can leverage commonality among queries in the workload. Our technique for exploiting commonality among queries in the workload is different.

Some papers also gave formal descriptions for view

selection. Chirkova et al. [3] gave a formal perspective on the view selection problem and pointed out the quality of the size estimator function plays a crucial role in the complexity of the view selection. Theodoratos et al. [6] gave a general framework for the view selection problem for data warehousing and evolution.

6. Conclusions

In this paper we mainly focus on view merging. We present a merging tree and a fast and scalable algorithm for view merging based on this tree. The merging tree can significantly reduce the search space of potential views to be merged. Our approach is significantly more scalable than the alternative of sequentially merging all pairs of views every time. View merging can be a useful tool in view selection to improve quality. It can also be used in the context of cached query results. After view merging, views can be further pruned by different design goals such as the minimization the query evaluation cost, the constraint of the storage space.

This algorithm can be extended to deal with two views with just the same base tables and the same join conditions. It can also be extended to deal with views with extra tables having lossless joins.

References

[1] S. Agrawal, S. Chaudhuri, V. R. Narasayya, Automated Selection of Materialized Views and Indexes in SQL Databases, VLDB 2000, 496-505.

[2] E. Baralis, S. Paraboschi, and E. Teniente, Materialized views selection in a multidimensional database, VLDB 1997, 156-165.

[3] R. Chirkova, A. Halevy, and D. Suciu, A formal perspective on the view selection problem. In Proc. of VLDB 2001, 59-68.

[4] J. Yang, K. Karlapalem, and Q. Li, Algorithms for materialized view design in data warehousing environment, VLDB 1997, 136-145.

[5] S. Chaudhuri, V. Narasayya, Index Merging, ICDE 1999, 296-303.

[6] D. Theodoratos, M. Bouzeghoub, A General Framework for the View Selection Problem for Data Warehouse Design and Evolution, DOLAP 2000, 1-8.

[7] H. Gupta, V. Harinarayan, A. Rajaraman, and J. D. Ullman, Index selection for OLAP, ICDE 1997, 208-219.

[8] J. Goldstein and P. Larson, Optimizing queries using materialized views: a practical, scalable solution. SIGMOD 2001, 331-342.

[9] H. Gupta and I. S. Mumick, Selection of views to materialize under a maintenance cost constraint, ICDT 1999, 453-470.

[10] H. Gupta, Selection of views to materialize in a data warehouse, ICDT 1997, 98-112.

[11] V. Harinarayan, A. Rajaraman, and J. D. Ullman, Implementing data cubes efficiently, SIGMOD 1996, 205-216.

[12] W. Lehner, B. Cochrane, H. Pirahesh, fAST Refresh using Mass Query Optimization, ICDE 2001, 391-398.

[13] D. Srivastava, S. Dar, H.V. Jagadish, A. Levy, Answering Queries with Aggregation Using Views, VLDB 1996, 318-329.

[14] A. Shukla, P.M. Deshpande, J.F. Naughton, Materialized View Selection for Multidimensional Datasets, VLDB 1998, 488-498.

[15] A. Shukla, P.M. Deshpande, J.F. Naughton, K. Ramaswamy, Storage Estimation for Multidimensional Aggregates in the Presence of Hierarchies, VLDB 1996, 522-531.

Paper Session II

(Mobile Data)

Nearest Neighbor and Reverse Nearest Neighbor Queries for Moving Objects

Rimantas Benetis   Christian S. Jensen   Gytis Karčiauskas   Simonas Šaltenis

Department of Computer Science
Aalborg University
DK-9220 Aalborg Øst, DENMARK
{rbenetis,csj,gytis,simas}@cs.auc.dk

Abstract

With the proliferation of wireless communications and the rapid advances in technologies for tracking the positions of continuously moving objects, algorithms for efficiently answering queries about large numbers of moving objects increasingly are needed. One such query is the reverse nearest neighbor (RNN) query that returns the objects that have a query object as their closest object. While algorithms have been proposed that compute RNN queries for non-moving objects, there have been no proposals for answering RNN queries for continuously moving objects. Another such query is the nearest neighbor (NN) query, which has been studied extensively and in many contexts. Like the RNN query, the NN query has not been explored for moving query and data points.

This paper proposes an algorithm for answering RNN queries for continuously moving points in the plane. As a part of the solution to this problem and as a separate contribution, an algorithm for answering NN queries for continuously moving points is also proposed. The results of performance experiments are reported.

1 Introduction

We are currently experiencing rapid developments in key technology areas that combine to promise widespread use of mobile, personal information appliances, most of which will be on-line, i.e., on the Internet. Industry analysts uniformly predict that wireless, mobile Internet terminals will outnumber the desktop computers on the Internet.

This proliferation of devices offers companies the opportunity to provide a diverse range of e-services, many of which will exploit knowledge of the user's changing location. Location awareness is enabled by a combination of political developments, e.g., the de-scrambling of the GPS signals and the US E911 mandate, and the continued ad-vances in both infrastructure-based and handset-based positioning technologies.

The area of location-based games offers good examples of services where the positions of the mobile users play a central role. In the recently released BotFighters game, by Swedish company It's Alive, players get points for finding and "shooting"other players via their mobile phones. Only players close by can be shot. In such mixed-reality games, the real physical world becomes the backdrop of the game, instead of the world created on the limited displays of wireless devices [5].

To track and coordinate large numbers of continuously moving objects, their positions are stored in databases. Here, the conventional assumption, that data remains constant unless it is explicitly modified, no longer holds. An update is needed when the real position of an object deviates from that stored in the database by an application-dependent threshold. Modeling the position of an object as a static point either leads to very frequent updates or a very outdated database. To reduce the amount of updates needed, the positions of moving point objects have instead been modeled as functions of time. This makes the recorded positions more resilient to object movement, so that they may be expected to approximately capture the actual positions for longer time periods.

We consider the computation of nearest neighbor (*NN*) and reverse nearest neighbor (*RNN*) queries in this setting. In the *NN* problem, which has been investigated extensively in other settings, the objects in the database that are nearer to a given query object than any other objects in the database have to be found. In the *RNN* problem, which is new and largely unexplored, objects that have the query object as their nearest neighbor have to be found. In the example to the left in Figure 1, the *RNN* query for point 1 returns points 2 and 5. Points 3 and 4 are not returned because they have each other as their nearest neighbors. Note that even though point 2 is not a nearest neighbor of point 1, point 2 is the reverse nearest neighbor of point 1 because point 1 is the closest to point 2.

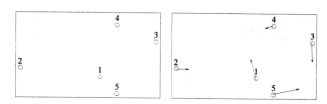

Figure 1. Static and Moving Points

A straightforward solution to computing reverse nearest neighbor (RNN) queries is to check for each point whether it has a given query point as its nearest neighbor. However, this approach is unacceptable when the number of points is large.

The situation is complicated further when the query and data points are moving rather than static and we want to know the reverse nearest neighbors during some time interval. For example, if points are moving as depicted to the right in Figure 1, then after some time, point 4 becomes a reverse nearest neighbor of point 1, and point 3 becomes a nearest neighbor of point 5, meaning that point 5 is no longer a reverse nearest neighbor of point 1.

Reverse nearest neighbors can be useful in applications where moving objects agree to provide some kind of service to each other. Whenever a service is needed an object requests it from its nearest neighbor. An object then may need to know how many objects it is supposed to serve in the near future and where those objects are. The examples of moving objects could be soldiers in a battlefield, tourists in dangerous environments, or mobile communication devices in wireless ad-hoc networks. In mixed-reality games like the one mentioned earlier, players may be "shooting" their nearest neighbors. Then a player may be interested to know who are her reverse nearest neighbors in order to dodge their fire.

There are proposed solutions for efficiently answering reverse nearest neighbor queries for non-moving points [12, 23, 25], but we are not aware of any algorithms for moving points. While much work has been conducted on algorithms for nearest neighbor queries, we are aware of only one work that has explored algorithms for a moving query point and static data points [22] and of no solutions for moving data and query points in two or higher dimensional space.

This paper proposes an algorithm that efficiently computes RNN queries for a query point during a specified time interval assuming the query and data points are continuously moving in the plane. As a solution to a subproblem, an algorithm for answering NN queries for continuously moving points is also proposed.

In the next section, the problem addressed by the paper is defined and related work is covered in further detail. In Section 3 our algorithms are presented. In Section 4 the results of the experiments are given, and Section 5 offers a

summary and directions for future research.

2 Problem Statement and Related Work

We first describe the data and queries that are considered in this paper. Then we survey the existing solutions to the most related problems.

2.1 Problem Statement

We consider two-dimensional space and model the positions of two-dimensional moving points as linear functions of time. That is, if at time t_0 the coordinates of a point are (x, y) and its velocity vector is $\bar{v} = (v_x, v_y)$, then it is assumed that at any time $t \geq t_0$ the coordinates of the point will be $(x + (t - t_0)v_x, y + (t - t_0)v_y)$, unless a new (position, velocity) pair for the point is reported.

With this assumption, the nearest neighbor (NN) and reverse nearest neighbor (RNN) query problems for continuously moving points in the plane can be formulated as follows.

Assume (1) a set S of moving points, where each point is specified by its coordinates (x, y) and its velocity vector (v_x, v_y) at some specific time; (2) a query point $q \in S$; and (3) a query time interval $[t^\vdash; t^\dashv]$, where $t^\vdash \geq t_{current}$, and $t_{current}$ is the time when the query is issued.

Let NN_j and RNN_j denote sets of moving points and T_j denote a time interval. The NN query returns the set $\{\langle NN_j, T_j\rangle\}$, and the RNN query returns the set $\{\langle RNN_j, T_j\rangle\}$. These sets satisfy the conditions $\bigcup_j T_j = [t^\vdash; t^\dashv]$ and $i \neq j \Rightarrow T_i \cap T_j = \emptyset$. In addition, each point in NN_j is a nearest neighbor to q during all of interval T_j, and RNN_j is the set of the reverse nearest neighbors to q during all of interval T_j. That is, $\forall j \; \forall p \in NN_j \; \forall r \in S \setminus \{p\} \; (d(q, p) \leq d(q, r))$ and $\forall j \; \forall p \in RNN_j \; \forall r \in S \setminus \{p\} \; (d(q, p) \leq d(p, r))$ during all of T_j, where $d(p_1, p_2)$ is the Euclidean distance between points p_1 and p_2.

The requirement that the query point q belongs to data set S is natural for RNN queries—the points from S are "looking" for their neighbors among the other points in S. Nevertheless, none of the solutions presented in this paper rely inherently on this assumption. Thus, q could as well be a point not belonging to S.

Observe that the query answer is temporal, i.e., the future time interval $[t^\vdash; t^\dashv]$ is divided into disjoint intervals T_j during which different answer sets (NN_j, RNN_j) are valid. Some of these answers may become invalidated if some of the points in the database are updated before $t^\dashv$.

According to the terminology of Sistla et al. [20], we term queries with answer sets that are maintained under updates *persistent*. It may be useful to change the query time interval in step with the continuously changing current time, i.e., it may be useful to have $[t^\vdash; t^\dashv] = [now, now + \Delta]$, where *now* is the continuously changing current time. Such a query is termed *continuous*. Algorithms for updates and persistent and continuous queries are available in the extended version of this paper [2].

2.2 Related Work

Reverse nearest neighbor queries are intimately related to nearest neighbor queries. In this section, we first overview the existing proposals for answering nearest neighbor queries, for both stationary and moving points. Then, we discuss the proposals related to reverse nearest neighbor queries.

2.2.1 Nearest Neighbor Queries

A number of methods were proposed for efficient processing of nearest neighbor queries for stationary points. The majority of the methods use index structures. Some proposals rely on index structures built specifically for nearest neighbor queries [3]. Branch-and-bound methods work on index structures originally designed for range queries. Perhaps the most influential in this category is an algorithm for finding the k nearest neighbors proposed by Roussopoulos et al. [16]. In this solution, an R-tree [6] indexes the points, and traversal of the tree is ordered and pruned based on a number of heuristics. Cheung and Fu [4] simplified this algorithm without reducing its efficiency. Other branch-and-bound methods modify the index structures to better suit the nearest neighbor problem [10, 24]. A number of incremental algorithms for similarity ranking have been proposed that can efficiently compute the $(k + 1)$-st nearest neighbor, after the k nearest neighbors are returned [9, 8]. They use a global priority queue of the objects to be visited in an R-tree.

Kollios et al. [11] propose an elegant solution for answering nearest neighbor queries for moving objects in one-dimensional space. Their algorithm uses a duality transformation, where the future trajectory of a moving point $x(t) = x_0 + v_x t$ is transformed into a point (x_0, v_x) in a so-called dual space. The solution is generalized to the "1.5-dimensional" case where the objects are moving in the plane, but with their movements being restricted to a number of line segments (e.g., corresponding to a road network). However, a query with a time interval predicate returns the single object that gets the closest to the query object during the specified time interval. It does not return the nearest neighbors for each time point during that time interval (cf. the problem formulation in Section 2.1). Moreover, this solution cannot be straightforwardly extended to the two-dimensional case, where the trajectories of the points become lines in three-dimensional space.

Most recently, Song and Roussopoulos [22] have proposed a solution for finding the k nearest neighbors for a

moving query point. However, the data points are assumed to be static. In addition, in contrast to our approach, time is not assumed to be continuous—a periodical sampling technique is used instead. When computing the result set for some sample, the algorithm tries to reuse the information contained in the result sets of the previous samples.

2.2.2 Reverse Nearest Neighbor Queries

To our knowledge, three solutions exist for answering *RNN* queries for non-moving points in two and higher dimensional spaces. Stanoi et al. [23] present a solution for answering *RNN* queries in two-dimensional space. Their algorithm is based on the following observations [21]. Let the space around the query point q be divided into six equal regions $S_i (1 \leq i \leq 6)$ by straight lines intersecting at q, as shown in Figure 2. Assume also that each region S_i includes only one of its bordering half-lines. Then, there exist at most six *RNN* points for q, and they are distributed so that there exists at most one *RNN* point in each region S_i.

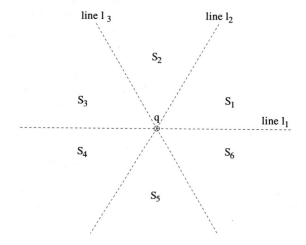

Figure 2. Division of the Space Around Query Point q

The same kind of observation leads to the following property. Let p be a *NN* point of q among points in S_i. Then, either q is the *NN* point of p (and then p is the *RNN* point of q), or q has no *RNN* point in S_i. Stanoi et al. prove this property [23].

These observations enable a reduction of the *RNN* problem to the *NN* problem. For each region S_i, an *NN* point of q in that region is found. We term it an *RNN* candidate. If there are more than one *NN* point in some S_i, they are not *RNN* candidates. For each of the candidate points, it is checked whether q is the nearest neighbor of that point. The answer to the $RNN(q)$ query consists of those candidate points that have q as their nearest neighbor.

In another solution for answering *RNN* queries, Korn and Muthukrishnan [12] use two R-trees for the querying, insertion, and deletion of points. In the RNN-tree, the minimum bounding rectangles of circles having a point as their center and the distance to the nearest neighbor of that point as their radius are stored. The NN-tree is simply an R*-tree [1] where the data points are stored. Yang and Lin [25] improve the solution of Korn and Muthukrishnan by introducing the Rdnn-tree, which makes possible to answer both *RNN* queries and *NN* queries using a single tree. Structurally, the Rdnn-tree is an R*-tree where each leaf entry is augmented with the distance to its nearest neighbor (dnn) and where a non-leaf entry stores the maximum of its children's dnn's.

None of the above-mentioned methods handle continuously moving points. In the next section, before presenting our method, we discuss the extendibility of these methods to support continuously moving points.

3 Algorithms

This section first describes the main ideas of the TPR-tree [18], which is used to index continuously moving points. Then, we briefly discuss the suitability of the methods described in Section 2.2.2 as the basis for our solution. The algorithms for answering the *NN* and *RNN* queries using the TPR-tree are presented next, followed by a simple example of a query.

3.1 TPR-tree

We use the TPR-tree (Time Parameterized R-tree [18]) as an underlying index structure. The TPR-tree indexes continuously moving points in one, two, or three dimensions. It employs the basic structure of the R*-tree [1], but both the indexed points and the bounding rectangles are augmented with velocity vectors. This way, bounding rectangles are time parameterized—they can be computed for different time points. The velocities of the edges of bounding rectangles are chosen so that the enclosed moving objects, be they points or other rectangles, remain inside the bounding rectangles at all times in the future. More specifically, if a number of points p_i are bounded at time t, the spatial and velocity extents of a bounding rectangle along the x axis is computed as follows:

$$x^{\vdash}(t) = \min_i\{p_i.x(t)\}; \quad x^{\dashv}(t) = \max_i\{p_i.x(t)\};$$
$$v_x^{\vdash} = \min_i\{p_i.v_x\}; \quad v_x^{\dashv} = \max_i\{p_i.v_x\}.$$

Figure 3 shows an example of the evolution of a bounding rectangle in the TPR-tree computed at $t = 0$. Note that, in contrast to R-trees, bounding rectangles in the TPR-tree are not minimum at all times. In most cases, they are minimum only at the time when they are computed. Other than

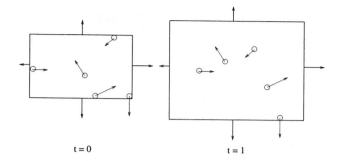

Figure 3. Time-Parameterized Bounding Rectangle

that, the TPR-tree can be interpreted as an R-tree for any specific time, t. This suggests that the algorithms that are based on the R-tree should be easily "portable" to the TPR-tree.

3.2 Preliminaries

Our *RNN* algorithm is based on the proposal of Stanoi et al. [23], described in Section 2.2.2. This algorithm uses the R-tree and does not require any specialized index structures. The other two proposals mentioned in Section 2.2.2 store, in one form or another, information about the nearest neighbor(s) of each point. With moving points, such information changes as time passes, even if no updates of objects occur. By not storing such information in the index, we avoid the overhead of its maintenance.

The sketch of the algorithm is analogous to the one described in Section 2.2.2. Our *RNN* algorithm first uses the *NN* algorithm to find the *NN* point in each S_i. For each of these candidate points, the algorithm assigns a validity time interval, which is part of the query time interval. Then, the *NN* algorithm is used again, this time unconstrained by the regions S_i, to check when, during each of these intervals, the candidate points have the query point as their nearest neighbor.

3.3 Algorithm for Finding Nearest Neighbors

Our algorithm for finding the nearest neighbors for continuously moving points in the plane is based on the algorithm proposed by Roussopoulos et al. [16]. That algorithm traverses the tree in depth-first order. Two metrics are used to direct and prune the search. The order in which the children of a node are visited is determined using the function $mindist(q, R)$, which computes the minimum distance between the bounding rectangle R of a child node and the query point q. Another function, $minmaxdist(q, R)$, which gives an upper bound of the smallest distance from q to points in R, assists in pruning the search.

Cheung and Fu [4] prove that, given the $mindist$-based ordering of the tree traversal, the pruning obtained by Roussopoulos et al. can be achieved without use of $minmaxdist$. Their argument does not seem to be straightforwardly extendible to our algorithm, where $mindist$ is extended to take into account temporal evolution. Nevertheless, because the $minmaxdist$ function is based on the assumption that bounding rectangles are always minimum [16], which is not the case in the TPR-tree (cf. Figure 3), we cannot adapt this function to our need.

In describing our algorithm, **FindNN**, the following notation is used. The function $d_q(p, t)$ denotes the square of the Euclidean distance between query point q and point p at time t. Similarly, function $d_q(R, t)$ indicates the square of the distance between the query point q and the point on rectangle R that is the closest to point q at time t.

Because the movements of points are described by linear functions, for any time interval $[t^\vdash; t^\dashv]$, $d_q(p, t) = at^2 + bt + c$, where $t \in [t^\vdash; t^\dashv]$ and a, b, and c are constants dependent upon the positions and velocity vectors of p and q. Similarly, any time interval $[t^\vdash; t^\dashv]$ can be subdivided into a finite number of non-intersecting intervals T_j so that $d_q(R, t) = a_k t^2 + b_k t + c_k$, where $t \in T_j$ and a_k, b_k, and c_k are constants dependent upon the positions and velocity vectors of R and q. Function $d_q(R, t)$ is zero for times when q is inside R. The details of how the interval is subdivided and how the constants a_k, b_k, and c_k are computed can be found elsewhere [2].

Nearest Neighbor Algorithm

FindNN$(q, [t^\vdash; t^\dashv])$:
1: $\forall t \in [t^\vdash; t^\dashv]$, set $min_q(t) \leftarrow \emptyset$ and $dmin_q(t) \leftarrow \infty$.
2: Do a depth-first search in the TPR-tree, starting from the root. For each visited node:
2.1: If it is a non-leaf node, order all rectangles R in the node according to the metric $M(R, q) = \int_{t^\vdash}^{t^\dashv} d_q(R, t)dt$. The entries corresponding to rectangles with smaller $M(R, q)$ are visited first. For each R:
2.1.1: If $\forall t \in [t^\vdash; t^\dashv](d_q(R, t) \geq dmin_q(t))$, prune rectangle R.
2.1.2: Else, go deeper into the node corresponding to R.
2.2: If it is a leaf node, for each p contained in it, such that $p \neq q$:
2.2.1: If $\forall t \in [t^\vdash; t^\dashv](d_q(p, t) \geq dmin_q(t))$, skip p.
2.2.2: If $\forall t \in T', T' \subset [t^\vdash; t^\dashv](d_q(p, t) < dmin_q(t))$, set $\forall t \in T' (min_q(t) \leftarrow \{p\}, dmin_q(t) \leftarrow d_q(p, t))$. If $\forall t \in T', T' \subset [t^\vdash; t^\dashv](d_q(p, t) = dmin_q(t))$, set $\forall t \in T' (min_q(t) \leftarrow min_q(t) \cup \{p\})$.

The algorithm maintains a list of intervals T_j as mentioned in Section 2.1. Initially the list contains a single interval $[t^\vdash; t^\dashv]$, which is subdivided as the algorithm progresses. Each interval T_j in the list has associated with it (i) a point p_j, and possibly more points with the same distance from q as p_j, that is the nearest neighbor of q during this interval among the points visited so far and (ii) the squared distance $d_q(p_j, t)$ of point p_j to the query point expressed by the three parameters a, b, and c. In the description of the algorithm, we represent this list by two functions. For each $t \in [t^\vdash; t^\dashv]$, function $min_q(t)$ denotes the points that are the closest to q at time t (typically, there will only be one such point), and $dmin_q(t)$ indicates the distance between q and $min_q(t)$ at time t.

Steps 2.1.1, 2.2.1, and 2.2.2 of the algorithm involve scanning through a list (or two) of time intervals and solving quadratic inequalities for each interval. In step 2.2.2, new intervals are introduced in the answer list. After the traversal of the tree, for each T_j in the answer list, $\forall t \in T_j(NN_j = min_q(t))$.

The idea behind metric M in step 2.1 is to visit first parts of the tree that are on average the closest to the query point q. The rectangle is pruned if there is no chance that it will contain a point that at some time during the query interval is closer to the query point q than the currently known closest point to q at that time.

3.4 Algorithm for Finding Reverse Nearest Neighbors

In this section, we describe algorithm **FindRNN** that computes the reverse nearest neighbors for a continuously moving point in the plane. The notation is the same as in the previous section. The algorithm produces a list $LRNN = \{\langle p_j, T_j \rangle\}$, where p_j is the reverse nearest neighbor of q during time interval T_j. Note that the format of $LRNN$ differs from the format of the answer to the RNN query, as defined in Section 2.1, where intervals T_j do not overlap and have sets of points associated with them. To simplify the description of the algorithm, we use this new format. Having $LRNN$, it is quite straightforward to transform it into the format described in Section 2.1 by sorting end points of time intervals in $LRNN$, and performing a "time sweep" to collect points for each of the formed time intervals.

To reduce the disk I/O incurred by the algorithm, all the six sets B_i are found in a single traversal of the index. Note that if, at some time, there is more than one nearest neighbor in some S_i, those nearest neighbors are nearer to each other than to the query point, meaning that S_i will hold no RNN points for that time. We thus assume in the following that, in sets B_i, each interval T_{ij} is associated with a single nearest neighbor point, nn_{ij}.

Reverse Nearest Neighbor Algorithm

FindRNN$(q, [t^\vdash; t^\dashv])$:

1: For each of the six regions S_i, find a corresponding set of nearest neighbors B_i by calling **FindNN**$(q, [t^\vdash; t^\dashv])$ for region S_i only. A version of algorithm **FindNN** is used were step 2.2.2 is modified to consider only time intervals when p is inside S_i.

2: Set $LRNN \leftarrow \emptyset$.

3: For each B_i and for each $\langle NN_{ij}, T_{ij} \rangle \in B_i$, if $|NN_{ij}| = 1$ (and $nn_{ij} \in NN_{ij}$), do:

3.1: Call **FindNN**(nn_{ij}, T_{ij}) to check when during time interval T_{ij}, q is the NN point of nn_{ij}. The algorithm **FindNN** is modified by using $min_{nn_{ij}}(t) \leftarrow q$, $dmin_{nn_{ij}}(t) \leftarrow d_{nn_{ij}}(q, t)$ in place of $min_{nn_{ij}}(t) \leftarrow \emptyset$, $dmin_{nn_{ij}}(t) \leftarrow \infty$ in step 1. In addition, an interval $T' \subset T_{ij}$ is excluded from the list of time intervals and is not considered any longer as soon as a point p is found such that $\forall t \in T' \, (d_{nn_{ij}}(p, t) < d_{nn_{ij}}(q, t))$.

3.2: If **FindNN**(nn_{ij}, T_{ij}) returns a non-empty answer, i.e., $\exists T' \subset T_{ij}$, such that q is an NN point of nn_{ij} during time interval T', add $\langle nn_{ij}, T' \rangle$ to $LRNN$.

All the RNN candidates nn_{ij} are also verified in one traversal. To make this possible, we use $\sum_{i,j} M(R, nn_{ij})$ as the metric for ordering the search in step 2.1 of **FindNN**. In addition, a point or a rectangle is pruned only if it can be pruned for each of the query points nn_{ij}.

Thus, the index is traversed twice in total.

When analyzing the I/O complexity of **FindRNN**, we observe that in the worst case, all nodes of the tree are visited to find the nearest neighbors using **FindNN**, which is performed twice. As noted by Hjaltason and Samet [9], this is even the case for static points ($t^\vdash = t^\dashv$), where the size of the result set is constant. For points with linear movement, the worst case size of the result set of the NN query is $O(N)$ (where N is the database size). The size of the result set of **FindNN** is important because if the combined size of the sets B_i is too large, the B_i will not fit in main memory. In our performance studies in Section 4, we investigate the observed average number of I/Os and the average sizes of result sets.

3.5 Query Example

To illustrate how an RNN query is performed, Figure 4 depicts 11 points, with point 1 being the query point. The velocity of point 1 has been subtracted from the velocities of all the points, and the positions of the points are shown at time $t = 0$. The lowest-level bounding rectangles of the index on the points, R_1 to R_5, are shown. Each node in the TPR-tree has from 2 to 3 entries. As examples, some

distances from point 1 are shown: $d_{P_1}(P_8, t)$ is the distance between point 1 and point 8, $d_{P_1}(R_1, t)$ is the distance between point 1 and rectangle 1, and $d_{P_1}(R_2, t)$ is the distance between point 1 and rectangle 2.

If the RNN query for the time interval $[0; 2]$ is issued, $dmin_{P_1}(t)$ for region S_1 is set to $d_{P_1}(P_3, t)$ after visiting rectangle 2, and because $d_{P_1}(R_4, t) > d_{P_1}(P_3, t)$ for all $t \in [0; 2]$, rectangle R_4 is pruned.

With the purpose of taking a closer look at how the RNN query is performed in regions S_2 and S_3, Figure 5 shows the positions of the points in regions S_2 and S_3 at time points $t = 0$, $t = 1$, and $t = 2$. Point 7 crosses the line delimiting regions S_2 and S_3 at time $t = 1.5$.

After the first tree-traversal, the NN points in region S_2 are $B_2 = \{\langle P_4, [0; 1.5] \rangle, \langle P_7, [1.5; 2] \rangle\}$, and in region S_3, they are $B_3 = \{\langle P_7, [0; 1.5] \rangle, \langle P_8, [1.5; 2] \rangle\}$. However, the list of RNN points $LRNN$, which is constructed during the second traversal of the TPR-tree while verifying candidate points 4, 7, and 8, is only $\{\langle P_7, [0; 1.5] \rangle, \langle P_7, [1.5; 2] \rangle\}$. This is because during time interval $[0; 1.5]$, point 10, but not point 1, is the closest to point 4, and, similarly, during time interval $[1.5; 2]$, point 7, but not point 1, is the closest to point 8.

4 Performance Experiments

The experimental setting for the performance experiments is described initially. Then follows an account for results of experiments that aim to elicit pertinent properties of the proposed algorithms.

4.1 Experimental Setting

The algorithms presented in this paper were implemented in C++, using a TPR-tree implementation based on GiST [7]. Specifically, the TPR-tree implementation with self-tuning time horizon was used [17]. We investigate the performance of algorithms in terms of the number of I/O operations they perform. The disk page size (and the size of a TPR-tree node) is set to 4k bytes, which results in 204 entries per leaf node in trees. An LRU page buffer of 50 pages is used [14], with the root of a tree always pinned in the buffer. The nodes changed during an index operation are marked as "dirty" in the buffer and are written to disk at the end of the operation or when they otherwise have to be removed from the buffer. In addition to the LRU page buffer, we use a main-memory resident storage area for recording the temporary answer sets of the first tree-traversals of RNN queries (the B_i lists).

The performance studies are based on synthetically generated workloads that intermix update operations and queries. To generate the workloads, we simulate N objects moving in a region of space with dimensions 1000×1000

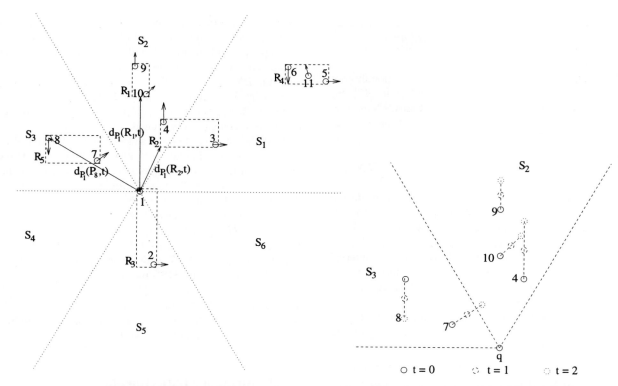

Figure 4. Example Query

Figure 5. Simplified Example Query

kilometers. Whenever an object reports its movement, the old information pertaining to the object is deleted from the index (assuming this is not the first reported movement from this object), and the new information is inserted into the index.

Two types of workloads were used in the experiments. In most of the experiments, we use uniform workloads, where positions of points and their velocities are distributed uniformly. The speeds of objects vary from 0 to 3 kilometers per time unit (minute). In other experiments, more realistic workloads are used, where objects move in a network of two-way routes, interconnecting a number of destinations uniformly distributed in the plane. Points start at random positions on routes and are assigned with equal probability to one of three groups of points with maximum speeds of 0.75, 1.5, and 3 km/min. Whenever an object reaches one of the destinations, it chooses the next target destination at random. The network-based workload generation used in these experiments is described in more detail elsewhere [18].

In both types of workloads, the average interval between two successive updates of an object is equal to 60 time units. Unless noted otherwise, the number of points is 100,000. Workloads are run for 120 time units to populate the index. Then, queries are introduced, intermixed with additional updates. Each query corresponds to a randomly selected

point from the currently active data set. Our performance graphs report average numbers of I/O operations per query.

4.2 Properties of the Nearest Neighbor and Reverse Nearest Neighbor Algorithms

In the first round of the experiments, a variety of the properties of the algorithms computing nearest and reverse nearest neighbors are explored.

Figure 6 shows the average number of I/O operations per query when varying the number of points in the database. In this experiment, after the initial phase of 120 time units, the workloads are run for an additional 10 time units. During this period, 500 queries are issued. For each query, its time interval starts at the time of issue, and the length of the interval varies from 0 to 30 time units.

The number of I/O operations increases almost linearly with the number of data points. Figure 7 shows that the size of an average result increases similarly.

It is interesting to observe that the second traversal of the tree, in which the candidates produced by the first traversal are verified, is more expensive than the first traversal, in which these candidates are found. The main reason for this behavior is that while there is only one query point during the first traversal, during the second traversal, there is a number of *RNN* candidates (from the different regions S_i

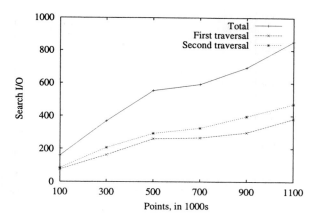

Figure 6. Query Performance for Varying Number of Points

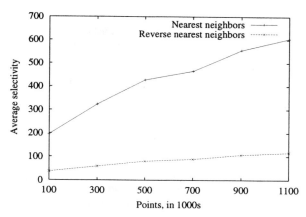

Figure 7. Average Selectivity of Queries for Varying Number of Points

and during different parts of the query interval) that serve as *NN* query points. This argument alone would perhaps lead us to expect a larger difference between the costs of the two traversals.

The relatively small difference between the two traversals occurs because during the first traversal, there is no initial upper bound for the distance between the query point q and the *RNN* candidate point, i.e., $dmin_q(t)$ is initially set to ∞ in the **FindNN** algorithm. The second traversal only needs to determine whether the point q is an *NN* point to the candidate points; and for each candidate point, there is an initial upper bound for $dmin_{nn_{ij}}(t)$, namely the distance between the point q and that candidate point, nn_{ij}. Further, since nn_{ij} is the *NN* point to q in some region S_i at some time, the distance between q and nn_{ij} is typically small. This enables a more aggressive pruning of tree nodes during the second traversal of the TPR-tree.

To learn whether the nearest neighbor (and reverse nearest neighbor) algorithm could possibly be significantly improved by changing the tree traversal order or by somehow improving the pruning, we explored how many of the visited bounding rectangles actually contained the query point at some time point during the corresponding query time interval. If several queries were performed in one tree traversal, we observed whether the bounding rectangle contained any of the query points. Tree nodes corresponding to such bounding rectangles must necessarily be visited by any *NN* algorithm to produce a correct answer. Thus, given a specific TPR-tree, the number of such bounding rectangles gives the lower performance bound for a corresponding nearest neighbor query.

In experiments with 100,000 points, during the first traversal, a total of 32 I/Os out of the average of 75 I/Os corresponded to "necessary" bounding rectangles. For the second traversal, the numbers were 39 I/Os out of 83 I/Os.

This shows, that under the most optimistic assumptions, the algorithm can be improved by no more than approximately a factor of two.

Figure 7 plots the average number of entries in the result sets of queries after the first traversal of the tree, which finds nearest neighbors, and after the second traversal, which finds reverse nearest neighbors. Note that a single point in the answer set may have more than one time interval associated with it. The graphs show that on average, only one out of five candidate *RNN* points is found to be a real *RNN* point. To investigate how much memory is needed for storing candidate *RNN* points (the B_i lists), we also recorded the maximum size of the answer sets in our experiments. It was no more than five times the average sizes reported in Figure 7 (i.e., at most ca. 100k bytes).

Figure 8 shows the average number of I/O operations per query when the number of destinations in the simulated network of routes is varied. "Uniform" indicates the case when the points and their velocities are distributed uniformly, which, intuitively, corresponds to a very large number of destinations. Each workload contained 500 queries, generated in the same way as for the previous experiment.

The number of I/O operations tends to increase with the number of destinations, i.e., as the workloads get more "uniform." The results are consistent with, although not as pronounced as, those reported for range queries on the TPR-tree [18]. Observe that while the performance of the second traversal shows the above-mentioned trend, data skew seems to not affect the performance of the first traversal. A possible explanation is that when moving points are concentrated on a small number of routes, the good quality of the TPR-tree is offset by the fact that there can be regions S_i that have no points inside of them, but contain parts of bounding rectangles. In such cases, $dmin_q(t)$ in **FindNN** always remains ∞ and those bounding rectangles cannot be

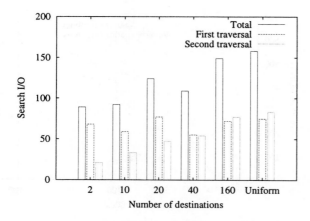

Figure 8. Query Performance for Varying Number of Destinations

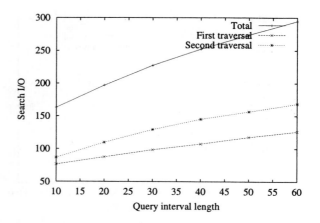

Figure 9. Query Performance for Varying Query Interval Length

pruned.

Figure 9 shows the average number of I/O operations per query for varying query interval lengths. The number of I/O operations increases approximately linearly with the query interval length. The experiment also showed that the number of results returned increases linearly.

5 Summary and Future Work

Rapidly advancing technologies make it possible to track the positions of large numbers of continuously moving objects. Because of this, efficient algorithms for answering various queries about continuously moving objects are needed. Algorithms have previously been suggested for answering *RNN* and *NN* queries for non-moving objects, but no solutions have been proposed for efficiently answering these queries when large numbers of objects are moving continuously. In this paper, we have proposed an algorithm for answering *RNN* queries for large numbers of continuously moving points in the plane. As a solution to a sub-problem, an algorithm for answering *NN* queries for continuously moving points in the plane has been proposed. An experimental study was performed that revealed a number of interesting properties of the proposed algorithms.

As the indexing structure for continuously moving points, the TPR-tree [18] has been used. This means that the same index structure can be used for range queries, nearest neighbor queries, and reverse nearest neighbor queries.

The presented *RNN* query algorithm is suitable for the *monochromatic* case [12] only—all the points are assumed to be of the same category. In the *bichromatic* case, there are two kinds of points (i.e., "clients" and "servers," corresponding to tourists and rescue workers), and an *RNN* query asks for points that belong to the opposite category than the

query point and have the query point as the closest from all the points that are in the same category as the query point. The approach of dividing the plane into six regions does not work for the bichromatic case—a point can have more than six *RNN* points. An interesting future research direction is to develop an algorithm for efficiently answering *RNN* queries for continuously moving bichromatic points.

Sometimes it is important to know not only the objects that have the query object as their nearest neighbor (a simple *RNN* query) but also the objects that have the query object as their second nearest, third nearest neighbor (second, third order *RNN* query), etc. Processing of higher order *RNN* queries could be another possible extension of the proposed algorithm.

In reality, the objects most often move along some underlying route structure, for example, cars in a road network. Even if objects move freely, another type of infrastructure could exist that prohibits movement in some areas, such as lakes or mountains. How to handle the complexities arising from the non-Euclidean distance functions inherent to such environments is an interesting research direction.

Acknowledgments

This research was supported in part by the Danish Technical Research Council through grant 9700780, by the Wireless Information Management network, funded by the Nordic Academy for Advanced Study through grant 000389, and by a grant from the Nykredit corporation.

References

[1] N. Beckmann, H.-P. Kriegel, R. Schneider, and B. Seeger. The R*-Tree: An Efficient and Robust Ac-

cess Method for Points and Rectangles. In *Proceedings of the 1990 ACM SIGMOD International Conference on Management of Data*, pp. 322–331, 1990.

[2] R. Benetis, C. S. Jensen, G. Karciauskas, and S. Šaltenis. Nearest Neighbor and Reverse Nearest Neighbor Queries for Moving Objects. TimeCenter TR-66, avaiable via <www.cs.auc.TimeCenter>.

[3] S. Berchtold, B. Ertl, D. A. Keim, H.-P. Kriegel, and T. Seidl. Fast Nearest Neighbor Search in High-Dimensional Space. In *Proceedings of the 14th International Conference on Data Engineering*, pp. 209–218, 1998.

[4] K. L. Cheung and A. W. Fu. Enhanced Nearest Neighbour Search on the R-tree. *SIGMOD Record*, 27(3): 16–21, 1998.

[5] J. Elliott. Text Messages Turn Towns into Giant Computer Game. *Sunday Times*, April 29, 2001.

[6] A. Guttman. R-Trees: A Dynamic Index Structure for Spatial Searching. In *Proceedings of the 1984 ACM SIGMOD International Conference on Management of Data*, pp. 47–57, 1984.

[7] J. M. Hellerstein, J. F. Naughton, and A. Pfeffer. Generalized Search Trees for Database Systems. In *Proceedings of the 21st VLDB Conference*, pp. 562–573, 1995.

[8] A. Henrich. A Distance Scan Algorithm for Spatial Access Structures. In *Proceedings of the Second ACM Workshop on Geographic Information Systems*, pp. 136–143, 1994.

[9] G. R. Hjaltason and H. Samet. Distance Browsing in Spatial Databases. In *ACM Transactions on Database Systems*, 24(2): 265–318, 1999.

[10] N. Katayama and S. Satoh. The SR-tree: An Index Structure for High-Dimensional Nearest Neighbor Queries. In *Proceedings of the 1997 ACM SIGMOD International Conference on Management of Data*, pp. 369–380, 1997.

[11] G. Kollios, D. Gunopulos, and V. J. Tsotras. Nearest Neighbor Queries in a Mobile Environment. In *Proceedings of the International Workshop on Spatio-Temporal Database Management*, pp. 119–134, 1999.

[12] F. Korn and S. Muthukrishnan. Influence Sets Based on Reverse Nearest Neighbor Queries. In *Proceedings of the 2000 ACM SIGMOD International Conference on Management of Data*, pp. 201–212, 2000.

[13] F. Korn, N. Sidiropoulos, C. Faloutsos, E. Siegel, and Z. Protopapas. Fast Nearest Neighbor Search in Medical Image Databases. In *Proceedings of the 22nd VLDB Conference*, pp. 215–226, 1996.

[14] S. T. Leutenegger and M. A. Lopez. The Effect of Buffering on the Performance of R-Trees. In *Proceedings of the 14th International Conference on Data Engineering*, pp. 164–171, 1998.

[15] F. P. Preparata and M. I. Shamos. *Computational Geometry. An Introduction*. Texts and Monographs in Computer Science. 5th corrected ed., Springer, 1993.

[16] N. Roussopoulos, S. Kelley, and F. Vincent. Nearest Neighbor Queries. In *Proceedings of the 1995 ACM SIGMOD International Conference on Management of Data*, pp. 71–79, 1995.

[17] S. Šaltenis and C. S. Jensen. Indexing of Moving Objects for Location-Based Services. In *Proceedings of the 18th International Conference on Data Engineering*, pp. 463–472, 2002.

[18] S. Šaltenis, C. S. Jensen, S. T. Leutenegger, and M. A. Lopez. Indexing the Positions of Continuously Moving Objects. In *Proceedings of the 2000 ACM SIGMOD International Conference on Management of Data*, pp. 331–342, 2000.

[19] T. Seidl and H.-P. Kriegel. Optimal Multi-Step k-Nearest Neighbor Search. In *Proceedings of the 1998 ACM SIGMOD International Conference on Management of Data*, pp. 154–165, 1998.

[20] A. P. Sistla, O. Wolfson, S. Chamberlain, and S. Dao. Modeling and Querying Moving Objects. In *Proceedings of the 13th International Conference on Data Engineering*, pp. 422–432, 1997.

[21] M. Smid. Closest Point Problems in Computational Geometry. In J.-R. Sack and J. Urrutia, editors, *Handbook on Computational Geometry*. Elsevier Science Publishing, pp. 877–935, 1997.

[22] Z. Song and N. Roussopoulos. K-Nearest Neighbor Search for Moving Query Point. In *Proceedings of the 7th International Symposium on Spatial and Temporal Databases*, pp. 79–96, 2001.

[23] I. Stanoi, D. Agrawal, and A. El Abbadi. Reverse Nearest Neighbor Queries for Dynamic Databases. In *Proceedings of the ACM SIGMOD Workshop on Research Issues in Data Mining and Knowledge Discovery*, pp. 44–53, 2000.

[24] D. A. White and R. Jain. Similarity Indexing with the SS-tree. In *Proceedings of the 12th International Conference on Data Engineering*, pp. 516–523, 1996.

[25] C. Yang and K.-Ip Lin. An Index Structure for Efficient Reverse Nearest Neighbor Queries. In *Proceedings of the 17th International Conference on Data Engineering*, pp. 485–492, 2001.

Continual Neighborhood Tracking for Moving Objects Using Adaptive Distances

Yoshiharu Ishikawa[†]   Hiroyuki Kitagawa[†]   Tooru Kawashima[‡*]
[†]Institute of Information Sciences and Electronics
[‡]Master's Program in Science and Engineering
University of Tsukuba
{ishikawa,kitagawa}@is.tsukuba.ac.jp

Abstract

Based on the recent progress of digital cartography, global positioning systems (GPSs), and hand-held devices, there are growing needs of technology that provides neighborhood information to moving objects according to their locations and trajectories. In this paper, we propose spatial query generation models that take account of the current position and the past/future trajectories of a moving object to provide appropriate neighborhood information to it. For this purpose, we introduce an influence model of trajectory points and derive neighborhood query generation models using adaptive ellipsoid distances. We describe query processing strategies for these query generation models and show incremental query update procedures to support continual query facilities with low processing cost. Finally, we present experimental results to show the effectiveness of our approach.

1. Introduction

Mobile computing technology has gained much interest recently because of the advances of wireless communication, electronics, and positioning systems. The growth of mobile computing has brought a new field of database research area—*moving object* support based on database technology [1, 7, 12, 16, 21, 22, 28, 33, 34]. In this paper, we focus on the retrieval and presentation of neighborhood information for moving objects such as a vehicle equipped with a GPS and a navigation system, and people with hand-held mobile devices. By cooperating with forthcoming technology of intelligent traffic systems (ITSs), such *neighborhood tracking* functionalities would realize new types of applications that have "location- and situation-awareness".

We briefly explain the proposed idea using Fig. 1. Suppose that a vehicle, which came from the left side of the map, is now approaching the position x. Its future trajectory is represented by the dotted arrow. Then consider the problem: "for the vehicle at the point x, what is an appropriate *spatial query* to retrieve neighborhood information from a spatial database?" A simple approach would be to use the Euclidean distance from x to obtain objects in neighborhood as shown by the circle in Fig. 1; the query can be formulated as a *range query* or a *k-nearest neighbor query* (*k-nn query* for short). Although this approach is simple and clear, it often loses useful information since it does not consider the *trajectory* of the moving object, namely, the past locations and the predicted future ones. In contrast to this Euclidean approach, we use an ellipsoid region to retrieve neighborhood information. The ellipsoid region shown in Fig. 1 is computed based on the past and future trajectories of the object and slightly biased toward

---
[*]Current affiliation: Hitachi Corporation

the "future"; namely, the center of the ellipsoid region is located at a predicted future position of the moving object and the shape of the region reflects the future trajectory than the past one.

Figure 1. Retrieval of Neighborhood Information

Neighborhood queries in our framework are formalized as spatial queries based on the *ellipsoid distances* [2, 3, 19, 30] that have elliptic isosurfaces. We call such queries *ellipsoid queries*. Two benefits of using ellipsoid queries are summarized as follows:

- **Adaptiveness**: As shown in the following sections, ellipsoid queries can have arbitrary "shapes" that reflect the trajectories and the current positions of moving objects. By tuning query centers and ellipsoid distances adaptively for each trajectory point, our query generation method can generate neighborhood queries that retrieve appropriate neighborhood information along the trajectory of a moving object. Figure 2 illustrates the idea. Suppose that the moving object is located at the point $x_{\tau-1}$ at the time $t = \tau - 1$. After one unit time later (i.e., when $t = \tau$), the object moves to x_τ, then it goes to $x_{\tau+1}$ at $t = \tau + 1$. Each ellipsoid shown in the figure is the isosurface of the spatial query issued at each trajectory point. As shown in the figure, three ellipsoids have different shapes in terms of rotation and thickness, and focus on the "neighborhood" of the moving object. Our proposed approach shown below provides such an adaptive neighborhood query generation facility for continuously moving objects. Additionally, our method offers some user-specifiable parameters to reflect users' preferences to the query generation.

- **Efficiency and simplicity**: For the efficient retrieval of neighborhood information from a huge spatial database, effective use of spatial indexes [13] is indispensable. Fortunately, there exist some query evaluation techniques proposed for ellipsoid distances that can effectively use spatial indexes [2, 30]. In this paper, we extend these techniques and apply them to our context. The retrieval algorithm shown below is implementable using conventional spatial indexes such as R-trees [17].

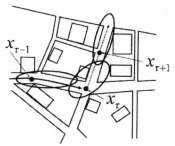

Figure 2. Adaptive Query Generation

As an alternative approach of neighborhood information retrieval, we could utilize spatial networks, consisting of spatial points, line-segments, and polygons, to process connectivity-based retrieval rather than proximity-based retrieval [31]. Although this approach may be able to perform a more detailed computation using connectivity information, it has to manage huge spatial network information and requires specialized data structures.

Our method has an additional feature: the support of *continual queries* [24]. The task to generate and process queries for a moving object along its trajectory is considered as a continual query task for the object. To generate and process queries continuously, we preserve the internal state used in the previous query generation and update the state incrementally. Since this proposed method has low update and storage costs, we can process continuous queries in an efficient manner. This feature would enhance real-time "tracking" capabilities often used in the analyses of spatio-temporal data [4].

The rest of the paper is organized as follows. In Section 2, we introduce some basic notions. The *influence model of trajectory points*, an important concept in this paper, is defined there. In Section 3, we derive some neighborhood query generation models taking account of the influence model. Section 4 introduces the notion of "continual query" task and presents query processing procedures to use spatial indexes efficiently, and Section 5 presents incremental query update methods. Section 6 shows experimental results and Section 7 describes the related work. Finally, Section 8 concludes the paper.

2. Basic Notions

In this section, we introduce basic notions used in the following discussion. Symbols and their meanings are shown in Table 1. Although our approach mainly targets geographical applications in low-dimensional space (two- or three-dimension), we derive formulas for arbitrary d dimension for the generality.

2.1. Representation of Trajectories

In our framework, neighborhood queries are generated based on the trajectory of a moving object, consisting of the past trajectory, the current position, and the future trajectory. Let the start time of a moving object be $t = 1$ and the current time be $t = \tau$. We denote each position of the object at time t ($t = 1, \ldots, \tau$) by a vector $\boldsymbol{x}_i = [x_{i1}, \ldots, x_{id}]^T$ in a d-dimensional space, where 'T' denotes vector transposition. Next, let the predicted time to arrive at the destination be $t = \tau + \tau'$; namely, we will need τ' unit times to arrive at the destination from the current position. The predicted positions of the object at $t = \tau + 1, \ldots, \tau + \tau'$ are also repre-

Table 1. Symbols and Their Definitions

Name	Definition
d	number of dimensions
$\boldsymbol{x}_i$	location vector ($t = 1, \ldots, \tau, \ldots \tau + \tau'$)
τ	current time
τ'	predicted time to arrive at the destination from the current position
σ	"look ahead" parameter
μ	decay factor for past trajectory points
ν	decay factor for future trajectory points
$\alpha(t)$	influence value of the location information at time t
$\boldsymbol{q}$	query center
$\bar{\boldsymbol{x}}$	weighted average of location information
$\mathbf{A}, \mathbf{M}$	distance matrix and derived distance matrix
$\mathbf{C}, \bar{\mathbf{C}}$	covariance matrices
$\mathcal{D}_{\text{Euclid}}(\cdot, \cdot)$	the Euclidean distance function
$\mathcal{D}_{\mathbf{A}}(\cdot, \cdot)$	ellipsoid distance function
s^-, s^+	(past and future) state vectors
$\mathbf{C}^-, \mathbf{C}^+$	(past and future) covariance matrices

sented by d-dimensional vectors $\boldsymbol{x}_{\tau+1}, \ldots, \boldsymbol{x}_{\tau+\tau'}$. Figure 3 illustrates the definition.

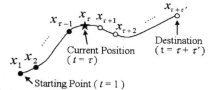

Figure 3. Representation of Trajectory

2.2. Influence Model of Trajectory Points

In the following, we utilize the past (and current) trajectory points $\boldsymbol{x}_1, \ldots, \boldsymbol{x}_\tau$ and the predicted future trajectory points $\boldsymbol{x}_{\tau+1}, \ldots, \boldsymbol{x}_{\tau+\tau'}$ for the generation of the neighborhood query for the moving object located at $\boldsymbol{x}_\tau$. For this purpose, we introduce the *influence model of trajectory points*. This model is based on a simple idea that the influence of a trajectory point is the highest for the "current" position and decays gradually towards past and future. To realize this idea, we incorporate the following three parameters σ, μ, and ν:

- *"look ahead" parameter σ*: This parameter σ ($\sigma \geq 0$) is used to reflect user's preference such that the predicted position $\boldsymbol{x}_{\tau+\sigma}$, at where the moving object will arrive after σ unit times, is the most influential position to generate a neighborhood query. Consider an example: suppose that a car driver driving a vehicle has high interest to the neighborhood of the location at where he will arrive one minute later. In this case, he can set $\sigma = 1$ to reflect his preference, then $\boldsymbol{x}_{\tau+1}$ will have the highest influence.

- *decay factor for past trajectory points μ*: The parameter μ ($0 \leq \mu \leq 1$) is used to set exponential influence values for the past trajectory points. The influence values exponentially decay from $t = \tau + \sigma$ to $t = 1$.

- *decay factor for future trajectory points ν*: The parameter ν ($0 \leq \nu \leq 1$) is used to set exponential influence values for the future trajectory points. The influence values exponentially decay from $t = \tau + \sigma$ to $t = \tau + \tau'$.

By using the three parameters, the influence model of trajectory points is formally defined as follows:

Definition 2.1 The *influence value* for each trajectory point x_t $(t = 1, \ldots, \tau + \tau')$ is given by

$$\alpha(t) = \begin{cases} \mu^{\tau+\sigma-t} & (t = 1, \ldots, \tau + \sigma) \\ \nu^{t-\tau-\sigma} & (t = \tau + \sigma, \ldots, \tau + \tau'). \end{cases} \quad (1)$$

Figure 4 illustrates the notion of influence values. By tuning σ, μ, and ν appropriately, users can reflect their preferences in various situations. The query generation models shown in the next section are based on this model.

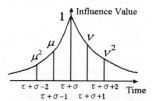

Figure 4. Influence Values

3 Query Generation Models

In the following, we derive neighborhood query generation models for a moving object at position x_τ. The neighborhood queries are constructed as spatial queries that retrieve data points from a spatial database. In general, queries in spatial databases can be specified in terms of the following three factors: 1) *query center* q, 2) *distance function* $\mathcal{D}$, and 3) *query task* (e.g., range query and k-nn query). In this section, we focus on how to derive an appropriate query center q and a distance function $\mathcal{D}$ from the given trajectory information. Query tasks are discussed in Section 4.

3.1. Query Center Derivation Models

We introduce two derivation models of a query center. We intend that a user will select an appropriate one based on his or her requirement.

Model cur The model **cur** is a simple approach and does not use past/future trajectories except for $x_{\tau+\sigma}$, the highest influence position. The query center is given by

$$q = x_{\tau+\sigma}. \quad (2)$$

Model avg The model **avg** fully uses the trajectory information and derives the query position as the weighted average of the trajectory points:

$$q = \bar{x} = \frac{\sum_{t=1}^{\tau+\tau'} \alpha(t) x_t}{\sum_{t=1}^{\tau+\tau'} \alpha(t)}. \quad (3)$$

Note that the query center is determined by considering the recent and the near future trajectories, because the influence values ($\alpha(t)$'s) set high weights on the trajectory points around $x_{\tau+\sigma}$.

3.2. Distance Function Derivation Models

We introduce three derivation models of distance functions.

Model EU The model **EU** is based on the ordinary Euclidean distance and introduced only for the comparison purpose. The Euclidean distance has less computational cost and clear semantics, but is not adaptive. In this approach, first a query center q is derived based on either of the query center derivation models, then a distance is computed for each object x by using the Euclidean distance $\mathcal{D}_{\text{Euclid}}(x, q)$. In the following, we denote a combination of a query center derivation model and a distance function derivation model such as **EU(cur)** and **EU(avg)**.

Model OV In this model **OV** ('OV' stands for "oval"), we use ellipsoid distances as the distance functions. By setting parameters appropriately, we can tune the "shape" of a distance function based on the application need. The *ellipsoid distance* (also called elliptic or ellipsoidal distance) is often used in various application areas such as image retrieval [9], pattern recognition and classification [8], and statistics [20]. It is defined as follows:

Definition 3.1 An *ellipsoid distance* has the following *quadratic form*

$$\mathcal{D}_{\mathbf{A}}^2(x_i, q) = (x_i - q)^T \mathbf{A}(x_i - q), \quad (4)$$

where $\mathbf{A}$ is a *symmetric positive definite matrix* ($\mathbf{A}^T = \mathbf{A}$ and $x^T \mathbf{A} x > 0$ for any $x \neq \mathbf{0}$). We call $\mathbf{A}$ the *distance matrix* for $\mathcal{D}_{\mathbf{A}}(\cdot, \cdot)$.

An ellipsoid distance $\mathcal{D}_{\mathbf{A}}(\cdot, \cdot)$ defined by the above formula has arbitrary-rotated ellipsoidal isosurfaces. In a special case, if $\mathbf{A}$ is a unit matrix $\mathbf{I}$, the induced distance $\mathcal{D}_{\mathbf{I}}(\cdot, \cdot)$ agrees with the Euclidean distance (i.e., model **EU**).

An ellipsoid distance can be tuned by setting $\mathbf{A}$ appropriately. In this model **OV**, we derive an appropriate distance matrix based on the trajectory of a moving object using the influence model of trajectory points. For the derivation, we consider the following *penalty* formula:

$$P(\mathbf{A}, q) = \sum_{t=1}^{\tau+\tau'} \alpha(t) \mathcal{D}_{\mathbf{A}}^2(x_t, q) \quad (5)$$

Since the influence factor $\alpha(t)$ is incorporated in the summation, the position $x_{\tau+\sigma}$, the most important position, exert the highest influence on the penalty, and the effects of other positions decay gradually towards past and future.

To derive the optimal distance matrix $\mathbf{M}$ according to the penalty (Eq. (5)), we apply the optimization technique used in [19]; $\mathbf{M}$ is derived as the matrix that minimizes the penalty:

$$\mathbf{M} = \underset{\mathbf{A}}{\text{argmin}} \, P(\mathbf{A}, q). \quad (6)$$

Since $\mathbf{M} = \mathbf{O}$ ($\mathbf{O}$ represents the null matrix) is obtained when we do not restrict $\mathbf{M}$, we set a constraint on $\mathbf{M}$ such that

$$\det(\mathbf{M}) = 1, \quad (7)$$

where $\det(\mathbf{M})$ is the determinant of $\mathbf{M}$. From this formulation, $\mathbf{M}$ can be derived as follows (the proof is shown in [18]).

Theorem 3.1 The matrix $\mathbf{M}$ that minimizes Eq. (5) under the constraint Eq. (7) can be derived as

$$\mathbf{M} = \det(\mathbf{C})^{\frac{1}{d}} \mathbf{C}^{-1}, \text{ where} \quad (8)$$

$$\mathbf{C} = \sum_{t=1}^{\tau+\tau'} \alpha(t)(x_t - q)(x_t - q). \quad (9)$$

$\mathbf{C} = [c_{jk}]$ is called the *(weighted sample) covariance matrix* and $\det(\mathbf{C})$ is the determinant of $\mathbf{C}$. ∎

56

The distance derived as above is a variation of *statistical distance* (also called *Mahalanobis distance*) often used in pattern analysis and multivariate statistics [8, 20]. In [19], we used a similar technique to derive distance functions based on user-specified examples for feedback-based interactive information retrieval. The statistical distance takes the spatial correlation of sample points into consideration and puts appropriate bias on each dimension so that it gains elliptic isosurfaces.

Now we mention the relationship between the **EU** model and the **avg** model. In Eq. (6), we have treated q as a constant, but we can treat q as an another optimization variable such as $(\mathbf{M}, q_{\text{opt}}) = \operatorname{argmin}_{\mathbf{A}, q} P(\mathbf{A}, q)$. In this case, we obtain $q_{\text{opt}} = \bar{x}$ and the result coincides with **OV(avg)**. This would be a good property to give a theoretical foundation to the **avg** model.

Model HB   The model **OV** derived above has a benefit that it can utilize trajectory information to derive distance functions, but it lacks of robustness compared to the Euclidean distance. For example, if an object continuously moves along a straight line, the covariance matrix $\mathbf{C}$ becomes an ill-conditioned matrix, then the derived distance $\mathcal{D}_{\mathbf{M}}(\cdot, \cdot)$ tends to have too narrow isosurfaces. Moreover, in an extreme case, $\mathbf{C}$ approaches to a singular matrix and we cannot derive $\mathbf{M}$ using Eq. (8). This is because the model **OV** uses the spatial correlation of trajectory points; it requires d-dimensional spatial spreading of sample points.

To alleviate this problem, we introduce a hybrid model **HB** that integrates two models **EU** and **OV**; it inherits the robustness feature from **EU** and the adaptivity feature from **OV**. The idea is based on the heuristics to *regularize* ill-conditioned matrices to obtain non-singular covariance estimates [26]. In this model, we use the following matrix $\tilde{\mathbf{C}}$, instead of $\mathbf{C}$, as the covariance matrix:

$$\tilde{\mathbf{C}} = \lambda \frac{\mathbf{C}}{\|\mathbf{C}\|} + (1 - \lambda) \frac{\mathbf{I}}{\|\mathbf{I}\|}, \qquad (10)$$

where $\|\cdot\|$ is the Frobenius matrix norm [15] and works as weight normalization factors. The parameter λ ($0 \leq \lambda \leq 1$) specifies how to set weights to **EU** and **OV**. In this model, as in the case of **OV**, the distance matrix $\mathbf{M}$ is derived as follows:

$$\mathbf{M} = \det(\tilde{\mathbf{C}})^{\frac{1}{d}} \tilde{\mathbf{C}}^{-1}. \qquad (11)$$

Note that when $\lambda = 0$ and 1, the **HB** model reduces to **EU** and **OV**, respectively. Therefore, we can say that **HB** is a generalized version of **EU** and **OV**.

4. Query Processing

In this section, we describe the query processing strategies for the query derivation models shown in Section 3.

4.1. Query Task

First, we introduce the notion of a query task. A *query task* specifies what should be retrieved when a query center q and a distance function $\mathcal{D}$ are given. As described in Section 3, a spatial query is fixed by specifying a query center, a distance function, and a query task. In our framework, query centers and distance functions are variables and change according to the movement of an object, while a query task is usually fixed throughout the movement. Therefore, we can say that a query task specifies a *continual query* for the moving object.

In this paper, we consider the following two query tasks:

- **range query task (equi-volume query task)**: On each movement, data objects within distance ε from the current query center q are retrieved. When a query center q, a distance matrix $\mathbf{M}$, and a distance value ε is given, we denote the ellipsoid region, centered at q and enclosed by the isosurface of distance ε, by

$$\text{ellip}(\mathbf{M}, q, \varepsilon) = \{p \mid p \in \mathcal{R}^d, \mathcal{D}_{\mathbf{M}}^2(p, q) \leq \varepsilon^2\}. \quad (12)$$

- **k-nn query task**: For each movement, k nearest objects from q are retrieved.

Here we mention an important property of the range query task. The volume of an ellipsoid region $\text{ellip}(\mathbf{M}, q, \varepsilon)$ is given by the following formula [6]:

$$vol(\text{ellip}(\mathbf{M}, q, \varepsilon)) = \frac{\pi^{\frac{d}{2}}}{\Gamma(\frac{d}{2} + 1)} \frac{\varepsilon^d}{\det(\mathbf{M})^{\frac{1}{2}}}, \qquad (13)$$

where $\Gamma(\cdot)$ is the gamma function. Since our ellipsoid distance derivation models **OV** and **HB** assure that $\det(\mathbf{M}) = 1$ as shown in Eq. (7), if ε is constant, the volume of each ellipsoid calculated on each object movement also becomes constant. Namely, if ε is constant, we can assure that the volume of the ellipsoid region for each range query is also constant throughout the movement. Therefore, we can say that the range query task is also an *equi-volume continual query* task.

4.2. Use of Bounding Regions

It is indispensable to use *spatial indexes* [13] effectively for the efficient query processing in spatial databases. Although we have to process ellipsoid queries for the **OV** and **HB** models, spatial indexes such as R-tree only support Euclidean distance-based queries and rectangle-based range queries in general. Therefore, we incorporate the approach proposed in [2] into our framework. The idea of the approach is to calculate the bounding region (bounding box or bounding sphere) that tightly bounds the given ellipsoid region then retrieve candidate objects using spatial indexes.

The *MBB (minimum bounding box) region* $\text{MBB}(\mathbf{M}, q, \varepsilon)$ that tightly bounds the ellipsoid region $\text{ellip}(\mathbf{M}, q, \varepsilon)$ (Eq. (12)) is given as follows [2]:

$$\text{MBB}(\mathbf{M}, q, \varepsilon)_i = \left[q_i - \varepsilon \sqrt{\mathbf{M}_{ii}^{-1}}, \; q_i + \varepsilon \sqrt{\mathbf{M}_{ii}^{-1}} \right], \quad (14)$$

where $\text{MBB}(\mathbf{M}, q, \varepsilon)_i$ ($i = 1, \ldots, d$) denotes the range that $\text{MBB}(\mathbf{M}, q, \varepsilon)$ takes in the i-th dimension. $\mathbf{M}_{ii}^{-1}$ means the (i, i) entry of the matrix $\mathbf{M}^{-1}$. This is illustrated in Fig. 5. The *MBS (minimum bounding sphere) region* $\text{MBS}(\mathbf{M}, q, \varepsilon)$ that tightly bounds the ellipsoid region $\text{ellip}(\mathbf{M}, q, \varepsilon)$ is derived as follows [2]:

$$\text{MBS}(\mathbf{M}, q, \varepsilon) = \left\{ p \mid p \in \mathcal{R}^d, \mathcal{D}_{\text{Euclid}}^2(p, q) \leq \frac{\varepsilon^2}{\lambda_{\min}} \right\}, \qquad (15)$$

where $\lambda_{\min}$ is the smallest eigenvalue of $\mathbf{M}$. Therefore, the radius of the MBS is given by $\varepsilon/\sqrt{\lambda_{\min}}$. This is illustrated in Fig. 6. The selection of the bounding region approximation method depends on the available spatial indexes; for example, if an R-tree index is available, we should use the MBB approximation.

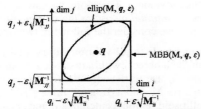

Figure 5. MBB-based Approximation

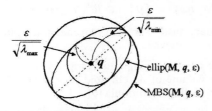

Figure 6. MBS-based Approximation

4.3. Query Processing Algorithms

In this subsection, we show query processing algorithms to process neighborhood queries using spatial indexes. We assume that the underlying spatial index module provides the following functions:

- `rect_search(r)`: retrieves all the objects within a d-dimensional rectangle region r.

- `dist_search(q, ε)`: retrieves all the objects p that satisfies $\mathcal{D}_{\mathrm{Euclid}}(p, q) \leq \varepsilon$.

- `knn_search(q, k)`: retrieves the nearest k objects from q based on the Euclidean distance.

Since these search functions can be easily supported by traditional spatial indexes, the query processing procedures shown below are considered to be general ones.

Processing range queries The processing of a range query task is basically based on the approach in [2]. If we use the MBB-based approximation, we first issue a range query `rect_search(MBB(M, q, ε))` for the filtering; note that according to the nature of the bounding region, the retrieved objects may contain *false alarms* but there are no *false dismissals* [11]. Therefore, we check whether each retrieved object p satisfies the original condition $\mathcal{D}_{\mathbf{M}}(p, q) \leq \varepsilon$ and discard false alarms to obtain the final result. If we use the MBS-based approximation, the query `dist_search(q, ε/√λ_min)` is issued as the filtering query considering the spherical bounding relationship shown in Fig. 6.

Processing k-nn queries For k-nn queries based on ellipsoid distances, processing algorithms that effectively use conventional spatial indexes are shown in [2, 30]. However, these algorithms directly use the internal structures of spatial indexes. Instead of them, we use the following k-nn query processing procedure that is implementable using only the three basic search functions described above.

1. Issue `knn_search(q, k)`, then get k-nn objects in terms of the Euclidean distance $\mathcal{D}_{\mathrm{Euclid}}(\cdot, \cdot)$. Let the Euclidean distance from q to the k-th object be δ.

2. Apply the range query procedure shown above to retrieve objects within the ellipsoid region $\mathrm{ellip}(\mathbf{M}, q, \delta\sqrt{\lambda_{\max}})$.

3. Select k nearest objects in terms of the ellipsoid distance $\mathcal{D}_{\mathbf{M}}(\cdot, \cdot)$ from the objects retrieved in step 2.

The ellipsoid region $\mathrm{ellip}(\mathbf{M}, q, \delta\sqrt{\lambda_{\max}})$ in Step 2 is an ellipsoid centered at q and tightly bounds a sphere centered at q with radius δ, as shown in Fig. 7. According to Step 1, we can find at least k objects within the ellipsoid $\mathrm{ellip}(\mathbf{M}, q, \delta\sqrt{\lambda_{\max}})$. Therefore, it is assured that all the result objects of the original k-nn query are contained in this ellipsoid region. Therefore, we issue a range query to retrieve all the objects within $\mathrm{ellip}(\mathbf{M}, q, \delta\sqrt{\lambda_{\max}})$ using the above procedure, then rank them in terms of the ellipsoid distance $\mathcal{D}_{\mathbf{M}}(\cdot, \cdot)$ to obtain the k-nn objects.

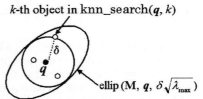

Figure 7. Processing k-NN Query

A similar k-nn query processing strategy is used in [23] to retrieve medical images with similar shapes based on the morphology concept. They used a cost-effective lower-bounding distance function instead of a costly morphological shape similarity function to determine the upper bound distance for the efficient k-nn query processing.

5. Incremental Query Update

5.1. Our Approach

When an object moves to the next position, we have to recalculate a new query center and a new distance function to generate the next neighborhood query. However, it is costly to recalculate all the required information from scratch and to maintain a long sequence of trajectory points permanently. In this section, we show incremental query update strategies which are efficient in terms of storage and computation costs.

Note that we do not reuse the previous query result for the next query processing. We simply process a new query without considering the previous query result. The reasons as follows:

1. If the spatial indexes are well-organized, page caching will reduce the I/O cost because continual object movement usually has page access locality.

2. It is difficult to reuse previous query result with low cost in our context since query centers and distance functions change every retrieval time.

3. Although ellipsoid distances are criticized by their computation costs in high dimensional spaces [2, 27, 30], our main target areas are low dimensional spaces such as $d = 2$ and 3 so that the calculation cost of ellipsoid distances in query processing is not the bottleneck of query processing.

5.2. Incremental Update Procedures

In this subsection, we assume that a moving object, which is located at x_τ at $t = \tau$, actually arrives at the predicted next point $x_{\tau+1}$ in time. Namely, the predicted arrival point $x_{\tau+1}$,

Table 2. Changes of Influence Values

	x_1	$\cdots$	x_τ	$x_{\tau+1}$	$\cdots$	$x_{\tau+\sigma}$	$x_{\tau+\sigma+1}$	$\cdots$	$x_{\tau+\tau'}$
$t=\tau$	$\mu^{\tau+\sigma-1}$	$\cdots$	μ^σ	$\mu^{\sigma-1}$	$\cdots$	1	ν	$\cdots$	$\nu^{\tau'-\sigma}$
$t=\tau+1$	$\mu^{\tau+\sigma}$	$\cdots$	$\mu^{\sigma+1}$	μ^σ	$\cdots$	μ	1	$\cdots$	$\nu^{\tau'-\sigma-1}$

the point where the object was supposed to reach at $t = \tau+1$, is approximately equal to the point $\tilde{x}_{\tau+1}$ where the object is actually located at $t = \tau + 1$ ($x_{\tau+1} \approx \tilde{x}_{\tau+1}$).

Changes of influence values When a moving object arrives at $x_{\tau+1}$, we have to update the influence values on the trajectory points for the next query generation. When the current time changes from $t = \tau$ to $t = \tau+1$, the influence decay factors change as shown in Table 2. After the change, $x_{\tau+\sigma+1}$ has the highest influence value for the query generation.

Update procedures for query centers and distance functions shown below have to reflect these changes of influence values.

Updating query centers For the model **cur**, we can simply set $x_{\tau+\sigma+1}$ to the new query center q. For the model **avg**, we can obtain an incremental update algorithm as follows. First, we translate Eq. (3) into

$$\bar{x}|_\tau = \frac{s^-|_\tau + s^+|_\tau}{w|_\tau}, \tag{16}$$

where vectors $s^-|_\tau$ and $s^+|_\tau$ are defined as

$$s^-|_\tau = \sum_{t=1}^{\tau+\sigma} \mu^{\tau+\sigma-t} x_t \tag{17}$$

$$s^+|_\tau = \sum_{t=\tau+\sigma+1}^{\tau+\tau'} \nu^{t-\tau-\sigma} x_t. \tag{18}$$

The notation "$|_\tau$" represents that the variable is as of $t = \tau$. Scalar values $w|_\tau$ is defined by

$$w|_\tau = w^-|_\tau + w^+|_\tau \tag{19}$$

$$w^-|_\tau = \sum_{t=1}^{\tau+\sigma} \mu^{\tau+\sigma-t} = \frac{1-\mu^{\tau+\sigma}}{1-\mu} \tag{20}$$

$$w^+|_\tau = \sum_{t=\tau+\sigma+1}^{\tau+\tau'} \nu^{t-\tau-\sigma} = \frac{\nu(1-\nu^{\tau'-\sigma})}{1-\nu}. \tag{21}$$

When the object moves to $x_{\tau+1}$ at $t = \tau+1$, we can update the state vectors by

$$s^-|_{\tau+1} = \mu s^-|_\tau + x_{\tau+\sigma+1} \tag{22}$$

$$s^+|_{\tau+1} = \frac{1}{\nu} s^+|_\tau - x_{\tau+\sigma+1}. \tag{23}$$

Then we can derive the update formula of the query center for the model **avg** as follows:

$$\bar{x}|_{\tau+1} = \frac{s^-|_{\tau+1} + s^+|_{\tau+1}}{w|_{\tau+1}}. \tag{24}$$

For this algorithm, we have to store *only* two d-dimensional vectors s^- (Eq. (17)) and s^+ (Eq. (18)) as internal states. When the object arrives at $x_{\tau+1}$, we can update the query center using Eqs. (22), (23), and (24). The algorithm has a benefit that we do not have to maintain a long sequence of trajectory points; we can update q in *constant time* for fixed dimensionality d.

Updating distance functions For the models **OV** and **HB**, we have to update the distance matrix $\mathbf{M}$ according to the movement of an object. As shown in Eq. (9) and Eq. (10), an update of $\mathbf{M}$ can be reduced to an update of the covariance matrix $\mathbf{C}$. In the following, we show an incremental update procedure for the covariance matrix $\mathbf{C}$ when query centers are calculated by the **avg** model. Based on the similar approach, we can also derive the update procedure for the **cur** model [18].

Now we show only the derived update procedure for the **avg** model. Details of the derivation are described in [18]. First, we separate $\mathbf{C}|_\tau$ into two "past" and "future" covariance matrices $\mathbf{C}^-|_\tau = [c_{jk}^-|_\tau]$ and $\mathbf{C}^+|_\tau = [c_{jk}^+|_\tau]$:

$$\mathbf{C}|_\tau = \mathbf{C}^-|_\tau + \mathbf{C}^+|_\tau, \tag{25}$$

which are defined as

$$c_{jk}^-|_\tau = \sum_{t=1}^{\tau+\sigma} \mu^{\tau+\sigma-t}(x_{tj} - \bar{x}_j|_\tau)(x_{tk} - \bar{x}_k|_\tau) \tag{26}$$

$$c_{jk}^+|_\tau = \sum_{t=\tau+\sigma+1}^{\tau+\tau'} \nu^{t-\tau-\sigma}(x_{tj} - \bar{x}_j|_\tau)(x_{tk} - \bar{x}_k|_\tau) \tag{27}$$

Updates are processed as follows. First d-dimensional vectors m and r are calculated:

$$m = \frac{-w^+|_\tau s^-|_\tau + w^-|_\tau s^+|_\tau}{w|_\tau} \tag{28}$$

$$r = \frac{(\mu w|_\tau - w|_{\tau+1})s^-|_\tau + (\frac{1}{\nu}w|_\tau - w|_{\tau+1})s^+|_\tau}{w|_\tau w|_{\tau+1}} \tag{29}$$

Then a differential vector $\Delta x = [\Delta x_1, \ldots, \Delta x_d]^T$ is calculated by

$$\Delta x = x_{\tau+\sigma+1} - \bar{x}|_\tau, \tag{30}$$

and the state covariance matrices are updated:

$$\mathbf{C}^-|_{\tau+1} = \mu\left[\mathbf{C}^-|_\tau + rm^T + mr^T + w^-|_\tau rr^T\right] + (\Delta x - r)(\Delta x - r)^T \tag{31}$$

$$\mathbf{C}^+|_{\tau+1} = \frac{1}{\nu}[\mathbf{C}^+|_\tau - rm^T - mr^T + w^+|_\tau rr^T] - (\Delta x - r)(\Delta x - r)^T \tag{32}$$

For this distance function update algorithms, we have to maintain only two $d \times d$ matrices $\mathbf{C}^-$ (Eq. (26)) and $\mathbf{C}^+$ (Eq. (27)) as the state matrices and the update costs are *constant* for a fixed d. When the object arrive at $x_{\tau+1}$, we can update the covariance matrix $\mathbf{C}|_\tau$ to $\mathbf{C}|_{\tau+1}$ using the above formulas. Similar to the case of the query centers, this algorithm has a benefit that we do not have to maintain a long sequence of trajectory points.

After the updates of the query center and the distance function, we invoke the neighborhood object retrieval procedure shown in Section 4 to perform the specified query task. Finally, we increment the current time as $\tau \leftarrow \tau + 1$. Then we can use the same update procedure for the next point.

5.3. Practical Update Procedures

Unfortunately, the incremental update procedures shown above have two problems:

1. If $x_{\tau+1}$, the predicted point for the time $t = \tau + 1$, and $\tilde{x}_{\tau+1}$, the actually arrived point at $t = \tau + 1$, are quite different, the calculated query center and the distance function will drift from the "true" ones. This situation is caused by two reasons: 1) the moving object came to the point $x_{\tau+1}$ earlier or later than expected, or 2) the moving object has changed its route.

2. The query center derivation model **avg** and the distance function derivation models **OV** and **HB** have a noise problem: even if $x_{\tau+1} \approx \tilde{x}_{\tau+1}$ is satisfied, the use of Eq. (18) and Eq. (32) to update s^+ and $\mathbf{C}^+$ causes the amplification of small noises because $\nu < 1$. Therefore, repeated use of Eq. (18) and Eq. (32) for a number of incremental updates will result in incorrect query generation.

The practical solution for this problem is as follows:

- If the actual point $\tilde{x}_{\tau+1}$ at $t = \tau + 1$ is mostly equal to the prediction ($\tilde{x}_{\tau+1} \approx x_{\tau+1}$), or the user allow small errors, apply the ordinal update procedure in Subsection 5.2.

- Otherwise, get a new prediction of future trajectory points $x_{\tau+2}, x_{\tau+3}, \dots$ from the route calculation module (e.g., a car navigation system) then recompute statistics values s^+ (required only for **avg**) and $\mathbf{C}^+$ (required for **OV** and **HB**).

This update strategy seems to be costly, but remember the role of the future decay factor ν; it sets high weights on the "near future" positions and discards far future ones. Therefore, the route calculation module has to calculate only a small number of trajectory positions that will be reached in the near future. Additionally, the recomputation cost of s^+ and $\mathbf{C}^+$ would not be higher than the cost to estimate future trajectories often recalculated by the route calculation module in typical mobile applications.

Finally, we have to remind the benefit of our approach: we can "forget" the past information freely; in contrast to x^+ and $\mathbf{C}^+$, we do not incur additional processing cost for x^- and $\mathbf{C}^-$.

6 Experimental Results

6.1. Behaviors of Query Generation Models

In the first experiment, we examine the difference between query generation models and their behaviors under different parameter settings. Figure 8 shows a trajectory of a moving object from A to B, and the object is currently located at x. We assume that the object is moving with constant velocity and 35 trajectory points are taken along the trajectory. The figure shows the isosorfaces of queries generated by **EU(cur)** and **OV(cur)** under the conditions $\sigma = 0$ (no look ahead) and $\mu = \nu = 0.5$ (same decay late for the past and the future) for the range query task. As shown in the figure, the model **OV**, represented by an ellipse, is well conformed along the trajectory as expected.

Figure 9 shows isosurfaces of queries generated by **OV(cur)** under the conditions $\sigma = 0$ (no look ahead: represented by the solid ellipse centered at q_1) and $\sigma = 5$ (highest

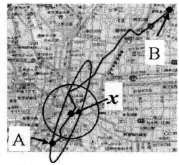

Figure 8. Comparison of EU and OV

weight on five unit times later: represented by the dotted ellipse centered at q_2). Other conditions are the same as Fig. 8. The query center q_1 for $\sigma = 0$ is approximately equal to the point x, the current location of the moving object. We can easily observe that q_2 is more biased towards the future trajectory because of the look ahead parameter σ.

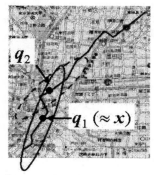

Figure 9. Comparison of Different σ-values ($\sigma = 0, 5$)

Figure 10 shows the behaviors of **OV(avg)** under two different ν values $\nu = 0.4$ (middle influence weights on future points: represented by the solid ellipse centered at q_1) and $\nu = 0.9$ (high influence weights on future points: represented by the dotted ellipse centered at q_2). Other parameters are set as $\mu = 0.4$ and $\sigma = 0$. The query center q_1 is approximately the same as x, the current location of the moving object. As shown in the figure, query q_2 is more biased to the future because of the parameter setting of ν.

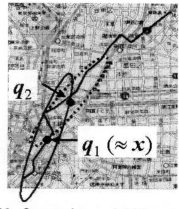

Figure 10. Comparison of Different ν-values ($\nu = 0.4, 0.9$)

Figure 11 shows the behaviors under different λ values for **HB(cur)**: $\lambda = 1.0$ (the solid ellipse) and 0.7 (the dotted ellipse). The former case corresponds to **OV(cur)** since $\lambda = 1$. The small circle is an isosurface of **EU(cur)**. As shown in the figure, **OV(cur)** has a narrow isosurface for this case because the trajectory nearby x is almost on the straight line. It may be an excessive behavior for a user who has interests only for the neighborhood information. In contrast to this, **HB(cur)** with $\lambda = 0.7$ has a more mild behavior; we can observe that the **HB** model has a mixed behavior of **OV** and **EU**.

Figure 11. Comparison of Different λ-values ($\lambda = 1.0, 0.7$)

6.2. Continual Neighborhood Tracking

In this experiment, we perform a trace-based simulation of continual neighborhood tracking. Figure 12 shows a driving route from the point A to C via the intermediate point B. We assume that a vehicle make a short stop at B. From A, it takes about thirteen minutes to reach C. For this route, we collected real driving trace data, represented by the positions of a car, obtained for every five seconds of the drive. We put small circles on the trajectory for every thirty seconds based on the trace data. As shown in the figure, the driving speed is slow nearby B because the road is congested around there, and the vehicle has to turn down a side road to stop by the intermediate point B.

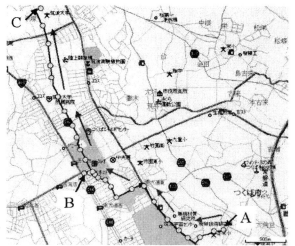

Figure 12. Driving Trace Data

In Fig. 13, the isosurfaces of neighborhood queries for the driving trace data is shown. To make the presentation understandable, isosurfaces are presented for every one minute of the driving. The neighborhood tracking is based on the range query task and the **OV(cur)** model with the parameters $\sigma = 1$, $\mu = 0.8$, and $\nu = 0.8$. As shown in the figure, each neighborhood query captures the local trajectory around it. Note that, for the straight roads driven with high speed, the isosurfaces take narrower shapes, and for the curved and crowded roads (especially around the point B) driven with slow speed, the isosurfaces take more rounded shapes. Based on this experiment, we can say that the proposed method can adaptively modify spatial queries according to the situation (the direction and the speed) of the moving object.

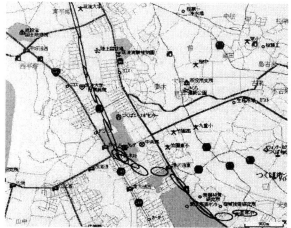

Figure 13. Neighborhood Tracking Result

6.3. Retrieval Cost

Finally we report the analysis of the retrieval cost. We use the Montgomery County dataset [10] with mid-points of road segments from the Montgomery County of Maryland that consists of 27,282 points (Fig. 14). We compare three approaches: sequential scan, the Euclidean distance-based approach, and the ellipsoid distance-based approach (**OV(cur)** is used). As the spatial index facility, we use the R*-tree extension of GiST [14]. We assume that an object moves along the road as shown in the figure; the road runs from south (Washington D.C.) to north and there are 62 mid-points of road segments on it. We also assume that the moving object specifies the k-nn query task ($k = 1, 10, 50, 100, 150$) and a k-nn query is issued on each of the 62 mid-points. We examine the number of page accesses to process k-nn queries.

Figure 15 shows the average number of page accesses to process k-nn queries on each query point. The x-axis represents the parameter k ($k = 1, 10, 50, 100, 150$) and the y-axis shows the number of page accesses in log-scale. In this experiment, we do not assume the existence of page caches. As shown in the figure, the page access cost of ellipsoid queries is slightly higher than that of the Euclidean distance-based queries (this property always holds because of the k-nn query procedure shown in Section 4), but quite lower than that of sequential scan. As shown in this experiment, the use of a spatial index based on the algorithms shown in Section 4 reduces the processing cost, and is indispensable in our context. Although this experiment does not assume the existence of a page cache, if a spatial index is well-organized and

Figure 14. Montgomery County Dataset

the spatial locality is well preserved in each leaf page of the index, page caching will further reduce redundant page I/Os since the trajectories of moving objects have spatial contiguity. Based on this experiment we can say that our use of a spatial index facility will support the neighborhood tracking task with low cost.

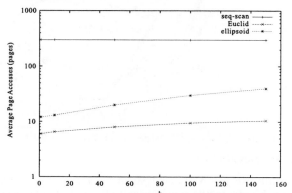

Figure 15. Average Page Accesses for k-nn Query

7. Related Work

Recent years, database technologies according to moving objects have been extensively developed: the main topics are data modeling issues [12, 16, 34] and efficient indexing and retrieval methods. In [1, 7, 21, 22, 28, 33], indexing methods are proposed to query moving objects stored in a database. In a typical setting, the trajectory of a moving object is represented by a function $x(t)$ parameterized by time t. In many cases, a linear function is used as $x(t)$ for its simplicity. In contrast to these indexing approaches aiming for efficient retrieval of moving objects stored in a database, we intend to provide neighborhood information for a moving object along its trajectory. Moreover, most of the indexing approaches for moving objects only consider static cases such that trajectories of objects are fixed beforehand. In contrast to this, we have considered a more dynamic situation and proposed adaptive query generation and processing strategies. And note that our approach is applicable to the parameterized representation of trajectories by transforming $x(t)$ into a sequence of points using sampling.

The influence model of trajectory positions proposed in this paper is a model to set the highest importance to the current position and to discount the importance of past and future trajectory points exponentially. The approach setting exponential weights to past samples then focusing mainly on recent data samples is used in various areas that process time-varying data in an online manner, for example, in signal processing and control [5, 25], time-series analysis [35], and machine learning [32]. The approach is often called *exponential forgetting* or *exponential discounting* and the past decay parameter μ is called a *forgetting factor* or a *discount-rate parameter*. Our approach shares the same idea with these approaches but we also set exponential weights to future predicted positions to focus on the "near future". Sample weighting is also used in statistics, for example, to estimate covariance matrices in a robust manner by excluding the effects of outliers [29].

8. Conclusions and Future Work

In this paper, we proposed a new approach to retrieve and provide neighborhood information to moving objects. Our approach use the past and future trajectories of a moving object to generate an appropriate query that mainly focuses on the current (or near future) neighborhood of the object. For this purpose, we introduced the influence model of trajectory points to discount past and future positions gradually. In our context, queries are formulated as ellipsoid queries that can be tuned by considering the trajectories of moving objects and users' preferences. Since ellipsoid queries can be supported efficiently using conventional spatial indexes, our approach can be implemented with low overhead. Also, we presented the incremental query update procedures to generate the next query from the previous query states in an incremental manner. Therefore, our approach would be highly adaptive in practical situations.

In future work, we would like to develop a semi-automatic parameter tuning scheme that incorporates sensory inputs from the external devices to tune the parameters to realize "situation-aware" neighborhood information presentation systems.

Acknowledgments

This research is supported in part by the Grant-in-Aid for Scientific Research from the Japan Society for the Promotion of Science and the Ministry of Education, Culture, Sports, Science and Technology (#12480067 and #12780183). Also, financial support from Secom Science and Technology Foundation is gratefully acknowledged.

References

[1] P. K. Agarwal, L. Arge, and J. Erickson. Indexing Moving Points. In *Proc. ACM PODS*, pages 175–186, 2000.

[2] M. Ankerst, B. Braunmüller, H.-P. Kriegel, and T. Seidl. Improving Adaptable Similarity Query Processing Using Approximations. In *Proc. of VLDB*, pages 206–217, 1998.

[3] M. Ankerst, H.-P. Kriegel, and T. Seidl. A Multistep Approach for Shape Similarity Search in Image Databases. *IEEE TKDE*, 6:996–1004, 1998.

[4] ArcView Tracking Analyst Extension. http://www.esri.com/software/arcview/extensions/trackingext.html.

[5] K. J. Åström and B. Wittenmark. *Adaptive Control*. Addison-Wesley, 2nd edition, 1995.

[6] H. Cramér. *Mathematical Methods for Statistics* (10th printing). Princeton University Press, 1963. (first published in Sweden, Uppsala 1945, by Almqvist & Wiksells).

[7] O. Devillers, M. Golin, K. Kedem, and S. Schirra. Queries on Voronoi Diagrams of Moving Points. *Computational Geometry*, 6:315–327, 1996.

[8] R. O. Duda, P. H. Hart, and D. G. Stork. *Pattern Classification*. Wiley, 2nd edition, 2000.

[9] C. Faloutsos, R. Barber, M. Flickner, J. Hafner, W. Niblack, D. Petkovic, and W. Equitz. Efficient and Effective Querying by Image Content. *Journal of Intelligent Information Systems*, 3(3/4):231–262, July 1994.

[10] C. Faloutsos and I. Kamel. Beyond Uniformity and Independence: Analysis of R-trees Using the Concept of Fractal Dimension. In *Proc. ACM PODS*, pages 4–13, 1994.

[11] C. Faloutsos. *Searching Multimedia Databases by Content*. Kluwer Academic Publishers, 1996.

[12] L. Forlizzi, R. H. Güting, E. Nardelli, and M. Schneider. A Data Model and Data Structures for Moving Objects Databases. In *Proc. ACM SIGMOD*, pages 319–330, 2000.

[13] V. Gaede and O. Günther. Multidimensional Access Methods. *ACM Computing Surveys*, 30(2):170–231, 1998.

[14] The GiST Indexing Project. http://gist.cs.berkeley.edu:8000/gist/.

[15] G. H. Golub and C. F. Van Loan. *Matrix Computations*. Johns Hopkins University Press, Baltimore, MD, 3rd edition, 1996.

[16] R. H. Güting, M. H. Böhlen, M. Erwig, C. S. Jensen, N. A. Lorentzos, M. Schneider, and M. Vazirgiannis. A Foundation for Representing and Querying Moving Objects. *ACM TODS*, 25(1):1–42, 2000.

[17] A. Guttman. R-Trees: A Dynamic Index Structure for Spatial Searching. In *Proc. ACM SIGMOD*, pages 47–57, 1984.

[18] Y. Ishikawa, H. Kitagawa, and T. Kawashima. Continual Neighborhood Tracking for Moving Objects Using Adaptive Distances. Technical Report, ISE-TR-02-188, Institute of Information Science and Electronics, University of Tsukuba, Apr. 2002. (available from http://www.kde.is.tsukuba.ac.jp/)

[19] Y. Ishikawa, R. Subramanya, and C. Faloutsos. MindReader: Querying Databases through Multiple Examples. In *Proc. of VLDB*, pages 218–227, 1998.

[20] R. A. Johnson and D. W. Wichern. *Applied Multivariate Statistical Analysis*. Prentice Hall, 3rd edition, 1992.

[21] G. Kollios, D. Gunopulos, and V. J. Tsotras. Nearest Neighbor Queries in a Mobile Environment. In *Proc. of Intl. Workshop Spatio-Temporal Database Management (STDBM'99)*, volume 1678, pages 119–134, LNCS.

[22] G. Kollios, D. Gunopulos, and V. T. Tsotras. On Indexing Mobile Objects. In *Proc. ACM PODS*, pages 261–272, 1999.

[23] P. Korn, N. Sidiropoulos, C. Faloutsos, E. Siegel, and Z. Protopapas. Fast Nearest Neighbor Search in Medical Image Databases. *IEEE TKDE*, 10(6):889–904, 1998.

[24] L. Liu, C. Pu, and W. Tang. Continual Queries for Internet Scale Event-Driven Information Delivery. *IEEE Trans. on Knowledge and Data Engineering*, 11(4):610–628, 1999.

[25] L. Ljung and T. Söderström. *Theory and Practice of Recursive Identification*. MIT Press, 1983.

[26] T. Musha and Y. Okamoto. *Inverse Problems and Their Solutions*. Ohmsha, Ltd., Tokyo, Japan, 1992. (in Japanese).

[27] R. T. Ng and D. Tam. Multilevel Filtering for High-Dimensional Image Data: Why and How. *IEEE TKDE*, 11(6):916–928, 1999.

[28] D. Pfoser, C. S. Jensen, and Yannis Theodoridis. Novel Approaches in Query Processing for Moving Objects. In *Proc. VLDB*, pages 395–406, 2000.

[29] P. J. Rousseeuw and A. M. Leroy. *Robust Regression and Outlier Detection*. Wiley, 1987.

[30] T. Seidl and H.-P. Kriegel. Efficient User-Adaptable Similarity Search in Large Multimedia Databases. In *Proc. of VLDB*, pages 506–515, 1997.

[31] S. Shekhar and D.-R. Liu. CCAM: A Connectivity-Clustered Access Method for Networks and Network Computations. *IEEE TKDE*, 9(1):102–119, 1997.

[32] R. S. Sutton and A. G. Barto. *Reinforcement Learning: An Introduction*. MIT Press, 1998.

[33] S. Šaltenis, C. S. Jensen, S. T. Leutenegger, and M. A. Lopez. Indexing the Positions of Continuously Moving Objects. In *Proc. ACM SIGMOD*, pages 331–342, 2000.

[34] O. Wolfson, B. Xu, S. Chamberlain, and L. Jiang. Moving Objects Databases: Issues and Solutions. In *Proc. 10th SSDBM*, pages 111–122, Capri, Italy, 1998.

[35] B.-K. Yi, N. D. Sidiropoulos, T. Johnson, H. V. Jagadish, C. Faloutsos, and A. Biliris. Online Data Mining for Co-Evolving Time Sequences. In *Proc. ICDE*, pages 13–22, 2000.

Energy-Efficient Data Broadcasting in Mobile Ad-Hoc Networks[**]

Le Gruenwald, Muhammad Javed, Meng Gu

The University of Oklahoma, School of Computer Science, Norman, OK 73019

Abstract

Energy saving is the most important issue in wireless mobile computing due to power constraints on mobile units. Data broadcasting is the main method of information dissemination in wireless networks as its cost is independent of the number of mobile hosts receiving the information. A number of data broadcasting techniques have been proposed for mobile wireless networks, where servers have no energy restrictions, but little research has been done to address the issue of data broadcasting in mobile ad-hoc networks where both servers and clients are nomadic. In this paper, we propose two groups of broadcast scheduling algorithms called adaptive broadcasting and popularity based adaptive broadcasting that consider time constraints on requests as well as energy limitation on both servers and clients. We also present the simulation experiments that compare the algorithms.

1. Introduction

In a mobile ad-hoc network (MANET), mobile units can communicate with each other directly via wireless links in the absence of a fixed wired infrastructure [6][10]. MANET is different from a wireless mobile network which usually consists of a static wired part, in which fixed hosts and base stations are interconnected through a high speed wired network, and a mobile wireless part, in which mobile units communicate with the base stations through wireless connections. A base station can only communicate with the mobile units moving within its coverage area called cell. Mobile units can communicate with each other only through at least one base station. Mobile units run on batteries while base stations are supplied by stable system power from static networks. In MANET, every mobile unit can move freely and communicate directly with another mobile unit as long as that mobile unit is in its communication coverage area.

In a mobile computing environment, bandwidth and power limitations impose significant restrictions on data management [8]. These limitations require frequent disconnection and inspire the need for energy-efficient data access methods. While research in mobile computing has received growing interest in recent years due to the large number of potential applications, research in mobile ad-hoc network is still in its infancy.

Data broadcasting is considered as a main method of information dissemination in mobile wireless networks and can also be adopted for information distribution in mobile ad-hoc networks. However, in a MANET environment, both servers and clients are mobile. Therefore, energy conservation issues must be considered in developing broadcasting strategies for both servers and clients. In this paper, we propose two groups of broadcast scheduling algorithms for MANET called adaptive broadcasting and popularity based adaptive broadcasting which address the issues of client and server energy limitation and timing constraints on requests. The performance of the proposed algorithms is analyzed using simulation.

This paper is organized as follows. Section 2 reviews related work. Section 3 describes our architecture. Sections 4 and 5 present our broadcasting algorithms. Section 6 analyzes the simulation experiments. Section 7 provides conclusions and future research.

2. Related Work

The existing studies on data broadcasting are limited to mobile network environments, where only clients are nomadic. They attempt to save energy for clients but not for servers. Below is a brief discussion of the three most recent data broadcast algorithms for mobile networks.

Askoy et. al. [1] have presented a large-scale low-overhead on-demand broadcasting model called RxW (Requests time Wait). In RxW, at each broadcast tick, the

---

[**] This research is supported in part by National Science Foundation grant No. EIA-9973465

server chooses an item with the highest value of (R * W) where R is the number of outstanding requests and W is the waiting time for the first request. The entry for this data item is then removed from the queue that keeps track of the number of requests and earliest request time for data. The algorithm makes no assumptions regarding access probabilities of data items. However, the size of the queue is equal to the size of the database, therefore, large databases will require a significant overhead in terms of time to find the highest value of R * W and space to store frequency and time.

Xuan et. al. [16] have proposed two on demand broadcast scheduling strategies, which consider deadlines attached to requests to decide the next item to be broadcast. In the first strategy, the server always broadcasts a request with the earliest deadline first (EDF) and every request is scheduled once no matter how frequently the same request is encountered. The second strategy is called EDF-batch, in which the server broadcasts an item according to EDF but after broadcasting, it removes the other entries for the same request.

Datta et. al. [8] have proposed the protocols that dynamically change the contents of broadcast according to client requests. In these protocols the broadcast data and index are organized using the (1,m) indexing strategy [9]. The server decides the data item to be included in the broadcast on the basis of priority, which is given by (IF^N*PF), where IF is Ignore Factor, PF is the Popularity Factor, and N is an adaptive scaling factor. PF makes sure that most popular data items are included in the broadcast and IF makes sure that less popular long neglected data items are also broadcast. In the Constant Broadcast Size protocol, the broadcast size is fixed, and after each broadcast cycle, the server calculates the priority of data items, sorts them in descending order of priority and adds them to the broadcast until it is full. In the Variable Broadcast Size protocol, all the items with PF > 0 are added to the broadcast set.

3. Architecture

Depending on communication capacity, computing power, disk storage, size of memory and energy limitation, MHs can be classified into two groups: 1) computers with reduced memory, storage, power and computing capabilities called *Small Mobile Hosts* (SMHs) *or Clients*, and 2) classical workstations equipped with more storage, power, communication and computing facilities than the SMHs called *Large Mobile Host* (LMHs) *or Servers*. Each MH has a radius of influence. An MH can directly communicate with other MHs within its radius of influence. If two MHs are outside each other's radius of influence, they will be able to indirectly

communicate with each other in multiple hops using intermediate MHs [2] as shown in Figure 1.

To conserve energy, an MH can operate in Active, Doze or Sleep mode. In active mode, the MH's CPU is working and its communication device can transmit and receive signals. In doze mode, the CPU of the MH will be working at a lower rate, but it can receive and examine messages from other MHs; so the MH can be awaken by a message from other MHs [3]. In sleep mode, both the CPU and the communication device of the MH are suspended. Due to energy and storage limitations, we will assume that only LMHs will store the whole DBMS (Data Base Management System) and SMHs will store only some modules of the DBMS that allow them to query their own data, submit transactions to LMHs and receive the results.

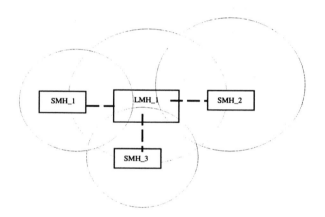

Figure 1. Architecture

This proposed architecture can be used to support many applications, such as battlefields and disaster recovery. In battlefields, portable computing devices with soldiers will work as SMHs while computers stored in tanks and humvees will work as LMHs. Note that tank/humvee computers are usually battery-powered so that they can easily be moved to other tanks/humvees, and these vehicles do not have to be turned on in order for their computers to function. These LMHs can store tactical information regarding enemy and other units in a database and the SMHs can communicate with the LMHs to get this information (e.g. location and strength of enemy units). In a disaster recovery operation, the palmtops carried by rescuers act as the SMHs and the computers in mobile hospitals can be viewed as the LMHs. The LMHs can keep the information about medical equipments in their databases, and the SMHs can query about the inventory.

4. The Proposed Adaptive Broadcast Scheduling Algorithms

The ultimate goal of broadcast scheduling is to minimize the average response time for clients' requests, but for MANET, broadcast scheduling must also address the issue of energy restriction on both servers and clients. In MANET, clients' requests will typically require fast responses with short soft deadlines [14].

Broadcast scheduling among the distinguished servers is possible in the assumed MANET. In MANET the movement patterns of the servers and the clients and the network topology are unpredictable. The simplest case is that in a certain area, there exist one server and multiple clients. These clients can communicate with the server if the server's radius of influence covers them. However, in the more complicated and practical cases, multiple servers and multiple clients exist in some areas. A client may communicate and receive broadcast from one or more servers depending on its location. Therefore, it is not energy-efficient that these servers broadcast the same data. On the other hand, a client who can communicate with one server only will prefer to have that server broadcast as many data items as possible so that it can benefit from broadcasting.

Based on the above considerations, we develop the broadcast scheduling algorithms applicable to the case where multiple servers and multiple clients exist in a certain area. We assume full data replication among the servers and the data in a server's local database can be divided into two groups: frequently requested data, called hot data and less frequently requested data, called cold data. The server's power level and location information are two hottest data items that are broadcast by all the servers. All requests from the clients are "read-only". Each request asks for one data item only.

Each server keeps the power level and location information of all the other servers in the network in its local database. It does periodic broadcasting for some hot data items only and offers cold data on-demand in one broadcast cycle. We assume one broadcast cycle takes T units of time and T is large enough to broadcast all hot data as in traditional periodic broadcast. A broadcast cycle should also have some time slots to serve data on-demand. The on-demand data items fill this part spontaneously. Thus, a broadcast cycle, in terms of time, consists of time to broadcast the indices and data, the time for on-demand data and maybe some idle time. The $(1, m)$ indexing scheme [9] is used in our algorithm. The periodic broadcast size varies within the range of T. The algorithm consists of two parts: Part 1 is performed by the leader server and Part 2 is performed by all the servers in the system.

4.1. Part 1: Leader Protocol

When a broadcast cycle starts, the server with the highest power level will be the leader and schedule data broadcast. The other servers will follow the instructions from the leader to arrange their broadcasting schedules. The idea is that the server with the highest power level will try to schedule data broadcasting for the other servers. It will partition the hot data, except for the power level and location information, into portions. The amount of data in each portion, which will be assigned to a server for broadcasting, will depend on the power level of the server. The server with less energy available broadcasts a smaller portion of hot data but these data are more frequently accessed than those broadcast by the server with more energy. This way the server with less energy will not have to accommodate too many on-demand requests. The algorithm is presented below.

Adaptive Broadcast Scheduling Algorithm (Part 1 - Leader Protocol): for the server with the highest power level:

Let P_1, P_2, ..., P_i, ..., P_n denote the power levels of all n servers. i represents a server's id number. Let $d = \{d_1, d_2, ..., d_j, ..., d_N\}$ denote the set of the more frequently requested data items, except power levels and locations of servers. N is the total amount of data items in set d.
Sort P_1, P_2, ..., P_n in increasing order, with $P_1 < P_2 < ... < P_n$;
If the power level of the server who is running this algorithm is the maximum power level among all the servers {
for $i = 1, ..., n$
   Calculate the ratio $R_i = P_i/P$, where P is the sum of P_1, P_2, ..., P_n;
Sort d_j in set d in decreasing order of the request frequency $f_1, f_2, ..., f_j$, which are associated with d_1, d_2, ..., d_N respectively;
for $i = 1, ..., n$
   Assign the first $R_i * N$ amount of data items in set d to server i;
}
else
   Send an appointment message to the server with the highest power level to notify it to start this algorithm for the next broadcast cycle;

Initially, each server will broadcast its power level and location to start the communication. The server with the highest power level becomes the leader and runs this algorithm every C broadcast cycles. The leader may change since after some time, the leader may have lower energy than other servers because of its heavier duty of broadcasting. To restart the algorithm, a routing algorithm in the mobile ad-hoc network is also assumed to be available [10].

4.2. Part 2: All Server Protocol

All the servers in the network will change their broadcast schedules after receiving a message from the leader. According to our scheme, the broadcast content of a server is only a portion of the more frequently requested data so the number of requests for data items not in the broadcast content from the clients may increase. We have to dynamically change a server's broadcast content so that broadcast data can satisfy as many requests as possible. Consequently, the server will save its energy by not serving the data on demand for many identical requests. A client will also save energy by going into doze mode to wait for the broadcast and directly retrieving data from the "air". The client can follow the provided index to find the data items it wants if the broadcast can satisfy its deadline. Otherwise, the client has to submit a request to the nearest server available.

We assume that the server always keeps track of the request frequency (RF) for each data item. The Exponential Weighted Moving Average (EWMA) method [11] given below will be used for calculating request frequencies.

$$f_{i(n)} = (f_{i(n)} + \alpha * f_{i(n-1)} + \alpha^2 * f_{i(n-2)} + ... + \alpha^{n-1} * f_{i(1)})/S$$

Here $S = (1 + \alpha + \alpha^2 + ... + \alpha^{n-1})$; f_i is the RF of data item i, $f_i(n)$ is the RF of data item i in the current broadcast cycle n. α amounts to an exponential reduction in the weight

If the RF for a particular hot data item is higher than that of a data item in the current broadcast, this hot data item should be included in the next broadcast. There are two alternatives to accomplish this. In alternative 1, this data item can replace the data item with the least RF in the current content of the periodic broadcast. After some time, the content of the periodic broadcast is getting more and more matching with the clients' access patterns through this self-learning process.

Adaptive Broadcast Scheduling Algorithm (Part 2, Alternative 1): for all servers

Any server in the assumed mobile ad-hoc environment, S_i, will run this algorithm.
For each broadcast cycle do the following:
  if S_i receives a broadcast assignment message from another server which is running our proposed adaptive broadcast scheduling algorithm (part 1) {
    if the number of data items in the assignment is less

than the number of data items in the current broadcast content
    cut down the number of data items in broadcast to the number of data items in assignment by "drop-tail";
  else
    add data items from the more frequently requested data group to the broadcast, up to the number of data items in the assignment;
  }
  if S_i receives a data request from a client {
    if S_i can satisfy the request within the deadline serve the data on demand based on "earliest deadline first" rule;
    else
      reject the request;
  }
  for each data item that was requested in this broadcast cycle {
    calculate the request frequency for this data item;
    if the request frequency of this data item i is greater than the least request frequency of a data item in the current broadcast content and this data item is in more frequently requested data group {
      replace the data item with the least request frequency in the current broadcast with the newly requested data item i;

      sort the data items in broadcast content according to the decreasing order of request frequency;

      reconstruct the index;

    }

  }

In alternative 2, when the RF of a hot data item gets higher than the RF of a data item in the current broadcast it is simply added to the broadcast.

The adaptive broadcast scheduling algorithm, which consists of part 1 and part 2 with alternative 1, is called *the adaptive replacement broadcast scheduling algorithm* (ARBSA). The adaptive broadcast scheduling algorithm which consists of part 1 and part2 with alternative 2 is called *the adaptive addition broadcast scheduling algorithm* (AABSA).

5. The Proposed Popularity Based Adaptive Broadcast Scheduling Algorithms

The EWMA based algorithms presented above require a global update when a request arrives. This requires a lot of communication among servers resulting in excessive energy consumption. Also data items to be broadcast are selected according to the global RF ignoring requests submitted to a server locally. Request deadlines and client movements are also not considered in calculating request frequencies. If the leader server leaves the network or fails, it is not clear who will run Part 1 of the algorithms. Servers that do not have any clients may waste energy since they are not required to switch to doze mode. Also, EWMA is used to calculate the RF of a data item. EWMA is a good forecasting technique where more recent values have greater influence than older data values. Therefore, if request frequencies are calculated using EWMA, data items requested in the current broadcast cycle will have more influence on the calculated request frequencies. Therefore, some of the less popular requests that were requested earlier may starve or the clients who requested the data item may leave the area.

To address the above-mentioned drawbacks, we propose two algorithms based on popularity factor [8]. They make the same assumptions about the network and the database as the EWMA based algorithms.

5.1. Broadcast Assignment

When a broadcast cycle starts, the server with the highest power becomes the leader and assigns the amount of data to be broadcast by each server according to the server's power level like the EWMA based algorithms. A server with less power will broadcast fewer data but more frequent data. The main difference is that the leader server informs the other servers only about the amount of the data they should broadcast, and the data items to be broadcast are taken by these servers from their local databases. The other difference is that the leader checks if a server will be able to broadcast the assigned data or not. If a server cannot broadcast the assigned data then it will broadcast the data and index from the previous broadcast so that it does not have to sort data and reconstruct index. A broadcast cycle in terms of time will consist of time to broadcast data and index and time to serve data on demand. A server goes into doze mode after broadcasting data and index and serving data on demand until its time to start the next broadcast cycle. The server is allowed to receive clients' requests during this period, but the number of such requests is expected to be low since data that has high access frequency is broadcast by the server. Similar to the EWMA based algorithms, the popularity based adaptive broadcast scheduling algorithms consist of two parts: leader protocol and all server protocol.

5.2. Part 1: Leader Protocol

Let P_1, P_2, P_3,...........,P_j, ...P_n be the power levels of
the servers S_1, S_2, S_3,........,S_j, ...Sn currently in the network,' n' is the number of servers currently in the network.
Let' j' be amount of energy required to broadcast one data item and 'd' be the total number of hot data items.
Sort the power levels in ascending order such that $P_1 <$ P_2 where P_1 and P_2 are power levels of S_1 and S_2 and the power level of S_1 is less than S_2
If the server running this algorithm has the highest power level among all the servers {
   calculate the sum of power levels of all the severs 'P';
   for i = 1,..........,n {
      calculate the amount of data to be broadcast by server S_i as $X_i = (Pi / P) * d$;
      if $J * X_i$ is greater than P_i then
         send a message to P_i , informing that it has to broadcast the previous broadcast set;
      else
         assign the' X_i' amount of data to be broadcasted by server S_i ;
   }
   appoint a backup leader server, which has the 2nd highest power level;
}
else
   send an appointment message to the server with the highest power level to start this algorithm

The leader server will run the above algorithm whenever a change occurs in the sorted list of power levels maintained by the leader. The back up leader is assigned so that if the leader moves out of the network or fails, it will act as the new leader.

5.3. Part 2: All Server Protocol

The servers, which accept the instructions from the leader, change their broadcast schedules accordingly. These servers will sort the hot data items in descending order of their request frequencies kept in their local database. After sorting, the servers will take the amount of data assigned by the leader from their local database and start broadcasting it. Similar to the argument we have made for ABRSA's and AARSA's part 2, the servers must dynamically change their broadcast content so that broadcasting can satisfy most of the requests. In these algorithms, the servers keep track of the number of requests for all the *hot* data items and use this information to calculate the *popularity factor* (PF) of data items as defined below [8].

The popularity factor *PFA* of a data item *A* is defined as the number of clients interested in *A* at a particular time *T* [8]. When a client requests for *A*, the popularity factor is incremented by 1 and the system records the corresponding time *TSA*. A corresponding decrement of 1 will be performed at *TSA + RL* to reflect the departure of the client who requested *A*, where *residence latency* (RL) is defined as the average time a mobile unit spends in a cell. RL will be computed a *priori* based on the advance knowledge of user movement patterns and cell geography [8]. Requests have deadlines, so whenever the deadline of a request for *A* expires, a decrement of 1 is performed to the popularity factor. The idea is to include only those data items in the broadcast that can satisfy the requests of clients currently in the cell within the associated deadlines. This way the server has to keep track of only those requests, which were received during the interval *current_time −RL* [8].

If the popularity factor of a *hot* item becomes higher than that of a data item in the current broadcast then it is added to the broadcast using the two alternatives described in Section 4.2. Below is the algorithm's part 2 using alternative 1.

Real Time Popularity Based Adaptive Replacement Broadcast Scheduling Algorithm (Part2, Alternative 1):

Every server Si will run this algorithm.
For each broadcast cycle do the following:
  If Si receives a message to broadcast the previous broadcast set
    broadcast the previous broadcast set and index
  else {
    sort the hot data items in descending order according to popularity factor;
    take the first Ri amount of data from the local database;
    while a new assignment message is not received {
      broadcast the data using (1, m) indexing technique;
      if Si has received a data request for a cold item
        serve data on demand based on the basis of earliest deadline first;
      for each data item requested in (current_time - RL) period {
        calculate the popularity factor;
        if the popularity of this data item becomes greater than the popularity of any of the data items in the current broadcast content {
          replace the data item with the least popularity factor in the current broadcast with this data item;
          reconstruct index;
        }
      }
    if Si did not receive any requests in the previous C broadcasts
      broadcast a greeting message to clients and wait for a reply;

  if no reply received
    switch to doze mode until a request is received;
  if this is the backup leader
    if the power level of the leader was received continue;
  else
    assume control and run the algorithm part 1;
  }
}

The proposed popularity based algorithm that uses alternative 1 for part 2 is called the real-time Popularity Based Adaptive Replacement Broadcast Scheduling Algorithm (PBARBSA), while the one that uses alternative 2 for part 2 is called the real-time Popularity Based Adaptive Addition Broadcasting Scheduling Algorithm (PBAABSA).

6. Simulation Model

6.1. Simulation Model Description

In order to measure the performance of the proposed algorithms, simulation experiments are conducted. The simulation model is implemented using Visual Slam as the simulation language and Awesim as the simulation tool [13]. Global transactions are created with a fixed inter-arrival time using an exponential distribution. Each transaction has a creation time, ID, data item requested, and ID of the mobile unit requesting the data. The data item requested is generated using the Gaussian random distribution and is assigned randomly to a mobile unit. Then the data item generated is checked against the broadcast of the servers within the area of influence of the mobile unit. If the data item is found it is downloaded, otherwise a request is issued and the mobile unit goes into doze mode. And it tunes into subsequent broadcasts to find out if the requested data item is included in the broadcast or not. If the request was made for a cold data item then the client tunes into the on demand portion of the data to find out whether the desired data item is being served on demand. The mobile servers are defined as resources in the simulation model.

The attributes associated with each server are ID, X and Y coordinates, energy level, radius of influence, time in active mode, and time in doze mode.

6.2. Performance Metrics

Below are the four performance metrics we have used to evaluate the performance of the proposed algorithms:

Energy Consumed by Mobile Units

(Time Spend by Mobile Unit in Active Mode * Energy Consumed per unit Time in Active Mode) + (Time Spend by Mobile Unit in Doze Mode * Energy Consumed per Unit Time in Doze Mode)

Energy Consumed by Server

(Time Spend by Server in Active Mode * Energy Consumed per Unit Time in Active Mode) + (Time Spend by Server in Doze Mode * Energy Consumed per unit Time in Doze Mode)

Access Time

The time interval between the submission of a request to the server and the moment the client receives a reply.

Broadcast Hit Ratio

Broadcast Hit Ratio =

$$Broadcast\ Hit\ Ratio = \frac{The\ Total\ Number\ of\ Requests\ Satisfied\ by\ Broadcast}{The\ Total\ Number\ of\ Requests\ Generated\ by\ Clients}$$

6.3. Simulation Parameters

Table 1. Static parameters of simulation model

Parameter	Meaning	Default
Bandwidth LMH	Bandwidth of wireless medium [16]	1 Mbps
Bandwidth SMH	Bandwidth of wireless medium [10]	100 kbps
CPU_power_LMH	CPU Power of LMH [5]	140 MIPS
CPU_power_SMH	CPU Power of SMH [9]	4 MIPS
LMH_power	LMH Power Dissipation Rate [12]	170W per hour
Mem_access_time	Main Memory [5] access time per word	0.00018 m
Data_item_size	Data Item Size	25 KB
Req_size	Size of request	1 KB
SMH_power	SMH Power Dissipation Rate [9]	7W per hour
Word_size	Number of bytes per word [5]	8
Radius_SMH	Radius of influence of SMH	100 unit
Radius_LMH	Radius of influence of LMH	200 unit
Inter-arrival Time	Time between requests	0.02
D_SIZE	Database Size	1800
Hot_data	Number of hot data Items	20% of database

Table 2. Dynamic parameters of simulation model

Parameter	Meaning	Default	Range
Num_LMH	Number of LMH	3	3-5
Ratio_cold_hot	Ratio of cold to hot requests	5 % of database	5% to 35%

The simulation parameters are summarized in Tables 1 and 2. The number of SMHs in the system is 1000. The positions of LMH and SMH are assumed to be inside a 500unit X 500unit square region. The initial locations (i.e. X and Y coordinates) of all the MHs are obtained using a random distribution within a 500 X 500 square units region. The Gaussian distribution [15] is used to generate the workload. Sample runs were performed initially to get the hot data items.

6.4. Simulation Results

The experiments were conducted using 3 servers and 4 servers. In Fig. 2-5, ARBSA3 and ARBSA4 mean Adaptive Replacement Broadcast Scheduling Algorithm tested using 3 servers and 4 servers, respectively. Similarly for The Adaptive Addition Broadcast Scheduling Algorithm (AABSA), the real time Popularity Based Adaptive Replacement Broadcast Scheduling Algorithm (PBARBSA), and the real time Popularity Based Adaptive Addition Broadcast Scheduling Algorithm (PBAARBSA).

Broadcast Hit Ratio

Fig. 2 shows the effect of number of requests for cold data on the broadcast hit ratio. Broadcast hit ratio is obtained by dividing the number of *hot* data requests satisfied by the periodic broadcast by the total number of requests. The broadcast hit ratio for addition algorithms is higher than that for the replacement algorithms. In the addition algorithms, a data item is added to the broadcast if its RF becomes higher than that of any of the data items in the current broadcast. Therefore, the periodic broadcast contains more of the hot data items and most of the requests are satisfied by the periodic broadcast. In the replacement algorithms, the periodic broadcast size is fixed, so in order to include a data item in the broadcast, one of the data items in the current broadcast has to be dropped. It is possible that the dropped data item is more popular than the added data item; so the number of broadcast hits decreases. Fig. 2 also shows that the popularity-based algorithms provide a better broadcast hit ratio than the EWMA based algorithms. Since the popularity based algorithms consider local RF in deciding which data items to include in the broadcast. So it is possible to include the requested data items in the broadcast more quickly than in the case of the EWMA based algorithms, in which the RF of a requested data item has to compete against the global request frequencies of the data items currently in the broadcast. This makes it difficult to include requested data items in the broadcast.

Another important observation from Fig. 2 is that, as the number of servers increases, the broadcast hit ratio increases. This is possible because clients can receive broadcasts from multiple servers and the likelihood that one of the servers is broadcasting the desired data item also increases. The figure also reveals that as the number of requests for hot data increases, the hit ratio drops in the addition algorithms simply because fewer requests for hot data items are being generated. But in the case of the replacement algorithms, the ratio increases when the number of requests for hot data items decreases up to a certain point and then it starts decreasing again. This happens because initially when there are too many requests, the servers cannot schedule all of them since the broadcast size is fixed, but as the rate drops, the servers are able to schedule more data items in the broadcast. Later on, the rate drops simply because there are not enough requests coming to increase the RF of less popular hot data items to a level that they can be included in the broadcast.

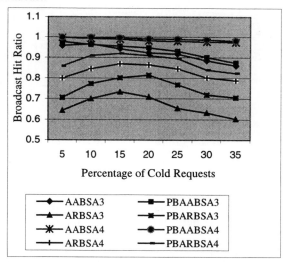

Figure 2. Broadcast hit ratio vs. percentage of cold requests

Power Consumed by Clients

Fig 3 shows that the energy consumed by clients increases as the number of requests for cold data items increases. A client can issue a request only after finding out that the desired data item is not in the broadcast of all the servers within its area of influence. In the proposed algorithms, only hot data items are served through periodic broadcast; so for cold data items, clients must issue a request and then monitor the periodic broadcast and on demand broadcast until the desired data item arrives. So, clients have to spend more time in active mode if the number of requests issued for cold data items is high. The figure also shows that the addition algorithms cause clients to consume more energy than the replacement algorithms. The reason is that, as more and more data items are added to the periodic broadcast, the index size becomes larger, and thus the clients consume more energy as they have to search through a larger index. At the same time, as the number of data items in the periodic broadcast increases, more requests are satisfied by periodic broadcast, and thus energy consumed by clients decreases. Higher energy consumption by clients occurs when the addition algorithms are used suggests that searching a larger index offsets the energy savings achieved from including more data items in the broadcast.

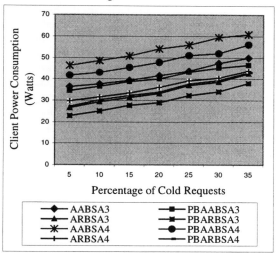

Figure 3. Total power consumed by clients vs. percentage of cold requests

Also obvious from Fig. 3 is that if there are more servers in the area of influence of clients, then energy consumption by clients increases. This occurs because a client has to check the broadcast of multiple servers to get the desired data item, so it has to spend more time in active mode, which results in higher energy consumption. Finally, the energy consumed by clients is less when the popularity based algorithms are used. These algorithms consider the local request frequencies to schedule data items for periodic broadcast. Therefore, it is easier to include a data item in the broadcast and clients have to tune into fewer subsequent broadcasts to obtain the desired data items. The difference in energy consumption between the popularity based algorithms and the EWMA based algorithms increases when the replacement algorithms are used. In the replacement algorithms, the method used to calculate RF has more influence on performance since the broadcast size is fixed, and a scheduling algorithm that can fill the periodic broadcast with data items that are more desired by clients will perform better.

Access Time

Fig 4 shows that when the number of requests for the cold data items increases, the average access time for hot data decreases. When the number of requests for cold data items increases, there is a corresponding decrease in the number of requests for hot data items. Therefore, it becomes faster for a server to include data items in the periodic broadcast as fewer data items are waiting to be scheduled in the broadcast. This figure also depicts that the average access time is lower when there are more servers in the network as this increases the likelihood that one of the servers is broadcasting the desired data item. Therefore, the clients can get data faster and the average access time is lower. It is also obvious from Fig. 4 that the addition algorithms provide a lower average access time since they keep on adding data items to the broadcast, which results in the requests being satisfied faster. Also the popularity based algorithms provide better access time than the EWMA based algorithms since with the former algorithms, it is faster to include a requested data item in the broadcast, which results in the clients requests being satisfied faster.

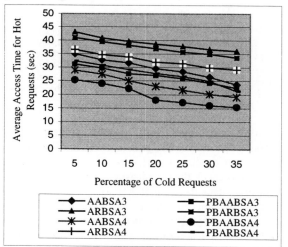

Fig. 4. Average access time for hot requests vs. percentage of cold requests

Power Consumed By Servers

Fig. 5 shows the average power consumed by a server in the network. The behavior of servers is very complex. The energy consumed by servers depends upon the following three factors: energy required to broadcast data items, energy required to handle requests, and energy required to perform computations in doze mode. The average energy consumption by a server is relatively stable although the mix of hot and cold requests is being changed. The reason for getting the stable results is that when the number of cold requests is increased, there is a corresponding decrease in the number of hot requests, so energy saved by not receiving hot requests is balanced by receiving cold requests. The servers have to perform fewer calculations when changing the broadcast content since there are fewer hot requests in the queue. But because there are more requests in the on demand queue, the energy saved by performing fewer calculations on hot requests is balanced with that saved by performing more calculations on the cold requests.

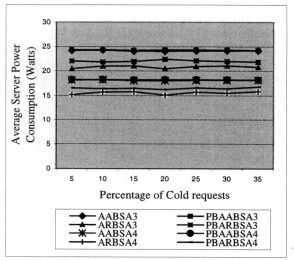

Figure 5. Average power consumed by a server vs percentage of cold requests

In performing calculations for energy consumption for servers, the cost involved in sending messages to other server has been ignored since a routing table must be available to perform these calculations. So when an update in the global table is performed, the cost involved in exchanging messages is ignored, but it is expected to be significant. This is one of the main reasons that the popularity based techniques perform poorly in terms of energy consumption. The other reason is that when its time to update the broadcast, in the EWMA based techniques, the server considers only those requests that were received in the current broadcast cycle. But in the case of popularity based techniques, the server has to consider requests received during the interval *current_time-RL*, which is larger than the broadcast cycle. Therefore, more requests have to be considered when scheduling broadcast in the popularity-based techniques than in the EWMA based techniques. Fig. 5 also shows that the average energy consumed by servers is higher when the addition algorithms are used. When a data item is added to the broadcast the broadcast size increases, so does the energy consumed by servers. Also, if there are more servers present in the network then the average energy consumed by a server is less since each server has to broadcast fewer data items as well as it has to serve fewer data items on demand.

7. Conclusions and Future Work

This paper has proposed data broadcasting algorithms for mobile ad-hoc networks (MANET). These algorithms consider three issues in scheduling broadcasts: energy consumed by mobile clients, energy consumed by mobile servers, and real-time constraints on client requests. The algorithms differ from each other based on how much data should be assigned to individual servers to broadcast, how request frequencies are computed, how the broadcast contents is dynamically changed, and how mobility of client and servers is considered. Simulation experiments conducted to study the performance of the proposed algorithms show that the popularity-based algorithms provide better broadcast hit ratio, access time, and client energy consumption, but more energy consumption than the EWMA based algorithms. The addition algorithms provide better broadcast hit ratio and access time but they are not energy-efficient for servers and clients. The replacement algorithms provide better energy consumption for clients and servers but do not give good broadcast hit ratio and access time. If there are more servers in a MANET, then the broadcast hit ratio, access time, and energy consumed by servers improve but the energy consumed by clients becomes worse.

The choice of an appropriate strategy will depend on the requirements of the environment. If access time and broadcast hit ratio are of prime importance, then the addition algorithms can be used. But if the main aim is to conserve energy consumed by clients and servers, then the replacement algorithms should be employed.

For future work, simulation experiments studying the effects of client and server mobility will be conducted.

8. References

[1] Askoy, D. and Franklin, M., "Scheduling for Large Scale On-Demand Data Broadcasting", Proceedings of the 12th International Conference on Information Networking, pp. 656-659, Jan 1998.

[2] Bandyopadhyay, S., and K. Paul, "Evaluating the Performance of Mobile Agent-Based Communication among Mobile Hosts in Large Ad-Hoc Wireless Network", MSWIM 1999.

[3] Barbara D., T. Imielinski, "Sleepers and Workaholics: Caching Strategies in Mobile Environments", ACM SIGMOD, May 1994.

[4] Datta, A., VanderMeer, D. E., Kim, J., Celik, A., and Kumar, V., "Adaptive Broadcast Protocols to Support Efficient and Energy Conserving Retrieval from Databases in Mobile Computing Environments", A TimeCenter Technical Report, University of Arizona, April, 1997.

[5] DECdirect Workgroup Solutions Catalog, winter 1993.

[6] Hong X., et al, "A Group Mobility Model for Ad Hoc Wireless Networks", MSWIM 1999.

[7] Imielinski, T. and Viswanathan, S., "Adaptive Wireless Information Systems", in Proceedings of SIGDBS (Special Interest Group in Database Systems) Conference, October 1994.

[8] Imielinski, T., Viswanathan, S., and Badrinath, B. R., "Power Efficient Filtering of Data on Air", Proc of 4th Intl Conference on Extending Database Technology, Cambridge, March 1994, pp. 245-258.

[9] Imielinski, T., Viswanathan, S., and Badrinath, B. R., "Data on Air: Organization and Access", IEEE Transactions on Knowledge and Data Engineering, Vol. 9, No. 3, May 1997, pp. 353-372.

[10] Ko, Y., Vaidya, N., "Loacation-Aided Routing (LAR) in Mobile Ad-hoc Networks", MOBICOM 1998.

[11] Lam, K., Chan, E. and Yuen, C. H., "Data Broadcast for Time-Constrained Read-Only Transactions in Mobile Computing Systems", Proceedings of the First International Workshop on Advance Issues of E-Commerce and Web-Based Information Systems, April 1999.

[12] Michael, C. et. al., "Aspects of Energy Conservation on the St. George University of Toronto Campus", A Report by Division of Environment at the University of Toronto, 1996/97.

[13] Pritsker A. Alan B, O'Reilly Jean J., "Simulation with Visual SLAM and Awesim", Systems Publishing Corp., 1999.

[14] Ramamritham K., "Real-Time Databases", Distributed and Parallel Databases, Vol. 1, No. 2, April 1993, pp 199-226.

[15] Stathatos, K., Roussopoulous, N. and Baras, J. S., "Adaptive Data Broadcast in Hybrid Networks", 23rd VLDB 1997.

[16] Xuan, P., Sen, S., Gonzalez, O., Fernandez, J., and Ramamritham K., "Broadcast on Demand: Efficient and Timely Dissemination of Data in Mobile Environments", 3rd IEEE Real-Time Technology Application Symposium, 1997.

A Location Dependent Benchmark with Mobility Behavior

Ayşe Y. Seydim, Margaret H. Dunham *
Department of Computer Science and Engineering
Southern Methodist University
Dallas, TX 75275-0122
{yasemin, mhd}@engr.smu.edu

Abstract

Location dependent benchmarking with mobility behavior is a necessary step in the evolution of improvements of wireless and computing technology. The components needed for a mobile computing benchmark include specifications for data, queries, mobile unit behavior, and execution guidelines. One of the most unique types of queries present in the mobile computing environment is a Location Dependent Query where its result depends on the issue location. In this paper, we describe the main features of a Location Dependent Benchmark including the execution guidelines. While targeted to location dependent applications, it contains more general queries as well. As such, it can be viewed as the first benchmark targeted to the general mobile computing environment.

1 Introduction

Benchmarking has been a powerful tool for evaluation and comparison of computer systems. The benchmarking of database systems is recognized as extremely difficult due to the breadth of application domains, types of database systems, and hardware alternatives involved. One of the first database system benchmarks was the Wisconsin Benchmark which targeted relational database systems [2], [3]. Predefined queries are used for testing the major components of the database system. There have been many successors to this approach which improved on it. Current accepted transaction processing benchmarks, TPC Benchmarks, are mainly based on determining the transaction per second (TPS) processing rate for sets of queries [4], [8]. They are loosely based on debit and credit banking applications.

The primary purpose of any database benchmarking tool

is to determine reasonable ways to compare the performance of different implementations of the same set of queries. However, queries are usually assumed to be domain specific. Typically, a benchmark consists of three features:

- **Queries:** These are typically simplistic versions of real life queries which could be executed to evaluate the necessary components for query processing.

- **Data:** Data may be artificial data that is created to represent typical data in that domain. Thus, data sets should be general enough to be used in various test environments.

- **Execution Guidelines:** Execution guidelines indicate specifically how the benchmark is to be executed, what performance metrics are to be used, and how these metrics are to be generated. These guidelines should be applicable for evaluating a real implementation, a testbed, a prototype, or even a simulation of a proposed implementation.

Although these features are the main ones for a benchmarking tool, generally there is no specific definition provided for the networking or connectivity characteristics of the environment. Today, mobile computing has become necessary for the applications to serve the mobile (and also stationary) users who want to be able to process from anywhere, anytime. Existing benchmarking tools though are simply not adequate for such a mobile computing environment. Data, queries and execution guidelines are not directly applicable to the environment and do not include the architectural and connectivity issues that are specific to mobility. There is no "typical" application for mobile computing, even a debit credit banking application does not seem to be a reasonable choice under the mobility circumstances. It is obvious that a major reason the existing benchmarks are inadequate is because the mobility aspect is completely ignored. If a query is requested from a Mobile Unit (MU),

*This material is based upon work supported by the National Science Foundation under Grant No. IIS-9979458

the way to test the movement of the MU should be specified in the benchmark. In this paper, we propose the first benchmark targeted to the mobile computing environment.

We assume that the queries are requested from the MU and executed at a node in the fixed wired network. Although different types of queries should be included in a mobile computing benchmark, those that highlight the uniqueness of that environment are those where data and application are location dependent, called Location Dependent Queries (LDQs) [10]. LDQs are often issued by mobile users, whose locations will also determine the results of the queries. Applications that manipulate Location Dependent Data (LDD) [7] might be seen as special case of spatial applications, however, most of the spatial data properties are not necessary in general location dependent applications. Although the Sequoia 2001 spatial database storage benchmark[11] can be partially used, a more simplified benchmark is needed for the location dependent applications. The benchmark must characterize typical applications with the mobility characteristics. Therefore, a Location Dependent Benchmark should include the following features:

- **Queries:** Queries should be targeted to location aware applications including (but not limited to) LDQs.

- **Data:** Data may be artificial that is created to represent any location dependent data.

- **Mobile Unit Behavior:** A method to abstract MU behavior including movement and connectivity should be specified.

- **Execution Guidelines:** These are similar to traditional benchmarking guidelines, but should be targeted to the wireless environment with queries requested from an MU and executed at a fixed data server.

In this paper, the main features of a location dependent benchmark are presented. Description of the database, which relations form the benchmark, are given in Section 2. Queries, their types and how they are going to be used, are discussed in Section 3. Section 4 explains the mobility behavior description in this first mobile application benchmark. Execution guidelines and the metrics to evaluate the system are in Section 5 to describe the usage of the former features. We summarize the first mobile computing benchmarking in the last section.

2 Benchmark Data

The benchmark for location dependent applications should involve database relations which will give different results depending on the location attributes in the query

predicates. The resulting LDD are usually not prone to frequent changes. On the other hand, moving objects data have dynamic attributes to represent the movement involving the frequent change in location data. The LDQs issued usually on the move are read-only queries that ask for information dependent on the query issuer's location. One can notice that most cited types of LDQs are for hotel and restaurant information. Thus, it would make sense to use this data as the benchmark data.

For the hotel and restaurant datasets, we assume the database is updated by the application/content provider and further each dataset is maintained by different providers. Initially, we create performance metrics for read-only queries, and leave the update transactions to a further study. Therefore, only selection and projection operations are defined.

As many actual implementations of mobile computing data will use different location granularities, it is important to have different location granularities defined in the data. Rather than using complex data types (i.e. spatial), such as line and polygon data definitions, we use the obvious relationships between the location concepts. For example, a State totally covers the Cities in it, but there is no need to keep all spatial data to represent this. The attributes are differentiated according to their location relatedness which is discussed in our previous work [10]. To have the flexibility in the benchmark, we define various location related attributes. We assume that the location data included follows the location concept hierarchy shown in Figure 1. Here the address and latitude/longitude are viewed to be at the same level.

Figure 1. Location Granularity Hierarchy

The schemas for Hotels and Restaurants tables are shown in Table 1. Hotel and Restaurant relations have unique keys as the ID number, and they are also accessed by some nonunique keys which are also specified as location related. The two relations have different candidate (secondary) keys as the location granularity difference is another testing criteria in the benchmark. Hotels relation has a nonunique key of City, and Restaurants relation has the Zipcode. For simplicity, length of the lattitude/longitute attributes are chosen similar to the most commonly used TIGER (Topological Integrated Geographic Encoded Referencing) data [12] in United States Postal Services. The specification of these attributes can also be integrated with the ones given in the Mobile Location Protocol Specification of Location Interoperability Forum [5].

Table 1. Schemas for Hotels and Restaurants

Attribute	Type	Relation
Restaurant ID/ Hotel ID	integer(5), NLR, Unique	Both
Restaurant Name/ Hotel Name	char(60), NLR	Both
Address	char(45), LR	Both
City	char(20), LR, Non-Unique	Hotel
State Code	char(2), LR	Both
Zipcode	char(10), LR Non-Unique	Rest.
Country Code	integer(3), LR	Both
Latitude	integer(9), LR	Both
Longitude	integer(10), LR	Both
Occupancy	integer(5), NLR	Hotel
Number of Tables	integer(5), NLR	Rest
Other	char(50), NLR	Both

2.1 Data Generation

The data values for the Hotels and Restaurants relations may be obtained from real database relations or artificially generated. Here, it is important that Location Related attributes exist in the data and they imply a hierarchy. All LDD points lie in a **Workspace** or **Test Area** which is defined as a rectangular area represented by upper right corner and lower left corner coordinate values in a Cartesian coordinate system. The lower left corner point is assumed to be at the origin (0,0) for simplicity, so it is enough to give maximum x and maximum y values to define the Test Area.

During artificial data generation, a number of area centric points are chosen in the Workspace to emulate the hypothetical city centers. x and y coordinate value pairs (latitude, longitude) are created for the hotel and restaurant point data. Figure 2 shows the center points with C's and other point data (x, y) pairs with dots. These data points can be distributed randomly in the workspace with any type of distibution, such as a Gaussian distribution. With Gaussian distribution, points will be scattered more densely towards each area center. For the hotels having restaurants, randomly chosen hotel point data should be added to restaurant point data.

Our benchmark assumes an artificial workspace. This 2-dimensional space could be overlayed on a real area (such

as a state) to provide a more realistic approach. If the benchmark is to be realized in a real world mobile computing environment, this artificial workspace concept can not be implemented precisely but it is to be a reasonable alternative for this benchmark.

Values of the attributes are also assigned randomly from a finite set of values. The value of City, State, Zipcode, Country Code are all from set-valued domains. For example, we can use the set CityTX = { Austin, Dallas, Houston, San Antonio, ... }, for cities in Texas. These values can be real values, so we are not restricting the assignments from a predefined set of values that is given in the benchmark. For each location granularity, the definition of area boundaries are defined. We envision this to be done by some grid representation. These definitions should be done during the benchmark preparation.

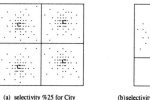

(a) selectivity %25 for City   (b)selectivity %35, %35 and %30 for Zipcode

Figure 2. Selectivities in a Test Area

Selectivity of Data   The result of a query depends on the selection criteria, sometimes all records will be desired, sometimes only the records in one area, so the number of records that is returned is going to change. The number of records returned is defined by the Selectivity factor of the attributes of relations [6]. If all hotel data is equally divided in a Test Area, in Figure 2, then the Selectivity factor of a query for a City will be at most 25% of the records. The distribution of hotel and restaurant data points in each location attribute (City, Zipcode, State, Country) will determine the Selectivity of the queries. Two example test area partitions are shown in Figure 2. In Figure 2 (a), we defined 4 cities, with equal numerical distribution, with Selectivity of City attribute value 25% each. In (b), we defined 3 centers where Selectivity of the attribute Zipcode is 35%, 35% and 30% for 3 different zipcodes.

The Selectivity defined here is due to the selection predicates when every location related attribute is given in the query and there is no need for binding. When mobility is the case, there might be a mismatch problem when the user's current location value is needed in the query. Mobile user's location is determined by a Location Service, either network oriented or handset oriented approaches, and assigned to the location predicate, i.e. Location Binding [9]. The LDQ becomes an LAQ after this Location Binding process. Location Granularity Mismatch has been defined as the mismatch between the location granularity assigned in Location Binding and the location granularity kept in the data store [9]. In the benchmark, Binding Location (BL) is different from the candidate (secondary) key of the data set when there is a Location Granularity Mismatch. Therefore, Selectivity after Location Binding (e.g. Zipcode) and the Selectivity after translation to the Data Loocation (DL) (e.g. City) might be different. This results in a satisfiability measure which is discussed in Section 5.

3 Queries

The application for the benchmark includes location dependent, location aware and non-location related queries issued to hotel and restaurant databases. A **Location Aware Query (LAQ)** is a query that includes at least one Location Related (LR) attribute in its predicates [10]. However, the location value is not dependent on the MU location. A **Location Dependent Query (LDQ)** is one where the results depend on the MU location. Once the MU location is bound to the LDQ, it can be viewed as an LAQ. LDQs are stated by special location related operators (closest, north east, etc.). Finally, a **Non-Location Related Query (NLR-Q)**, does not have any location related attributes.

The benchmark queries are a mix of these three basic types. LDQs are not traditional queries. The location to which the query is related must be determined (Location Binding [9]), prior to processing the query (since the user is moving) where the location dependence is implied by an LR-Operator (closest, etc.). The number of relations, and the number of predicates used in the query determines the query as being a **Simple(S)**, **Multi-Relation(M)** or **Compound(C)** query. A Simple query has only one relation and one simple selection predicate. A Compund query involves more than one simple selection predicate or one selection predicate and a location dependence keyword. In a Multi-Relation query, one query is directed against two separate relations where a preprocessing is necessary.

3.1 Base Query Set

Benchmark queries can be created randomly for each run of the experiment. The query model is shown in Figure 3. To create a query for the benchmark each of the five parts of the model, explained below, must be completed.

Projected Attributes. To determine the attributes to be shown to the user, either ALL (*) or one attribute must be chosen. A projection operation is implied and the DISTINCT keyword is issued by default.

Relations. Attributes can be selected from one relation, either Hotels or Restaurants, or both. When we have two

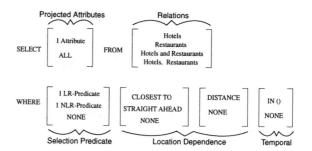

Figure 3. Query Model

relations with the same Projection Attributes and Selection Predicates, we refer to this query as being a Multi-Relation query and we need to issue the same query for the second relation.

Selection Predicate. The Selection Predicate might include a Location Related (LR) predicate, or a Non-Location Related (NLR) predicate or nothing at all. An LR predicate is one associated with a location related attribute while an NLR predicate is associated with a traditional attribute.

Location Dependence. The location dependence portion of the query model contains the two operators "CLOSEST TO" and "STRAIGHT AHEAD" with a "DISTANCE" keyword. These are defined as Location Related (LR) Operators, where they imply an area within which the MU stands [10]. CLOSEST implies a circular area within the specified distance, where the other STRAIGHT AHEAD implying a rectangular area in the direction of movement (Figure 4). Unless a DISTANCE is specified, the value of the radius(longer side) of the circular (rectangular) area should be set to a default. If additional operators are going to be used by a tester, the meaning of the operators should be defined explicitly.

Temporal. We also define a time parameter at the end of the query test model. This parameter should be used in the test of Prediction Queries. When the keyword IN is used, the time value specified is added to the current timestamp to estimate the predicted location of the mobile user. Otherwise, the current time is assumed.

Figure 4. LR Operator Meanings

Using this basic query model gives us the following basic types of queries for the benchmark:

- **Traditional or Non-Location Related Query:** (SELECT Occupancy FROM Hotels)

- **Location Aware Query:** LAQ has at least one LR predicate. (SELECT Name FROM Restaurants WHERE Zipcode = "12345%")

- **Location Dependent Query:** LDQ requires Location Binding, and has special LR operators. (SELECT all FROM Hotels WHERE CLOSEST TO (5 miles))

- **Prediction Query (PQ):** PQ is an LDQ which is issued for a future time. (SELECT all FROM Hotels WHERE CLOSEST TO (5 miles) IN (10 min))

Using the basic query model, the Base Query Set determined for the benchmark is shown in Table 2. We also give the type of queries to guide the tester, abbreviations are self explanatory. Note that, the Hotels and Restaurants relations are Location Related since they have at least one Location Related attribute in their schemas. Therefore, when we select all attributes from any of these relations,(e.g.Q21 and Q22), the query can be viewed as an LAQ. The binding location (BL) [1] granularity is also given to be used in evaluating the quality of results. **Continuous Query (CQ)** is an LDQ which has been issued continuously during the movement of a mobile user, i.e. the overlapping frequency between queries is not zero. [2] OverlapRate will be given as a benchmark parameter and at least one of the LDQs will be tested as CQ test.

A query which is not a part of this query model but used during Location Binding is Location Query [9]. **Location Query (LQ)** can be viewed as a special case of LDQ, which includes inherently a location related attribute. LQ is issued to obtain current MU position[3] from a Location Service (e.g. SELECT CurrentLocation). We have also added an LQ to the query set since it will be used for Location Binding.

4 Mobility Behavior Description

The most remarkable part of the benchmark is the Mobile Unit (MU) behavior. There are two behavioral compo-

nents to be considered for modeling the mobility and exploring query processing performance of location dependent applications under this condition. The first one is the *connectivity* of the mobile device. Mobile devices have limitations compared to fixed devices. Due to limited bandwidth, wireless network conditions and energy limitations, mobile devices are more prone to disconnections. Planned and unplanned disconnections can be modeled in the benchmark. For the planned disconnections, frequent voluntary disconnections are considered to be "sleepers" type of users, and infrequent voluntary disconnections are "workaholics" type of users [1]. If we assume that we have the same number of involuntary disconnections, the total disconnections should be larger for "sleepers" than "workaholics". Figure 5 shows the ratios in a pictorial manner. In this Location Dependent Benchmark, we concentrate on modeling movement and we assume the MU is connected all along its path after its activation. Thus, we do not explicitly model disconnections.

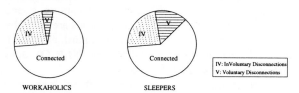

Figure 5. Sleepers and Workaholics Connectivity Ratios

The second item for the MU behavior is *modeling of movement* to locate the MU in a geographical space. There are three dimensions to the movement modeling: speed, direction and movement pattern. At any time, an MU will have a direction and a driving speed towards that direction. When a mobile user is going along a path, probably its direction and average speed will not change. Therefore, if a Location Service knows the current location of the MU, its speed and direction, then the new location for a specific time can be estimated depending on its movement pattern.

In general, moving objects follow predefined paths which can be different routes to specific places in a geography. If we are going from our house to work, we normally drive on the roads, streets which exist before. Every path consists of small pieces of road which can be treated as straight line segments. With this particular thought in mind, movement patterns for each mobile user can be modeled in a reference region within which all the movement occurs. Thus, each distinct path can be given a Path ID.

Depending on his mobility pattern, a user can drive from one place to another by using only one line segment, and/or come back to his original place with the same segment. She/he can also stop at intermediate points. As a result,

---

[1]It is given in italics if Location Leveling is required. When the location is bound to the query with a different granularity that its candidate key's granularity, we say, there is a need for a translation process, called *Location Leveling (LL)*[9].

[2]The rate of two consecutive queries being the same can be represented by overlap frequency, which we call the OverlapRate.

[3]Location Service can be implemented in various ways and this benchmark does not test the location determination. The benchmark relations are not used for this implementation.

we view the movement pattern or path of a mobile user to be **One-Way**, **Round Trip** or **Random**. While One-Way and Random trip paths both have different source and destination locations, Round Trip path has the same source and destination point. A Random Trip path can be considered to be constructed by more than one One-Way trips. We view the Workspace in 2-dimensions and model the location of the mobile unit in a 2-dimensional space. Figure 6 shows each movement examples in a Test Area. Thus, the sufficient movement patterns, where two points, s and t, are randomly generated in a benchmarking Test Area can be summarized as follows:

- **One-Way:** MU moves from point s to t at a uniform speed (MU1, PATH1, 1 line segment).

- **Round Trip:** MU moves from point s at a uniform speed to point s_1, waits a certain time at point s_1, then moves from point s_1 to point $s=t$ at a uniform speed (MU2, PATH2, 2 line segments).

- **Random:** MU moves in a set of One-Way segments. Assuming there are n of these segments we label the endpoints as s_i, where $1 \leq i \leq n$. There is a waiting time between the segment activations. The waiting time at each intermediate point may be different as with random assignments within a range. The entire set of segments defines the movement pattern. Thus, we have the following segments: $< s, s_1 >, < s_1, s_2 >, ..., < s_{n-1}, s_n > = < s_{n-1}, t >$. The ending point of segment i is the starting point of segment $i + 1$ (MU3, PATH3, 5 line segments).

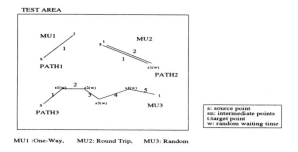

MU1 :One-Way,   MU2: Round Trip,   MU3: Random

Figure 6. Movement Patterns

In the benchmark execution, a given Path ID can be taken by any MU at any time. There is a speed associated with each path. The speed for the paths are chosen randomly within a range and associated with the path number. The basic assumption here is the mobile user keeps an average speed within this limit. A real location database can be used for the location determination, but our approach is simpler and serves the purposes of this benchmark.

4.1   Moving Object Path Generation

When the benchmark is used in a simulated movement environment, the MU movements can be generated according to the predefined paths. In a real world implementation, the MU will be required to move in one of these patterns. In this case, the entire movement pattern of the MU causes some concerns as this is difficult to duplicate from one implementation to another. The discussions below assume that a simulated MU movement is used. Use of this benchmark with real world MU movement needs future research.

All the experiments have queries which will need to access a Location Service to estimate the location of the mobile user at a given time with the given parameters. We assume the available paths are stored in a Location Service/Location Identification Service component. This way, Location Service gives an estimation for the position of a mobile user using the specified path at a given time. If the Location Service (LCS) knows the Path ID, it can estimate the location when the starting time from the source point is given. This point of view is realistic since street maps imply predefined paths from one destination to another.

Location Service   No matter how it is implemented, a Location Service calculates and returns the location of a mobile user for the specific time asked. MU's assigned Path ID, the Id of the MU and the starting time for that drive has to be provided to the component. Also, the time for the requested location should also be provided to the Location Service. In return, Location Service estimates the position by calculating the distance from the source point by using the starting time and the required time (query time). The granularity of the location to be bound to the issued query is chosen as geographic coordinates - latitude/longitude. When the mobile unit reaches its final destination according to the given time (which must be greater than the total travel time), the same x, y coordinates are returned. This can also be used for testing queries issued by stationary users. In a way, location service provides a table look-up calculation for the position of a mobile user at a given time.

A more realistic way of location estimation can be performed real-time by the help of wireless network or the wireless device (GPS) in the Location Service. However, the intent here is to obtain a location independent from a Location Service of any kind. To provide a simple Location Service simulation, it is sufficient to assume a third party Location Service which provides a position in granularity of latitude/longitude pairs for a certain path and for a given time.

The benchmark uses predefined movement pattern sets for testing. For each set of paths, the maximum number of users in the mobile environment determines the number of paths for each type of movement. That is, for each type of movement, number of paths is equal to the maximum number of mobile users. For instance, if the benchmark accommodates 100 separate mobile users, there will be 100 One-Way, 100 Round-Trip and 100 Random movement paths created in one path set before the benchmark is executed. The same path can be used by more than one mobile user as in real life.

During path generation, every path should have source and destination points which are chosen within certain area of geography, namely the Workspace. The limits of the Test Area are given as the path generation parameter besides the maximum number of mobile units (number of paths). The source and destination points are to be generated uniformly. As a future extension to the benchmark, the source and destination points can be chosen with certain Gaussian distributions closer to city centers. Similarly, distribution of travel types has a significant role during the benchmark testing in case of evaluating a caching or prefetching strategy. However, in this benchmark, we do not intend to evaluate caching or prefetching issues.

5 Execution Guidelines

The basic benchmark queries are tested in an architecture consisting of any wireless network, connected to a fixed network, where the data servers belong. Queries are issued from a mobile unit and the data sets are stored on fixed host servers. The general benchmark architecture is shown in Figure 7. The mobility of the users and the Location Service is simulated with the predefined communication costs.

It is obvious that there is a need for preprocessing or translation for processing an LDQ. After the query (or MU) is bound to location, the current/future location values are embedded in the query, then the new query is sent to the related database server. Note that, there may be Location Granularity Mismatch between the LDQ stated and the new location embedded query, which becomes an LAQ. However, there is no restriction on the implementation of Location Binding and query translation. There should be some metrics to evaluate these discrepancies, because the result set of the query will differ from the desired query results if the binding is not exact.

5.1 Benchmark Activities

Mobile users and their movement patterns (paths) constitute the **Activity Sets** of this benchmark execution. These MUID-PathID pairs in actuality corresponds to movement patterns of each MU in their profiles. Each mobile unit, then, submits queries from a **Query Set** along the travel during a run. Therefore, a set of MUID-PathID assignment pairs are to be generated before the benchmark starts. These

Activity Sets are saved to create the same inputs to the system when needed.

For generating an Activity Set, the distribution of the travel types (One-Way, Round-Trip, Random) are given to create the corresponding percentages for each type.

Number of mobile units, Mobile Unit ID's range, Path Group ID to choose the paths from, and Percentages of each movement type are the basic Activity Set generation parameters, but one can add more to it depending on their implementation.

The file name of the activity set can be created by adding the number of the activity set to a predefined name. At least three activity sets for each path group should be created during benchmark preparation process. The set of queries are chosen from the Base Query Set (at least one from each) and put together in a Query Set file. Total time period to run the queries, mean arrival time between queries, distribution of each query type, and the overlap frequency between consecutive queries (OverlapRate) are needed to prepare a Query Set file.

5.2 Benchmark Execution

After preparation of the data, the benchmark is executed with the Activity Set, Query Set, and the Path Group file under the given parameters. These parameters include: number of queries in each Query Set, maximum number of mobile units, mean activation time between the mobile units for each Activity Set, random number seeds, mean arrival time of queries, overlap percentage between consecutive queries, benchmark run period. We can summarize the input to an execution as:

- Benchmark workspace definition (at least 400 x 400 units)

- Area (Zipcode regions, City boundaries) definitions (overlaying areas on workspace)

- Hotels data set (at least 2 City centers, 50-150 hotel point data)

- Restaurants data set (at least 2 Zipcode area centers, 100-200 restaurant point data)

- Path Group files (at least 2 Path group)

- Activity Set files (at least 3 MUID-PathID pair file for each Path Group)

- Query Sets (at least 3 sets with different distributions of query types, including the Base Query Set in each)

A universal time counter should be set before the execution. MUs are to be activated (simulated) at random points using a uniform distribution with the given mean activation

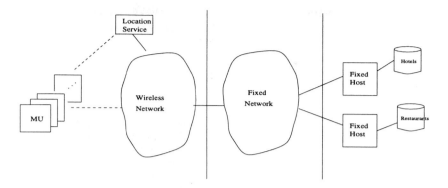

Figure 7. Benchmark Architecture

time from the Activity Set. Each MU should issue queries from the Query Set with the mean query issue time interval. MUs continue to move until reaching their destinations. Queries continue to be issued until all the queries have finished. This may mean that some queries are actually issued when the corresponding MU has finished its movement and is at its destination point. After all mobile units are stopped and all queries are executed, benchmark reports should be prepared from history files.

5.3 Metrics

In this benchmark setting, **Response Time (RT)** for each query is the first to consider among the performance evaluation criteria. RT is calculated using all of the following parts:

- Any processing time on MU after issue of the query, M_p,

- Transfer time from MU to network, M_c,

- Time within network before the query reaches to communication interface, N_{p1},

- Transfer time of the query from network to Fixed Host, F_c,

- Processing time (access time) for the query results, F_p,

- Transfer time of results from Fixed Host to network, $F_c * n$,

- Time within network until the query results arrive to the MU, $N_{p2} * n$,

- Transfer time from network to MU, $M_c * n$,

- Time to display the results to the user, M_d.

Here, n is the number of records that is returned as the result of the query. The multiplication with n means that there is a factor depending on the number of resulting records. Thus, the total Response Time (RT) for one query can be written as :

$$\mathbf{RT} = M_p + M_c + N_{p1} + F_c + F_p + (F_c * n) + (N_{p2} * n) + (M_c * n) + M_d$$

For a traditional, Simple query, there will be no processing cost on MU, within the network, so M_p, N_{p1}, N_{p2} will be almost zero. However, there might be some processing cost for the LDQs, since they need Location Binding and query translation on the way to the Fixed Host. The processing cost of LDQs, either on MU or in the network, depends on different implementations, so it is left flexible to add in this evaluation. Communication cost from MU to network, M_c, is to be set to a fixed value, but if the tests are run from a wired (stationary) terminal, this value is updated. Note that, RT is also affected by the resulting number of records that is determined by the Selectivity factor of the attributes mentioned in Section 2.

Not only does an architecture have to provide a basic framework for Location Dependent applications but also it must provide the best answers to the queries in these. The response of the query Q31 will be a set of hotels. Different implementations of the query may obtain different results. This could be based on how and when the MU is bound to a location. It may also be based on how "closest" is calculated and what location granularities are used. The quality of the answers depends on the Binding Location (BL) and Data Location (DL) granularities and the processing provided. If there is no granularity mismatch for an application, then we can definitely conclude the best quality of the results are provided by the application. Otherwise, if BL is either a fine or coarse granularity, the data accessed will give better results if DL is closer to that fine or coarse granularity. Table 2 also has the BL granularities to evaluate this semantic differences.

To measure the quality of service (QoS), what the user wants versus what he receives, the precision/recall metrics from the Information Retrieval area can be used. **Precision** is the ratio of the number of items in the result set (hotels or restaurants) which should have been retrieved to those that were retrieved. **Recall** is the ratio of the number of items which were retrieved to the total number that should have been retrieved. The calculation of these is based upon knowledge of the actual relations as well as the desired results from each executed query.

The required granularity and the supplied granularity difference will also tell the user how far his expectations can be satisfied. We introduce a metric called the *satisfiability* measure, but to avoid confusing with the "satisfiability" of query results, we call it **Location Mismatch Satisfaction Ratio (LMSR)**.

When, there is no Location Granularity Mismatch, LMSR should be 0, meaning there is nothing left to be satisfied. So, for traditional, NLR-Queries and LAQs, this measure is 0, therefore quality can be accepted as good. When a query is an LDQ, there is a higher chance of BL is different than the DL. For instance, Zipcode is finer than State according to the hierarchy in Figure 1. If the BL is assigned as Zipcode, and DL is State, then LMSR will be less than 0. That is, the resulting data will be more general for the user, so the precision will be low. In contrast, when BL is assigned as State, more detailed data will be returned, then LMSR is expected to be greater than 0. We summarize this formulation as follows:

- BL granularity $= DL$ granularity $\rightarrow$ LMSR $= 0$,

- BL granularity $< DL$ granularity $\rightarrow$ LMSR < 0,

- BL granularity $> DL$ granularity $\rightarrow$ LMSR > 0.

In the Location Dependent benchmark, we assumed a Location Service is estimating the location of MU as latitude/longitude pair. Unless otherwise this granularity is defined/assigned different, LMSR will be always less than 0. The amount or convergence to zero will be the measure of quality of service during the benchmark runs. However, the processing needed for any effort to build this quality will definitely affect the total Response Time. We leave the details of this performance metric to future refinements of the benchmark.

6 Conclusion

We have argued the need for a benchmark targeting the location dependent query processing domain. We have also presented our preliminary guidelines concerning the query, data, and MU behavior components of such a benchmark.

Our future work will refine these ideas and use them in evaluating the performance of a testbed under development at SMU.

References

[1] D. Barbara and T. Imielinski. Sleepers and workaholics:caching strategies in mobile environments. In *ACM SIGMOD International Conference on Management of Data*, pages 1–12, Minneapolis, Minnesota, USA, May 1994.

[2] D. Bitton, D. DeWitt and C. Turbyfill. Benchmarking database systems, a systematic approach. In *9th International Conference on Very Large Data Bases, VLDB'83*, pages 8–19, Florence, Italy, November 1983.

[3] D. J. DeWitt. *The Wisconsin Benchmark: Past, Present, and Future*, pages 269–315. In Gray [4], second edition, 1993.

[4] J. Gray, editor. *The Benchmark Handbook for Database and Transaction Processing Systems*. Morgan Kaufmann Publishers, Inc., San Mateo, CA, USA, second edition, 1993.

[5] Location Interoperability Forum (LIF). Location Interoperability Forum home page. web page, http://www.locationforum.org, 2000.

[6] P. E. O'Neil. *The Set Query Benchmark*, pages 361–395. In Gray [4], second edition, 1993.

[7] Q. Ren and M. H. Dunham. Using semantic caching to manage location dependent data in mobile computing. In *Sixth Annual International Conference on Mobile Computing and Networking, MobiCom 2000*, pages 210–221, Boston, MA, USA, August 2000. ACM SIGMOBILE.

[8] O. Serlin. *The History of DebitCredit and the TPC*, pages 21–40. In Gray [4], second edition, 1993.

[9] A. Y. Seydim, M. H. Dunham, and V. Kumar. An architecture for location dependent query processing. In *4th International Workshop on Mobility in Databases and Distributed Systems (MDDS'01) in 12th International Conference on Database and Expert System Applications (DEXA 2001)*, Munich, Germany, June 2001.

[10] A. Y. Seydim, M. H. Dunham, and V. Kumar. Location dependent query processing. In S. Banerjee, P. Chrysanthis, and E. Pitoura, editors, *Second ACM International Workshop on Data Engineering for Mobile and Wireless Access, MobiDE'01*, pages 47–53, Santa Barbara, California, USA, May 2001.

[11] M. Stonebraker, J. Frew, K. Gardels, and J. Meredith. The SEQUOIA storage benchmark. In *ACM SIGMOD International Conference on Management of Data*, pages 2–11, Washington, DC, USA, May 1993.

[12] U. S. P. S. USPS. Tiger-topological integrated geographic encoded referencing/zip-zone improvement plan technical guide. USPS - National Customer Support Center, web page, http://www.usps.com/ncsc/addressmgmt/tiger_print.htm, 1999.

Table 2. Base Query Set for Location Dependent Benchmark

#	Query	Type	BL
Q11	SELECT Occupancy FROM Hotels WHERE HotelID = 12345	NLR-Q, S	N/A
Q12	SELECT NumberofTables FROM Restaurants WHERE RestaurantID = 67890	NLR-Q, S	N/A
Q21	SELECT all FROM Hotels	LAQ, S	N/A
Q22	SELECT all FROM Restaurants	LAQ, S	N/A
Q23	SELECT all FROM Hotels WHERE City = "Dallas"	LAQ, S	N/A
Q24	SELECT all FROM Restaurants WHERE Zipcode = "75275-0000"	LAQ, S	N/A
Q25	SELECT Zipcode FROM Hotels WHERE City = "Richardson"	LAQ, S	N/A
Q26	SELECT Zipcode FROM Restaurants WHERE City = "Richardson"	LAQ, S	N/A
Q27	SELECT all FROM Hotels and Restaurants WHERE City = "Richardson"	LAQ, M	N/A
Q31	SELECT all FROM Hotels WHERE CLOSEST TO DISTANCE(5 miles)	LDQ, S	*Zip*
Q32	SELECT all FROM Hotels WHERE CLOSEST TO DISTANCE(5 miles)	LDQ, S	City
Q33	SELECT all FROM Restaurants WHERE CLOSEST TO DISTANCE(5 miles)	LDQ, S	*City*
Q34	SELECT all FROM Restaurants WHERE CLOSEST TO DISTANCE(5 miles)	LDQ, S	Zip
Q35	SELECT all FROM Hotels and Restaurants WHERE CLOSEST TO DISTANCE(5 miles)	LDQ, S	*Zip*
Q41	SELECT all FROM Hotels STRAIGHT AHEAD DISTANCE(10 miles)	LDQ, S	City
Q42	SELECT all FROM Hotels STRAIGHT AHEAD DISTANCE(10 miles)	LDQ, S	*Zip*
Q43	SELECT all FROM Restaurants STRAIGHT AHEAD DISTANCE(10 miles)	LDQ, S	Zip
Q44	SELECT all FROM Restaurants STRAIGHT AHEAD DISTANCE(10 miles)	LDQ, S	*City*
Q45	SELECT all FROM Hotels and Restaurants WHERE STRAIGHT AHEAD DISTANCE()	LDQ, M	*Cell*
Q51	SELECT all FROM Hotels WHERE Name like "Marriot%' and CLOSEST TO DISTANCE(5 miles)	LDQ, C	*Zip*
Q52	SELECT all FROM Restaurants WHERE Name like "Blue%" and CLOSEST TO DISTANCE(5 miles)	LDQ, C	*City*
Q53	SELECT all FROM Hotels WHERE Zipcode = "75275-0000" and CLOSEST TO DISTANCE(5 miles)	LDQ, C	City
Q54	SELECT all FROM Restaurants WHERE City = "Dallas" and CLOSEST TO DISTANCE(5 miles)	LDQ, C	Zip
Q61	SELECT all FROM Hotels WHERE CLOSEST TO DISTANCE() IN(2 min)	LDQ, PQ	*Zip*
Q62	SELECT all FROM Restaurants WHERE CLOSEST TO DISTANCE() IN(2 min)	LDQ, PQ	*City*
Q63	SELECT all FROM Hotels and Restaurants WHERE CLOSEST TO DISTANCE() IN(2 min)	LDQ, PQ, M	*Zip*
Q71	SELECT all FROM Hotels, Restaurants WHERE Hotels.Zipcode = Restaurants.Zipcode and CLOSEST TO DISTANCE(5 miles)	LDQ, C	*Zip*
Q72	SELECT all FROM Hotels, Restaurants WHERE Hotels.Address = Restaurants.Address and CLOSEST TO DISTANCE(5 miles)	LDQ, C	*City*
Q81	SELECT CurrentLocation	LDQ (LQ)	Any

Paper Session III

(XML & OO)

XGL: a graphical query language for XML

S. Flesca, F. Furfaro, S. Greco

DEIS, Università della Calabria,
87036 Rende (CS), Italy
{flesca,furfaro,greco}@si.deis.unical.it

Abstract

In this paper we present a graphical query language for XML. The language, based on a simple form of graph grammars, permits us to extract data and reorganize information in a new structure. As with most of the current query languages for XML, queries consist of two parts: one extracting a sub-graph and one constructing the output graph.

The semantics of queries is given in terms of graph grammars. The use of graph grammars makes it possible to define, in a simple way, the structural properties of both the subgraph that has to be extracted and the graph that has to be constructed. By means of examples, we show the effectiveness and simplicity of our approach.

1. Introduction

The problem of developing query languages for XML, the emerging new standard for the representation of semistructured data on the Web, has been investigated widely. XML documents are composed of a sequence of nested elements: each element is delimited by a pair of tags giving a formal description of their content and a semantics to the enclosed information. Most of the languages proposed so far are declarative languages [13], although there have been proposals for graphical [7] and procedural languages [12].

In this paper we present a declarative, graphical language, called $\mathcal{XGL}$ (XML Graphical Language), for querying XML data. The basic idea underlying our language is that XML and semistructured data can be represented by means of graphs [1, 2, 6]; thus the query problem is basically the extraction of subgraphs and the creation of a new graph. It is widely accepted that, for this kind of query, graphical notations are more natural [9, 10].

As with most of the proposed languages for XML, $\mathcal{XGL}$ queries consist of two parts used, respectively, for extracting information from data and restructuring information into novel XML documents. Our language provides (graphical) constructs to express nesting of elements, variables associated with both tags and values, path expressions, grouping,

and permits us to collect and integrate information coming from different documents.

With respect to other graphical languages [7, 8], the main difference of $\mathcal{XGL}$ is that graphs are defined by means of (extended) graph grammars and the semantics of the language is based on the theory of graph grammars. A graph grammar is a graph rewriting system consisting of a set of rewriting rules (or *productions*). Just as a production of a standard grammar defines how to substitute a non terminal symbol (or a group of symbols) with a string, a production of a graph grammar defines how to replace a node (or an edge) in a graph with a sub-graph. A graph grammar defines a class of graphs which have common structural properties (e.g. the class of complete graphs, the class of trees, etc.).

Thus an $\mathcal{XGL}$ query consists of a set of (graphical) production rules which describe the structural property of the graphs which we want to extract and construct. More specifically, the structure of an $\mathcal{XGL}$ query on a set of XML documents is a set of extended graph grammars. Each (extended) graph grammar is described by means of a sequence of extended production rules describing how graphs can be expanded (each rule says how and under which conditions a node of a given graph can be replaced by a specified graph).

In our opinion, the use of (extended) graph grammar production rules makes the language more flexible and usable since they make it possible to describe the structural properties of the graph to be extracted in a simple, compact and intuitive way.

2. $\mathcal{XGL}$ in a nutshell

In this section we informally present the $\mathcal{XGL}$ query language. We use a classical XML document containing bibliography entries conforming to the following DTD [13]

```
<!ELEMENT book (title, author+,
                publisher)>
<!ATTLIST book year CDATA>
<!ELEMENT title     PCDATA>
<!ELEMENT author    PCDATA>
<!ELEMENT publisher PCDATA>
```

The main features of the language are described by means of Example 1, where some queries over the document below, called `"bib.xml"` and graphically represented in Fig. 1, are described.

```
<bib>
  <book year="1997">
    <title> A First Course in
            Database Systems </title>
    <author> Ullman </author>
    <author> Widom  </author>
    <publisher> Prentice-Hall </publisher>
  </book>
  <book year="1988">
    <title> Principles of Database and
            Knowledge-Base Systems </title>
    <author> Ullman </author>
    <publisher> C. S. Press </publisher>
  </book>
  <book year="1999">
    <title> Data on the Web </title>
    <author> Abiteboul </author>
    <author> Buneman </author>
    <author> Suciu   </author>
    <publisher> Morgan Kaufmann </publisher>
  </book>
</bib>
```

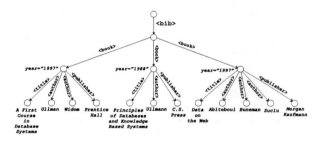

Figure 1. XML graph

The structure of a $\mathcal{XGL}$ query consists of two parts: one querying and one constructing XML data graphs. The querying part is defined by means of a simplified form of graph grammar, which is made user-friendly by adding some syntactic simplifications to standard graph grammars.

The constructing part is defined by a graph which describes the structure and the content of the document which has to be created.

The querying and constructing parts are correlated by means of variables, which are defined in the querying part (where it is specified what kind of information each variable identifies) and then used in the constructing part (where variables refer to the extracted information).

In the extraction of graphs, graph grammars are coupled with first order formulas on such variables, in order to express conditions on data and filter them. In particular, every production rule is associated to a (possibly empty) first order formula which states under which conditions (regarding the data contained in the source graph) the rule can be applied.

Also the constructing rule defining the output graph is associated to a first order formula, which filters the extracted information and defines how to re-assemble it.

In the representation of graphs of both the querying and constructing part, the language provides shortcuts associated to nodes and arcs. In particular, in order to identify paths in the source graph during the extraction phase, arcs may be labelled with regular expressions defined on a vocabulary of tags. On the other side, nodes may be marked with the symbol '+': such a marked node (called *grouping node*) represent a (possibly empty) set of nodes matching one or more nodes of the input graph.

Like most of the query languages for XML, $\mathcal{XGL}$ queries consist of a "WHERE" clause defining the querying part (extraction of a subgraph) and a "CONSTRUCT" clause defining the constructing part.

The following example presents four queries on the document of Fig. 1. Here, each graph grammar consists of only one production rule. We shall use, respectively, the symbol **S** to denote the axiom (start symbol) of the graph grammar used to extract sub-graphs, and the symbol **T** to denote the constructing rule which defines how to build the output document. Thus the form of all the queries presented in the following examples will be:

```
WHERE S IN "bib.xml"
CONSTRUCT T
```

Example 1

1. *Construct a document containing the titles of all books printed by Prentice-Hall from 1992 on.* We first ex-

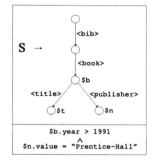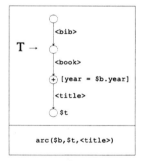

Figure 2. $\mathcal{XGL}$ Query 1

tract for each book the pairs t/n, where t denotes the title and n the publisher of the book satisfying the condition that the year of the book is after 1991 and the publisher is "Prentice-Hall" ($b.year > 1991 \land \$n =$ "Prentice−Hall"). The symbol "+" inside the node labelled with b means that we are interested in all books. In the matching with the input graph, the node is expanded into a list of notes to match a maximal number of nodes. The output graph is constructed by means of the constructing rule denoted by the symbol **T** on the right side of Fig. 2. Here we construct an XML document having a structure similar to that of the input document, but where each book contains only the attribute *year* and the element *title*. The symbol "+" inside the node ending the arc with label `<book>` means that we are interested in all books and, therefore, the output graph may contain more arcs with tag `<book>`. The variables $\$b$ and $\$t$ are used to pass data from the input graph to the output graph. The condition `arc($b, $t, <title>)` states that we consider pairs ($\$b, \$t$) which in the extracted graph are connected by an arc with label `<title>`.

2. *Construct a document containing for each book and for each author of the book, the pairs (title,author).* The query reported in the figure below extracts, for each book, the title and the set of all authors. The symbol "+" inside the node ending the arc with tag `<book>` means that we are interested in all books, and the same symbol marking the nodes at the end of the arc with tag `<author>` means that we want to collect, for each book, all of its authors. Thus, a set of results is constructed and each result contains a pair $\$t/\$a$, where $\$t$ denotes a title of book and $\$a$ an author.

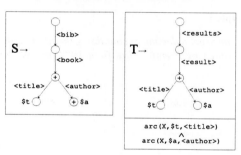

Figure 3. $\mathcal{XGL}$ Query 2

The condition `arc(X, $t, <title>) ∧ arc(X, $a, <author>)` states that we are only interested in pairs ($\$t, \$a$) identifying, respectively, the title and the author of the same book (X).

3. *Construct a document containing, for each book, the title and the set of all authors.* This query can be expressed by a simple variation of the rule **T** in Fig. 3. In particular, by putting the symbol "+" inside the node ending the arc marked with `<author>`, we collect for each book all of its authors.

4. *Construct a document containing, for each author, the titles of the books written by him.* Also this query can

be expressed by a simple variation of the rule **T** in Fig. 3. In particular, by putting the symbol "+" inside the node ending the arc marked with `<title>`, we collect for each author all the titles of the books he has written.

3. Preliminaries: NR Graph Grammars

Let Γ be an alphabet of node labels and Σ an alphabet of edge labels. A graph over Γ and Σ is a tuple $D = (N, E, \lambda)$ where N is a set of nodes, $E \subseteq \{(u, \sigma, v)|u, v \in N, \sigma \in \Sigma\}$ is a set of labelled edges and $\lambda : N \rightarrow \Gamma$ is a node labelling function. We identify a subset $\Delta \subseteq \Gamma$ as the set of *terminal* node labels. A node x of a graph D is said to be terminal if $\lambda(x) \in \Delta$ and we say that D is terminal if all its nodes are terminal. An arc from u to v with label σ is denoted by $u \xrightarrow{\sigma} v$. The components of an edge e will be denoted by $e[1]$, $e[2]$ and $e[3]$, respectively.

Given two data graphs A and B, we say that A is a subgraph of B iff i) $N_A \subseteq N_B$, ii) $\forall x \in N_A \ \lambda_A(x) = \lambda_B(x)$, and iii) $\forall x, y \in N_A, (x, \sigma, y) \in E_A$ only if $(x, \sigma, y) \in E_B$.

Graph grammars generalize standard grammars and *context-free* graph grammars are the natural generalization of context-free grammars: standard grammars generate strings whereas graph grammars generate graphs [14]. Two main types of context-free graph grammars have turned out to be the most natural, robust, and easy to handle: the *Hyperedge Replacement (HR) grammars* and *Node Replacement (NR) grammars*. In this paper we consider NR context-free graph grammars.

Node Replacement grammars generate labelled, directed graphs. A production of a graph grammar is of the form $X \rightarrow (D, C)$ where X is a nonterminal node label, D is a graph and C is the set of connection instructions. A rewriting step of a graph H according to such a production consists of removing a node u labelled X from H, adding D to H and adding edges between D and H as specified by the connection instructions in C. The pair (D, C) can be viewed as a new type of object, and the rewriting step can be viewed as the substitution of the object (D, C) for the node u in the graph H. Intuitively, these objects are quite natural: they are graphs ready to be embedded in an environment. Their formal definition is as follows.

Let Γ be an alphabet of node labels and Σ an alphabet of edge labels. A *graph with embedding* is a pair $K = (H, C)$ where H is a graph over Γ and Σ and $C \subseteq \Gamma \times \Sigma \times \Sigma \times N \times \{in, out\}$ is the connection relation of K. Each element $(\gamma, \sigma_1, \sigma_2, v, d) \in C$ is a connection instruction of K and is generally written as $(\gamma, \sigma_1/\sigma_2, v, d)$. The components of a graph with embedding K will be denoted as N_K, E_K, λ_K and C_K.

Intuitively, for a graph with embedding K, the meaning of a connection instruction $(\gamma, \sigma_1/\sigma_2, v, out)$ is as follows: if there was a σ_1-labelled edge from a node u which has been substituted by K to a γ-labelled node w, then the embedding mechanism defines a σ_2-labelled edge from v

to w. Similarly, the meaning of a connection instruction $(\gamma, \sigma_1/\sigma_2, v, in)$ is as follows: if there was a σ_1-labelled edge from a γ-labelled node w to a node u which has been substituted by K, then the embedding mechanism defines a σ_2-labelled edge from w to v. The feature which replaces edge labels is called *dynamic edge labelling*.

Let H be a graph over Γ and Σ, K be a graph with embedding over the same alphabets, and let $v \in N_H$. The substitution of K for v in H is denoted by $H[v/K]$.

In the following, connection rules of the form $(\gamma, \sigma/\sigma, v, a)$ (i.e. rules which do not re-label edges) are simply written as (γ, σ, v, a).

Example 2 The grammar G defined by the productions in Fig.4 describes a language containing chains. Connection rules can be incorporated into the left and right parts of production rules, as shown in Fig.5.

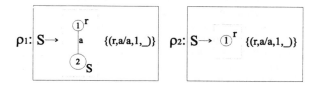

Figure 4. A graph grammar producing chains

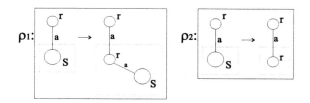

Figure 5. A graph grammar equivalent to that of Fig.4

Fig.6 illustrates a chain derivation by means of G productions.

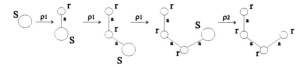

Figure 6. Derivation of a chain

Definition 1 *A node replacement (NR) grammar is a tuple $G = (\Gamma, \Delta, \Sigma, P, S)$ where Γ is the alphabet of node labels, $\Delta \subseteq \Gamma$ is the alphabet of terminal node labels, Σ is the alphabet of edge labels, P is the finite set of productions,*

and $S \in \Gamma - \Delta$ is the initial nonterminal symbol (axiom). A production is of the form $X \rightarrow (D, C)$ where $X \in \Gamma - \Delta$ and (D, C) is a graph with embedding over the alphabets Γ and Σ. □

The graph appearing in the right side of a production can be empty, and a production of the form $X \rightarrow (\emptyset, \emptyset)$ will be simply denoted as $X \rightarrow \epsilon$.

Let $G = (\Gamma, \Delta, \Sigma, P, S)$ be an NR grammar. Let H and H' be two graphs, let $v \in N_H$ and let $p : X \rightarrow (D, C)$ be a production of G. Then, we say that H' is directly derived from H (and write $H \Rightarrow_{v,p} H'$, or just $H \Rightarrow H'$), if $\lambda_H(v) = X$ and $H' = H[v/(D, C)]$. Moreover, we say that H' is derived from H if there is a finite sequence $H \Rightarrow H_1 \Rightarrow \cdots \Rightarrow H'$.

A graph grammar G defines a class of graphs which have common structural properties. The set of graphs generated by G is called *graph language* and denoted $\mathcal{L}(G)$.

4. Querying Data Graphs

We start by defining a simple graph model on an alphabet with three different types of symbol labelling nodes: constants, variables and nonterminal symbols. A variable can take any value and, therefore, it can be associated to any constant. In the following, constants are represented by strings starting with digits or lowercase letters (e.g. $b1$), variable names are denoted by strings preceded by a dollar (e.g. $\$b1$) and non terminal symbols are denoted by strings starting with uppercase letters (e.g. X). Given an alphabet of node labels Γ we will denote with Γ_c, Γ_v and Γ_{nt} the subsets of Γ which contain, respectively, constant symbols, variable symbols and non terminal symbols. A graph over the two alphabets $\Gamma = \Gamma_c \cup \Gamma_v \cup \Gamma_{nt}$ and Σ will be called *query graph*. A query graph whose nodes are labelled only with constant symbols (i.e. $\Gamma = \Gamma_c$) will be called *data graph*. A query graph which does not contain any non terminal nodes (i.e. $\Gamma_{nt} = \emptyset$) is called *terminal query graph*.

Thus, data graphs only contain constants and are used to represent the input database; terminal query graphs are used to denote graphs which can be 'mapped' on data graphs (by associating variables appearing in the terminal query graph to the constants labelling nodes of the data graph, or by associating nodes of the terminal query graph labelled with a constant to nodes of the data graph labelled with the same constant). General query graphs are used to represent the intermediate steps of the derivation of the query graphs obtained applying graph grammars.

Given a query graph α, we shall denote with $Terminal(\alpha)$ the sub-graph derived from α by deleting nodes marked with non terminal symbols and arcs connected to deleted nodes.

Example 3 The graph grammar G consisting of the productions of Fig. 7 defines a language consisting of trees.

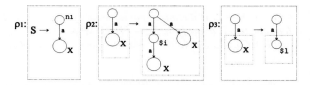

Figure 7. Graph grammar defining trees

Fig. 8 illustrates a tree derivation by means of G productions. Note that the root nodes of the trees in the language

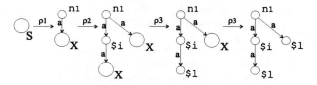

Figure 8. Graph derivation

defined by this grammar have a specific data label (n_1), the internal nodes have label $\$i$ and the leaf nodes have label $\$l$. □

Since in this context we are not interested in generating new graphs, but only in identifying sub-graphs of a given data graph, we shall not consider the whole language generated by a grammar, but only a subset containing graphs which identify some portion of the input data graph. To this purpose we define a mapping from terminal query graphs (obtained at the end of a graph grammar derivation) to subgraphs of a given data graph.

Definition 2 Let $\alpha = (N, E, \lambda)$ be a terminal query graph over Γ and Σ, and $D = (N_D, E_D, \lambda_D)$ a data graph over Γ_c and Σ. A *mapping* φ from α to D is a total function mapping, respectively, nodes in N to nodes in N_D and edges in E to edges in E_D such that i) for each node $n \in N$ either $\lambda(n) = \lambda_D(\varphi(n))$ or $\lambda(n)$ is a variable label, ii) for each arc $(u, \sigma, v) \in E$ there is an arc $(\varphi(u), \sigma, \varphi(v)) \in E_D$, and iii) there are no two nodes u and v such that $\lambda(u) = \lambda(v)$ and $\varphi(u) = \varphi(v)$ (i.e. two nodes with the same label cannot by associated to the same node in D). □

A data graph D is recognized by a graph grammar G if there exists a derivation from S to a terminal query graph α ($S \Rightarrow^* \alpha$) and a mapping from α to D. The set of data graphs recognized by G is denoted $\mathcal{DL}(G)$. The set of sub-graphs of a given data graph D recognized by G is denoted $\mathcal{DL}(G, D)$.

Definition 3 Let D be a data graph. A *mapping pair* on D is a pair (α, φ) where α is a query graph and φ is a data mapping from $Terminal(\alpha)$ to D. □

Observe that $Terminal(\alpha)$ is a terminal query graph (i.e. a graph whose node labels can be either constants or variables). Moreover a mapping pair (α, φ) is said to be *terminal* if α is a terminal query graph. Like an embedded graph, a mapping pair can be seen as a new type of object consisting of a query graph (derived from a graph grammar) mapped over a given data graph. The derivation of query graphs from parsing grammars can be extended to mapping pairs. Let D be a data graph, G a graph grammar and (α, φ) a mapping pair over D. We say that a mapping pair (β, ψ) is directly derived from (α, φ) through a production ρ of PG (and write $(\alpha, \varphi) \Rightarrow^\rho (\beta, \psi)$) if and only if $\alpha \Rightarrow^\rho \beta$ and ψ extends φ (i.e. $\varphi \subseteq \psi$). Moreover, we say that a mapping pair (α_n, φ_n) is derived from a mapping pair (α_0, φ_0) over a data graph D if $(\alpha_0, \varphi_0) \Rightarrow^{\rho_1} (\alpha_1, \varphi_1) \Rightarrow^{\rho_2} \cdots \Rightarrow^{\rho_n} (\alpha_n, \varphi_n)$. Given a graph grammar G and a data graph D, $\Phi(G, D)$ defines the set of terminal mapping pairs derived from $(S, \emptyset)$ where $\emptyset$ denotes an empty mapping.

A terminal mapping pair applied to a data graph D allows us to identify a subgraph of D having the property defined by the grammar. Each node of the extracted subgraph can be associated to more than one node of the query graph, if these nodes have different labels (roles). Different labels are used to distinguish different classes of nodes (e.g. in a tree internal nodes and leaf nodes may have different labels).

Example 4 Consider the parsing grammar of Example 2, the derivation shown in Fig. 8 and the data graph shown in Fig.9:

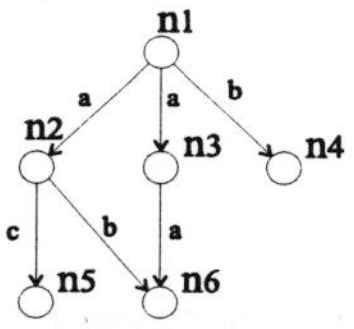

The query graphs produced respectively at the third and last steps of the derivation can be mapped on D, as shown in Fig.10.

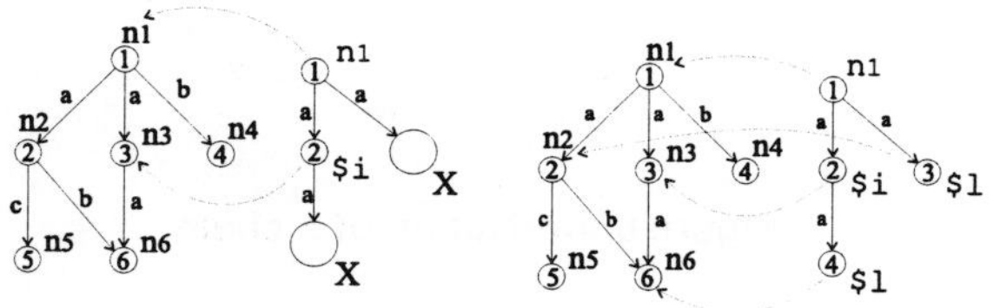

Figure 9. A data graph

Figure 10. Mapping of query graphs to a data graph

Note that the production defining the axiom (start symbol of the graph grammar) contains an arc whose source node is marked with the constant label $n1$. This means that all derived query graphs are trees whose root node is marked with $n1$. Therefore, every tree generated by such grammar can be mapped only to a tree whose root node has label $n1$. In the above mapping $\lambda(1) = \lambda(\varphi(1)) = n1$ whereas all other nodes in the query graph have associated a variable. Although not represented in the figure, the arcs in the query graph are mapped to arcs in the data graph; for instance the arc $e = (1, a, 2)$ and the arc $\varphi(e)$ have the same label a (i.e. $\varphi(e) = (\varphi(1), a, \varphi(2))$). $\qquad\square$

4.1. Parsing grammars

We now introduce a new type of graph grammars, called *parsing grammars*, which are specialized in extracting information from data graphs. Parsing grammars have the following characteristics:

- the set of production rules is linearly ordered (in order to drive the derivation process and reduce the nondeterminism);

- a rule can only be applied if a certain condition on the extracted data is satisfied.

Definition 4 A *Parsing (Graph) Grammar* is a tuple $PG = (\Gamma, \Sigma, P, S)$, where: Σ is the alphabet of edge labels, Γ is the alphabet of node labels ($\Gamma \cap \Sigma = \emptyset$) and $S \in \Gamma_{nt}$ is the axiom. P is a linearly ordered set of productions of the form $X \to (\alpha, C, \Theta)$, where

1. $X \in \Gamma_{nt}$ is a non-terminal symbol,

2. α is a query graph over Γ and Σ,

3. C is a set of connection rules, i.e. a set of tuples (γ, σ, v, d) where $d \in \{in, out\}$, $\gamma \in \Gamma$, $\sigma \in \Sigma$ and v is a node,

4. Θ is a first order formula on $\Sigma, \Gamma_c, \Gamma_v$ without quantifiers,

5. for each symbol $X \in \Gamma_{nt}$ there is a production $X \to \epsilon$ in P,

6. for each pair of productions $\rho_i : X \to (\alpha, C, \Theta)$ with α not empty and $\rho_j : X \to \epsilon$ is $\rho_i < \rho_j$,

7. for each production $\rho : X \to (\alpha, C, \Theta)$ with α not empty, D contains at least one terminal node. $\quad\square$

Thus, a parsing grammar is a restricted form of graph grammar. The restrictions have been introduced to reduce the nondeterminism (item 5-7 in Definition 4). The formula Θ states under which condition the rule can be applied.

Parsing grammars generate terminal query graphs without allowing edge re-labelling. The formal semantics of production rules can be done by extending the definition of the derivation of mapping pairs.

Let (β, φ) be a mapping pair, $\rho : X \to (\alpha, C, \Theta)$ a parsing grammar production rule and $\rho' : X \to (\alpha, C)$ the corresponding "standard" rule. We say that a mapping pair (γ, ψ) directly derives from (β, φ) through ρ (written $(\beta, \varphi) \Rightarrow^\rho (\gamma, \psi)$) if $(\beta, \varphi) \Rightarrow^{\rho'} (\gamma, \psi)$ and Θ is true w.r.t. the pair (α, ψ)[1]. The formula Θ is true w.r.t. (α, ψ) if by replacing the variables in Θ with the constants associated with ψ the resulting formula is satisfied.

The order of the productions of a parsing grammar PG defines an order on the mapping pairs derived from PG. Given a data graph D, a parsing grammar PG, and two productions ρ and ν of PG such that $\rho < \nu$, we say that a derivation d_1 of a pair (α_1, φ_1) from a pair (α, φ) precedes a derivation d_2 of a pair (α_2, φ_2) from (α, φ) (written $d_1 \prec d_2$), if 1) $d_1 = (\alpha, \varphi) \Rightarrow^\rho (\alpha_i, \varphi_i) \overset{*}{\Rightarrow}(\alpha_1, \varphi_1)$, $d_2 = (\alpha, \varphi) \Rightarrow^\nu (\alpha_j, \varphi_j) \overset{*}{\Rightarrow}(\alpha_2, \varphi_2)$, or 2) there are three derivations d, d_3 and d_4 such that $d_1 = dd_3$ and $d_2 = dd_4$ and $d_3 \prec d_4$.

The above defined ordering criterion on the derivations defines a preference criterion on the mapping pairs that are generable from a parsing grammar. Given a set of mapping pairs $P \subseteq \Phi(PG, D)$, a mapping pair $M \in P$ is said to be *founded* for P if there is a derivation $d = (S, \emptyset) \overset{*}{\Rightarrow} M$ such that there is no derivation $d' = (S, \emptyset) \overset{*}{\Rightarrow} M'$ of a terminal mapping pair $M' \in P$ with $d' \prec d$.

Theorem 1 *[17] Let PG be a parsing grammar and D a data graph. The non-deterministic selection of a terminal mapping pair founded for $\Phi(PG, D)$ can be computed in polynomial time.* $\quad\square$

5. Graph grammars for XML data

In this section we present a data model for representing XML documents by means of graphs, and then specialize parsing grammars to extract data from XML graphs.

An XML document can be represented as an ordered, labelled and oriented graph where:

- the containment relation between two elements is represented by an arc labelled with the tag of the sub-element;

- references are represented by arcs connecting the referencing element to the referenced one which are labelled with the name of the reference attribute;

- each node contains the set of the attributes of the corresponding element;

- if an element contains text and does not contain any sub-elements, the text is assimilated to the value of an attribute *value*;

- if an element contains both sub-elements and text strings, each string is assimilated to the attribute *string = "string-value"* of a sub-element <text>.

---

[1] The mapping ψ replace variables in α with constants in the input data graph.

The representation that we adopt in this paper can be easily understood by examining the document and the corresponding graph shown in Section 2.

In the following definition we formally identify the structure of an *XML Graph*.

Definition 5 Let A be a set of attribute names, T a set of tag names, and V a set of attribute values. An unordered XML graph is a labelled oriented graph $G = \langle N, E_r \cup E_t, f, r \rangle$ where:

- N is the set of nodes,
- $E_r \subseteq \{(u, \sigma, v) | u, v \in N \text{ and } \sigma \in A\}$ is a set of reference arcs,
- $E_t \subseteq \{(u, \sigma, v) | u, v \in N \text{ and } \sigma \in T\}$ is a set of tag arcs,
- $f : N \to 2^{A \times V}$ is the function associating a set of attribute/value pairs to each node.
- $\langle N, E_t \rangle$ is a tree with root r.

An ordered XML graph is a quintuple $G = \langle N, E_r \cup E_t, f, g, r \rangle$ where N, E_r, E_t, f and r are defined as above and $g : E_t \to Z^+$ is a function associating an unique ordinal number to each arc in E_t. □

In the previous sections, we showed that parsing grammars can be used to extract information from a source data graph. Now we 'specialize' parsing grammars to extract information from XML graphs.

The only difference with respect to the querying of graphs introduced in the previous section is that each node in an XML graph has a set of attributes and a value. Attributes and values can be identified by using a 'dot' notation as shown in the examples of Section 2. Thus, the attribute *year* of the element *book* identified by the variable b, is denoted by $b.year$. The text contained in the element b is denoted by $b.value$.

The following example shows how XML sub-graphs can be extracted from XML documents.

Example 5 A parsing grammar extracting from the document described in Section 1 the titles of the books published after 1991 by "Prentice-Hall" (equivalent to the $\mathcal{XGL}$ parsing grammar of Example 1) is reported in Fig. 11. □

The characterization of graphs given in Section 4 can be easily extended to XML-like graphs. Thus, XML data graphs are XML graphs whose labels are constants, XML query graphs may have both constants and variables as labels, and terminal XML query graphs are XML query graphs which do not contain non terminal nodes. For instance, the graphs used by production rules (see Fig. 11) are (non terminal) XML query graphs.

The derivation process of an XML parsing grammar applied to a source XML data graph XD, leads to a terminal mapping pair (α, φ) where φ associates each variable of α to a set of nodes of XD.

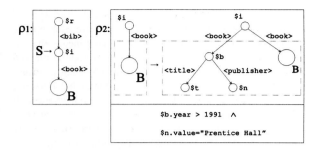

Figure 11. XML parsing grammar

6. $\mathcal{XGL}$: a graphical language for XML

XML parsing grammars can be used for extracting data from XML documents. Here, we further extend graph grammars for extracting data making them more user-friendly, and introduce simple construction rules to restructure information into new documents. Thus, we present the language $\mathcal{XGL}$ which is a graphical language derived from the grammars introduced in the previous section by adding new features to simplify the process of extracting subgraphs and to construct the output graph.

An $\mathcal{XGL}$ query is of the form[2]

WHERE	S_1 IN $F_1, ..., S_n$ IN F_n
CONSTRUCT	T [($u_1 \to v_1, ..., u_k \to v_k$)] [AS F_0]

where $F_0, ..., F_n$ are file names, $S_1, ..., S_n$ are axiom symbols corresponding to $\mathcal{XGL}$ parsing grammars, T is an $\mathcal{XGL}$ constructing rule and $u_j \to v_j$ means that the variable u_j appearing in the WHERE clause is renamed as v_j in the CONSTRUCT clause.

Thus, the WHERE clause is used to extract and mark information from the specified XML documents, whereas the CONSTRUCT clause specifies how to re-organize the extracted information in the XML document which results.

In the following, given an $\mathcal{XGL}$ query Q and a set of XML documents $D_1, ..., D_k$, $Q(D_1, ..., D_k)$ denotes the set of all documents which can be constructed by applying Q to $D_1, ..., D_k$.

6.1. $\mathcal{XGL}$ parsing grammars

Definition 6 An $\mathcal{XGL}$ parsing grammar is an XML parsing grammar where:

1. nodes may be marked with the symbol "+"; these nodes, called *grouping nodes*, denote sets of nodes labelled with the same symbol;

2. arcs may be labelled with general regular expressions denoting not empty strings.

---

[2]A this level we use the same syntax of XML-QL [13].

92

Moreover, if the regular expression associated to a given arc contains the union symbol "|" or the closure symbols "⋆" and "+", the ending node must be a grouping node labelled with a terminal symbol. □

Observe that the restriction on arcs with regular expressions has been introduced to avoid ambiguity in the result. General regular expressions denoting not empty strings may be rewritten into regular expressions without ϵ and ⋆ symbols. Therefore, in the following we assume that our regular expression denoting not empty paths does not contain both symbols ϵ and ⋆.

The formal semantics of $\mathcal{XGL}$ parsing grammars can be done in terms of XML parsing grammars by defining how production rules containing shortcuts (grouping nodes and arcs labelled with regular expressions) are rewritten into XML production rules. We first show how production rules with regular expressions are rewritten, and next consider the rewriting of production rules with grouping nodes.

Each rule ρ containing shortcuts is rewritten into one or two standard rules denoted, respectively, by r and r_1, r_2. For the sake of simplicity, in our rewriting rules we do not consider the contexts associated with the rules, and assume that each node labelled with X in $r_1, ..., r_k$ has the same context of the node marked with X in ρ.

Rewriting of productions with regular expressions

A production rule with a regular expression is rewritten into a set of equivalent rules as follows:
- *Concatenation.* The rewriting of a production rule containing an arc labelled with the concatenation $p.q$ is reported in Fig.12 where the rules ρ_1 and ρ_2 are replaced, respectively, by the rules r_1 and r_2. Observe that there

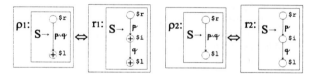

Figure 12. Rewriting arcs with concatenation

are two different re-writings, respectively, for arcs ending with simple nodes and grouping nodes.
- *Union.* The rewriting of a production rule containing an arc labelled with the union $p \mid q$ is shown in Fig. 13 where the rule ρ is replaced by the rule r.
- *Closure.* The rewriting of a production rule containing an arc labelled with the positive closure l^+ is shown in Fig. 14 where the rule ρ is replaced by the two rules r_1 and r_2.

Rewriting of productions with grouping nodes

The rewriting of a production rule containing grouping nodes is shown in Fig. 15 where the rule ρ is replaced by the two rules r_1 and r_2, and T is a new non terminal symbol.

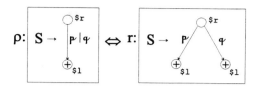

Figure 13. Rewriting arcs with union

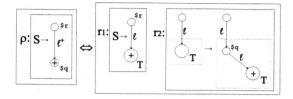

Figure 14. Rewriting arcs with closure

Example 6 The rewriting of the parsing grammar in the first query of Example 1 (Fig. 2) is reported in Example 6 (Fig. 11). □

6.2. $\mathcal{XGL}$ constructing rules

In the previous section we have shown that $\mathcal{XGL}$ parsing grammars can be used to extract information from an XML data graph, allowing us to specify the structure of the subgraph containing such information.

In this section we now show that in a similar way, using the graph containing the extracted information, it is possible to build a new document. The process of creating a new XML graph is carried out by defining a tree structure containing information from the extracted graph which satisfies a given condition. The new graph is defined by means of an $\mathcal{XGL}$ constructing rule whereas the condition is defined by means of a first order formula.

Syntax The first order formula is based on the ternary predicates *arc* and *path* storing, respectively, information about arcs and paths in the extracted graph. The arguments of the predicates *arc* and *path* may be constants, variables representing node labels (denoted by lowercase strings preceded by $) and *general variables* representing node identifiers, and edge labels (denoted by strings starting with an uppercase letter). For instance, the fact `arc(X, $t, <title>)` states that there is an arc labelled <title> from a generic node to a node labelled t. Analogously, the fact `path(X, $t, <title>*)` states that there is a path whose first arc is labelled <title> from a generic node to a node labelled t.

Definition 7 Let D be an XML data graph, (β, φ) a terminal mapping pair on D. An $\mathcal{XGL}$ *constructing rule* has the form $T \rightarrow (\alpha, \Theta)$, where α is an XML query graph, and Θ is a *FO* formula on $\{arc, path\}$ evaluated on D. □

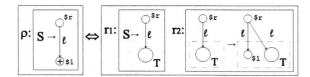

Figure 15. Rewriting grouping nodes

It is worth noting that instead of FO it is possible to use alternative languages such as SQL, logic languages or graphical notations.[3]

Semantics We now present the semantics of constructing rules. At the end of the parsing process we have produced a mapping pair (β, φ) over an XML data graph D, where each variable symbol $\$v$ in β is associated to a (possibly empty) set of nodes in D. The association between variables and nodes is represented by means of a ternary relation $Node$ where a tuple $(id, val, \$v)$ states that a node in β labelled with $\$v$ is associated (by φ) to the node with identifier id and value val in D[4]. Moreover, we assume that the graph D is stored by means of the ternary predicate Arc which is different from the predicate arc used in the FO formula: Arc corresponds to the set E_D (i.e. $Arc(id_1, l, id_2)$ is true iff $(id_1, l, id_2) \in E_D$). Analogously, the predicate $Path$ denotes the transitive closure of Arc, and corresponds to the predicate $path$ which defines the transitive closure of arc.

The query graph α, in a constructing rule (α, Θ), defines the structural properties of the output XML document, while the first order formula Θ expresses a condition defining which nodes in the data graph extracted in the WHERE clause will be used in the construction of the output graph.

Observe that in the FO formula Θ, the predicates arc and $path$ take as arguments i) variables representing node identifiers and edge labels, denoted by capital letters (e.g. X), ii) variables representing node labels, denoted using the symbol $\$$ (e.g. $\$x$), and iii) constants. To explain the semantics of the construction rule we first rewrite the condition Θ, translating the predicates arc and $path$ in an equivalent formula containing only the predicates Arc and $Path$ in order to obtain a formula Θ' which is directly verifiable on D. Before introducing the formal rewriting we present an example.

Example 7 Consider the construction rule of the second query in Example 1. The condition

$$\texttt{arc(X, \$t, <title>)} \land \texttt{arc(X, \$a, <author>)}$$

---

[3]In the prototype of the language under development we use FO_R^{agg} formulas. FO_R^{agg} denotes first order logic over the signature of the real field with aggregation operators[19].

[4]Formally, since variables in the extracted graph may be renamed, we should use an additional predicate storing the mapping between variables in the extracted graph and (renamed) variables in the output graph.

is rewritten as

$$\texttt{Node(Id_a, V_a, \$a)} \land \texttt{Node(Id_t, V_t, \$t)} \land$$

$$\texttt{Arc(X, Id_t, <title>)} \land \texttt{Arc(X, Id_a, <author>)}$$

The variables $\$a$ and $\$t$ in the graph are replaced, respectively, by V_a and V_t. □

The formal rewriting of construction rule $T \rightarrow (\alpha, \Theta)$ into a rule $T \rightarrow (\alpha', \Theta')$ is as follows:

1. α' is derived from α by replacing every occurrence of $\$x$ with V_x;
2. Define Θ'' as the first order formula derived from Θ by replacing i) all occurrences of the predicate arc with Arc, ii) all occurrences of the predicate $path$ with $Path$ and iii) every variable $\$x$ with Id_x;
3. $\Theta' = \bigwedge_{\substack{\$x\ in\ \Theta \\ \$x\ in\ \alpha}} Node(Id_x, V_x, \$x) \land \Theta''$.

Using the rewritten constructing rule we obtain the output graph by expanding the grouping nodes and replacing variables with constants satisfying the condition Θ'. The expansion of a grouping node appearing in an $\mathcal{XGL}$ constructing rule can be explained as similar to the expansion of a grouping node in the application of a parsing grammar production. When, in a parsing grammar rule, a node n is marked with the symbol "+" all the (maximal) sub-trees rooted in n and matching the specified structure have to be extracted.

Analogously, the presence of a grouping node m in the query graph specified in a constructing rule implies that the subtree rooted in m must be replicated for all the possible instances of the variables labelling the node in the subtree.

The formal semantics of the construction rule is given expressing, by means of logical rules with complex terms and nested sets, the structure of the output graph. Complex terms and nested sets are used to describe the nesting of elements and grouping elements. (For the formal semantics of logic languages with sets we address readers to [5]). Before introducing the semantics of construction rules we present an example.

Example 8 Consider the second query of Example 1. The logic rule defining the output graph is the following:

```
Tree(xml(results(⊥, ≪ result(⊥, title(T),
                 author(A)) ≫))) ← Theta(T, A).
```

where $\bot$ is the null value which denotes that the element $<$ results $>$ does not have any attributes and contains only a set of subelements $<$ result $>$. The condition Θ is defined by the following rule:

```
Theta(T, A) ← Node(Id_A, A, $a) ∧ Node(Id_T, T, $t)
         ∧ arc(X, Id_A, <author>) ∧ arc(X, Id_T, <title>).
```

Analogously, the logic rule defining the output graph for the fourth query of Example 1 is as follows:

```
Tree(xml(results(⊥, ≪ result(⊥, ≪title(T)≫,
                  author(A)) ≫))) ← Theta(T, A).
```
□

The logic program associated to a rewritten $\mathcal{XGL}$ constructing rule (α', Θ') consists of a logical program defining two predicates $Tree$ and $Theta$. The predicate $Tree$ defines the structure of the resulting document, whereas $Theta$ is the translation of the FO formula Θ' into a logic program.

The predicate $Tree$ is defined by a rule of the form $\texttt{Tree}(\texttt{xml}(\texttt{TR}(\alpha')) \leftarrow \texttt{Theta}(\texttt{V}_1, ..., \texttt{V}_\texttt{n})$, where $V_1, ..., V_n$ are the variables appearing in α, and $\texttt{TR}(\alpha')$ denotes the translation of α' into a nested structure defined as follows:

- if α' is a leaf node with label n, $\texttt{TR}(\alpha')$ denotes the label of n;

- if the root of α' is a non leaf node n, $T_1, ..., T_q$ are the subtrees connected to n whose root is not a grouping node and $T'_1, ..., T'_r$ are the subtrees connected to n whose root is a grouping node, then $\texttt{TR}(\alpha')$ denotes $\texttt{X}, \texttt{l}_1(\texttt{TR}(\texttt{T}_1)), ..., \texttt{l}_\texttt{q}(\texttt{TR}(\texttt{T}_\texttt{q})), \ll \texttt{l}'_1(\texttt{TR}(\texttt{T}'_1)) \gg, ..., \ll \texttt{l}'_\texttt{r}(\texttt{TR}(\texttt{T}'_\texttt{r})) \gg$ where X is the label of $root(\alpha')$ and $l_1, ..., l_q, l'_1, ..., l'_r$ are the labels of the arcs connecting $T_1, ..., T_q, T'_1, ..., T'_r$ to n.

Observe that if a node of α' is labelled with a variable V, V also appears as an argument of the atom $Theta(V_1, ..., V_n)$, even if it does not appear in the original condition Θ.

Example 9 Consider the constructing rule of Fig. 16 where the condition Θ has not been reported. The associated logic

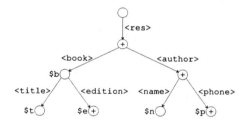

Figure 16. Graph of a construction rule

rule is as follows:

$$
\begin{aligned}
\texttt{Tree}(\texttt{xml}(\bot, \ll \texttt{res}(\bot, \texttt{book}(\texttt{B}, \texttt{title}(\texttt{T}), \ll \texttt{edition}(\texttt{E}) \gg), \\
\ll \texttt{author}(\bot, \texttt{name}(\texttt{N}), \ll \texttt{phone}(\texttt{P}) \gg) \gg \gg)) \\
\leftarrow \texttt{Theta}(\texttt{B}, \texttt{T}, \texttt{E}, \texttt{N}, \texttt{P}).
\end{aligned}
$$

$\square$

References

[1] Abiteboul, S. Semistructured Data. *Proc. Int. Conf. on Database Theory*, 1997.

[2] Abiteboul, S., Buneman, P., and Suciu, D. *Data on the Web: From Relations to Semistructured Data and XML*. Morgan Kauffman, 1999.

[3] Abiteboul S., Hull R., and Vianu V. *Foundations of Databases*. Addison-Wesley, 1994.

[4] Abiteboul S., Quass, D., McHugh, J., Widom, J., Wiener, J. L., The Lorel Query Language for Semistructured Data. Journal of Digital Libraries 1(1), 1997. pages 68-88.

[5] Beeri, C., Naqvi, S., Shmueli, O., Tsur, S.: Set Constructors in a Logic Database Language, *Journal of Logic Programming*, **10**, 3 & 4, 1991.

[6] Buneman, P., Semistructured Data. *Proc. Int. Symp. on Principles of Database Systems*, 1997.

[7] Ceri S., Comai S., Damiani E., Fraternali P., Paraboschi S., Tanca L. XML-GL: A Graphical Language for Querying and Restructuring XML Documents. *Computer Networks* 31(11-16), 1999. pages 1171-1187.

[8] Ceri, S., Comai, S., Damiani, E., Fraternali, P., and Tanca, L., Complex Queries in XML-GL. *ACM Symp.m on Applied Computing* (2) 2000. pages 888-893.

[9] Ceri, S., Fraternali, P., Paraboschi, S.. XML: Current Developments and Future Challenges for the Database Community. *Proc. Int. Conf. EDBT*, 2000, pages 3-17.

[10] Consens, M, and Mendelzon, A., GraphLog: a Visual Formalism for Real Life Recursion. *Proc. Ninth ACM Symposium on Principles of Database Systems*, 1990. pages 404-416.

[11] Damiani, E., and Tanca, L., Blind Queries to XML Data. *Proc. Int. Conf. on Database and Expert Systems Applications*, 2000. pages 345-356.

[12] Boag, S., Chamberlin, D. Florescu, D., Robie, J., Siméon, J., and Stefanescu, M., XQuery 1.0: An XML Query Language, http://www.w3.org/TR/xquery, 2002.

[13] Deutsch, A., Fernandez, M. F., Florescu, D., Levy, D. A., and Suciu, D., A Query Language for XML. *Computer Networks* 31(11-16), 1999. pages 1155-1169.

[14] Engelfriet J. Context-Free Graph Grammars. In *Handbook of Formal Languages, Volume 3: Beyond Words (G. Rozenberg, A. Salomaa, eds.)*, Springer-Verlag, 125-213, 1997.

[15] Fernandez, M.F., Florescu, D., Kang, J., Levy, A. Y., and Suciu, D., STRUDEL: A Web-site Management System. *Proc. ACM SIGMOD Conf. on Management of Data*, 1997. pages 549-552.

[16] Fernandez, M. F., Simeon, J., Wadler, P. An Algebra for XML Query. *Int. Conf. on Found. of Software Technology and Theoretical Computer Science*, 2000. pages 11-45.

[17] Flesca, S., Furfaro, F., Greco, S. Graph Grammars for querying graph-like data. *Workshop on Graph Transformation and Visual Modeling Techniques (GT-VMT)*, 2001

[18] Flesca, S., and Greco, S. Querying Graph Databases. *Proc. Int. Conf. on Extending Database Technology* 2000. pages 510-524.

[19] Grumbach, S., Rafanelli, M., Tininini, L., Querying Aggregate Data, *Proc. PODS* 1999, pages 174-184

[20] Konopnicki, D., and Shmueli, O., W3QS: A Query System for the World-Wide-Web, *Proc. Int. Conf. VLDB*, pages 54-65, 1995.

[21] Kuper, G. M.: Logic Programming with Sets, Journal of Computer and System Science, **41**, 44-64, 1990.

[22] Mecca, G., Atzeni P., Masci, A., Merialdo, P., and Sindoni, G., The Araneus Web-Base Management System. *Proc. of SIGMOD Conference*, 1998, pages 544-546.

[23] Mendelzon, A., Mihaila, G., and Milo, T., Querying the World Wide Web, *Journal of Digital Libraries*, 1997.

[24] Paredaens, J., Peelman, P., and Tanca, L., G-Log: A Declarative Graphical Query Language. *Proc. Int. Conf. DOOD*, 1991. pages 108-128.

Parallel Processing XML Documents

Kevin Lü, Yuanling Zhu and Wenjun Sun
School of Computing, Southbank University
London SE1 OAA UK
{lukj,zhuy,sunw@sbu.ac.uk}

Shouxun Lin, Jianping Fan
Institute of Computing Technology, Chinese
Academy of Sciences, 100080, Beijing, China
{sxlin,fan@ict.ac.cn}

Abstract

As Web applications are time vulnerable, the increasing size of XML documents and the complexity of evaluating XML queries pose new performance challenges to existing information retrieval technologies. This paper introduces a new approach for developing a purpose-built XML data management system to improve the system performance of a Web site with XML support by using parallel data processing techniques. To improve the system performance, we proposed a parallelisation model for XML data processing, where the data storage strategies, data placement methods and query evaluation techniques have been studied. Other related issues are also presented.

Key words: XML, data management, query processing

1   Introduction

The extensible markup language XML has recently emerged as a new standard for information representation and exchange on the Internet. It can be expected that a large amount of data represented in XML format will be available throughout the Web in the near future [7]. Most of the current studies on XML documents processing are based on uniprocessor environment. To assess the feasibility and importance of the project, we studied the features of available XML database products and conducted some experiments. We tested several available XML database products, including Tamino, Xset and Lore [10]. The system performance deteriorates when the size of data sets increased, in particular, when complex queries (including join operations and multiple path expressions) are involved [14]. A large number of disk I/O is the direct reason for the high

cost of query processing, that is because the processing regular path expression is based conventional tree traversal approaches, and such approaches can be inefficient if complex queries are involved.

Parallelism is an attractive solution to improve system performance. The use of parallelism has shown good scalability in traditional database applications. XML documents can be distributed onto several processing nodes so that a reasonable query response time can be achieved by retrieving the related data in parallel. With the advent of inexpensive microprocessor and high bandwidth interconnet, coupling a large number of processors to form a highly parallel system has become an increasingly popular method for improve system performance.

In order to investigate the suitable approaches of using parallel techniques to manage XML documents, a purpose-built data management system – where features of XML documents are appropriately modelled - called Parallel XML Database System, PXDS, is developed. PXDS provides a practical approach to the modelling and managing of XML documents taking into account considerations on performance. In this paper, in stead to describing the details of algorithms developed for PXDS and the evaluations of these algorithms, we present an overall system introduction, the main features of each component and the unfinished work ahead.

Two important issues in the design of a parallel shared-nothing data management system are data placement and query processing. A suitable data placement strategy is essential to utilise the resources of a multiple processor system and query processing must exploit the potential parallelism available with declustered data placement in order to achieve good response-time/throughput trade-off and overall high performance. In this paper, our efforts on these two issues are presented. In addition, other system design issues are also discussed. This paper is organised as follows. Section 2 introduces the data model, data storage and data placement strategies used in PXDBS. Section 3 discusses various aspects about query evaluation, and concluding remarks are presented in Section 4.

2   Data model and data storage strategies

2.1   Data model

The latest W3C working draft on XML Information Set (InfoSet) provides a data model for describing the logical structure of a well-formed XML document. Similar to the data model used in Lore [10]. We extended the InfoSet data model to a directed labelled graph, where the vertices in the graph represent the information items and arcs represent the semantic links between the information items. Each vertex in the graph has an associated *oid* and each arc has a label attached. Figure 1 gives an example for directed labelled graphs, which illustrate the data model in our research. The definition for the data model can be found in [15].

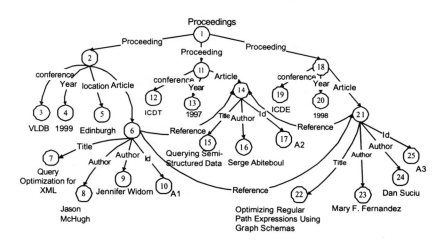

Figure 1 The graph presentation for an XML document

2.2   Query language

The query language used PXDS is XQuery [13]. One reason of using XQuery is that it is becoming the standard query language for XML documents and it satisfies the requirements of PXDS. XQuery is a functional language in which query is represented as an expression. It supports several kinds of expressions, such as path expression and regular path expression. XQuery relies path expressions for navigating in hierarchic documents.

2.3   Data storage strategies

To store an XML document, we firstly parse it into a DOM tree and assign an *oid* to each vertex and an *arcid* to each arc in the tree. ID/IDREF pairs are identified and corresponding oids are linked together by adding new arcs. The resulted graph can be mapped into a relation describing the properties of each arc in the graph, including its source vertex, its target vertex, its label, and its value. Figure 2 illustrates the relational representation for the XML document shown in figure 1. We implemented our data repository for XML on Linux using the Libxml as the parser and the Berkeley DB Library [3] as the database primitives.

Arc_id	Source_id	Target_id	Label	Value
1	1	2	Proceeding	-
2	2	3	Conference	VLDB
3	2	4	Year	1999
4	2	5	Location	Edinburgh
5	2	6	Article	-
6	6	7	Title	Query Optimisation for XML
7	6	8	Author	Jason McHugh
8	6	9	Author	Jennifer Widom
9	6	10	Id	A1
10	6	14	Reference	-
11	6	21	Reference	-
12	1	11	Proceeding	-
13	11	12	Conference	ICDT
14	11	13	Year	1997
15	11	14	Article	-
16	14	15	Title	Querying Semi-structured Data
17	14	16	Author	Serge Abiteboul
18	14	17	Id	A2
19	1	18	Proceeding	-
20	18	19	Conference	ICDE
21	18	20	Year	1998
22	18	21	Article	-
23	21	22	Title	Optimising Regular Path Expressions Using Graph Schemas
24	21	23	Author	Mary F. Femandez
25	21	24	Author	Dan Suciu
26	21	25	Id	A3
27	21	14	Reference	-

Figure 2 The relational representation for the XML document listed in figure 1

2.4   Data placement strategies

The data placement strategy for parallel systems is concerned with the distribution of data between different nodes in the system. A poor strategy can result in a non-uniform distribution of the load and the formation of bottlenecks. In general, determining the optimal placement of data across nodes for performance is a difficult problem even for the relational data model. XML documents introduce additional complexity because they do not have a rigid, regular, and complete structure.

2.4.1   Vertical fragmentation

To store the directed labelled graph representation of XML documents, we use a binary table model to improve I/O parallelism and avoid the retrieval of data not needed by the query. The Berkeley DB Library [3] provides a kernel of DBMS primitives on binary tables. The binary table model has the drawback that queries must spend extra effort in recombining fragmented data, i.e. they must do extra joins. However, the extra joins needed on a vertical fragmented data model are not mere 'random' joins.

Vertical fragments of the same table contain identical tuple sequences, and if the join operator is aware of this, it does not need to spend effort in finding matching tuples at all. In the binary table model, the vertical fragmentation has been exploited. This model has the advantages of simplicity and flexibility because it provides a uniform representation. As shown in figure 3, attributes of each arc are vertically partitioned into four binary tables. By storing theses pairs of columns in different tables, different queries accessing different attribute values of the same arc can be evaluated concurrently.

Source Node Table

Arc_id	Source_id
1	1
2	2
3	2
...	...
27	21

Target Node Table

Arc_id	Target_id
1	2
2	3
3	4
...	...
27	25

Arc_id	Label
1	Proceeding
2	Conference
3	Year
...	...
27	Reference

Arc_id	Value
2	VLDB
3	1999
4	Edinburgh
...	...
26	A3

Figure 3 Vertical partitioning of the labelled directed graph

2.4.2 Horizontal partitioning

In addition to the vertical partitioning, we also exploit the horizontal partitioning to improve the query parallelism. The idea of our data placement strategy [15] for XML data is similar to those in parallel object-oriented databases [12]. But we focus on how to construct the weighted graph from the original XML document, which forms the basis of the graph partitioning algorithm. Each arc in the graph is associated with a weight to describe the frequency of traversals on it. The weight information is included in the file of "Query Profile", which is generated during Web log analysis. During this process, the query pattens are recognised and query arrival frequencies (which determine the frequency of traversals within a data model) are accumulated. The objective of horizontal partitioning is trying to find a nearly optimal data distribution so that the system throughput and resource utilisation can be maximised. A new algorithm is proposed for deriving the weighted graph from the labelled directed graph by using the implied schema information from XML queries. According to our approach, entities to be accessed by navigation in a query should be assigned to the same processing node, and instances accessed by the same query are distributed as evenly as possible along all the processing nodes. Our graph partition algorithm is based on the multilevel graph partition algorithm for its efficiency and accuracy [6]. The unique features of XML documents and XML queries have been studied to provide the foundation for the graph partition. In the coarsening phase of the multilevel graph partitioning algorithm, all vertices in the neighbourhood of the selected matching vertex are coalesced based on their edge weight. This criterion speeds up the procedure of the coarsening and reduces the possibility of assigning vertices to be accessed by navigation to different processing nodes. In the partitioning phase, the weights of multivertices are used to evenly distribute the workload of a query. The performance analysis being conducted on the DBLP data set shows that the partition produced by our algorithm could greatly reduce the communication cost and lower workload skew [15].

After the data is partitioned into a number of fragments and is distributed to different processing elements, we used two data dictionaries to store the information describing where the data is located. One dictionary describes the location of each arc, which is also a binary table indexed on the *arcid* with the processing element identification (*PE_id*) specified. Another dictionary describes the distribution of the *boundary nodes*. The boundary nodes refer to the nodes that belong to multiple partitions. As shown in figure 4, the labelled directed graph is partitioned into three fragments and the nodes 1, 14, 21 are the boundary nodes. The corresponding boundary node data dictionary is shown in figure 5. The value of flag field in the dictionary indicates the property of the boundary node: source node (1), target node (2), and both (3). This information is needed while evaluating regular expression queries. Each processing element has a replication of the global dictionaries so that it can easily know with which processing element it needs to communicate.

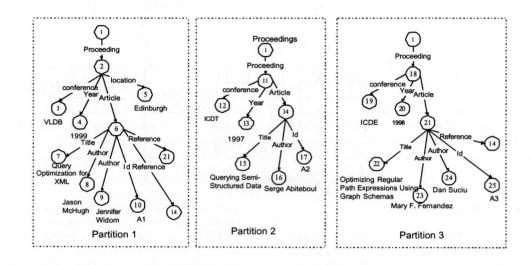

Figure 4. An example for XML document partitioning

Arc Data Dictionary

Arc_id	Partition_id
1	1
2	1
...	...
12	2
13	2
...	...
19	3
...	...
27	3

Boundary-node Data Dictionary

PE_id	Partition_id	Flag
1	1	1
1	2	1
1	3	1
14	1	2
14	2	3
14	3	2
21	1	2
21	3	3

Figure 5. Data dictionaries for the partitioning presented in figure 4

2.5 Indexing

In addition to the indexes used to speed up data search within these tables, the XML graph numbering scheme [8] is introduced. One unique feature of this approach is able to determine the ancestor-descendant relationship quickly and without traversal of the data graph. A set of order-range pairs are assigned to a node in the XML graph Numbering Scheme (XNS) that. The *numbering set* $\{(n^x_{order}, n^x_{size})\}$ of each node x of the graph consists of:

- A *primary numbering pair* $(n_{x\ order}, n_{x\ size})$ that is assigned to the node x during extended numbering of the XML containment tree. This pair is denoted as $(n^x_{x\ order}, n^x_{x\ size})$;

- A *linked numbering pair* is referred to as a primary numbering pair $(n_{y\ order}, n_{y\ size})$ of any node y that is linked by x directly or indirectly (through its descendants). Such a pair is denoted as $(n^x_{y\ order}, n^x_{y\ size})$.

The new linked pair $(n_{y\ order}, n_{y\ size})$ will be included into the numbering set only if it refers to the range not reachable through any other pair in the set, i.e. interval $[n_{y\ order}, n_{y\ order} + n_{y\ size}]$ is not contained in any interval $[n^x_{i\ order}, n^x_{i\ order} + n^x_{i\ size}]$ from the set $\{(n^x_{order}, n^x_{size})\}$. Note that the numbering set of each node will never be empty and consists at least of one numbering pair, the primary numbering pair. The

ancestor-descendant relationship between two nodes is determined as follows. Given nodes x and y and their numbering sets $\{(n^x_{order}, n^x_{size})\}$ and $\{(n^y_{order}, n^y_{size})\}$ respectively, x is an ancestor of y (y is a descendant of x), iff $\exists i, (n^x_{i\ order}, n^x_{i\ size}) \in \{(n^x_{order}, n^x_{size})\}$, that $n^x_{i\ order} < n^y_{y\ order}$ and $n^x_{i\ order} + n^x_{i\ size} = n^y_{y\ order} + n^y_{y\ size}$. In other words, there exist such a node i, which is referenced by x and the ancestor of the node y. An example of the graph numbering is given on f0, b. The primary pairs are shown in bold. Node o_8 has the linked pair (50, 90), corresponding to node o_5 and representing the link: $o_8 ? o_5$. Nodes o_2, o_4 have the linked pair (1, 100), corresponding to node o_1 and representing the reference $o_4 ? o_1$ (node o_2 as parent of o_4). Lastly, node o_3 has the linked pair (65, 71), corresponding to node o_7 and representing the reference $o_3 ? o_7$. Nodes o_2, o_4 are ancestors of the node o_3 but do not have the linked pair (65, 71) as they can reach node o_7 via their linked pair (1, 100). The root node o_1 has not any linked pairs: every node of the graph is reachable through its primary pair.

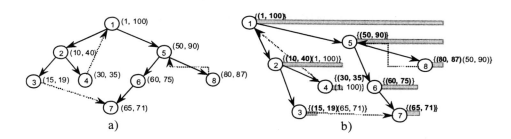

Figure 6 Numbering and extended numbering of the XML graph.

3 Parallel query processing XML documents

3.1 XML query representations

Like semistructured data [11], XML documents usually don't have rigid structure information, so the query language for XML documents utilises *path expressions* to exploit the information stored in XML documents. Path expressions are algebraic

representations of sets of paths in a graph and are specified by a sequence of nested tags. For example, the path expression *"proceedings.article.title"* for the XML document in figure 1 refers to all the titles of article published in all the conference proceedings.

As shown in [2], an XML query can also be presented by a labelled directed graph. Figure 7 shows two typical XML queries and their corresponding graph based presentattions.

The first query in figure 7 can be represented as: $V = \{v1,v2,v3,v4\}$; $A = \{a1,a2,a,3\}$; $S\{(a1,v1), (a2,v2), (a3,v3)\}$; $T = \{(a1,v2), (a2,v3), (a3,v4)\}$; $L = \{(a1,'Article'),(a2,'Auther'), (vs,'Jenifer Widom'), (a3,'Titl')\}$. Where, V denotes the set of vetices, A denotes the set of arcs, S denotes the souce vertex of each arc in A, T denotes the target vertex of each arc in A, and L denotes the label constraints on the vertices and arcs. The graphs in figure 6 can act as schemas, which partly describe the structure of the XML document. The answer to a query of XML

documents is the union of instances conformed to the schema. In the other words, we need to find the match between the database and the variables $v_i \in V$, $a_j \in A$ in the schema. Figure 8 shows the the query results for the queries illustrated in figure 7. It can be figured out that the match m between the schema of the first query and the database is as follows: $m = \{(v1,2), (v2,6), (v3,9), (v4,7), (a1,5), (a2,7),(a3,6)\}$.

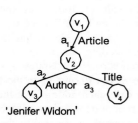

Q$_1$: select all papers authored by 'Jenifer Widom'   Q$_2$: select all papers that are cited by the papers autored by 'Jenifer Widom'

Figure 7. Two typical XML queries and their corresponding graph based presentation

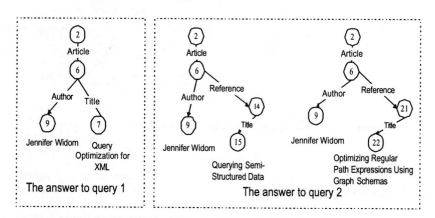

Figure 8. The query results for the queries illustrated in figure 6

3.2   Query processing methods

XML data is represented as a graph, evaluating queries involves navigating paths where the operations of traversing graphs are required.

Although a number of indexes have been proposed to speed up query processing, however, it is essential that a purpose built system to have the facilities to evaluate queries. For example, in the cases where indexes are not applicable, the traversing graphs for answering queries are the inevitable method to be used.

Four new parallel query evaluation algorithms have been developed in PXDS [14]. The Parallel Top-down Query Processing Strategy (PTDQ) follows the path from the root to the target collections using the depth first graph traversal algorithm. It processes the path expression by navigating through object references following the order of the collections in path expressions. If there are multiple references from one object to the objects in the next collection, the navigation follows the depth first order. The Parallel Bottom-up Query Processing Strategy (PBUQ starts with identifying all objects via the last edge in the input path and check if the objects satisfying the predicate, then traverses backwards through the path, going from children to parents. Similar to the top-down strategy, if it finds that the next object is in another *PE*, it will send an *search instruction (SI)* to it. The advantage of this approach is that it starts with objects guaranteed to satisfy at least part of the predicate, and it does not need examine the path any further if the path does not satisfy the predicate. The Parallel Hybrid Query Processing Strategy (PHQ) starts to evaluate a query from both top down and bottom up directions at the same time, and processes from both directions will meet somewhere in the middle. This will increase the degree of parallelisation for query processing. On the direction of top down, the PHQ uses the PTDQ algorithm to create a temporary result which satisfying the predicate so far. Meanwhile, on the other hand, this algorithm traverses up from the bottom vertex using the PBUQ algorithm and reaches the same point as the top-down thread does. A join between the two temporary results yields the complete set of satisfying paths.

One drawback of the PTDQ, PBUQ and PHQ algorithms is the possible large number of communication requests as during the query processing messages need to be passed amongst processing elements. The communication cost is much more expensive compare other data operation costs and it should be kept as less as possible. The other drawback is causing additional waiting time due to excessive coherence traffic on the network. The Parallel Partial Match Query Processing Strategy (PPMQ) is designed to overcome the drawbacks of these three algorithms by using the pre-fetch technique to reduce the communication cost. The idea of the fourth method is that every processing element searches the path in parallel. When a processing element finds an object in the path outside local partition, it will record the *id* of the processing element hosting the object instead of sending a message to that processing element instantly. After all possible *partial matched routes* have been produced, they will be sent to one processing element to merge the *partial matched route* to match the whole path expression. Although this method can greatly reduce the amount of messages among processing elements, it may demand extra time for merging the partial query results.

3.4 Other sources of parallelism in XML data processing

The evaluation of path expressions discussed so far is based on the pointer navigation approach. An XML query is represented as a query graph consisting several paths. The evaluation of a path can start from any node on the path, not necessarily only from the root or the leaf nodes. These four algorithms mainly focus on exploiting the intra-path parallelism, which is achieved by data partitioning. There are also other types of path parallelism in the XML parallel query processing: *intra-path parallelism*. The intra-path parallelism is achieved by data partitioning, and the inter-path parallelism refers to the parallelism among different paths. Two paths are called *intersected* if they share one common *joint* node. The intersected paths can be evaluated in a pipelined fashion, where the bindings to the variables of the joint node on the first path can act as an input to the evaluation of the second path. In this case, *pipelined inter-path parallelism* is achieved. Two different paths can also be evaluated independently, and additional intersection operations need to be conducted on the joint node. Two paths are called *independent* if they share no common node variables. Independent paths can be evaluated concurrently by multiple threads working independently. This type of parallelism is referred as to *independent inter-path parallelism*.

4. Discussion

In this section, outlook of future work and a summary are presented.

Analytical analyses – It is crucial to select a suitable query evaluation method for a specific application, because the efficiency of the query evaluation methods could be varied greatly as there are many factors could affect the way a query be executed. An analytical performance estimator is currently under development; it will take the features of platform, the features of data, queries and their frequencies and data placement strategies as the input. Based the input and use set of cost formulas for each evaluation method, a suitable query processing algorithm will be selected with estimated system throughput and average responsible time.

Utilising DTD information - The presence of DTDs can help the understanding of the structures of XML documents, therefore can provide the basis for initial data partitioning. In the current version of PXDS, the structure information of semi-structured data is not being sufficient used during data placement process and query evaluation. The appropriate use of DTD and other structure information would improve the system efficiency.

Multimedia data processing – XML language is used in MPEG – 7 Standard to describe multimedia data [9]. As the amount of multimedia data is normally very large, to bring parallel techniques to resolve the performance problem seems a natural solution. In order to do so, a number of fundamental question need to be answered. The data placement strategies for multimedia data need to consider the features of multimedia data queries. For example, the contents that are likely to be required by the same query should be put together in order to reduce the communication cost. Therefore, the semantics, and other features of multimedia data must be taken consideration during the design of data placement strategies. It is also applicable to query process methods.

Summary - PXDS is designed for storing, indexing and querying XML data. The outline features of PXDS are introduced in this paper. Most of algorithms of PXDS have been implemented and evaluated. It is based on a shared-nothing parallel computing environment. The architecture consists of a set of processing elements, each containing its own processor, main memory, and disks. The processing elements are interconnected by an interconnection network which is on 10/100MB/s Ethernet at present. One or more processing elements are selected as the co-ordinator of the system, which is in charge of tracking user requests, decomposing the query into several sub-tasks, scheduling tasks, collecting the query results and sending them back to the clients. Initial tests and performance analysis being conducted on the DBLP data set [4] and Internet movie database (IMDB) [5]. Work is currently being carried out to enhance the functionality of PXDS. This includes designing and implementing algorithms transitive-closure and recursive query processing. It is planned to extend index methods therefore the advantages of multi-processor systems can be explored and integrate data placement strategies with index methods.

Acknowledgments

This work is partly supported by Wang Kuan Cheng Foundations of China.

References

[1] The Apache XML project. Xerces-C++ is a validating XML parser. At http:// xml. apache. org/ xerces-c

[2] A. Bergholz, *Querying Semistructured Data Based on Schema Matching*, Doctoral dissertation, Humboldt University Berlin, Berlin, Germany, January 2000

[3] Berkeley DB, http://www.sleepycat. com/ docs/ index.html. Visited at May 2001

[4] [Dblp00] DBLP maintained by M. Ley. http: //www.informatik.uni-trier.de/~ley/db/index.html, December 2000.

[5] Internet Movie Database Inc. At http://www.imdb.com.

[6] George Karypis and vipin Kumar, *A Fast and High Quality Multilevel Scheme for Partitioning Irregular graphs*, SIAM Journal on Scientific Computing, Vol. 20 Number 1, pp359-392. 1998.

[7] A. Kotok, *An Updated Survey of XML Business Vocabularies*, http ://www.xml.com/lpt/a/2000/ 8 /02/ ebiz/extensible.html, August 2000

[8] O. Logvynovskiy, K. J. Lü, An efficient indexing technique for XML documents. http://www.sbu.ac.uk/~lukj/papers/paper32.pdf

[9] J. M. Martinez, "Overview of the MPEG-7 Standard (v4.0)", ISO/IECJTCI/SC29/WG N3752, La Baule, 2000 http://www.cselt.it/mpeg

[10] J. McHugh, J. Widom, *Query Optimisation for XML*, Proceedings of VLDB'99

[11] D. Suciu, *Distributed Query Evaluation on Semi-structured Data*, Technical Report, AT&T, 1998

[12] D. Taniar, *Toward an Ideal Data Placement Scheme for High Performance Object-Oriented Database Systems*, Proceedings of HPCN Europe, 1998.

[13] XQuery 1.0: An XML Query Language. http://www.w3.org/TR/xquery/. Visited 17 January 2002

[14], W. Sun, K. J. Lü *Parallel Query Processing Algorithms for Semi-structured Data*. Accepted by The Fourteenth International Conference on Advanced Information Systems Engineering (CAiSE'02). The extended version can be found http://www.sbu.ac.uk/~lukj/papers/paper1.pdf

[15] Y. Zhu, K. J. Lü. An Effective Data Placement Strategy for XML documents. In the proceedings of 18th British National Conference On Databases (LNCS 2097), 2001

Yet Another Query Algebra For XML Data*

Carlo Sartiani   Antonio Albano

Dipartimento di Informatica - Università di Pisa

Corso Italia 40, Pisa, Italy

{sartiani,albano}@di.unipi.it

Abstract

XML has reached a widespread diffusion as a language for representing nearly any kind of data source, from relational databases to digital movies. Due to the growing interest toward XML, many tools for storing, processing, and querying XML data have appeared in the last two years.

Three main problems affect XML query processing: path expression evaluation, nested query resolution, and preservation of document order. These issues, which are related to the hierarchical structure of XML and to the features of current XML query languages, require compile-time as well as run-time solutions.

This paper describes a query algebra for XML data. The main purpose of this algebra, which forms the basis for the Xtasy database management system, is to combine good optimization properties with a good expressive power that allows it to model significant fragments of current XML query languages; in particular, explicit support is given to efficient path expression evaluation, nested query resolution, and order preservation.

1. Introduction

XML has reached a widespread diffusion as a language for representing nearly any kind of data source, from relational databases to digital movies. While the usual application for XML is data exchange, there exist many application fields where direct manipulation of XML is needed, e.g., the management of medical data. Therefore, many tools for storing, processing, and querying XML data have appeared in the last two years: some of these tools are based on existing database management systems [18] extended with the ability to store XML data into relational tables and to process XML queries, while others [17, 1] are designed from scratch for XML data. Systems in the first class are designed and implemented by middleware layers that store XML documents into relational tables or collections of objects, and that directly map XPath [8] and XQuery [5] queries into special-purpose SQL queries, endowed with some code needed to fill the expressive gap between XQuery and SQL (even SQL3). Systems in the second class, instead, represent an attempt to build XML-tailored database systems, i.e., systems designed to manage ordered tree-structured data; nevertheless, most of these systems are just based on existing relational, object-oriented, or even *hierarchical* database engines on top of which XML functionalities are built.

Whatever class of systems you are considering, three key problems affect query processing over XML data: *evaluation of path expressions*; *evaluation and resolution of nested queries*; *order preservation*. These problems are related both to the tree structure of XML and to the features offered by current XML query languages.

Path expressions   Path expression evaluation requires to traverse a tree according to a given path specification. This specification usually gives only a partial description of the path, by using *wildcards* and recursive operators (e.g., $*$ in GPE [21] and // in XPath). There exist many approaches to path expression optimization. The most popular (and maybe the most effective) ones are based on path indexes or full-text indexes [14, 6], and on path expression minimization [11]. The former approach is based on the massive use of path indexes or full-text indexes, hence trying to solve this optimization problem at the physical level only; the latter approach, instead, is based on the fusion of the path expression automaton with schema information. Both kinds of approaches exploit structural information about XML data (usually DTD-like schemas).

Another interesting approach tries to expand path expressions at compile-time [19], by replacing recursive operators with real paths being present in the data; substitution information is taken from a *DataGuide* [15], a graph containing each path being present in the database. As a matter of fact, this technique can be considered as a special case of

*Research partially supported by the MURST DataX Project and by Microsoft Research

path expression minimization.

Nested queries   Current XML query languages impose no restriction on query nesting: indeed, they generalize the "free nesting philosophy" of OQL, and allow one to put a query or a complex expression returning a *well-formed* document wherever a well-formed XML document is expected. This feature allows one to easily formulate complex queries, e.g., queries containing esoteric joins, or queries changing the structure of data (see [5] and [12] for a discussion on how to use nested queries for grouping and reshaping XML elements). As a consequence, nested query resolution has become more and more important, at least to transform annoying d-joins into more tractable ordinary joins.

Ordering   Unlike relational data models, XML is an **ordered** data format, i.e., a total order is defined among elements of the same document, as well as a total order among the children of a given node. A common requirement in XML applications, such as the managing of digital movies, is the preservation of document order among elements extracted from the database; still, there are many application fields (e.g., database publishing and semistructured database management) that do not require to retain document order. Most XML query languages support these requirements, and also allow the user to specify an arbitrary order among elements in query results (the way document order and user-defined order combine together is unclear).

The order preservation problem also has another face. Some query languages, such as XQuery, express tree navigation by means of d-joins, which are inherently ordered, e.g., $A < B > \neq B < A >$. Unfortunately, d-joins are also used for connecting independent path expressions. XQuery formal semantics imposes that d-joins are evaluated in the query order, until an explicit statement by the user is given. As a result, order preservation in XML queries requires one to deal with these three issues: document order, user-defined order, and join order preservation.

Our contribution   This paper shows a query algebra for XML data. This algebra, which forms the basis for the Xtasy database management system [10], has been defined as an extension of object-oriented and semistructured query algebras [9, 7, 4]; it retains common relational and OO optimization properties (e.g., join commutativity and associativity), and gives explicit support to efficient path expression evaluation, nested query resolution, and order preservation. In particular, the algebra provides general rewriting rules for transforming d-joins into ordinary joins, as well as a general approach for preserving order in XQuery queries.

The paper is structured as follows. Section 2 describes the Xtasy data model; next, Section 3 describes the alge-

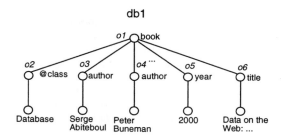

db1

Figure 1. A data model instance

bra operators. Then, Sections 4 introduces some algebraic equivalences. Next, Section 5 contains a review of related works. Finally, in Section 6 we draw our conclusions.

2. Data model and term language

The Xtasy query algebra employs a data model similar to the W3C XML Query Data Model [13]. A data model instance is a *well-formed* XML document represented as an unordered forest of *node-labeled* trees, the global ordering being preserved by a special-purpose function *pos*; internal nodes are labeled with constants (tags and attribute names), and leaves with atomic values. Each internal node has a unique *object identifier* (oid) that can be accessed by the special-purpose function *oid*; an algebraic support operator ν is used to generate new oids and to refresh existing ones, hence allowing the algebra to support *copy* semantics as well as *reference* semantics operations.

Example 2.1   Consider the XML fragment shown below:

```
<book class = "Database">
    <author> Serge Abiteboul </author>
    <author> Peter Buneman </author>
    <author> Dan Suciu </author>
    <title> Data on the web: from ... </title>
    <year> 2000 </year>
    <publisher> ... </publisher>
</book>
```

This fragment can be represented by the tree depicted in Figure 1.
∎

3. Algebra operators

Xtasy algebra is an extension of common object-oriented and semistructured query algebras to XML. The starting point of the algebra is the object-oriented algebra described in [9]; from that the Xtasy algebra borrows the idea of relational-like intermediate structures, hence extending to XML common relational and OO optimization strategies, as well as the presence of *border* operators, which insulate other algebraic operators from the technicalities of XML. The algebra provides two border operators, namely *path* and *return*, which respectively build up intermediate structures from XML documents and publish these structures into XML.

In addition to *path* and *return*, the Xtasy algebra provides quite common operators such as *Selection*, *Projection*, *TupJoin*, *Join*, *DJoin*, *Map*, *Sort*, *TupSort*, and *GroupBy*.

There exist both *set-based* and *list-based* versions of the algebraic operators: list-based operators should ease the management of the forthcoming XPath 2.0 path language [20]. For the sake of brevity, in the following sections only set-based algebraic operators will be presented.

3.1. *Env* structures

As already stated, algebraic operators manipulate relational-like structures. These structures, called *Env*, are very similar to YAT Tab structures [7], and contain the variable bindings collected during query evaluation. As in [9] and YAT, *Env* structures allow one to define algebraic operators that manipulate sets of tuples, instead of trees; hence, common optimization and execution strategies (which are based on tuples rather than trees) can be easily adapted to XML without the need to redefine all that stuff.

An *Env* structure is a collection of *flat* tuples, each tuple describing a set of variable bindings. With the only exception of sorting operators, each algebraic operator manipulates unordered *Env* structures, e.g., tuples order is irrelevant.

The following example shows a sample *Env* structure.

Example 3.1 Consider the *Env* structure shown below:

$\$b : o_1$	$\$a : o_3$
$\$b : o_1$	$\$a : o_4$
$\$b : o_1$	$\$a : o_5$
...	...

This structure is a set of tuples, where each tuple consists of two fields. The first field ($\$b : ...$) contains the **oid** of a **book** element, while the second contains the **oid** of a related **author** element. Since the book o_1 has three authors, the *Env* structure contains three tuples referring to o_1. ∎

In order to ensure the closure of the algebra, intermediate structures are themselves represented as node-labeled trees conforming to the algebra data model; this kind of representation also allows one to apply useful optimization properties to border operators. Hence, *Env* structures can be represented as terms like this:

$$env[\quad tuple[label_1[t_{11}], \ldots, label_n[t_{1n}]],$$
$$\ldots,$$
$$tuple[label_1[t_{k1}], \ldots, label_n[t_{kn}]]]$$

Each **tuple** element describes a binding tuple, where $label_i$ are variable names and t_{ji} the corresponding values.

3.2. *path* **and** *return*

path The main task of the *path* operator is to extract information from the database, and to build variable bindings. The way information is extracted is described by an *input filter*; a filter is a tree, describing the paths to follow into the database (and the way to traverse these paths), the variables to bind and the binding style, as well as the way to combine results coming from different paths. Input filters are described by the following grammar:

$$
\begin{array}{llll}
F & ::= & F_1, \ldots, F_n & \text{conjunctive filters} \\
  & | & F_1 \vee \ldots \vee F_n & \text{disjunctive filters} \\
  & | & (op, var, binder)label[F] & \text{simple input filter} \\
  & | & \emptyset & \text{empty filter}
\end{array}
$$

$$
\begin{array}{ll}
\text{where} & op \in \{/, //, \_\} \\
 & var \in String \cup \{\_\} \\
 & binder \in \{\_, in, =\}
\end{array}
$$

A simple filter $(op, var, binder)label[F]$ tells the *path* operator a) to traverse the current context by using the navigational operator op, b) to select those elements or attributes having label $label$, c) to perform the binding expressed by var and $binder$, and d) to continue the evaluation by using the nested filter F.

The *path* operator takes as input a single data model instance and an input filter, and it returns an *Env* structure containing the variable bindings described in the filter. The following example shows a simple input filter and its application to a sample document.

Example 3.2 Consider the following fragment of XQuery query:

```
FOR $b in book,
    $a in $b//author,
```

This clause traverses the path **book//author** into the sample document, binding each **book** and **author** element to $\$b$ and $\$a$, respectively. This clause can be translated into the following *path* operation:

$$path_{(\_, \$b, in)book[(//, \$a, in)author[\emptyset]]}(db1)$$

which returns the following *Env* structure:

$\$b : o_1$	$\$a : o_3$
$\$b : o_1$	$\$a : o_4$
$\$b : o_1$	$\$a : o_5$

∎

Input filters provide a simple but rich path language, containing common path operators, such as / and // (/l takes as input a collection of nodes, and returns the children of these nodes labeled by l, while $//l$ returns the descendants of these nodes labeled by l). No direct support, instead, is given to the resolution of ID/IDREF attributes, e.g., `a/b/@c=>/d` is represented by using joins. Moreover, input filters provide two binding styles (in and $=$), which directly correspond to XQuery binders.

The following example shows the grouping binder $=$.

Example 3.3 Consider the following XQuery clause:

```
FOR $b in book,
LET $a_list := $b//author,
```

This clause traverses the path book//author; each book element is bound to b, and, for each book element, the whole set of author sub-elements is bound to a_list. This clause can be expressed by using the following *path* operation:

$$path_{(\_,\$b,in)book[(//,\$a\_list,=)author[\emptyset]]}(db1)$$

which returns the following Env structure:

$\$b : o_1$	$\$a : \{o_3, o_4, o_5\}$

∎

As shown by the filter grammar, multiple input filters can be combined to form more complex filters. Xtasy algebra allows filters to be combined in a *conjunctive* way, or in a *disjunctive* way. In the first case, the Env structures built by simple filters are joined together, hence imposing a product semantics; in the second case, partial results are combined by using an *outer union* operation. Therefore, disjunctive filters can be used to map XPath union paths into input filters (e.g., book/(author|publisher)), as well as more sophisticated queries; the use of outer union ensures that the resulting Env has a uniform structure, i.e., all binding tuples have the same fields.

The following examples show the use of disjunctive filters.

Example 3.4 Consider the following XQuery clause:

```
FOR $b in book,
    $p in $b/(author|publisher),
```

This clause binds the p variable to publishers and authors of each book. It can be expressed by using the following *path* operation:

$$path_{(\_,\$b,in)book[(/,\$p,in)author[\emptyset]\vee(/,\$p,in)publisher[\emptyset]]}(db1)$$

∎

Due to the presence of disjunction, a precedence order among combinators has to be established: we chose to give precedence to disjunction, i.e., $f_1 \vee f_2, f_3 \vee f_4$ is evaluated as $(f_1 \vee f_2),(f_3 \vee f_4)$.

return While the *path* operator extracts information from existing XML documents, the *return* operator uses the variable bindings of an Env to produce new XML documents. *return* takes as input an Env structure and an *output filter*, i.e., a skeleton of the XML document being produced, and returns a data model instance (i.e., a well-formed XML document) conforming to the filter. This instance is built up by filling the XML skeleton with variable values taken from the Env structure: this substitution is performed once per each tuple contained in the Env, hence producing one skeleton instance per tuple.

Output filters satisfy the following grammar:

$$\begin{aligned} OF \quad &::= OF_1, \ldots, OF_n \\ &\mid label[OF] \\ &\mid @label[val] \\ &\mid val \\ val \quad &::= v_B \mid var \mid \nu var \end{aligned}$$

An output filter may be an *element constructor* ($label[OF]$), which produces an element tagged $label$ and whose content is given by OF, an *attribute constructor* ($@label[val]$), which builds an attribute containing the value val, or a combination of output filters ($OF_1, \ldots, OF_n$). The second production needs further comments. The algebra offers two way to publish information contained in an Env structure: by copy (νvar) and by reference (var). Referenced elements are published as they are in query results; in particular, their object ids are not changed, thus allowing support for the definition and management of views over the database. Copied elements, instead, are published with *fresh* oids, hence losing the ties with their originating databases.

The following example shows the use of the *return* operator.

Example 3.5 Consider the following XQuery query:

```
FOR $b in book
    $t in $b/title,
    $a in $b/author
RETURN
    <entry> $t, $a </entry>
```

This query returns the title and the authors of each book. This query can be represented by the following algebraic expression:

$$return_{entry[\nu\$t,\nu\$a]}(\\ path_{(\_,\$b,in)book[(/,\$a,in)author[\emptyset],(/,\$t,in)title[\emptyset]]}(db1))$$

∎

The following example shows the use of the *return* operator to define a view over the database.

Example 3.6 Assume that you want to define a database view restricting the access to only those books published before 2001. By using a reference output filter this task can be accomplished by the following algebraic expression:

$$return_{view[\$b]}(\sigma_{\$y<2001}($$
$$path_{(\_,\$b,in)book[(/,\$y,in)year[\emptyset]]}(db1)))$$

∎

3.3. Basic operators

Xtasy algebra basic operators manipulate *Env* structures only, and perform quite common operations. They resemble very closely their relational or object-oriented counterparts, thus allowing the query optimizer to employ usual algebraic optimization strategies. This class contains *Map*, *TupJoin*, *Join*, *DJoin*, *Selection*, *Projection*, *GroupBy*, *Sort*, as well as *Union*, *Intersection*, *Difference*, *OuterUnion*, and their list-based counterparts. In the following the most important operators will be presented.

Selection *Selection* σ takes as input an *Env* and a boolean predicate P, and returns a new *env* structure where binding tuples not satisfying P are missing. The predicate language of the Xtasy algebra is quite rich, offering existential as well as universal quantification over variables. These quantifications are required for easily translating universally quantified XQuery queries, and can be optimized by using quite standard rewriting techniques.

TupJoin *TupJoin* $\bowtie_P$ is the Xtasy counterpart of standard join operators. So, it takes as input two *Env* structures e_1 and e_2 as well as a boolean predicate P; it evaluates the predicate P over each pair of tuples $(t_1, t_2) \in e_1 \times e_2$, returning only the pairs satisfying P. The primary use of the *TupJoin* operator is to combine *path* operations over independent data sources, and it is also introduced during query unnesting. The following example shows the typical use of *TupJoin*.

Example 3.7 Consider the following query fragment:

```
FOR $b in book,
    $a in $b/author,
    $b1 in document("amazoncatalog.xml")/book,
    $t in $b1/title
```

This query accesses two data sources, an internal one (*db1*) and an external one (`catalog.xml`). This fragment can be represented by the algebraic expression shown below.

$$(path_{(\_,\$b,in)book[(/,\$a,in)author[\emptyset]]}(db1)) \bowtie_{true}$$
$$(path_{(\_,\$b1,in)book[(/,\$t,in)title[\emptyset]]}(extdb))$$

∎

The previous example requires further comments. Unlike XQuery joins, Xtasy algebra joins are unordered, e.g., $e_1 \bowtie_P e_2 \equiv e_2 \bowtie_P e_1$. This is a significant divergence from XQuery Formal Semantics, since XQuery Formal Semantics joins are (unless otherwise stated by the user) *non-commutative*, even on independent operands, i.e., $e_1 \bowtie_P e_2 \neq e_2 \bowtie_P e_1$. This divergence imposes the use of a *Sort* operation before the *return* operation, as it will be shown in the next paragraphs; we chose this approach since we believe that the join efficiency improvement might overcompensate for the cost of the additional *Sort* operation.

DJoin Unlike the *TupJoin* operator, which joins together two independent *Env* structures, the $DJoin < \cdot >$ performs a join between two *Env* e_1 and e_2, where the evaluation of e_2 may depend on e_1. This operator comes from object-oriented query algebras, and it is used to translate **for** and **let** clauses of XQuery and, in particular, to combine an inner nested block with the outer one.

The only way to evaluate a *DJoin* is to perform a nested loop among operands, hence one major goal of the optimization process is to transform, whenever possible, *DJoins* into more tractable *TupJoin* operations.

Sort The *Sort* operator is used for dealing with the three sorting issues described in the Introduction: translating the **sortby** clause of XQuery (and similar clauses of other languages), preserving document order, and retaining join order. *Sort* takes as input an *Env* structure e and an ordering predicate P, and returns e sorted according to P. Ordering predicates are binary predicates defined on binding tuples, and used to impose the desired order; they have signature: $tuple \times tuple \rightarrow boolean$. The following example shows the use of *Sort* for translating **sortby** clauses.

Example 3.8 Consider the following query:

```
UNORDERED(
    FOR $b in book
    RETURN $b
    SORTBY (title))
```

This query just returns the list of all books sorted by title. To translate this query, we need to define an appropriate predicate, as the following: $Pred(u, v) \equiv u.\$t < v.\$t$, where u and v ranges over *Env* tuples, and $\$t$ is bound to book titles. Thus, this query can be represented by the following algebraic expression:

$$return_{v\$b}($$
$$Sort_{u.\$t<v.\$t}($$
$$path_{(\_,\$b,in)book[(/,\$t,in)title[\emptyset]]}(db1)))$$

∎

For preserving join order and order among elements a specialized version of *Sort* is used (called *TupSort*). *TupSort* takes as input an ordered list of variables $(\$x_1, \ldots, \$x_n)$, and an *Env* e; it returns a new *Env* e' obtained by sorting e according to the position of values of the variables $\$x_1, \ldots, \$x_n$. Hence, the algebra can mimic the behavior of XQuery joins, whose semantics requires to retain the order in which variables are bound, unless the programmer qualifies the query with the keyword UNORDERED. The following example shows how *TupSort* can be used to preserve order among variables and XML elements.

Example 3.9 Consider the following query:

```
FOR $b in book,
    $t in $b/title,
    $a in $b/author
RETURN <entry> $t, $a </entry>
```

XQuery semantics [12] prescribes that joins should be executed in an ordered fashion. Hence, a correct translation of this query should contain the *TupSort* operation $TupSort_{(\$b,\$t,\$a)}(\ldots)$, which sorts tuples in the *Env* structure according to the order specified in the query. ∎

n-ary **sortby** clauses can be translated by using a n-ary ordering predicate, or by a combination of unary *Sort* operations. The following example shows the translation of such **sortby** clauses.

Example 3.10 Consider the query of Example 3.8 and assume that we want to return books ordered by title and by author.

```
UNORDERED(
    FOR $b in book
    RETURN $b
    SORTBY (title, author))
```

Unlike [12], the Xtasy algebra offers two ways to translate this query. The first augments the ordering predicate of the *Sort* operation: $(u.\$t < v.\$t) \lor (u.\$t = v.\$t \land u.\$a = v.\$a)$ where $\$a$ is bound to each book author; the second one breaks the **sortby** clause into two smaller clauses, as shown below:

$$return_{\nu\$b}(Sort_{u.\$t<v.\$t}(Sort_{u.\$a<v.\$a}($$
$$path_{(\_,\$b,in)book[(/,\$t,in)title[\emptyset],(/,\$a,in)author[\emptyset]]}(db1))))$$

∎

GroupBy The *GroupBy* operator Γ of Xtasy takes as input an *Env* structure e, and partitions it according to the following definition: $\Gamma_{g;A;f_1;f;\theta}(e) = \{y.A\bullet[g:G] \mid y \in e, G = f(\{x \mid x \in e, f_1(x)\theta f_1(y)\})\}$ where $A \subseteq Att(e)$ and $y \notin Att(e)$.

As shown by the definition (very close to that of [9]), Xtasy *GroupBy* projects e tuples over A, and augments them with the corresponding groups G, obtained by applying the function f to the set of related tuples.

4. Optimization properties

Three classes of algebraic equivalences can be applied to the Xtasy query algebra. The first class contains *classical* equivalences inherited from relational and OO algebras (e.g., *push-down* of *Selection* operations and commutativity of joins); the second class consists of path decomposition rules, which allows the query optimizer to break complex input filters into simpler ones; the third class, finally, contains equivalences used for unnesting nested queries. In the next sections, the following notation will be used: (i) $Att(e)$ is the set of labels of an *Env* structure e; (ii) $FV(exp)$ is the set of free variables occurring in an algebraic expression exp; (iii) $symbols(of)$ is the set of node labels used in the output filter of.

4.1. Classical equivalences

Given the close resemblance of Xtasy algebraic operators to relational and OO operators, the Xtasy algebra supports a wide range of classical equivalences. In particular, *Selection*, *Projection*, *Map*, *TupJoin*, and even *return* are linear, so common *reordinability* laws can be easily applied to these operators.

Here follows a brief (and quite incomplete) list of supported algebraic equivalences.

$$\sigma_{P_1 \land P_2}(e) \equiv \sigma_{P_1}(\sigma_{P_2}(e)))$$
$$\sigma_{P_1}(\sigma_{P_2}(e)) \equiv \sigma_{P_2}(\sigma_{P_1}(e))$$
$$\sigma_{P_1}((e_1) \bowtie_{P_2} (e_2)) \equiv (e_1) \bowtie_{P_1 \land P_2} (e_2)$$
$$(e_1) \bowtie_{Pred} (e_2) \equiv (e_2) \bowtie_{Pred} (e_1)$$

4.2. *path* decompositions

As already stated, *path* is the most important operator in the algebra, since it performs the basic tasks of evaluating path expressions and binding variables (both in an iterative fashion and in a grouping fashion). As a result, its efficiency affects the efficiency of the whole query processing. An efficient evaluation of *path* relies on the ability of the query compiler to simplify path expressions and to exploit existing access support structures, indexes in particular, which can dramatically speed up the evaluation. To this purpose the ability to decompose a complex filter into smaller ones is crucial, since it allows to match existing access structures as well as to replace expensive filters (i.e., filters involving //) with less expensive ones. By using decomposition laws, optimization techniques based on path indexes and full-text indexes can be safely applied.

The Xtasy algebra provides three decomposition laws for *path* operations: the first works on the nested structure of a filter, while the remaining ones work on the horizontal structure of a filter.

Proposition 4.1 *Vertical decomposition of path operations*

$$path_{(op,var,binder)label[F]}(t)$$
$$\equiv$$
$$path_{(\_,\_,in)env[(/,\_,in)tuple[(/,\_,in)var[(/,var,binder)\_[F]]]]}\big(path_{(op,var,binder)label[\emptyset]}(t)\big)$$

The following example shows how this decomposition law can be exploited during query optimization.

Example 4.2 Consider the following XQuery clause:

```
FOR $b in library/book,
    $a in $b/author,
    $y in $b/year,
```

This clause retrieves the sub-elements of each **book** element, binding them to a corresponding variable. This clause can be mapped into the following *path* operation.

$$path_{(\_,\_,in)library[(/,\$b,in)book[F]]}(db_2)$$
where
$$F \equiv (/,\$a,in)author[\emptyset], (/,\$y,in)year[\emptyset]$$

Assume now that a path index on **library/book** is available. To exploit the presence of this index, the previous *path* operation should be decomposed into a *path* operation with filter $(\_,\_,in)library[(/,\$b,in)book[\emptyset]]$ and a new *path* operation, which further explores the subtrees bound to $\$b$. This decomposition is shown below.

$$path_{F_1}\big(path_{(\_,\_,in)library[(/,\$b,in)book[\emptyset]]}(db2)\big)$$
where
$$F_1 \equiv (\_,\_,in)env[(/,\_,in)tuple[(/,\_,in)b[F_2]]]$$
$$F_2 \equiv (/,\$b,in)\_[(/,\$a,in)author[\emptyset], (/,\$y,in)year[\emptyset]]$$

∎

Proposition 4.3 *Horizontal decomposition of conjunctive input filters*

$$path_{f_1,\ldots,f_m}(t)$$
$$\equiv$$
$$(path_{f_1,\ldots,f_{i-1}}(t)) \bowtie_{true} (path_{f_i,\ldots,f_m}(t))$$

Proposition 4.4 *Horizontal decomposition of disjunctive input filters*

$$path_{f_1 \vee \ldots \vee f_m}(t)$$
$$\equiv$$
$$(path_{f_1 \vee \ldots \vee f_{i-1}}(t)) OuterUnion(path_{f_i \vee \ldots \vee f_m}(t))$$

The Xtasy query algebra supports also decompositions of *path* via d-joins; those decompositions allow the compiler to translate XQuery for and let clause by using arbitrarily complex filters, or simple filters only (as in XQuery Formal Semantics).

Proposition 4.5 *Dependent decomposition of input filters*

$$path_{(op,var,binder)label[F]}(t)$$
$$\equiv$$
$$path_{(op,var,binder)label[\emptyset]}(t) < path_F(var) >$$

4.3. Nested queries equivalences

This Section presents some equivalence rules that can be used to transform d-joins induced by nested queries into $TupJoin$ operations. These rules are not intended to be exhaustive, nor to be the most efficient transformations; they just rewrite $DJoins$ induced by nested queries into more tractable joins, and do not exploit *special-purpose* algebraic operators such as binary grouping. Before presenting our rewriting rules a brief introduction to the problem of query unnesting is necessary. In the reference paper about nested queries in object databases [9], authors extend Kim's taxonomy of relational nested queries by defining three classification criteria: the *kind of nesting*, i.e., queries of type A, N, J, JA; the *nesting location*, i.e., the presence of nested queries into the *select*, *from*, or *where* clause of OQL queries; the *kind of dependency*, i.e., the location of references to external variables. Referring to such classification, our rewriting rules apply to queries of type J (nested dependent queries returning sets of elements/attributes/values), and deal with the three kinds of dependencies (**projection** dependency, **range** dependency, and **predicate** dependency). In the next paragraphs these three kinds of dependencies will be discussed in more detail.

A typical query has the following structure:

$$return_{of}(Sort_{P_1}(\sigma_{P_2}(path_f(db))))$$

The output filter of, the selection predicate P_2 as well as the input filter f can define dependencies with an outer query by referring to external variables. Depending on where these references are located into the nested query, **projection** dependencies (of), **range** dependencies (db), or **predicate** dependencies (P_2) may occur.

Predicate dependency Predicate dependencies occur when an external variable is referenced into the *where* clause of the inner query, i.e., into the predicate P_2. Consider, for example, the following query returning authors and the list of their papers.

```
FOR $a in library//author
RETURN $a, <publist> FOR $p in library/*,
```

```
            $aa in $p/author
            WHERE $aa = $a
            RETURN $p
      </publist>
```

This query contains a nested block (FOR $p ... RETURN $p) that scans the papers and returns only those papers written by a given author (WHERE $aa = $a). This query can be represented by the following algebraic expression.

$$return_{\nu\$a,publist[\nu\$\_var]}\big(\\ path_{(\_,\_,in)library[(//,\$a,in)author[\emptyset]]}(db) < q >\big)$$
where
$$q \equiv path_{(\_,\$\_var,=)\_[\emptyset]}\big(return_{\$p}(\sigma_{\$aa=\$a}\big(\\ path_{(\_,\_,in)library[(/,\$p,in)\_[(/,\$aa,in)author[\emptyset]]]}(db)\big)\big)\big)$$

In this kind of dependency the predicate P_2 has the form $Pred(\$X,\$Z,\$Y)$, where $\$X$ are external variables, and $\$Y$ and $\$Z$ local variables. In order to remove this dependency (and the related $DJoin$ operation), we need to decompose $Pred(\$X,\$Z,\$Y)$ into $Pred_{Glob}(\$X,\$Z) \wedge Pred(\$Y,\$Z)$, i.e., to separate local variables from global ones, and to transform the $return$ filter.

Proposition 4.6 *Predicate Dependency*

$$e_1 < (path_{(\_,\$var,=)}(return_{of}(\\ \sigma_{Pred(\$X,\$Z,\$Y)}(path_{f_1}(db))))) >$$

$$\equiv$$

$$\Gamma_{\$var;Att(e_1);\lambda x.(x.\$Z);id;=}(e_1 \bowtie_{Pred_{Glob}(\$X,\$Z)}\\ (path_{f'}(return_{of'}(\sigma_{Pred_{Loc}(\$Y,\$Z)}(path_{f_1}(db))))))$$

where

- $of' = \_nested[\_result[of], \_env[z_1[\$z_1], \ldots, z_k[\$z_k]]]$

- $f' = (\_,\$\_n,in)\_nested[(/,\$\_res,=)\_result[\emptyset],\\ (/,\_,in)\_env[(/,\_,in)z_1[(/,\$z_1,=)\_[\emptyset],\\ \ldots,(/,\_,in)z_k[(/,\$z_k,=)\_[\emptyset]]]]]$

if $FV(of) \cap Att(e_1) = \emptyset$, $FV(f_1) \cap Att(e_1) = \emptyset$, $\$X \subseteq Att(e_1)$, $\$z_1, \ldots, \$z_k \notin Att(e_1)$, $\$Y \notin Att(e_1)$, $z_1, \ldots, z_k \notin symbols(of)$

By applying this transformation the predicate dependency is brought out of the inner query, hence the previous algebraic expression can be rewritten as follows.

$$return_{\nu\$a,publist[\nu\$\_var]}\big(\\ \Gamma_{\$\_var;\$a;\lambda x.(x.\$aa);id;=}\big(\\ path_{(\_,\_,in)library[(//,\$a,in)author[\emptyset]]}(db) \bowtie_{\$a=\$aa} q'\big)\big)$$
where
$$q' \equiv path_{(\_,\$\_n,in)\_nested[F_1,F_2]}\big(\\ return_{\_nested\_[result[\$p],\_env[aa[\$aa]]]}\big(\\ path_{(\_,\_,in)library[(/,\$p,in)\_[(/,\$aa,in)author[\emptyset]]]}(db)\big)\big)$$
and
$$F_1 \equiv (/,\$_res,=)\_result[\emptyset]$$
$$F_2 \equiv (/,\_,in)\_env[(/,\_,in)aa[(/,\$aa,=)\_[\emptyset]]]$$

Range dependency In this form of dependency, the input filter of the inner query is applied to variables coming from the outer query. Consider, for example, the following query associating each paper with the list of its Italian authors.

```
FOR $p in library/*
RETURN <italianrd>
          $p,
          FOR $a in $p/author
          WHERE $a/country/data() = "Italy"
          RETURN $a
       </italianrd>
```

This query contains an inner block (FOR $a ... RETURN $a) retrieving, for each given paper p, the list of Italian authors (if any). This query can be translated as follows.

$$return_{italianrd[\$p,\$\_var]}\big(\\ path_{(\_,\_,in)library[(/,\$p,in)\_[\emptyset]]}(db) <\\ path_{(\_,\$\_var,=)\_[\emptyset]}(return_{\$a}(\sigma_{\$c="Italy"}(\\ path_{(/,\$a,in)author[(/,\$c,=)country[\emptyset]]}(\$p)))) >\big)$$

Object-oriented rewriting rules for range dependencies are based on the use of *type extents*; in particular, if the domains of the external variables referenced by the inner block are covered by type extents, their references are replaced by scans over these extents, and results are then combined through object equality predicates. Such transformations cannot be applied to data without extents, therefore we rely on a different rewriting technique, whose main idea is to **copy** the left part of the $DJoin$ into the nested query, hence transforming it into a constant block, and then to combine results by using an equality predicate.

Proposition 4.7 *Range dependency*

$$e_1 < (path_{(\_,\$var,=)\_[\emptyset]}(return_{of}(\\ \sigma_P(path_{f_1,\ldots,f_k}(\$x_1,\ldots,\$x_k))))) >$$

$$\equiv$$

$$\Gamma_{\$var;Att(e_1);\lambda y.(y.\$X);id;=}(e_1 \bowtie_{\$X=\$X}\\ (path_{f'}(return_{of'}(\sigma_P(path_{f''}(e_1))))))$$

113

where

- $f'' \equiv (\_, \$\_tuple, in) tuple[(/,\_,in)x_1[$
  $(/, \$x_1, =)\_[f_1]], \ldots, (/, \_, in)x_k[(/, \$x_k, =)\_[f_k]]]]$

- $of' \equiv \_nested[\_result[of], \_env[x_1[\$x_1], \ldots, x_k[\$x_k]]]$

- $f' \equiv (\_, \$\_n, in)\_nested[(/, \$\_res, in)result[\emptyset],$
  $(/, \_, in)\_env[(/, \_, in)x_1[(/, \$x_1, =)\_[\emptyset]], \ldots,$
  $(/, \_, in)x_k[(/, \$x_k, =)\_[\emptyset]]]]]$

if $FV(of) \cap Att(e_1) = \emptyset$, $FV(f_1, \ldots, f_k) \cap Att(e_1) = \emptyset$, $FV(P) \cap Att(e_1) = \emptyset$, $FV(db) = \$X \subseteq Att(e_1)$, $x_1, \ldots x_k \notin symbols(of)$

By applying Proposition 4.7, the previous query can be rewritten as follows.

$return_{italianrd[\nu\$p, \nu\$\_var]}(\Gamma_{\$var;\$p;\lambda y.(y.\$p);id;=}($
$path_{(\_,\_,in)library[(/,\$p,in)\_[\emptyset]]}(db) \bowtie_{\$p=\$p} q_1))$
where
$q_1 \equiv path_{(\_,\$\_n,in)\_nested[F_1,F_2]}($
$return_{\_nested[\_result[\$a],\_env[p[\$p]]]}(\sigma_{\$c="Italy"}($
$path_{(/,\$\_tuple,in)tuple[(/,\_,in)p[(/,\$p,=)\_[F_3]]]}($
$\pi_{\$p}(path_{(\_,\_,in)library[(/,\$p,in)\_[\emptyset]]}(db))))))$
and
$F_1 \equiv (/, \$\_res, in)\_result[\emptyset]$
$F_2 \equiv (/, \_, in)\_env[(/, \_, in)p[(/, \$p, =)\_[\emptyset]]]$
$F_3 \equiv (/, \$a, in)author[(/, \$c, =)country[\emptyset]]$

Projection dependency In this form of dependency the output filter of the inner block refers to external variables. As these variables may be deeply nested into complex XML skeleton and mixed with local variables (user abruptness has no limits), the output filter cannot be decomposed into a local part and a global one. A rule to unnest such dependencies is based on the *copy&join* technique used for range dependencies, as well as on the introduction of cross products. Therefore, the unnested expression may be (much) more expensive than the nested one, hence making this transformation not convenient. For the sake of brevity, this (almost useless) unnesting rule is omitted.

5. Related work

Several algebras for semistructured data and XML have been proposed in the past years. Here we briefly review the most important ones.

YAT YAT [7] is an integration system based on a semistructured tree data model. Its query algebra, largely based on [9], manipulates relational-like intermediate structures. The novelty of this approach is represented by two *frontier* operators, *bind* and *tree*, which are similar to Xtasy *path*

and *return*: *bind* expresses binding, vertical navigation, horizontal navigation, as well as grouping operations; *tree*, instead, is used to create new trees, and can perform grouping and sorting operations.

As already stated, the Xtasy query algebra derives from [9], so it is not surprising that they share many common features. However, differences are still present, in particular in the frontier operators and in the sorting policy; while Xtasy *path* and *return* are simpler than YAT *bind* and *tree* (even though the notation is awkward), YAT *bind* cannot directly evaluate recursive XPath pattern. Moreover, YAT does not deal with the order preservation problem emerged in the XML context, being mainly intended for virtual data integration.

SAL SAL [4] is a query algebra for XML data based on an ordered data model. SAL is quite similar to the YAT query algebra, even though it requires Map operations to perform variable bindings. One key feature of SAL is the ρ operator, which is used to evaluate general path expressions.

TAX TAX [16] is a query algebra developed in the context of the TIMBER project [2]. TAX data model is based on unordered collections of ordered data trees, and each TAX operator takes as input collections of data trees, and produces as output collections of data trees. Unlike YAT and SAL, TAX directly manipulates trees without the need for an explicit intermediate structure. Data extraction and binding are performed by using *pattern trees*: pattern trees, which resemble Xtasy input filters, describe the structure of the desired data, and impose conditions on them.

Even though TAX is very promising, its optimization properties and sorting policy remain unclear; in particular, the way document and join order is preserved is not well defined, and exposes the algebra to possible clashes between unordered collections and ordered trees. Moreover, the way existing optimization properties may be extended to TAX operators is far from being self-evident.

XQuery Formal Semantics (former XML Query Algebra) XML Query Algebra [12] comes from the activity of the W3C XML Query Working Group, being one of the building blocks of the W3C XML Query suite. That algebra is mainly intended for the formal definition of query languages semantics, and its main contribution is an interesting and powerful type system used for statically inferring query result type. The algebra itself is an abstract version of XQuery, where high-level operators (e.g., n-ary for and sortby clauses) are mapped into low-level algebraic operators. Rewriting rules are provided resembling functional programming languages rules and nested relational rules.

While the XML Query algebra would be very useful in defining query language formal semantics and in studying typing problems on XML queries, it appears unlikely that it will form the basis for effective implementations of XML query languages.

Other algebras In [3] authors present a query algebra for ordered XML data, which are modeled as rooted graphs. The distinctive feature of this algebra, very influential in the XML community, is the use of ordered algebraic operators; in particular, joins are ordered, i.e., $A \bowtie B \neq B \bowtie A$, even when A and B are independent.

6. Conclusions and future work

This paper describes a query algebra for XML data, as well as some basic optimization properties; this algebra is used in the Xtasy database management system, which is currently under development.

Our future work moves along three lines. First, we are currently implementing a persistent version of Xtasy, and we are exploring the dark world of run-time query processing. Second, we need to investigate further the problem of query unnesting: we believe that a classification of nested queries over XML data could be very useful. Finally, we plan to explore further the problem of order preservation and its effects on query execution costs.

7. Acknowledgments

Authors would like to thank Dario Colazzo for his precious suggestions and his continuous support during the writing of the paper.

References

[1] http://www.tamino.com.

[2] http://www.eecs.umich.edu/db/timber/.

[3] D. Beech, A. Malhotra, and M. Rys. A formal data model and algebra for xml. Note to the W3C XML Query Working Group, 1999.

[4] C. Beeri and Y. Tzaban. Sal: An algebra for semistructured data and xml. In *Proceedings of the ACM SIGMOD Workshop on The Web and Databases (WebDB'99), June 3-4, 1999*, Philadelphia, Pennsylvania, USA, June 1999.

[5] D. Chamberlin, J. Clark, D. Florescu, J. Robie, J. Siméon, and M. Stefanescu. XQuery 1.0: An XML Query Language. Technical report, World Wide Web Consortium, June 2001. W3C Working Draft.

[6] V. Christophides, S. Cluet, G. Moerkotte, and J. Siméon. Optimizing generalized path expressions using full text indexes. *Networking and Information Systems Journal*, 1(2):177–194, 1998.

[7] V. Christophides, S. Cluet, and J. Siméon. Semistructured and Structured Integration Reconciled: YAT += Efficient Query Processing. Technical report, INRIA, Verso database group, November 1998.

[8] J. Clark and S. DeRose. XML Path Language (XPath) Version 1.0. Technical report, World Wide Web Consortium, Nov. 1999. W3C Recommendation.

[9] S. Cluet and G. Moerkotte. Classification and optimization of nested queries in object bases. Technical report, University of Karlsruhe, 1994.

[10] D. Colazzo, P. Manghi, and C. Sartiani. Xtasy: A typed xml database management system. Available at http://www.di.unipi.it/~sartiani/papers/mementomori.pdf, 2001.

[11] A. Deutsch and V. Tannen. Optimization Properties for Classes of Conjunctive Regular Path Queries. In *Proceedings of the 8th Biennial Workshop on Data Bases and Programming Languages (DBPL'01), Frascati, Rome, September 8-10, 2001*, 2001.

[12] P. Fankhauser, M. Fernandez, A. Malhotra, M. Rys, J. Simeon, and P. Wadler. XQuery 1.0 Formal Semantics. Technical report, World Wide Web Consortium, June 2001. W3C Working Draft.

[13] M. Fernandez and J. Robie. XML Query Data Model. Technical report, World Wide Web Consortium, May 2000. W3C Working Draft.

[14] T. Fiebig and G. Moerkotte. Evaluating Queries on Structure with eXtended Access Support Relations. In *Proceedings of the third International Workshop WebDB 2000*, pages 125–136, 2000.

[15] R. Goldman and J. Widom. DataGuides: Enabling query formulation and optimization in semistructured databases. In *VLDB'97, Proceedings of 23rd International Conference on Very Large Data Bases, August 25-29, 1997, Athens, Greece*, pages 436–445. Morgan Kaufmann, 1997.

[16] H. Jagadish, L. V. S. Lakshmanan, D. Srivastava, and K. Thompson. Tax: A tree algebra for xml. In *Proceedings of the 8th Biennial Workshop on Data Bases and Programming Languages (DBPL'01), Frascati, Rome, September 8-10, 2001*, 2001.

[17] C.-C. Kanne and G. Moerkotte. Efficient storage of xml data. In *Proceedings of the 16th International Conference on Data Engineering, 28 February - 3 March, 2000, San Diego, California, USA*, 2000.

[18] I. Manolescu, D. Florescu, D. Kossmann, F. Xhumari, and D. Olteanu. Agora: Living with xml and relational. In A. E. Abbadi, M. L. Brodie, S. Chakravarthy, U. Dayal, N. Kamel, G. Schlageter, and K.-Y. Whang, editors, *VLDB 2000, Proceedings of 26th International Conference on Very Large Data Bases, September 10-14, 2000, Cairo, Egypt*, pages 623–626. Morgan Kaufmann, 2000.

[19] J. McHugh and J. Widom. Compile-time path expansion in Lore. Technical report, Stanford University Database Group, November 1998.

[20] S. Muench, M. Scardina, and M. Fernandez. XPath Requirements Version 2.0. Technical report, World Wide Web Consortium, Feb. 2001. W3C Working Draft.

[21] D. Quass, A. Rajaraman, Y. Sagiv, and J. Ullman. Querying semistructured heterogeneous information. In *Deductive and Object-Oriented Databases, Fourth International Conference, DOOD'95, Singapore, December 4-7, 1995*, pages 319–344, 1995.

Distributing CORBA Views From an OODBMS

Eric Viara
SYSRA
523, place des Terrasses
91000 EVRY, France.
Eric.Viara@sysra.com

Guy Vaysseix
CRI INFOBIOGEN
523, place des Terrasses
91000 EVRY, France
Guy.Vaysseix@infobiogen.fr

Emmanuel Barillot
GENOPLANTE
523, place des Terrasses
91000 EVRY, France
Emmanuel.Barillot@infobiogen.fr

Abstract

The need to distribute objects on the Internet and to offer views from databases has found a solution with the advent of CORBA. Most database management systems now offer CORBA interfaces which are generally simple mapping of the database schema to the CORBA world. This approach does not address all the problem of database interoperation because (i) such a view is static (ii) its semantic is completely bound to the semantic of the schema and it is not possible to re-model it (iii) only one view per database can be offered (iv) access may be limited to reading and no mechanism is given to write in the database through the view. To solve these problems, we have designed a language, the Interface Mapping Definition Language (IMDL) and some tools, grouped in the Interface Mapping Service (IMS). IMDL is used to define CORBA views from OODBMS, while IMS generates an IDL construct and a full CORBA implementation from an IMDL construct and a database schema.

1. Introduction

The problem of data interoperation remains one of the greatest challenge in the domain of database science. To tackle this issue, the Object Management Group [17] promotes the Common Object Request Broker Architecture (CORBA) [9, 15, 17, 18, 20, 23] for several years. CORBA specifies a common language and protocol for the description and distribution of objects: the Interface Definition Language (IDL) and the Internet Inter-ORB Protocol (IIOP). They allow for a language and platform independence of servers and clients. Besides, CORBA offers a great variety of services such as Naming or Trading. For all these reasons, CORBA has been successfully adopted in several domains as different as banking, electronic commerce, scientific research and transportation.

Most database management systems (DBMS) now pro-
vide a CORBA interface. This interface allows the manipulation of objects (or rows) from a database through an ORB layer. Generally, the interface is schema oriented in the sense that the IDL interface is a direct mapping of the database schema. Each class (or table) is mapped on a CORBA interface in a one-to-one mapping: each class attribute is mapped to an interface attribute and each class method is mapped to an interface method.

This approach enables a standardized distribution of objects but does not address all the requirements of database interoperation. For example, it may be preferable not to export some parts of the schema (some classes, attributes, or methods) which have only an internal purpose. When dealing with biological information, the domain whose database interoperation needs drove our developments, it is often necessary to offer several views from one database, simply because Biology is not yet a unified science but presents many facets : for example a physician, a molecular biologist and a geneticist would not be interested in the same aspect of the information known on a given gene. Also there are a myriad of databases storing data on the same knowledge domain but with a different perspective, which means that the database schemas present a semantic gap that has to be bridged. To address this issue, the different data providers may wish to use a common interface definition, or a standard interface may preexist that will enforce the database manager to map a database schema to a given target IDL. All these points are not addressed by a one-to-one mapping of the database schema to an IDL.

To solve these problems, we have designed a language, Interface Mapping Definition Language (IMDL) and tools, grouped in the Interface Mapping Service (IMS), to define and produce CORBA views from an OODBMS [2, 26, 14] in an automated and flexible way.

The current work has been designed to be as generic as possible: ideally, the IMDL language and IMS should not depend neither on the OODBMS nor on the ORB used. This is true for IMDL: the IMDL language is quite independent from the OODBMS and the ORB used. However, the Interface Mapping Services (IMS), whose main purpose is to generate the CORBA bridge for the given OODBMS and ORB, both depend on the OODBMS and the ORB used.

Because ORBs follow the CORBA standard, there is a large common denominator to all the ORB implementations: the differences appear essentially in the form of the provided API and the quantity of services provided. IMS has been designed so that only a couple of days is necessary to port IMS from one ORB to another.

The diversification in the set of the OODBMS is larger: although ODMG specifies and promotes a standard for OODBMS (see 2.2), only a few OODBMS are ODMG compliant and very few of them implement strictly the C++ language binding. IMS can be adapted to any OODBMS that supports at least single inheritance and provides a query language, but the adaptation time is far more important than for an ORB adaptation.

The EYEDB OODBMS has been choosen to realize the first implementation of the Interface Mapping Services for two main reasons: the first one is that EYEDB is closely based on the ODMG concepts and so, it makes future ODMG-based OODBMS adaptation easier; the second more pragmagtic reason is that the designers of IMDL and IMS are the designers of the EYEDB OODBMS.

The actors of the problem of distributing CORBA views are presented in section 2, while those intervening in the solution (IMDL and IMS) are described section 3. Section 4 exposes the details of use of IMDL and IMS through a basic example and section 5 discusses about related work and approaches.

2. CORBA view distribution: Actors of the problem

2.1. CORBA

CORBA specifications have been designed by the Object Management Group (OMG) at the beginning of the '90. These specifications mainly include:

1. **architecture specification**: the OMG Object Management Architecture (OMA). The major components of this architecture are the clients, the servers and the Object Request Broker (ORB) which is the inescapable mediator between clients and servers.

2. **interface specification**: services provided by servers to clients are described in a platform independent interface language named Interface Definition Language (IDL),

3. **protocol specification**: object are distributed accross the network using a standard protocol named Internet Inter-ORB Protocol (IIOP).

4. **standard services**: a great variety of standard services gathered in a set called *CORBAservices* are specified: Lifecycle, Relationship, Persistent Object, Externalization, Naming, Trading, Event, Transaction, Concurrency, Property, Query, Security and Licensing Services.

CORBA specifications are currently implemented by many ORB products: `Orbix`, `Orbacus`, `VisiBroker`, `HP ORB Plus`, `SUN Neo` and so on. All this products implements the OMA, the IDL and the IIOP protocol but, generally, do not implement currently all the standard services gathered in the *CORBAservices*.

2.2. Object Oriented Database Management Systems

The domain of the Object Oriented Database Management Systems (OODBMS) is large and diversified; the OODBMS concept includes several meanings. However, all the OODBMS have a number of common points:

1. they provide an object model which allows for the definition of complex data:

   (a) single or multiple inheritance is provided,

   (b) classes include both attributes and methods,

   (c) class attributes can take the form of literal types, arrays, collections or object references.

   (d) one-to-one, one-to-many and many-to-many relationships are often supported.

2. each database object is identified in a unique way by an Object IDentifier (OID),

3. integration with at least one programming language: C++, Smalltalk, Java,

4. a query language adapted to the object model.

Because of the great diversity of the OODBMS, the Object Data Management Group (ODMG) [11] has been created in the early 1990 whose aim is to specify and promote a standard for the OODBMS. ODMG gathers the main actors of the OODBMS. ODMG standard (currently version 2.0) specifies mainly the following points:

1. an object model,

2. an object definition language (ODL),

3. an object query language (OQL),

4. C++, Java and Smalltalk language bindings.

ODMG specifies several level of compliance: object model compliance, ODL compliance, OQL compliance, C++ binding compliance and so on.

Several product databases are currently partially compliant with the ODMG standard: O2[2], ObjectStore [10], POET [24], VERSANT [12], ONTOS [4], Objectivity [16], EYEDB [30] and so on.

2.3. The EYEDB OODBMS

The EYEDB OODBMS [30] is an OODBMS based on the ODMG concepts. It is currently used in several projects related to genetics and molecular biology and undergoes testing in several locations, including industrial companies. Online information and a trial version of EYEDB can be obtained from http://www.eyedb.com.

The key features of the EYEDB OODBMS are

- **standard OODBMS features** [2, 26, 14]: persistent typed data management; client/server model; transactional services; recovery system; expressive object model; inheritance; integrity constraints; methods; triggers; query language; application programming interfaces,

- **language orientation**: a definition language based on the ODMG [11] Object Definition Language (ODL); a query language based on the ODMG Object Query Language (OQL); C++ and Java bindings; PHP and PERL bindings,

- **genericity and orthogonality of the object model**: inspired by the SmallTalk, LOOPS, Java and ObjVlisp object models (i.e. every class derives from the class `object` and can be manipulated as an object); type polymorphism; binary relationships; literal and object types; transient and persistent objects; method and trigger overloading; template-based collections (set, bag and array); multi-dimensional and variable size dimensional arrays,

- **support for data distribution**: CORBA binding; multi-database objects,

- **support for large databases**: databases up to several Tb (terabytes),

- **efficiency**: database objects are directly mapped within the virtual memory space; object memory copies are reduced to the minimum; clever caching policies are implemented,

- **scalability**: programs are able to deal with hundred of millions of objects without loss of performance.

2.4. Distributing CORBA Views from an OODBMS

2.4.1 What is a CORBA View?

A database CORBA view (named CORBA view for shortcut) allows the user to manipulate database objects through an ORB. A CORBA view is mainly composed of an interface definition (using the IDL language) and an implementation of this IDL dealing with an OODBMS.

We call this a view by analogy to the well known relational database management systems (RDBMS) view concept, but there are some conceptual differences between an RDBMS and a CORBA view.

An RDBMS view is a table-oriented exportation of the RDBMS content through an SQL statement: a relational view denotes a set of rows on which queries can be performed.

A CORBA view is essentially an instance-oriented interface to the DBMS: objets are built on the fly by the CORBA server and one cannot restrict the extension of a class, every instance in the DBMS from a mapped class will be accessible through the interface. Differently said, the production rules are separated from the view and reside in factories, where the filtering is done if needed. As a consequence, no query is possible in CORBA views.

The main other differences between are:

1. the CORBA view allows for the distribution of database objects,

2. the CORBA view allows for the manipulation of object in different databases with different schemas,

3. the CORBA view allows read and write access to the database objects,

4. the CORBA view does not depend on the DBMS used,

5. the creation of a CORBA view is done outside the DBMS.

To define and distribute CORBA views from an OODBMS, we provide two approaches whose spirit differ fundamentally. The first approach is driven by the OODBMS source schema, while the second is driven by the target CORBA view defined in IDL. The first approach is named *source schema driven* and the second one is named *target view driven*.

2.4.2 Source Schema driven CORBA views

From a database schema, one defines, using the IMDL language, hints about the view to be built, for example:

- class, attribute or method visibility restrictions,

- class, attribute or method renaming,

- interface attribute or method mapping to an OQL construct,

- interface attribute or method mapping to a C++ construct,

- addition of attributes or methods in a target interface.

In this case, as shown in Figure 1, the starting point is:

1. a database schema,

2. hints about the view to be built expressed as an IMDL construct.

the result is:

1. a generated IDL,

2. a full or partial CORBA implementation.

2.4.3 Target View driven CORBA views

In this case, the target view is given a priori in IDL. From a database schema, one defines, using IMDL, the way to map the target IDL from the source schema.

In this second case, as shown in Figure 2, the starting point is:

- a database schema,

- an IDL,

- hints about the way to map the target view from the input schema expressed as an IMDL construct.

the result is:

- a full or partial CORBA implementation of the IDL.

The mapping hints are expressed using IMDL and the CORBA view is generated using IMS services.

3. CORBA view distribution: Actors of the solution

3.1. The Interface Mapping Definition Language (IMDL)

IMDL is a strict superset of the OMG IDL [17, 18]. A few constructs have been added to specify the mapping from the database schema to the IDL view. These constructs allow the user to give the following directives to IMS compiler:

1. to hide database classes, database class attributes or methods in the target CORBA view,

2. to rename database classes, database class attributes or method in the target CORBA view,

3. to extend database classes in the CORBA view by adding new attributes or methods in the target CORBA view,

4. to map an IDL interface attribute from a specific database class attribute,

5. to map an IDL interface attribute from an Object Query Language (OQL) construct,

6. to map an IDL interface attribute from a C++ expression or C++ code.

7. to map an IDL interface method from a database method,

8. to map an IDL interface method from an OQL construct,

9. to map an IDL interface method from a C++ expression or C++ code.

Note that IMDL does not depend on the OODBMS nor on ORB used: as soon as the OODBMS provides a data description language and a query language, IMDL can be used.

3.2. The Interface Mapping Services (IMS)

The main actor of IMS is the IMS compiler which generates an IDL and a full or partial CORBA implementation for a given ORB from a database schema and an IMDL construct (Figure 1) or which generates a full or partial CORBA implementation from a target IDL, a database schema and an IMDL construct (Figure 2). The IMS compiler may generate also a standard interface factory to build instances of any generated interface.

The IDL generated with IMS does not depend on the OODBMS nor on the ORB used; but the generated C++ code depends on both the OODBMS and the ORB. IMS has been implemented for the Orbix and Orbacus ORBs and for the EYEDB [27, 30] OODBMS.

3.3. CORBA View Runtime Architecture

The main actors of the runtime architecture of a CORBA view are (Figure 3):

1. the clients of the CORBA view using the services defined in the IDL,

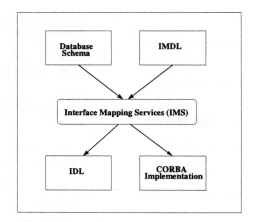

Figure 1. Principles of a source schema driven CORBA view

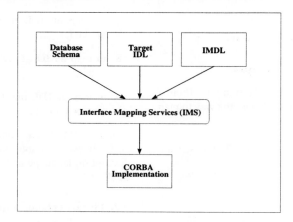

Figure 2. Principles of a target IDL driven CORBA view

2. the Object Request Broker,

3. the server implementing the CORBA IDL; the clients dialog with this server through the ORB layer; this server is a client of the OODBMS server,

4. the OODBMS server.

Clients manipulate CORBA objects while the server manipulates both CORBA and OODBMS objects. More precisely, there are three kind of objects: (Figure 3):

1. The CORBA objects, instances of the IDL interfaces: for each client CORBA object, there is one corba object in the server side which is the implementation of the client corba object. Those objects are denoted as client and server corba objects.

2. The OODBMS runtime objects, instances of the ODL classes, bound to the database objects. There is one

oodbms object in the server side for each oodbms object in the client side. Those objects are denoted as client and server oodbms objects.

3. The OODBMS database objects residing in a database. Those objects are denoted as database objects. Note that the oodbms objects and the database objects are tightly linked together through the OODBMS runtime layer.

A corba object *cobj* is said to be mapped from an oodbms object *iobj* when:

1. at least one attribute selection or modification on *cobj* refers to *iobj* <u>or</u>

2. at least one method invocation on *cobj* refers to *iobj*.

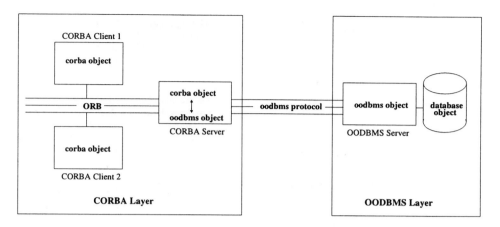

Figure 3. CORBA View Runtime Architecture

4. Designing a CORBA View from an OODBMS

As presented previously, to design a CORBA view from an OODBMS, one needs to define the mappings from the database classes to the target CORBA interfaces using the IDML language. The IMS compiler then generates the CORBA implementation for a given ORB and OODBMS from the IMDL construct.

To illustrate this paper and give more details on the principles of IMS, let's consider a simple schema that is described here using the EYEDB Object Definition Language (ODL) close to the ODMG ODL [11].

4.1. A Simple Schema

```
enum CivilState {
  Lady = 0x10,
  Sir  = 0x20,
  Miss = 0x40
};

class Address {
  attribute string street;
  attribute string<32> town;
};

class Person {
  attribute string name;
  attribute int age;
  attribute Address addr;
  attribute CivilState cstate;
  relationship Person * spouse
    inverse Person::spouse;
  attribute set<Car *> * cars;
  attribute Person *children[];
```

```
};

class Car {
  attribute string brand;
  attribute int num;
};

class Employee extends Person {
  attribute long salary;
};
```

This ODL construct defines one enumerated type, CivilState, and four classes, Address, Person, Car and Employee. The class Adress is composed of a variable size literal attribute, street, and one fixed size literal attribute town. As specified by the ODMG, a literal attribute value has no identifier, while an object attribute value has an identifier.

The class Person is composed of four literal attributes, name, age, addr, and cstate, a relationship object attribute, spouse, a collection object attribute, cars, and a variable size object attribute array, children. Note that as the spouse attribute is a relationship, the OODBMS maintains its referential integrity. This means that if an object that participates in a relationship is removed, then any traversal path to that object is also removed.

As the object attributes cars and children are not relationships, the OODBMS does not maintain their referential integrity. Such a unidirectionnal reference is called an object-valued attribute.

4.2. Source Schema driven study

4.2.1 Creating a CORBA view with IMDL

From the previous database schema, we want to build a CORBA view where several attributes are hidden, some others are renamed and some methods are created; for example, we want:

- to hide the following attributes:

  - `cstate` and `children` in the class `Person`,

  - `street` in the class `Address`.

- to rename the following attributes:

  - `name` in the class `Person` renamed as `last-name`,

  - `age` in the class `Person` renamed as `how_old_is_he`

- to add an updatable attribute in the class `Person` named `spname` mapped from the `name` of the `spouse` of the calling instance of `Person`,

- to add a readonly attribute in the class `Person` named `same_age_person_list` which gives the list of the instances of `Person` which have the same age as the calling instance of `Person`.

- to add a method in the class `Employee` named `is_he_rich()` which returns `true` if the salary of the instance of `Employee` is greater than a constant amount.

- to add an updatable attribute in the class `Employee` named `euro_salary` mapped from the `salary` attribute converted to the *euro* currency,

IMDL and IMS allow the user to implement such a CORBA view in a quite automatic and simple way. The user only has to define hints in IMDL and to invoke IMS compiler to generate both the target IDL and the CORBA implementation of that IDL for `Orbix` or `Orbacus`.

Using IMDL, the description of the hints for the CORBA view proposed above is as follows:

```
module People {

  implicit *;

  hide Person::cstate,
       Person::children,
       Address::street;

  rename Person::name to Person::lastname;
  rename Person::age to
                  Person::how_old_is_he;

  typedef sequence<Person> PersonList;

  extend Person {
    map attribute spname
      from spouse.name;
```

```
    map readonly attribute
      PersonList same_age_persons
      from %oql{select x from Person x where
                    x.age = this.age; %};
  };

  extend Employee {
    map boolean is_he_rich() from
        expr("return salary() > 10000");
    map attribute euro_salary from
        // get C++ expression
        expr("salary() / 6.55957")
        : // token delimiter
        // set C++ expression
        expr("salary(euro_salary * 6.55957)");
  };
};
```

Let's explain each detail of the previous IMDL construct:

- this IMDL construct is composed of an IDL module, named `People`, in which view hints are defined.

- the first statement within the module declaration is `implicit *`. This statement means that all the database schema types defined in the input ODL will be mapped in an implicit way. An implicit mapping for an ODL class is a one-to-one mapping:

  - the ODL class has a corresponding generated IDL interface with the same name,

  - each of its attributes (resp. methods) has a corresponding attribute (resp. method) within the generated IDL interface with the same name and the corresponding type (resp. signature).

For example, the implicit mapping of the ODL class `Address` is:

```
interface Address {
  attribute string street;
     // mapped from Address::street
  attribute string town;
     // mapped from Address::town
};
```

The directive `implicit *` ensures a one-to-one mapping between each ODL class and each generated IDL interface. Nevertheless, the IMDL directives `hide`, `rename` and `extend` may be used to alter this implicit mapping.

- the `hide` directive allows the user to hide an ODL class, an ODL class attribute or method: this means that the pointed class, attribute or method will not be present in the generated IDL. In our example, three attributes are hidden in the generated IDL view: `Person::cstate`, `Person::children` and `Address::street`. This means that the previously shown IDL interfaces becomes:

```
interface Address {
  attribute string town;
};

interface Person {
  attribute string name;
  attribute long age;
  attribute Address addr;
  attribute Person spouse;
  attribute CarList cars;
  // ...
```

- the `rename` directive allows the user to rename an ODL class, an ODL class attribute or method: this means that the pointed class, attribute or method will be renamed in the generated IDL. In our example, the interface `Person` becomes:

```
interface Person {
  attribute string lastname;
      // mapped from Person::name
  attribute long how_old_is_he;
      // mapped from Person::age
      ...
```

- the `extend` directive allows the user to extend an existing mapping by adding some attributes or methods to it. In our example, an attribute named `same_age_persons` of type sequence of `Person` is added to the interface `Person` and a method named `is_he_rich()` is added to the interface `Employee`.

- the `map from IMDL` directive allows the user to map an IDL attribute or method from one of the following constructs:

  1. an ODL attribute,
  2. an OQL construct,
  3. a C++ expression,
  4. some C++ code.

This example introduces the first, the second and the third mapping:

1. mapping from an attribute:

As we have seen previously, the attributes of the `Person` IDL interface are mapped from attributes of the ODL `Person` class thanks to the `implicit *` and `rename` directives. These view attributes are updatable as they are directly mapped to well identified mono valued database attributes.

The attribute `spname` is also mapped from an attribute, more exactly from an attribute path expression (path expression for shortcut): `spouse.name`. A path expression is a sequence of attribute names separated by dots. It can also contain array modifiers under the form `[const_int_expr]`. For instance, the following path expression mapping construct is valid:

```
map attribute long xage from
    spouse.children[(2+3)>>1].spouse.age;
```

Note that an IDL attribute mapped from an ODL path expression is always updatable unless it has the `readonly` qualifier.

2. mapping from an OQL construct:

```
map readonly attribute
    PersonList same_age_persons
    from %oql{select x from Person x
             where x.age =
                 this.age; %};
```

This construct means that the `same_age_persons` attribute is assigned to the evaluation of the OQL statement `select x from Person x where x.age = this.age` where `this` denotes the corresponding database object. For instance, if the age of the database person object is 32, the executed OQL statement `select x from Person x where x.age = 32` will return the list of persons in the database whose age is equal to 32, including of course, the calling person; this returned list will be bound onto the attribute `same_age_persons`.

Contrary to the mapping from an attribute, such an attribute is not updatable for two reasons:

- this attribute is `readonly`. Although this reason is sufficient to forbid the update, this is not the structural reason.
- the structural reason is that this attribute is mapped from an arbitrary OQL construct (in this case a `select` statement) and the system is not able to convert automatically any OQL statement to a "reverse" `update` statement. Furthermore, even if it will be able, the update of all the person instances in the list is perharps not wanted.

To allow the user to update the `same_age_persons` attribute, one has to give explicitly the OQL construct for update in the IMDL. For example:

```
map attribute
    PersonList same_age_persons
```

```
from // the get OQL construct:
 %oql{ select x from Person x where
       x.age = this.age; %}
: // token delimiter
// the set OQL construct:
%oql{ for (x in
          (select x from Person x
           where x.age = this.age))
         x.age := same_age_persons; %}
```

Note that the IMS does not perform any semantic control of the update function: you can do whatever you want in the update function.

3. mapping from a C++ expression:

```
map boolean is_he_rich() from
  expr("return salary() > 10000");
```

This construct means that the is_he_rich() method is assigned to the evaluation of the C++ expression salary() > 10000 Note that the function call salary() returns the salary attribute value of the calling instance. So, if the salary attribute value is greater than 10000, the calling instance is said to be a rich person instance, and poor otherwise.

The euro_salary is an attribute mapped from a C++ expression: it is an updatable attribute as a C++ expression for update has been explicitly given in the IMDL as follows:

```
map attribute euro_salary from
   // get C++ expression
   expr("salary() / 6.55957")
   :
   // set C++ expression
   expr("salary(euro_salary * 6.55957)");
```

The euro_salary attribute is mapped from the evaluation of the C++ expression salary() / 6.55957 for reading and from salary(euro_salary * 6.55957) for writing.

4.2.2 The generated IDL

The complete generated IDL is as follows (forward declaration are skipped):

```
#include <eyedb/corba/eyedb.idl>

module People {
  typedef sequence<People::Car>
    CarList;
  typedef sequence<People::Person>
    PersonList;
  typedef sequence<People::Address>
```

```
    AddressList;
  typedef sequence<People::Employee>
    EmployeeList;

  enum CivilState {
    Lady,
    Sir,
    Miss
  };

  interface Address : EyeDB_ORB::idbStruct {
    attribute string town;
  };

  interface Person : EyeDB_ORB::idbStruct {
    attribute string lastname;
    attribute long how_old_is_he;
    attribute string spname;
    attribute People::Address addr;
    attribute People::Person spouse;
    attribute People::CarList cars;
    readonly attribute
      People::PersonList same_age_persons;
  };

  interface Car : EyeDB_ORB::idbStruct {
    attribute string brand;
    attribute long num;
  };

  interface Employee : People::Person {
    attribute People::CivilState cstate;
    attribute People::PersonList children;
    attribute long salary;
    attribute euro_salary;
    boolean is_he_rich();
  };

  interface Factory {

    People::Address AddressQueryFirst
      (in EyeDB_ORB::idbDatabase db,
       in string query);

    People::AddressList AddressQuery
      (in EyeDB_ORB::idbDatabase db,
       in string query);

    People::Address asAddress
      (in EyeDB_ORB::idbObject o);

    People::Address AddressCreate
      (in EyeDB_ORB::idbDatabase db);

    // similar methods for Person,
    // Car and Employee
  };
};
```

124

This generated IDL calls for a few remarks:

1. as previously introduced, the generated IDL includes by default the file `eyedb.idl` which contains the generic interface of EYEDB. Each generated interface inherits directly or indirectly from the `EyeDB_ORB::idbObject` interface.

2. by default, an interface factory is generated which contains a few methods for each generated interface:

   (a) the method `Address AddressQueryFirst(db, query)` returns the first `Address` instance which matches the input OQL `query` argument.

   (b) the method `AddressList AddressQuery(db, query)` returns all the instances of `Address` which matches the input OQL `query` argument.

   (c) the method `Address asAddress(EyeDB_ORB::idbObject o)` builds an `Address` instance from a generic `idbObject` instance if and only if the generic instance is of dynamic type `Address`. Otherwise a null object is returned.

   (d) the method `Address AddressCreate(db)` creates an empty runtime `Address` instance.

4.2.3 Using the generated CORBA view

To use the CORBA view, the user must:

1. generate the CORBA view by giving the database schema and the IMDL construct to the IMS compiler.

2. generate the CORBA stubs and skeleton by giving the generated IDL to the ORB IDL compiler,

3. compile all the generated code,

4. write and compile the client programs.

Here is a simple example of a client program to get, display and update all the instances of the class `Employee`:

```
// making a OQL query
EyeDB_ORB::idbObjectSeq_var obj_seq =
  db->queryObjects("select Employee");

for (int i = 0; i < obj_seq-
>length(); i++) {
  // building an IDL SpecialEmployee from
  // an ODL Employee
  People::Employee_var empl =
    person_factory->asEmployee(obj_seq[i]);
  // displaying Employee attributes
```

```
  cout << "Employee #" << i << endl;
  cout << "\tname = '" << empl->lastname()
       << "';\n";
  // making this Employee rich
  while (!empl->is_he_rich())
    empl->salary(empl->salary() + 100)
  cout << "\tsalary = " << empl->salary()
       << ";\n";
  cout << "\teuro_salary = " <<
          empl->euro_salary()
       << ";\n";
  // incrementing his age
  empl->age(empl->age() + 1);
  cout << "\tage = " << empl->age()
       << ";\n";
}
```

And to create an instance of `Person` and store it in the database:

```
// creating a Person instance
People::Person_var p =
    person_factory->PersonCreate(db);

// setting the person lastname
p->lastname("martin");

// setting martin's age
p->how_old_is_he(32);

// storing martin into the database
p->store();
```

5. Related work and approaches

There have been other proposals for view support in the context of OODBMS [1, 21, 22, 3].

The O2 approach [1] is based on the concept of *virtual class*: a *virtual class* is populated with objets selected through a query in the OQL language on the root class extension. Part of the information visible in the original base class may be hidden in the view and some renaming may also take place. Furthermore, virtual attributes, defined by OQL constructs, may be added to the view. This view mechanism (O2 Views) is based on the query language - at least to define the extension of the virtual class - and on a specific view language to add virtual attributes, hide or rename attributes in the original base class. A mechanism for updating views in OODBMS, implemented on top of O2 Views, is exposed in [3].

Another view approach, implemented on top of the COCOON model, is presented in [22] and [21]: contrary to the O2 Views approach, this view system uses the standard way of defining views by nothing else than query language expressions.

In those both approaches, as in the traditionnal RDBMS view approach and contrary to our approach, the view gathers "production" and "filtering" rules:

- the "production" rules, expressed in the query language, are used to select objets from one or several classes.

- the "filtering" rules are used to filter objets by, for instance, adding virtual attributes, hiding or renaming attributes in the original base class. The filtering rules are expressed in the query language or in a specific language depending on the system.

In our approach, the production rules are separated from the filtering rules: the production rules "reside" in factories while the filtering rules "reside" in the view interface. The production mechanism is orthogonal to the filtering (or view) mechanism: one produces an object using a factory and then one applies the filter (view) to this object, keeping its original database identifier.

About this point, our approach is conceptually more similar to *aspects* [19] which provides mechanisms to extend existing objects with new state and new behavior while maintaining the same object identity.

On the other hand, our approach for the update of views is close to the O2 one described in [3]. In the both approaches:

- one keeps the original database identifier (OID) in the "viewed" object: this is the core of the update process.

- some attributes can be straightforwardly updated: O2 allows update of any attribute for which the reverse mapping method can be automatically derived from the mapping expression. Our approach allows update of any attribute mapped from an ODL path expression, which is, in a certain sense, more restrictive than the O2 approach.

- the user must supply update methods for other attributes: in our approach, the user must supply an update method for the attributes mapped from an OQL or a C++ expression.

Lastly, our approach has a structural difference with the previous ones: our view management is done "outside" the DBMS, thus, our system is structurally more independent from the DBMS used than the other systems and it can be - more or less easily - ported to other DBMS included relational DBMS. Futhermore, the choice of CORBA as our view architecture made our "viewed" objects easily and standardly distributable.

6. Conclusion

We have defined a powerful language, IMDL, and tools named IMS that enable the distribution of CORBA views from an OODBMS. As opposed to the traditional RDBMS views, our approach allows one to customize with flexibility the CORBA views, and to offer several different views or to map a database schema onto a pre-existing IDL definition. Another important improvement on traditional views lies in a mechanism that enables an update access to the objects mapped in the view.

The IMDL language and IMS service were used at Infobiogen to develop a standard interface to a database of human genome maps: HuGeMap [8, 6]. This database was built with the EyeDB OODBMS. A common IDL for genome maps was defined as a consensus by the genome community [7] and HuGeMap had to offer a CORBA view implementing this IDL. This target IDL consists of 19 interfaces that were mapped to the database schema in a 170 line IMDL file. The resulting generated implementation of the CORBA server contains about 1,500 lines of code. Only two man-days were spent to implement this CORBA view using the IMDL language and IMS compiler. Without this tool, the realization of such an implementation is estimated to take about two man-weeks.

IMS was implemented for the EYEDB OODBMS and the Orbix and Orbacus ORBs. But IMDL is a language that does not depend on the ORB or on the DBMS. The concepts and the language presented here can be used with any ORB and any DBMS, relational or object-oriented.

We now plan to extend IMDL and IMS to allow for the definition and implementation of a single and integrated CORBA view of several databases with different schemas. This will achieve a real interoperation of multiple databases with heterogeneous and complementary semantics.

More information on the IMDL language, the Interface Mapping Services and the EYEDB OODBMS can be found at the EYEDB home page [27, 30]. This page contains the full online programming manual, links to related publications and a trial version for Solaris can be downloaded. The page http://www.eyedb.com/corba_views [29] encloses material related to this paper: the IMDL grammar, the source schema driven example given in this paper, a target view driven example, the common IDL for genome maps and the IMDL file used to map the HuGeMap database to this IDL.

7. Acknowledgements

The Interface Mapping Definition Language (IMDL) and the Interface Mapping Services (IMS) have been developped at CRI Infobiogen [25] with funding from the European Commission (BIO4-CT96-0346).

The EYEDB OODBMS has been developped at Sysra [28] with partial funding from the Agence National de la Valorisation de la Recherche (ANVAR) [5] and the Conseil Regional d'Ile de France [13].

References

[1] S. Abiteboul and A. Bonner. Objects and views. pages 238–247, 1991.

[2] M. Adiba and C. Collet. *Objets et bases de données, le SGBD O2*. Hermès, 1993.

[3] S. Amer-Yahia, P. Breche, and C. S. dos Santos. Object views and updates.

[4] T. Andrews and all. *The ONTOS Object Database*. Ontologic, Inc, Burlington, Massachusetts, 1989.

[5] ANVAR. L'Anvar, votre partenaire pour l'innovation. http://www.anvar.fr/, 1998.

[6] E. Barillot. The Hugemap Home Page. http://www.infobiogen.fr/services/Hugemap/, 1998.

[7] E. Barillot, U. Leser, P. Lijnzaad, C. Cussat-Blanc, K. Jungfer, F. Guyon, G. Vaysseix, C. Helgesen, and P. Rodriguez-Tomé. A proposal for a CORBA interface for genome maps. *BIOINFORMATICS*, 15, 1999.

[8] E. Barillot, S. Pook, F. Guyon, C. Cussat-Blanc, E. Viara, and G. Vaysseix. The HuGeMap database: Interconnection and Visualisation of Human Genome Maps. *Nucleic Acids Research*, 27:119–122, 1999.

[9] R. Ben-Natan. *CORBA a Guide to Common Object Request Broker Architecture*. Computing McGraw-Hill, 1995.

[10] C. Lamb et al. The objectstore database system. *Communications of the ACM, 34(10)*, pages 50–63, 1991.

[11] C. G. Cattell and al. *Object Database Standard, ODMG 2.0*. Morgan Kaufmann, 1997.

[12] V. Corporation. Versant Corporation. http://www.versant.com/.

[13] CRIF. Conseil Régional d'Ile de France. http://www.cr-ile-de-france.fr/, 1998.

[14] H. F. Korth and A. Silberschatz. *Database system concepts*. MacGraw-Hill, 1991.

[15] T. J. Mowbray and R. Zahavi. *The Essential CORBA*. John Wiley & Sons, Inc., 1995.

[16] Objectivity. Welcome to objectivity. http://www.objectivity.com/.

[17] OMG. Object Management Group Home Page. http://www.omg.org/, 1997.

[18] A. L. Pope. *The CORBA Reference Guide*. Addison Wesley, 1998.

[19] J. Richardson and P. Schwarz. Aspects: Extending objects to support multiple, independent roles. pages 298–307, 1991.

[20] D. H. Robert Orfali and J. Edwards. *The Essential Distributed Objects, Survival Guide*. John Wiley & Sons, Inc., 1996.

[21] M. H. Scholl, C. Laasch, and M. Tresch. Updatable Views in Object-Oriented Databases. (566), 1991.

[22] M. H. Scholl and H.-J. Schek. Supporting views in object-oriented databases. *Data Engineering Bulletin*, 14(2):43–47, 1991.

[23] J. Siegel. *CORBA Fundamentals and Programming*. John Wiley & Sons, Inc., 1996.

[24] P. Software. Data management for the Internet Age. http://www.poet.com/.

[25] I. Staff. The INFOBIOGEN Home Page. http://www.infobiogen.fr/, 1998.

[26] M. Stonebraker and J. M. Hellerstein, editors. *readings in database systems*. Morgan Kaufmann, 1998.

[27] E. Viara. The EYEDB Home Page. http://www.eyedb.com/, 1998.

[28] E. Viara. The SYSRA Home Page. http://www.sysra.com/, 1998.

[29] E. Viara. Material for the article *Distributing CORBA Views from an OODBMS*. http://www.eyedb.com/corba_views/, 2001.

[30] E. Viara, E. Barillot, and G. Vaysseix. The EYEDB OODBMS. *IEEE publications*, 1999. International Database Engineering and Applications Symposium (IDEAS), Montreal, 2-4 August 1999.

Paper Session IV

(Applications I)

Completing CAD Data Queries for Visualization

Milena Gateva Koparanova and Tore Risch
Uppsala Database Laboratory
Department of Information Technology
Uppsala University
Sweden
{firstname.lastname}@it.uu.se

Abstract

A system has been developed permitting database queries over data extracted from a CAD system where the query result is returned back to the CAD for visualization and analysis. This has several challenges. First, CAD data representations use complex object-oriented schemas and the query language must be object-oriented too. Second, the query system resides outside the CAD system and must therefore use standardized data exchange formats for interoperability with the CAD. ISO STEP standard exchange formats are used for the exchange. Third, a CAD system cannot import an arbitrary object structure but places restrictions on the imported objects to be acceptable. Therefore, the query system must complement the query results in order to produce an acceptable CAD model, called the model completion of the query. These problems have been solved using an extensible object-relational query processor. The system also supports queries combining CAD data with data from other data sources.

1. Introduction

CAD systems such as I-DEAS [30] and Pro/ENGINEER [27] allow engineers to build design models that may contain very large amounts of data with complex object-oriented structures. During the engineering design process there is often need to analyze these models and select components and sub-models having certain properties. One way to support this is to regard the contents of such engineering models as databases that are queried using a database query language. A system offering techniques for query processing of engineering data extracted from CAD models has been developed, which is called the Engineering Mediator Query system (EMQ). EMQ allows data to be extracted from CAD models for subsequent analysis and querying.

Data in CAD systems are represented using complex Object-Oriented (OO) data representations. In order to minimize information loss and maximize query expressibility, the query system needs also to be OO. EMQ therefore uses an OO data model and query language based on an extended subset of SQL-99. The main enabling technology for querying engineering data is the kernel of the Amos II mediator database system [28]. EMQ uses the query language AmosQL of Amos II, with certain extensions.

The engineering queries can contain functions that match and select objects in the original CAD model. Different query types are possible, including queries on the hierarchical product structure and administrative information, as well as queries on the geometric and topological data defining the shape of a product. For the latter class of queries it is important to be able to return the query results back to a CAD system for visualization and further analysis. However, the CAD system can only visualize data that forms a complete geometric representation of the shape of some part. EMQ therefore has to extend the query result with certain objects that the CAD requires in order to make the former an acceptable CAD model. We call such an extended query result *model completion* of the query. An algorithm for the CAD data query completion has been developed and implemented in EMQ in order to accomplish the full cycle from CAD representation through a query system and back to the query result visualized in the original or other CAD system.

Such a system needs tools for data exchange with CAD systems. The ISO-10303 Standard for Product Data Representation and Exchange [14], known as STEP, provides standardized formats for data exchange with CAD and other engineering systems. The STEP standards use separate meta-data descriptions (schemas) of the exchanged data formally expressed in the EXPRESS information modeling language [31]. For a given meta-data description the data can then be exchanged using the STEP/Part 21 standard format [17] for data exchange files. In database terminology, EXPRESS is a *data model*, while an EXPRESS *information model* contains meta-data descriptions of data about some portion of the real world and corresponds to a *schema* (possibly with subschemas).

Our system can read an information model in EXPRESS and translate it to a corresponding OO database schema. Given this OO schema, the EMQ system can then access standard data exchange files exported from the CAD using its standardized STEP exportation facilities. In our experiments we exchanged CAD data whose meta-data were described by both the STEP standards AP203, Configuration Controlled 3D Design of Mechanical Parts and Assemblies [15], and AP214, Core Data for Automotive Mechanical Design Processes [16]. The experiments were made using two of the most widespread CAD systems, namely, I-DEAS and Pro/ENGINEER. In particular, we used their modules for development of part geometry in the initial design of product parts. However, EMQ is general and can work with any EXPRESS information model and Part 21 data exchange file.

The EXPRESS data representation requires multiple inheritance which is supported by the data model and the query language of Amos II [29] on which EMQ is based. Queries retrieving all components in a hierarchical product structure as well as the model completion require transitive closure operations. The transitive closure facility of AmosQL allows for repeated application of a function with the same argument and result type until either no further application is possible, or a specified number of repetitions has been reached.

Furthermore, EMQ uses the mediator/wrapper approach [8, 9, 23, 32, 33] to allow queries and views that combine STEP/EXPRESS based data with other kinds of data, such as relational databases [7] and XML-based data [24]. These facilities rely on the techniques developed for OO mediation in Amos II [18, 19], a discussion of which is outside the scope of the present paper.

This paper first discusses related work. Section 3 describes the architecture of EMQ, while Section 4 provides certain examples of how EMQ queries are expressed and visualized. Section 5 describes the model completion implementation, and Section 6 concludes.

2. Related work

Early work on CAD databases [1, 4, 3, 10] concentrated on object storage rather than high-level queries and [22] discussed various approaches to the geometric data modeling. In contrast, our contribution is a query system for high-level user queries to complex standardized CAD data, where the system provides *model completion* of the query result for visualization by means of a CAD system. The management of engineering data in Amos II and querying using AmosQL is discussed in [26] with no consideration of problems involved in the visualization and completion of the query result.

EQL [20] is an EXPRESS query language intended for ad hoc queries on data in STEP/Part 21 data files. The language is not closed, i.e., the query result can not be queried and it has no geometric model completion. The aim of the EXPRESS-X language [12] and its predecessor BRIITY [11] is to translate data (e.g., Part 21 files) represented in one EXPRESS information model into the corresponding data in another, thereby reconciling heterogeneous and conflicting data. Its ability to construct views of EXPRESS data provides basic query facilities. EXPRESS-X is primarily intended to be a schema translation language and is not a general query language for CAD data. Unlike EMQ, it does not deal with the problem of the model completion of query results that is needed in order to make the result of an ad hoc query acceptable to a CAD system.

We have not intended to develop a new query language, but rather to extend an existing OO query language with certain required operations, such as geometric model completion.

[25] discusses certain approaches for optimizing a PDM system that resides on top of a relational DBMS. DIVE [21] is a database integration tool for virtual engineering applications providing for separate storage and management of product structure data (in a relational database) and spatial data (in ORDBMS). The system provides query facilities on both kinds of data, i.e., structural queries through CAD DB and advanced spatial queries, but it does not send query results to the CAD system for visualization. While we do not consider such special representations for spatial data, nor the implementation of spatial operations, we do address the querying of geometric and topological data concerning the shape and size of product parts in standardized object-oriented engineering schemas and representations. Whereas a spatial query result is a set of existing spatial objects, a query on OO representation of geometric and topological data may result in an object structure non-complete in a spatial sense. This type of queries therefore requires a completion algorithm for the query results.

Several systems have been developed for visualizing the results of database queries [5, 2]. Rather than connecting the visualization directly to the DBMS, we utilize a general CAD system for this purpose. This requires standardized data exchange between EMQ and the CAD, along with our model completion methods that modify the results of a query such that they can be visualized by the CAD system. In addition to visualization, this technique allows for the use of the query result in further analysis and in other operations inside a CAD system.

3. EMQ Architecture

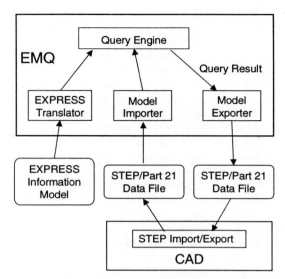

Figure 1. The EMQ architecture

illustrates the EMQ architecture. Since the data models of EXPRESS and Amos II differ, we need to translate meta-data from EXPRESS into Amos II. This is performed by the *EXPRESS Translator* module. This module reads any EXPRESS information model and translates it into a corresponding Amos II database schema. The translator carries out certain mappings between the data representations in EXPRESS and Amos II (for more details see http://www.csd.uu.se/~milena/Mapping.pdf). Since both EXPRESS and Amos II have OO data models, the mapping is straightforward.

Once an EXPRESS schema has been imported into EMQ, the *Model Importer* makes it possible for the system to access any Part 21 data exchange file using that schema generated by a CAD system. It creates new database objects and sets relationships between them in order to fully represent the CAD data in Amos II.

The OO query language AmosQL allows for general database queries over CAD data, and the result of such a query is a set of database objects. In order to export this result back into the CAD, the *Model Exporter* generates a new Part 21 exchange file representing the result of the query. This is sent back to the CAD system for visualization or further analysis.

Queries that result in geometric and topological data are of particular interest for visualization. However, encoding this type of query result as a Part 21 file is not sufficient for representing it in a CAD system since it

must be enclosed by an object structure rooted in an object that represents a specific geometric model. We have therefore developed a generic *Model Completion* framework as a part of the model exporter. Additional objects are created within this framework which, together with the query result, form a CAD model that is a shape representation of a fictional product part. The architecture of the Model Exporter is illustrated in Figure 2.

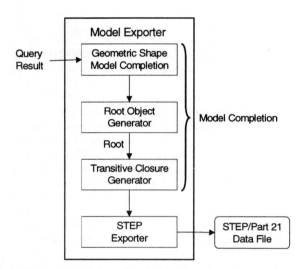

Figure 2. The Model Exporter

The Model Completion framework follows the STEP standard requirements for representing a product shape. First, *Geometric Shape Model Completion* (GSMC) performs the task of creating an enclosing structure for a given query result with an appropriate root object. GSMC deals with two kinds of problems, namely, different result sets need different root objects, and more than one type of root object is possible for certain result sets. This module is generic and table driven.

The root object of the enclosing structure must be one of the Geometric Shape Models (GSMs) defined in the STEP standard [13]. Two classic types of geometric modeling of solid objects are included in this standard: constructive solid geometry and boundary representation. The latter, for example, is presented by *Manifold_solid_brep* and its subtypes. Certain models in the standard, such as *Geometric_set* and *Shell_based_surface_model*, represent less complete descriptions of the geometry of a product. They allow for communication with systems whose capabilities differ from those of solid modeling systems. They are particularly useful for communicating the results of a DB query with a CAD system that accepts certain incomplete solid models.

The second step in the model completion framework is

executed by the *Root Object Generator (ROG)*. The ROG creates additional *root* objects whose roles are to place the GSM structure that has been created within a context, e.g., the dimensionality of the coordinate space and units of measurement. Together they form a CAD model acceptable to the CAD system. One of the objects plays the role of a root object for the entire model exported to the CAD.

The exported data set needs to be closed. For example, an object representing a surface needs to be exported together with the objects that represent points on this surface. The query result, the objects created by GSMC, the root objects, and all objects representing attributes of the query result are collected by the *Transitive Closure Generator* (TCG). They form the closure of the root object of the CAD model.

Finally, the data in the object set collected by TCG is encoded by *STEP Exporter* into a file in STEP/Part 21 standardized format that is sent to the CAD system. While the GSMC and the ROG modules depend on the EXPRESS information model for a particular application domain, the TCG and the STEP exporter are domain independent.

4. CAD data example queries

In general, AmosQL queries are expressed as
select <result>
from <type specification>
where <condition>
The *<type specification>* defines variables bound to the extent of types. The conditional expression in the where clause restricts the cartesian product of the type extents. The select clause specifies a result tuple that is calculated for every variable binding in the restricted cartesian product of the type extents.

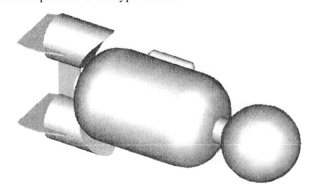

Figure 3. Space ship

Let us consider a simplified CAD model of a space ship, shown in Figure 3. We export the data in STEP/Part 21 data format from the CAD system into an EMQ database where the corresponding AP203 schema is already loaded. A subset of the schema relevant to the given example is shown in Figure 4 as an extended entity-relationship (EER) diagram. The relationships have a logical direction (i.e., they are *functional relationships*), but can still be queried in the inverse direction.

Although the query facilities of EMQ are general, we focus in the present discussion on queries over CAD data with geometric and topological results. EMQ can query and send to the CAD system the geometric representation of any component of an assembly. For example, the object structure that represents a component named "tail turbine" in Figure 5a is extracted by calling a predefined query function *get_component*[1]:
select get_component("s1_tail_turbine");
Given the name of a component, this function returns a *shape_representation* object (Figure 10) that is a root of the object structure defining the component geometry.

Data can be extracted by geometric condition in the query. For instance, in order to see all planar faces in the tail turbine component, we specify the following query that retrieves all faces in the tail turbine having an associated plane surface geometry[2]:
select fs from ST_face_surface fs, ST_plane pl
where face_geometry(fs) = pl and
fs =[3] entclosure(get_component("s1_tail_turbine"));
The *fs* and *pl* variables are bound to the extents of *ST_face_surface* and *ST_plane* types respectively. The first condition selects those *ST_face_surface* objects that are related to geometric surfaces of type *ST_plane* through the relationship *face_geometry*. The second condition restricts the selection to only those objects of type *ST_face_surface,* that occur in the component named "s1_tail_turbine". The *entclosure* function implements a transitive closure operation. Applied on the root object of type *ST_shape_representation,* it returns all objects in the structure defining the component geometry.

In order to import the result of the example query into a CAD system, the model exporter module of the EMQ is called, which is implemented as a system query function:
export_model (Bag of Entity query_result)
The function *export_model* creates a new complete CAD model representation for the result of an ad hoc CAD data query. For example:
export_model(select fs
from ST_face_surface fs, ST_plane pl
where face_geometry(fs) =pl and
fs= entclosure(get_component ("s1_tail_turbine")));

---

[1] *get_component* is defined through a rather complex query. It is omitted here for the sake of brevity.
[2] The names of the mapped EXPRESS types have the prefix 'ST_' in order to avoid name collisions with other Amos II types.
[3] In our system '=' is overloaded to denote set membership when an operand denotes a set.

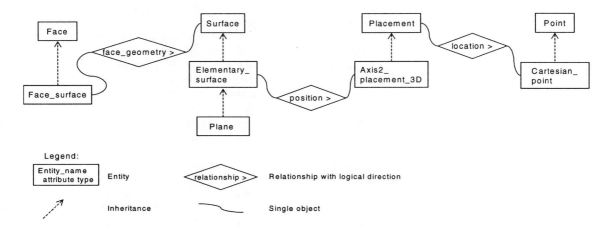

Figure 4 EER diagram of subset of AP203 for the examples

Figure 5 (a) Tail Turbine, (b) Plane faces in Tail Turbine, (c) Plane faces with more than 4 edges in Tail Turbine

The function first calls the GSMC module in order to find an appropriate geometric model for the query result type and construct an object structure that encloses the result set. The algorithm for GSMC is presented below in Section 5.

The system has information about the GSMs required to contain the query result. It automatically determines which of these models can be containers for the particular query result by using the relationships between types. Since more than one GSM is possible for certain result types, EMQ uses a system table that prioritizes the models in order to resolve ambiguities. In our example, data of type *Face_surface* can be contained in several geometric shape models and EMQ prioritizes the least limiting *Shell_based_surface_model*.

The user can override the automatic selection of the GSM by explicitly specifying the name of the model as an optional second argument of *export_model*:

> *export_model (Bag of Entity query_result,*
> *Character geom_model)*

After creating the GSM structure, the necessary root objects of the CAD model are added by the root object generator. The root of the model is passed to the transitive closure generator that collects all objects composing the complete CAD model. For the example query this means that *Plane* objects will be added to the model together with *Face_surface* objects because of the *face_geometry* relationship.

The collected object set is then sent to the STEP Exporter, which creates a Part 21 data exchange file encoding the model. The CAD system visualization of the model containing only the plane faces of the tail turbine component of the ship as selected by our query can be seen in Figure 5b.

In a similar way we can extract all faces with planar geometry and more than four edges in some of their boundaries from the tail turbine component (Figure 5c), combining in one query structural, geometrical, and topological criteria:

> *export_model(select fs*
> *from ST_face_surface fs, ST_plane pl,*
> *ST_edge_loop l*
> *where fs =*
> *entclosure(get_component("s1_tail_turbine"))*
> *and face_geometry(fs) = pl and*
> *bound(bounds(fs)) = l and count(edge_list(l))>4);*

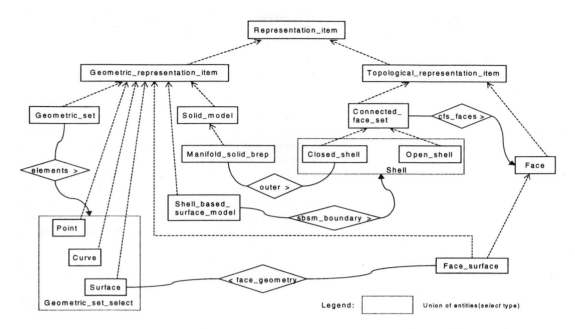

Figure 6. Subset of AP203 and AP214 illustrating model completion

5. Model Completion

In this section we will consider in detail the model completion framework and, in particular, the algorithm for geometric model completion.

5.1 Geometric Shape Model Completion

Geometric model completion is needed for geometrical and/or topological query results. STEP standards require this type of data to be enclosed by a structure rooted in some GSM, such as *Shell_based_surface_model*, *Geometric_set* and *Manifold_solid_brep* explained in Sec. 3 and illustrated in Figure 6. Different parts of the standard define different valid geometric models; for example, *Face_based_surface_model* is included in the AP214 schema, but is not used in AP203. Since the choice of the container for the query result is application dependent, we provide the system with information about the valid GSMs in a generic way through a system function called *priority table*:

valid_geom_models() -> Vector of Type t;

The system administrator shall set the function value to a vector (ordering) of all types representing GSMs for a particular standard schema ordered by how general the models are.

Since different GSMs are appropriate for different kinds of geometric and topological data, the work of GSMC depends on the type of the query result. The system needs knowledge of which GSM is appropriate for every kind of geometric and topological data. Following the relationships between types in the database schema, the system automatically determines which of the GSMs can be a root for the enclosing structure of the particular query result. The fact that more than one GSM is possible for certain result types is resolved through an ordering of the models by priority in the value of the *valid_geom_models()* function. GSMs that are less restrictive according to STEP standard constraints have a higher priority.

The example query on page 9 returns a collection of *Face_surface* objects. From the diagram in Figure 6 we see that possible GSMs for a *Face_surface* object are *Shell_based_surface_model* and *Manifold_solid_brep*. The system chooses the first one since it has fewer constraints and precedes the other in the priority table.

The system automatically finds a path through the schema from the GSM type determined to the query result type, creates instances of the types along this path, and connects these instances by setting functional relationships. In this way a new structure is created that contains the query result and has a root of GSM type. In our example, the system finds a path from *Shell_based_surface_model* through *Open_shell* to the result type *Face_surface*, creates one instance of each (except the result type), and connects the *Shell_based_surface_model* instance to the *Face_surface* result objects by setting the *sbsm_boundary*

135

and *cfs_faces*.

There may at times be several paths when searching for one that connects the GSM and the query result type. In the example above there are ambiguous paths between *Shell_based_surface_model* and *Face_surface*, and the system does not know whether to choose the one through the *Closed_shell* type or the one through the *Open_shell* type. The GSMC therefore contains an *ambiguity table* as guidance for how to relate types when there are ambiguities.

amb_table(Type tstart, Type tend) -> Type t;

The ambiguity table specifies the next edge in the path, given the start and end types. In the simplified schema in Figure 6, the ambiguity table contains an element for the path from *Shell_based_surface_model* to *Face* type through the *Open_shell* type.

Queries returning objects of certain GSM types (*geometric_set*, *manifold_solid_brep*, etc.) do not require geometric completion. Thus, when the system automatically recognizes such types using the model priority table, it directly calls the ROG and TCG modules.

5.2   Algorithm for GSM completion of CAD data query

Figure 7 presents the main steps in the algorithm for the geometric model completion of a given query result.

Input: set of database objects that are result of an ad hoc query.
Output: the root GSM object of the constructed object structure that encloses the query result.
Algorithm:
1.   Analyze the query result to determine whether it needs a model completion. If model completion is needed:
1.1. The user has provided a GSM type as an argument. Either check its validity and continue with step 2, or raise an error message when the type is not a valid GSM;
1.2. The GSM is not provided. Run the algorithm in step 2 for one or more valid GSMs starting with the model with highest priority. Stop when an appropriate GSM has been found or when all models have been checked without success.
2.   Search a path in the entity type graph between a valid GSM type and the query result type (we assume that the objects in the query result have the same type).
3.   Construct an object structure with a root that is an instance of a GSM type using the path found in step 2.

Figure 7 The algorithm for the geometric shape model completion of the query result

The algorithm consists of three steps: determine the GSM type for the particular query result, search the path between the GSM type and the query result type, and construct the object structure enclosing the query result. The root of the constructed structure is then sent to the ROG module (section 5.4).

The goal of the first step is to find a GSM type appropriate for the root of the enclosing object structure. The second step searches for a path between this type and the query result type. The algorithm used is a graph algorithm for an instance of the single-pair path problem [6] with additional modifications. The graph $G = (V, E)$ has a set of vertices V that correspond to entity types in a given EXPRESS schema. The set of edges E includes the functional relationships between types in V. Since the functional relationships have logical direction, the edges in G are oriented:

$E = \{f_{t \to u}\}, t, u \in V;$

The graph is defined in a generic way in the system as follows:

- metaqueries to the metatype Type provide the definition of vertices V;
- the set of edges is modeled by a derived metafunction *contain_types*:

Contain_types(Type t)-> bag of <Type u, Function f>;

The function returns a pair <Type, Function> for each functional relationship defined on the argument type that connects it to other entity type, including functions whose result is an array or a union type since they can have an entity type as an element.

Modifications of the basic single-pair path algorithm are needed because of type inheritance and ambiguity when more than one path is possible. Let A and B be entity types for which a functional relationship is established in the schema: $f_{A \to B}$. The functional relationships are inherited: for each type A' subtype of A, the set of the functional relationships on A' includes $f_{A \to B}$ although f is defined only once - on type A. This property is automatically provided by the system through the inheritance mechanism. The functional relationship $f_{A \to B}$ is also a relationship to every type B' that is subtype of B, since every instance of B' is an instance of B. The inheritance of the function result type is not automatically provided and must be modeled by the algorithm or by the edge definition.

Another modification of the algorithm is needed because of the ambiguity. Since the algorithm should provide exactly one path for the construction in step 3, it needs tools for resolving ambiguity when more than one path exists for a given pair of vertices. We assume that different paths can have different values from the GSMC point of view. Instead of arbitrarily choosing one of the possible paths, the algorithm checks the ambiguity table to recommend a path between the current pair of vertices. This check is required only when more than one edge exits the current vertex and, therefore, the table contains elements for only such pairs of vertices. The function *Recommended_path(Type t, Type q)* checks the contents of the ambiguity table for the current pair of vertices and returns a pair $< u, f_{t \to u} >$ of the preferred vertex u (type) and the edge (function) to it where the path should continue.

```
Input:   current type and end type to which a path is
         looked for;
Output: boolean value True if a path exists and False
         otherwise. Global variable P contains the arcs in
         the path found;
Function:
boolean Search_path (t, end_type)
    S ← contain_types(t)
    if |S| = 0 return False
    for each s ∈ S, s = <u, f t→u >
        if (u = end_type) or Subtype(end_type, u)
        Append(P, <t, f t→u >)
        return True
    if |S| =1
        Extract element u from S
    else u ← Recommended_path(t, end_type)
        S₁ ← S - {u}
    if Search_path(u, end_type)
        Append(P, <t, f t→u >)
        return True
    else for each u ∈ S1
        if Search_path(u, end_type)
            Append(P, <t, f t→u >)
            return True
    return False
```

Figure 8 Algorithm for recursive searching for a path between types in the entity type graph

In the pseudocode for searching the path in Figure 8, we assume that a global list variable P is defined in order to store pairs of kind $< t, f_{t \to u} >$ that define the arcs $f_{t \to u}$ in the path found. A new arc is appended at the end of the list (Append (P,x)) after previous successful recursive calls of Search_path function have already constructed the rest of the path to the end_type. As a result the list P starts with the arc leading to the end_type as needed by the next step.

The algorithm for the third step, presented in Figure 9, constructs an object structure that encloses the query result. The object structure is built in a bottom-up fashion. The list P is processed from the beginning using Pop(P) operation. For each pair $< t, f_{t \to u} >$ in the path P an instance of type t is created and the functional relationship $f_{t \to u}$ is set to the object of type u created in the previous step. The first "lowest" functional relationship is set to the

query result objects. The output is the root of the constructed object structure, which is of the type specified in the first step GSM type. The algorithm presented here is simplified since the setting of the functional relationships

```
Input: the query result and the path specification
        stored in the global variable P.
Output: the GSM root of the builded structure
        enclosing the query result.
Function:
GSMtype Create_model(query_result)
    e ←query_result
    while P ≠ 0
        <t,f> ← Pop(P)
        create o of type t
        f(o) ← e
        e ← o
    return e
```

Figure 9 Construction of the object structure enclosing the query result

of kind 1:1 and 1:M require special treatment.

In the current implementation, the analysis of the possible GSMs and the search for the path between types in the schema do not take into account the STEP standard facility for constraints that express restrictions on properties to ensure data validity and logical consistence. Through the GSM priority table and the ambiguity table we implement a way to provide the system with knowledge of how to work correctly, replacing information in the constraints. Constraints could be used to ignore certain formally incorrect geometric models. However, a large number of requirements are formulated only as *informal propositions* and the STEP standard does not provide formal algorithms (if such exist) to check them. For example, the requirement that the union of the domains of the faces that are contained in a *Connected_face_set* object should be connected is described only in the form of an informal proposition. Furthermore, the constraints provide restrictive but not constructive information for how to build a GSM (based on the fact that the construction is made always by a CAD or other engineering system). In addition, the experiments have shown that CAD systems accept (on different levels) models in which formal constraints and/or informal propositions are not satisfied.

It is thus impossible to assess the correctness of a constructed GSM structure if only STEP constraints are used, even if EMQ would have supported formal constraints. We instead currently rely only on the GSM priority table and the ambiguity table to automatically construct the model completion, which, as the experiments have shown, is accepted by the CAD systems.

5.3   Root Object Generator

A CAD model of a product shape requires specific types of the root objects defined in the standard. For example, both in AP203 and AP214 the main root object is an instance of type *Shape_representation* (Figure 10). As all GSM types are subtypes of the *Representation_item* (Figure 6), the GSM structure enclosing the query result has to be connected to the root object through the functional relationship *items*. Other attributes of the root object, such as the dimensionality of the coordinate space and measurement units, describe characteristics of the context in which the shape geometry is defined.

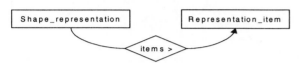

Figure. 10 Root object structure

This root object is in fact sufficient to construct a model that the experimental CAD systems import with warning messages about missing definitional data. In order to construct a model that is accepted by the CAD without any warnings, a wider set of root objects has been implemented as well. They describe a fictional product part and are beyond the present scope of discussion.

5.4   Transitive Closure Generator

Finally, the model has to be *closed*, which means that all assigned attributes of the exported objects must also be exported. This is a transitive closure operation that, according to the STEP/Part 21 encoding requirements, follows every functional relationship defined in the STEP/EXPRESS schema. The algorithm for the transitive closure is generic and does not depend on the query result or the particular EXPRESS schema.

Input parameter for the TOG is the root object created by the previous module. The TOG collects all objects that compose a complete model capable of being represented in the CAD system. This set includes the query result, GSMC objects, root objects, and all other objects reachable through functional relationships from these objects. For example, in our query the objects of type *Face_surface* require the objects of type *Surface* that are values of the functional relationship *face_geometry* to be included in the model. The latter objects in their turn require objects of type *Axis2_placement_3D* to be added as values of the functional relationship *position*, and *Cartesian_point* objects to be included as values of the *location* function. The object closure set is then passed to the STEP/Part-21 file exporter for encoding into an exchange file.

6.   Conclusions and Future Work

The main results of the current work are the following:

An ad hoc OO query facility has been developed for data in CAD systems.

A query result can be exported to a CAD system using an ISO standardized format (STEP Part 21).

By means of the exportation facility the result of a query can be visualized or analyzed through a CAD system.

A model completion algorithm is implemented for extending a query result such that it becomes a model acceptable by a CAD system.

The mediator facilities permit queries combining CAD data with other types of data.

The model completion algorithm is driven by the STEP/EXPRESS information model complemented by two system tables. One prioritizes possible geometric shape models, and the other resolves ambiguous paths between types in the information model.

Possible future work includes:

Implementation of remaining EXPRESS features as functions, procedures, etc., needed for constraint checking. The constraints in STEP standards would complement but not replace our model completion system tables.

Investigation of the ability to specify queries with functions that make advanced calculations over engineering data. The foreign function mechanism of Amos II can be used for this purpose.

Enhancing performance by developing new data representations and indexing techniques for complex EXPRESS data structures.

7.   References

[1]   R. Ahmed and S.B. Navathe: Version Management of Composite Objects in CAD Databases, *SIGMOD'91*, 218-227, 1991.

[2]   L. Bouganim, T.C-S. Ying, T-T. Dang-Ngoc, J-L. Darroux, G. Gardarin, and F. Sha: MIROWeb: Integrating Multiple Data Sources Trough Semistructured Data Types. In *Proc. of the 25th VLDB Conference*, Edinburgh, Scotland, 1999.

[3]   A.P. Buchmann and C.P. de Celis: An Architecture and Data Model for CAD Databases, In *Proc. of the 11th VLDB Conference*, 105-114, 1985.

[4]   D.S. Batory and W. Kim: Modeling Concepts for VLSI CAD Objects. *ACM Trans. on Database Systems*, 10(3):322-346, 1985.

[5]   M. Carey, L. Haas, V. Maganty, and J.Williams: PESTO: An Integrated Query/Browser for Object Databases. In *Proc. of the 22nd VLDB Conference*, pages 203-214, Mumbai, India, 1996.

[6]   T. Cormen, C. Leiserson, R. Rivest, *Introduction to Algorithms*, The MIT Press, 1990.

[7]   G. Fahl and T. Risch: Query Processing over Object

Views of Relational Data, *The VLDB Journal*, 6 (4): 261-281, 1997.

[8] H. Garcia-Molina, Y. Papakonstantinou, D. Quass, A. Rajaraman, Y.Sagiv, J. Ullman, V. Vassalos, and J. Widom. The TSIMMIS Approach to Mediation: Data Models and Languages. *Journal of Intelligent Information Systems (JIIS)*, Kluwer, 8(2): 117-132, 1997.

[9] L. Haas, D. Kossmann, E.L. Wimmers, and J. Yang: Optimizing Queries across Diverse Data Sources. In *Proc. of the 23rd VLDB Conference*, pages 276-285, Athens, Greece, 1997.

[10] M. Hardwick and D. Spooner: The ROSE Data Manager: Using Object Technology to Support Interactive Engineering Applications, *IEEE Trans. on Knowledge and Data Engineering*, 1(2): 285-289, 1989.

[11] T. Härder, G. Sauter, and J. Thomas: The intrinsic problems of structural heterogeneity and an approach to their solution. *The VLDB Journal*, 8: 25-43, 1999.

[12] International Organization for Standardization:. *ISO 10303-14, Industrial automation systems and integration - Product data representation and exchange- Part 14: Description methods: The EXPRESS-X Language Reference Manual*. ISO Document TC 184/SC4/WG11 N117, 2000.
http://www.nist.gov/sc4/step/parts/part014/CD/doc/

[13] International Organization for Standardization: *ISO 10303-42:2000, Industrial automation systems and integration - Product data representation and exchange - Part 42: Integrated generic resources: Geometric and topological representation*. Second Edition. ISO Document TC 184/SC4/ WG12 N 540, 1994.
http://www.nist.gov/sc4/step/parts/part042e2/is/n540/

[14] International Organization for Standardization: *ISO 10303-1:1994, Industrial automation systems and integration - Product data representation and exchange - Part 1: Overview and fundamental principles*, 1994.

[15] International Organization for Standardization: *ISO 10303-203:1994, Industrial automation systems and integration — Product data representation and exchange — Part 203: Application protocol: Configuration controlled 3D design of mechanical parts and assemblies*, 1994.

[16] International Organization for Standardization: *ISO 10303-214:1998, Industrial automation systems and integration - Product data representation and exchange - Part 214: Core Data for Automotive Mechanical Design Processes*. ISO Document TC 184/SC4/WG3, 1996.

[17] International Organization for Standardization: *ISO/DIS 10303-21:1999, Industrial automation systems and integration - Product data representation and exchange - Part 21: Clear text encoding of the exchange structure*. ISO Document TC 184/SC4/WG11 N102, 1994.

[18] V. Josifovski and T. Risch: Functional Query Optimization over Object-Oriented Views for Data Integration, *Journal of Intelligent Information Systems (JIIS)*, 12(2-3), 1999.

[19] V. Josifovski and T. Risch: Integrating Heterogeneous Overlapping Databases through Object-Oriented Transformations, In *Proc. of the 25th VLDB Conference*, Edinburgh, Scotland, 1999.

[20] D. Koonce, L. Huang, and R. Judd: EQL an EXPRESS Query Language, *Computers and Industrial Engineering*, 35(1-2),1998.

[21] H.P. Kriegel, A. Muller, M. Pötke, and T. Seidl: DIVE: Database Integration for Virtual Engineering, *Demo session on 17th International Conference on Data Engineering*, Heidelberg, Germany, 2001.

[22] A. Kemper and M. Wallrath: An Analysis of Geometric Modeling in Database Systems, *ACM Computing Surveys*, 19(1), 1987.

[23] L.Liu and C. Pu: An Adaptive Object-Oriented Approach to Integration and Access of Heterogeneous Information Sources. *Distributed and Parallel Databases*, Kluwer, 5(2), 167-205, 1997.

[24] H. Lin, T. Risch, and T. Katchaounov: Adaptive data mediation over XML data. To be published in special issue on "Web Information Systems Applications" of *Journal of Applied System Studies (JASS)*, Cambridge International Science Publishing, 2002.

[25] E. Muller, P. Dadam, J. Enderle, and M. Feltes: Tuning an SQL-Based PDM System in a Worldwide Client/Server Environment. In *Proc. of the 17th International Conference on Data Engineering*, Heidelberg, Germany, 2001.

[26] K. Orsborn: Management of Product Data Using an Extensible Object-Oriented Query Language, *International Conference on Data and Knowledge Systems for Manufacturing and Engineering*, Phoenix, Arizona, USA, 1996.

[27] PTC Corporation: Pro/ENGINEER, http://www.ptc.com/products/proe/index.htm, 2001.

[28] T. Risch and V. Josifovski: Distributed Data Integration by Object-Oriented Mediator Servers, *Concurrency and Computation: Practice and Experience J.*, 13(11), John Wiley & Sons, 2001.

[29] T. Risch, V. Josifovski, and T. Katchaounov: *AMOS II Concepts*, Department of Information Science, Uppsala University, 2000, http://www.dis.uu.se/~udbl/amos/.

[30] SDRC Corporation: *Introducing I-DEAS*. http://www.sdrc.com/ideas/index.html, 2001

[31] D. Schenck and P. Wilson: *Information Modeling: The EXPRESS Way*. Oxford University Press, 1994.

[32] A. Tomasic, L. Raschid, and P. Valduriez: Scaling Access to Heterogeneous Data Sources with DISCO. *IEEE Transactions on Knowledge and Date Engineering*, 10(5), 808-823, 1998.

[33] G. Wiederhold: Mediators in the architecture of future information systems, *IEEE Computer*, 25(3), 38–49, 1992.

An index structure for improving closest pairs and related join queries in spatial databases

Congjun Yang
Division of Computer Science
Department of Mathematical Sciences
The University of Memphis
Memphis, TN 38152, USA.
yangc@msci.memphis.edu

King-Ip Lin
Division of Computer Science
Department of Mathematical Sciences
The University of Memphis
Memphis, TN 38152, USA.
linki@msci.memphis.edu

Abstract

Spatial databases have grown in importance in various fields. Together with them come various types of queries that need to be answered effectively. While queries involving single data set have been studied extensively, join queries on multi-dimensional data like the k-closest pairs and the nearest neighbor joins have only recently received attention.

In this paper, we propose a new index structure, the b-Rdnn tree, to solve different join queries. The structure is similar to the Rdnn-tree for the reverse nearest neighbor queries. Based on this new index structure, we give the algorithms for various join queries in spatial databases. It is especially effective for the k-closest pair queries, where earlier algorithms using R*-tree can be very inefficient in many real life circumstances. To this end we present experimental results on k-closest pair queries to support the fact that our index structure is a better alternative.

1 Introduction

Applications from navigation to mobile networks to multimedia require handling of spatial and multidimensional data. It is paramount for database systems to be able to efficiently answer queries about these data, especially in a dynamic environment.

Many queries on these kind of data are on a single table. These include point location, range, nearest neighbor, and reverse nearest neighbor queries [7]. However, another type of queries involves relating data from multiple tables – a 'join' query in database terms. These queries look for pairs of tuples in different tables that satisfy various conditions. A naive join algorithm that examines all possible pairs is prohibitively expensive. Thus, we need to devise more effective index and algorithm for these queries.

We illustrate various join queries by the following example. Suppose we have a table of residential houses in a certain state, with location information stored as x,y-coordinates. Also, we have a separate table of factories or other sources of pollution, again with location information. Various groups of people, from homeowners to environment workers, need to determine the level of pollution the factories are creating to the residents and determine what actions are needed. We can ask various queries:

1. *(Distance-based) Spatial joins*: for each house, list all factories within 100 miles. If the effect of pollution is negligible beyond 100 miles, potential homeowners can use this to determine the suitability of a house.

2. *k Closest nearest neighbor pairs*: list the top k houses, together with the corresponding closest factory to each house, in the order of closeness to the factory. This can be another metric to measure the effect of pollution, especially if we assume the effect of pollution is non-additive – i.e. the effect of pollution is primarily due to the factory closest to the house. If k equals the total number of houses, this query is also called *all pair nearest neighbors*.

3. *k Closest pairs*: find the top k factory-house pairs ordered by the closeness to one another. This gives us a measure of the seriousness of the effect of individual factory on individual household, and can give environmental workers a priority on which pair to tackle first.

All the above queries require some kind of join. Hence, it is imperative that such queries be performed effectively. As mentioned, the naive algorithm requires examining every pair of objects, which is impractical for large tables. Thus, one would like to use various techniques – such as indexes – to speed up the queries considerably.

Distance-based spatial join has been studied extensively. Many existing join algorithms are based on the R-trees [2, 3], the Seed-trees [9]; or the Breadth-First approach [6]. Other spatial join techniques exist, such as spatial merge-join [11], spatial hash-join [10], size-separation spatial join [8], and scalable sweeping-based spatial join [1]. However, closest pair related join problems have only recently been in the spotlight. For instance, Hjaltason and Samet [5] as well as Corral et al [4] propose various algorithms to solve the k-Closest pair problem. They assume that each data set is indexed using an R^*-tree (or similar index structure). Their methods traverse the indexes to find the closest pairs. This works well in cases where the two data sets do not 'overlap' – i.e. the two data sets reside in completely disjoint regions of a multidimensional space. However, in many real life applications, this assumption is invalid. For instance, in the example above, it is more likely that the houses and the factories are in the same geographic proximity. In such cases, their methods perform poorly. We believe that there is room for significant improvement.

In this paper, we propose a new index structure, the bichromatic Rdnn-Tree (bRdnn-Tree), to solve the closest pair join problem. The structure uses information about nearest neighbors to help prune the search path more effectively. Moreover, the index structure is also very efficient on various types of join queries, such as spatial join, closest nearest neighbor pairs, and all pairs nearest neighbor.

The rest of the paper is organized as follows: Section 2 defines the various problems mentioned above, discusses previous solutions to the closest pair problems, and outlines the potential for improvement. The bRdnn-Tree is presented in Section 3. Section 4 provides experimental results. Section 5 discusses future directions.

2 Problem Definitions and Existing Algorithms

In what follows, we assume that S, T are sets of points in d dimensional space. $D(p, q)$ is the distance between two points p and q. R_S denotes the R-tree containing data set S. For an R-tree, we use N_S to denote a node of the tree containing data set S.

2.1 Problem Definitions

Here we give the formal definitions of the problems we handle in this paper. Our focus is the nearest neighbor related problems. Given two data sets S and T and a query point in one data set S, one can search the nearest neighbor of a point in $p \in S$ in the other data set T. Let us call it the bichromatic nearest neighbor search. Formally, we have the following:

DEFINITION: (Bichromatic Nearest Neighbor Query) Given two data sets S and T of points in some d dimensional space and a query point $q \in S$, the bichromatic nearest neighbor query is to find a point $p \in T$ such that $D(q, x) \geq D(q, p) \quad \forall x \in T$

In the above definition, we call (q, p) a nearest neighbor pair (NN pair) with respect to q. The problem of finding k-closest such pairs with respect to k points in one data set is hence called the k Closest NN pairs.

DEFINITION: (k Closest NN Pairs Query) Given two data sets S and T of points in d dimensional space, the k-closest NN pair query (with respect to S) is to find k points $s_1, s_2, \cdots, s_k \in S$ and the nearest neighbor $t_i \in T$ for each s_i such that $\forall s \in S \setminus \{s_1, \cdots, s_k\}$ and its nearest neighbor t in T we have $D(s, t) \geq D(s_i, t_i) \quad \forall i \in \{1, 2, \cdots, k\}$

In other words, the k-closest NN pair problem with respect to a data set is to find k points in the data set that have smaller nearest neighbor distances than any other points in the same data set. If k is the same as the size of the data set, the problem can also be viewed as the bichromatic version of the all pair nearest neighbor problem. Another common join query is called the k-closest pair problem, which we formally give the definition as follows:

DEFINITION: (k-Closest Pair Join) Given two data sets S and T of points in some d dimensional space, the k-Closest Pairs (k-CPs) of S and T is a collection of k ordered pairs $KCP = \{(s_1, t_1), (s_2, t_2), \cdots, (s_k, t_k)\}$ where $s_i \in S$ and $t_i \in T$ $\forall i \in \{1, 2, \cdots, k\}$, such that for any $(s, t) \in S \times T - KCP$ we have $D(s, t) \geq D(s_i, t_i) \quad \forall i \in \{1, 2, \cdots, k\}$

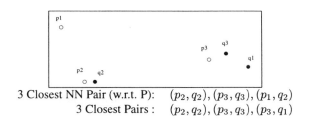

| 3 Closest NN Pair (w.r.t. P): | $(p_2, q_2), (p_3, q_3), (p_1, q_2)$ |
| 3 Closest Pairs : | $(p_2, q_2), (p_3, q_3), (p_3, q_1)$ |

Figure 1. Example: k Closest Pair vs. k Closest NN Pair

Figure 1 shows that the k-closest NN pairs is not necessarily the k closest pairs and vice versa. The main difference is that the closest NN pairs is always with respect to one of the data set involved. For that set, each object can only appear in the result once. For closest pairs queries, there is no such restriction. The difference in applications has been outlined in section 1. However, the two types of queries are closely related to each other, as shown by the following theorem (it will be used in section 3):

THEOREM 2.1 *Given two data sets P and Q of points from some d dimensional space, assume $\{(p_1, q_1), (p_2, q_2), \cdots, (p_k, q_k)\}$ is the k-closest NN pairs with respect to P (or Q) $\forall i \in \{1, 2, \cdots, k\}$, and (p, q) is one of the k Closest Pairs. Then we have*

$$p \in \{p_1, p_2, \cdots, p_k\} \quad (or \ q \in \{q_1, \cdots, q_k\})$$

Proof: Without loss of generality, we assume that $D(p_1, q_1) \leq D(p_2, q_2) \cdots \leq D(p_k, q_k)$ since (p, q) is one of the k-closest pairs in $P \times Q$, it is clear that $D(p, q) \leq D(p_k, q_k)$. Suppose $p \notin \{p_1, p_2, \cdots, p_k\}$, then (p, q) is not an NN pair with respect to p. In other words, q is not the nearest neighbor of p in Q. Assume q' is the nearest neighbor of p in Q, then we have $D(p, q') \leq D(p, q) \leq D(p_k, q_k)$ and hence (p, q') is one of the k-closest NN pairs with respect to p. Therefore, $p \in \{p_1, p_2, \cdots, p_k\}$, a contradiction. This proves that $p \in \{p_1, p_2, \cdots, p_k\}$. Similarly, we can show that $q \in \{q_1, q_2, \cdots, q_k\}$. *QED*

2.2 Existing Algorithms

The significant work in this field has been described in two separate papers. Hjaltason and Samet [5] introduced several incremental distance join algorithms, while Corral et al. [4] introduced various algorithms based on the R-tree family. Due to space limitation we focus on the methods by Corral. The interested reader is directed to [4] for a comparison between the two algorithms.

In [4], it is assumed that for each data set there is an R-tree (or one of its variants) constructed, and the indexes are used to avoid the naive nested-loop join. The basic algorithm traverses the two trees together using a branch-and-bound approach. The search starts at the root of the two trees, and it keeps track of the current best solution (which is ∞ initially). At any stage, if a pair of internal nodes are retrieved, the algorithm examines the bounding rectangles of all pairs of branches (one from each tree) and decides which pairs need to be traversed and which pairs can be pruned; when a pair of leaves is reached, all data in the nodes are examined to update the current solution. This continues until all possible pairs are either traversed or pruned. Various measures are used to decide which pairs to prune: MINMINDIST (lower bound of minimum distance between of the bounding rectangles), MINMAXDIST (upper bound of minimum distance), and MAXMAXDIST (upper bound of maximum distance). These provide bounds for the distances between any pair of objects that are descendents of the nodes. Also, various order of traversal like the Depth-First and the Best-Firest are explored. Furthermore,

the number of available buffers affects the performance of algorithms: small buffer size favors using a priority queue while depth-first traversal benefits from a larger number of buffers.

However, an even more important factor of the performance of the join algorithm, not mentioned in previous papers, is the amount of "overlap" of the data in the two sets. This can be defined as the overlapping area of the bounding rectangles of the two data sets S and T. For example, with their proposed technique, we run experiments joining two 2D data sets with 80,000 data points each. We build an R-tree (with 2K page size) for each data set and apply the join algorithms. Table 1 shows the result:

Overlap %	0%		100%	
k	1	12,500	1	12,500
Pairs compared, DFS	1	21.6	5074.4	5504
Pairs compared, PQ	1	21.6	5073	5312.8
Page faults, DFS	2	14.8	2570.4	2592
Page faults, PQ	2	14.8	3164.2	3320.8

DFS : depth-first search; PQ : Priority queue (160 buffers)
Average number of leaf nodes per tree : 1080

Table 1. Comparison of join performance with different overlap

In table 1, the "pairs compared" corresponds to the total number of pairs of leaf nodes compared. This measures the performance when there is no buffer available. The "page faults" measures the actual cost with LRU buffering. The table shows that the performance of the algorithms vary significantly with respect to the difference in overlap, regardless of whether buffering is available. When the overlap is 100%, practically both trees have to be completely traversed 2-3 times (depending on k and the traversal method). The poor performance is due to the inability of the join algorithm to prune nodes. For example, when the two dataset has 100% overlap, for each node N_1 (with bounding rectangle R_1) in the R^*-tree corresponding to one data set, it is highly likely that there is at least another node N'_1 (with bounding rectangle S_1) in the other R^*-tree such that R_1 and S_1 intersects. In fact, one can expect R_1 to intersect with bounding rectangles of quite a few nodes in the other tree. However, the join algorithms have to examine all pairs of overlapping nodes. This leads to the poor performance of the algorithm. The same effect occurs in the incremental algorithms by Hjaltason and Samet, as their algorithms tranverse the tree based on increasing distance, thus all the overlapping pairs must be traversed.

The above discussion suggests that a new indexing scheme for join queries over multiple data sets is needed.

3 The Index Structure and Algorithms

3.1 Proposed Index Structure: bichromatic Rdnn-Tree (bRdnn-Tree)

As Theorem 2.1 shows, the k-closest pair and the k-closest NN pair problems are closely related. Thus, if we can solve the k-closest NN pair problem effectively, we can use it to find the k-closest pairs. One way to solve the k-closest NN pair problem is to try to pre-compute and store the nearest neighbor information in an index. We propose a new index structure, the bichromatic Rdnn-Tree (bRdnn-Tree), that dynamically maintains the nearest neighbor pair information. The structure is similar to the Rdnn-tree for the Reverse Nearest Neighbor problem [12]. Recall that the reverse nearest neighbor (RNN) of a point p in a data set S is a collection of points in S that have p as their nearest neighbor. In this case, as we are given two data sets, we construct two trees, one for each data set. In what follows, we denote them as the Red tree and the Blue tree. For a point p in R, $NN_S(p)$ denotes its nearest neighbors in data set S, and $RNN_S(p)$ its reverse nearest neighbors in S.

In each tree, a leaf node contains entries of the form (pt, dnn), where pt refers to a d-dimensional point in the data set and dnn is the distance between the NN pair with respect to pt. In other words, the dnn of a leaf entry in the Blue tree is the distance from a blue point pt to its nearest neighbor in the Red tree. Formally, for a blue point b we have $dnn = dnn_R(b) = \min_{r \in R} D(b, r)$. The dnn can be defined similarly for any red points.

A non-leaf node contains an array of branches of the form $(ptr, Rect, max\_dnn, min\_dnn)$; ptr is the address of a child node in the tree. If ptr points to a leaf node, $Rect$ is the minimum bounding rectangle of all points in the leaf node. If ptr points to a non-leaf node, $Rect$ is the minimum bounding rectangle of all rectangles that are entries in the child node; max_dnn (min_dnn) is the maximum (minimum) distance of each point to its nearest neighbor in the other data set. More specifically, for a node N of the Red tree containing data set R we have $max\_dnn = \max_{p \in N}\{dnn_B(p)\}$; ($min\_dnn = \min_{p \in N}\{dnn_B(p)\}$). Similarly, we can define max_dnn (min_dnn) for any node in the Blue tree.

3.2 Algorithms

Insertion and Deletion When a point p' is to be inserted into the Red tree, we first perform an NN and a RNN search on the Blue tree to find the nearest neighbor ($NN_B(p')$) and the reverse nearest neighbor of p' ($RNN_B(p')$) respectively. With $NN_B(p')$, we can compute $dnn(p')$ to create the entry for p'. It is easy to see that $RNN_b(p')$ are the points that are affected as they are the points in the Blue

tree that have the new red point p' as their nearest neighbor. Typically, their dnn field and hence the max_dnn and min_dnn in their parent nodes need to be updated. Therefore, we have a pre-insertion phase to search the blue tree for $NN_B(p')$ and $RNN_B(p')$ for a red point p' before we insert p' into the Red tree, and vice versa. We update the entries for $RNN_B(p')$ and their parent nodes while searching for $NN_B(p')$ and hence finish two tasks in one pass. Formally, we have the following Pre-insert algorithm.

Algorithm 1 Pre-insert (blueNode n, redPoint p')
Input: The root n of the blue tree and a red point p'
Output: the adjusted blue tree and $NN_B(p')$
1) Initialize the candidate nearest neighbor c
2) If n is a leaf node, then for each entry (pt, dnn) do: If $D(p', pt) < D(p', c)$, then let $c = pt$; If $D(p', pt) < dnn$, output pt and return $D(p', pt)$
3) If n is a non-leaf node, then for each branch $Bch = (ptr, Rect, max\_dnn, min\_dnn)$ do: If $D(p', Rect) < max\_dnn$ or $D(p', Rect) < D(p', c)$ call Pre-Insert(ptr, p'); If ptr was adjusted, adjust max_dnn and min_dnn for Bch.

After finding $NN_B(p')$, the nearest blue neighbor of a red point p', it is straightforward to insert the point p' in the Red tree since each tree is essentially an R-tree with embedded "bichromatic" nearest neighbor distance. Here we formally present the following Insertion algorithm.

Algorithm 2 Insert (blueNode bn, redNode rn, redPoint p')
Input: Root nodes bn rn and red point p' to be inserted
Output: the red tree with p' inserted and blue tree adjusted
1) Pre-Insert(bn, p')
2) Call R^*-tree insertion algorithm to insert entry $(p', dnn_S(p'))$ into rn

---

Now we turn to deletion. Notice that deleting a point from the Red (Blue) tree also affects the reverse nearest neighbors in the Blue (Red) tree. In order to maintain the integrity of the trees while deleting a red (blue) point p'', an NN search needs to be done for each point in $RNN_B(p'')$ ($RNN_R(p'')$). As with the Rdnn-tree, we can do a Batch-NN search[12], finding the nearest neighbors for multiple query points in one pass. To remove the point, the standard R^*-tree deletion algorithm can be applied.

Algorithm 3 Delete (redPoint p'')
Input: a red point p'' to be deleted
Output: p'' deleted red tree and blue tree adjusted
1) Call R^*-tree algorithm to delete p'' from red tree
2) Call RNN-Search(p'') to find $RNN_B(p'')$
3) Call Batch-NN-Search($RNN_B(p'')$) on the red tree
4) Adjust the dnn for each point in $RNN_B(p'')$ and propagate the change up to the root

Spatial Join Any standard distance-based spatial join algorithms can be applied to the bRdnn-tree. Moreover, the min_dnn value (the minimum distance of any point under the subtree to its nearest neighbor in the other tree) in each node provides extra pruning power. Assuming d being the distance threshold for a spatial join query, if for a node N we have $min\_dnn > d$, then N can be pruned since no pairs with distance less that d can be formed from any point contained under N.

k Closest NN Pairs Since we pre-compute the "bichromatic" nearest neighbor distance for each point while building the bRdnn-Tree, searching for the k-closest NN pairs in our index structure is straight forward. Each non-leaf node contains a number min_dnn, the minimum of the distances from each point in the subtree to it's nearest neighbor in the other data set. In a leaf node, each point is accompanied by such a nearest neighbor distance of its own. On an index structure with the above properties, a branch-and-bound approach for the k-closest NN pairs is natural. During the search, k candidate pairs are kept in a priority queue with the pair of largest distance on the top. Starting from the root of one tree with empty candidate pairs, select one branch with the smallest min_dnn to descend the tree. Prune any branch whose min_dnn field is larger than the distance of the pair on the queue top. Here we formally give the algorithm for the k-closest NN pairs as follows:

Algorithm 4 k Closest NN Pairs
1) Start from the root of the red tree with an empty candidate queue.
2) Sort the branches in ascending order according to the min_dnn field.
3) Recursively visit each branch in the order. Prune the branches that have min_dnn larger than the distance of the pair on the queue top.
4) If a leaf node is reached, retriete each entry. If the dnn of the entry is smaller than that of queue top element, insert it into the queue.
5) Repeat the above steps on the blue tree.

k Closest Pairs From Theorem 2.1 we can see that the k-closest NN pairs with respect to each data set gives us the end points for the k-closest pairs. To find the k-closest pairs, we first find the k-closest NN pairs (as shown above), then apply the following method:

Given two data sets R and S, after performing the k-closest NN pair search in the bRdnn-Tree containing S, we get k NN pairs $(p_1, q_1), (p_2, q_2), \cdots, (p_k, q_k)$ with respect to R, in ascending order according to the distance $D(p_i, q_i)$ for $i \in \{1, 2, \cdots, k\}$. Note that for $i \neq j$, p_i and p_j are not necessarily different. Hence, if we let $P = \{p'_1, \cdots, p'_{k_s}\}$ ($\subseteq R$) be the set of distinct points among $p_1, p_2, \cdots, p_k$, we have $k_s \leq k$. Similarly, if we interchange R and S, we can get the corresponding subset Q in S such that $Q = \{q'_1, q'_2, \cdots, q'_{k_t}\}$. With these two sets of points P and Q, we can derive the k-closest pairs. By theorem 2.1, we know that if (p, q) is one of the k-closest pairs, then $p \in P$ and $q \in Q$. Hence, to find k-closest pairs in R and S, we only need to examine possible pairs from P and Q to build the k pairs incrementally in the following way. For any two points $p'_i \in P$ and $q'_j \in Q$ where $1 \leq i \leq k_s$ and $1 \leq j \leq k_t$:

- Case 1: (p'_i, q'_j) is an NN pair. If it is the kth pair, stop the search. Otherwise, for all $i' < i$ and $j' < j$, consider $(p'_{i'}, q'_{j'})$. If it is better than the worst of the current candidate solution set, insert it into the candidate solution.

- Case 2: (p'_i, q'_j) is not an NN pair. If it is better than the worst of the current candidate solution set, insert it into the candidate solution.

Algorithm 5 k Closest Pairs
1) Perform k NN pair search on the blue tree to find the subset P of points that form the k NN pairs.
2) Repeat the above on the red tree to find the corresponding subset Q
3) If (p'_i, q'_j) is an NN pair, then do:
   If it's the kth pair, stop the search.
   Else, for all $i' < i$ and $j' < j$ do:
     If $(p'_{i'}, q'_{j'})$ is better than the worst of the current candidate solution set, insert it into the candidate solution.
4) If (p'_i, q'_j) is not an NN pair, than if it is better than the worst of the current candidate solution set, insert it into the candidate solution.

Theorem 2.1 shows that, in any of k-closest pair (p, q), point p and q come from the k-closest NN pairs. Some of the k closest pairs are NN pairs while some are not. In the above algorithm, we search for the non-NN pairs from points in the NN pairs to find the k-closest pairs. The worst case is a nested loop of k iterations. For large k, this may not be desirable. However, for small k, our experiments show that this algorithm is much more efficient than the existing solutions, especially when the data spaces overlap.

4 Experimental results

This section presents the results of our experiments. We focus on the k-closest pair query as we can compare with previously designed algorithms. Also note that, when k is small enough so that the k closest NN pairs can be put in the buffer, the k closest pair and the k closest NN pair query have the same number of disk accesses.

We ran our tests on a machine with two 500-MHz Pentium II processors with 512 MB RAM under SCO UNIX. For comparison, we implemented the R*-tree and both algorithms mentioned in [4], the depth-first branch and bound (DFS) (called sorted-distance recursive algorithm in [4]) and the heap algorithm. For those algorithms, we also included a LRU buffer[1], and measured the number of page faults. For the bRdnn-Tree, since we never have to revisit a leaf node, we do not have to rely on the buffer (except one to store the solution).

We experimented with different types of data sets. They included uniformly distributed data, clustered data, as well as real geographical 2D data from the US National Mapping Information web site (URL: http://mappings.usgs.gov/www/gnis/). For each type, we generated data sets of various sizes. For each size, we generated five different pairs of data and ran experiments on them. The average number of leaf node access is the main measure of search cost. We also measured the total number of nodes accessed. However, the two measures behave similarly, so in this paper we mainly show the leaf accesses.

4.1 Uniformly distributed data sets

We first present the results on uniform data with 100% overlap. We measure the number of leaf page faults (i.e. number of page faults caused by reading data from disk). We have similar results when we consider the total page faults (including non-leaf pages). Figure 2 shows the results for the three different approaches: the bRdnn-Tree, the depth-first-search with R^*-tree (DFS), and the heap algorithm with R^*-tree (Heap). The DFS and Heap algorithms are given a buffer of 10 or 80 pages.

From figure 2, we can see that our index structure consistently outperforms both the depth-first and the heap algorithm, even when they are given a 10 or 80 page buffer

---
[1]Strictly speaking, it is level-wise LRU buffer – i.e. each level of a tree has an LRU buffer

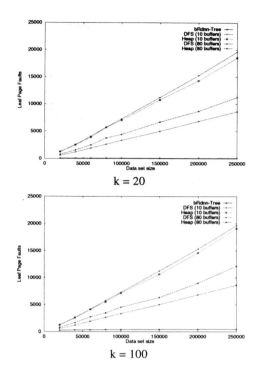

k = 20

k = 100

Figure 2. Comparison of performance for 2D data (fixed k)

advantage. When k is small, where our algorithm is most beneficial, the savings can be of a couple of order of magnitude. For instance, with $k = 20$ and data set size 80,000, the depth-first search takes more than 2,600 leaf page faults while our index requires less than 80 leaf accesses. (The numbers are similar on total node accesses).

As we mentioned, the R^*-tree based algorithms fail due to the overlap between the two data sets. This implies the upper-level nodes cannot be pruned, as each node intersects with some other nodes of the other index. In fact, in all the experiments conducted on overlapping data sets, every node of the two R^*-trees has to be accessed. However, by storing the nearest neighbor distance, our method can prune each bRdnn-Tree index separately at a high level. Thus, it outperforms the R^*-tree algorithm by a large margin.

Also note that in our approach, one page is retrieved at a time. In that page, the dnn or the max_dnn of each leaf entry or branch is compared with the current candidates. In the R^*-tree algorithm, a pair of nodes from each tree is read and the distances between pairs of branches or leaf entries are computed before compared to the current candidate solution set. This is a nested loop and hence computationally expensive.

From the figure, we also notice that the performance of the R^*-tree algorithms is sensitive to the number of buffers available. However, as we mentioned earlier, our index is very robust in terms of buffer dependency.

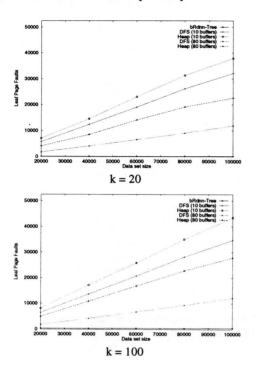

k = 20

k = 100

Figure 3. Comparison of performance for 4D data (fixed k)

Next, we tested the applicability of the index in multimedia applications in higher dimensions by experimenting with 4D data, Figure 3 shows that the bRdnn-Tree still outperforms the existing R^*-tree algorithms consistently.

The performance with varied k is also measured. Figure 4 shows the results for 2D data. (Similar results are obtained for 4D data sets.)

Comparing the results, we see that for reasonably sized k, the bRdnn-Tree performs exceptionally well. With overlapping data sets, even for a small k, both R^*-tree based algorithms, DFS and Heap, need to search the whole tree. This is because, with overlapping regions, each node from one tree very likely overlaps with a node from the other tree. This means that this pair cannot be pruned away (because the distance between the bounding regions is 0). Thus even if $k = 1$, one has to traverse both trees completely. On the other hand, when k is small, the pruning power of the nearest neighbor distance is very strong. Thus, our algorithm prevails when k is not too large.

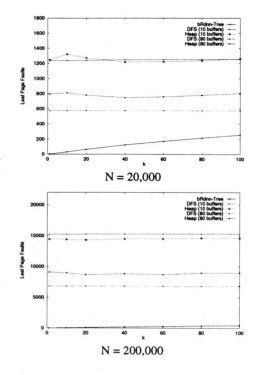

N = 20,000

N = 200,000

Figure 4. Comparison of performance for 2D data (varying k)

We also ran experiments on larger values of k. Typically, the performance of the R^*-tree catches up with our structure when k is around 10,000 if there is a large number of buffers. For instance, with data set size equal to 200,000, the R^*-tree only catches up when $k = 10,000$. Even then, it requires some buffer size (in this case, 80 buffer pages). For smaller buffer size (like 10-20 buffers), the bRdnn-Tree beats the R^*-tree based algorithms.

We also experimented with non-overlapping data sets. In this case, the R^*-tree based algorithms become more effective, since many branches can be pruned away at the root level (as the bounding rectangles are non-overlapping). This is true when k is large. However, when k is small, the performance of the two structures are similar.

4.2 2D clustered data sets

We also experimented with clustered data as they arise often in spatial databases. For instance, locations of houses are often highly clustered.

In our experiments, we created pairs of data sets. Each set contains 5 small clusters of radius 10 inside a 1000 x 1000 box. The center of a cluster was randomly generated.

	Leaf Page Fault		Total Page Fault	
	$k = 20$	$k = 100$	$k = 20$	$k = 100$
bRdnn-Tree	2 - 4	6 - 11	6 - 8	10 - 15
DFS (80 buffer)	3 - 1090	5 - 1091	7 - 1120	9 - 1121
Heap (80 buffer)	2 - 1090	3 - 1091	6 - 1120	7 - 1121

Table 2. Performance with 2D clustered data (N = 80,000)

At the same time, we also ensure that no two clusters in any pair of data sets intersect with each other. For each data set size, we generated 5 separate pairs of data sets and ran tests on them. Table 2 shows some representative results with a data set of 80,000 points.

While the bRdnn-Tree produces consistently excellent results, the search costs on the R^*-tree with the DFS and the Heap algorithm vary greatly. This is due to the bounding regions of the data set, which may or may not overlap in our data sets. When they do not overlap, the performances of the various methods are comparable. However, if the bounding regions overlap significantly, then even though the data is well clustered, the R^*-tree based algorithms still take much longer to execute. Thus, we can see the robustness of the bRdnn-Tree with regard to some non-uniform data distributions.

4.3   2D Real data set

We also experimented on the US geographical data set. It contains more than 160,000 populated places in the USA, represented by latitude and longitude coordinates. We split the set into pairs of smaller sets of various sizes. Each pair of the data sets has no location in common.

We ran tests on the various data sets and the results are shown in figure 5. We can see that the bRdnn-Tree once again outperforms the R^*-tree based algorithms.

4.4   Index maintenance

While the bRdnn-tree outperforms the R^*-tree based algorithms in queries, it does require extra cost in terms of index maintenance, like insertion. This is because inserting a point into the bRdnn-tree requires finding the reverse nearest neighbors of the point to be inserted, which means one has to traverse both trees, as opposed to the case of the R^*-tree, where only one tree need to be inserted.

We measure the cost of index maintenance by inserting 2D points one at a time. We measure the average cost of insertion for the last 1,000 points. We also assume that there is a 10-page buffer for each tree. (For comparison's sake, for 200,000 data points, each bRdnn-tree has more than 4,000 nodes). The results in Table 3 are the averages of 5 different data sets.

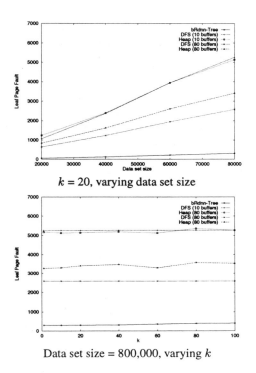

$k = 20$, varying data set size

Data set size = 800,000, varying k

Figure 5. Comparison of performance on real data set

From Table 3 we see that an insertion into the bRdnn-tree takes around 2.4 times that of the R^*-tree. However, this is easily offset in the case when the two data sets overlap, as the bRdnn-tree requires an order of magnitude less time than the standard R^*-tree based joins.

4.5   Is an index worthwhile?

So far, we have been comparing the bRdnn-tree with the standard R^*-tree. However, a more fundamental question needs to be answered: is an index necessary at all?

If both data sets are static, one obvious option is to pre-compute the result once and store it in a separate file for

Data points	60,000	100,000	150,000	200,000	250,000
R^*-tree	1.7072	1.8233	1.8944	1.922	1.9449
bRdnn-tree	4.0556	4.2388	4.2895	4.6779	4.7525
ratio bRdnn-tree/R^*-tree	2.38	2.325	2.264	2.433	2.44

Table 3. Comparison of insertion cost for 2D data

later retrival. This is especially useful if an upper bound of k can be reasonably estimated or assumed. For instance, for 2D data, a page of size 2K can store around 125 pairs of points. Thus, if we assume $k \leq 500$, we can run the nested loop algorithm once and store the top 500 pairs. Subsequently, all queries with $k \leq 500$ require only reading four pages, cheaper than any indexing methods. Moreover, for small data sets, a simple nested loop is typically less costly than building the two indexes from scratch. Thus, in such cases, it is better to apply a simple nested loop for the first query and then cache the results.

However, when the data set size grows, the cost of a simple nested loop query grows very fast – $O(n \times m)$, where m and n are the sizes of the data sets. However, the cost of building the index grows in a much slower pace. Figure 6 illustrates this fact.

We performed tests with different data sets of up to 3,000,000 points and built the tree with 10 buffers for each bRdnn-tree. We measure the cost per insertion. Figure 6 (b) shows that the cost per insertion grows logarithmically. As mentioned previously, an insertion requires both a reverse nearest neighbor search and placing the point in the corresponding tree. The cost of the latter is proportional to the height of the tree. The former depends on the cost of finding the reverse nearest neighbor of the point to be inserted. We observe that the number of neighbors is small, and the reverse nearest neighbor search typically requires traversing only a couple of branches of the tree. Thus, when the data set size becomes large, it is worthwhile to build the index, instead of using the nested loop, even if it is just for precomputing results.

Now we turn our attention to the dynamic case. One can still decide to simply precompute and cache the list of current k closest pairs. However, when a new point is inserted, we need to compare it with all the points of the other set and update the list accordingly. Here, one needs to read one of the data set sequentially. This is costly when the data set becomes large, as illustrated by table 4.

To interpret the results of table 4, let's assume that a new query comes after 250 points (1 page of data for 2K page size) have been inserted into one table. If we precompute and cache the results without an index, then we have to compare the pairwise distances between the new points and the existing table. The cost is that of a linear scan on one table, which corresponds to the third row in table 4. In order to

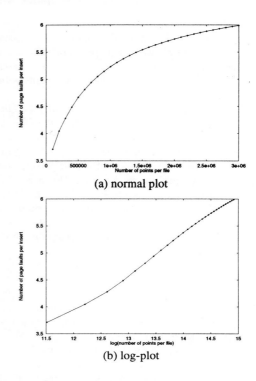

(a) normal plot

(b) log-plot

Figure 6. Per insertion cost of building the bRdnn-tree

use the index, one needs to do 250 seperate insertions to the index. This corresponds to the second row of the table. As it can be seen from the table, when the database becomes large, the index becomes a far more cheaper choice. Notice that querying the index takes about a few hundred page accesses, for a million data points – still much cheaper than a sequential scan. Thus, it is crucial in the dynamic case to maintain an index.

In summary, in a relatively static environment with a relatively small data set, it is appropriate to use the naive nested-loop algorithm and cache the closest pairs. However, in a dynamic environment or with large amount of data, it is preferable to use the bRdnn-tree.

148

Data set size ($\times 1000$)	100	500	1,000	1,500	2,000
Average Cost per insert (bRdnn-tree)	4.2388	5.4905	6.0437	6.2576	6.4212
Cost for inserting 250 points to the bRdnn-tree	1059.7	1372.62	1510.92	1574.4	1605.3
Cost for sequential scan of a table	391	1954	3907	5860	7813

Table 4. Comparing indexing vs. caching cost for dynamic case

5 Conclusion and future work

In this paper, we present the bRdnn-Tree - a new index structure suitable for many kinds of join queries. The index structure keeps track of the nearest neighbor distance for each data point. This is shown to be a powerful pruning method for various kinds of queries, such as k-closest pairs and k-closest NN pairs. We experimented with k-closest pair queries and the results show that our index is efficient as well as robust – it can handle various distributions as well as work with limited resources.

Our immediate attention is to explore the possibility of efficiently bulk-loading the bRdnn-Tree. As we stated, for large data sets, it is worthwhile to build the index. Currently in our experiments, we built the tree by inserting the data point by point. If the data set is given beforehand, there should be many ways we can make use of it to build the index faster.

One other direction we would look at is to incorporate our structure into a query optimization and automatic index maintenance environment. As stated, our structure works extremely well when the data sets to be joined are overlapping, while the R^*-tree works well when the data is non-overlapping. Thus, an interesting question is how our index can provide hints and information to the system as to when to use or build such a structure and when to use the R^*-tree instead. This will have tremendous impact on automatic database tuning and other query optimization processes.

Acknowledgments

We would like to thank Diane Mittelmeier and Janis Dublin for proofreading the manuscript.

References

[1] L. Arge, O. Procopiuc, S. Ramaswamy, T. Suel, and J. S. Vitter. Scalable sweeping-based spatial join. In *Proceedings of the Twenty-fourth International Conference on Very Large Databases*, pages 570–581, 1998.

[2] T. Brinkhoff, H.-P. Kriegel, R. Schneider, and B. Seeger. Multi-step processing of spatial joins. In *Proceedings of the 1994 ACM SIGMOD International Conference on Management of Data*, pages 197–208, Minneapolis, MN, May 1994.

[3] T. Brinkhoff, H.-P. Kriegel, and B. Seeger. Efficient processing of spatial joins using R-trees. In *Proceedings of the 1993 ACM SIGMOD International Conference on Management of Data*, pages 237–246, Washington, D.C., May 1993.

[4] A. Corral, Y. Manolopoulos, Y. Theodoridis, and M. Vassilakopoulos. Closest pair queries in spatial databases. In *Proceedings of the 2000 ACM SIGMOD International Conference on Management of Data*, pages 189–200, May 2000.

[5] G. R. Hjaltason and H. Samet. Incremental distance join algorithms for spatial databases. In *Proceedings of the 1998 ACM SIGMOD International Conference on Management of Data*, pages 237–248, 1998.

[6] Y.-W. Huang, N. Jing, and E. A. Rundensteiner. Spatial joins using r-trees: Breadth-first traversal with global optimizations. In *Proceedings 23th International Conference on Very Large Data Bases*, pages 396–405, Aug. 1997.

[7] F. Korn and S. Muthukrishnan. Influence sets based on reverse nearest neighbor queries. In *Proceedings of 2000 ACM SIGMOD International Conference on Management of Data*, pages 201–212, May 2000.

[8] N. Koudas and K. C. Sevcik. Size separation spatial join. In *Proceedings of 1997 ACM SIGMOD International Conference on Management of Data*, pages 324–335, 1997.

[9] M.-L. Lo and C. V. Ravishankar. Spatial joins using seeded trees. In *Proceedings of the 1994 ACM SIGMOD International Conference on Management of Data*, pages 209–220, Minneapolis, MN, May 1994.

[10] M.-L. Lo and C. V. Ravishankar. Spatial hash-joins. In *Proceedings of the 1996 ACM SIGMOD International Conference on Management of Data*, pages 247–258, Montreal, Quebec, Canada, 4–6 June 1996.

[11] J. M. Patel and D. J. DeWitt. Partition based spatial-merge join. In *Proceedings of the 1996 ACM SIGMOD International Conference on Management of Data*, pages 259–270, 1996.

[12] C. Yang and K.-I. Lin. An index structure for efficient reverse nearest neighbor queries. In *Proceedings of the 17th IEEE International Conf. on Data Engineering*, pages 485–492, Apr. 2001.

Management of Multiply Represented Geographic Entities

Anders Friis-Christensen[1,2]   David Skogan [3,4]   Christian S. Jensen[1]   Gerhard Skagestein [3]   Nectaria Tryfona[1,5]

[1]Department of Computer Science, Aalborg University, Denmark, {afc,csj}@cs.auc.dk
[2] Product Development, National Survey and Cadastre, Denmark
[3]Department of Informatics, University of Oslo, Norway, gerhard@ifi.uio.no
[4]SINTEF Telecom and Informatics, Norway, david.skogan@sintef.no
[5]Computer Technology Institute, Athens, Greece, tryfona@cti.gr

Abstract

Multiple representation of geographic information occurs when a real-world entity is represented more than once in the same or different databases. In this paper, we propose a new approach to the modeling of multiply represented entities and the relationships among the entities and their representations. A Multiple Representation Management System is outlined that can manage multiple representations consistently over a number of autonomous databases. Central to our approach is the Multiple Representation Schema Language that is used to configure the system. It provides an intuitive and declarative means of modeling multiple representations and specifying rules that are used to maintain consistency, match objects representing the same entity, and restore consistency if necessary.

Keywords: data modeling, geographic information system, multiple representation, consistency rules, data integration, data management

1 Introduction

Geographic information is needed in a wide range of application domains. This information is often managed independently by various parties and in specialized geographic information systems (GISs). Often, the same real-world *entity* (e.g., a river or a building) is represented by different *objects* in the same or different databases[1]. This phenomenon is called multiple representation, and is a key problem in managing geographic information [3].

Multiple representation may be caused by different approaches in data collection, different semantic definitions, varying levels of detail, or differing application purposes. It may be intended, in that an entity is represented at more than one scale, e.g., the same road can be represented in

---

[1]Here object is used when an entity is represented in a database.

the scale of 1:10,000 and 1:50,000, or it may be accidental, e.g., when two unrelated databases represent the same entity. In both cases, no tradition exists for maintaining relations among objects representing the same entity, and this may lead to inconsistencies. For example, this happens when a new building is added to a register database, but not to a corresponding topographical map database.

Geographic databases are often developed with a specific application in mind. Data are either captured or copied from another source database and are possibly altered to fit the application. Traditionally, little concern is given to the fact that the source database may change. Since it is not feasible to import the complete source database every time a change occurs, procedures for detecting changes and updating dependent objects should be developed.

Several characteristics of geographic information complicates the process of keeping objects consistent in a multiple representation context. An example is that the spatial extent of an entity may vary depending on the given abstraction. The spatial extent is a complex attribute, e.g., a point, line, or polygon. Consider a city which can be represented as either a point or a polygon depending on the abstraction level used. Fundamental for the representation of geographic information is the scale. Entities may be represented at different scales, which again influences the level of detail of an object being represented. To ensure consistency in a multiple representation context, it is necessary to specify the relationship between the geographic objects. Since these relationships seldom are exact, we need to utilize generalization functions and spatial or topological operators to bridge the gaps among the different abstraction levels. A factor that complicates this process is the varying accuracy of the objects that is to be compared.

The National Survey and Cadastre in Denmark is responsible for a wide range of geographic databases. Previous administrative reorganizations and decisions have led to a range of independent geographic databases describing the same entities at different scales for various juridical and planning purposes. Thus, a need exists for an effective approach to the management of multiply represented geographic entities. To address this need, we introduce the notion of a Multiple Representation Management System (MRMS), the purpose of which is to maintain consistency over selected autonomous databases storing geographic information. The problem of multiple representation is here studied in the context of geographic information. However, it is our belief that the general principles of an MRMS may be applied to other subject areas as well. In connection with the MRMS, we present a Multiple Representation Schema Language (MRSL) that allows users to model multiply represented entities, and to specify consistency and consistency restoration rules in a Multiple Representation Schema (MRSchema). The MRMS operates according to an MRSchema, and it protects prior investments in application development and employee training by operating nonintrusively on top of existing database management systems. A system fulfilling these requirements will ensure geographic representation databases with higher data quality.

Our contributions are threefold:

- We develop a novel concept for modeling multiply represented entities and their consistent representations.
- We outline the Multiple Representation Management System.
- We describe the Multiple Representation Schema Language in detail.

The MRSL is based on an extension to the Unified Modeling Language (UML) and on UML's accompanying Object Constraint Language (OCL).

We assume that the objects representing the same entity (called representation objects) exhibit semantic similarities that enable us to model their correspondences. It is fundamental to our approach to describe how the objects correspond to the entity they represent, rather than to describe the correspondence among objects that represent the same entity. We thus introduce a new type of object that represents the entity (called an integration object), and we describe the correspondence between the integration object and its representation objects. The representation objects can then be seen as "roles" of the integration objects. The need to be able to model multiple representations and roles of geographic entities is described in previous work [9].

Multiple representation of geographic entities has been subject to research especially in the field of cartographic and model based generalization [27]. Kilpeläinen [14] investigates the principles of a system of databases called a multiple representation database. Her work focuses on generalization where there is an exact dependency among representation objects, whereas we focus on multiple representation from a more general point of view.

A subfield of multiple representation databases concerns multi-scale databases. Jones et al. [12] propose a single multi-scale database that is capable of storing geographic objects with multiple geometries. This approach requires an integrated database and does not take into account heterogeneous independent databases. Another approach by Devogele et al. [7] bears similarities with ours. They propose a multi-scale database that maintains scale-transition relationships between objects at different scales. However, they focus mainly on integration and only consider relationships between pairs of objects, whereas our approach handles consistency among more than two representation objects. A current research initiative is the MurMur project, described by Spaccapietra et al. [24, 23]. Its focus is to extend commercial data management software (DBMS or GIS) to support multiple representation, which is similar to our goal. However, no result of this work has been published yet.

The paper is organized as follows. Section 2 presents an example to be used throughout the paper. Section 3 describes the MRMS, and Section 4 describes the MRSL, which is the main contribution of the paper. Finally Section 5 concludes and identifies future work.

2 Case Study

The following section presents an example that illustrates the challenge of managing multiple representation. Excerpts of three databases with their respective schemas in UML are shown in Figure 1. We assume that the reader is familiar with the UML notation [2].

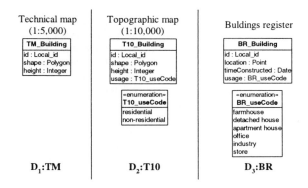

Figure 1. Representation Classes

The scopes of the different databases are described as the follows:

- The technical map database (TM) is used as a digital basis for administrative considerations and register information. It is based on aerial photo interpretation and on-site registrations. All buildings greater than 10m² are stored as polygons. Updates happen regularly and whenever administrative changes occur.

- The topographic map database, 1:10,000, (T10) is used for analysis purposes and furthermore provides source data for the production of maps in smaller scales. It is based on aerial-photo interpretation. All buildings greater than 25m² are stored as polygons, but with less geometric detail than in the technical map database. Buildings smaller than 25m² are not represented. Updates occur every fifth year.

- The buildings register (BR) gives access to various kinds of juridical information about buildings. A building is stored as a point and defined by its usage. Only buildings of a certain size are registered, i.e., small sheds and outbuildings are not registered. Updates occur regularly.

The classes in the three schemas describe the same entity. Because their objects represent an entity in a specific database, we call these classes representation classes (r-classes). The r-classes all have spatial attributes. The `shape` is of the spatial type polygon and the `location` is of the spatial type point. The attribute domains for the `usage` attribute in T10_BUILDING and BR_BUILDING are based on two different enumerations. The `height` attribute in T10_BUILDING is in meters above sea level, whereas the `height` attribute in TM_BUILDING is the exact height of the building. Finally there is an attribute `timeConstructed` in the BR_BUILDING, which tells us when the building was constructed.

The inexpedience in this multiple representation scenario is that the three databases have been developed separately. There is for example no explicit correspondence between the usage of a building in T10 and BR, even though precise information about the usage exists in BR and could be used in T10 instead of using aerial photo interpretation to resolve the usage. If we can describe the exact correspondence and ensure consistency between these two representations, it would save maintenance efforts and would improve data quality.

An example of building objects can be seen in Figure 2. Here we have a building in TM and the same building in T10 with less detail. In BR, two building objects exist because the extent of the building overlaps two different properties. The `usage` in BR is "store" and "office", respectively. In T10 the `usage` is "non-residential". The height of the building location in T10 is 50 meters above sea level, whereas the exact height of the building itself in TM is 5 meters. The example uncovers several potential consistency requirements:

1. The shape of the building in T10 should be a simplification of the corresponding building in TM.

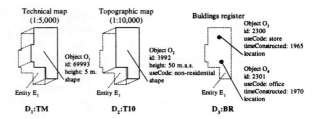

Figure 2. Examples of Building Objects

2. The location of the building in BR should be inside the shape of the corresponding building in TM.

3. The height of the building in T10 should correspond to the sum of the height of the terrain and the building in TM.

4. The usecode enumeration in T10 should correspond to the enumeration in BR. Since two different value domains exist, transformation from one to the other is needed.

These requirements are later specified in a Multiple Representation Schema, which can be used to configure the Multiple Representation Management System described next.

3 Multiple Representation Management System

The aim of this section is to present the motivation and context of our approach. We do this by describing a Multiple Representation Management System (MRMS). It is not our intention to describe the system in detail, but rather to introduce important requirements to such a system.

The main purpose of the MRMS is to actively maintain multiply represented entities with respect to a set of consistency rules. The MRMS can be seen as a loosely coupled, federated database system [21], as it is a collection of cooperating, but autonomous component database systems. The component database systems encapsulate the representation databases. We use the term representation object (r-object) to refer to an object stored in a representation database. The MRMS is loosely coupled since it does not require full control over the representation databases, and neither does it require a complete integrated federated schema. A federated schema usually provides an integrated view of the underlying representation databases. The purpose of the MRMS, however, is different and its schema is called the Multiple Representation Schema (MRSchema). Related work can be found in the field of distributed integrity constraint maintenance [11, 13].

The MRSchema is central to the MRMS. This schema defines a number of consistency, matching, and restoration rules expressed in the Multiple Representation Schema Language (MRSL) specified in Section 4. The representation databases are assumed to be part of GISs that are maintained by independent parties. As a result, it is technically and politically difficult, if not impossible, to change the schemas or the data manipulation interfaces of the representation databases to accommodate the MRMS. Therefore, the MRMS must operate on top of the representation databases and must be non-intrusive so that the autonomies of the representation databases are maintained.

We identify the following requirements as essential for the management of multiple representations. The MRMS must:

- Be configurable according to the rules defined in the MRSchema.

- Be able to match r-objects located in different representation databases and identify multiply represented entities according to the matching rules stated in the MRSchema.

- Provide a repository over the multiply represented entities in order to keep track of the entities that are consistent and those that are not.

- Evaluate the consistency rules with respect to a multiply represented entity.

- Monitor the representation databases for changes to the r-objects that may affect the consistency of the multiply represented entities managed by the MRMS.

- Send requests for consistency restoration actions to the relevant representation database when an inconsistency is detected. The requests are based on the restoration rules given in the MRSchema.

The MRMS will maintain an acceptable level of consistency among the representation databases. The MRMS also needs efficient access to the rules expressed in the MRSchema to be operational. Since the MRMS is non-intrusive, the consistency restoration actions must be forwarded to the representation databases. Based on the type of the restoration action, it is up to the representation database manager to decide whether the request can be performed automatically or whether it should be handled manually.

Figure 3 shows the architecture of an MRMS. It consists of six components and is associated with a set of component database systems containing representation databases $D_1, \ldots, D_n$. The MRSchema component represents the MRSchema, which defines the multiply represented entities to be managed. The Multiple Representation Engine is the main processing component and is responsible for evaluating the consistency rules given by the MRSchema. It uses the MR Repository to store necessary information about the multiply represented entities managed, and their

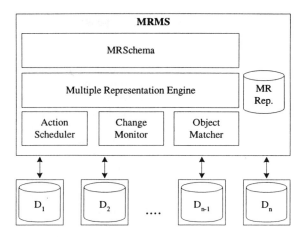

Figure 3. Example MRMS Architecture

current consistency state. The Multiple Representation Engine uses the Object Matcher, Change Monitor and Action Scheduler helper components, to interact with the representation databases. The Object Matcher is responsible for finding corresponding representation objects in the underlying databases that form multiply represented entities. The Change Monitor component is responsible for monitoring the representation databases for changes. If a change occurs, that may lead to an inconsistent state, it notifies the Multiple Representation Engine, which re-evaluates the consistency rules for the respective multiply represented entity. The Action Scheduler is used if an inconsistent is detected. It is mainly responsible for dispatching consistency restoration action requests to the underlying representation databases.

4 Multiple Representation Schema Language

This section presents the multiple representation schema language (MRSL) that is used to model multiply represented entities with consistency rules, matching rules, and restoration rules. We first present the main concepts behind the language. Then the semantics of the most important constructs are explained together with two concrete language syntaxes, a graphical one and a lexical one. The graphical language syntax is based UML and the lexical language syntax is based on OCL [26]. UML and OCL are chosen because of their expressive power and because they can be extended to suit our needs. Further they are platform independent and not tied to a specific implementation. To realize a MRMS system we therefore need to create mappings to specific implementation platforms.

4.1 Towards Integration

To enable a functional MRMS, we need to define pertinent correspondences among the representation databases. Traditional methods of defining correspondences among databases—used, e.g., by Rusinkiewicz et al. [18] and Ceri and Widom [5]—employ data dependency descriptors to describe how objects of a source class are related to objects of a target class in another database. An r-class is typically defined in the context of one database, which stores representation objects (r-objects). It is assumed that r-classes are defined in a common schema language, in our case UML. A dependency from a source class to a target class is denoted by an arrow, which states that a source object is dependent on the existence of a target object and on some of the target object's properties. Figure 4(a) shows a complex depen-

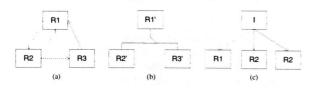

Figure 4. Approaches to Define Correspondence

dency scenario. The r-classes R1, R2, and R3 are from different schemas describing a similar concept, i.e., a multiply represented entity. We can see that R2 is dependent on R1 and R3, that R1 is dependent on R2 and that R3 is dependent on R1. If for example R1 or R3 are updated, R2 might need to be updated as well. A problem with this method is that it is only possible to specify dependencies between pairs of source and target classes. This may be sufficient in the field of data warehousing and geographic generalization [27], where the target representation classes are controlled by derivation rules. The main problem, however, is when the r-classes constitute a multiply represented entity that depends on more than one class. This is illustrated by the complex dependencies among the three classes shown in Figure 4(a). No common concept exists that binds the classes together and controls the priority and sequence of updates. Thus we cannot maintain multiple representation using dependency descriptors alone.

Another approach is model integration where the aim is to remove inconsistencies in both schema and data. Sheth [20] gives an overview of the interoperability area in which schema [6] and data [7] integration have central parts. Figure 4(b) illustrates the model integration approach. Our three classes R1, R2, and R3 are here integrated in a class hierarchy by modifying the existing classes resulting in three new classes R1', R2', and R3'. The actual instances

then must be converted into the new, integrated schema and inconsistencies resolved.

4.2 Integration Class

The two approaches presented above do not comply with our needs. First, we want to ensure the consistency among multiply represented entities without changing the representation database schemas. Second, we want only binary dependency descriptions to avoid complex correspondence scenarios. The main concept behind our language is the *integration class* (i-class). It allows us to explicitly model multiply represented entities and use them as a basis for defining consistency rules. An i-class is a special class that describes how semantically similar r-classes are related to a multiply represented entity.

Figure 4(c) shows an i-class, I, that controls the dependencies to its r-classes, R1, R2, and R3. It forms a partial integration of its r-classes and constitutes a concept of a multiply represented entity that covers, or includes more than one r-class, because integration is not possible if we have only one r-class. Notice that only the i-class knows of its r-classes—no dependencies among the r-classes exist.

The r-classes associated with the i-class bear similarities to the object-oriented concept of roles [17, 10]. The r-classes can be seen as roles to an i-class and is similar to the description of roles as being adjunct instances, which carries role specific characteristics [25]. In our modeling approach the roles (r-classes) are specified beforehand and then an i-class is created based on a synthesis of the r-classes. This is similar to the role model synthesis in the OOram methodology [16].

An instance of the i-class, the i-object, is a proxy for a multiply represented entity and is responsible for maintaining links to its r-objects and for keeping them consistent with respect to a set of rules. These consistency rules are divided into object correspondences and value correspondences and will be described in Sections 4.3 and 4.4. An i-object is created in a matching process where it is associated with its r-objects. The matching rules will be described in Section 4.5.

Figure 5(a) shows the i-class concept modeled as a metaclass in UML. It defines generic attributes for identifying the i-object, representing object and value correspondences, and for storing matching and restoration rules. It further defines generic operations for evaluating the rules. The metaclass defines a stereotype called <<i-class>>, which is used to model user-defined i-classes where application-dependent attributes and operations are specified. An example is shown in Figure 5(b). The i-class' attributes and operations are essential for the specification and evaluation of the consistency rules. Graphically, a new specification compartment for expressing value correspondences is added to an i-class. This is an extension to the three standard specification compartments of a UML class.

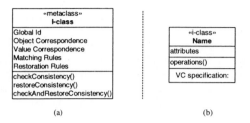

Figure 5. Integration Class

An *multiple representation association* (mr-association) is a directed association from an i-class to an r-class. An i-class has mr-associations to its r-classes to indicate which r-classes are its roles. Similar to the UML association we specify the role name and the multiplicity of the end of an mr-association close to the r-class, as shown in Figure 6. The multiplicity specifies the minimum and maximum number of r-objects needed to form a complete i-object. It is important to emphasize that an mr-association is not an ordinary association, as in the UML terminology, but combines a UML dependency relation (dashed directed line) and an ordinary UML association (normal line). The mr-association is expressed using a dot-dashed, directed line as shown in Figure 6. If the r-class in an mr-association

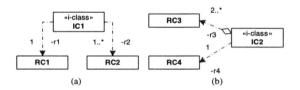

Figure 6. Multiple Representation Associations

is a subordinate concept and perceived as an aggregation, e.g., a built-up area is an aggregation of buildings, this can be symbolized by attaching the UML aggregation symbol to the end of the mr-association, as shown in Figure 6(b).

An *integration attribute* (i-attribute) holds the authoritative value on which value correspondences are evaluated. When an i-class is instantiated, its i-attributes are assigned values from the r-class attributes. It has to be decided which r-attributes that are to be used in this assignment, and the ones chosen are denoted as master r-attributes. The i-attributes are assigned according to the following procedure. Let $\mathcal{A}$ be the set of all attributes of the r-classes that correspond to the i-class. Identify subsets of semantically similar attributes in $\mathcal{A}$. For each subset $A_i \subseteq \mathcal{A}$, define an

i-attribute α_i. Define the initial and authoritative value of an i-attribute based on the attributes in A_i. In most cases it can be defined as $\alpha_i = a_j$, where the i-attribute is assigned to exactly one r-attribute. The more general definition is $\alpha_i = f(a_1, \ldots, a_n)$, where $f()$ is a function using more r-attributes $(a_1, \ldots, a_n)$, which all are considered as master attributes to α_i. The type and resolution of the i-attribute are defined by the master r-attribute.

The next two sections describe how to define consistency rules among the i-class and the r-classes at two levels: the object correspondence level and the value correspondence level. These are similar to the existence dependency and value dependency [5, 15].

4.3 Object Correspondence

An *object correspondence* (OC) specifies how an object of one class should be related to an object of another class. Here object correspondences define existence dependencies between the instantiation of the i-class and its associated r-objects. An OC specifies which r-objects that must be present to form a complete i-object, and it is described by the mr-association. The OC can be restricted by attaching constraints to the mr-association indicating that only r-objects satisfying the constraints will form i-objects. OCL is used to specify these constraint, and an example is seen in Figure 7 where a building has two roles to TM_BUILDING and T10_BUILDING. The constraint on the tm role specifies that only TM_BUILDINGs with an area larger than or equal to 25 m^2 should be considered. The multiplicity of the mr-associations indicates that we require at least one T10_BUILDING and at least one TM_BUILDING to be present to form an i-object. If the OC is not satisfied

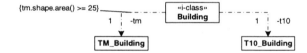

Figure 7. Example of Object Correspondences

then both the i-object and its other corresponding r-objects should be deleted. Alternatively a new r-object could be created to satisfy the OC. See Section 4.6 for a further description of restoration rules. In our lexical language, we can specify the OC as:

```
Object Correspondence:
    tm  [1] : TM_Building
                { tm.shape.area() >= 25 }
    t10 [1] : T10_Building
```

4.4 Value Correspondence

A *value correspondence* (VC) specifies how attribute values of the i-object and the r-objects should be related. We have previously introduced a special form of value correspondence, which describes how the i-attributes are related to their master r-attributes. Here we describe how the r-attributes, which are not used as master attributes, are related to the i-attributes. In brief, we denote this relationship as $a_j \sim \alpha_i$, where the r-attribute, a_j, has some form of similarity to the corresponding i-attribute, α_i.

A VC is described as an OCL constraint. An OCL constraint is an OCL expression that is Boolean-valued. Thus, if the constraint evaluates to true the VC holds. If the constraint evaluates to false the VC is not satisfied, which indicates that an inconsistency exists. OCL defines a number of different operators. It provides access to object's attributes and operations, as well as navigation of associations and it has mechanisms to iterate over many valued collections. Examples of OCL operators include $\leq, =, \geq$, `forAll`, `exists`, `and`, `or`, and `xor`. We extend these with spatial and topological comparison operators that allows us to compare spatial attributes, e.g., `overlaps`, `inside`, and `touches`. Furthermore it is necessary to provide derivation functions that can be applied to the attributes, e.g., $simplify(\alpha_i)$ where `simplify` is a special generalization function that simplifies a curve or a polygon by removing certain points according to a specific algorithm. The most simple form of a VC is of course the comparison operator = with no functions applied to the attributes. A more complex VC can use a combination of the above operations.

Examples of VCs are given in Table 1 that summarizes the VCs of an i-class, I, that integrates the three r-classes R_1, R_2, and R_3. The left hand side of the table defines

Table 1. Value Correspondences

I $(\alpha_1 \ldots \alpha_4)$	R_1 $(a_1 \ldots a_4)$	R_2 $(a_5 \ldots a_8)$	R_3 $(a_9 \ldots a_{12})$
$\alpha_1 = f(a_9, a_{10})$	$a_1 \sim \alpha_1$	$a_5 = \alpha_1$	a_9
$\alpha_2 = a_6$	$a_2 \sim \alpha_2$	$\underline{a_6}$	a_{10}
$\alpha_3 = a_{12}$	$\underline{a_3}$	$a_7 \sim \alpha_3$	a_{11}
$\alpha_4 = a_3$	$a_4 = \alpha_4$	$a_8 = \alpha_4$	$\underline{a_{12}}$

four i-attributes $\alpha_1, \ldots, \alpha_4$ and how they are assigned to the respective attributes of the r-classes. The right hand side of the table defines how the r-attributes correspond (= or $\sim$) to the i-attributes. Notice that the VC ($\sim$) needs further specification. In the example, the master of α_1 is defined as a function that aggregates a_9 and a_{10}. The master of α_2, α_3, and α_4 is equal to a_6, a_{12}, and a_3, respectively. The VCs corresponding to R_1's attributes specify that a_1 and a_2 are similar ($\sim$) to α_1 and α_2, respectively, that a_3 is a master

(denoted by the underline), and that a_4 has an exact (=) VC to α_4. The rest of the table can be read in the same way. An attribute a_n with no underline is not included as a master attribute, and neither does it have a correspondence to any i-attribute.

If a VC is not satisfied the MRMS needs to restore consistency. If a master r-attribute is changed, the restoration procedure is to change the corresponding i-attribute and then reevaluate the affected VCs. This implies that a comparison operation = will be interpreted as an assignment if the constraint is not satisfied. The restoration procedures will be further described in Section 4.6.

In UML we specify the value correspondence between an i-attribute and its master r-attribute as an initial value in the attribute compartment. A dedicated specification compartment is used to express the other VCs. For the r-class we use a different specification compartment to specify which attributes are used as master and which are included in the VC. Each VC is associated with an identifier. Figure 8 shows an example of an i-class with value correspondences which model the consistency requirements given in Section 2. References to the requirements are given in parentheses. VC `v1` specifies that `t10.shape` must be a simplification of the i-attribute `shape`. The VC is expressed as `t10.shape = g1.simplify(shape)`, where `simplify` is included in a generalization library `g1`. VC `m1` indicates that the `shape` attribute should correspond exactly to the its master value `tm.shape`. VCs `v1` and `m1` jointly satisfy requirement 1. VC `v4` requires that `br.location` is inside `shape` (requirement 2). VCs `m3` and `v2` specify that the `height` attribute is assigned to the terrain height of the building plus the buildings height taken from `tm` and furthermore that `t10` height is required to be equal to this value (requirement 3). VCs `m2` and `v3` resolve the possibly many usages of `br` and map this to the `t10` usage (requirement 4).

An example of the VC is given below where the i-class `Building` is specified in the lexical language. In the VC, the `<<master>>` keyword indicates that the i-attribute has the corresponding r-attribute as master.

```
iclass Building
Attributes:
    shape  : Polygon
    usage  : BR_useCode
    height : Integer
Operations:
    resolveUsage(set<BR_useCode>) : BR_useCode
    mapUsage(BR_useCode) : T10_useCode
Object Correspondence:
    tm  [1] : TM_Building
                    { tm.shape.area() >= 25 }
    t10 [1] : T10_Building
    br  [1..*] : BR_Building
Value Correspondence:
    m1: shape = <<master>> tm.shape
    m2: usage = <<master>> resolveUsage(br.usage)
```

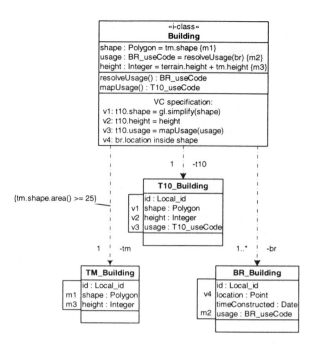

«i-class»
Building

shape : Polygon = tm.shape {m1}
usage : BR_useCode = resolveUsage(br) {m2}
height : Integer = terrain.height + tm.height {m3}

resolveUsage() : BR_useCode
mapUsage() : T10_useCode

VC specification:
v1: t10.shape = gl.simplify(shape)
v2: t10.height = height
v3: t10.usage = mapUsage(usage)
v4: br.location inside shape

{tm.shape.area() >= 25}

1   -t10

T10_Building

id : Local_id
v1   shape : Polygon
v2   height : Integer
v3   usage : T10_useCode

1   -tm

TM_Building

id : Local_id
m1   shape : Polygon
m3   height : Integer

1..*   -br

BR_Building

id : Local_id
v4   location : Point
     timeConstructed : Date
m2   usage : BR_useCode

Figure 8. Integration class with VC

```
m3: height = <<master>> terrain.height(shape)+
                        tm.height
v1: t10.shape = gl.simplify(shape)
v2: t10.height = height
v3: t10.usage = mapUsage(usage)
v4: br.location inside shape
end iclass
```

4.5 Object Matching Rules

To create an i-object, we need to identify the r-objects that form a multiply represented entity. This process is called object matching, and it is controlled by object matching rules associated with the i-classes. An *object matching rule* specifies a strategy for how to find corresponding r-objects.

The object matching process for an i-class follows certain steps. The first step is to identify the r-objects that are candidates to be matched. The mr-associations together with additional constraints can be used to select the initial set of r-objects, one set for each mr-association. The next step is to select an mr-association as the starting point for the match and to create an incomplete i-object with attributes instantiated with the master r-attributes. Then, for each remaining mr-association, we need to find the r-objects that match the i-object under construction. The process is continued until all r-objects have been associated with an i-object.

Three different matching criteria can be used: global

object identifier, attribute comparison, and manual inspection. The *global object identifier* approach provides an exact match criterion. It is assumed that the r-objects share a common unique global identifier that exactly identifies the entity represented. Thus if two or more r-objects have the same global identifier, matching becomes trivial. The need for global identifiers in the management of geographic information is described in previous work [1, 19].

The *attribute comparison* approach involves finding objects based on similar attribute values. The selection of the attributes and the comparison operators can be based on the value correspondences, but also on other criteria. Spatial attributes may provide a basis for matching, because we normally can assume that two objects that are spatially overlapping represent the same entity. The attributes' resolution differences may complicate the matching criteria, and there is a need to define tolerances and operations that take into account the resolution difference between two objects [8, 22]. Attribute comparison may fail due to poor data quality or resolution differences among the r-objects. In such cases the r-objects may still be matched by *manual inspection*. These rules can in their simplest form rely on visual interpretations.

An example is a matching rule for the i-class BUILDING shown in Figure 7. The mr-association to TM_BUILDING is selected as a source, and a set of tm buildings greater than 25 m² is prepared. For each tm building, a match is attempted in the t10 set using VC v1 as a matching criterion. After all tm objects are associated with an i-object then the possibly remaining unmatched t10 objects are also associated with an i-object.

The result of the matching process is a set of i-objects, where each i-object is associated with a number of r-objects; the consistency rules can then be evaluated. If the OCs are not satisfied, the i-object is incomplete, i.e., all the required r-objects have not been found. This means that further consistency checks cannot be performed. If the i-object on the other hand has a valid OC then it can be evaluated against its VCs. If the VCs or the OCs are not satisfied we say that the i-object is inconsistent. After the object matching process, we may end up with a set of inconsistent i-objects. In the next section, we describe restoration rules that can be used to restore an i-object's consistency.

4.6 Restoration Rules

If an i-object is inconsistent, we need to identify the reason behind the problem and apply appropriate restoration actions that will restore the i-object to a consistent state. A *restoration rule* specifies not only the actions needed for restoring consistency but also the conditions that should trigger an update action. The restoration rules define the core set of restoration actions that can be applied when an

OC or VC is not satisfied. This may happen when changes occur in the representation databases.

Changes to the r-objects involve insertion of new r-objects and update or deletion of existing r-objects. The restoration actions are highly dependent on the representation databases and what correspondence statements that have been violated. They involve everything from simple requests for actions, such as insert, update, and delete, to complex combinations of such requests. Restoration rules may be automatically generated by analyzing the MRSchema, following the principles described in Ceri and Widom [4].

If an OC is not satisfied, it means that the expected correspondence among the i-object and its r-objects no longer exists. Two strategies can be applied: Either the inconsistent i-object and the remaining r-objects can be deleted, or the absent r-objects can be inserted and then the i-object can be updated. For example if a required r-object has been deleted, a restoration action can be to delete the i-object and its other r-objects altogether. The actions when violating an OC seem straightforward, but the difficult part is to decide which of the two restoration strategies to follow.

If a VC is not satisfied, it means that a value or several of the values of the r-attributes no longer correspond with the i-attributes. There are two ways of restoring an i-object's consistency, either by updating the i-attributes or by changing the i-objects' respective r-objects. An example of the former is if a master r-attribute has changed. Then the respective i-attributes must be updated accordingly. If a VC is violated then the restoration action can be extracted from the VC. This results in a modification request to change the respective r-object.

The restoration actions can either be directly applied to the representation database or they can be applied indirectly, by notifying the representation database manager about the inconsistency and request necessary restoration actions to be made.

An example of a restoration rule for the BUILDING i-class shown in Figure 7 is: if a TM_BUILDING object exists and no corresponding object is found in the T10 representation database, then a T10_BUILDING object shall be created using the VC v1.

5 Conclusion

In this paper we have presented a new approach to the modeling and management of multiply represented entities in the context of a Multiple Representation Management System. We have described a Multiple Representation Schema Language (MRSL) that enables users to express their consistency requirements across a system of autonomous databases. Our approach provides a solution to the consistency problems that arise from the multiple representation of entities among geographic information systems.

The MRSL is a comprehensive and expressive language that makes it possible to model multiple representation as well as specifying consistency rules, matching rules, and restoration rules. In addition, it is extendible so that user-defined operations can be specified. A key concept in our approach is the integration class (i-class). Its use permits us to manage multiply represented entities by integrating heterogeneous representation objects via a single integration object. The i-object is responsible for keeping its r-objects consistent according to the consistency rules given by its class. The i-class concept comprises an intuitive approach to multiple representation modeling and it enables us to model the consistency requirements described in the case study. Compared to the traditional dependency description approaches, the i-class reduces the complexity of handling correspondences among several semantically similar r-classes.

Our approach is non-intrusive, which fulfills the requirement that the databases are to be kept autonomous. We use UML and OCL as the basis for our graphical and lexical language syntaxes, and we have found that the extension mechanisms in UML have been sufficient for our needs.

Future work involves formalization of the MRSL, where matching rules and restoration rules must be addressed in particular. We further want to investigate methods to ensure correctness of the rules specified in the MRMS to avoid discrepancies among them. Finally, to test the efficacy of our approach, we need to design and implement a prototype MRMS and evaluate it with respect to a more comprehensive case study.

Acknowledgements

This work was supported in part by a mobility scholarship from the Nordic Academy for Advanced Study (NorFA), the Norwegian Research Council's DYNAMAP-I project 118048/223, the Wireless Information Management network, funded by NorFA through grant 000389, and by a grant from the Nykredit corporation. The authors wish to thank Bjørn Skjellaug for helpful comments.

References

[1] Y. Bishr. A Global Unique Persistent Object ID for Geospatial Information Sharing. In *Proceedings of the 2nd International Conference on Interoperating Geographic Information Systems*, Volume 1580 of *Lecture Notes in Computer Science*, pages 55–64. Springer, 1999.

[2] G. Booch, J. Rumbaugh, and I. Jacobson. *The Unified Modeling Language User Guide*. Object Technology Series. Addison-Wesley, USA, 1st edition, 1999.

[3] B. P. Buttenfield and J. S. DeLotto. Multiple Representations – Scientific Report for the Specialist Meeting. Report 89-3, National Center for Geographic Information Analysis, NCGIA, Department of Geography, SUNY at Buffalo, Buffalo, NY 14260, 18-21 Februrary 1989.

[4] S. Ceri and J. Widom. Deriving Production Rules for Constraint Management. In *Proceedings of the 16th International Conference on Very Large Data Bases*, pages 566–577, Brisbane, Queensland, Australia, 13-16 August 1990. Morgan Kaufmann.

[5] S. Ceri and J. Widom. Managing Semantic Heterogeneity with Production Rules and Persistent Queries. In *Proceedings of the 19th International Conference on Very Large Data Bases*, pages 108–119, Dublin, Ireland, 24–27 Aug. 1993.

[6] T. Devogele, C. Parent, and S. Spaccapietra. On Spatial Database Integration. *International Journal of Geographic Information Systems*, 12(4):335–352, 1998.

[7] T. Devogele, J. Trevisan, and L. Raynal. Building a Multiscale Database with Scale-transition Relationships. In *Proceedings of the 7th International Symposium on Spatial Data Handling*, pages 337–351, Delft, Netherlands, 1996.

[8] M. J. Egenhofer, E. Clementini, and P. D. Felice. Evaluating Inconsistencies Among Multiple Representations. In *Proceedings of the 6th International Symposium on Spatial Data Handling*, pages 901–920, Edinburgh, Scotland, UK, 1994.

[9] A. Friis-Christensen, N. Tryfona, and C. S. Jensen. Requirements and Research Issues in Geographic Data Modeling. In *Proceedings of the 9th ACM International Symposium on Advances in Geographic Information Systems*, pages 2–8, Atlanta, Georgia, November 2001.

[10] G. Gottlob, M. Schrefl, and B. Röck. Extending Object-Oriented Systems with Roles. *ACM Transactions on Information Systems*, 14(3):268–296, July 1996.

[11] P. W. P. J. Grefen and J. Widom. Protocols for Integrity Constraint Checking in Federated Databases. *Distributed and Parallel Databases*, 5(4):327–355, 1997.

[12] C. Jones, D. Kidner, L. Luo, G. Bundy, and J. Ware. Database Design for a Multi-scale Spatial Information System. *International Journal of Geographic Information Systems*, 10(8):901–920, 1996.

[13] G. Karabatis, M. Rusinkiewicz, and A. Sheth. Interdependent Database Systems. In A. Elmagarmid, M. Rusinkiewicz, and A. Sheth, editors, *Management of Heterogeneous and Autonomous Database Systems*, Data Management Systems, Chapter 8, pages 217–252. Morgan Kaufman, 1999.

[14] T. Kilpeläinen. *Multiple Representation and Generalization of Geo-databases for Topographic Maps*. PhD thesis, Finnish Geodetic Institute, 1997. ISBN 951-711-211-4.

[15] Q. Li and D. McLeod. Managing Interdependencies among Objects in Federated Databases. In *Proceedings of the IFIP Database Semantics Conference on Interoperable Database Systems (DS-5)*, IFIP Transactions A-25, pages 331–347, Lorne, Victoria, Australia, Nov. 1992.

[16] T. Reenskaug. *Working With Objects : The OORAM Software Engineering Method*. Manning Publications Co., USA, 1996.

[17] J. Richardson and P. Schwarz. Aspects: Extending Objects to Support Multiple, Independent Roles. In *Proceedings of the ACM SIGMOD International Conference on Management of Data*, pages 298–307, Denver, Colorado, USA, May 1991.

[18] M. Rusinkiewicz, A. Sheth, and G. Karabatis. Specifying Interdatabase Dependencies in a Multidatabase Environment. *Computer*, 24(12):46–53, Dec. 1991.

[19] P. Sargent. Features Identities, Descriptors and Handles. In *Proceedings of the 2nd International Conference on Interoperating Geographic Information Systems*, Volume 1580 of *Lecture Notes in Computer Science*, pages 41–53. Springer, 1999.

[20] A. P. Sheth. Changing Focus on Interoperability in Information Systems: From System, Syntax, Structure to Semantics. In M. F. Goodchild, M. J. Egenhofer, R. Fegeas, and C. A. Kottman, editors, *Interoperating Geographic Information Systems*. Kluwer, 1998.

[21] A. P. Sheth and J. A. Larson. Federated Database Systems for Managing Distributed, Heterogeneous, and Autonomous Databases. *ACM Computing Surveys*, 22(3):183–236, 1990.

[22] D. Skogan. Managing Resolution in Multi-Resolution Databases. In *Proceedings of the 8th Scandinavian Research Conference*, pages 99–113, Ås, Norway, 2001.

[23] S. Spaccapietra, C. Parent, and C. Vangenot. GIS Databases: From Multiscale to MultiRepresentation. In B. Choueiry and T. Walsh, editors, *Proceedings of the 4th International Symposium on Abstraction, Reformulation, and Approximation*, Volume 1864 of *Lecture Notes in Artificial Intelligence*, pages 57–70. Springer, July 2000.

[24] S. Spaccapietra, C. Vangenot, C. Parent, and E. Zimanyi. MurMur: A Research Agenda on Multiple Representations. In *Proceedings of the International Symposium on Database Applications in Non-Traditional Environments*, Kyoto, Japan, November 1999.

[25] F. Steimann. On the Representation of Roles in Object-Oriented and Conceptual Modelling. *Data & Knowledge Engineering*, 35(1):83–106, 2000.

[26] J. B. Warmer and A. G. Kleppe. *The Object Constraint Language : Precise Modeling with UML*. Object Technology Series. Addison-Wesley, USA, 1st edition, 1999.

[27] R. Weibel and G. H. Dutton. Generalising Spatial Data and Dealing with Multiple Representations. In P. Longley, M. Goodchild, D. Maguire, and D. Rhind, editors, *Geographic Information Systems - Principles and Technical Issues*, Volume 1, pages 125–155. John Wiley & Sons, 2 edition, 1999.

Integrating HTML Tables Using Semantic Hierarchies and Meta-Data Sets

Seung-Jin Lim
Computer Science Dept.
Brigham Young University
Provo, Utah 84602, U.S.A.

Yiu-Kai Ng
Computer Science Dept.
Brigham Young University
Provo, Utah 84602, U.S.A.

Xiaochun Yang
Computer Science Dept.
Northeastern University
Shenyang, China

Abstract

As the Internet is a global network, there is a demand on accessing closely related data without browsing through different Web documents. A significant amount of these data are presented in HTML documents. Since data contents of HTML documents are intervened by markups, it is not trivial to integrate and provide a unified view of closely related data in different HTML documents. In this paper, we present an approach for integrating semantically related data in any HTML tables that belong to a particular domain of interest (ID), such as house/apartment rental, by using the semantic hierarchies generated from the tables and the predefined meta-data sets that indicate related column names in ID. In our approach, we capture each data source as semistructured data, called semantic hierarchy, *and the end result of integrating different HTML tables of ID is a* unified view *of data in the tables, which is presented in an XML document. Besides HTML tables, our approach can be adopted by any system that integrates semi-structured data across different platforms.*

1 Introduction

The Internet is perceived as a global network of heterogeneous data sources. As the Internet and Web technologies are driving the ways of accessing data sources beyond the intranet boundaries, we witness an increasing demand on methods for accessing (closely) related data available on the Internet. It is, however, a challenging task to determine the similarity of data in different Web documents. Any two data objects with the same data content may be represented by different names, types, and/or structures in general, which makes the integration of data sets challenging. For instance, *last name* in one data set and *surname* in another may represent the same data. The data object representing *address* may be a single object in one data set, whereas it may consist of multiple data objects such as *street address*, *city*, *postal code*, and *state* in another. Furthermore, *postal code* may be a numeric data type in one data set versus an alphanumeric data type in another.

There are a wide spectrum of approaches to meet the demand of integrating heterogeneous data sets. At one end of the spectrum is the integration of different data sources by providing a precompiled global view of the data. Data warehouse repository [9] is such an approach where different data sources are maintained at a central location and are presented as materialized views. World View in the Information Manifold [5] is another approach where information sources are 'tagged' for efficient searching before the information is served to the user. In [2], (semi-)structured data sources are analyzed beforehand and the data fields that are declared using different terminologies, but carry the same or closely related information, are manually integrated together to provide an integrated view to the user. At the other end of the spectrum is the approach which processes queries against heterogeneous data sources on-the-fly, where queries are decomposed into subqueries that are sent to relevant data sources. The answers to subqueries are merged afterwards. The approach in [10] falls into this category. In reality, this method is not widely adopted since the time for processing queries on demand against heterogeneous data sources is longer than the time for processing queries against pre-configured repositories in general, and the integrated systems based on this approach may suffer lagging. Between these two different approaches, there exist hybrid approaches where data that do not change over time are pre-configured onto a repository and data that frequently change are fetched on demand [7]. Other integration approaches also appear in [3]

In either approach for integrating data sources, the architecture of the integrated systems tends to be a typical 3-tier architecture: (i) the user interface at the top that composes and initiates queries, (ii) data sources at the bottom, and (iii) the middle-tier that processes queries and controls data flows. The middle-tier is usually called *integrator* or *mediator*, which often incurs human intervention for the analysis of data sources and the refinement of integrated views of data until the system becomes operational.

In this paper, we propose an HTML-table integration

approach, called HTI, for integrating data from different HTML tables. Inputs of HTI are tables presented in HTML documents. HTI, however, can process any data sets, such as relational tables, as long as their format is known to HTI. In HTI, an XML wrapper and its corresponding DTD are constructed as the end result of each integration. HTI generates and displays the *unified/integrated view* of the integration that is a mapping between data items in different HTML tables configured according to the column names defined in the tables.

We adopt XML as the data exchange format for data integrated from HTML tables. Using XML we enhance the adoptability of the unified views generated by HTI to other data integration applications on various platforms since XML is a platform-independent, W3C standard, and widely accepted. We provide a visual integration assistant tool that generates tree view of the given data sources as well as the integrated unified view.

We proceed to present our results as follows. In Section 2, we justify the necessity of data acquisition using semantic hierarchy which is our data model for encapsulating semi-structured data. In Section 3, we present an approach for constructing the semantic hierarchy of any HTML table. In Section 4, we propose a method for matching column names in different HTML tables to be integrated and provide the complexity analysis of the entire integration process. In Section 5, we give the concluding remarks.

2 Preliminaries

We are interested in retrieving textual data that are hierarchically structured, such as data in HTML documents. Although the primary purpose of HTML is to define appearance of data in a browser, we notice that the creator of an HTML document often imposes, either intentionally or unintentionally, certain hierarchies among the data contents in the document by using *block markups*. Consider the simple HTML document that includes a table as shown in Figure 1(a). The (hierarchical) relationships among the data components average height, males, and merged cells are not precisely preserved in the document, as shown in Figure 1(b). It is difficult to determine the relationships among these data components without considering the meaning of their corresponding tags, such as TR, TH, TD, and TABLE. Existing approaches [1] for extracting hierarchical data are based on *syntactic hierarchies* in which HTML *tags* and *contents* are included in the hierarchical structures, and source documents must be analyzed before hierarchical data are extracted, or HTML tags in the documents are extensibly used to determine the data hierarchy. In contrarily, our proposed hierarchy, called *semantic hierarchy*, of an HTML document H preserves the hierarchical relationships of data contents in H such that the hierarchy of data contents in H is determined without using tags in H.

(a) A table in Netscape   (b) The source code of the table in Figure 1(a)

Figure 1. A table and its source code

Note that table-related HTML elements are often chosen by document creators for encapsulating hierarchical data and are commonly being used. Our recent survey shows that 52% of the sampled HTML documents include some tables[1]. (In the survey, we chose a number of Web sites of common interest and fetched more than 30,000 documents that were linked from referencing HTML documents within four hyperlinks.)

Given an HTML table T as input, we generate the semantic hierarchy (SH) of T as output. SH captures the data hierarchy (excluding HTML tags) of T and is generated without requiring the internal structure of T to be known beforehand at the source code level (such as which HTML markups are used and how they are used) or at the conceptual level (such as how many columns and rows are declared in T, whether headings and the caption of T exist, etc.). A semantic hierarchy captures the hierarchy of the given data contents, whereas a syntactic hierarchy captures the hierarchical relationships of data contents and their tags. Existing data collection methods, such as wrappers and integrators for data warehousing systems, which frequently access a large number of HTML tables for extracting structured data, such as stock quotes, can benefit from our method of data acquisition using semantic hierarchies.

3 Construction of semantic hierarchies

In this section, we present our method in constructing the semantic hierarchy of data contents in an HTML table embedded in a given HTML document. Prior to presenting our approach, we first discuss table-specific HTML elements.

3.1 Table-specific elements

Among the table-specific elements, TR determines the number of rows, whereas TH and TD determine the number of columns in an HTML table (table in short). A TH element declares one or more headings, whereas a TD element

---

[1]Even though these days an increasing number of HTML tables are created by filling out HTML forms to access the underlying data sources, the automatic data extraction method developed by [6] can be adopted for retrieving dynamically generated HTML tables.

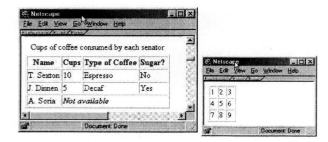

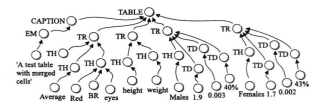

Figure 3. The syntactic hierarchy of the table in Figure 1(a)

(a) An HTML table with a first-row heading

(b) An HTML table without heading

Figure 2. Two prominent types of HTML tables

asserts data of a table cell. The data contents of TD elements are called *table data* since they are the data instances in their respective cells. In contrast, the data contents of TH elements are either column or row headings that are not considered as table data. The data content of either element, however, renders the content of its respective cell by a visual HTML user agent, such as a Web browser. (A visual HTML user agent, however, may not explicitly indicate that a cell is a heading cell while another is a data cell.) Besides TH and TD, THEAD (TBODY, respectively) implicitly designates certain rows as headings (data cells, respectively).

According to the experimental survey (as mentioned in Section 1), we observe that (i) a typical HTML table has at least one heading row at the top of the table and at least one heading column on the left, such as the table shown in Figure 1(a). We call this type of tables *column-row-wise*; (ii) another typical table contains at least one heading row at the top of the table, such as the table shown in Figure 2(a). We call this type of tables *column-wise*. In a column-wise table, the heading rows yield the schema of the table; and (iii) other than these two types of tables, we notice that a large number of tables do not make use of table-specific elements other than TABLE and TD, as the one rendered in Figure 2(b). In such a table, every cell is in fact a data cell (according to the HTML grammar), and the intended hierarchy of the data cells is very difficult, if not impossible, to be determined by an automaton at the source code level using the HTML grammar alone. We conclude from our survey that the creator of this type of tables often implicitly designates the first row as a heading. Thus, we treat this type of tables as column-wise.

Among the table-specific elements, two attributes of TH and TD, ROWSPAN and COLSPAN, play significant roles in determinating the data hierarchy of an HTML table. To better understand the roles of these attributes, consider Figure 3. The table, as graphically captured in the figure, has four rows (i.e., four TRs) as rendered in Figure 1(a). Note that the first TR contains three TH elements, implying that the row is a heading which includes three cells (i.e., three

columns). The second row contains two TH elements, implying that there are two heading cells, whereas each of the last two TRs contains one TH and three TDs, implying that there are one heading cell on the left and three data cells in each row underneath the heading rows. Apparently, the numbers of columns of the first two rows are not equal, nor with that of the last two rows. The attributes ROWSPAN and COLSPAN remedy the mismatch of the number of columns among different rows in a table. When a TH or TD includes ROWSPAN="n" (COLSPAN="n," respectively), the associated cell is supposed to span n rows downward (n columns to the right, respectively). We consider these attributes in the construction process of the semantic hierarchy of a given HTML table.

3.2 Semantic Hierarchy

In order to create the semantic hierarchy (SH), which is an enhancement of the syntactic tree, of an HTML table T, we first determine the hierarchical dependencies among the data contents in T (instead of the hierarchy of the data contents and tags in T). Once the hierarchical dependencies among the data contents in T are determined, we retain data objects, but exclude all the tag objects, in SH. This is because tags are markups for defining the rendered appearance of data in a visual HTML user agent, and they are not shown to the user.

A semantic hierarchy is defined on top of the notion of p-table (see Definition 1 below) since the properties of a p-table are easy to understand. A p-table can be considered as a special type of HTML tables for expressing either a column-row-wise table or a column-wise table. In constructing the semantic hierarchy of an HTML table T we first transform T to its p-table and then obtain the semantic hierarchy of T from the p-table.

Definition 1 A *p-table* $T = \{(a_{1,1}, \ldots, a_{1,n}), \ldots, (a_{m,1}, \ldots, a_{m,n})\}$ with column headings $C_1, \ldots, C_n$ and caption C, is a two-dimensional table, where each C_i ($1 \leq i \leq n$) or table data $a_{i,j}$ ($1 \leq i \leq m, 1 \leq j \leq n$) may be null. If a column heading or data d is null, then the name of the object representing d is the empty string. We assume that values under the first column in different rows of T are different. □

Note that dependency constraints of HTML objects in a syntactic hierarchy are determined by the container-content

162

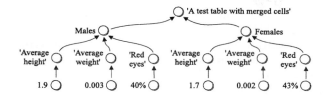

Figure 4. The semantic hierarchy of the table in Figure 1(a)

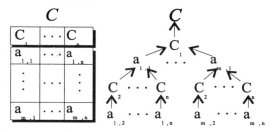

Figure 5. A p-table T and its corresponding SH_T

$h_{1,1}$	$\cdots$	$h_{1,n}$		$C_1 =$	$\cdots$	$C_n =$
				$h_{1,1} \cdots h_{k,1}$		$h_{1,n} \cdots h_{k,n}$
$h_{k,1}$	$\cdots$	$h_{k,n}$				
$d_{k+1,1}$	$\cdots$	$d_{k+1,n}$	$\Leftrightarrow$	$a_{1,1} = d_{k+1,1}$	$\cdots$	$a_{1,n} = d_{k+1,n}$
$\vdots$		$\vdots$		$\vdots$		$\vdots$
$d_{k+m,1}$	$\cdots$	$d_{k+m,n}$		$a_{m,1} = d_{k+m,1}$	$\cdots$	$a_{m,n} = d_{k+m,n}$

A single dot (.) is the dot operator, which is the separator of two names.

Figure 6. Mapping from a column-wise HTML table to a p-table

relationships of tags and data contents according to the HTML grammar as illustrated in Figure 3. We define the notion of dependency for p-tables differently since there are no tags in a p-table. Dependency constraints on p-tables are defined over captions, column headings, and table data as given in Definition 2. Since column headings and table data may be null in a p-table, we consider a special case of dependency constraints: given a dependency constraint $o_1 \leftarrow o_2 \leftarrow o_3$, where o_i ($1 \leq i \leq 3$) is either a column heading or table data, it is reduced to $o_1 \leftarrow o_3$ if o_2 is the empty string.

Definition 2 Given an n-ary p-table $T = \{(a_{1,1}, \ldots, a_{1,n}), (a_{2,1}, \ldots, a_{2,n}), \ldots, (a_{m,1}, \ldots, a_{m,n})\}$ with column headings $C_1, \ldots, C_n$ and caption C, the semantic hierarchy $SH = (V, E, g)$ of T, denoted by SH_T, is a directed tree, where

- $V_R \in V$ is the root node of SH_T, labeled by C, and each node $v \in V$, other than V_R, denotes a non-empty $a_{i,j}$ (C_j, respectively) ($1 \leq i \leq m$, $1 \leq j \leq n$) of T, and is labeled by $a_{i,j}$ (C_j, respectively).
- E is a finite set of *directed* edges.
- g: $E \rightarrow V \times V$ is a function such that $v_2 \leftarrow v_1$ if $g(e) = (v_1, v_2)$, and $V_R \leftarrow C_1 \leftarrow a_{i,1} \leftarrow C_j \leftarrow a_{i,j}$ ($1 \leq i \leq m$, $2 \leq j \leq n$) hold. $\square$

Since the caption of a p-table T often indicates its content, we choose the caption as the root node of the corresponding SH_T. SH_T contains subtrees rooted at $a_{1,1}, \ldots, a_{m,1}$ with the constraints $V_R (C) \leftarrow C_1 \leftarrow a_{i,1}$ ($1 \leq i \leq m$) since each row can be uniquely identified from the other rows by the first column (i.e., $a_{i,1}$) in T (see Definition 1). Figure 5 shows a p-table and its corresponding semantic hierarchy constructed according to Definition 2, which captures the process of constructing the semantic hierarchy from a p-table. In the following sections, we discuss how to obtain each row, i.e., $a_{i,1}, \ldots, a_{i,n}$ ($1 \leq i \leq m$), and column, i.e., $a_{1,j}, \ldots, a_{m,j}$ ($1 \leq j \leq n$), from the corresponding HTML table, which is either column-wise or column-row-wise. Note that by the HTML specification, an HTML table contains at most one CAPTION element. If it exists, it becomes the caption C of the p-table; otherwise, the string value "TABLE" is the caption C.

3.2.1 Column-wise tables

Consider a given column-wise HTML table $T = \{(h_{1,1}, \ldots, h_{1,n}), \ldots, (h_{k,1}, \ldots, h_{k,n}), (d_{k+1,1}, \ldots, d_{k+1,n}), \ldots,$

$(d_{k+m,1}, \ldots, d_{k+m,n})\}$, where each $h_{i,j}$ ($1 \leq i \leq k$, $1 \leq j \leq n$) is the data content of a TH element and each $d_{i,j}$ ($k+1 \leq i \leq k+m$, $1 \leq j \leq n$) is the data content of a TD element. T, similar to a p-table, is a collection of rows such that each data row contains the data instances corresponding to the respective column headings, and hence we treat each data row (column, respectively) in T as a row (column, respectively) in a p-table by mapping $d_{l,j}$ to $a_{i,j}$ in a p-table such that $a_{i,j} = d_{l,j}$, $1 \leq i \leq m$, $1 \leq j \leq n$, $k+1 \leq l \leq k+m$. By definition of a column-wise table, the first k rows specify the column headings $C_1, \ldots, C_n$ of a p-table. Since the first k rows in a column-wise HTML table are headings, concatenating the first k rows of a particular column yields the content of the column. Thus, the column heading of $C_j = concat(\ldots(concat(h_{1,j}, h_{2,j}), \ldots), h_{k,j})$, $1 \leq j \leq n$. Figure 6 illustrates how the data contents of THs and TDs in a column-wise HTML table are mapped to C_js and $a_{i,j}$s in a p-table, respectively.

3.2.2 Column-row-wise tables

Consider a column-row-wise HTML table $T = \{(hh_{1,1}, \ldots, hh_{1,n}), \ldots, (hh_{k,1}, \ldots, hh_{k,n}), (hv_{k+1,1}, \ldots, hv_{k+1,l}, d_{k+1,l+1}, \ldots, d_{k+1,l+n-1}), \ldots, (hv_{k+m,1}, \ldots, hv_{k+m,l}, d_{k+m,l+1}, \ldots, d_{k+m,l+n-1})\}$, where each $hh_{i,j}$ ($1 \leq i \leq k$, $1 \leq j \leq n$) and $hv_{i,j}$ ($k+1 \leq i \leq k+m$, $1 \leq j \leq l$) is the data content of a TH element, and each $d_{i,j}$ ($k+1 \leq i \leq k+m$, $l+1 \leq j \leq l+n-1$) is the data content of a TD element. Just like column-wise tables, we concatenate the first k rows in a column-row-wise table column-by-column since they are the headings of columns in the table, and assign the jth concatenated heading to be the jth column heading $C_j =$

163

$hh_{1,1}$		...	$hh_{1,n}$	
$\vdots$			$\vdots$	
$hh_{k,1}$		...	$hh_{k,n}$	
$hv_{k+1,1}$	... $hv_{k+1,l}$	$d_{k+1,l+1}$	...	$d_{k+1,l+n-1}$
$\vdots$	$\vdots$	$\vdots$		$\vdots$
$hv_{k+m,1}$	... $hv_{k+m,l}$	$d_{k+m,l+1}$	...	$d_{k+m,l+n-1}$

$$\Updownarrow$$

$C_1 =$ $hh_{1,1}.\ldots.$	...	$C_n =$ $hh_{1,n}.\ldots.$
$a_{1,1} = hv_{k+1,1}.$	...	$a_{1,n} =$
$\vdots$		$\vdots$
$a_{m,1} = hv_{k+m,1}.$ $\ldots.hv_{k+m,l}$	...	$a_{m,n} =$ $d_{k+m,l+n-1}$

A single dot (.) is the dot operator, which is the separator of two names.

Figure 7. Mapping from a column-row-wise HTML table to a p-table

$concat(\ldots(concat(hh_{1,j}, hh_{2,j}),\ldots), hh_{k,j}), 1 \leq j \leq n$, in the corresponding p-table. The concatenation of the first l columns of each row, starting from the $(k+1)$th row, yields the heading of the row in this type of tables. Hence, the first column of the ith data row in the p-table is $a_{i,1} = concat(\ldots(concat(hv_{i,1}, hv_{i,2}),\ldots), hv_{i,l}), k+1 \leq i \leq k+m$, and $a_{i,j} = d_{i,l+j-1}, k+1 \leq i \leq k+m, 2 \leq j \leq n$. Figure 7 illustrates the concatenation of data contents of THs and TDs in a column-row-wise HTML table to C_js and $a_{i,j}$s in a p-table, respectively.

3.2.3 Colspan and rowspan

As mentioned in Section 3.1, an HTML table may not have the same number of columns in each row, and COLSPANs and ROWSPANs play an important role in transforming an HTML table to its p-table. In this section, we discuss how to manipulate COLSPANs and ROWSPANs in THs or TDs.

If a TH or TD element in an HTML table contains COLSPAN = "n," the particular cell of the TH or TD is supposed to be expanded to n columns and occupy n cells, including the current cell in the current row. Hence, at the current row, we insert $n-1$ cells to the right of the current cell and replicate the data content of the current cell $n-1$ times to the new cells. ROWSPAN, however, is processed differently. If a TH element contains ROWSPAN = "n," the particular cell of the TH element is supposed to be expanded to the next $n-1$ rows and occupy n cells, including the current cell and the new $n-1$ cells in the current column. We push the data content h of the current cell all the way down to the $(n-1)$th new cell, rather than replicating h to the underneath rows $n-1$ times. As a result, h appears at the $(n-1)$th new cell, and each of the cells above the $(n-1)$th new cell in the same column is left as the empty string. This is necessary for retaining the correct association among the table data across all the rows in a column while avoiding repetition of the same heading label. If the data content, say d, of the cell is replicated in the next $n-1$ cells vertically, the identical heading label will repeatedly

appear n times in its corresponding column heading C_i of a p-table, which yields $d.d.\ldots.d$, because the data content of these n cells are to be concatenated, and subsequently in the name of the node representing C_i in the corresponding SH. However, if ROWSPAN is contained in a TD, we insert $n-1$ new cells underneath the current TD cell, and replicate the data content of the TD to the inserted cells since each table data in different rows of the same column is meant to represent a data entry with the same content. After COLSPANs and ROWSPANs are properly processed, the given table conforms to the definition of p-table as given in Definition 2.

Example 1 Consider the source code in Figure 1(b), where the first TH contains null data, the second TH contains the data content "Average," and the third TH contains the data content "Red eyes." Here, we demonstrate the process of constructing the semantic hierarchy of the HTML table in Figure 1(a). Since the first and third TH both contain ROWSPAN="2", the null data of the first one is pushed down to the next row in the corresponding p-table T. At a glance, it may look like that this action has no effect to the table since the pushed-down value is a null data. With this action the pushed-down null data is inserted into cell(2, 1) in T and subsequently the TH with *height* (*weight*, respectively) is moved to the new location which is cell(2, 2) (cell(2, 3), respectively) in T. This is desirable since the correct association among "height," "weight," and other table data are now in place in T. Furthermore, the second TH contains COLSPAN = "2" and thus its data content "Average" is replicated once to the right, and "Red eyes," which is originally in the third TH, is moved to the forth column and pushed onto the forth column of the next row in T because of the existence of the attribute ROWSPAN = "2."

Note that there are two heading rows, and each column heading C_i ($1 \leq i \leq 4$) is constructed by concatenating the data contents of the two rows in the ith column (see Definition 2 for the definition of C_i). As a result, C_1 is the empty string, C_2 = Average.height, C_3 = Average.weight, and C_4 = 'Red eyes.', whereas the caption of T is the caption of the HTML table in Figure 1(a). The resulting p-table T is shown in Figure 8.

We now transform the resulting p-table T to its corresponding semantic hierarchy SH. Since T contains the caption C (i.e., *A test table with merged cells*), C forms the root node of the resulting SH according to Definition 2. Next, consider C_1. Since C_1 is empty, we skip C_1 in the hierarchy $V_R \leftarrow C_1 \leftarrow a_{i,1} \leftarrow \ldots$ and create two child nodes of the root node C by using $a_{1,1}$ (i.e., Males) and $a_{2,1}$ (i.e., Females). The rest of the cells $a_{i,j}$ ($1 \leq i \leq 2$, $2 \leq j \leq 4$) in the last two rows of T yield nodes and edges in SH as follows: $a_{1,1} \leftarrow C_2 \leftarrow a_{1,2}$; $a_{1,1} \leftarrow C_3 \leftarrow a_{1,3}$; $a_{1,1} \leftarrow C_4 \leftarrow a_{1,4}$; $a_{2,1} \leftarrow C_2 \leftarrow a_{2,2}$; $a_{2,1} \leftarrow C_3 \leftarrow a_{2,3}$; $a_{2,1} \leftarrow C_4 \leftarrow a_{2,4}$. We render the resulting SH as shown under the root node "[ROOT=E:\Table5.xml]" in

A test table with merged cells			
	Average.height	*Average.weight*	*Red eyes*
Males	1.9	0.003	40%
Females	1.7	0.002	43%

Figure 8. *P*-table of the HTML table in Figure 1(b)

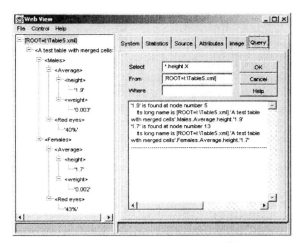

Figure 9. *SH* of the HTML table in Figure 1(a), rendered in WebView, and a sample query

the left pane of Figure 9, where each node label is enclosed within angle brackets except the leaf nodes. Note that the association of a table data *D* with another, i.e., the intended hierarchy of *D* in the table, can be conceived by examining the name of *D*. For instance, `'A test table with merged cells'.Males.Average.height.'1.9'` captures the intended hierarchy of "1.9". □

4 Semantic Matching of HTML Tables

In previous sections, we have proposed a transformation method from HTML tables to their semantic hierarchies. In this section, we present a semantic matching approach for integrating HTML tables using their semantic hierarchies.

It is a challenging task to integrate different data sources on the Web because of their differences in structures and semantics. However, it is our desire to pursue a solution of integrating HTML tables belonged to a particular domain of interest, which provides a view that captures the contents of all tables. We are particularly interested in integrating HTML tables because they are still widely used on the Web for posting information from multiple sources. Integration of HTML tables is a difficult task since (i) HTML tables enforce no particular structure of data in the tables (compare the HTML tables in Figures 10, 11, and 12, as an example), and (ii) table elements in an HTML document must first be analyzed prior to extracting the table content. In summary,

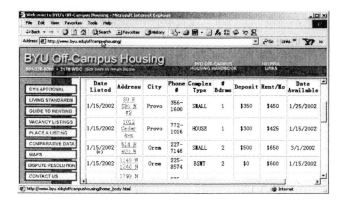

Figure 10. BYU off-campus housing

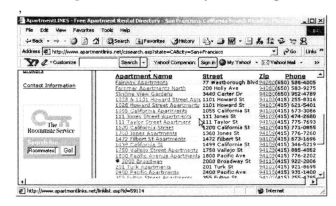

Figure 11. House rental in San Francisco

- compared with relational databases, HTML tables do not have a rigid schema definition, and hence the integration of HTML tables is more complicated than the integration of relational tables; and

- compared with different data-sensitive applications [4], most of the HTML tables are designed individually and independently. Designers of these tables may adopt different structures to organize data and use different terms to name the same or semantically equivalent data items.

It is well-known that determining the relevance of any two data items without considering their context is a very difficult, if not impossible, task. Occasionally, thesaurus and WORDNET, which are archives of precompiled lists of related words, can be used for determining the synonymous relationships among different words. However, a synonym may provide an unmatched meaning of different words. For example, the term *address* in thesaurus has seven different meanings and one of them is *destination*, whereas another one is *speech*. Even though *destination* and *speech* are two irrelevant words, they are relevant with respective to *address* in thesaurus.

165

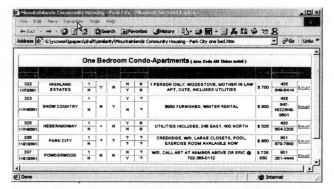

Figure 12. Mountainlands Community Housing - Park City

In this paper we assume that all HTML tables to be integrated by using our semantic matching method come from a number of "related" sources, and they belong to a particular application domain, e.g., house/apartment rental, car advertisement, etc. Without knowing a particular application domain, it is more difficult to determine the semantic of a column name in an HTML table. However, it is clear that the term *address* in an advertisement of house/apartment rental denotes a *location* rather than *speech*. Most of the existing integration methods [8] assume that each term in an integrated view has a common meaning. This assumption is impractical for HTML tables or most of the Web data in general. Our integration method, however, can be adopted in real world situation to determine whether different column names of various HTML tables that belong to a particular domain of interest are (ir)relevant. Our integration method is semi-automatic since it follows the steps below.

1. It is required that (synonymous) relationships among different (ir)relevant terms (i.e., column names in HTML tables) belong to a particular domain of interest (DOI) are *manually* determined, which yields a number of disjointed meta-data sets of terms.

2. Using the meta-data sets computed in Step 1, any two HTML tables belonging to the same DOI can be integrated *automatically*.

4.1 Computing meta-data sets of column names in related HTML tables

For a particular domain of interest DOI, we manually collect and examine a significant number of HTML tables belonged to DOI downloaded from various Web sites. Column names of these tables are extracted from their corresponding semantic hierarchies, and the set of extracted column names is called the *sample data* set of DOI. Hereafter, we create a collection of disjointed *meta-data sets* of column names from the sample data set such that each meta-data set contains a number of *semantically related* or

equivalent column names. Each element in a meta-data set is either a singleton set (i.e., a set contains only one column name) or a set of column names. For instance, in a meta-data set S consisting of column names that represent the *address* of house/apartment rental, an element in S can be {*location, city*}, whereas another element in S can be {*street, city*} or simply {*address*}.

For each meta-data set S we choose a particular element in S as the `primary name` of S, which is either a column name or a number of column names in S. The primary name of S is the most representative element in S that indicates the semantic of elements in S. For example, if $S =$ { *location, city, street, city, address* }, *address* is chosen as the primary name of S, assuming that *address* includes the information of *street*, *city*, *state*, and *ZIP*, whereas *location* includes only *apartment/unit number* and *street*. During the process of integrating HTML tables, whenever there is a collection of (one or more) column names C in a table that is included in a meta-data set M, then C is replaced by the primary name of M.

After all the meta-data sets for a particular application domain have been constructed, elements in each set are sorted in a lexicographical order, e.g., sorted by alphabetic order. Searching for column names in an HTML table to be integrated against sorted meta-data sets can be performed using binary search, which is a $\mathcal{O}(log_2 n)$ searching method, where n is the number of elements in a meta-set.

4.2 Integration of HTML tables

Algorithm 1 integrates HTML tables by using their corresponding semantic hierarchies and predefined meta-data sets.

Algorithm 1 (Integration of HTML tables).
Input: A collection of sorted meta-data sets MDS and an HTML table HT to be integrated.
Output: The integrated view of HT.

1. FOR each column name C in HT, DO
1.1.   REPEAT
1.2.   Consider the next meta-data set S in MDS.
1.3.   IF $C \in S$, THEN
1.4.   Assign the *primary name* of S to C.
1.5.   UNTIL ($C \in S$) OR (each meta-data set in MDS has been examined).
   END_FOR
2. Cluster all column names in HT that have been assigned the same *primary name*.
2.1.   Each cluster yields a single column named after the primary name.
2.2.   Each non-cluster column name is either the assigned name (i.e., the primary name) or the original column name in HT.
3. The end-result of Step 2 is the integrated view of HT.

We use the following example to illustrate the step-by-step procedure of Algorithm 1. In the example, we consider HTML tables that contain data of *house/apartment rental*, a particular domain of interest.

Example 2 Consider the three HTML tables displayed in a browser as shown in Figure 10, 11, and 12. Figure 10 is an HTML table extracted from the Brigham Young University Off-campus Housing HTML page, Figure 11 displays an HTML (house renting) table that lists rental unites in the *San Francisco* area, and Figure 12 includes information apartment rental in Park City, Utah, managed by *Mountainlands Community Housing*.

Prior to integrating the tables in Figures 10, 11, and 12, meta-data sets of *House/Apartment Rental* should have been constructed. The meta-data set of *Address* contains *Address*, *Street*, *Location*, *City*, and *Resident Location*, etc., and *Address* is selected as the primary name of the metadata set, whereas elements in the meta-data set of *(Contacted) Phone* are *Phone*, *Telephone*, *Phone#*, etc.

We first create the semantic hierarchies of the three extracted tables. Hereafter, by using metadata sets of the *House/Apartment Rental* application domain, which include *Address*, *Phone*, *Rent*, *Deposit*, *Unit Type*, etc., we integrate different column names in the tables by using metadata sets. Column names that capture relevant or equivalent meaning of *Address* include *Address* and *City* in Figure 10, *Street* and *Zip* in Figure 11, and *Location* in Figure 12. Our integration algorithm is able to determine that column names *Date Listed* (in Figure 10) and *Date Listing#* (in Figure 12) are relevant to the primary name *Date* in the meta-data set *Date*. The integrated view of the three HTML tables is partially shown in Figure 13, where the symbol '&' denotes the linked address to the corresponding data item. Note that the integrated view is just a conceptual view of the integration. The actual integrated view can be displayed using various data format. Our integration tool also provides an XML version of any integration so that the integrated data are presented in an XML document (see Section 4.4 for a sample XML document). □

4.3 Complexity analysis of our integration approach

Our approach for constructing the semantic hierarchy of an HTML table is a "one-pass" approach, meaning that the approach processes the given source table in the left-to-right, top-to-bottom, object-by-object manner, and it never reads the same object in the given table more than once. Upon detecting an object in the source table, our semantic-hierarchy construction method takes appropriate actions and process the next object until no more object is found in the table. Furthermore, no preprocessing step is required. Hence, the time complexity for constructing the semantic

hierarchy of an HTML table is proportional to the number of objects n in the given table, i.e., $\mathcal{O}(n)$.

The time complexity of creating the integrated view of a number of HTML tables is determined by Step 1 of Algorithm 1, i.e., it is the dominated step of the entire integration process. Step 1 considers each column name C in an HTML table HT to be integrated and attempts to assign C the primary name of a meta-data set, if one exists. The time complexity of this step is $\mathcal{O}(m \times Log_2\, p)$, where $Log_2\, p$ is the time complexity of performing a binary search on a pre-sorted meta-data set with p elements, and m is the number of columns in HT. Therefore, processing each column in HT is $\mathcal{O}(m \times m \times Log_2\, p)$. To cluster all the assigned primary names of original column names in Step 2 comes with $\mathcal{O}(m)$ time complexity. Hence, the time complexity for generating an integrated view of a number of HTML tables is $\mathcal{O}(n) + \mathcal{O}(m \times m \times Log_2\, p) + \mathcal{O}(m) = \mathcal{O}(m^2 Log_2\, m)$.

4.4 XML Documents of Integrated Views

We capture the integrated table of HTML tables (IHT) using the XML grammar such that the hierarchical structure of IHT is represented in its DTD.

According to the XML recommendation, the core construct of XML document type declaration is the *markup declarations*, which is DTD, a grammar for a class of documents. Among all the markup declarations, we only need *element type* and *attribute-list* declarations to obtain the DTD representation of IHT. Our strategy in generating the DTD of the given IHT is to pursue "a best guess" since reverse engineering from a data instance to its original specification is often impossible.

Element declarations. An element declaration is of the form <!ELEMENT *Name contentspec*>, where *Name* is the name of an XML element e and *contentspec* specifies whether e has #PCDATA and/or other elements as content. In our integration approach, during the process of generating the element type declaration of a node N in the given IHT, *contentspec* is replaced by (i) (#PCDATA), if N contains constant child nodes only; (ii) the list of the names of children of N, if N has non-constant child nodes only such that each name is distinguished from its adjacent name by the *choice* symbol, i.e., '|', in the list; or (iii) (#PCDATA | *children*), if N has both non-constant and constant child nodes, where *children* is the list of non-constant children's names of N as described in (ii). We group node names by *choice*, instead of a sequence of node names, because *choice* is less restrictive.

Element-content model. Given a node in an IHT, there may exist more than one child node (i.e., cnode) of node with the same name, i.e., cnode[1], cnode[2], etc. In this case, cnode in *contentspec* of <!ELEMENT node *contentspec*> is immediately fol-

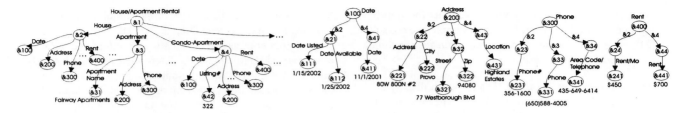

Figure 13. A portion of the integrated view of tables in Figures 10, 11 and 12

lowed by an occurrence symbol '?,' '*,' or '+,' which denotes that the preceding content particle, i.e., cnode, may occur one or more times (+), zero or more times (*), or at most once (?). If cnode occurs just once in an IHT, either `<!ELEMENT node (cnode?)>`, `<!ELEMENT node (cnode*)>`, `<!ELEMENT node (cnode+)>`, or even `<!ELEMENT node (cnode)>` is a valid declaration.

Attribute-list declarations. When a node with name cnode in an IHT comes with auxiliary information of the form *:text*, we leverage this information in its corresponding DTD. We create an attribute-list declaration `<!ATTLIST cnode AttrSpec>`, where *AttrSpec* is of the form (i) *AttrName* CDATA #IMPLIED for each string pattern *AttrName* = ..., and each one is delimited by a semicolon from its neighboring pattern in *:text* of *label(cnode)*, or (ii) attribute CDATA #IMPLIED for other patterns.

Based on the discussion above, we define the transformation from an IHT to a DTD.

Definition 3 Given a hierarchical data tree $IHT = (V, E, g)$, the DTD of IHT contains

i) an element type declaration `<!ELEMENT leaf EMPTY>` for all the non-constant leaf nodes with the same name *leaf*;

ii) an element type declaration `<!ELEMENT inode (`c_1` | ... | `c_n` | #PCDATA)>` with associated occurrence symbol that conforms to the element-content model for all the internal nodes (including the root node) with the same name *inode*, where c_i $(1 \leq i \leq n)$ denotes the non-constant child nodes of *inode* with name c_i, if any exists, and #PCDATA denotes any constant child node of *inode*, if any exists; and

iii) an attribute-list declaration `<!ATTLIST inode AttrSpec>`, where *AttrSpec* consists of zero or more (1) *AttrName* CDATA #IMPLIED for each *AttrName* = ... pattern, or (2) attribute CDATA #IMPLIED for each pattern other than *AttrName* = ... in *:text* of *label(inode)*.

The element type declaration of the root node appears at the beginning of the wrapper. □

Example 3 Consider the integrated table as partially shown in Figure 13. Since the root node is House/Apartment Rental that has more than one child nodes, i.e., House, Apartment and Condo-Apartment, with the same respective name (for each tuple), the element-type declaration of the root `<!ELEMENT HouseApartmentRental (House | Apartment | Condo-Apartment)+>` is attached to the corresponding DTD D. For the child nodes of House, since each House node has a child node with name Date, Address, Phone, Rent, etc., we obtain `<!ELEMENT House (Date | Address | Phone | Rent | ...)>`. Hence, the DTD D of IHT House/Apartment Rental is

```
<!ELEMENT HouseApartmentRental (House |
   Apartment | Condo-Apartment)+>
<!ELEMENT House (Date | Address | Phone |
   Rent | ...)>
<!ELEMENT Apartment (ApartmentName | Address
   | Phone | ...)>
<!ELEMENT Condo-Apartment (Date | Address |
   Phone | Rent | ...)>
<!ELEMENT Date (#PCDATA)>
<!ELEMENT Address ((Address, City) |
   (Street, Zip) | Address | (#PCDATA))>
<!ELEMENT City (#PCDATA)>
<!ELEMENT Street (#PCDATA)>
<!ELEMENT Zip (#PCDATA)>
<!ELEMENT Phone (#PCDATA)>
<!ELEMENT Rent (#PCDATA)>
```

: □

Definition 4 Given a hierarchical data tree IHT, the XML wrapper of IHT is an XML document of IHT that conforms to the DTD of IHT according to Definition 3. □

Example 4 Consider the integrated view shown in Figure 13 and its DTD computed in Example 3. The XML wrapper X of *House/ Apartment Rental* is constructed by plugging each node in IHT into X according to the DTD. The root *HouseApartmentRental* is attached to X as `<HouseApartmentRental>`, `</HouseApartmentRental>`, and the first House is then attached to X, which yields `<HouseApartmentRental> <House> </House> </HouseApartmentRental>`. Figure 14 shows the final XML wrapper. □

```
<HouseApartmentRental>
 <House>
  <Date> <Date Listed> 1/5/2002 </Date Listed>
   <Date Available> 1/25/2002 </Date Available>
   </Date>
  <Address> <Address> 80W 800N #2 </Address>
   <City> Provo </City> </Address>
  <Phone> 356-1600 </Phone>
  <Rent> <RentMo> $450 </RentMo> </Rent>...
 </House>
 <Apartment>
  <ApartmentName> Fairway Apartments </Apartment-
  Name>
  <Address> <Street> 77 Westborough Blvd </Street>
  <Zip> 94080 </Zip> </Address>
  <Phone> (650)588-4005 </Phone>...
 </Apartment>
 <Condo-Apartment>
  <Date> 11/1/2001 </Date>
  <Listing#> 322 </Listing#>
  <Address> Highland Estates </Address>
  <Phone> 435-649-6414 </Phone>
  <Rent> $700 </Rent>...
 </Condo-Apartment>
 ...
</HouseApartmentRental>
```

Figure 14. The XML wrapper of the integrated view in Figure 13

4.5 Experimental results

By using Google, we randomly retrieved fifty HTML tables chosen from 13 Web sites throughout the country. These HTML tables form the meta-data set of the application domain *house/apartment rental*, and they were manually examined to determine relevant column names to be clustered. For example, there are ten distinct column names in a cluster that are relevant to *Address*. Some of these Web sites provide static HTML pages, e.g., *BYU off-campus housing*, whereas others are generated dynamically using a database or data repository according to user queries, e.g., the table *House rental in San Francisco* in Figure 11.

Out of the fifty HTML tables, we randomly selected thirty as the training data set and use the other twenty as the test data set. We clustered the 20 tables into 10 different groups and ran a total of 25 test cases. Figure 15 shows the results of the experimental data. Note that for some of the incorrect results, there are column names that do not belong to the predefined column names determined by the training data set, e.g., column name *property* in some tables is relevant to *address*. The result is significantly affected by the chosen meta-data set.

5 Concluding remarks

In this paper, we propose a method for integrating HTML tables. Since HTML tables have different structures and naming conventions, it is necessary to identify and resolve the differences. In solving this problem, we first cre-

Name	T	C	I	P	R
Address	250	219	31	87.6%	87.6%
Rent	215	212	3	98.6%	98.6%
Deposit	203	197	6	97%	97%
Bedrooms	192	182	10	94.8%	94.8%
Available Date	97	97	0	100%	100%
Email	103	81	22	78.6%	78.6%
Note	72	72	0	100%	100%

T (Total); C (Correct); I (Incorrect); P (Precision); R (Recall)

Figure 15. Experimental Results for the House Rental Application Domain

ate the semantic hierarchies of HTML tables embedded in different HTML documents. The constructed semantic hierarchies are integrated by matching the "closely" related column names in the original HTML tables, and the end-result is an integrated view. The integrated view is stored in an XML document, with its well-defined DTD representation. The pre-processing step of matching column names requires human intervention; however, the process of constructing semantic hierarchies of HTML tables and hereafter the actual integrated of multiple HTML tables are fully-automatic. Since the integrated view is given in XML, our approach can be adopted across various platforms and data modeling paradigms.

References

[1] G. O. Arocena and A. O. Medelzon. WebOQL: Restructuring Documents, Databases and Webs. In *Proceedings of the 14th ICDE*, February 1998.

[2] S. Bergamaschi, S. Castano, and M. Vincini.Semantic Integration of Semi- structured and Structured Data Sources. *SIGMOD Record*, 28(1):54–59, 1999.

[3] S. Castano, V. D. Antonellis, M. Fugini, and B. Pernici. Conceptual Schema Analysis: Techniques and Applications. *ACM TODS*, 23(3):286–333, 1998.

[4] M. Fernandez, D. Suciu, and W. Tan. SilkRoute: Trading between relations and XML. In *Proc. of 9th Intl. Conf. on WWW*, 2000.

[5] A. Levy, A. Rajaraman, and J. Ordille. Querying Heterogeneous Information Sources Using Source Descriptions. In *Proc. of VLDB*, pages 251–262, 1996.

[6] S. Liddle, S. Yau, and D. Embley. On the Automatic Extraction of Data from the Hidden Web. In *Proceedings of the Intl. Workshop on Data Semantics in Web Information Systems*, pages 106–119, 2001.

[7] J. McHugh and J. Widom. Integrating Dynamically-Fetched External Information into a DBMS for Semistructured Data. *SIGMOD Record*, 26(4), 1997.

[8] J. D. Ullman. Information Integration Using Logical Views. In *Proceedings of ICDT '97*, pages 19–40, 1997.

[9] J. Widom. Research Problems in Data Warehousing. In *Proceedings of the 4th ACM CIKM*, 1995.

[10] G. Wiederhold. Mediators in the Architecture of Future Information Systems. *IEEE Computer*, 25(3):38–49, 1992.

Paper Session V

(Modelling)

YAM² (Yet Another Multidimensional Model): An extension of UML

Alberto Abelló
U. Politècnica de Catalunya (UPC)
Dept. de Llenguatges i Sistemes Informàtics
aabello@lsi.upc.es

José Samos
U. de Granada (UGR)
Dept. de Lenguajes y Sistemas Informáticos
jsamos@ugr.es

Fèlix Saltor
U. Politècnica de Catalunya (UPC)
Dept. de Llenguatges i Sistemes Informàtics
saltor@lsi.upc.es

Abstract

This paper presents a multidimensional conceptual Object-Oriented model, its structures, integrity constraints and query operations. It has been developed as an extension of UML core metaclasses to facilitate its usage, as well as to avoid the introduction of completely new concepts. YAM² allows the representation of several semantically related star schemas, as well as summarizability and identification constraints.

1 Introduction

A "Data Warehouse" (DW) is roughly a huge repository of data used on the decision making process. To help on the management and study of that enormous quantity of data appeared "On-Line Analytical Processing" (OLAP) tools. The main characteristic of this kind of tools is multidimensionality. They represent data as if these were placed in an n-dimensional space, allowing a study in terms of facts subject of analysis, and dimensions showing the different points of view according to which data can be analyzed.

There are several papers about multidimensional modeling (see [11] and [16] for two surveys of multidimensional models), but few of them place the discussion at conceptual level. Moreover, most of them focus on the representation of isolated star schemas, i.e. the representation of only one kind of facts surrounded by its analysis dimensions. In spite of the dominant trend in data modeling is the "Object-Oriented" (O-O) paradigm, there exist only a couple of proposals on O-O multidimensional modeling: [15] and [8]. These proposals use "Unified Modeling Language" (UML) standard (defined in [9]) in some way, but none of them proposes an extension of it to include multidimension-

ality. Just the "Common Warehouse Metamodel" (CWM) standard (defined in [10]) extends UML metaclasses to represent some multidimensional concepts. However, it is too general, and not conceived as a conceptual model.

Next section explains the main contributions of our multidimensional model. Then, sections 3, 4, and 5 present its structures, inherent integrity constraints, and operations, respectively. Finally, section 6 shows the metaclasses of the model and their relationships with UML metaclasses.

2 *YAM²* is not JAM² (Just Another Multidimensional Model)

As stated in [3], a "database model" provides the means for specifying particular data structures, for constraining the data sets associated with these structures, and for manipulating the data. It is also explained there that, as Relations are the data structures of the Relational model, so graphs are the structures of O-O models. We provide a precise, easily understandable semantics for graphs in our O-O model, by defining *YAM²* structures as an extension of a wide accepted modeling language, i.e. UML (each and every *YAM²* metaclass is a subclass of a UML metaclass). There are some multidimensional models that use UML notation, but no one extends its concepts for multidimensional purposes. By using UML as a base for the definition of structures of *YAM²*, we build our model on solid, well accepted foundations, and avoid the definition of basic concepts.

"Expressiveness" or "Semantic Power", as it is defined in [12], is the degree to which a model can express or represent a conception of the real world. It measures the power of the elements of the model to represent conceptual structures, and to be interpreted as such conceptual structures. The most expressive a model is, the better it represents the real world, and the more information about the data gives to the user. As outlined in [5], due to the presence of multidimensional aggregation, data warehouse - and specially OLAP - applications ask for the vital extension of the expressive power and functionality of traditional conceptual modeling formalisms. Therefore, this is crucial for conceptual multidimensional models like YAM^2. We will define different kinds of nodes and arcs in the graphs to improve the "Expressiveness" of our model. The applicability of the different kinds of relationships supported by UML has been systematically studied.

Another important point for a data model is its "Semantic Relativism". It is defined in [12] as the degree to which the model can accommodate not only one, but many different conceptions. This is really important, because ,since different persons perceive and conceive the world in different ways, the data model should be able to capture all of them. The information kept in the DW should be shown to users in the form they expect to see it, independently of how it was previously conceived or is actually stored. Therefore, YAM^2 also provides mechanisms (derivation relationships) to model the same data from different points of view.

Our model also pays special attention to show how data can be classified and grouped in a manner appropriate for subsequent summarization. Summarized data can be reflected in a YAM^2 schema, as well as the ways to obtain it. For instance, this information can be used at later design phases to decide materialization.

Therefore, main advantages of YAM^2 are its expressiveness and semantic relativism, besides the flexibility offered in the definition of summarization constraints (it generalizes the work in [6]). Moreover, from the separate study of characteristics of analysis dimensions and factual data in [1] and [2], we ensure that it is defined on solid foundations.

3 Structures

In this section, we define the structures in our O-O model (i.e. nodes and arcs).

3.1 Nodes

Multidimensional models are based on the duality "fact-dimensions". Intuitively, a "fact" represents data subject of analysis, and "dimensions" show different points of view we can use in analysis tasks. The "facts" represent measurements (in a general sense), while "dimensions" represent given information we already have before taking the measurements. Now we are going to give the definition of the different nodes we find in a multidimensional O-O schema.

Definition 1 *A* Level *represents the set of instances of the same granularity in an analysis dimension. It is an specialization of* Class *UML metaclass.*

Definition 2 *A* Descriptor *is an attribute of a* Level, *used to select its instances. It is an specialization of* Attribute *UML metaclass.*

Definition 3 *A* Dimension *is a connected, directed graph representing a point of view on analyzing data. Every vertex in the graph corresponds to a* Level, *and an edge reflects that every instance of target* Level *decomposes into a collection of instances of source* Level *(i.e. edges reflect part-whole relationships between instances of* Levels*). It is an specialization of* Classifier *UML metaclass.*

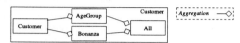

Figure 1. *Levels* **in a** *Dimension*

Figure 1 shows an example of *Dimension*. It contains four *Level*s: Customer, AgeGroup, Bonanza, and All. Every instance of Customer *Level* represents a customer, which can be aggregated in two different ways to obtain either age or bonanza groups of customers. At top we have All level with exactly one instance representing the group of all customers in the *Dimension*. The structure of graphs of *Dimension* forms a lattice, and due to the transitive property of part-whole relationships, some arcs are redundant, so that they do not need to be explicited (for instance, Customer being aggregated into All).

Definition 4 *A* Cell *represents the set of instances of a given kind of fact measured at the same granularity for each of its analysis dimensions. It is an specialization of* Class *UML metaclass.*

Definition 5 *A* Measure *is an attribute of a* Cell *representing measured data to be analyzed. Thus, each instance of* Cell *contains a (possibly empty) set of measurements. It is an specialization of* Attribute *UML metaclass.*

Definition 6 *A* Fact *is a connected, directed graph representing a subject of analysis. Every vertex in the graph corresponds to a* Cell, *and an edge reflects that every instance of target* Cell *decomposes into a collection of instances of source* Cell *(i.e. edges reflect part-whole relationships between instances of* Cell*s). It is an specialization of* Classifier *UML metaclass.*

Figure 2 shows an example of the structure of a *Fact* with two orthogonal *Dimension*s: Customer, already depicted in figure 1; and Clerk, composed by Clerk, Team, and All *Level*s. We can see that there is a *Cell* in the *Fact* for every combination of *Level*s in the *Dimension*s. Thus, a *Fact* contains all data regarding the same subject at any granularity. Having two independent *Dimension*s with 4 and 3 *Level*s respectively, means that the *Fact* will have 12

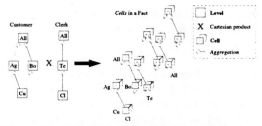

Figure 2. *Cell*s in a *Fact* **with two** *Dimension*s

different *Cell*s. These *Cell*s and the part-whole relationships between them form a lattice. It is not necessary to represent all those *Cell*s in the schema. *Cell*s just containing derived data are optional, and should only be explicited to emphasize the importance of summarized data at a given aggregation level.

These six kinds of nodes are grouped in three pairs. At intermediate level, there are *Cell*s and *Level*s. Looking at lower detail we see *Measure*s and *Descriptor*s. Moreover, at this level, we also define *KindOfMeasure* to show that several *Measure*s in different *Cell*s correspond to the same measured concept at different aggregation levels. Moreover, at upper detail level, we have *Fact*s and *Dimension*s (one *Fact* and the *Dimension*s associated to it compose a *Star*).

Definition 7 *A* Star *is a modeling element composed by one* Fact, *and several* Dimension*s that can be used to analyze it. It is an specialization of* Package *UML metaclass.*

3.2 Arcs

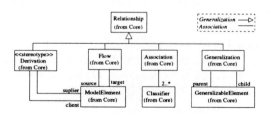

Figure 3. UML Relationships

Once the nodes have been defined, in this section, we are going to see the different kinds of arcs we could find between them. UML provides different subclasses and stereotypes of *Relationship*. As depicted in figure 3, *Generalization* relationships relate two *GeneralizableElement*s, one with a more specific meaning than the other. *Classifier*s and *Association*s are *GeneralizableElement*s. *Flow* relationships relate two elements in the model, so that both represent different versions of the same thing. *Association*, as defined in UML specification, defines a semantic relationship between *Classifier*s. By means of a stereotype of *AssociationEnd*, UML allows to use a stronger type of *Association* (i.e. *Aggregation*), where one classifier represents

parts of the other. It shows part-whole relationships. Finally, UML allows to represent different kinds of *Dependency* relationships between *ModelElement*s like *Binding*, *Usage*, *Permission*, or *Abstraction*. We are not going to consider the three first, because they are rather used on application modeling, and *YAM*[2] is just a data model. Moreover, due to the same reason, out of the different stereotypes of *Abstraction* we are only going to use *Derivation*. Derivability, also known as "Point of View", helps to represent the relationships between model elements in different conceptions of the UoD.

In this section, we systematically see how those relationships can be used to relate multidimensional constructs at every detail level. For every pair of constructs at each detail level we will show whether they can be related by a given kind of *Relationship* or not. Moreover, if two constructs can be related, we will also show whether they must belong to the same construct at the level above, or not (i.e. inter or intra relationships, respectively).

3.2.1 Upper detail level

	Fact-Fact	Fact-Dimension	Dimension-Fact	Dimension-Dimension
Generalization	Inter	-	-	Intra/Inter
Association	Intra/Inter	Intra/Inter	Intra/Inter	Intra/Inter
Aggregation	Intra/Inter	-	-	Intra/Inter
Flow	Inter	-	-	Intra/Inter
Derivation	Inter	Intra/Inter	-	Intra/Inter

Table 1. Relationships at upper detail level

Table 1 shows the different relationships we can find at this detail level. Since a *Star* only contains one *Fact*, in order to have two related *Fact*s, they must belong to different *Star*s. Therefore, relationships between *Fact*s will always be inter-stellar, but for reflexive *Association*s and *Aggregation*s. However, we can have inter-stellar as well as intra-stellar relationships between two *Dimension*s, because a *Star* contains several *Dimension*s, which can be related.

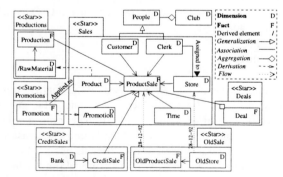

Figure 4. *YAM*[2] **schema at upper detail level**

Figure 4 shows examples of most relationships at this level. Firstly, corresponding to the upper-left corner of the table, we see that two *Fact*s can be related by *Generalization* (i.e., ProductSale and CreditSale). We will

174

have different information for the more specific *Fact* (for example, number of credit card). Thus, analysis dimensions are inherited from the more general *Fact*, but others could be added, like `Bank`. `ProductSale` and `Production` are related by *Association* to show the correspondences between produced and sold items. We can also find *Aggregation* relationships between *Facts*. A *Fact* in a *Star* can be composed by *Facts* in another *Star*. For instance, a `Deal` is composed by several individual `ProductSale`. Notice that it is not always possible to calculate all measurements of `Deal` from those of `ProductSale` (for instance, discount in the deal). Data sources, measure instruments, or calculation algorithms are probably going to change, and these changes should be reflected in our model by means of *Flow* relationships between *Facts*. All these changes are not reflected by just relating our *Facts* to `Time` *Dimension*, since we actually have different *Cells*. On `December 28th of 1992`, we started recording discount checks in `ProductSale`, so that we kept both incomes (i.e. cash, and discount checks). From that day on, we have different *Facts* containing the same kind of data before and after the acceptance of the checks (i.e. `OldProductSale`, and `ProductSale`). Finally, two *Facts* could also be related by *Derivation* relationships to show that they are the same concept from different points of view.

In the upper-right corner of table 1, we can see that there exist *Generalization* relationships between *Dimensions*. For instance, `People` *Dimension* generalizes `Clerk` and `Customer` ones. Notice that if we suppose that all people are customers, both related *Dimensions* would belong to the same *Star*. It is also possible to have analysis dimensions related by *Association*. Thus, `Clerk` is associated with `Store` *Dimension* to show that clerks are assigned to stores. We can also find stronger associations between analysis dimensions, if we join more than one to give rise to another. For example, `People` *Dimension* is used to define `Club` by means of an *Aggregation* relationship. Every instance of `Club` is composed by a set of people. Several years ago, when our local business grew, `Store` *Dimension* was changed to reflect the new *Level* `Region`. At conceptual level, those changes are represented by a *Flow* relationship between `OldStore` and `Store`. *Derivations* allow to state that there are different views of the same *Dimension*. We could find that the same concept has different names depending on the subject we are. Thus, a *Dimension* could be used in different *Stars*. For example, `Product` is considered `RawMaterial` in a different context. Therefore, the same *Dimension*, with exactly the same instances, needs a different name depending on the context. These *Dimensions* could even have different aggregation hierarchies or attributes of interest to the users. For example, studying the raw material grouped by profit margin can be meaningless.

The middle columns in table 1 show how a *Fact* can be related to a *Dimension* and vice versa. Firstly, we see that a *Fact* is related to its analysis dimensions by means of *Association* relationships. Moreover, they can also be associated to *Facts* in another *Star* as shown in the example, where `Promotion` *Fact* is associated to `Product` *Dimension* in the `Sales` *Star*. A *Dimension* can be obtained by deriving it from a *Fact*. The name can be changed, some aggregation levels added or removed, others modified, some instances selected, etc. in order to adapt it to its new usage. In our example, some people is interested in the analysis of promotions. Thus, the promotions selected by studying `Promotion` *Fact*, can be used as *Dimension* to study `ProductSale`. Notice the difference between deriving a *Dimension* and associating it to a *Fact* in another *Star*. The former allows to study the sales performed during a promotion, while the latter shows all promotions that have been applied to a kind of product. That *Derivation* between a *Fact* and a *Dimension* uses to be an inter-stellar relationship (i.e. from a *Fact*, we derive a *Dimension* to analyze another *Fact*). However, we could also use information derived from a *Fact* to analyze the same *Fact*. It is also important to say that a *Fact* cannot be derived from a *Dimension*, because *Facts* represent measurements, so that they cannot be found a priori in the form of *Dimension*. The rest of relationships (i.e. *Generalization*, *Aggregation*, and *Flow*) cannot be found between a *Fact* and a *Dimension*, nor vice versa. All three imply obtaining a new element based on a preexisting one, and the difference between *Fact* and *Dimension* is so important that obtaining of one from the other should be restricted to derivation mechanisms. For instance, a *Fact* cannot eventually become a *Dimension*.

3.2.2 Intermediate detail level

	Cell-Cell	Cell-Level	Level-Cell	Level-Level
Generalization	Inter	-	-	Inter
Association	Intra/Inter	Inter	Inter	Intra/Inter
Aggregation	Intra/Inter	-	-	Intra/Inter
Flow	Inter	-	-	Inter
Derivation	Inter	Inter	-	Inter

Table 2. Relationships at intermediate detail level

Table 2 shows the relationships we can find at this level. Most of them are exemplified in figure 5. Our company (resulting from the fusion of preexisting smaller companies) is organized in autonomous regions. Thus, the information systems in one of these regions collect data that those in other regions do not, so we specialize our *Cells* (i.e. `AtomicSale`) depending on the region. This specialization is due to the specialization of the kind of fact they are representing. Therefore, we can see in the upper-left corner of the table that two *Cells* can be related by *Generalization*, but they must belong to different *Facts* (i.e. it is an inter-factual relationship). *Cell*s in different *Fact*s can be associated (for instance, each *Cell* representing a sale with its corresponding *Cell* representing the production of what was sold). Moreover, we can also have *Association* relationships between *Cell*s in the same *Fact* (for instance, computers are associated to those other products that are plugged to them). In general, we only have intra-factual *Aggregation* relationships, which correspond to those relationships between *Level*s, and are not necessary in the schema. However, we could also find that different *Cell*s are aggregated to obtain a *Cell* about a different kind of fact (when both *Fact*s are also related like `ProductSale` and `Deal`). In this case, we do not group *Cell*s along any analysis dimension, i.e. it does not generate coarser *Cell*s in the same *Fact*, but *Cell*s in another *Fact* (i.e. `AtomicDeal`). If a new *Measure* would appear for a kind of fact, we would obtain a new *Cell* related to the old one by means of a *Flow*. Both would represent the same concept. However, they would belong to different versions of the same *Fact* (it is an inter-factual relationship). *Derivation* relationships can be used to hide information, change names, or *Measure*s in the *Cell*s, giving rise to new *Fact*s.

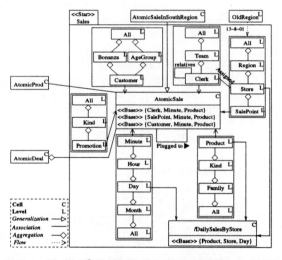

Figure 5. *YAM²* **schema at intermediate detail level**

The rightmost column shows that we could also find *Generalization* relationships between two *Level*s. As in the case of *Cell*s, it must be an inter-dimensional relationship, because both *Level*s cannot be related, at the same time, by *Generalization* and part-whole relationships. *Association*s between *Level*s can be intra- as well as inter-dimensional. The *Level* representing clerks is associated with other clerks (his/her relatives) in the same *Dimension*, and with stores in another *Dimension*. Intra-dimensional *Aggregation*s define the graph of the *Dimension*. However, we could also find inter-dimensional *Aggregation*s between *Level*s, if two *Di-*

*mension*s are so related. When the company was restructured and the regional division changed, the aggregation level showing it also changed. Both, new and old *Level*s are related by means of a *Flow* (although they represent the same concept, they belong to different versions of the same *Dimension*). Finally, as for any other concept, a *Level* could be derived from another one to show it from a different point of view.

All relationships in the central columns must be inter-structure, because *Cell*s and *Level*s always belong to different structures (i.e. *Fact*s and *Dimension*s, respectively). As for relationships at upper detail level, a *Cell* cannot be converted into a *Level* nor vice versa by means of *Generalization*, *Aggregation*, or *Flow*. It must always be done using derivation mechanisms. Moreover, because of the same reason that a *Fact* cannot be derived from a *Dimension*, a *Cell* cannot be derived from a *Level*. Nevertheless, if a *Dimension* is derived from a *Fact*, its *Level*s are also derived from the *Cell*s of the *Fact*. *Association*s exist between *Cell*s and *Level*s, and vice versa (showing the granularity of the *Cell*s).

3.2.3 Lower detail level

	Measure-Meas.	Measure-Descr.	Descriptor-Meas.	Descriptor-Descr.
Flow	Inter	-	-	Inter
Derivation	Intra/Inter	Inter	Inter	Intra/Inter

Table 3. Relationships a lower detail level

Since elements at this level are neither *Classifier*s nor *GeneralizableElement*s, but just *Attribute*s, as it is shown in table 3, they can only be related by those relationships between *ModelElement* (i.e. *Derivation*, and *Flow*).

If a change affects a *Measure* or *Descriptor*, they will belong to new versions of their *Cell* and *Level*, respectively. Thus, *Flow* relationships are in both cases inter-structure. Moreover, evolution cannot convert a *Measure* into a *Descriptor*, nor vice versa.

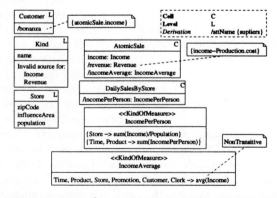

Figure 6. *YAM²* **schema at lower detail level**

It is always possible to define derived *Measure*s from

other *Measure*s in the same *Cell*, as well as *Descriptor*s from other *Descriptor*s in the same *Level*. Moreover, in both cases, supplier *Attribute*s could also be in other *Classes*. *Measure*s in a *Cell* could be obtained by applying some operation to *Measure*s in other *Cell*s. For instance, looking to lower detail level elements in figure 6, we see that measurements of `revenue` in `AtomicSale` are obtained from subtracting `cost` in `Production`. What is more, a *Descriptor* can be obtained from some *Measure*s (for example, the goodness of a customer from the income of his/her purchases), or vice versa (for example, impact of sales obtained by dividing incomes by the population of the influence area of the store). This figure does not show arcs between *Cell*s and *Level*s, because they are at intermediate detail level.

4 Inherent integrity constraints

The metaclasses of the model define constraints on multidimensional schemas, but constraints should also be defined on their instances. In this section, we are going to address that kind of constraints, paying special attention to two important aspects in multidimensional modeling, namely placement of data in an n-dimensional space, and summarizability of data.

The main contribution of multidimensionality is the placement of data in an n-dimensional space. This improves the understanding of those data and allows the implementation of specific storage techniques. It is important that the n dimensions of the space (i.e. *Cube*) are orthogonal. If not, i.e. if a *Dimension* determines others, the visualization of data will be unnecessarily complicated (we are showing more information than it is needed and it will be more difficult for users to understand it); moreover, storage mechanisms are affected, as well, because they are not considering that several combinations of dimension values are impossible, maybe resulting in a waste of space. This does not mean that all *Dimension*s in a *Star* must be orthogonal. Nevertheless, those defining *Cube*s (which are used for visualization as well as storage purposes) should be, or at least the user should know whether they are.

A *Cell* instance is related to one object or set of objects (if it is an *Association* with upper-bound multiplicity greater than one) at each associated analysis dimension, and those objects or sets of objects completely identify it. Thus, regarding placement of data in n-dimensional spaces, we could say that the set of *Level*s a *Cell* is associated with form a "superkey" (in Relational terms) of that *Cell*. We call *Base* to every minimal set of *Level*s being "superkey" (i.e. "key" in the Relational model) of a *Cell*. When one of these *Base*s (that define spaces of orthogonal *Dimension*s) is associated to a *Cell*, we obtain a *Cube*. For instance, `AtomicSale` (in figure 5) can be associated with points in the 3-dimensional space defined by *Level*s `Clerk`, `Minute`, and `Product`,

so that `AtomicSale` is fully functionally determined by those three *Level*s (a *Base* of the space).

Definition 8 *A* Cube *is an injective function from an n-dimensional finite space (defined by the cartesian product of n functionally independent* Level*s), to the set of instances of a* Cell *(C_c).* $c : L_1 \times .. \times L_n \to C_c$

If the *Level*s were not functionally independent (i.e. they did not form a *Base*), we would use more *Dimension*s than strictly needed to represent the data, and would generate empty meaningless zones in the space.

Another interesting group of constraints to deal with is that related to summarization anomalies and how to solve (or prevent) them. In multidimensional modeling, it is essential to know how a given kind of measure must be aggregated to obtain it at a coarser granularity. [6] identifies three necessary (intuitively also sufficient) conditions for summarizability:

1. Disjointness: the subsets of objects to be aggregated must be disjoint.

2. Completeness: the union of subsets must constitute the entire set.

3. Compatibility: category attribute (i.e. *Level*), summary attribute (i.e. *KindOfMeasure*), and statistical function (i.e. *Summarization*) must be compatible.

The first two conditions are absolutely dependent on constraints over cardinalities in the part-whole relationships in the *Dimension*s, because these define the grouping categories. Therefore, let us briefly talk also about this third group of integrity constraints of our model.

To avoid those anomalies on summarizing data, some models forbid "to-many" relationships in the aggregation hierarchies. This means that instances of a *Part Level* can only belong to one *Whole*. Nevertheless, there is no mereological axiom forbidding the sharing of parts among several wholes. A given product `Kinder Surprise` (at *Level* `Product`) belongs to two different kinds of products at the same *Level* `Kind` (i.e. `Candies`, and `Toys`). We argue that this case should not be ignored by a multidimensional model. Therefore, non-strict hierarchies are allowed in the *Dimension*s, and they need to be taken into account to decide summarizability of *Measure*s.

The other problem on cardinalities is that of "non-onto" and "non-covering" hierarchies (as presented is [11]). That is, having different part-whole structures for instances at the same *Level* is allowed. For example, if we would have a state-city (like `Monaco` in a `Geographic` linear *Dimension* with *Level*s `City`, `State`, and `All`), we could generate both situations. If we consider that `Monaco` is a city, we have a "non-covering" hierarchy (we are skipping `State`

Level). On the other hand, if it is considered a state, we obtain a "non-onto" hierarchy (we have different path lengths from the root to the leaves depending on the instances). In this case, we propose the usage of what some authors call "Dummy Values" to guarantee the existence of at least one part for every whole in the hierarchy. These values are not dummy at all. `Monaco` being a state-city does not mean it is either a state or a city, but a state and a city at the same time. Thus, both instances will represent city and state facets of the same entity. Therefore, in YAM^2, cardinalities in aggregation hierarchies are "1..*" parts for every whole, and "*" wholes for every part, on the understanding that *Dimension* instances can always be defined so that there are "1..*" wholes for every part.

Going back to the group of constraints regarding summarizability, in our model, there are three different elements to deal with that problem (all exemplified in figure 6). These elements allow to represent summarizability conditions in a more flexible way than just distinguishing "additive", "semi-additive", and "non-additive" *Measure*s. Firstly, we have that some *Level*s are an *InvalidSource* for the calculation of a given *KindOfMeasure* (for example, `Kind` is an invalid source for `Income` and `Revenue`). This means that measurements at an aggregation level cannot be used to obtain data at higher aggregation levels. We must go to *Level*s below to obtain the source of data for the calculation.

This can be due to the fact that the instances of that *Level* are not disjoint or not complete (i.e. summarizability conditions 1 and 2 mentioned above). A *Level* being invalid or not cannot be deduced just from the cardinalities of its associations, but also depends on the *KindOfMeasure*. For instance, if a *Measure* is obtained as the minimum of a set of measurements, it does not matter whether the source sets of instances are disjoint or not.

Moreover, *Induce Association* shows the summarization that must be performed on aggregating a given *KindOfMeasure* along a *Dimension*. This constraint regards the third condition mentioned above. Along a given analysis dimension we use a summarization operation, while along a different analysis dimension we use a different function. For instance, we aggregate `IncomePerPerson` along `Time` and `Product` by means of sum, while along `Store` it needs to be recalculated from `Incomes`. Incompatibilities are not always associated to `Time` *Dimension*. Furthermore, instances of *Induction* could be partially ordered, if necessary, to show that operations are not commutative, and must be performed in a given order, as pointed out in [14]. For example, sums along a *Dimension* must be performed before averages along another one, so that, we aggregate up to the desired *Level* in a *Dimension*, and then we aggregate along the other.

Finally, another point to take into account, usually overlooked in other models, is that of transitivity. If a summarization operation is not transitive, we cannot use precalculated aggregates at a given *Level* to obtain those at higher levels. Going to the atomic source is mandatory (for instance, we should not perform the average of averages, if we want to obtain the average of raw data).

5 Operations

The multidimensional model is just a query model, i.e. it does not need operations for update, since this is not directly performed by final users. YAM^2 operations focus on identifying and uniformly manipulating sets of data, namely *Cube*s. In a *Cube*, data are identified by their properties. Thus, these operations are separated from the physical storage of the data. Moreover, they are not presentation oriented like those in [13].

Detail level	Subject of analysis	Point of view
Upper	Drill-across	ChangeBase
Intermediate	-	Roll-up
Lower	Projection	Dice

Table 4. YAM^2 **operations**

As everything in a multidimensional model, operations are also marked by the duality "fact-dimensions". Table 4 shows the operations in two columns. The first one contains those operations having effect on the subject of analysis (i.e. *Fact*, *Cell*, and *Measure*). They select the part of the schema we want to see. In the other column, there are those operations affecting the point of view we will use in the analysis (i.e. *Dimension*, *Level*, and *Descriptor*). They allow to reorganize the data, modify their granularity, and focus on a specific subset, by selecting the instances we want to see.

Figure 7. Multidimensional operations as composition of functions

In the sense of [3], these operations are conceptually a "procedural language", because queries are specified by a sequence of operations that construct the answer. We generally say that a query is from (or over) its input schema to its output schema. Thus, there exists an input m-dimensional *Cube* (c_i), and we want to obtain an output n-dimensional *Cube* (c_o). Since we defined a *Cube* as a function (see definition 8), operations must transform a function into another function. Operations in the first column work on the image of the function (i.e. *Cell*), while operations in the second column change its domain (i.e. *Base*). As depicted in figure 7, we have three families of functions (i.e. f, g, and h), that can be used to transform a *Cube*.

Obtaining c_o from c_i, can be seen as mathematical composition of functions ($c_o = \psi \circ c_i \circ \phi$, with ψ and ϕ belonging to the families of functions g and f, respectively). Firstly, we can see how *ChangeBase*, given c_i and ϕ (a function belonging to a family of functions f between the finite spaces defined by cartesian product of *Level*s of each *Cube*), we obtain a new *Cube* ($c_o = c_i \circ \phi$). Nevertheless, *Drill-across* does change the *Cell*. Thus, it works in the opposite way, in the sense that it needs a *Cube* c_i and the function ψ (belonging to a family of functions g from a *Cell* to another *Cell*) to obtain the new *Cube* ($c_o = \psi \circ c_i$).

Unfortunately, it is not possible to define all operations in such a way. *Roll-up* changes the space as well as the *Cell*. Thus, obtaining it as a composition of functions is not possible, because a coordinate in the space of c_o corresponds to several points in c_i. Therefore, there is no ζ, so that c_o is a composition of ζ and c_i. It can neither be defined as an homomorphism (like those in [4]), because the problem is not the conversion of a set of instances into one instance (which is always performed by union), but deciding which is the set of instances to be converted (defined by a function of family h).

Drill-across: This operation changes the image set of the *Cube* by means of an injective function ψ of the family g (relationships in section 3.2 can be used for this purpose). The space remains exactly the same, only the cells placed in it change. This function relates instances of a *Fact* to instances of another one. $\psi : C_c^i \to C_c^o$, *injective* so that $c_o(x) = \delta_\psi(c_i) = \psi(c_i(x))$

Projection: This just selects a subset of *Measure*s from those available in the selected *Cell*. Since it works at the attribute level, it is absolutely equivalent to the homonym operation in Relational algebra. $c_o(x) = \pi_{m_1,..,m_k}(c_i) = c_i(x)[m_1,..,m_k]$

ChangeBase: This operations reallocates exactly the same *Cell* in a new space. It changes the domain set of the *Cube* by means of an injective function ϕ of the family f (i.e. ϕ relates points in an n-dimensional finite space to points in an m-dimensional finite space). Thus, it actually modifies the analysis dimensions used. $\phi : L_1^o \times .. \times L_n^o \to L_1^i \times .. \times L_m^i$, *injective* so that $c_o(x) = \gamma_\phi(c_i) = c_i(\phi(x))$

Roll-up: It groups cells in the *Cube* based on an aggregation hierarchy. This operation modifies the granularity of data, by means of an exhaustive function φ of the family h (i.e. φ relates instances of two *Level*s in the same *Dimension*, corresponding to a part-whole relationship). It reduces the number of cells, but not the number of *Dimension*s. $c_o(x) = \rho_\varphi(c_i) = \bigcup_{\varphi(y)=x} c_i(y)$

Dice: By means of a predicate P over *Descriptor*s, this operation allows to choose the subset of points of interest out of the whole n-dimensional space. Like *Projection*, it is absolutely equivalent to an operation of Relational algebra. In this case, the operation is "Selection". $c_o(x) = \sigma_P(c_i) = \begin{cases} c_i(x) & if\ P(x) \\ undef & if\ \neg P(x) \end{cases}$

Looking to the empty cell in table 4, it is clear that there is another operation missing, which would allow to select the *Cell* we want to query in the same way we choose *Measure*s or *Fact*s. However, the specific *Cell* we analyze cannot be selected by itself, but it is absolutely determined by the selected aggregation levels in every *Dimension*.

If we want to know the production cost of every product sold under a given promotion, by month and plant, we should perform the following operations over our `AtomicSale` schema: 1) *Dice* to select promotion "A", 2) *Drill-across* to "Production" *Fact*, 3) *Projection* to see just the desired *Measure* "cost", 4) *Roll-up* to obtain data at "Month" *Level* (notice that summarization operation is not explicited, because a YAM^2 schema shows how a given *KindOfMeasure* must be summarized along each *Dimension*), and finally 5) *ChangeBase* to choose the appropriate n-dimensional space to place data.

$$\gamma_{Month \times Plant \times Product}(\rho_{Month}(\pi_{cost}(\delta_{Production}($$
$$\sigma_{Promotion="A"}(AtomicSale))))))$$

These operations allow to build *Cube*s on solid mathematical foundations. Semantic relationships in the multidimensional schema define functions between *Classes*. By composing those functions appropriately, we can obtain the desired vision of data. If we want to analyze instances of a given *Class* in the space defined by the cartesian product of a set of *Classes*, all we have to do is find the appropriate composition of functions. If that "chain" of functions exists, we can analyze data in the desired way. Thus, properties of mathematical functions can be applied.

It is also important to outline that this set of operations is minimal (i.e. none can be expressed in terms of others, nor can any be dropped without affecting their functionality) and the operations are atomic (i.e. each operation performs exactly one task). This can be easily inferred from the explanation above, and table 4. Each operation works inside only one detail level. Moreover, they work either on factual or dimensional data. *Roll-up* could be thought as working on both sides, however, it really operates only on factual data based on dimensional data.

6 Metaclasses

When analysts want to study a given subject, they want to see together all data regarding it. Thus, we propose a

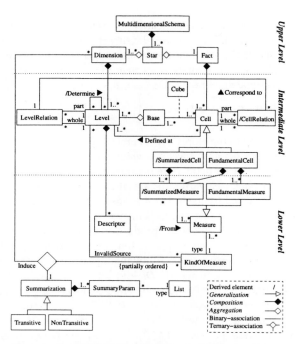

Figure 8. *YAM²* **metaclasses in UML notation**

subject-oriented model, where all *Class*es related to a subject are shown together in the multidimensional schema. For this purpose we use the upper detail level which, as depicted in figure 8, shows that a *Star* is composed by one *Fact* and several *Dimension*s. Subject-oriented does not imply subject-isolated. Therefore, relationships between different *Star*s will exist, as it was shown in section 3.2.

At the intermediate detail level, we can see that *Dimension*s are composed by *Level*s related by *LevelRelation*s, representing part-whole relationships. Hence, a *Dimension* is a lattice stating how measured data can be aggregated. On the other hand, we see that a *Fact* is composed by a set of *Cell*s. Each of those *Cell*s is defined at an aggregation level for each of the analysis dimensions of its *Fact*. If there is a *Level* (l_2) whose elements are obtained by grouping those of another *Level* (l_1) at which a *Cell* (c_1) is defined, then we have another *Cell* (c_2) related to l_2 whose instances are composed by those of c_1. *Cell*s c_1 and c_2 are related by a *CellRelation*, which corresponds to the *LevelRelation* between l_1 and l_2. A set of functionally independent *Level*s form a *Base*, and the pair *Base-Cell* (where the *Base* fully determines instances of the *Cell*) is a *Cube*.

Some data must be physically stored while other will or could be derived. In the same way, some model elements must be explicited in the schema, while other (for instance, *CellRelation*) can be derived. In this sense, we distinguish those *Cell*s that need to be explicited (i.e. *FundamentalCell*s), from those that do not (i.e. *SummarizedCell*s), because all data they contain can be derived.

At lower detail level, we can see information regarding the attributes of the concepts we are representing. The *Level*s contain *Descriptor*s, and the *Cell*s contain *Measure*s. *SummarizedCell*s only contain data that can be derived (i.e. *SummarizedMeasure*s), and *FundamentalCell*s can contain derived or not derived data. *SummarizedMeasure*s are obtained from other *Measure*s, while *FundamentalMeasure*s are not. Notice that it is possible to obtain one *Measure* from more than one supplier (for instance, to be able to weigh an average).

Every *Dimension* induces a *Summarization* over a given *KindOfMeasure*. In general, *SummarizedMeasure*s are obtained by sum of other. However, this is not always the case, product, minimum, maximum, average, or any other operation could be used. It depends on the *KindOfMeasure* and the *Dimension* along which we are summarizing ([6] studies the influence of the temporal dimension on three different kinds of attributes). Thus, when we want to obtain a *SummarizedMeasure* in a *Cell* (c_1), from a *Measure* in another *Cell* (c_2), the *Summarization* performed is that induced by the *Dimension* that contains the *LevelRelation* to which the *CellRelation* between c_1 and c_2 corresponds.

*Summarization*s over a *KindOfMeasure* are partially ordered to state that some must be performed before others. Moreover, some data at an aggregation level could be an invalid source to summarize some *KindOfMeasure*s, which is also captured in a *YAM²* schema. A summarization operation being non-transitive, implies that any summarization that uses it must be done from the atomic data.

Figure 9 shows how all these multidimensional concepts perfectly fit into UML. A *Star* is a *Package* that contains a subject of analysis. *Fact*s and *Dimension*s are *Classifier*s containing *Class*es (i.e. *Cell*s, and *Level*s respectively). Finally, *Measure* and *Descriptor* are just *Attribute*s of the *Class*es. All other elements in *YAM²* have also been placed as specialization of a UML concept. Maybe, the most relevant ones are *CellRelation* and *LevelRelation* that are *Aggregation*s. Moreover, a *Base* is just a *Constraint* stating that a set of functionally independent *Level*s fully determine instances of a *Cell*.

This proves that multidimensional modeling is just an specialization of general data modeling. We could roughly say that all we are doing is splitting elements in the model based on whether they refer to factual or dimensional data. It can be seen that some specific concepts are defined, besides properties and constraints of the new structures. [7] claims that E/R provides the complete functionality and support necessary for OLAP applications. Here, we can see that UML also provides such support. However, it is well known that the more specific the *Class*es in a schema are, the better they represent reality. In the same way, the more specific our data model is, the better it will represent reality.

180

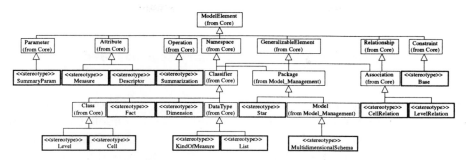

Figure 9. Extension of UML with stereotypes

7 Conclusions

In the last years, lots of work have been devoted to OLAP technology in general, and multidimensional modeling in particular. However, there is no well accepted model, yet. Moreover, in spite of the acceptance of the O-O paradigm, only a couple of efforts take it into account for conceptual modeling.

In this work, we have presented YAM^2, a multidimensional conceptual model, which allows the usage of semantic O-O relationships between different *Stars*. The model has been defined as an extension of UML to make it much more understandable, and avoid its definition from scratch. As a side effect, this shows that multidimensional modeling is just an special case of data modeling.

Structures in the model have been defined by means of metaclasses, which are specialization of UML metaclasses. Thus, possible relationships among multidimensional elements have been systematically studied in terms of UML relationships among its elements, so that they allow to show semantically rich multi-star schemas. The inherent integrity constraints of the model pay special attention to identification of data, and summarizability (providing much more flexibility than those of previous multidimensional models). Finally, a set of intuitive, algebraic operations on *Cubes* have been defined in terms of operations over mathematical functions.

Acknowledgements

Our work has been partially supported by the Spanish Research Program PRONTIC under projects TIC2000-1723-C02-01 and TIC2000-1723-C02-02, as well as the grant 1998FI-00228 from the Generalitat de Catalunya.

References

[1] A. Abelló, J. Samos, and F. Saltor. Understanding Analysis Dimensions in a Multidimensional Object-Oriented Model. In *3rd International Workshop on Design and Management of Data Warehouses (DMDW)*. SwissLife, 2001.

[2] A. Abelló, J. Samos, and F. Saltor. Understanding Facts in a Multidimensional Object-Oriented Model. In *4th Int. Workshop on Data Warehousing and OLAP (DOLAP)*. ACM, 2001.

[3] S. Abiteboul, R. Hull, and V. Vianu. *Foundations of Databases*. Addison-Wesley, 1995.

[4] L. Fegaras and D. Maier. Towards an Effective Calculus for Object Query Languages. In *Proc. of the ACM SIGMOD Int. Conf. on Management of Data*. ACM Press, 1995.

[5] E. Franconi, F. Baader, U. Sattler, and P. Vassiliadis. *Fundamentals of Data Warehousing*, chapter Multidimensional Data Models and Aggregation. Springer-Verlag, 2000. M. Jarke, M. Lenzerini, Y. Vassilious and P. Vassiliadis editors.

[6] H.-J. Lenz and A. Shoshani. Summarizability in OLAP and Statistical Data Bases. In *Proc. of the 9th Int. Conf. on Scientific and Statistical Database Management (SSDBM)*. IEEE Computer Society, 1997.

[7] J. Lewerenz, K. Schewe, and B. Thalheim. Modelling Data Warehouses and OLAP Applications by Means of Dialoge Objects. In *Proc. of the 18th Int. Conf. on Conceptual Modeling (ER1999)*, volume 1728 of *LNCS*. Springer, 1999.

[8] T. B. Nguyen, A. M. Tjoa, and R. R. Wagner. An Object Oriented Multidimensional Data Model for OLAP. In *Int. Conf. on Web-Age Information Management (WAIM)*, volume 1846 of *LNCS*. Springer, 2000.

[9] OMG. *Unified Modeling Language Specification*, June 1999. Version 1.3.

[10] OMG. *Common Warehouse Metamodel*, February 2001. Version 1.0.

[11] T. B. Pedersen and C. S. Jensen. Multidimensional data modeling for complex data. In *Proc. of 15th Int. Conf. on Data Engineering (ICDE)*. IEEE Computer Society, 1999.

[12] F. Saltor, M. Castellanos, and M. García-Solaco. Suitability of Data Models as Canonical Models for Federated DBs. *ACM SIGMOD Record*, 20(4), 1991.

[13] O. Teste. Towards Conceptual Multidimensional Design in Decision Support Syste ms. In *Proc. of the East-European Conference on Advances in Databases and Information Systems (ADBIS)*, 2001.

[14] E. Thomsen. *OLAP Solutions*. John Wiley & Sons, 1997.

[15] J. C. Trujillo, M. Palomar, J. Gomez, and I.-Y. Song. Designing Data Warehouses with OO Conceptual Models. *IEEE Computer*, 34(12), 2001.

[16] P. Vassiliadis and T. Sellis. A survey of logical models for olap databases. *SIGMOD Record*, 28(4), December 1999.

Authorization Model for Summary Schemas Model

Sudsanguan Ngamsuriyaroj   Ali R. Hurson*
Department of Computer Science & Engineering
The Pennsylvania State University
University Park, PA 16802
{*ngamsuri, hurson*}@cse.psu.edu

Thomas F. Keefe[†]
Oracle Corporation
500 Oracle Parkway
Redwood Shores, CA 94065
thomas.keefe@oracle.com

Abstract

Security issues in multidatabases are complicated due to autonomy and heterogeneity of local databases. Deriving global authorizations by integrating underlying local authorizations is difficult since subjects and objects at each local database may not be compatible. In addition, local authorizations may conflict and could not be combined to form common global authorizations.

This paper proposes an authorization model for a multidatabase system. The Summary Schemas Model (SSM) is used as the underlying paradigm. The SSM resolves name differences in multidatabases using word relationships defined in a standard dictionary. Hypernyms and hyponyms of access terms exported from local databases are the main components of the SSM as they form a hierarchical metadata structure. SSM global authorizations tagged to hypernyms are derived from local authorizations using global roles and a role hierarchy defined in multidatabases. The model considers roles as common global subjects onto which local subjects can be mapped. Since the mapping can be done independently and autonomously among local databases, authorization autonomy is preserved.

The paper also evaluates the performance of the proposed model. The simulation results show that the proposed model offers better performance than the original SSM since user queries with insufficient authority are rejected earlier. This results in fewer communication and less query response time.

1 Introduction

Unlike a typical homogeneous distributed database, a multidatabase system (MDBS) integrates existing and pos-sibly heterogeneous databases while preserving their local autonomy [15]. The motivation is to join individual and independently developed databases without any modification and hence to save the existing investment. The MDBS will act as a front end to local databases and facilitate any operation performing across them.

Local autonomy in an MDBS allows local databases to maintain complete control over their local resources [15]. Local autonomy comes in the form of communication autonomy, execution autonomy, design autonomy, and authorization autonomy. In other words, after joining the global information sharing environment, individual local database can continue to maintain its current data model and query language. It can decide to globally share its local resources. Moreover, it should be able to execute its local operations without interference from external sources. Finally, *authorization autonomy* [7] allows a local database to accept or reject any request from others that accesses its data.

Due to local autonomy, each local database can join or depart an MDBS at any time without major changes. It simply adds global functions to access the MDBS while its local functions remains unchanged. However, each database joining an MDBS may be heterogeneous. Specifically, they often have different data models and different query languages. The MDBS must be able to map various data models to a common and canonical model. In addition, semantically similar data may have different names and representations while different data may have identical names. The MDBS must resolve these differences and similarities based on the semantics of data. These overhead may degrade global performance significantly as the MDBS has no control over local databases.

There are two general approaches to resolve multidatabase heterogeneity [4]. In the first approach, local schemas are integrated to form a global schema representing common data semantics. The process of integration is rather complicated, labor intensive, and probably requires manual manipulation. The global schema is usually maintained at every site to allow simple and fast accesses to the

---
*This work in part is supported by Office of Naval Research under the contract N00014-02-1-0282.

[†]Opinions expressed in this paper are solely those of the authors and are not necessarily those of the Oracle Corporation. This paper must not be construed to imply any product commitment on the part of the Oracle Corporation.

data. Duplication of the global schema, however, raises the consistency problem in the case of updates at local databases [1].

In the second approach, the integration of local schemas is achieved through a common multidatabase language which interprets and transforms a query to data represented and maintained at local databases. There is no global view of shared data. Thus, a user must know the location and the representation of data being queried. The approach is naturally less transparent than the global schema approach, but it is more efficient and less complicated.

The Summary Schemas Model (SSM) [3] is proposed as an adjunct to multidatabase language systems for supporting the identification of semantically similar data entities. The model resolves name differences using word relationships defined in a standard dictionary such as Roget's Thesaurus. It builds a hierarchy structure of metadata based on access terms exported from underlying local databases.

While most research in multidatabases have been focused on update issues [1], consistency and concurrency control [10], and query optimization [12], security issues in multidatabases have received a little attention. A number of authorization models for multidatabases have been proposed [5, 7, 13, 16] which mainly focused on authorization models for a system based on global schema integration approach.

In a multidatabase environment, authorization models of local databases must be preserved because of local autonomy. With the addition of heterogeneity, enforcing a single authorization model globally in an MDBS is quite a challenge. One approach is to derive a global authorization model from underlying local authorizations of local databases [5]. Authorizations can be derived for integrated or imported objects based on the similarity between subjects. However, subjects among local databases are unlikely to be compatible and may have conflicting access authorizations to the same object. As a result, no global authorization can be derived for those subjects. Another approach is to propagate defined global authorizations to local databases when local data accesses are requested [8]. However, local databases may accept or reject any global request.

In this paper, we propose an authorization model for the SSM. The model proposed is based on role-based access control (RBAC) [14]. The motivation is to define a global authorization model that not only is independent of local authorizations, but also inherits common entities which individual local authorization is mapped onto without changing local authorizations. We consider a role as a common representative for users or subjects in local databases since a role represents a job function defined by an organization which accommodates local databases and the MDBS. Each local database may map some of its local subjects to a global role defined at the MDBS level. In addition, no local subject

identification is maintained at the global level.

Due to the hierarchical structure of the SSM, when more general access terms are formed at a higher level, less degree of authorization is required for accessing those terms. Hence, a global authorization model should be expressed in a hierarchical form. In RBAC, roles can form a role hierarchy and may suite the hierarchical structure of the SSM.

There are two major motivations in enhancing the SSM model by an authorization policy and, hence, limiting accesses to access terms in the SSM hierarchy: (i) Each term has its own degree of sensitivity and should not be accessed by unauthorized subjects. For example, "salary of an employee" in a company should not be publicly accessible while "name of an employee" may be publicly accessible, (ii) any unauthorized access detected as early as possible reduces network traffic and computation which result in increasing the query bandwidth.

Imposing security structure on top of the SSM adds both time and space overhead to the system. It obviously affects the performance of the SSM. The goal of this work is to show the feasibility of such an attempt and to evaluate the performance gain of the enhanced SSM. The remainder of the paper is organized as follows. Section 2 gives background of the SSM and RBAC. Section 3 presents our proposed model. Section 4 describes the simulation model and experiments used to evaluate the performance of the two SSM models. We also discusses the experimental results. Section 5 explains related work to authorization models for multidatabases. Section 6 concludes our work and suggests some future research directions.

2 Background

A brief background of Summary Schemas Model (SSM) and role-based access control (RBAC) are given in this section. More details for SSM and RBAC are referred to [3, 14].

2.1 Summary Schemas Model

Summary Schemas Model (SSM) is proposed to resolve name differences among similar data in multidatabase systems [3]. Basically, it uses word relationship defined in a standard thesaurus such as Roget's Thesaurus to build a hierarchical metadata of local access terms exported from underlying local databases. Users can submit *imprecise* queries at any site without knowing the location of requested access terms. The SSM maps imprecise query terms with precise access terms found at local databases.

Access terms can be related to each other as synonyms, hypernyms or hyponyms. The SSM forms a hierarchical structure by linking hypernyms and hyponyms and by connecting synonyms on the same level.

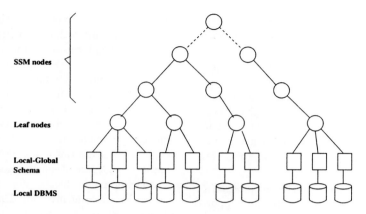

SSM nodes

Leaf nodes

Local-Global
Schema

Local DBMS

Figure 1. SSM Architecture

The hierarchical structure of the SSM consists of local database schemas as leaf nodes and summary schemas as internal nodes. The architecture of the SSM is shown in Figure 1. A schema at each node is a list of access terms. A summary schema node is created by mapping access terms at lower nodes to the corresponding hypernyms. Obviously, summary schemas are smaller and more abstract than their lower schemas. Semantic similarity between any two terms is measured in terms of *Semantic Distance Metric* (SDM) computed using the number of hypernyms-hyponyms and synonyms linked between them. An SDM value indicates how closely two terms are [3]. Particularly, the smaller the SDM, the more similarity between the terms.

The SSM intelligently resolves user queries when precise access terms and/or their locations are unknown. A user can submit a query with imprecise terms at any node. The SSM will search upward or downward in the hierarchy for more precise terms based on computed SDM values. If the query is not originated at leaf nodes, the search is conducted downward to its hyponyms until it reaches a leaf node. If the query term does not match with its precise term at leaf nodes, the search is then upward to its parent node which contains its hypernym. The search is complete when all query terms are matched with precise terms at leaf nodes, or after the entire hierarchy has been searched and no matching precise term is found.

The SSM model was simulated and its prototype architecture supported by DARPA was developed [2, 6]. The performance of the model was evaluated under various schema distributions, query complexity and network topology. The simulation results show that both precise and imprecise queries incur comparable cost, and hence have compatible performance. In certain cases, the SSM imprecise query processing even outperforms a precise query processing [2]. In summary, the SSM model provides many benefits as follows.

- The SSM provides global accesses to data without re-

quiring precise knowledge of data names or locations.

- The SSM incurs infinitesimal memory overhead compared to global schema approach. As a result, it gives good performance.

2.2 Role-Based Access Control

Role-Based Access Control (RBAC) model [14] is based on three sets of entities: *users*, *roles* and *access permissions*. A role represents a job function in an organization and embodies a specific set of authorizations and responsibilities for the job. In practice, a user is created when a person has a role in an organization. As a member of a role, the user also inherits the same privileges to access objects accessible by the role. If a person no longer works for the organization, the corresponding user must be deleted and his/her privileges are revoked by removing his/her membership from the role.

RBAC model as described represents a many-to-many relation as shown in Figure 2. In the model, a user can be a member of many roles and a role can be assigned to many users. Also, a role can have many access permissions and one permission can be assigned to many roles. Furthermore, roles can form a role hierarchy to reflect lines of authority and responsibility in an organization (chain of commands). Thus, a role can inherit permissions assigned to another role in a role hierarchy. But, some pairs of roles in a hierarchy may be incomparable. Three different forms of role hierarchies [11] are:

- *isa role hierarchy*. This hierarchy is based on generalization. Roles are defined by qualification where one role is more specific than its *isa* role and the role inherits all permissions assigned to its *isa* role and also has its own extra permissions.

- *Activity role hierarchy*. This hierarchy is based on aggregation where a role is defined as an aggregation of

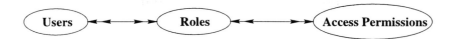

Figure 2. RBAC Many-to-Many Relations

its component roles. Thus, the role inherits all permissions given to its components.

- *Supervision role hierarchy.* This hierarchy is based on organizational hierarchy of positions where a role at a higher position inherits all permissions of roles at its lower positions.

The corresponding examples of the three role hierarchies are shown in Figure 3.

3 Authorization Model for the SSM

We propose a global authorization model for Summary Schemas Model based on role-based access control (RBAC). The main idea is to map an individual subject in local databases to a common role defined at MDBS level, and to tag access terms in the SSM hierarchy with a set of roles allowed to access those objects.

3.1 Subjects and Objects

The proposed authorization model specifies subjects and objects both at local databases and at MDBS level. At local databases, there are local subjects and local objects. Local subjects are defined and managed by local databases. Local objects are objects created and maintained at local databases. Each local subject can access its own local objects according to access control rules defined locally and independently at local databases. In addition, we do not make any assumption about authorization models used at local databases.

At MDBS level, access terms in the hierarchy are global objects exported access terms from underlying local schemas. Higher terms are populated in a hierarchical structure according to their word relationships. Thus, there is no composite object at MDBS level. Since global subjects are allowed to access objects across multiple local databases, it is natural to assume that only a subset of local subjects is allowed to be global subjects. Mapping individual local subjects to global subjects is a tedious and error prone task. However, using roles as global subjects simplifies the task. In addition, local databases are responsible for mapping their local subjects to corresponding global roles. Local databases may maintain a table that keeps track of which subject is mapped to which global role. If a new role is added or an existing role is deleted, all local database will

be informed and their local subjects can be remapped. Nevertheless, we do not anticipate frequent changes of global roles. In addition, when a user logs in at any node, the authentication can be done at a local database where a user has an account. No global authentication is needed.

3.2 Populating Global Authorizations

When a local database joins the SSM, it registers itself to the SSM so that its semantic contents can be captured in SSM metadata. A local database provides the SSM a list of its exported access terms and a list of its local subjects mapped onto global roles. Mapped global roles are then tagged to each exported access term of a node.

When hypernyms of exported access terms are captured in the SSM hierarchy, a list of authorized global roles is also tagged to those hypernyms. However, since more general SSM access terms are populated at higher level closer to the top of the SSM hierarchy, roles with less privileges are allowed to access those SSM metadata. As a result, if two roles from lower nodes are partially ordered in the role hierarchy, only the minimum role between the two is tagged to the higher node. But, if two roles are uncomparable, both are tagged to the higher node. Note that if a role has higher privileges than the minimum role at a node, the role does not need to be tagged to the node since it is implicitly allowed to access summary schema terms.

The algorithm for populating authorized SSM nodes is iterative in nature as described in Figure 4. The algorithm can be generalized for higher number of local databases and access terms. Also, there is no assumption about how roles are related in a role hierarchy.

Figure 5 illustrates how global authorizations are populated at SSM nodes based on the role hierarchy shown in Figure 3(c). The figure exemplifies a hypernym relationship among words related to personal income of employees in an organization. Each term is tagged with an authorized role based on the hierarchy of employees' role given in Figure 3(c). Since, in a supervision role hierarchy, roles at a lower level have less privileges than roles at the higher level, roles tagged to higher terms are the combination of minimum roles tagged at lower terms. For example, at Node 2.A, roles tagged to the node are [Personnel, Employee, Engineer] since they represent all minimum roles at lower nodes (Node A and Node B). The role [Project Manager] and [Payroll] are implicitly allowed to access the term "Earnings" at Node 2.A, but only the roles [Project

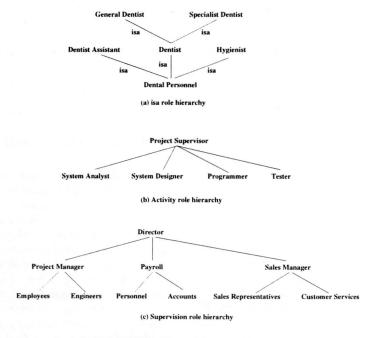

(a) isa role hierarchy

(b) Activity role hierarchy

(c) Supervision role hierarchy

Figure 3. Examples of Role Hierarchies

Assume that we have two local databases. One database exports an access term x accessible to a role r1 and the other exports an access term y accessible to a role r2. An SSM metadata or access term is formed according to the semantic contents of x and y and r1 and r2 role relationship.

(a) If x and y are semantically different, then two SSM entries: [hypernym of x, r1] and [hypernym of y, r2] are formed at higher level.

(b) If x and y are semantically similar and z is a hypernym of x and y, then we consider r1 and r2 as follows:

  (i) If r1 and r2 are partially ordered in the role hierarchy, an SSM node is formed as [z, minimum(r1, r2)].

  (ii) If r1 and r2 are not related, an SSM node is formed as [z, r1 or r2].

Figure 4. Algorithm for Populating Global Authorizations

Manager] and [Employee] are allowed to access the term "Wage" at Node A. Both roles [Project Manager] and [Payroll] can access the term "Salary" at Node B.

3.3 User Query Processing

The algorithm presented in [3] for imprecise query processing is based on SDM values computed at each node in the SSM hierarchy. Since accesses to terms are now limited to only some authorized roles, the algorithm must be modified so that a query submitted by users of different roles will be properly responded according to role privileges of users. As a result, submiting the same query by different roles may not get the same result. The modified query algorithm is described in Figure 6.

4 Performance Evaluation

A simulator was developed to study the feasibility and efficiency of the proposed authorization model within the scope of the SSM. Performance metrics such as query response time and throughput are used to compare and contrast the enhanced SSM model against the original baseline SSM which imposes no security restriction.

4.1 Generating SSM Hierarchy

For the purpose of simulation, an SSM hierarchy is generated statically. The SSM hierarchy is generated based on the number of local nodes (`lnode`) and the maximum number of levels in the hierarchy (`mlevel`). The maximum number of children per SSM node (`nchild`) is computed as `lnode / mlevel + 1`. The number of children per SSM node is randomly generated between two and `nchild`.

For authorized SSM, a number of roles are generated. Each role is given a rank defined in a role hierarchy as a partial order. A rank is simply indicated by a number where zero is the highest rank with the most authority. Initially, each local node is randomly assigned a rank. Ranks are assigned to the SSM nodes according to the algorithm described in Section 3.2. As a result, each SSM node may contain the minimum rank or a number of ranks from lower nodes.

Since access terms at higher level nodes are more general than their children at lower level nodes, an imprecise query has higher probability to match with access terms at higher level nodes than with those at lower level nodes. The idea of using Semantic Distance Metric (SDM) in searching for a precise match can be emulated by assigning higher probability of successful match for higher level nodes than that for lower level nodes. Thus, the probability of 1.0 is equally divided and accumulated across levels. Each level

is then assigned a specific *level probability*. For example, if the hierarchy has four levels, *level probabilities* ranged from the lowest level to the highest level are 0.25, 0.5, 0.75, and 1.0, respectively. We assume that all nodes at the same level have the same level probability.

4.2 Processing a query

When a query is submitted at a node, a randomly generated matching probability is assigned to the query. At each origin node, matching probability of the query is compared with level probability of the node. A matching probability less than or equal to the level probability represents a successful match; otherwise, it is an unsuccessful match. A successful match at a level sends the query to the lower level node(s) and an unsuccessful match sends the query to a higher level node in the SSM hierarchy. An unsuccessful match at the top level of the hierarchy rejects the query. The query is accepted only when it is matched at local nodes.

For authorized SSM, a randomly generated rank is also assigned to a query so that it can be used to compare against ranks at each node in the query's searching path. However, the query's rank is examined only after a match is found at a node. If the query has lower rank than the node's rank, the query is rejected immediately at that node. The query is *invalid* if it is matched, but has insufficient authorization for accessing the requesting term. Hence, the output of a query can be either *accepted* at local nodes, *rejected* at the top level, or *invalid* due to insufficient authority.

4.3 Workload

The workload to the system is composed of precise queries and imprecise queries submitted to any node in the SSM hierarchy. Precise queries are executed at local nodes only. Imprecise queries are moved up or down in the hierarchy until they are either accepted, rejected, or invalidated. At each node, there are a fixed number of processes (*nprocs*) running concurrently. Each process generates its own queries. When a query is resolved, a new query is generated immediately. To simplify our measurement, we assume that a query contains only one access term so that the effect of query size to the performance would be eliminated.

System parameters related to a generated SSM hierarchy are the number of local nodes, the total number of levels including the local level, the maximum number of children per SSM node, and *level probabilities* assigned to all levels. We assume that each node takes the average of *proc_time* for processing one query. Each node also maintains a queue of queries submitted from its child nodes or its parent node. Moreover, it takes the average of *comm_time* for sending a query between any pair of nodes in the hierarchy. We assume that there is one communication link connecting a

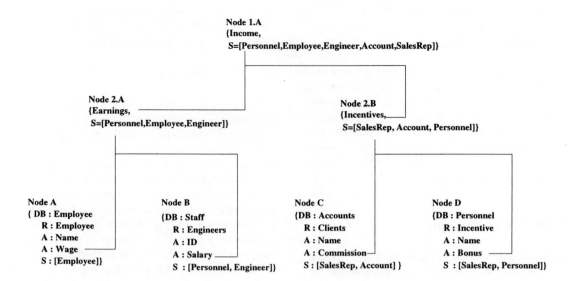

where DB : Database name, R : Relation name, A : Attribute name, S : Subject role

Figure 5. Sample SSM Hierarchy with Role Authorization

Assumptions:

(1) An imprecise query is submitted at any node in the SSM hierarchy.

(2) If one access term is rejected due to insufficient authority,
    the whole query is also rejected.

At query origin node, a query is parsed to identify access terms..

A submitted query is also tagged with a valid global role of the user.

```
1. FOR each imprecise term in the query DO
2.      Compute SDM of each term
3.      IF a match is found and accessible by the user role
4.      THEN IF this is a local node
5              THEN replace imprecise term with its corresponding precise term
6              ELSE  send it to lower node and continue at line 2
7      ELSE IF a match is found, but inaccessible by the user role
8              THEN reject the access and the whole query is rejected
9              ELSE IF this is the top-level node
10.                THEN reject the access and the whole query is rejected
11.                ELSE send it to higher node and continue at line 1
```

Figure 6. Modified Query Algorithm for the Enhanced SSM Model

188

parent-child pair. All parameters and their default values are summarized in Table 1.

Table 1. Workload and System Parameters

Parameters	Default values	Description
lnode	15	number of local databases
mlevel	5	total number of levels
nchild	3	maximum number of children per SSM node
nprocs	1-4	number of processes per node
level_prob	0.2-1.0	level probability of each level
invalid_prob	0.1	probability that a query is invalid
rank_level	6	number of ranks in role hierarchy
proc_time	0.001	processing time of a node per query
comm_time	0.003	communication time between nodes

4.4 Performance Measurement

The performance of the enhanced SSM model (i.e., authorized SSM) is measured and compared against the original SSM model in terms of the response time and the throughput of accepted queries. Since the throughput and the response time are reciprocal, only the response time is reported. In addition, each response time reported is the average of 30 simulation runs where each run takes 3000 time units.

The response time of an imprecise query depends on several factors: i) the structure of the SSM hierarchy - Even though the algorithm presented in section 4.1 can generate SSM hierarchy with different height and structure, the same SSM hierarchy organization is used for all experiments reported in this paper. ii) the location and the level of the originating node within the SSM hierarchy - Based on our experiences, the response time of queries originated at the same level of the SSM hierarchy also varies slightly. However, for the sake of simplicity, we assume that this effect is insignificant and the response time of all nodes in the same level is approximately the same. Hence, the averaged query response time of individual level, not node, is reported in this paper. iii) the workload of each summary schema node is the sum of queries at that node and queries transferred from its parent and/or children nodes. As a result, the query response time is affected by the workload of each node, and consequently, on the frequency of imprecise queries generated at that node and the network traffic.

In the enhanced SSM model, imprecise queries with insufficient authority may be rejected as early as possible. This reduces the workload of each node and the network traffic in the SSM hierarchy. Consequently, the response time of accepted queries is decreased. Finally, we assume that the time taken for authorizing a query at each node is negligible.

4.5 Experiments and Results

We report on two experiments to show the effect of having authorization control in the SSM hierarchy under various conditions. For both experiments, precise queries are submitted and executed only at local nodes. Additionally, the results reported are the average response time of accepted queries.

4.5.1 Experiment 1

This experiment measures the query response time of the same set of imprecise queries submitted to different SSM levels. The experiment is conducted for both the enhanced SSM model and the original SSM model.

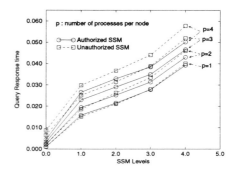

Figure 7. Response time of Single SSM levels

As anticipated, in spite of the overhead due to the authorization control, the response time of accepted queries for the original SSM is mostly higher than that of the enhanced SSM (Figure 7). The main reason is that invalid queries in the original SSM model are travelling longer distance in the SSM hierarchy before being rejected, whereas invalid queries in the enhanced SSM model are detected and rejected earlier. As a result, both the workload at each SSM node and the network traffic in the hierarchy of the enhanced SSM model are lower than those of the original SSM model, and hence lower response time.

Figure 7 also shows that increasing number of queries submitted simultaneously per node (*nprocs*) results in higher response time as workload at each SSM node is increased. In the enhanced SSM model, there are two factors contributing to query response time: i) the distance between the originating node and local nodes for accepted queries, and ii) invalid queries submitted at lower levels are rejected earlier than the same queries submitted at higher levels, since security at lower levels is more restrictive.

4.5.2 Experiment 2

This experiment investigates the effect of the percentage of *invalid* queries to the query response time at each level. We define *invalid probability* as the ratio of invalid queries to the total number of queries submitted at all nodes of a particular SSM level. Hence, we run this experiment only for the enhanced SSM model. Moreover, for demonstration purposes, the experiments are run only for SSM level 1 and level 2.

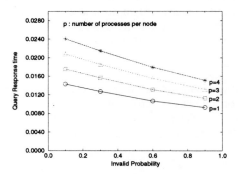

Figure 8. Response time of First SSM level

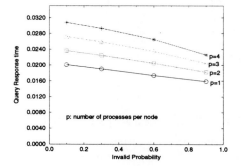

Figure 9. Response time of Second SSM level

The results are shown in Figure 8 and Figure 9, respectively. Both figures illustrate that increasing invalid probability reduces the query response time since invalid queries are detected and rejected from the SSM hierarchy earlier. The results also illustrate the same trend regardless of the number of queries submitted per node. Eventually, we can conclude that nodes at higher SSM levels are less sensitive to the invalid probability factor.

5 Related Work

The first work that addressed security issues in heterogeneous databases was presented in [17]. The authors addressed the problem of authorization inconsistency incurred when a user granted some privileges to another user at the global level, but the granting was not realized at participating local databases. As a result, a query submitted by a grantee to access data at local databases was denied. The authors modified the protection mechanism normally used in centralized databases to realize global grantings at local databases.

Most of the research in this area is directed toward the application of the security policy in traditional distributed databases and federated databases, while our work is directed toward the multidatabases (heterogeneous databases) within the scope of the SSM.

In federated databases, import/export schemas at each node classifies objects and subjects into local and global levels where authorizations are specified at both levels. Local authorizations are specified at individual local database. There are three general approaches to derive global authorizations [7]. The first approach [7] considers that global and local authorizations are independently specified. It assumes that global objects are created and owned by the federation at the global level. Thus, global authorizations must be specified when accessing those global objects. If objects are imported from local databases, they are not replicated at the global level and global accesses to those objects must be authorized again at local databases. Moreover, global subjects must be authenticated at the global level. To avoid inconsistent authorizations between levels, security administrators of both levels must corporate with each other.

The second approach [8] proposes a top-down derivation that global authorizations are propagated to local databases when accesses to local objects are necessary. However, local databases may choose to accept or reject any global request. Hence, global requests may not be granted. The main problem is that global subjects defined as groups are known only at global level. They may not be mapped to local subjects or may be mapped to many authorizations at local databases.

The third approach [5] presents a bottom-up derivation that global authorizations are derived from local authorizations for integrated and imported objects using word similarity. In addition, a dictionary is used to maintain mappings between local to global entities. Consequently, global authorizations are derived based on how closely two local subjects are. The closeness is calculated based on the similarity between access compatibility of objects and access permissions of local subjects to objects. As a result, if two local subjects are not compatible or have conflict accesses to the same object, no global authorization can be derived.

Our model uses a bottom-up approach, but local subjects are mapped to a global role and global authorizations are derived according to the roles defined in a role hierarchy. The mapping can be done independently and autonomously among local databases. As a result, authorization autonomy is preserved.

6 Conclusions and Future Directions

Similar to any other databases, enforcing security in multidatabases is an important issue. However, local autonomy and heterogeneity in multidatabases make this issue relatively more difficult to enforce since local databases may have diverse sets of users and may contain objects of varying degree of sensitivity. Deriving global authorizations by integrating underlying local authorizations may be unobtainable since subjects and objects at each local database may be incompatible. In addition, local authorizations may conflict and could not be combined to form common global authorizations.

This paper proposed an authorization model for Summary Schemas Model (SSM) which resolves imprecise queries based on the semantic contents of a request. Hypernym, hyponym, and synonym relationships among access terms exported from local databases are the main components of the SSM which form a hierarchical metadata structure. The proposed model derives global authorizations for the SSM from authorizations of local databases. The model defines global roles and a role hierarchy indicating how global roles are related to local subjects. When an access term is exported to the SSM, its mapped authorized role is also tagged to the term. Global authorizations are then automatically derived for metadata in the SSM hierarchy based on role definitions in the role hierarchy. Since local subjects and global roles can be modified independently and autonomously, authorization autonomy is preserved in our model.

Imposing authorization information to the SSM adds both space and time overhead and clearly affects the query resolution of the SSM. The paper evaluated the performance of the proposed model and compared it with that of the original SSM. The simulation results showed that the proposed model outperforms the original SSM model since user queries with insufficient authority are rejected earlier. The early rejection of unauthorized queries reduces the network traffic and workload at both SSM nodes and at local databases. Thus, the response time of valid queries in the proposed model is lower than that of the original SSM.

The SSM platform was extended to include mobility and wireless communication [9]. A mobile computing environment introduces extra requirements such as disconnectivity and limited bandwidth to the model. Even though the issues of its concurrency control, recovery and replication have been studied [9], security issues in mobile environment under the scope of the SSM have not been addressed. We intend to integrate mobile data accesses to the proposed authorization model as our future work.

References

[1] Y. Breitbart and A. Silberschatz. Multidatabase Update Issues. In *Proceedings of the Conference of Management of Data*, pages 135–142, 1988.

[2] M. Bright, A. Hurson, S. Pakzad, and H. Sarma. The Summary Schemas Model - An Approach for Handling Mul-

tidatabases: Concept and Performance Analysis. In *Multidatabase Systems: An Advanced Solution for Global Information Sharing*, pages 199–216. IEEE Computer Society Press, 1999.

[3] M. W. Bright, A. R. Hurson, and S. Paksad. Automated Resolution of Semantic Heterogeneity Multidatabases. *ACM Transactions on Database Systems*, 19(2):212–253, June 1994.

[4] O. Bukhres and A. Elmagarmid. *Object-Oriented Multidatabase Systems*. Prentice-Hall, Englewood Cliffs, NJ, 1996.

[5] S. Castano. An Approach to Deriving Global Authorizations in Federated Database Systems. In *Proceedings of the IFIP Working Conference on Database Security*, pages 58–75, Como, Italy, July 1996.

[6] K. Dash, A. Hurson, S. Phoha, and C. Chehadeh. Summary Schemas Model: A Scheme for Handling Global Information Sharing. In *Proceedings of the International Conference on Intelligent Information Management Systems*, pages 47–51, 1994.

[7] S. di Vimercati and P. Samarati. An Authorization Model for Federated Systems. In *Proceedings of 4th European Symposium on Research in Computer Security*, pages 99–117, Rome, Italy, September 1996.

[8] D. Jonscher and K. Dittrich. An Approach for Building Secure Database Federations. In *Proceedings of the 20th VLDB Conference*, Santiago, Chile, 1994.

[9] J. Lim and A. Hurson. Transaction Processing in a Mobile, Multi-Database Environment. *Multimedia Tools and Applications*, 15:161–185, 2001.

[10] S. Mehrotra, H. Korth, and A. Silberschatz. Concurrency Control in Hierarchical Multidatabase Systems. *The VLDB Journal*, 6(2):152–172, 1997.

[11] J. D. Moffett and E. C. Lupu. The Uses of Role Hierarchies in Access Control. In *Proceedings of 4th ACM Workshop on Role-Based Access Control*, pages 153–160, Fairfax, VA, October 1999.

[12] T. Morzy and Z. Krolikowski. Query Optimization in Multidatabase Systems: Solutions and Open Issues. In *Proceedings of 10th International Conference in Database and Expert Systems Applications*, pages 6–11, September 1999.

[13] S. Osborn. Database Security Integration using Role-Based Access Control. In *Proceedings of the IFIP Working Conference on Database Security*, pages 1–15, Schoorl/Amsterdam, Netherlands, August 2000.

[14] R. Sandhu, E. Coyne, H. Feinstein, and C. Youman. Role-based Access Control Models. *IEEE Computer*, 19(5):38–47, February 1996.

[15] A. Sheth and J. Larson. Federated Database Systems for Managing Distributed, Heterogeneous, and Autonomous Databases. *ACM Computing Surveys*, 22(3):183–236, 1990.

[16] Z. Tari and G. Fernandez. Security Enforcement in the DOK Federated Database System. In *Proceedings of the IFIP Working Conference on Database Security*, pages 23–42, Como, Italy, July 1996.

[17] C. Wang and D. Spooner. Access control in a heterogeneous distributed database management system. In *Proceedings of the 6th Symposium on Reliability in Distributed Software and Database Systems*, Williamsburg, VA, March 1987.

Implementing Federated Database Systems by Compiling SchemaSQL

François Barbançon, Daniel P. Miranker
Department of Computer Sciences
The University of Texas at Austin
{francois, miranker} @cs.utexas.edu

Abstract

Federated systems integrating data from multiple sources must cope with semantic heterogeneity by reasoning over both the data and meta-data of their sources. SchemaSQL is one of a number of related higher-order languages, which have been proposed for succinctly expressing integrated views over heterogeneous sources.

We define a method for compiling SchemaSQL into standard SQL. We show that the output of the compilation algorithm is of size $O(m+p)$ where m is the size of the catalogs and p the size of input queries. The resulting code may be executed by existing conventional SQL query engines without modification. We extend our basic compilation method by including type driven optimizations which, empirical evaluation shows, yield an effective execution by native query engines. Prior efforts do not provide feasible guarantees on the size of the compiled programs or require the development of new query engines encompassing higher-order query operators.

1   Introduction

Krishnamurthy, Litwin and Kent [8], hereafter referred to as Krishnamurthy, showed that to concisely express federating views declaratively over heterogeneous databases requires special, *higher-order*, syntactic features. The features consist of *metadata-variables* ranging over schema elements: database, tables and columns. *Metadata-variables* bridge schematic discrepancies where information in one source appears as explicit data and the same information in another source has been integrated into the schema definition. Starting with Krishnamurthy's IDL, several forms of higher order extensions for SQL and Datalog have been included in a number of heterogeneous database architectures. SchemaSQL is probably the best known of these ([11, 10]).

We are using SchemaSQL as the meta-representation language for a federated database architecture, which we review in Section 2. The goals of that architecture include simplifying the development of heterogeneous databases through active machine learning of federating transforms, and ensuring system independence to the extent of portability. The logical foundation of SchemaSQL in declarative semantics provides the ideal framework for an abstract machine learning algorithm to federate heterogeneous databases.

We present a compilation and optimization method for translating higher-order features of SchemaSQL into simple first-order SQL queries. The method takes as input both the higher order program and the database catalogs from the source databases. The size of the target code produced by our method is a $O(m+p)$, where m is the catalog size, and p the input size. A compilation method has been previously proposed for SchemaSQL ([11]), but no analysis was provided per the size of the resulting program. However that method was clearly at least polynomial, and perhaps even exponential in a set of plausible worst-case scenarios (see related work section).

The construction of our target code amounts to carefully substituting the meta-variables with strings from the catalog. The bound on target size is achieved, in part, by noting the primary keys in the source databases and exploiting those keys to sidestep multiplicative aspects of blind substitutions.

To our knowledge, all previous efforts to implement higher-order query languages started by building new query optimizers on top of existing databases. This is obviously not a portable approach compatible with multi-database systems ([11]). By compiling SchemaSQL to SQL, our method enables the development and execution of higher-order query languages in a layered architecture where the impact of higher-order operators is isolated and rendered executable by existing query engines.

The implementation we report on includes static optimizations using data types and schema elements. Further, after additional basic semantic optimizations, it encapsulates higher order operators into simple SQL joins such that a query engine executing the target code can optimize them. The space bounds on the size of the target code are a necessary guarantee on the efficiency of the compilation. Still, the target code may contain multi-way joins, which if executed using poor query-plans may prove expensive. However section 6 contains some relevant empirical results which show that by including static optimizations, our compiler produces target code, which is executed effectively by a standard SQL engine.

2   Adopting SchemaSQL for Data Federation architectures

We offer the architecture shown in Figure 1 as an illustrative example of an architecture leveraging SchemaSQL as the language to define the warehouse's federating queries. In this architecture, a graphical user interface, in the spirit of modern query interfaces, shields the operator from the abstraction and most of the complexity of SchemaSQL view definitions. This interface uses *active learning* to drive the user interaction towards precise definitions of the federated views and is described in detail in a separate document ([3]). A similar graphical interface, but using a passive learning approach to define schema mappings, is proposed by Miller et al. ([12]). In our system SchemaSQL semantics form the basis, used for selection and exploration by the system. The system can then provide provable guarantees that the learning mechanism has converged to a correct result.

The federated view definitions are then compiled into SQL queries over the source databases. The data extraction process can then directly leverage the native SQL interface of the local databases to perform data extraction. Our compilation method exploits the built-in optimizers of the component query engines blended with static optimization. A standard SQL query engine is also sufficient at the warehouse level to receive the data and perform the integration.

3   Higher Order Database Languages

In this paper, for accessibility, we speak to the syntax of SchemaSQL introduced by Lakshmanan in [11]. Like other higher order languages such as IDL ([8]) and SchemaLog ([9]), SchemaSQL syntax is characterized by letting variables substitute in place of meta-data elements: database, table and columns.

Our presentation will leverage the same running example presented by Krishnamurthy. The example speaks to integrating stock market data from three actual sources of stock market quotes, code named Euter, Ource and Chwab. Data comprises the daily closing price of individual stocks. Figure 2 illustrates the schema of the three sources. Note that only Ource is properly normalized. Although one may debate the merits of each representation, the debate is moot. These are real sources

and they embody issues commonly faced in practice. In this example a stock symbol may appear as data, the name of a column, or the name of a table. Thus, variables are necessary, in order to bridge schematic discrepancies when federating heterogeneous databases.

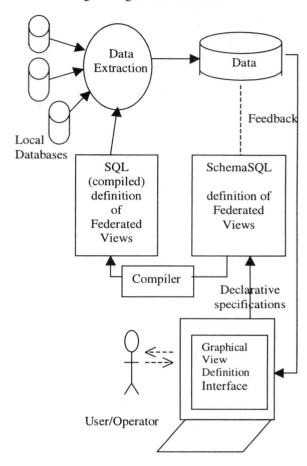

Figure 1 – User Friendly Data Federation Architecture.

Figure 3 illustrates two queries over the database Ource. While they do not represent meaningful queries, they were chosen because they contain multiple meta-data variables in the same Select/From/Where statement, which will allow us to clearly illustrate our algorithm and the resulting complexity of the compiled program.

The first query returns all stock triplets such that for some date, the price of the first stock is greater than the price of the other two combined. The second query returns all pairs of stock, ordered by their price on a given date. These queries are written in the usual SQL syntax for Database Ource in Figure 3. The syntax *"From Ource::Table1 T "* denotes that T stands for a row in Table 1, in database Ource.

Euter Database

Table1

Pkey	Date	IBM	Apple	Microsoft
P01	Monday	110	75	80
P02	Tuesday	100	85	90

Ource Database

Table 1

Pkey	Date	Company	Price
P01	Friday	IBM	105
P02	Friday	Apple	70
P03	Friday	Microsoft	105
P04	Monday	IBM	115
P05	Monday	Apple	65
P06	Monday	Microsoft	100

Chwab Database

Table IBM

Pkey	Date	Price
P01	Wednesday	95
P02	Thursday	100

Table Microsoft

Pkey	Date	Price
P01	Wednesday	95
P02	Thursday	90

Table Apple

Pkey	Date	Price
P01	Wednesday	80
P02	Thursday	85

Figure 2- Krishnamurthy's stock market databases

The same queries over databases Chwab and Euter cannot be written out with simple SQL statements. Alternatively SchemaSQL can be used to express these queries concisely because variables are allowed to be defined and to range over database tables or table columns. In Figure 4, q1 and q2 are expressed using C1, C2 and C3. In SchemaSQL, the expression *"From Euter::Table-> C"*, marks C to be a variable ranging over the set of columns of table Euter::Table1. The expression *"C isa 'StockColumn'"* is a selection predicate, which ensures that C belongs to the type: 'StockColumn'. In this instance, type 'StockColumn' is made up of the set: {"Euter", "Ource", "Chwab"}. Similarly in Figure 5, the

same two queries are expressed over the database Chwab using T1, T2 and T3, variables ranging over the set of tables: {"Euter", "Ource", "Chwab"} which form the type 'StockTable'. Note that the syntax *"From Chwab-> T"* , indicates that T is a variable ranging over the tables of database Chwab.

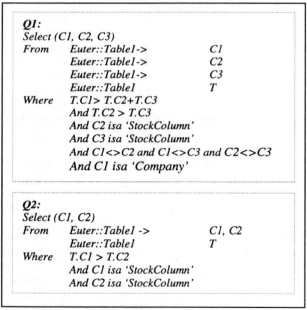

Q5:
Select (T1.Company, T2.Company, T3.Company)
From   Ource::Table1   T1
            Ource::Table1   T2
            Ource::Table1   T3
Where   T1.Price>T2.Price+T3.Price
And T2.Price > T3.Price
And T1.Date=T2.Date=T3.Date
And T1.Company <> T2.Company
And T1.Company <> T3.Company
And T2.Company <> T3.Company

Q6:
Select (T1.Company, T2.Company)
From   Ource::Table1   T1
            Ource::Table1   T2
Where   T1.Price > T2.Price
            T1.Date = T2.Date

Figure 3 – Standard SQL queries over the Ource Database

Q1:
Select (C1, C2, C3)
From   Euter::Table1->   C1
            Euter::Table1->   C2
            Euter::Table1->   C3
            Euter::Table1   T
Where   T.C1> T.C2+T.C3
            And T.C2 > T.C3
            And C2 isa 'StockColumn'
            And C3 isa 'StockColumn'
            And C1<>C2 and C1<>C3 and C2<>C3
            And C1 isa 'Company'

Q2:
Select (C1, C2)
From   Euter::Table1 ->   C1, C2
            Euter::Table1   T
Where   T.C1 > T.C2
            And C1 isa 'StockColumn'
            And C2 isa 'StockColumn'

Figure 4 – SchemaSQL queries over the Euter Database

4   Query Compilation

Compiling is done in three steps: creation of intermediate views over the source database, and translation of higher order queries into standard SQL and optimizing the results. The intermediate views are an "unskolemized" form of the source database's system catalog and other meta-data such that a data element is generated for each meta-data element. The compiler then substitutes meta-data variables in the input program with first-order variables ranging over the Skolem constants. The term "unskolemization" was introduced for a similar construction in automatic theorem proving [1]. This compilation method is proven correct in a separate and more detailed exposition ([3]).

```
Q3:
Select (C1, C2, C3)
From      Chwab->           T1, T2, T3
          Chwab::T1         R1
          Chwab::T2         R2
          Chwab::T3         R3
Where     R1.Price > R2.Price+R3.Price
          And R2.Price > R3.Price
          And R1.Date = R2.Date = R3.Date
          And T1<>T2 and T1<>T3 and T2<>T3
          And T1 isa 'StockTable'
          And T2 isa 'StockTable'
          And T3 isa 'StockTable'
```

```
Q4:
Select (C1, C2)
From      Chwab->           T1, T2
          Chwab::C1         R1
          Chwab::C2         R2
Where     R1.Price > R2.Price
          And R1.Date = R2.Date
          And T1 isa 'StockTable'
          And T2 isa 'StockTable'
```

Figure 5 – SchemaSQL queries over the Chwab Database

As a starting point, every table, in every database, is assumed to contain one column that can be used as a primary key. Without loss of generality that assumption could be relaxed by assuming that for every table, a group of columns can be identified as a candidate key. In our running example, we introduced one column, named Pkey, to each table to serve this purpose (see Figure 2). Our algorithm leverages primary keys in order to rewrite expressions containing meta-data variables into joins. This allows standard SQL engines to optimize complex expressions mixing several meta-data variables, as a normal set of join expressions.

For the purpose of this exposition, without loss of generality we will assume that there are no database variables involved in the SchemaSQL queries submitted to the compiler.

4.1   Defining the Intermediate Views

There are two kinds of intermediate views in our construction. Both kinds exploit the notion of types. In SchemaSQL, meta-data variables can be typed by predicates such as "*var isa TypeName*". Types can be viewed as enumerations of uniform catalog elements that serve as the range for meta-data variables. If types are not defined by the user, they must be inferred by default. In the default typing system, the type of a column is inferred from its SQL type: all the columns of each table which are of identical SQL type form an enumeration, which column variables can range over. The type of a table is defined by the juxtaposition of the type of its columns. All the tables of identical type in a given database can form an enumeration that table variables are allowed to range over. More details on types in SchemaSQL can be found in [11].

The first kind of intermediate view is defined by augmenting each table with its corresponding catalog information. Database and Table elements are mapped into data fields using Skolem constants to represent them with the following algorithm:

- For every class of table TypeTC of arity n, such that there is at least one table T, of type TC:
  Create View TypeTC (Database, Table, Value$_1$, Value$_2$, ..., Value$_n$, Key)
  As Union [U_{TC}]

- For every table T of type TypeTC (Pkey, Col$_1$, Col$_2$, ..., Col$_n$) insert into Union U_{TC}:
  Select ('DB', 'T', r.Col$_1$, r.Col$_2$, ..., r.Col$_n$, r.Pkey)
  From   DB::T   r

This intermediate view is defined by creating one row per relevant table in the source databases. Its purpose is to help retrieve row values defined in expressions such as "*From DB::T row*" when T is itself a variable. This algorithm applied to type StockTable is shown in Figure 6. Note that in this construction the Skolem constant introduced for table T, is simply the string T containing the name of the table. In certain cases, when all the tables within a database are of the same type, such as in database Chwab, the syntax allows the selection predicate isa(type..) to be omitted. As we discussed earlier, in such an instance, the compiler has to create a default type for the database, which will contain all the tables in it.

The second part is the creation of intermediate views for column types. For every column type CC the same algorithm has to be applied:

- For every column class of type CC such that there is at least one column C of type TypeCC:
  Create View TypeCC (Database, Table, Column, Value, Pkey) As Union [U_{CC}]

- For every column C insert into Union Ucc:
Select ('DB', 'T', 'C', r.C, r.Pkey)
From DB::T   r

This intermediate view is defined by creating one row for every relevant cell in the source tables. Its purpose is to help retrieve the proper value of expressions involving column variables such as: row.colvar. The value of such expressions can be retrieved from the appropriate row in NewTable by selecting on the Database, Table, Column and Pkey fields. Figure 7 illustrates the algorithm for StockColumn.

View TypeStockTable:
Create View TypeStockTable (database, table, value1, value2, pkey) AS
Select ('Chwab', 'IBM', r.Date, r.Price, r.Pkey)
From   Chwab.IBM   r
Union
Select ('Chwab', 'Apple', r.Date, r.Price, r.Pkey)
From   Chwab.Apple   r
Union
Select ('Chwab', 'Microsoft', r.Date, r.Price, r.Pkey)
From   Chwab.Microsoft   r

Figure 6 – Intermediate View for TypeStockTable (comprising Chwab::IBM, Chwab::Apple, Chwab::Microsoft)

View TypeStockColumn:
Create View TypeStockColumn (Database, Table, Column, Value, Pkey) As
Select ("Euter", "Table1", "IBM", r.IBM, r.Pkey)
From   Euter.Table1   r
Union
Select ("Euter", "Table1", "Apple", r.Apple, r.Pkey)
From   Euter.Table1   r
Union
Select ("Euter", "Table1", "Microsoft", r.Microsoft, r.Pkey)
From   Euter.Table1   r

Figure 7 – Intermediate View for TypeStockColumn (comprising IBM: int, Apple: int, Microsoft: int)

4.2   Generating the First-Order Queries

The second step is to rewrite the higher order queries in the input program. Those queries must be rewritten so as to derive their answers from the appropriate intermediate view whenever an expression involving a meta-data variable appears. Meta-data variables will no longer appear in the rewritten queries since the necessary catalog information from the database sources has been incorporated into the intermediate tables and can be accessed with regular variables. Thus the resulting queries become simple select/from/where statements in standard SQL.

The following algorithm takes each select/from/where statement appearing in the higher order "extended" SQL program and translates it into a standard SQL statement. In order to achieve this result, the principal substitutions that occur are:
- row variables ranging over a table which is itself a variable are substituted by a row ranging over the appropriate intermediate view for the table's type
- row.cv expressions, where cv is an column variable, are retrieved from the Value column of the intermediate view for that column's type by selecting on the Database, Table, Column and Pkey fields.
- table variables are substituted by a projection on the Table column of the appropriate view for that variable's type.

The full four-step algorithm 'Compile' follows. In every step of this algorithm, "r_1" will represent a newly generated variable name. Figure 8 shows the application of this algorithm to queries q1 through q6 of our running example.

4-Step Algorithm Compile:

Step 1. For every row variable r
Input:
In the From clause, r's range is *DB::T*, where T is a table variable of type TypeT (col$_1$, col$_2$, … , col$_n$)
Action:
In the From clause, replace *DB::T* with *TypeT* as a range for r
In the Where clause, insert as a selection "*r.Database = DB*"
In the Where clause, insert as a selection "*r.Table = T*"
In the Select and Where clauses, replace every *r.column* expression, with *r.value$_i$* where column is the ith column in DB::T

Step 2. For every expression r.cv where r is a row variable and cv is a column variable of type TypeC
Input:
cv is of type TypeC
Action:
In the From clause, introduce r1 with Range TypeC: "*TypeC r1*"
In the Where clause, insert as a join "*r1.Database = r.Database*"
In the Where clause, insert as a join "*r1.Table = r.Table*"
In the Where clause, insert as a join "*r1.Pkey = r.Pkey*"
In the Where clause, insert as a join "*r1.Column = cv*"
In the Select and Where clauses, replace every occurrence of "*r.cv*" with "*r1.col*"

Step 3. For every column variable cv such that cv is of type TypeC
Input:
In the From clause cv appears with range *DB::T*, where cv is a column of type TypeC
Choose appropriate case:
Case 1:
If step 2 was executed at least twice for expressions of type "$row_1.cv$" and "$row_2.cv$"
Action for Case 1:
In the From clause, remove the entry for cv: "$DB::T\ cv$"
In the Where clause, replace all expressions "$row_1.Column\ =\ cv$", "$row_2.Column=cv$", …, "$row_n.Column=cv$" with the n-1 following join predicates "$row_1.Column\ =row_2.Column\ =…=\ row_n.Column$"
In the Select and Where clause replace remaining occurrences of "cv" with "$row_1.Column$"

Case 2:
If step 2 was executed exactly once for the expression "$row_1.cv$"
Action for Case 2:
In the From clause, remove the entry for cv: "$DB::T\ cv$"
In the Select and Where clause replace remaining occurrences of "cv" with "$row_1.Column$"

Case 3:
If step 2 was never executed for any expression of type "$row.cv$"
Action for Case 3:
In the From clause replace "$DB::T\ cv$" with "$TypeC\ r1$"
In the Where clause, insert as a join "$r1.Database = DB$"
In the Where clause, insert as a join "$r1.Table = T$"
In the Select and Where clauses, replace every occurrence of "cv" with "$r1.Column$"

Step 4. For every table variable T such that T is of type TypeT (col_1, col_2, … , col_n)
Input:
In the From clause, T appears with range *DB*.
Choose appropriate case:
Case 1:
If steps 1 and steps 3 combined to form two or more expressions of type "$row_1.Table = T$", "$row_2.Table = T$", … "$row_n.Table=T$" in the Where clause
Action for Case 1:
Replace with (n-1) join predicates: "$row_1.Table = row_2.Table = …row_n.Table$"
In the From clause remove the entry "$DB\ T$"
In the Select and From clause replace every remaining occurrence of "T" with "$row_1.Table$", preferably where row_1 is a variable over TypeT rather than a TypeColumn.

Case 2:
If steps 1 and steps 3 combined to form exactly one expression of type "$row1.Table = T$" in the Where clause
Action for Case 2:
In the From clause remove the entry "$DB\ T$"
In the Select and From clause replace every remaining occurrence of "T" with "$row_1.Table$".

Case 3:
If steps 1 and steps 3 never produced an expression of type "$row.Table = T$" in the Where clause.
Action for Case 3:
In the From clause replace the entry "$DB\ T$" with "$TypeT\ r1$"
In the Where, insert as a selection "$r1.Database =DB$"
In the Select and Where clause, replace all occurrence of "T" with "$r1.Table$"

4.3   Optimizing Intermediate Views

The intermediate view definitions algorithms are exhaustive, resulting in much larger tables than acceptable. Following is an optimization method useful when the views are to be materialized or the target query engine is incapable of optimizing queries over views. The optimization amounts to pushing predicates down from the generated SQL into the intermediate view definitions.

This algorithm is executed by examining every statement produced by the four-step algorithm 'Compile' described in the previous Section.

Step 1. For TypeTable views,

If "TypeTable   row" is a line in the From clause of a compiled statement sfw,
Then every selection predicate SP(row) which appears in that statement sfw is used to form
Create View TypeTableOptimized-sfw-row
     As   Select *
          From TypeTable t
          Where SP(t)
Then in the From clause of statement sfw, replace "*TypeTable   row*"with "*TypeTableOptimized-sfw-row* row".

Step 2. For TypeColumn views,

If "TypeColumn col" is a line in the From clause of compiled statement sfw,
Then every selection predicate SP(col) which appears in that statement sfw is used to form
Create View TypeColumnOptimized-sfw-col
     As   Select *
          From TypeColumn c
          Where SP(c)

Then in the From clause of statement sfw, replace *"TypeColumn col"* with *"TypeColumnOptimized-sfw-col col"*.

Further, the SQL compiler should be directed to materialize these optimized views into tables whenever it is appropriate and the space is available. When possible, materializing will save on the number of run-time union operations performed by the query engine, which is the best policy in the absence of a cost-based model. The views should only materialized right before a query; and there is of course an incurred cost, which is negligible for large queries.

5   Size and Complexity

To validate the feasibility and practicality of our compilation algorithm, two aspects of the generated output are considered here. The first one is the size of the compiled program as a character string. This size is directly related to the number of SQL statements generated and their individual size. Guaranteeing a non-exponential growth in size is a necessary but not sufficient condition to implement SchemaSQL by compilation. Our simple size metric, while not very sophisticated, is adequate and sufficient to provide this necessary guarantee on the validity of our compilation. The other and somewhat more empirical aspect of compiler performance is the complexity and performance of the output queries it generates. A compiler producing a small number of computation intensive S/F/W statements is just as inefficient as a compiler producing vast quantities of computationally simple S/F/W statements.

5.1   Size

Because higher order programs when compiled into SQL must include meta-data catalog elements in them, the size of the compiled program will be some function of m, size of the meta-data catalogs. To be feasible a compilation must produce a manageable number of select/from/where (S/F/W) statements. Obviously compilations yielding programs of size m^k, where k is allowed to grow arbitrarily with the input are unacceptable if queries such as q1 are to be implemented.

To measure the size of the output program we consider S/F/W statement to be made up of Select lines, From lines, and Where lines. The Select clause is considered to make up only one line. Every Range-Abbreviation combination in the From clause is also considered to make up one line. Finally, every predicate in the Where clause forms a line. Except for the select line, each line contains two expressions, and possibly a logical connective. This is the case for a predicate (i.e. a.b = c.d) or for a Range-Abbreviation combination (i.e.

Customer c). Expressions are the unit in which the size of S/F/W statements will be measured here.

```
Q1:      Select (R1.Column, R2.Column, R3.Column)
From     TypeStockColumn   R1, R2, R3
         Euter::Table1         R4, R5, R6
Where
R1.Database = R2.Database = R3.Database = 'Euter'
And R1.Table = R2.Table = R3.Table = 'Table1'
And R1.Value > R2.Value+R3.Value
And R2.Value > R3.Value
And R1.Column <>R2.Column
And R1.Column<>R3.Column
And R2.Column<>R3.Column
And R1.Pkey = R4.Pkey and R2.Pkey = R5.Pkey and
R3.Pkey = R6.Pkey
And R3.Date = R4.Date = R5.Date
```

```
Q2:      Select (R1.Column, R2.Column)
From     TypeStockColumn   R1, R2
         Euter::Table1        R3, R4
Where
R1.Database = R2.Database = 'Euter'
And R1.Table = R2.Table = 'Table1'
And R1.Value > R2.Value
And R1.Column <>R2.Column
And R1.Pkey = R3.Pkey and R2.Pkey = R4.Pkey
And R3.Date = R4.Date
```

```
Q3:      Select (R1.Table, R2.Table, R3.Table)
From     TypeStockTable    R1, R2, R3
Where
R1.Database = R2.Database = R3.Database = "Chwab"
And R1.Value1 = R2.Value1 = R3.Value1
And R1.Value2 > R2.Value2 + R3.Value2
And R2.Value2 > R3.Value2
And R1.Table<>R2.Table and R1.Table<>R3.Table and
R2.Table<>R3.Table
```

```
Q4:      Select (R1.Table, R2.Table)
From     TypeStockTable    R1, R2
Where
R1.Database = R2.Database = "Chwab"
And R1.Value1 = R2.Value1
And R1.Value2 < R2.Value2
```

Figure 8 – Compiled queries

Theorem:

The size of the meta-data catalog is measured by m, the size of the input program by p, then the size of the compiled program p' is bound by:

$p' < k*m + 16*p$. k is not dependent on the input, but is a constant factor of the compilation construction.

Overall if p' is the size of the entire output program, we have $p' < k*m+16*p$, where k is the maximum size of a select/from/where statement inserted by the first step algorithms. Thus p' is linear in m and p, and asymptotically is a $O(m)+O(p)$ and also a $O(m+p)$.

Proof: The first step of the compilation requires the creation of intermediate views. The optimized version of those views will not be considered here.

Creating a TypeColumn view requires one SQL statement of fixed size for all the columns in the type TypeColumn. Assuming that every column in the heterogeneous databases belongs to exactly one type, there is at most one SQL statement per column.

Creating the TypeTable views requires one SQL statement for each table in the type TypeTable. The size of each of these statements is bound by a linear function of the number of columns in that table. Again, we will assume that each table in the heterogeneous databases belongs to exactly one type.

Size (TypeTable SQL statement for each table T) < k1*(# of Column in T)

$\Rightarrow$ *Size (TypeTable view creations for all tables T) < k1*(# of Columns in the catalogs)*

Thus the size of the statements generated by the first compilation step can be bound by a $k*m$, where $m = m_1+m_2+..+m_n$, and m_i is the size of the catalog for database i in the federation.

The second step generates a standard SQL query for each input SchemaSQL query. Let p be the size of the input program (unit: number of expressions). Here are the worst-case bounds:

- For every row variable 1 line is removed and 3 lines are added (step **1**)
- For every distinct "*row.col*" row and column combination, 5 lines are added (step **2**)
- For every column variable, in the worst case 1 line is removed and 5 are added. (step **3**)
- For every table variable, in the worst case 1 line is removed and 3 are added (step **3**)

Note that the 'Compile' algorithm never inserts a higher order variable or a new "row.col" row/column combination. Therefore those numbers are not cumulative. Also, each line inserted by the algorithm contains at most two expressions and an equality sign. The size of the Select line is unchanged.

The worse case size increase is for row/column combinations, where every expression provokes the insertion of at most 5*(2 expressions + 1 equality sign). Thus a very gross linear bound for the output produce by the second step is p+15*p. (A more precise bound would be in fact much better).

The reader can verify that adding the optimizations described in Section 4.3 does alter the size guarantee.

5.2   Run-Time Complexity

Our complexity measure is relevant insofar as we measure the complexity of the compiler output versus that of the compiler input. Thus we are only interested in the additional complexity due to the compiler's work. In order to measure that quantity we will not examine precise cost functions relating to the complexity of each statement, but leave that evaluation work to the experimental Section. Instead, we identify here, each explicit join in the output program, subtract each explicit join, which was already present in the input program, which yields the joins "added" by the compiler.

The first step yields SQL statements, which do not contain joins. In the second step, the 'Compile' algorithm adds Selection predicates at many junctures. However, Joins are only added to a translated SQL statement whenever column or table variables appear.

Each Column variable can yield up to a (n-1)-way join of the form "$row_1.Column = row_2.Column \dots = row_n.Column$".

Each Table variable can yield up to a (n-1)-way join of the form "$row_1.Table = row_2.Table \dots = row_n.Table$".

Further, because of the construction, n is at most the number of variables in the input SchemaSQL statement.

The compiled program contains at most one additional join per meta-data variable in the input. Each of these joins is at most a (n-1)-way join where n is the number of variables in the input.

5.3   Lower Bound

If a O(m)+O(p) type bound is accepted by the reader as a trivial lower bound for output size: **i.e.** the compiled program can't be smaller than the input program, and it has to contain at least the meta-data since that is not otherwise accessible in SQL, then the algorithm can be considered optimal by that size measure.

From the point of view of complexity, the number of joins itself produced by the compilation can be seen as a trivial lower bound. Any fewer joins in the output program is impossible since the higher order program can contain implicit joins on meta-data variables, which appear in the From clause rather than the Where clause. These are the case when our algorithm insert an extra join for that meta-data variable. The size and complexity of each of these additional joins is another matter and can obviously be optimized further.

To make this simple 'optimality' argument requires abstracting many details as well as the optimization of selections and projections. In this argument we only considered join complexity, which is what is argued to be close to the trivial lower bound.

6   Experimental Results

The databases are generated according to a random formula, which can yield a wide fluctuation of catalog statistics for the selected queries. Measurements points shown in the graphs are averages in seconds on a Postgres server. The query optimizer uses default settings, recreating conditions in which only the static optimizations, described in section 4, are applied.

6.1   Comparative Complexity

A simple way to evaluate the performance of the compiler is to compare the execution time of the queries in our running example when they run on Ource (q5, q6), which is in normal form, and when they are expressed on Euter (q1, q2) and Chwab (q3, q4) in their higher order form. Figure 9, shows the computing time for each query against the number of rows in the Euter database. The numbers plotted in Figure 9 show a linear execution time for all queries. However compiled SchemaSQL queries q1, q2, q3 and q4 are slower by a constant multiplicative factor than their SQL counterparts: q5 and q6.

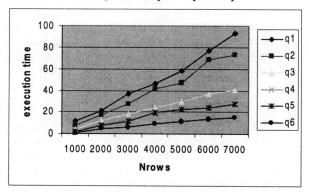

Figure 9 – execution time vs. number of rows

The difference is that on Ource (q5, q6), the queries are expressed with explicit joins using standard SQL. On Euter (q1, q2) and Chwab (q3, q4), the joins are implicit and occur at the interface between meta-data variables and standard SQL variables. This is easily seen in expressions such as *"From DB::T row"*. This expression represents an implicit join between meta-data variable *T* and the SQL variable *row*. The same argument is made in the previous section to justify the trivial lower bound on join complexity.

Thus comparing the performance of the queries in our running example can give an indication of how much the compiler costs in terms of complexity when implicit joins are compiled into explicit first-order joins.

The database Ource, which is in normal form, contains 50% more cells. The databases Chwab and Euter

are more compact since they do not contain the company names in their tables.

6.2   Complexity

An interesting measure of complexity is in terms of the compiler's performance when both the data and the meta-data catalogs grow. Our theorem and theoretical analysis would make us hope that the computation costs grow linearly with the size of the catalog. That theory is comforted by the results graphed in Figures 10 and 11. The catalogs are grown by increasing the number of stocks from 5 to 40. For Euter, the number of attributes grows with the number of stocks, for Chwab the number of tables grows with the number of stocks. Figure 10 groups q1, q3 and q5 together since they all correspond to a three-way join type of operation. Figure 11 groups q2, q4, and q6 together since these queries only represent two-way join. The experimental number show that, *in both cases*, compiled SchemaSQL queries on Euter and Chwab do perform slower than the SQL queries on Ource, but by no more than a constant linear factor. This is best seen in the logarithmic scales of Figures 10 and 11 by noting that the separation between the curves is either constant (Figure 11) or decreases (Figure 10).

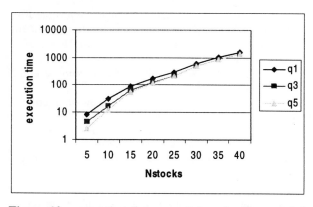

Figure 10 – execution time vs. catalog size (3 way join)

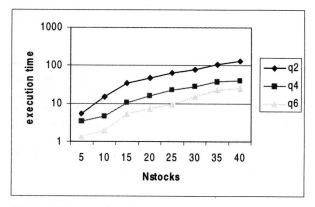

Figure 11- execution time vs. catalog size (2 way join)

7   Related Work

In [9] and [11] Lakshmanan et al. define SchemaLog and SchemaSQL as query languages derived from Datalog and SQL, and possessing, as suggested in [8], the higher order syntax necessary for schema restructuring. A query optimizer for SchemaSQL is implemented in [10]. The described implementation incorporates the operators necessary to deal with the higher order features of SchemaSQL. A compilation method for SchemaSQL is described in [11], where intermediate views called VITs are created to handle tuple variables. A single VIT can include instantiations for several meta-variables associated with a common tuple variable. In that scenario, expressing the VIT can require $O(m^k)$ SQL statements (k: number of meta-variables, m: schema constant). This approach lacks the necessary guarantee described in Section 5.1. This results in a very noticeable combinatorial effect on the size of the intermediate view definitions. Our approach associates intermediate views exclusively with meta-variables, guaranteed a linear complexity as the schema grows and allowing static optimizations.

Vassalos and Papakonstantinou introduce in [14] a higher order language, which specifies semantics for mediators. They compile that language into a first order logic language noted p-Datalog. In that compilation intermediate view definitions built using skolem constants, are guaranteed to remain of fixed size. That idea sets the direction which our work follows to implement SchemaSQL.

While SchemaSQL with a platform independent implementation is our concern for the reasons discussed in Section 2, there exists a large number of other schema integration architectures with declarative mediation languages and various query execution models: [6] (Tsimmis), [7] (Garlic), [13] (Disco), [15] (Aurora), [4] (YAT) to name a few (or see [5] for a brief overview).

8   Conclusion

We have presented a method to compile a subset of SchemaSQL (PSJ queries) into standard SQL. The compilation algorithm offers guarantees in terms of size and complexity of the resulting program. And experimental results suggest that those theoretical guarantees seem to hold in practice. This algorithm can be used to build portable federated database systems using higher order syntactic specifications. Native SQL engines can understand and optimize the resulting code like they would any normal join expression. Furthermore, the higher order operators we implement by compilation are associated with some necessary semantic optimizations. Experiments show that a few SchemaSQL queries, compiled solely with those semantic optimizations, do not fare much worse than comparable SQL queries. We leave open the problem of implementing a wider class of queries including aggregations and dynamic output schema, but are optimistic as evidenced by [11] that the basic scheme we introduced can be suitably adapted. We also leave open the issue of implementing cost-based optimization techniques for the compiled code, and reconciling them with the constraint of portability and platform independence.

References

[1] Bledsoe W., J. Minor: *Unskolemizing*. University of Texas at Austin, Math Department, technical report ATP-77.

[2] Barbançon F., D. Miranker: *Compiling Higher-Order Federating Queries for Execution on Relational Systems*. University of Texas at Austin, Computer Sciences Department TR-01-41. http://www.cs.utexas.edu/users/francois/tr01-41.pdf

[3] Barbançon F., D. Miranker: *Federated Database by Example*. University of Texas at Austin, Computer Sciences Department TR-01-42.
http://www.cs.utexas.edu/users/francois/tr01-42.pdf

[4] Cluet S., C. Delobel, J. Siméon, K. Smaga: *Your Mediators Need Data Conversion!* SIGMOD Conference 1998: 177-188.

[5] Florescu D., A. Levy, A. Mendelzon: *Database Techniques for the World-Wide Web: A Survey*. SIGMOD Record 27(3): 59-74 (1998)

[6] Garcia-Molina H., Y. Papakonstantinou, D. Quass, A. Rajaraman, Y. Sagiv, J. Ullman, V. Vassalos, J. Widom: *The TSIMMIS Approach to Mediation: Data Models and Languages*. JIIS 8(2): 117-132 (1997)

[7] Haas L., D. Kossmann, E. Wimmers, J. Yang: *Optimizing Queries Across Diverse Data Sources*. VLDB 1997: 276-285.

[8] Krishnamurthy R., W. Litwin, W. Kent: *Language Features for Interoperability of Databases with Schematic Discrepancies*. SIGMOD Conference 1991: 40-49.

[9] Lakshmanan L., F. Sadri, S. Subramanian: *Logic and Algebraic Languages for Interoperability in Multidatabase Systems*. JLP 33(2): 101-149 (1997)

[10] Lakshmanan L., F. Sadri, S. Subramanian : *On Efficiently Implementing SchemaSQL on an SQL Database System*. VLDB 1999: 471-482.

[11] Lakshmanan L., F. Sadri, S. Subramanian: *SchemaSQL – An Extension to SQL for Multi-database Interoperability*. To appear in TODS (2001).

[12] Miller R., L. Haas, M. Hernández: *Schema Mapping as Query Discovery*. VLDB 2000: 77-88.

[13] Tomasic A., L. Raschid, P. Valduriez: *Scaling Heterogeneous Databases and the Design of Disco*. ICDCS 1996: 449-457.

[14] Vassalos V., Y. Papakonstantinou: *Describing and Using Query Capabilities of Heterogeneous Sources*. VLDB 1997: 256-265.

[15] Yan L., T. Özsu, L. Liu: *Accessing Heterogeneous Data Through Homogenization and Integration Mediators*. CoopIS 1997: 130-139.

A multi-agent model for handling e-commerce activities

Domenico Rosaci, Giuseppe M.L. Sarné, Domenico Ursino

D.I.M.E.T. - Università Mediterranea di Reggio Calabria

Via Graziella, Località Feo di Vito, 89060 Reggio Calabria (RC), Italy

e-mail:{rosaci,sarne,ursino}@ing.unirc.it

Abstract

In this paper we propose a multi-agent model for handling e-commerce activities. In our model, an agent is present in each e-commerce site, managing the information stored therein. In addition, another agent is associated with each customer, handling her/his profile. The proposed model is based on the exploitation of a particular conceptual model, called B-SDR network, capable of representing and handling both information stored in e-commerce sites and customer profiles. The capabilities of the B-SDR network model are exploited to let customer and site agents to cooperate in such a way to support a customer to detect, whenever she/he accesses an e-commerce site, those products and services present in the site itself and better matching her/his interests.

1 Introduction

In the last decade e-commerce has emerged as a significant, both social and cultural, phenomenon; indeed, nowadays, a large number of vendors provide their customers with the possibility to buy their products also through the Internet; several trading companies (e.g., Amazon), even, exist, carrying out their activity only via Web.

Operations executed by a customer, whenever she/he buys a product or a service from an e-commerce site, can be grouped into two main activities, namely *(i)* the exploitation of a Web search engine (such as Altavista or Google) for finding potentially interesting sites; *(ii)* the use of a Web browser for navigating through the pages of a site she/he judged interesting. While a large variety of tools already exists over the Internet for helping a customer in the search of potentially interesting sites, only a little number of supports are available for assisting her/him in the navigation through an interesting site.

One of the most common of these supports are *recommender systems* [18, 19] which have been conceived for helping the customer of an e-commerce site in the purchase activity. In order to carry out its task, a recommender system provides the customer with the list of those products and services available on the site and appearing to be the most successful, according to the opinion and past purchases of other customers. Moreover, it could analyze the past behaviour of the customer on the site for predicting those issues which, presumably, will interest her/him in the future. Last, but not the least, it could classify a customer according to some demographic parameters and could make offers to her/him taking into account this classification. In order to perform these activities, a recommender system must process available data; this can be done by exploiting various computation tools such as cross-sell lists and information filters.

Another important tool present in a large number of e-commerce sites is a (usually rough) handler of customer profiles, exploited for proposing personalized offers. However profile construction requires a strong intervention of the customer who is required to provide information about her/his interests and desires; the profile is just intended as a summary of this information. This profile construction methodology causes some problems. Indeed, it requires that a customer spends a certain amount of time for constructing and/or updating her/his profile; in addition, it stores only information about the issues which the customer claims to be interested in, without considering other issues somehow related to those ones she/he already provided, possibly interesting her/him in the future and that she/he disregarded to take into account in the past.

In spite of recommender systems and customer profile handlers, generally, when accessing an e-commerce sites, the customer must personally search the issues of her/his interest through the site. As an example, consider the bookstore section of Amazon: whenever a customer looks for finding a book of her/his interest, she/he must carry out an autonomous personal search of the book throughout the pages of the site. We argue that, for improving the effectiveness of the e-commerce service, it is necessary to increase the interaction between the site and the customer, on the one hand, and to construct a rich profile of the customer, taking into account her/his desires, interests and behaviour, on the other hand. In order to obtain these results three main problems must be tackled.

First, a customer can access *many* e-commerce sites; a faithful and complete customer profile can be constructed only taking into account her/his behaviour on accessing all these sites. In other words, it should be possible to construct a *unique structure on the customer site*, storing her/his profile and, therefore, representing her/his behaviour on accessing *all these sites*. In addition, in order to construct the single customer profile, it would be possible to recognize semantically similar concepts represented by different constructs in the various sites and to represent them by a unique construct in the customer profile. In order to satisfy this requirement, a technique for deriving similarities between information stored in different sites appears to be compulsory.

Second, since e-commerce sites usually present various forms of heterogeneities, ranging from representation formats to data semantics, it is necessary to define a conceptual model capable of representing and handling heterogeneous information sources. This model might be exploited for representing information of the various sites visited by the customer; in addition, it would be capable to represent the customer profile, in particular her/his behaviour on accessing the various sites. In the literature some models have been proposed for uniformly representing and handling the contents of heterogeneous information sources (see, for example, [2, 6, 21]); however, none of them is capable to represent also the behaviour of a user on accessing the sources.

Third, for a given customer and e-commerce site, it is possible to compare the profile of the customer with the offers of the e-commerce site for extracting those issues that probably will interest the customer. Existing techniques for satisfying such a requirement are mainly based on the exploitation of either log files [4, 22] and cookies [17]. Techniques based on *log files* are capable to register only some information about the actions carried out by the customer on accessing the site; however, they are not capable to match customer preferences and site contents. Vice versa, techniques based on *cookies* are able to carry out a certain, even if primitive, matching; however they need to know and exploit some personal information that a customer might consider private.

In the past, various agent-based approaches have been proposed for solving some or all of the problems introduced above [1, 7, 8, 10, 11, 13, 14, 20]. In this paper we aim at providing a contribution in this setting by proposing a multi-agent based model for representing and handling e-commerce activities. Our model is capable to face the three problems discussed above. In particular, in our model, an agent is present in each e-commerce site, handling the information stored therein. In addition, an agent is associated

with each customer, handling her/his profile. Both the information relative to each e-commerce site and each customer profile is represented and handled by a particular conceptual model called *B-SDR network* [3]. This is able not only to uniformly manage heterogeneous data sources but it can handle also behavioural information, i.e., information about the behaviour of a customer on accessing data sources. The agents we exploit for handling e-commerce sites and customer profiles use the B-SDR network as their reference model for representing their ontologies; they are called *B-SDR agents*. The exploitation of both B-SDR network and B-SDR agents allows our model to satisfy the second requirement described above.

In our model, a profile is constructed and maintained for each customer, storing information about the visits she/he carried out on *all* e-commerce sites into consideration. Whenever a customer accesses an e-commerce site, her/his agent updates the profile. This operation is carried out by deriving similarities between concepts present in different e-commerce sites; each group of similar concepts is represented by a unique concept in the profile. As a consequence, also the first requirement discussed above is satisfied.

Finally, in order to satisfy also the third requirement above, our model behaves as follows. Whenever a customer accesses an e-commerce site, the site agent sends its B-SDR network to the customer agent. This latter activates a function for computing semantic similarities between portions of the B-SDR network relative to the site and portions of the B-SDR network representing the customer profile. Each of these similarities represents an issue of interest for the customer which is present in the e-commerce site; for each similarity both the site and the customer agents cooperate for presenting to the customer a B-SDR network illustrating what the site can offer to the customer as far as the issue associated with the similarity is concerned. We argue that this behaviour provides our model with the capability to support the customer in searching, in the e-commerce sites, those products satisfying her/his interests. In addition, as it will be clear in the following, the characteristics of the exploited conceptual model, along with the properties of the algorithm proposed for extracting sub-source similarities, allow to determine not only information probably interesting for the customer, according to both the interests she/he expressed in the past and her/his behaviour, but also other issues, somehow related to those ones she/he already considered appealing, possibly interesting for her/him in the future and that she/he disregarded to take into account in the past. As previously pointed out, we argue that this is a particularly interesting feature for a model devoted to handle e-commerce services. Last, but not the least, it is worth observing that, since the computation of semantic similarities between the e-commerce site and the customer profile is carried out at the customer side, no information about the customer profile is sent to the e-commerce site. In this way, our approach solves privacy problems left open by cookies.

2 The B-SDR network and the B-SDR agent models

In our approach both the information relative to e-commerce sites and customer profiles is represented and handled by a specific conceptual model, called B-SDR network [3]. Such a model is particularly suited not only because it is capable to uniformly handle heterogeneous data sources but also because, in its most general form, it stores and manages behaviour information, i.e., information about the behaviour of a user on accessing data sources. As a matter of facts, B-SDR network features have been conceived for them to be particularly suited for representing user profiles. Whenever it is not necessary to represent and handle information regarding user behaviour, thus reducing our interest to information typical stored and managed by a classical conceptual model, we can use a reduced version of the B-SDR network, called SDR network [16, 21]. Such a distinction is quite important in our model; indeed, as it will be clear in the following, in some steps of the interaction between site and customer agents, it is necessary to handle only information about concepts and their relationships whereas information about customer behaviour must not be elaborated; in all these steps, it appears more suitable to exploit the SDR network as the reference model for representing information to handle.

Let us define the B-SDR network. Consider a *universe* $\mathcal{U}$ of information sources, each encoding information both at *extensional* and *intensional* levels. The basic elements of the extensional level are *instances* whereas, at the intensional level we deal with *concepts*. We denote by I the set of instances relative to all concepts of $\mathcal{U}$ and by C the set of such concepts. We assume that each concept $c \in C$ has a name denoted by *name(c)*.

In its most general version, the B-SDR network is defined for a given user u and a given set of concepts in C. Given a subset of concepts $N \subseteq C$ and a user u, a *B-SDR network* (for u on N) is a rooted labeled direct graph $B\_Net(N, u) = \langle N, A \rangle$, where N is the set of nodes and $A \subseteq N \times N$ is the set of arcs. We denote by I_N the set of instances appearing in the concepts of N. Informally, N represents the set of concepts of interest for u. Since a B-SDR network node represents a concept of the corresponding information source, and vice versa, in the following, we use the terms B-SDR network node and concept interchangeably.

Arcs encode semantic relationships between concepts. Their labels define a number of properties associated with relationships of $BNet(N, u)$. More precisely, a label $\langle d_{st}, r_{st}, h_{st}, \tau_{st} \rangle$ is associated with an arc (s, t), where

both d_{st} and r_{st} belong to the real interval $[0, 1]$, h_{st} is a non negative integer and τ_{st} is a non negative real number. The four *label coefficients* introduced above encode different properties. In more detail:

- d_{st} is the *semantic distance coefficient*. It is inversely related to the contribution given by the concept t in characterizing the concept s. As an example, in an E/R scheme, for an attribute t of an entity s, d_{st} will be smaller than $d_{ss'}$, where s' is another entity related to s by a relationship. Analogously, in an XML document, a pair (s, t), where s is an element and t is one of its sub-elements, will have a semantic distance coefficient d_{st} smaller than $d_{ss'}$, where s' is another element which s refers to through an $IDREF$ attribute.

- r_{st} is the *semantic relevance coefficient*, indicating the fraction of instances of s whose complete definition requires at least one instance of t.

- h_{st} is the *hit coefficient*, counting the number of hits which the user u carries out on t coming from s.

- τ_{st} is the *(no-idle) time coefficient*, denoting the effective total time, measured in minutes, which u spent for consulting t coming from s.

Similarly to the relationship between concepts, also the membership of instances to concepts is weighed by labeling. In particular, we associate a label $\langle h_{st}, \tau_{st} \rangle$ with each pair (s, t) such that s is a node of the graph and t is an instance relative to s; in this case h_{st}, called *hit coefficient*, and τ_{st}, called *(no-idle) time coefficient*, are defined in an obvious way, coherently with the corresponding coefficients presented above.

In order to elaborate hit and time coefficients, for making more interpretable them, we define two functions $\theta, \rho : (N \times N) \cup (N \times I_N) \to [0, 1]$. These are partial functions since they are defined only on arcs (s, t) of $B\_Net(N, u)$ and on pairs concept-instance (s, t) such that t is an instance of s.

The function θ, computed on a given pair (s, t), exploits hit and time coefficients of (s, t) in order to give a measure of the "interest" the user u has for t when she/he accesses t through s. In particular:

$$\theta(s, t) = h_{st} + \lfloor \tfrac{\tau_{st}}{q} \rfloor$$

where q is a parameter devoted to modulate the importance of the effective access time w.r.t. the number of hits. Indeed, for high values of q, the interest measures just how many times the user contacted t. On the contrary, a small q cancels the effect of contact actions. The value q could be set taking into account several variables, like the connection bit rate, the expertise of the user and so on.

The function ρ, computed on a given pair (s,t), represents the preference the user u gives to t w.r.t. all the other concepts reachable in just one step coming from s, in case t is a concept, or all the other instances of s, in case t is an instance. The preference is computed as a fraction of the overall interest. More precisely, ρ is defined as:

$$\rho(s,t) = \frac{\theta(s,t)}{\sum_{t' \in A(s)} \theta(s,t')}$$

where $A(s)$ is *(i)* the set of nodes reachable in just one step coming from s, or s itself, if t is a concept; *(ii)* the set of instances relative to s, if t is an instance[1].

Unlike hit and time coefficients, the semantic distance coefficient provides us a way for measuring how much concepts are "structurally" related to each other, independently on the user behaviour. On the basis of such a notion, we can define the *neighborhood* of a given concept s as the set of concepts of the B-SDR network which s is sufficiently (i.e., up a suitable threshold) dependent on. To formally provide such a definition, we must extend the semantic distance measure to paths.

Let s and t be two nodes and let π be a path from s to t in a B-SDR network $B\_Net(N,u)$. The *path semantic distance* of t w.r.t. s by π, denoted by $\delta_{path}(s,t,\pi)$, is the sum of the semantic distance coefficients labeling the arcs of π. Let s and t be two nodes such that there exists a path in $B\_Net(N,u)$ from s to t. The *semantic distance* of t w.r.t. s, denoted by $\delta(s,t)$, is defined as $min\{\delta_{path}(s,t,\pi) \mid \pi$ is a path in $B\_Net(N,u)$ from s to $t\}$. Given a B-SDR network $B\_Net(N,u)$, a positive integer number k and a concept $t \in N$, the *k-neighborhood* of t in $B\_Net(N,u)$, denoted by $nbh(t,k)$, is the set of nodes $\{s \in N \mid \delta(s,t) \leq k\}$.

An example of a B-SDR network is shown in Figure 1; it represents the profile of a customer, say Jack. Due to space limitations, we do not show the instances associated with each concept. B-SDR network nodes, such as *Music*, *Book* and *Movie* represent the involved concepts. The arc $\langle Classic, Composer, [0.5, 0.7, 38, 34] \rangle$ denotes the existence of a relationship between classic music and composers; in particular, it indicates that *(i)* 70% of instances relative to classic music are related to at least one instance of composer; *(ii)* the user Jack accessed 38 times the concept *Composer* through the concept *Music*, and *(iii)* the total no-idle time that Jack spent for visiting the concept *Composer*, coming from the concept *Music*, is 34 minutes. The other arcs have an analogous semantics. The path semantic distance of *Lyric* w.r.t. *Music* by the path $[Music - Composer - Lyric]$ is 1. The semantic distance of *Lyric* w.r.t. *Music* is $min\{1, 0.5, 1\} = 0.5$. Finally, $nbh(Music, 1) = \{Classic, Composer, Lyric\}$.

[1]Recall that, due to the features of the B-SDR network model, also t is an instance of s.

The other semantic distances and neighborhoods can be computed in the same way.

As previously mentioned, in our approach, both e-commerce sites and user profiles are handled by agents exploiting the B-SDR network as the reference model for representing their ontologies; they are called *B-SDR agents*. It is worth pointing out that, in the B-SDR network associated with e-commerce sites, all behaviour coefficients are null since they are meaningful only for a user, and not for a site.

3 An overview of the proposed model

In this section we illustrate our multi-agent model for representing and handling e-commerce activities. It has been conceived for realizing an effective cooperation between customer and site agents in order to support the customer in the quick and complete search, through an e-commerce site, of those products and services appearing to be the most interesting ones, according to her/his profile.

Let $C = \{c_1, c_2, \ldots, c_n\}$ be a set of customers; let $S = \{s_1, s_2, ..., s_m\}$ be a set of e-commerce sites; assume that each customer of C and each site of S has an associated B-SDR agent and let $CA = \{CA_1, CA_2, \ldots, CA_n\}$ and $SA = \{SA_1, SA_2, ..., SA_m\}$ be the sets of these agents.

The B-SDR network associated with each agent $CA_i \in CA$ represents the profile of c_i. It stores concepts and instances which c_i visited in the past, as well as information about her/his behaviour on accessing them. The profile of c_i is updated by the corresponding agent whenever she/he visits an e-commerce site. In order to construct a starting profile associated with c_i, she/he is monitored during her/his navigation on the Web; the starting profile is obtained by suitably elaborating the information stored in the visited sources (see, below, Section 4.1). The duration of the monitoring activity depends on both the customer and the way she/he navigates on the Web; obviously, the longer the duration of the monitoring activity is, the higher the profile precision will be. It is worth pointing out that this initial profile is to be intended only as a way for "defining" the customer "world"; as a matter of facts, the profile is refined and, possibly, deeply modified by the subsequent dynamics of customer accesses. Figure 1, introduced in the previous section, illustrates the B-SDR network representing the profile of the customer Jack.

The B-SDR network handled by each agent $SA_j \in SA$ represents the content of the site s_j in terms of concepts and instances stored therein. The B-SDR network relative to s_j is created when this site is made available over the Internet and is updated asynchronously whenever a concept or an instance is either created or removed or updated in it. In Figure 2, the B-SDR network associated with an e-commerce site is depicted. Also in this case, due to space limitations, we do not show the associated instances.

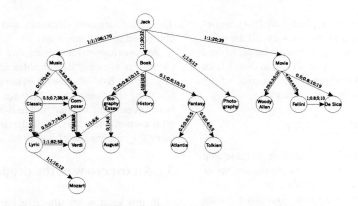

Figure 1. The B-SDR network representing a customer profile

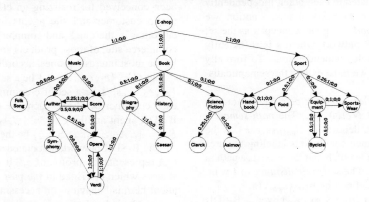

Figure 2. The B-SDR network representing an e-commerce site

We are now able to examine the behaviour of the proposed model. For each visit of a customer $c_i \in C$ to an e-commerce site $s_j \in S$, it carries out the following four steps:

1. The agent SA_j, associated with s_j, and having a corresponding B-SDR network $BSDR_j$, sends to the agent CA_i, associated with c_i, the SDR network SDR_j, representing, at the conceptual level, the content of s_j. SDR_j is derived from $BSDR_j$ by disregarding all instances and behaviour coefficients.

2. When c_i receives SDR_j, the associated agent CA_i, having a corresponding B-SDR network $BSDR_i$, constructs the SDR network SDR_i representing, at the *conceptual* level, the information about c_i's profile. After this, CA_i carries out a scheme match operation [12] on SDR_i and SDR_j. This is devoted to derive the set $SNSet$ of pairs of similar subnets $[SN_{i_u}, SN_{j_v}]$ such that SN_{i_u} belongs to SDR_i and SN_{j_v} belongs to SDR_j. Each sub-net similarity represents a correspondence between a customer interest and a piece of

information stored in the e-commerce site. Observe that the model considers sub-net similarities instead of node similarities because, this way, it is able to detect not only information that could be appealing to the customer, according to her/his past interests, but also related information that could interest c_i in the future and whose existence she/he possibly ignored. Figures 3(a) and 3(b) show a pair of similar sub-nets relative to the SDR network associated with the customer profile of Figure 1 and the SDR network corresponding to the e-commerce site of Figure 2. The technique for deriving sub-net similarities is described in Section 5.

3. From each pair $[SN_{i_u}, SN_{j_v}] \in SNSet$, such that SN_{i_u} belongs to SDR_i and SN_{j_v} belongs to SDR_j, the agent CA_i constructs a B-SDR network $BSDR_{uv}$. This contains all nodes, arcs, semantic distance and relevance coefficients of SN_{j_v}. In addition, for each arc a from s to t in $BSDR_{uv}$, if there exists an arc a' from s' to t' in $BSDR_i$ and s' and t' are either synonym or coincident with s and t, then h_{st} and τ_{st} are

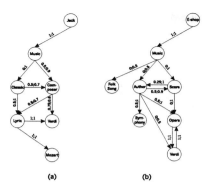

(a)   (b)

Figure 3. The similar sub-nets concerning the issue "Music" in the customer profile (a) and in the e-commerce site (b)

set equal to $h_{s't'}$ and $\tau_{s't'}$, respectively; otherwise h_{st} and τ_{st} are set equal to 0. All B-SDR networks thus constructed are sent by CA_i to SA_j. Figure 4 shows the B-SDR network derived by applying the method described above on the pair of SDR networks depicted in Figures 3(a) and 3(b).

As an example, in this figure, there is an arc $\langle Author, Opera, [0.5, 1, 76, 59]\rangle$ because *(i)* the arc $\langle Author, Opera, [0.5, 1]\rangle$ is present in the SDR network of Figure 3(b), *(ii)* there exists an arc $\langle Composer, Lyric, [0.5, 0.7, 76, 59]\rangle$ in the B-SDR network $BSDR_i$ of Figure 1, *(iii)* *Author* is synonym with *Composer*, *(iv)* *Opera* is synonym with *Lyric*. Analogously, in Figure 4, there is an arc $\langle Music, Folk\ Song, [0, 0.5, 0, 0]\rangle$ because *(i)* the arc $\langle Music, Folk\ Song, [0, 0.5, 0, 0]\rangle$ is present in the SDR network of Figure 3(b), *(ii)* there does not exist, in the B-SDR network $BSDR_i$ of Figure 1, an arc whose source and target nodes are either synonym or coincident with *Music* and *Folk Song*, resp.

4. SA_j receives the B-SDR networks sent by CA_i, representing those pieces of s_j information interesting for c_i. Let $BSDR_{uv}$ be one of these B-SDR networks. For each concept of $BSDR_{uv}$, SA_j associates the corresponding instances as stored in $BSDR_j$. In this way the whole concept and instance information stored in s_j, and interesting for c_i, is reconstructed. The B-SDR networks thus completed are sent to CA_i which presents them in a suitable format to c_i in order to let him carry out her/his choices. Whenever c_i makes a choice, and therefore accesses either a concept or an instance stored in s_j, her/his profile is suitably updated for registering this event. The technique for updating the profile of c_i is illustrated in Section 4.2.

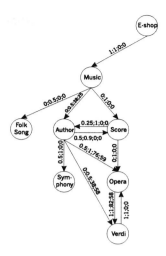

Figure 4. The final B-SDR network concerning the issue "Music" provided to the customer

This closes, briefly, the description of our model. In the next sections we illustrate into detail the most complex activities relative to it.

4 Handling Customer Profile

4.1 Customer Profile Construction

As pointed out in Section 3, in order to construct a starting profile, the customer is monitored for determining an initial set of sites visited by her/him and, therefore, presumably of interest for her/him. The starting profile is obtained by suitably elaborating the information stored in the sources of the set. In particular, for each source, a B-SDR network, representing the information stored therein, is constructed. After this, all these B-SDR networks are integrated and the global B-SDR network thus obtained is assumed as the starting customer profile.

Given a Web site, in order to obtain the corresponding B-SDR network, some translation rules must be applied. These depend on the format used for representing and handling the information stored therein; we do not describe all details of these rules here since this goes beyond the scope of this paper; however, the interested reader can find them in [15, 16, 21].

After the B-SDR networks associated with Web sites chosen by the customer have been obtained, it is necessary to integrate them for constructing the customer profile. B-SDR network integration is carried out by a suitable function that we call *Integrate*.

4.1.1 Function Integrate

Integrate receives two B-SDR networks B_1 and B_2 and integrates them for obtaining a global B-SDR network B_G.

In order to determine the topology of B_G, *inter-source properties* existing among concepts of B_1 and B_2 must be computed. Inter-source properties are terminological and structural properties relating concepts belonging to different information sources; here we consider two kinds of inter-source properties, namely synonymies and homonymies. A *synonymy* between two concepts indicates that they have the same meaning. A *homonymy* between two concepts, belonging to two different data sources, denotes that they have different meanings, yet having the same names. Derived synonymies and homonymies are stored in the Synonymy Dictionary SD and in the Homonymy Dictionary HD as tuples of the form $\langle C_x, C_y, f_{xy} \rangle$, where C_x and C_y are the involved concepts and f_{xy} is a plausibility coefficient, in the real interval $[0, 1]$, denoting the strength of the property[2]. In order to derive synonymies and homonymies, our approach exploits the B-SDR network based techniques presented in [16]. Such techniques exactly fit all our requirements; indeed, they are based on a *scheme match* approach [12], they take into account context information by computing and exploiting the neighborhood of involved concepts, they use semantic relevance coefficients and concept terminological similarities for computing the plausibility degree associated with each property; moreover, since they are based on the B-SDR network model, they can operate on information sources having different data representation formats.

After Synonymy and Homonymy Dictionaries have been constructed, B_1 and B_2 are juxtaposed for obtaining a roughly version of B_G, possibly containing redundancies and ambiguities.

The first step in refining B_G consists in deriving its root[3]; as far as this operation is concerned, if the roots of B_1 and B_2 are synonym, they must be merged; otherwise a new root is created and connected to the roots of B_1 and B_2.

The second step in refining B_G consists in the elimination of possible synonymies and homonymies. This step is, in its turn, composed by the following sub-steps:

Node normalization The first operation of this sub-step consists in examining the Synonymy Dictionary SD; for each tuple $\langle N_x, N_y, f_{xy} \rangle \in SD$, N_x and N_y are merged in a new node N_{xy} whose name is chosen between names of N_x and N_y. All arcs incoming into or outgoing from N_x and N_y are transferred to N_{xy}.

After this operation, all instances of N_x and N_y are transferred to N_{xy} without changing the associated hit and

---

[2]Actually, SD and HD contain only synonymies and homonymies whose plausibility coefficient is greater than a certain threshold.

[3]Recall that a B-SDR network is a rooted labeled graph.

---

time coefficients[4]. If there exist instance synonymies, these must be removed. In order to eliminate a synonymy between two instances i_x and i_y, a unique instance i_{xy}, representing both of them, is constructed by applying any of the techniques proposed in the literature for carrying out such a task (see, for example, [5]). Hit and time coefficients associated with i_{xy} are obtained by summing the corresponding ones relative to i_x and i_y.

Finally, the Homonymy Dictionary HD is examined for removing homonymies from B_G. In particular, for each tuple $\langle N_x, N_y, f_{xy} \rangle$ belonging to HD, N_x and N_y must be considered distinct in B_G and, consequently, at least one of them must be renamed. However, no change is necessary on instances of N_x and N_y, as well as on the corresponding hit and time coefficients.

Arc normalization Due to the transformations described above, values of semantic distance, semantic relevance, hit and time coefficients associated with arcs incoming to or outgoing from merged nodes could change. In addition, pairs of arcs could exist, sharing the same source and target nodes. For this reason, all arcs relative to a node derived from merging other nodes must be examined.

In case that only the target node of an arc derives from merging two nodes, it is possible to prove, from the definitions of arc coefficients introduced in Section 2, that no update is necessary on arc labels.

Analogously, if only the source node of an arc derives from merging two nodes, no change is necessary on semantic distance, hit and time coefficients. Vice versa, since the number of instances associated with the source node has changed, the value of the semantic relevance coefficient must be computed again; the computation can be carried out by directly applying the definition of this coefficient, as provided in Section 2.

If both the source node N_s and the target node N_t of an arc derive from a merge process, but no other arc exists from N_s to N_t, the reasoning and the consequent conclusions we have seen for the previous case are still valid.

Finally, if both the source node N_s and the target node N_t of an arc, say A_1, derive from a merge process and another arc, say A_2, exists from N_s to N_t, A_1 and A_2 must be merged into a unique arc A_{12}. The hit coefficient h_{12} (resp., time coefficient τ_{12}) of A_{12} is obtained by summing the hit coefficients (resp., time coefficients) h_1 (resp., τ_1) of A_1 and h_2 (resp., τ_2) of A_2. The semantic distance coefficient d_{12} of A_{12} is obtained by computing a weighed mean of the semantic distance coefficients d_1 of A_1 and d_2 of A_2, whose weights are the number of instances associated

---

[4]As previously pointed out, hit and time coefficients of B-SDR networks associated with e-commerce sites are null; we report here rules relative to their integration because the function *Integrate* is activated also for handling customer profiles (see below).

---

with the nodes whose merge originated N_t. The formulas we have provided for computing these three coefficients are justified by considering their definition, as provided in Section 2. Finally, the semantic relevance coefficient r_{12} of A_{12} is obtained directly from its definition, as introduced in Section 2.

4.2 Customer Profile Update

As pointed out in Section 3, whenever the customer accesses an e-commerce site, her/his profile must be updated for registering her/his behaviour on visiting this site. The first task of this activity consists in adding to the customer profile those concepts and instances represented in the e-commerce site and not yet registered. Furthermore, it may happen that some concepts and instances (or, equivalently, their synonyms) stored in the e-commerce site are already present in the customer profile; in this case, it is necessary to increase the corresponding hit and time coefficients for registering the new visit. Finally, in order to maintain the profile at a reasonable size, it is necessary to perform a pruning phase for removing from it those concepts and instances that appear to be no longer interesting for the customer.

In order to carry out the first two activities described above, at the end of Step 4 illustrated in Section 3, when the customer accesses the e-commerce site for navigating through it, a B-SDR network B_R, registering all customer activities on visiting the site, is constructed. After the conclusion of the customer visit, B_R is integrated with the B-SDR network representing the customer profile for registering into it the activities she/he carried out on accessing the site. The integration activity is performed by applying the technique described in Section 4.1.1.

Now, let us show how B_R is constructed. Initially it is empty. For each access a to a concept s:

- If a is the first access of the visit, then the root r and a node s are inserted into B_R, and an arc (r, s) is added. h_{rs} is set to 1 and τ_{rs} is set to the minutes the customer spent in visiting s. Semantic distance and relevance coefficients of the arc (r, s) are set to the corresponding values occurring in the B-SDR network associated with the e-commerce site.

- If a is not the first access of the visit, but s is accessed for the first time, and if the user accesses it coming from another concept s', then the node s is put into B_R and an arc (s', s) is added. $d_{s's}$, $r_{s's}$, $h_{s's}$ and $\tau_{s's}$ are set in a way analogous to that we have seen in the previous case.

- If s has been already accessed in the past and, presently, it is accessed through a concept s'[5], then the

---

[5]It is worth observing that s have been accessed in the past through concepts different from s'.

arc (s', s) is added in B_R, if not already present. $h_{s's}$ is increased of 1 and $\tau_{s's}$ is suitably updated for registering the time the customer spent for visiting s again.

For each access a to an instance t of a concept s

- If t is accessed for the first time, then it is added as an instance of s. The hit coefficient h_{st} is set to 1 and the time coefficient τ_{st} is set to the time the customer spent for visiting t.

- If t has been already accessed in the past, then the hit coefficient h_{st} is increased of 1 and the time coefficient τ_{st} is suitably increased for registering the time the customer spent for visiting t again.

After B_R has been constructed, it is integrated with the customer profile for registering into it the activities performed by her/him on the site.

Now, we consider how concepts and instances no longer interesting for the customer can be pruned from the corresponding profile. The pruning activity takes into account the preference function ρ and the semantic distance coefficient, described in Section 2. Recall that the preference function indicates how much a customer preferred a "target" concept (resp., an instance) w.r.t. the other ones that could be reached from the same "source" concept (resp., w.r.t. the other instances of the same concept).

Let us first examine concept pruning. A concept t can be pruned from the customer profile if it has been not particularly interesting for the customer in the nearest past and appears to be probably not interesting for her/him in the future. A concept t is considered not particularly interesting for the customer in the nearest past if, for all arcs (s, t), the value of $\rho(s, t)$ is small (i.e., under a certain threshold). A concept t appears to be probably not interesting for the customer in the future if the semantic distance of t w.r.t. all the other (sufficiently interesting) concepts is greater than a certain threshold. As far as instance pruning is concerned, given an instance t, we can consider only the past interest of the customer for t; as a consequence, only the function ρ must be taken into account; in particular, ρ is exploited in a way analogous to that we have previously seen for the concepts.

5 Deriving sub-net similarities

As pointed out in Section 3, sub-net similarities are derived for determining those e-commerce site offers which better satisfy customer interests. Recall that such similarities are computed at the customer site and are relative to (i) the SDR network extracted from the B-SDR network associated with the e-commerce site and representing, from a conceptual point of view, products and services which it offers, and, (ii) the SDR network derived from the B-SDR network representing the customer profile and, therefore, denoting, from a conceptual point of view, her/his interests.

The first step of sub-net similarity derivation consists in selecting the most promising pairs of sub-nets. Indeed, given an SDR-Network, the number of possible sub-nets that can be identified in it is exponential in the number of its nodes. To avoid the burden of analyzing such a huge number of sub-nets, it is necessary to define a technique for singling out only the *most promising* ones. Such a technique receives two SDR networks Net_1 and Net_2 and a Dictionary SD of Synonymies between nodes of Net_1 and Net_2. As previously pointed out, SD can be obtained by applying the approach presented in [16]. The technique carries out its task according to the following rules:

- For each tuple $\langle N_i, N_j, f_{ij} \rangle$ belonging to SD, it takes N_i and N_j as the "seeds" for the construction of a set of promising pairs of sub-nets.

- In order to select *the possible promising pairs of sub-nets*, associated with the seed nodes N_i and N_j, it takes into account only rooted sub-nets having N_i and N_j as roots. For determining the most promising ones among them, it takes into consideration maximum weight matchings computed on some bipartite graphs, obtained from the target nodes of the arcs composing the neighborhoods of N_i and N_j. In more detail, for each k such that both $nbh(N_i, k)$ and $nbh(N_j, k)$ are not empty, a promising pair of sub-nets $[SS_{i_k}, SS_{j_k}]$ is constructed by determining the set of promising pairs of arcs $[A_{i_k}, A_{j_k}]$, relative to N_i, N_j and k. Given two seed nodes N_i and N_j and an integer k, a pair of nodes $[A_{i_k}, A_{j_k}]$ is considered promising if: *(i)* A_{i_k} belongs to $nbh(N_i, l)$ and A_{j_k} belongs to $nbh(N_j, l)$, for some l in the integer interval $[0, k]$; *(ii)* the target nodes T_{i_k} of A_{i_k} and T_{j_k} of A_{j_k} are connected by an edge in the maximum weight matching computed on a suitable bipartite graph constructed from the target nodes of the arcs composing $nbh(N_i, l)$ and $nbh(N_j, l)$; *(iii)* the tuple $\langle T_{i_k}, T_{j_k}, f_{ij} \rangle$ belongs to SD.

The rationale underlying this technique is that of constructing promising pairs of sub-nets such that each pair is composed by the maximum possible number of pairs of concepts whose synonymy has been already stated. In this way, it is probable that the overall similarity degree, resulting for each promising pair of sub-nets, will be high.

After all promising pairs of sub-nets have been determined, it is necessary to derive similar sub-nets. The proposed technique for carrying out such a task consists of two steps. The first one computes the similarity degree relative to each promising pairs of sub-nets. The latter one constructs a Sub-net Similarity Dictionary SSD by selecting only those pairs of sub-nets whose similarity degree is greater than a certain, dynamically computed, threshold.

In order to derive the similarity degree associated with a promising pairs of sub-nets SS_i and SS_j, a function μ, computing the objective function associated with the maximum weight matching on a suitable bipartite graph, constructed from the nodes of SS_i and SS_j, is activated. The inputs of μ are: *(i)* two sets of nodes $P = \{p_1, \ldots, p_r\}$ and $Q = \{q_1, \ldots, q_s\}$, *(ii)* a set T of triplets of the form $\langle p_l, q_m, f_{lm} \rangle$, where, for each $p_l \in P$ and $q_m \in Q$, $0 \le f_{lm} \le 1$. The output of μ is a value in the real interval $[0, 1]$. The function behaves as follows: first it constructs the bipartite weighed graph $BG = (P \cup Q, E)$, where E is the set of weighed edges $\{(p_l, q_m, f_{lm}) \mid f_{lm} > 0\}$. After this, it determines the maximum weight matching for BG as the set $E' \subseteq E$ of edges such that, for each node $x \in P \cup Q$, there exists at most one edge of E' incident onto x and $\phi'(E') = \sum_{(p_l, q_m, f_{lm}) \in E'} f_{lm}$ is maximum. Finally, it computes the objective function associated with the matching as $\left(1 - \frac{|P| + |Q| - 2|E'|}{|P| + |Q|}\right) \frac{\phi'(E')}{|E'|}$.

After that the similarity degree associated with each pair of promising sub-nets has been determined, the Sub-net Similarity Dictionary SSD is constructed by selecting only those pairs of sub-nets whose similarity degree is greater than the, dynamically computed, threshold

$$th_{Sim} = min\left(\frac{f_{Sim}^{Max} + f_{Sim}^{Min}}{2}, th_M^{Sim}\right)$$

where f_{Sim}^{Max} (resp., f_{Sim}^{Min}) is the maximum (resp., the minimum) coefficient associated with derived sub-net similarities and th_M^{Sim} is a limit threshold value. The formula for th_{Sim} is justified by considering that the technique for selecting the set of promising pairs of sub-nets is defined in such a way that similarities between selected pairs will be probably high; for this reason it may happen that almost all sub-net pairs are to be considered interesting. If this really happens, all interesting pairs must be included in the Dictionary; the particular structure of the formula makes it possible.

6 Conclusions

In this paper we have proposed a multi-agent model for handling the activities in an e-commerce community. In particular, our model specifies that agents are associated with each e-commerce site, as well as with each customer of the community. We have seen that all these agents exploit a particular conceptual model, called B-SDR network, for representing and handling the associated ontology. After this, we have described into detail the behaviour of the proposed model. In particular, we have illustrated how the specific features of the B-SDR network can be exploited for supporting a customer to detect, whenever she/he accesses an e-commerce site, those offers appearing to be the closest to the her/his interests.

We have already implemented some parts of this approach, namely the construction of a B-SDR network from a given information source (in particular, we have implemented translation rules from E/R, OEM and XML to B-SDR network), the extraction of synonymies, homonymies, sub-sources similarities as well as the integration task. Presently we are working for implementing the remaining parts of the approach in order to construct a complete prototype.

As for future work, first we plan to test the thus obtained prototype on real cases. After this, we plan to study the possibility to enrich the proposed multi-agent model with other features capable to improve its effectiveness and completeness in supporting the various activities related to e-commerce. As an example, it may be interesting to cluster involved customers on the basis of their profiles, as well as involved e-commerce sites on the basis of their contents. As a further example of profitable features which the model could be enriched with, we consider extremely promising the derivation of association rules representing and predicting the customer behaviour on accessing one or more e-commerce sites.

ACKNOWLEDGMENTS. The Authors thank Francesco Buccafurri and Luigi Palopoli for many inspiring discussions about the arguments of the paper. This work has been partially funded by Italian "Ministero dell'Istruzione, dell'Università e della Ricerca" in the context of the project "D2I - Integrazione, Warehousing e Mining di sorgenti eterogenee".

References

[1] L. Ardissono, A. Goy, G. Petrone, M. Segnan, L. Console, L. Lesmo, C. Simone, and P. Torasso. Agent technologies for the development of adaptive web stores. *Agent Mediated Electronic Commerce, The European AgentLink Perspective*, pages 194–213, 2001.

[2] S. Bergamaschi, S. Castano, M. Vincini, and D. Beneventano. Semantic integration and query of heterogeneous information sources. *Data & Knowledge Engineering*, 36(3):215–249, 2001.

[3] F. Buccafurri, D. Rosaci, and D. Ursino. An agent modeling heterogeneous environments and user interactions. Submitted for Publication. Available from the Authors.

[4] A.G. Buchner and M.D. Mulvenna. Discovering internet marketing intelligence through online analytical web usage mining. *SIGMOD Record*, 27(4):54–61, 1998.

[5] A. Calí, D. Calvanese, G. De Giacomo, and M. Lenzerini. Accessing data integration systems through conceptual schemas. In *Proc. of International Conference on Conceptual Modeling (ER'01)*, pages 270–284, Yokohama, Japan, 2001. Lecture Notes in Computer Science. Springer Verlag.

[6] D. Calvanese, G. De Giacomo, M. Lenzerini, D. Nardi, and R. Rosati. Description logic framework for information integration. In *Proc. of International Conference on Principles of Knowledge Representation and Reasoning (KR'98)*, pages 2–13, Trento, Italy, 1998. Morgan Kaufman.

[7] Q. Chen, U. Dayal, M. Hsu, and M.L. Griss. Dynamic-agents, workflow and xml for e-commerce automation. In *Proc. of International Conference on Electronic Commerce and Web Technologies (EC-Web'01)*, pages 314–323, London, UK, 2001. Lecture Notes in Computer Science, Springer Verlag.

[8] L. Foner and I.B. Crabtree. Multi-agent matchmaking. *Software Agents and Soft Computing: Towards Enhancing Machine Intelligence, Concepts and Applications*, pages 100–115, 1997.

[9] Z. Galil. Efficient algorithms for finding maximum matching in graphs. *ACM Computing Surveys*, 18:23–38, 1986.

[10] P.H. Hanh, H. Nguyen, and N. Van Hop. Envrironment and means for cooperation and interaction in e-commerce agent-based systems. In *Proc. of International Conference on Internet Computing 2000 (IC'00)*, pages 253–260, Las Vegas, Nevada, USA, 2000. CSREA Press.

[11] J. Liu and Y. Ye. Introduction to e-commerce agents: Marketplace solutions, security issues,and supply and demand. *E-Commerce Agents: Marketplace Solutions, Security Issues,and Supply and Demand*, pages 1–6, 2001.

[12] J. Madhavan, P.A. Bernstein, and E. Rahm. Generic schema matching with cupid. In *Proc. of International Conference on Very Large Data Bases (VLDB 2001)*, pages 49–58, Roma, Italy, 2001. Morgan Kaufmann.

[13] A. Moukas. User modeling in a multi agent evolving system. In *Proceedings of the 6th International Conference on User Modeling*, Chia Laguna, Italy, 1997.

[14] E. Oliveira and A.P. Rocha. Agents advanced features for negotiation in electronic commerce and virtual organizations formation processes. *Agent Mediated Electronic Commerce, The European AgentLink Perspective*, pages 78–97, 2001.

[15] L. Palopoli, D. Rosaci, G. Terracina, and D. Ursino. Un modello concettuale per rappresentare e derivare la semantica associata a sorgenti informative strutturate e semi-strutturate. In *Atti del Congresso sui Sistemi Evoluti per Basi di Dati (SEBD 2001)*, pages 131–145, Venezia, Italy, 2001. In Italian.

[16] L. Palopoli, G. Terracina, and D. Ursino. A graph-based approach for extracting terminological properties of elements of XML documents. In *Proc. of International Conference on Data Engineering (ICDE 2001)*, pages 330–340, Heidelberg, Germany, 2001. IEEE Computer Society.

[17] J.S. Park and R.S. Sandhu. Secure cookies on the web. *IEEE Internet Computing*, 4(4):36–44, 2000.

[18] B.M. Sarwar, G. Karypis, J.A. Konstan, and J. Riedl. Analysis of recommendation algorithms for e-commerce. In *ACM Conference on Electronic Commerce 2000 (EC-00)*, pages 158–167, Minneapolis, USA, 2000. ACM Press.

[19] J. Schafer, J. Konstan, and J. Riedl. E-commerce recommendation applications. *Data Mining and Knowledge Discovery*, 5(1/2):115–153, 2001.

[20] S. Soltysiak and B. Crabtree. Knowing me, knowing you: Practical issues in the personalization of agent technology. In *Proc. of International Conference on the Practical Application of Intelligent Agents and Multi-Agent Technology (PAAM'98)*, pages 253–260, London, UK, 1998.

[21] G. Terracina and D. Ursino. Deriving synonymies and homonymies of object classes in semi-structured information sources. In *Proc. of International Conference on Management of Data (COMAD 2000)*, pages 21–32, Pune, India, 2000. McGraw Hill.

[22] O. Zaiane, M. Xin, and J. Han. Discovering web access patterns and trends by applying olap and data mining technology on web logs. In *IEEE Advances in Digital Libreries Conference (ADL'98)*, pages 19–29, Santa Barbara, California, USA, 1998. IEEE Computer Society Press.

Paper Session VI

(DW/DM)

Clustering Spatial Data in the Presence of Obstacles: a Density-Based Approach

Osmar R. Zaïane
University of Alberta
Database Laboratory
Edmonton, Canada
zaiane@cs.ualberta.ca

Chi-Hoon Lee
University of Alberta
Database Laboratory
Edmonton, Canada
chihoon@cs.ualberta.ca

Abstract

Clustering spatial data is a well-known problem that has been extensively studied. Grouping similar data in large 2-dimensional spaces to find hidden patterns or meaningful sub-groups has many applications such as satellite imagery, geographic information systems, medical image analysis, marketing, computer visions, etc. Although many methods have been proposed in the literature, very few have considered physical obstacles that may have significant consequences on the effectiveness of the clustering. Taking into account these constraints during the clustering process is costly and the modeling of the constraints is paramount for good performance. In this paper, we investigate the problem of clustering in the presence of constraints such as physical obstacles and introduce a new approach to model these constraints using polygons. We also propose a strategy to prune the search space and reduce the number of polygons to test during clustering. We devise a density-based clustering algorithm, DBCluC, which takes advantage of our constraint modeling to efficiently cluster data objects while considering all physical constraints. The algorithm can detect clusters of arbitrary shape and is insensitive to noise, the input order, and the difficulty of constraints. Its average running complexity is O(NlogN) where N is the number of data points.

1. Introduction

Unsupervised classification of objects into groups such that the similarity of objects in a group is maximized while the similarity between objects of different groups is minimized, is an interesting problem that has attracted the attention of statisticians for many years because of the numerous potential applications. Recently, we are witnessing a resurgence of interest in new clustering techniques in the data mining community, and many effective and efficient methods have been proposed in the machine learning and data mining literature. The rapid increase in digitized spatial data availability has prompted considerable research in what is known as spatial data mining [19]. Clustering analysis for data in a 2-dimensional space is considered spatial data mining and has applications in geographic information systems, pattern recognition, medical imaging, marketing analysis, weather forecasting, etc. Clustering in spatial data has been an active research area and most of the research has focused on effectiveness and scalability. As reported in surveys on data clustering [11, 14] clustering methods can be classified into Partitioning approaches [17, 21, 5, 22, 31], Hierarchical methods [26, 32, 10, 15], Density based algorithms [8, 2, 13], Probabilistic techniques [6], Graph theoretic [31], Fuzzy methods [4, 23], Grid-based algorithms [30, 25, 1], and Model based approaches [24, 18]. As pointed out earlier, these techniques have focused on the performance in terms of effectiveness and efficiency for large databases. However, almost none of them have taken into account constraints that may be present in the data or constraints on the clustering. These constraints have significant influence on the results of the clustering process of large spatial data. In medical imaging, for example, while 2 points could be close together according to a distance measure they should be restrained from being clustered together due to physical or biological constraints. In a GIS application studying the movement of pedestrians to identify optimal bank machine placements, for example, the presence of a highway hinders the movement of pedestrians and should be considered as an obstacle. To the best of our knowledge, only two clustering algorithms for clustering spatial data in the presence of constraints have been proposed very recently: COD-CLARANS [28] based on a partitioning approach, and AUTOCLUST+ [9] based on a graph partitioning approach. [29] introduces the taxonomy of constraints for clustering: Constraints on individual objects; Obstacle objects as constraints; Clustering parameters as constraints; and Constraints imposed on each individual cluster. Its primary discussion has been focused on SQL aggregate and existential constraints. Those constraints have

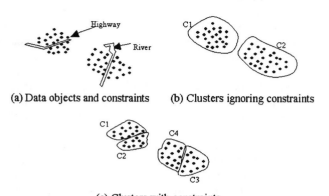

(a) Data objects and constraints   (b) Clusters ignoring constraints

(c) Clusters with constraints

Figure 1. Clustering data objects with constraints

considerable effect on clustering a database, taking into account the capacity of involved resource. COD-CLARANS [28] and AUTOCLUST+[9] propose algorithms to solve the problem of clustering in the presence of physical obstacles to cross such as rivers, mountain ranges, or highways, etc. [28] defines obstacles by building visibility graphs to find the shortest distance among data objects in the presence of obstacles. The graph has edges between data points that are visible to each other and the edge is eliminated if an obstacle obstructs the "visibility". The visibility graph is expensive to build and is considered as pre-processed in [28], thus making the approach look performing and scaling well since the pre-processing is taken out of the performance evaluation. [9] builds a Delaunay structure to cluster data points considering obstacles, a more scalable and efficient data structure. However, it is expensive to construct and is not flexible to combine a different kind of constraints. As an example, Figure 1 shows clustering data objects in relation to their neighbours as well as the physical constraints. Ignoring the constraints leads to incorrect interpretation of the correlation among data points. Figure 1(b) shows two clusters. The correct grouping (Figure 1(c)) visually generates four clusters, four clusters due to highway and river constraints, and one naturally grouped cluster.

The algorithm we propose in a 2-dimensional planar space, DBCluC (Density-Based Clustering with Constraints, pronounced DB-clu-see), is based on DBSCAN [8] a density-based clustering algorithm that clearly outperforms the effectiveness and efficiency of CLARANS [21], the algorithm used for COD-CLARANS. The performance is better not only in terms of time complexity, but also in terms of clustering performance; detection of natural cluster shapes and noise sensitivity.

In this paper, we also introduce a new idea for modeling constraints using simple polygons. Note that there are two classes of polygons with respect to mathematical context, as illustrated in the geometry lieterature [12, 27]: a simple polygon and a crossing polygon (see Obstacle Modeling). Polygons can represent obstacles of arbitrary shapes, lengths, thickness, etc. Given the potential large number of edges representing all the polygons in the space to cluster, we have reduced the size of the search space by introducing the idea of representing polygons with a minimum number of lines that preserve the connectivity and disconnectivity between points in space.

The remainder of the paper is organized as follows: In Section 2, we briefly introduce the notions of reachability and connectivity needed in the expansion process of DBSCAN [8] since the same reachability idea is adopted in our algorithm, and present the motivating concepts significant to this study. In Section 3, we show how we model the constraints, obstacles, and illustrate how the edges of the polygons are reduced to improve performance. The main clustering algorithm that considers constraints during the clustering is introduced with its complexity analysis in Section 4. Section 5 shows the performance of this algorithm and its clustering results. Finally, Section 6 concludes this study with some discussion of future work.

2. Background Concepts

While COD-CLARANS is based on the partitioning approach of CLARANS, which adopts Euclidean distances and considers only clusters with spherical shapes, we have selected the density-based idea behind DBSCAN that expands the neighbourhood of a point based on a fixed minimum number of points reachable within an area of a given radius. Unlike the partitioning approach, the density-based method we adopted does not require the a priori knowledge of the number of clusters in the data. In the following section, we present the important concepts of DBSCAN and define the important notions that motivate our clustering algorithm.

2.1. DBSCAN

DBSCAN is a clustering algorithm with two parameters, *Eps* and *MinPts*, utilizing the density notion that involves correlation between a data point and its neighbours. In order for data points to be grouped, there must be at least a minimum number of points called MinPts in Eps-neighbourhood, $N_{Eps}(p)$, from a data point p, given a radius *Eps*. Its intuition has focused on detecting natural clusters among data objects, while discriminating noises (outliers) from clusters. In DBSCAN, the following definitions are denoted.

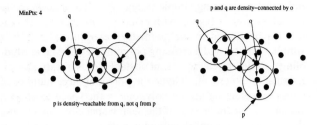

MinPts: 4

p is density-reachable from q, not q from p

p and q are density-connected by o

Figure 2. Density-reachable and Density-connected

Definition 1. (Directly density-reachable) A point *p* is directly density-reachable from a point q with respect to *Eps*, *MinPts* if

(1) p $\in$ N$_{Eps}$ (q)

(2) |N$_{Eps}$ (p)| $\geq$ MinPts, where |N$_{Eps}$ (p)| denotes the number of points in the circle of radius Eps and centre p.

Definition 1 is important to understand the difference between core points and border points, since border points have the less number of Eps-neighbourhood than core points do.

Definition 2. (Density-reachable) A point p is density-rea- chable from a point q with respect to Eps and MinPts, if there is a chain of points p_1, .., p_n, p_1 = q, , p_n = p such that p_{i+1} is directly density-reachable from p_i.

Definition 3. (Density-connected) A point p is density-connected to a point q with respect to Eps and MinPts, if there is a point o such that both, p and q are density-reachable from o with respect to Eps and MinPts.

Definition 4. (Cluster) Let D be a database of points. A cluster C with respect to Eps and MinPts is a non-empty subset of D satisfying the following conditions:

(1) Maximality: $\forall$ p, q if p $\in$ C and q is density-reachable from p with respect to Eps and MinPts, then q $\in$ C.

(2) Connectivity: $\forall$ p, q $\in$ C, p is density-connected to q with respect to Eps and MinPts.

Definition 5. (Noise) Let p $\in$ a database D. p is noise, if p $\notin$ C$_i$, where C$_i$ is ith cluster, 0 $\leq$ i $\leq$ k, k is the number of clusters in D.

Figure 2 illustrates the above definitions. The detailed figures and discussion are found in [8].

Once the two parameters *Eps* and *MinPts* are defined, DBSCAN starts to group data points from an arbitrary

point. If a cluster cannot be expanded with respect to the density reachable and density-connected definitions, it starts grouping data points for another cluster. This procedure is iterated until there is no data point to be expanded and all data points in the dataset clustered or labelled as a noise. One major issue with DBSCAN, as presented in [8], is the problem of high dimensionality of data objects when looking for range queries to quickly identify points in the neighbourhood of another point. In [8] the authors indexed data objects using the R*tree [3], but this structure has a dimensionality limitation of 16 dimensions with respect to efficiency, as reported in [7]. While we are only dealing with 2 dimensions for spatial data, we use SR-Tree structures [16] instead in our implementation of DBCluC, which allows us to do efficient range queries for neighbourhood data points.

2.2. Motivating Concepts

As briefly mentioned in the introduction, the existence of constraints may not only affect the efficiency but also the accuracy of the clustering. This leads us to investigate means to overcome these two problems while considering constraints. In the following, we characterize these physical constraints by introducing some definitions. We assume that obstacles are given in the form of polygons with rigid edges.

Definition 6. (Obstacle) An obstacle is a polygon denoted by P(V, E) where V is a set of k points from an obstacle: V = {v_1, v_2, v_3,..., v_k} and E is a set of k line segments: E = { e_1, e_2, e_3, ..., e_k} where e_i is a line segment joining v_i and v_{i+1} ,1$\leq$ i$\leq$ k, i+1=1 if i+1>k. There are two classes of obstacles: *convex* and *concave*. The distinction is important as we shall see later.

There are two classes of obstacles: *convex* and *concave*. The distinction is important as we shall see later.

Definition 7. (Visibility) Visibility is a relation between two data points, if the line segment drawn from one point to the other is not intersected with a polygon P (V, E) representing a given obstacle. Given a set D of n data points D ={d_1, d_2, d_3, ..., d_n}, a line segment *l* joining d_i and d_j where d_i, d_j $\in$ D, i$\neq$j, i and j $\in$ [1..n], and a line segment e_k $\in$ E, If $\nexists$ a point p that is an intersection point between two line segments *l* and e_k , then d_i is visible to d_j.

Definition 8. (Visible Space) Given a set D of n data points D={d_1, d_2, d_3, ..., d_n}, A visible space is a set S of k points S={s_1, s_2, s_3, ..., s_k} such that $\forall$ s_i,s_j $\in$ S, s_i and s_j are visible to each other, while s_k is not visible to s'$_k$ in S' , where S' is a visible space such that S' $\cap$ S = $\emptyset$, S' and S $\subseteq$ D, i$\neq$j, and i and j $\in$ [1..n].

216

Before defining the problem of clustering data points in the presence of obstacles, we need to redefine a cluster (Definition 4) that conforms to Definition 7.

Definition 9. (Cluster) Given a set D of n data points D=$\{d_1, d_2, d_3, \ldots, d_n\}$, a cluster is a set C of c points C=$\{c_1, c_2, c_3, \ldots, c_c\}$, satisfying the following conditions, where $C \subseteq D$, $i \neq j$, and i and $j \in [1..n]$. Let D be a database of points. A cluster C with respect to Eps and MinPts is a non-empty subset of D satisfying the following conditions:

(1) Maximality: $\forall d_i, d_j \in D$, if $d_i \in C$ and d_j is density-reachable from d_i with respect to Eps and MinPts, then $d_j \in C$.

(2) Connectivity. $\forall c_i, c_j \in C$, c_i is density-connected to c_j with respect to Eps and MinPts.

(3) $\forall c_i, c_j \in C$, c_i and c_j are visible to each other.

3. Modeling Constraints

We have defined the problem of clustering with constraints in the previous section. Considering the efficiency of the process of clustering, it is essential to model the constraints efficiently to limit the impact of the constraints on the cost-effectiveness of the clustering algorithm. As mentioned in Section 1, we have opted to model the physical constraints with polygons. However, with a large number of obstacles, we would have a large number of edges to test for the division of visibility spaces (Definition 8). We present herein a scheme to model polygons that minimizes the number of edges to take into consideration.

3.1. Obstacle Modeling

Many research areas such as spatial data mining, computational geometry, computer graphics, robot navigations, etc, have considered obstacles as polygons. The performance of the algorithms used is dependent on the size of inputs (i.e. the number of polygon edges). For instance, for finding a shortest path between a starting point and a destination in the presence of obstructions, it is required to evaluate obstacles to minimize a tour distance. Understanding connectivity among given data points is also necessary to evaluate obstacles. [28] and [9] discuss the clustering problem in the presence of obstacles, but [9] does not explicitly explain how to model obstacles but simply uses a Delaunay graph to model the whole data space. Even though [28] models obstacles using a visibility graph, the authors did not present how the types of obstacles are specified, since the classification of an obstacle type improve the searchin cost in [28]. In addition, the visibility graph is assumed to be given and never considered in the complexity analysis or execution time.

While we model obstacles with polygons, a polygon is represented with a minimum set of line segments, called obstruction lines, such that the definition of visibility (Definition 7) is not compromised. This minimum set of lines is smaller than the number of edges in the polygon. This in turn reduces the input size and enhances the searching task. The obstruction lines in a polygon depend upon the type of polygon: convex or concave. Note that an obstacle creates a certain number of visible spaces along with the number of convex points. Before we discuss the idea to convert a given polygon into a smaller number of line segments (obstruction lines), we need to test if a given polygon is convex or concave. If any point of the polygon is categorized as concave, the polygon is said to be concave. It is convex otherwise. The convexity test is fundamental in composing the obstruction lines. The problem then consists in determining whether polygon points are either concave or convex. The convex point test and the multifaceted process to determine the obstruction lines, representing a given polygon, is given in details in [20]. For the sake of brevity and lack of space, we only present the essential idea herein.

3.1.1. The Convexity test: Turning Directional Approach

The "Turning Directional" approach has been introduced by [27]. The intution of the Turning directioanl approach is to evaluate the convexity of polygons via the definition of a polygon that is mathematically defined. [27] classifies a polygon as either a simple polygon or a crossing polygon. A simple polygon is a polygon such that every edge in the polygon is not intersected with other edges that exist in the polygon. A crossing polygon is a polygon such that there is an edge that is intersected with other edges that exist in the polygon. Therefore, crossing polygons are not determined as convex. Note that this paper considers a simple polygon and a crossing polygon, as the former is a dominant object in spatial applications and the latter is simply dealt with set of simple polygon.

Now we claim that a polygon is a convex polygon, if and only if all points from the polygon make a same directional turn. The claim can be easily proved . Suppose a polygon P does not follow the claim. It then is obvious that P is not a convex. As desrcribed in Figure 3 (a), points b and c are concave verteces that make P a concave. Let P be a convex polygon. Then all possible line segment that join two non-consecutive points from P should be interior to P. Hence the vertex f must be pulled out at least up to the line l in order for P to be a convex. If the vertex f lies on the line l, then a convex is composed erasing one vertex. Note that a different shape of a polygon is drawn, if f lies over the line l.

In order to test a turning direction for 3 consecutive verteces, the sign of the triangle area of 3 points is exam-

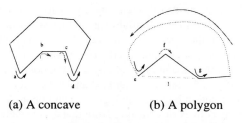

(a) A concave   (b) A polygon

Figure 3. Turning examples in polygons

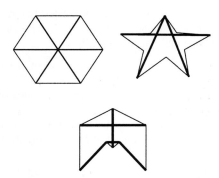

Figure 4. Simple polygons and generated obstruction lines

ined via a determinant. As a result, the sign of the determninant evaluates the turning direction either a clockwise or a counterclockwise. Note that we assume all points in a polygon are enumerated in an order either clockwise or a counterclockwise. Hence, we can easily identify a type of a polygon as well as a type of each vertex from the polygon in a linear time $O(n)$, where n is the number of points in a polygon.

3.1.2. Polygon Reduction

In order to generate obstruction lines for a given polygon, we first need to identify the type of the polygon. convex or concave. Notice that the number of obstruction lines depends on a polygon type. The convex point test on a point from a given polygon is based on testing whether the turning direction of all points is in a same way. Note that the Convex Hull algorithm in the graph theory literature is not applicable in this context. For instance, the polygon on the bottom of Figure 4 could be identified as a concave, whereas the Convex Hull algorithms can not recognize a type of a point. It is critical for Polygon Reduction algorithm to label a type of a point from a polygon. Once we categorize a polygon into a convex or a concave, we find the obstruction lines to replace the initial line segments from the polygon as we make sure the visibility spaces are not divided or merged. It is clear for a convex polygon to have the same number of visible spaces (Definition 8) as the number of its convex points since each line segment from the convex point blocks visibility of its neighbour visible spaces. In contrast, a concave point does not create two visible spaces, but does a visible space that is created by its nearest convex point. Accordingly, a convex point creates two adjacent visible spaces. We observe the fact that two adjacent line segments sharing a convex vertex in a polygon are interchangeable with two line segments such that one of which obstructs visibility in a dimension between two neighbour visible spaces that are created by the convex vertex and the other impedes visibility between two neighbour visible spaces and the rest of visible spaces created by the polygon. As a consequence, the initial polygon is to be represented as a lose-less set of primitive edges with respect to visibility. Now, it is sufficient to discover a set of obstruction lines

that impedes visible spaces for every convex vertex from a polygon minimizing the number of obstruction lines. It is obvious that we reduce n lines for a convex to $\lceil \frac{n}{2} \rceil$ obstruction lines. Due to a bi-partition method that divides a set of convex points into two sets by an enumeration order, it is straightforward to compose a set of obstruction lines by joining two points from each partition. In addition, the bi-partition method achieves the lose-less reduction of a polygon.

It is not, however, trivial for a concave due to its characteristic, whereas an obstruction edge is easily drawn between two convex vertex in a convex. It is required for a concave to check a possible obstruction line drawn by the bi-paritition method is intersected with a line segment from the concave polygon and is exterior to the polygon, which is a *"non-admissible"* obstruction line. If a possible obstruction line is non-admissible to a given concave polygon, then it is to be replaced with a set of obstruction lines that might be line segments from the concave or are interior to and not intersected with the concave polygon, which is a set of *"admissible"* obstruction lines. In order to construct a set of obstruction edges from a concave, as a possible obstruction edge candidate is not admissible, we employ a modified single-source shortest path algorithm [20] converting concave $P(V, E)$ into a weighted graph whose edges are all possible obstruction lines for each point in the concave and whose weight is the distance between a source and a destination. The distance on a path $\overline{vw}$ between two points v and w is not *Euclidean*, but the number of points on the path $\overline{vw}$. Note the source and the destination vertex are one of two end points from possible obstruction edge candidates. The detailed study is found in [20]. These measures should ensure that the generated number of obstruction lines is less than the original number of line segments from a polygon.

4. Algorithm

Once we have modeled obstacles using the polygon reduction algorithm, DBCluC starts the clustering procedure from an arbitrary data point. Hence it is not sensitive to an order of the data input. The clustering procedure in DB-CluC is quite similar to DBSCAN [8]. As illustrated in [8], the distance between clusters C_1 and C_2 is defined as a minimum distance between data objects in C_1 and C_2, respectively. Normally defined clusters that are not satisfied with Definition 9 or whose distance between clusters is larger than *Eps* are isolated.

A database is a set of data points to be clustered in Algorithm 1. Line 1 initiates the clustering procedure. In the course of clustering, Line 4 assigns a new cluster id for the next expandable cluster.

The ExpandCluster in Algorithm 2 may seem similar to the function in the DBSCAN. However, the distinction is that obstacles are considered in RetrieveNeighbours (Point, Eps, Obstacles) illustrated by Algorithm 3. Given a query point, neighbours of the query point are retrieved using SR-tree. In DBCluC, we have adopted the range neighbour query approach instead of the nearest neighbour query approach from SR-tree, since it is extremely difficult for the latter to expand a set of clusters if a density of data objects is high. Its average run time of a neighbour query is O(logN) where N is the number of data objects. Notice that the range search in SR-tree is very expensive, especially when the density is very high with a large database.

Once retrieving neighbours of a query point, it is trivial to evaluate visibilities between a query point and its neighbours. The visibility between two data objects in the presence of obstacles is computed using a line segment whose endpoints are the two data objects in question. If any line segment representing an obstacle is intersected with this line, then the two data points are not grouped together, since they are not visible to each other according to Definition 7. Those accepted neighbours defined as the SEED that are retrieved by RetrieveNeighbours of Algorithm 2 continue to expand a cluster from elements of the SEED, if the number of elements in the SEED is not less than MinPts. A data object is labeled by a proper cluster id, if retrieved neighbours are satisfied with the parameter *MinPts* discriminating outliers. Note that line 15 in Algorithm 2 does exclude a noise from being an element of the SEED in order to enhance query efficiency.

The "RESULT" in Algorithm 3 is a set of data objects that are neighbours of a given query objects. The elements in the RESULT is collected and the obstacles are evaluated by Alogorithm 3. The RESULT elements are constructed by removing data objects that are not visible each other because of the blockage of obstacles. This is performed by line 3 in Algorihtm 3. Notice that line 1 in Algorihtm 3

Input	: Database and Obstalces
Output	: A set of clusters

```
1  // Start clustering;
2  for Point ∈ Database do
3      if ExpandCluster(Database,Point,ClusterId,Eps,MinPts,Obstacles)
       then
4          │  ClusterId = nextId(ClusterId);
       endif
   endfor
```

Algorithm 1: DBCluC

retrieves neighbours of a given query point using SR tree [16].

4.1. Complexity

As discussed before, the polygon reduction algorithm models obstacles by classifying an obstacle into convex or concave. Let n be the number of points of a polygon p, and n_{cc} and n_{cv} are the number of concave points and the number of convex points respectively with $n = n_{cc} + n_{cv}$. The convexity test for p requires $O(n)$. The polygon reduction algorithm requires a weighted graph [20] to replace a non-adimissible obstruction line segment with a set of admissible line segments. The complexity in the replacement is in worst case $O(n\log n)$ with an indexing scheme to search line segments. It in turn creates a set with E number of edges including a set of line segments that lies in P. Notice that the number of E is less than $\alpha * n$, where $\alpha \ll n$. The polygon reduction algorithm for P requires $O(n\log n + n_{cv} I E)$ in the worst case where I is the number of non-admissible line segments to be replaced, while the lower bound is $\Omega(n)$. Hence, the upper bound of the polygon reduction algorithm is depicted by $O(n_{cv} I n)$. When we evaluate a set of polygons and n_{cc} and I that are on average far smaller than n, the complexity of the polygon reduction is on average in the order of $O(n)$. Polygon Reduction Algorithm is a pre-processing phase that precedes the clustering. The complexity of the clustering algorithm alone, is in the order of $O(N \cdot \log N \cdot L)$, where L is the number of obstruction lines generated by the polygon reduction algorithm, and N is the number of points in the database. The complexity can, however, be reduced to $O(N \cdot \log N)$, if we adopt an indexing method for obstacles. Currently, to check the visibility between two data points, all obstruction lines are tested. We could reduce the number of obstruction lines to be checked by evaluating only lines that traverse the point neighbourhood (see conclusions and future work).

```
Input    : Database, a data point Point, ClusterId,
           Eps, MinPts, and Obstacles
Output   : True or False
1  SEED = RetrieveNeighbours(Point, Eps, Obstacles);
2  if size of seed is less than MinPts then
3  |    Classify Point as NOISE;
4  |    Return False;
   endif
5  change clustered of all elements in SEED into Clus-
   terId;
6  delete Point from SEED;
7  while SEED.SIZE < 0 do
8  |    CurrentPoint = SEED.first();
9  |    RESULT = RetrieveNeighbours(CurrentPoint,
   |    Eps, Obstacles);
10 |    if RESULT.SIZE ≥ MinPts then
11 |    |    for element ∈ RESULT do
12 |    |    |    if element is UNCLASSFIED then
13 |    |    |    |    put it into SEED;
14 |    |    |    |    set its cluster id to ClusterId;
   |    |    |    endif
15 |    |    |    if element is NOISE then
16 |    |    |    |    set its cluster id to ClusterId;
   |    |    |    endif
   |    |    endfor
   |    endif
17 |    delete CurrentPoint from SEED;
   endw
18 Return True;
```

Algorithm 2: ExpandCluster

```
Input    : a data object Point, Eps, and Obstalces
Output   : A set of data points
1  RESULT = getNeighbour(Point, Eps);
2  for element RESULT do
3  |    if CheckVisibility_with(element, Obstacles) then
4  |    |    RESULT.delete(element);
   |    endif
   endfor
5  Return RESULT;
```

Algorithm 3: RetrieveNeighbours(Point, Eps, Obstacles)

5. Performance

In this section we evaluate the performance of the algorithm in terms of effectiveness and scalability. Although COD-CLARANS and AUTOCLUST+ discuss the clustering problem in the presence of obstacles, it is hard to compare quantitatively the performance with their respective approaches due to the difference in the datasets used. To realistically compare the algorithms, we ought to use the exact datasets with the same constraints. However, we did not have access to these datasets, even if they are synthetic datasets, we can not regenerated them . Yet it is known that density- based clustering algorithms such as DBSCAN [8] outperforms partitioning algorithms such as CLARANS [28] in terms of efficiency and effectivenss. It can be concluded that DBCluC would outperform COD-CLARANS with respect to the scalability and clustering quality. We have evaluated DBCluC by generating datasets with complex cluster shapes and by varying the size of data as well as the number and complexity of the physical constraints.

For the purpose of the experiments, we have generated synthetic datasets. We report three of them herein Dataset1, Dataset2, and Dataset3. Obstacles such as rivers, lakes, and highways are also simulated in these datasets. Dataset1 containing 434 data points with four obstacles is for illustration purposes. Figure 5 shows the 16 polygon line segments reduced to 8 obstruction lines. Since Dataset1 is sparse, it is primarily grouped into one cluster. Adding obstacles creates four distinct clusters (Figure 5(c)). Figures 6 and 7 illustrate the effectiveness of DBCluC in the presence of obstacles. For the convenience of comparison of clustering results, Figure 6 and 7 illustrate sequentially data points, and obstacles, before clustering (a); clustering results in the absence of constraints (b); clusters in the presence of obstacles (c). The red lines from obstacles in all datasets are the obstruction lines to replace initial polygons that are drawn in blue. Dataset2 has about 1063 data points with 4 obstacles. There are visually 6 clusters ignoring obstacles, as shown in Figure6 (b). Dataset2 represents the primary intuition of the problem we have investigated in this paper. The correct clustering shows 8 groups of data points. Dataset3 has 11775 data points with 6 obstacles that consist of 29 line segments. The initial 29 line segments from simulated obstacles are replaced with 15 obstruction lines.

We also conducted experiments varying the size of the dataset and the number of obstacles to demonstrate scalability of DBCluC. Figure 8 represents the execution time in seconds for eight datasets varying in size from 25K to 200K with an increment of 25K data points. The figure shows a good scalability. The execution time is almost linear to the number of data objects. Figure 9 presents the execution time in seconds for clustering 40K data objects but by varying the number of obstacles. The numbers in the X-axis represent

220

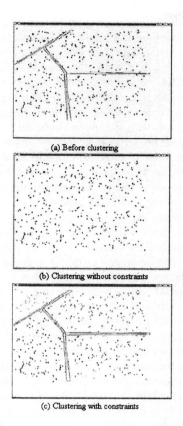

(a) Before clustering

(b) Clustering without constraints

(c) Clustering with constraints

Figure 5. Clustering dataset Dataset1

the total number of polygon edges and the respective obstruction lines. Notice that our polygon reduction algorithm manages to reduce the number of lines by approximately half each time. The differential in the increase of the polygon edges is not constant. However, in the proportion of the increase in the polygons, the execution time is almost linear. Thus DBCluC is scalable for large databases with complicated obstacles in terms of size of the database and in terms of the number of constraints.

6. Conclusions

In this paper we have addressed the problem of clustering spatial data in the presence of physical constraints. The constraints we considered are not only obstacles such as rivers, highways, mountain ranges, etc. We have proposed a model for these constraints using polygons and have devised a method for reducing the edges of polygons representing obstacles by identifying a minimum set of line segments, called obstruction lines, that does not compromise the visibility spaces. The polygon reduction algorithm reduces the number of lines representing a polygon by half,

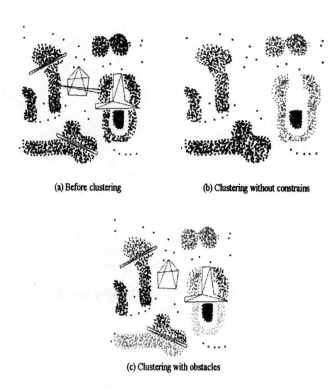

(a) Before clustering

(b) Clustering without constrains

(c) Clustering with obstacles

Figure 6. Clustering dataset Dataset2

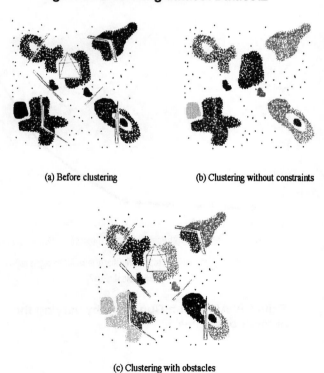

(a) Before clustering

(b) Clustering without constraints

(c) Clustering with obstacles

Figure 7. Clustering dataset Dataset3

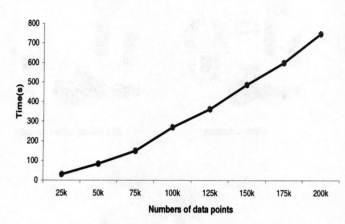

Figure 8. Algorithm Run Time by varying the number of data points

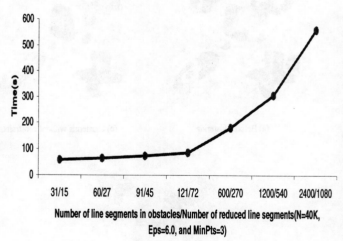

Figure 9. Algorithm Run Time by varying the number obstacles

and thus reduces the search space by half. We have also defined the concept of reachability in the context of obstacles and have used it in the designation of the clustering process. Finally, we have developed a density-based clustering algorithm, DBCluC, which takes constraints into account during the clustering process. Owing to the effectiveness of the density-based approach, DBCluC finds clusters of arbitrary shapes and sizes with minimum domain knowledge. In particular, it is not necessary to know the number of clusters to be discovered. In addition, experiments have shown scalability of DBCluC in terms of size of the database in number of data points as well as scalability in terms of number and complexity of physical constraints.

In the current implementation of DBCluC, obstacles are not indexed. This obliges a check of all obstruction lines before expanding the reachability of any point. While the number of line segments to test is reduced significantly thanks to the polygon reduction algorithm, this number can still be reduced with a better indexing of the obstruction lines. Indeed, it suffices to test only the lines traversing the neighbourhood of a data point to expand. However, since lines are represented by their end-points, and end-points of a close line can be relatively far, it is difficult to issue a range query for such lines. With a good indexing scheme of the obstruction lines, the complexity of the clustering algorithm can be reduced to $O(N \cdot \log N)$. Moreover, most of the execution time in the current implementation is spent in retrieving neighbours with range queries in the SR-tree structure indexing data points. SR-trees perform well for k- NN type of queries instead. For spatial databases, with an index structure optimized for range queries of 2- dimensional data objects, the run time of DBCluC could be dramatically improved.

We have addressed the problem of clustering in the presence of constraints such as physical obstacles but only in a 2-dimensional space. While the SR-tree structure allows us to cluster spaces of higher dimensionality, our model for constraints has not been tested at higher dimensionality and our polygon reduction algorithm is limited to two-dimensional plans. We believe that some consideration should be given to modeling constraints when clustering high dimensional spaces. We are currently investigating other constraints such as bridges and pedways that can invalidate obstacles such as rivers and highways at some given points or simply connect distant clusters. Moreover, operational constraints, not considered in this paper, have a key role with respect to the effectiveness of clustering results, even though they require expensive processing.

References

[1] R. Agrawal, J. Gehrke, D. Gunopulos, and P. Raghavan. Automatic subspace clustering of high dimensional data for

data mining applications. In *Proc. 1998 ACM-SIGMOD Int. Conf. Management of Data (SIGMOD'98)*, pages 94–105, 1998.

[2] M. Ankerst, M. M. Breunig, H.-P. Kriegel, and J. Sander. OPTICS: ordering points to identify the clustering structure. In *ACM-SIGMOD Int. Conf. Management of Data (SIGMOD' 99)*, pages 49–60, 1999.

[3] N. Beckmann, H.-P. Kriegel, R. Schneider, and B. Seeger. The R* tree: An efficient and robust access method for points and rectangles. In *Proc. of the 1990 ACM SIGMOD Intl. Conf.*, pages 332–331, 1990.

[4] J. Bezdek and R. Hathaway. Numerical convergence and interpretation of the fuzzy c-shells clustering algorithm. *IEEE Transactions on Neural Networks*, 3(5):787–793, 1992.

[5] P. S. Bradley, U. M. Fayyad, and C. Reina. Scaling clustering algorithms to large databases. In *Knowledge Discovery and Data Mining*, pages 9–15, 1998.

[6] V. Brailovsky. A probabilistic approach to clustering. *Pattern Recognition Letters*, 12(4):193–198, 1991.

[7] N. Colossi and M. Nascimento. Benchmarking access structures for high-dimensional multimedia data. In *Proc. IEEE Intl. Conf. on Multimedia and Expo (ICME'2000)*, pages 1215–1218, 2000.

[8] M. Ester, H.-P. Kriegel, J. Sander, and X. Xu. A density-based algorithm for discovering clusters in large spatial databases with noise. In *Knowledge Discovery and Data Mining*, pages 226–231, 1996.

[9] V. Estivill-Castro and I. Lee. Autoclust+: Automatic clustering of point-data sets in the presence of obstacles. In *International Workshop on Temporal and Spatial and Spatio-Temporal Data Mining (TSDM2000)*, pages 133–146, 2000.

[10] S. Guha, R. Rastogi, and K. Shim. CURE: an efficient clustering algorithm for large databases. In *ACM-SIGMOD International Conference Management of Data*, pages 73–84, 1998.

[11] J. Han and M. KamberK. *Data Mining: Concepts and Techniques*. Morgan Kaufman, 2000.

[12] P. S. Heckbert. *Graphics Gems(4)*. Academic Press, 1994.

[13] A. Hinneburg and D. A. Keim. An efficient approach to clustering in large multimedia databases with noise. In *Knowledge Discovery and Data Mining*, pages 58–65, 1998.

[14] A. K. Jain, M. N. Murty, and P. J. Flynn. Data clustering: a review. *ACM Computing Surveys*, 31(3):264–323, 1999.

[15] G. Karypis, E. Han, and V. Kumar. Chameleon: A hierarchical clustering algorithm using dynamic modeling. In *IEEE Computer*, pages 68–75, 1999.

[16] N. Katayama and S. Satoh. The SR-tree: an index structure for high-dimensional nearest neighbor queries. In *Proc. of the 1997 ACM SIGMOD Intl. Conf.*, pages 369–380, 1997.

[17] L. Kaufman. Finding groups in data: an introduction to cluster analysis. In *Finding Groups in Data: An Introduction to Cluster Analysis*. Wiley, New York, 1990.

[18] T. Kohonen. Self-organized formation of topologically correct feature maps. *Biological Cybernetics*, 43:59–69, 1982.

[19] K. Koperski, J. Adhikary, and J. Han. Spatial data mining: Progress and challenges survey paper, 1996.

[20] C.-H. Lee and O. R. Zaïane. Polygon reduction: An algorithm for minimum line representation for polygons. In *Submitted to 14th Canadian Conf. on Computational Geometry*, 2002.

[21] R. Ng and J. Han. Efficient and effective clustering methods for spatial data mining. In *Proc. of VLDB Conf.*, pages 144–155, 1994.

[22] H. Ralambondrainy. A conceptual version of the k-means algorithm. *Pattern Recognition Letters*, 16(11):1147–1157, 1995.

[23] E. H. Ruspini. A new approach to clustering. *Information and Control*, 15(1):22–32, 1969.

[24] J. W. Shavlik and T. G. Dietterich. *Readings in Machine Learning*. Morgan Kaufmann, 1990.

[25] G. Sheikholeslami, S. Chatterjee, and A. Zhang. Wavecluster: A multi-resolution clustering approach for very large spatial databases, 1998.

[26] P. Sneath and R. Sokal. Numerical taxonomy, 1973.

[27] M. Stone. A mnemonic for areas of polygons. *AMER. MATH. MONTHLY*, 93:479–480, 1986.

[28] A. K. H. Tung, J. Hou, and J. Han. Spatial clustering in the presence of obstacles. In *Proc. 2001 Int. Conf. On Data Engineering(ICDE'01)*, 2001.

[29] A. K. H. Tung, R. T. Ng, L. V. S. Lakshmanan, and J. Han. Constraint-based clustering in large databases. In *ICDT*, pages 405–419, 2001.

[30] W. Wang, J. Yang, and R. R. Muntz. STING: A statistical information grid approach to spatial data mining. In *The VLDB Journal*, pages 186–195, 1997.

[31] C. Zahn. Graph-theoretical methods for detecting and describing gestalt clusters. In *IEEE Transactions on Computers*, pages 20:68–86, 1971.

[32] T. Zhang, R. Ramakrishnan, and M. Livny. BIRCH: an efficient data clustering method for very large databases. In *ACM-SIGMOD International Conference Management of Data*, pages 103–114, June 1996.

Consistency in Data Warehouse Dimensions

Carolin Letz[1,2]
[1]IS Dept., Univ of Muenster
Leonardo-Campus 3
D-48149 Muenster
Germany

Eric Tobias Henn[2]
[2]zeb/information.technology
Hammer Strasse 165
D-48153 Muenster
Germany

Gottfried Vossen[1,3]
[3]PROMATIS Corp.
3223 Crow Canyon Rd., # 300
San Ramon, CA 94583
USA

Abstract

Data warehouses present a powerful framework for storing and analyzing huge amounts of data. In this context analyses focus on data that has been gathered over long periods of time, often between one and five years. A data warehouse can therefore be regarded as a specialized historical database. However, not only the data kept in a data warehouse has to be seen in a temporal context, but also the fact that dimension data may undergo changes during such a time period needs to be taken into consideration. In this paper, we focus on update operations on dimensions and establish a notion of consistency for guiding such operations. We devise algorithms for executing update operations that can be shown to preserve consistency, and we study their time complexity.

1. Introduction

Data warehouses in combination with online analytical processing (OLAP) applications present a powerful framework for storing and analyzing huge amounts of data. In this context analyses focus on data that has been gathered over long periods of time, often between one and five years. A data warehouse can therefore be regarded as a specialized *temporal* or even *historical* database. However, not only the data kept in a data warehouse has to be seen in a temporal context, but also the fact that dimension data may undergo changes during such a time period needs to be taken into consideration. Surprisingly, research in this direction has only recently begun, yet no complete solutions are in sight. In this paper, we focus on *update operations* (i.e., insertions, deletions, and modifications) on dimensions and establish a notion of *consistency* that has to guide them. Moreover, we devise algorithms for executing such update operations that can be shown to preserve consistency; finally, we study their time complexity.

As a motivating example, consider the following scenario which is taken from the financial industry: Let us consider the simplified organizational structure of a bank (as shown below in Figures 1 and 2): At a first level it is divided into two divisions, for doing business with private, respectively corporate customers. Below that, there are two organizational structures: Besides a regional structure with different branches for retail business there exists a central investment center with specialized advisors. Each customer belongs to a branch, where he or she handles everyday transactions and has a dedicated advisor in the investment center whom he or she consults for discussing investment strategies. Note that in this example every customer has to have such a specialized advisor. This organizational structure undergoes different changes; here we examine two representative examples: Advisors in the central investment center may change their responsibilities from private to corporate customers, due to business needs or personal preferences. Quite often, the customer base changes as well — new customers are acquired, customers change their local branch due to moving, or customers close their accounts.

In order to investigate changes in warehouse dimensions from a formal point of view, we will introduce dimension schemata and instances, as well as update, in particular insert and delete operations on the latter. These operations must preserve the *consistency* of a dimension, which will also be defined formally. In the above example, the customer dimension is consistent if every customer that is assigned to the corporate division by her branch affiliation must also be assigned to that division via her special advisor in the investment center; the corresponding has to hold for private customers. It will then be shown that consistency *violations* in a dimension instance can only occur if the schema meets certain conditions. Indeed, consistency violations are due to the existence of so-called *conflicting levels* in a dimension schema; fortunately, analyzing a schema to determine whether such levels exist can be done efficiently.

224

The organization of the paper is as follows: In Section 2, we introduce preliminaries and set the stage for our investigation from a formal point of view, in particular, we define a suitable notion of consistency. In Section 3 we define and study dimensional updates. In Section 4 we show applications of this notion in temporal as well as non-temporal warehouse design contexts. In Section 5, we survey related work, and in Section 6 we summarize our development and exhibit questions that deserve further study.

2. Consistency of Data Warehouse Dimensions

In this section, we provide preliminaries needed for understanding the remainder of the paper, and in particular introduce our notion of consistency formally. We assume the reader to have a basic understanding of data warehouses and their main ingredients (such as dimensions, facts, cube and roll-up operations, etc.), e.g., at the level of [3, 8, 15]. Following [4], *facts* represent atomic information elements in a multidimensional database. A fact consists of quantifying values stored in *measures* and a qualifying context which is determined through the *terminal attributes* of different *dimensions*. The hierarchy of a dimension specifies the possible *aggregation paths* of related measures. A given aggregation level along the path is defined through a *category attribute*. The terminal attribute of a dimension is the root category attribute of the corresponding dimension hierarchy.

In a multidimensional model for data warehouses, dimension schemata as well as dimension instances can be visualized as graph structures. Depending on the specific data model these graph structures have different properties. The following definitions of dimension schemata, instances, and their consistency are based on the multidimensional model introduced in [6].

A *dimension schema* is a directed acyclic graph $D_S = (\mathbf{L}_S, \mathbf{F}_S)$, where $\mathbf{L}_S$ is a fixed set of levels or nodes and $\mathbf{F}_S$ is a fixed set of directed edges between them. The graph has the following properties:

1. There exists a distinguished terminal node $l_t \in \mathbf{L}_S$ of indegree 0 and an implicit node $l_{All} \in \mathbf{L}_S$ of outdegree 0. The indegree and outdegree of all other nodes in $\mathbf{L}_S$ are greater than 0.

2. If level $l_i \in \mathbf{L}_S$ functionally determines level $l_j \in \mathbf{L}_S$ (i.e., if $l_i \to l_j$ in standard database notation), which means $(l_i, l_j) \in \mathbf{F}_S$, then there is no other path from l_i to l_j via one or more intermediate nodes.

3. Every dimension level has an associated value domain. In particular, the value domain of level l_{All} is {all}.

All paths of the graph start at level l_t and end at level l_{All}. If there is more than one path from l_t to l_{All}, the dimension schema is called a *multiple dimension schema*.

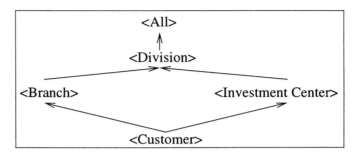

Figure 1. Dimension Schema of a Bank Organization.

As an example, Figure 1 shows the multiple dimension schema of our sample bank. The different dimension levels are denoted by "<...>".

A *dimension instance* $D_I = (\mathbf{L}_I, \mathbf{F}_I)$ of a dimension schema $D_S = (\mathbf{L}_S, \mathbf{F}_S)$ is a directed acyclic graph with the following properties:

1. $\mathbf{L}_I$ consists of pairwise disjoint sets $\mathbf{L}_I = V_{l_1} \cup \cdots \cup V_{l_n}$. Every V_{l_x} is a finite subset of the value domain of $l_x \in \mathbf{L}_S$.

2. If $(l_i, l_j) \in \mathbf{F}_S$ then every member of $V_{l_i} \subseteq \mathbf{L}_I$ is connected to exactly one member of $V_{l_j} \subseteq \mathbf{L}_I$.

A dimension over a multiple dimension schema is called a *multiple dimension*.

A sample dimension instance for our bank is shown in Figure 2. In the following, the terms *dimension instance* and *dimension* will be used interchangeably. This definition implies that leaf nodes in the dimension instance may occur at any level, not only at the terminal level. Nevertheless, summerizability [10] is not violated because it is assumed that the measures which are summarized are functionally determined by a combination of terminal levels of the relevant dimensions, and not by any other level further up in the hierarchy.

Adopting the notion of consistency introduced in [6], we say that a multiple dimension $D_I = (\mathbf{L}_I, \mathbf{F}_I)$ over a multiple dimension schema $D_S = (\mathbf{L}_S, \mathbf{F}_S)$ is *consistent* if the following conditions are satisfied:

1. If there is more than one path in the schema from level l_i to level l_j, where $l_i, l_j \in \mathbf{L}_S$, then the different paths

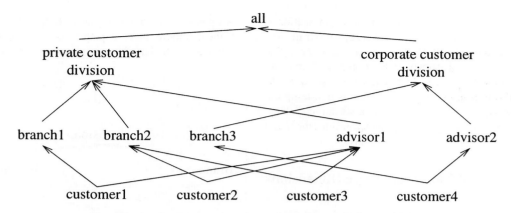

Figure 2. Dimension Instance of a Bank Organization.

from a member of l_i to a member of l_j must lead to the same element of l_j.

2. If there is just one path in the schema from level l_i to level l_j for $l_i, l_j \in \mathbf{L}_S$, then there is also just one path from every member of l_i to a member of l_j.

Notice that a dimension over a schema with just one path from level l_t to l_{All} is always consistent.

3. Update Operations on Dimension Instances

In this section, we study update operations on dimension instances, in particular insertions, deletions, and reclassifications. For each operation, we analyze the consistency violations they may cause and ways to detect such situations. It turns out that the respective conflicting dimension levels in either case can be determined efficiently.

3.1. Insertions into and Deletions from Dimension Instances

According to [5] and [2], all changes of dimension instances can be described as a series of insertions and deletions applied to level members. In particular, a level member may be deleted if the corresponding node in the graph D_I is a leaf node. Deleting a member m_x of level l_x also removes all outgoing edges. Obviously, the deletion of a leaf node m_x does not violate the consistency of the dimension. A level member may be inserted at any level except for level l_{All}. Inserting a member m_x into level l_x means adding a node to the graph and connecting this node to exactly one member of every level immediately above the level l_x.

Inserting a member m_x may or may not violate the dimension's consistency, as the following example demonstrates. Consider Figure 2 again and assume that a new customer, customer5, is inserted and assigned to branch2

as well as to advisor2. This insertion is a legal operation within the dimensional model, but it violates the consistency because branch2 belongs to the private customer division and advisor2 is working for the corporate customer division. Therefore, an insertion is only permitted if it preserves the consistency of the dimension.

In the following the notion of *conflicting* levels first introduced in [6] is adopted to properly capture conditions under which an insertion operation results in an inconsistent dimension. Informally, the insertion conflict of the above example arises because when inserting a customer more than one connection to a higher level has to be established, and the levels <Branch> and <Investment Center> immediately above the level <Customer> are connected to the level <Division> further up in the hierarchy which is not the level <All>. The example in particular shows that the schema itself already determines whether an insertion conflict is likely to arise in a given dimension instance. Indeed, in a dimension schema with just one aggregation path an insertion conflict cannot occur.

Before determining the conditions of an insertion conflict, we need to define two sets: Given a dimension schema $D_S = (\mathbf{L}_S, \mathbf{F}_S)$ as above. Then $D_S^+ = (\mathbf{L}_S, \mathbf{F}_S^+)$ denotes the transitive closure of D_S. The set of direct successors of a given level $l_i \in \mathbf{L}_S$ is defined as

$$Succ_{l_i} = \{l_x | (l_i, l_x) \in \mathbf{F}_S\}.$$

Moreover, the set of all successors of a given level $l_i \in \mathbf{L}_S$ is defined as

$$Succ_{l_i}^+ = \{l_x | (l_i, l_x) \in \mathbf{F}_S^+\}.$$

Definition 3.1 Given a dimension schema $D_S = (\mathbf{L}_S, \mathbf{F}_S)$ as described above with transitive closure $D_S^+ = (\mathbf{L}_S, \mathbf{F}_S^+)$. Then a level $l_j \in \mathbf{L}_S$ is a *conflicting* level for an insertion operation into level $l_i \in \mathbf{L}_S$ if the following conditions are satisfied:

1. $outdeg(l_i) = |Succ_{l_i}| > 1$

2. $\exists l_x, l_y \in Succ_{l_i}, l_x \neq l_y : l_j \in Succ^+_{l_x} \cap Succ^+_{l_y}$

□

Intuitively, Condition 1 states that level l_i must be directly connected to more than one higher level of the dimension hierarchy. Condition 2 says that an insertion conflict may arise at level l_j if level l_j can be reached from at least two direct successor levels of l_i.

The following theorem, the proof of which can be found in [12], says that there are efficient ways to detect conflicting levels for insertions within a dimension schema.

Theorem 3.1 The set of conflicting levels for insertions of a level l_i in a given dimension schema $D_S = (\mathbf{L}_S, \mathbf{F}_S)$ can be computed in time polynomial in the number of nodes. □

Once the conflict levels for every level of a dimension schema are known, this knowledge can be used to systematically check for insertion conflicts when inserting a new member into a given dimension instance. Indeed, suppose a level $l_i \in \mathbf{L}_S$ has the conflict level l_j. Before inserting an element into level l_i it must be computed if a conflict on level l_j will arise or not. As the conflict levels are known in advance, not all possible paths originating from the new element need to be tested but only those paths leading to elements on the conflict level. It is obvious that these computations can also be executed time polynomial in the number of nodes [12].

3.2. Properties of Insertion Conflicts

Knowing the levels of insertion conflicts, the next step must be to study how the different conflict levels of a dimension level influence each other during an insertion operation. To this end, consider the abstract dimension schema shown in Figure 3 (left) with a given dimension instance (right).

Levels <F>, <G>, and <H> are conflict levels for insertions into level <A>. Inserting a new element a3 into level <A> and assigning it to b1 and c2 causes a conflict on level <F> and <H>. Likewise, connecting a3 to d1 and e2 causes a conflict on level <G> and <H>. If f1, f2, g1 and g2 had all been assigned to the same element on level <H>, the conflicts on level <H> had not occurred. To solve the above conflict on level <F>, a3 is connected to b1 and c1. On level <H>, a3 is connected to h1 via b1 and c1. Assigning a3 to d2 and e2 also settles the conflict on level <G>. Via d2 and e2, a3 is connected to h2. Thus, the conflict on level <H> remains. Had a3 been assigned to d1 and e1 the conflict on level <H> had also been solved.

This example demonstrates important properties of insertion conflicts. Given a dimension schema $D_S =$

$(\mathbf{L}_S, \mathbf{F}_S)$ and a level l_i with conflict levels $l_{i_1} \ldots l_{i_n}$. The acyclic graph structure implies a partial order $\prec$ between these nodes, $\prec^+$ denotes the transitive closure of the relation.

- If $l_{i_x} \prec^+ l_{i_y}$ a conflict on level l_{i_x} may but need not be propagated onto level l_{i_y}.

- If $l_{i_x} \prec^+ l_{i_y}$ a conflict on level l_{i_y} may occur even if there is no conflict on level l_{i_x}.

- A level l_{i_y} is a n-fold conflict level if there are $(n-1)$ conflict levels $l_{i_1}, \ldots l_{i_{n-1}}$ such that $l_{i_j} \prec^+ l_{i_y} \forall j \in 1, \ldots, n-1$

In Figure 3, level <H> is a threefold conflict level. First, there can be a conflict on level <H>, without another conflict on levels <F> or <G>. Second, every conflict on level <F> may cause a conflict on level <H>, and third, every conflict on level <G> may also be propagated onto level <H>. This shows that detecting an insertion conflict once the conflict levels are known is straightforward, whereas actually solving the conflict is more complex. When correcting the original insertion operation all conflict levels have to be checked again. For example, in Figure 3 there are sixteen different ways of inserting a new element into level <A> but only two of them lead to a consistent dimension instance.

3.3. Reclassification of Level Members

Executing all possible changes within a dimension as a series of insertions and deletions can be quite tedious. Therefore, more complex operators have been defined in [6] and in [2]. One of these, *reclassification* of a level member, may also result in an inconsistent dimension. In the following it will be shown that the reclassification conflict first described in [6] is caused by an insertion conflict as defined above.

To this end, consider a dimension schema $D_S = (\mathbf{L}_S, \mathbf{F}_S)$ with $l_i, l_j \in \mathbf{L}_S, (l_i, l_j) \in \mathbf{F}_S$ and a dimension $D_I = (\mathbf{L}_I, \mathbf{F}_I)$ over this schema. Let m_i be a member of level l_i, and let m_{j_1}, m_{j_2} be members of level l_j s.t. $(m_i, m_{j_1}) \in \mathbf{F}_I$. The reclassification of member m_i from m_{j_1} to m_{j_2} is defined as deletion of the edge (m_i, m_{j_1}) followed by an insertion of the new edge (m_i, m_{j_2}), i.e.:

$$\mathbf{F}_I \setminus \{(m_i, m_{j_1})\} \cup \{(m_i, m_{j_2})\}.$$

As can be seen in the next example, such a reclassification may cause an inconsistency.

Assume, in our running example, that advisor2 in Figure 2 changes from the corporate to the private customer division. After this reclassification customer4 still belongs to branch3 which is part of the corporate customer division, but his advisor is no longer responsible for corporate customers. This reclassification of advisor2 can be executed as

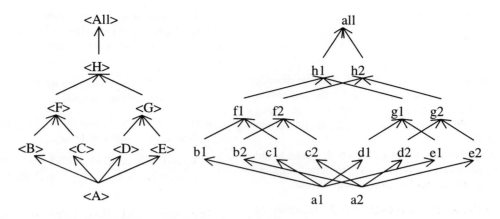

Figure 3. Abstract Dimension Schema and Instance.

a series of insertions and deletions. First customer4 has to be deleted, then advisor2 is deleted. After that, advisor2 is re-inserted with the new connection to the private customer division. Finally, customer4 is re-inserted with the old connections to advisor2 and branch3. At this point, an insertion conflict occurs.

In general, reclassification conflicts can always be explained as the consequence of an insertion conflict hidden in the reclassification operation. Therefore it is again the dimension schema that determines the possibility of reclassification conflicts. A schema without conflicting levels for insertions will never have conflicting levels for reclassifications either.

Definition 3.2 Given a dimension schema $D_S = (\mathbf{L}_S, \mathbf{F}_S)$ with $l_i, l_j \in \mathbf{L}_S, (l_i, l_j) \in \mathbf{F}_S$ as described above. $D_S^* = (\mathbf{L}_S, \mathbf{F}_S^*)$ denotes the reflexive-transitive closure of D_S. Level l_x is a conflict level for a reclassification between level l_i and level l_j if the following holds:

- Level l_x is above level l_j such that $(l_j, l_x) \in \mathbf{F}_S^*$,

- there is a level l_y underneath level l_i such that $(l_y, l_i) \in \mathbf{F}_S^*$, and

- level l_x is a conflict level for insertions into level l_y.

$\square$

If l_x is a conflict level for insertions into level l_y then there are at least two different paths from l_y to l_x, namely one via l_i and l_j and the other avoiding l_i and l_j. Therefore a reclassification between members of level l_i and l_j may result in an inconsistency.

The following theorem, the proof of which can again be found in [12], states that there are efficient ways to detect conflicting levels for reclassifications within a dimension schema:

Theorem 3.2 The set of conflicting levels for a reclassification between members of levels l_i and l_j in a given dimension schema $D_S = (\mathbf{L}_S, \mathbf{F}_S)$ can be computed in time polynomial in the number of nodes. This holds even without computing the conflict levels for insertions first. $\square$

On the other hand, given a dimension instance it is more difficult to decide whether a reclassification is allowed than to test for an insertion conflict. Indeed, given two levels l_i and l_j between which a reclassification of members is to take place, where level l_x is known to be a conflict level for the reclassification and a conflict level for an insertion into l_y as explained above. If a member m_i of level l_i is assigned to the element m_{j_1} on level l_j and shall be reclassified to m_{j_2}, a conflict arises if two prerequisites are fulfilled: First, m_{j_1} is connected to a different element of level l_x than m_{j_2}. Second, at least one element of level l_y is connected to m_i. Again, testing these prerequisites can be executed in polynomial time.

Returning to the bank example (cf. Figure 2), it is known that the level <Division> is a conflict level for a reclassification between the level <Investment Center> and the level <Division>. At the same time, it is a conflict level for insertions into the level <Customer>. Thus, the level <Division> plays the role of l_j and l_x at the same time. As a result, if advisor2 is reclassified from the corporate to the private customer division the first prerequisite for a reclassification conflict is met. The second is also satisfied because on the level <Customer> customer4 is connected to advisor2. If customer4 did not exist it would be perfectly fine to reclassify advisor2.

3.4. Properties of Reclassification Conflicts

As a reclassification conflict can always be explained as the result of an insertion conflict, the properties of in-

228

sertion conflicts determine the properties of reclassification conflicts.

Going back to our abstract example in Figure 3, reclassifications between levels <A> and <B> or <A> and <C> may cause inconsistencies on level <F>; analogously, reclassifications between <A> and <D> or <A> and <E> may invoke a conflict on level <G>. The conflicts on levels <F> and <G> may, but need not be propagated onto level <H>. Reclassifications between <B> and <F> as well as <C> and <F> might cause conflicts on level <F>, between <D> and <G> as well as <E> and <G> a reclassification might lead to an inconsistency on level <G>. Again, these conflicts may cause a conflict on level <H> as well. Finally, reclassifications between <F> and <H> as well as <G> and <H> can result in an inconsistency on level <H>. The levels below the two reclassification levels are not affected.

Assume, in that figure, that member d1 is reclassified from g1 to g2. Now element a1 is assigned to g1 and g2 on level <G> and to h1 and h2 on level <H>. To solve this conflict, different measures can be taken. First, the reclassification can be undone. Second, e1 is also reclassified from g1 to g2. This solves the conflict on level <G> but does not solve the conflict on level <H>. Moreover, further reclassifications must be carried out in order to return to a consistent state. Therefore, the second and all the other possible ways to solve the conflict are less efficient than undoing the original operation.

Given a dimension schema $D_S = (\mathbf{L}_S, \mathbf{F}_S)$ and two levels l_i, l_j between which a reclassification causes a conflict on the levels $l_{i_1} \ldots l_{i_n}$.

- If $l_{i_x} \prec^+ l_{i_y}$ a conflict on level l_{i_x} may but need not be propagated onto level l_{i_y}.

- Solving the reclassification conflict on one conflict level does not necessarily solve all conflicts caused by the reclassification.

In short, the manifestation of an inconsistency in a given dimension instance is determined by two factors, the dimension schema and the instance. The schema needs to be analyzed only once to determine conflict levels for insertions, respectively reclassifications whereas the dimension instance needs to be tested every time a modification is made which effects the known conflict levels. These tests can be executed in time polynomial in the number of nodes.

4. Applications

In this section, we exhibit applications of our consistency considerations from the previous section. We see two major applications, one in ordinary warehouses where dimensions undergo changes over time, the other in *temporal* warehouses that need to maintain a history of changes. We consider each application in turn.

4.1. Applications in Traditional Data Warehouses

The definitions of dimension schemata and dimension instances in Section 2 are rather restrictive. In reality, not every customer with an account in a local branch also needs a financial advisor. Other banks might want to split their customers into two groups and assign them either to a local branch or to a centralized investment center, but not to both. Therefore dimension schemata often allow the existence of *alternative* and *optional* aggregation paths [4].

In a schema with alternative aggregation paths every member of a level need not be connected to exactly one member of every level immediately above it. Going back to our bank example in Figure 2, customer1 might have an account in branch1 but does not need a financial advisor. If this constellation is allowed, summerizability is violated. This weakness can be remedied if every level has a special member "else". A customer without a specialized financial advisor will then be assigned to this element on the level <Investment Center>. Dimension instances with alternative aggregation paths can therefore always be transformed to meet the requirements of our instance definition. Hence, the definition of conflict levels applies to these schemata in just the same way as defined above. The detection of conflict levels for insertions and reclassifications can be carried out without taking into regard that some aggregation paths may not be in use in some dimension instances. Also the detection of conflicts in a given dimension instance is carried out in the same way as described above.

In a dimension schema with optional aggregation paths, only one of the different options can be chosen at a time. Indeed, in our bank example a customer may either have an account in a local branch or deal with the investment center. The dimension schema can then be split into two separate schemata,

$$\text{<Customer>} \rightarrow \text{<Branch>} \rightarrow \text{<Division>} \rightarrow \text{<All>}$$

and

$$\text{<Customer>} \rightarrow \text{<Investment Center>}$$
$$\rightarrow \text{<Division>} \rightarrow \text{<All>},$$

which now represent the different choices. Each of these schemata is a schema in the sense of Section 2. The separate schemata can be analyzed to detect conflict levels for insertion and reclassification as described above. Given a dimension instance over a schema with optional aggregation paths, the schema can be transformed into a number of separate schemata which meet the requirements of the schema definition in Section 2. In these schemata, insertion and reclassification conflicts are detected in the same way as for ordinary schemata. In our bank example, the original dimension schema was split into two separate schemata, each of which consists of just one aggregation path. Therefore, both schemata do not have any conflict levels at all. As a consequence, it is not necessary to search for insertion or reclassification conflicts in a given dimension instance over the combined schema with optional aggregation paths.

This illustrates that the results obtained above, which have been achieved by examining the consistency properties of a very restricted type of dimension schema, are also relevant for a broader group of schemata. The definition of conflicting levels and insertion respectively reclassification conflicts can be re-used with slight modifications to the given schemata and instances.

4.2. Applications in Temporal Data Warehouses

So far, schema properties have been the main focus of our analysis. It has been assumed that a conflict is likely to occur in a given dimension instance if a dimension schema has conflict levels for insertions. In that case, a test has to be executed for insertions and reclassifications in a given dimension instance. However, these conflicts will only occur if the initially consistent dimension undergoes changes at all. Therefore, dimensions can be partitioned into *changing* and *stable* dimensions [8]. Stable dimensions which are consistent when they are first built up will never become inconsistent. A schema analysis for finding conflict levels is superfluous if it is known in advance that the dimension instance will never be altered. However, this type of dimension is rare in practice. More often, modifications in dimensions substitute the original configuration as described in Section 3. In some cases, the history of changes needs to be maintained. Some data models use valid-time time-stamping to record the period of validity of the edges in the schema and the instance graph [13] to be able to reconstruct the dimension schema and the instance at a given point in time. In the following, terms referring to temporal databases are use in accordance with the definitions in [7].

To be able to reconstruct a dimension schema and dimension instances the definitions of Section 2 have to be extended. A *temporal* dimension schema consists of a directed acyclic graph $D_S = (\mathbf{L}_S, \mathbf{F}_S)$ and a set T of single points on a time axis of a fixed granularity. Every edge $(l_i, l_j) \in \mathbf{F}_S$ is labelled with the set of time points when this edge is valid. To simplify the notation, a set of consecutive time-points can be written as an interval. Here a closed-open interval representation is chosen. At every single point in time, the dimension schema must have the three properties as demanded in Section 2.

Considering again our sample bank, the business organization undergoes structural changes which are reflected in the development of the dimension schema; Figure 4 illustrates this. When the bank was founded at time t_0 it was organized in different branches which were grouped in divisions. At time t_5 the investment center was opened parallel to the branches. At time t_{10} the branches were given up and only the investment center remains until some time t_n in the future.

As long as the branches and the investment center exist in parallel, the level <Division> is a conflict level for insertions into the level <Customer>. Before the investment center was founded and after the branches are closed the dimension schema does not have any conflict levels.

The definition of conflict levels for insertions and deletions given in Section 2 can also be applied to temporal dimension schemata. To this end, at every single point in time the dimension schema is regarded as a non-temporal schema. Thus, the conflict levels for insertions and reclassifications can be identified for every snapshot of the dimension schema. In practice, the detection algorithm needs to be applied every time the dimension schema changes and not for every single point on the time axis. As long as the schema does not undergo any changes the conflict levels do not change either.

The same approach can be taken for the historization of dimension instances. Again the edges of the instance graph are labelled with the time points respectively intervals to indicate when the edge exists. In Figure 4, it is shown that the bank first started with one branch for private customers only. At time t_3 the division for corporate customers was founded together with a new branch. At time t_5 the investment center opened. At time t_{10} the branches were closed and only the investment center remains.

The historization does not prevent the occurrence of inconsistencies as the following example demonstrates. At time t_{11} a new customer is won and assigned to branch1 and advisor2. Then this customer belongs to the private and the corporate customer division at the same time. Also the reclassification of advisor2 from corporate to private customers leads to a reclassification conflict. Consequently, time-stamping does not prevent inconsistencies. As long as the dimension schema does not have any conflicting levels it is not necessary to check for insertion or reclassification conflicts. When the investment center is opened a consistency check is needed. When the branches are closed these tests can be abandoned.

Dimension schemata in temporal data warehouses may also posses alternative or optional aggregations paths. If the temporal dimension schema is analyzed every time it changes it is always reduced to a single point in time. Therefore the solutions for non-temporal dimension schemata with alternative and optional aggregation paths can be extended to cope with temporal dimension schemata as well.

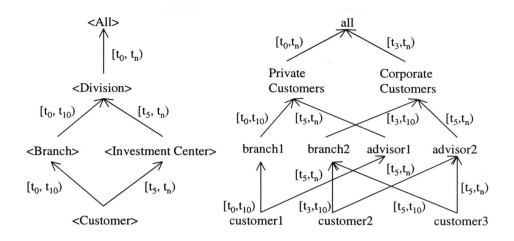

Figure 4. Temporal Dimension Schema and Instance.

In conclusion, the results obtained above are not only relevant for the restricted non-temporal definitions of schemata and instances but are also relevant for more flexible schemata and temporal data warehouse models. As only certain schemata are prone to consistency violations a schema check can already be performed during the data warehouse design process. As conflicting levels are already determined during the design phase, it is worth reconsidering the design decisions if too many conflict levels occur in a dimension schema that is known to have changing dimension instances. Furthermore, when the design phase is complete and the data warehouse is in use, the knowledge about the existence of conflicting levels within a dimension schema can be used to help maintain the consistency of the dimension data. Every time a dimension with conflict levels is updated, it can be tested automatically if conflicts occur. This is especially relevant if part of the dimensional data is not imported from the operational subsystems but is maintained manually or semi-automatically by the data warehouse administrators.

5. Related Work

In this section, we survey related work that has looked either at temporal warehouse aspects or at the problem of updating dimensions (or both). Up to now, properties of dimension schemata have mainly been examined under the aspect of summerizability, i.e., guaranteed correctness of aggregation results, in order to develop criteria for good schema design [11, 10]. The focus has been on functional dependencies between the different schema levels and different kinds of measures with different summerizability properties. Dimension instances have been treated as static or have not been considered important for correct aggrega-

tions.

Practical ways to handle changing dimensions without introducing a temporal data model have already been proposed by Kimball in [8]. Although the solutions presented there are rather pragmatic in nature and in many cases insufficient, they are still widely employed in practice if the OLAP system under consideration does not support changes in dimension instances. However, the issue of consistency has not been touched in this context.

Hurtado, Mendelzon, and Vaisman [5] have studied changes in dimension instances as well as in dimension schemata, and have defined operators to describe them; in their model, all operators have to transform the dimension from one consistent state to another. In [6] the reclassification conflict was first described and formally defined in order to develop a strategy to test for reclassification conflicts in a relational implementation of the dimension. However, a clear distinction between schema properties and dimension properties is not made. The focus is on a comparison of a normalized and a denormalized implementation of the proposed data model. Therefore, the algorithms for detecting reclassification conflicts are dominated by implementation issues. Still, a similar approach is missing for the insertion operation. The reclassification conflict is examined without relating it to the underlying insertion conflict. To simplify the test for consistency, Hurtado et al. define *minimal conflict levels*, these levels are conflict levels that cannot be reached via any other conflict levels. If a reclassification conflict occurs it will occur on the minimal conflict levels first but solving the conflict on the minimal conflict levels does not necessarily solve the conflict in the complete dimension instance.

Returning to our abstract dimension instance in Figure 3, the levels <F> and <G> are minimal conflict levels for reclassifications between the levels <A> and <B>, <A> and <C>, <A> and <D> or <A> and <E> whereas <H> is not a minimal conflict level. Reclassifying a1 from c1 to c2 causes a conflict on level <F>. Reclassifying a1 from b1 to b2 solves this conflict on level <F> but the conflict on level <H> remains. The dimensional model was further extended by the capability to historize dimensions [13] as briefly described in the above section without raising the question of consistency for temporal dimension instances in particular.

Changes in dimension instances are usually treated as part of the search for a temporal data model for data warehouses. A first approach to implement a temporal data model using a relational temporal star schema has been made in [1]. Other models have been proposed, for example, in [2] and in [14]. The center of attention of [14] rests on different time-representations and their suitability for temporal data warehousing. Modifications in dimensions are described but not examined any further. [2] concentrates on a temporal data model that enables the user to integrate different time aspects into his or her queries and to automatically convert facts according to changes within the dimensions. Again, modifications in dimension instances are defined but their properties are not studied in depth.

6. Conclusions

Driven by the observation that dimensions in a multidimensional data warehouse often undergo changes that have an impact on the consistency of the dimension, we have developed criteria to analyze the underlying dimension schema in order to detect levels where conflicts are likely to occur. The schema properties represent a necessary precondition for consistency violations during dimension modifications. Insertions and reclassifications are the two types of modifications that need to be executed in a controlled way to avoid inconsistencies. We have demonstrated that as a reclassification can be executed as a series of deletions and insertions the reclassification conflict can be explained as a hidden insertion conflict. These observations may also be transferred to historized dimensions and dimensions with optional or alternative aggregation paths.

Therefore it is worth considering to integrate the notion of insertion and reclassification conflict levels into methods for a systematic data warehouse design concept such as proposed in [9]. If the application scenario allows different ways to model the same information the solution with the least conflict levels might be of advantage. If there is only one reasonable way to design the data warehouse schema the conflict levels are still known in advance so that tests can be integrated.

References

[1] R. Bliujute, S. Salentis, C. S. Jensen, "Systematic Change Management in Dimensional Data Warehousing," Timecenter, Technical Report TR-23, 1998.

[2] J. Eder, C. Koncilia, "Evolution of Dimension Data in Temporal Data Warehouses," University of Klagenfurt, Technical Report, 2000.

[3] H. Garcia-Molina, J. D. Ullman, J. Widom, *Database System Implementation*, Prentice-Hall, 2000.

[4] B. Hüsemann, J. Lechtenbörger, G. Vossen, "Conceptual Data Warehouse Design," *Proc. 2nd International Workshop on Design and Management of Data Warehouses* (DMDW) 2000, Stockholm; Report No. 25, Swiss Life IT Research and Development Zurich, June 2000, pp. 6.1–6.11.

[5] C. A. Hurtado, A. Mendelzon, A. Vaisman, "Maintaining Data Cubes under Dimension Updates," *Proc. 15th Int. Conf. on Data Engineering* (ICDE) 1999, pp. 346–355.

[6] C. A. Hurtado, A. Mendelzon, A. Vaisman, "Updating OLAP Dimensions," *Proc. 2nd ACM Int. Workshop on Data Warehousing and OLAP* (DOLAP) 1999, pp. 60–66.

[7] C. S. Jensen, C. E. Dyreson (eds.), "The Consensus Glossary of Temporal Database Concepts, February 1998 Version", Springer LNCS 1399, pp. 367-405.

[8] R. Kimball, *The Data Warehouse Toolkit*, John Wiley & Sons, 1996.

[9] J. Lechtenbörger, "Data Warehouse Schema Design," Ph.D. thesis, Fachbereich Mathematik und Informatik, Universität Münster, 2001.

[10] W. Lehner, J. Albrecht, H. Wedekind, "Normal forms for multidimensional databases," *Proc. 10th Int. Conf. on Scientific and Statistical Database Management* (SSDBM) 1998, pp. 63–72.

[11] H. Lenz, A. Shoshani, "Summarizability in OLAP and statistical databases," *Proc. 9th Int. Conf. on Scientific and Statistical Database Management* (SSDBM) 1997, pp. 132–143.

[12] C. Letz, "Temporal Concepts in Data Warehousing," Diploma Thesis (in German), Fachbereich Mathematik und Informatik, Universität Münster, 2001.

[13] A. Mendelzon, A. Vaisman, "Temporal Queries in OLAP," *Proc. 26th Int. Conf. on Very Large Data Bases* (VLDB) 2000, pp. 242–253.

[14] S. Stock, *Modellierung zeitbezogener Daten im Data Warehouse*, Deutscher Universitäts-Verlag, 2001.

[15] G. Vossen, *Data Models, Database Languages and Database Management Systems*, 4th edition (in German), R. Oldenbourg Verlag, 2000.

DWS-AQA: A Cost Effective Approach for Very Large Data Warehouses

Jorge Bernardino
Institute Polytechnic of Coimbra
ISEC - DEIS, Portugal
jorge@isec.pt

Pedro Furtado, Henrique Madeira
University of Coimbra
DEI, Portugal
pnf, henrique@dei.uc.pt

Abstract

Data warehousing applications typically involve massive amounts of data that push database management technology to the limit. A scalable architecture is crucial, not only to handle very large amount of data but also to assure interactive response time to the users. Large data warehouses require a very expensive setup, typically based on high-end servers or high-performance clusters. In this paper we propose and evaluate a simple but very effective method to implement a data warehouse using the computers and workstations typically available in large organizations. The proposed approach is called data warehouse striping with approximate query answering (DWS-AQA). The goal is to use the processing and disk capacity normally available in large workstation networks to implement a data warehouse with a very reduced infrastructure cost. As the data warehouse shares computers that are also being used for other purposes, most of the times only a fraction of the computers will be able to execute the partial queries in time. However, as we show in the paper, the approximated answers estimated from partial results have a very small error for most of the plausible scenarios. Moreover, as the data warehouse facts are partitioned in a strict uniform way, it is possible to calculate tight confidence intervals for the approximated answers, providing the user with a measure of the accuracy of the query results. A set of experiments on the TPC-H benchmark database is presented to show the accuracy of DWS-AQA for a large number of scenarios.

1. Introduction

During the last decade, data warehouses have become increasingly important in many applications areas such as decision support, banking and financial services. However, one of the aspects that most restrict the introduction of data warehouses in the organizations is the large investment in powerful servers needed to support large amount of data and to assure the interactive response time necessary to the *ad-hoc* querying typically used in decision support activities.

With the advent of fast networking technologies, many organizations have today large networks of computers (typically, personal computers and workstations) in which only a small fraction of the processing power and disk capacity are normally used. The parallel processing community has been seduced by the huge processing power available in many networks for quite a long time. However, this potentially available processing power has proved to be very hard to be used, even for the most favorable parallel applications.

We decided to investigate the possibilities of using the processing power and disk capacity normally available in large networks to implement a data warehouse at very low infrastructure cost. To achieve this we propose a new method called DWS-AQA (Data Warehouse Striping with Approximate Query Answering) based on the clever combination of two simple ideas: 1) uniform data striping to partition the data warehouse facts over an arbitrary number of computers, in such a way that queries can be executed in a true parallel fashion (a query is actually split into many partial queries), and 2) an approximate query answering strategy to deal with the momentary unavailability of one or more computers in the network.

The data striping technique is in fact the well-known round-robin partitioning applied to the very low level of the data warehouse facts in such a way that assures uniform distribution of the partitioned data. This very simple and old partitioning technique proved to be very effective for the typical queries in data warehouses. In fact, using this partitioning technique we can convert one query into queries that compute partial results, and the global result can be computed very fast from these partial results. The (partial) queries are executed independently in the different computers, which is the necessary condition to achieve optimal load balance and performance scaleup. This partitioning technique, called "Data Warehouse Striping" (DWS), was thoroughly evaluated in a previous work [5].

The key aspect that makes it possible to use the available processing power and disk capacity in a network to implement a data warehouse is the combination of the DWS technique mentioned above with an approximated query answering scheme. Tight confidence intervals for the approximated answers are calculated, providing the user with a measure of the accuracy of the query results.

The main contributions of this paper are as follows:

- Proposes a framework to implement a large data warehouse in an affordable way. This approach has a very good scalability, as more computers can be added to the system as needed, and a nearly linear speedup can be obtained.

- Proposes methods that allow the computation of the different types of aggregation queries on an environment formed by a large number of computers. An efficient way to distribute the queries by all computers and merging the results is also presented.

- An exploration interface is proposed providing continuously feedback to the user and offering accurate estimates of the results, together with confidence intervals. This interface receives the partial answers from different nodes asynchronously, taking into account the unavailability of DWS-AQA.

- Presents an extensive set of experiments to establish the accuracy of DWS-AQA and provide statistical bounds for the errors contained in the estimations of final results.

The remainder of the paper is organized as follows. In the next section we review related work and discuss the problems associated with parallel and distributed data warehouses. Section 3 describes the different components of a DWS-AQA system. We present an experimental evaluation in Section 4 and the final section summarizes the conclusions from this work.

2. Related work

Today's commercial database systems support creation and use of indexes and materialized views. Materialized views are based on pre-computed answers to queries and are probably the most effective way to accelerate specific queries in a data warehouse. However, it only works when user queries can be correctly anticipated, which is not often possible [15]. Indexes also have limitations in what concerns their usage by the optimizer [9]. More recently, commercial systems have also added support for automatically picking indexes, provide tools to tune the selection of materialized views for a workload, and also tools that can recommend both indexes and materialized views [3]. It is worth noting that these techniques (indexes and materialized views) are general techniques that can (and should) be used with the data warehouse striping approach proposed in this paper.

There is a vast literature on query processing and load balancing in parallel database systems [e.g. 1, 14] and distributed databases [e.g. 17]. Many DBMS vendors claim to support parallel data warehousing to various degrees, e.g. Oracle8 [16], Red Brick Warehouse [20], IBM DB2 Universal Database [6], and the Advanced Decision Support Option of Informix Dynamic Server [13]. Similarly to our proposal Teradata system's parallel-processing architecture [7] divide a query workload among its processing nodes, which then execute the query in a true parallel and independent way. However, our approach is unique in what concerns the ability of using/sharing heterogeneous nodes and solving the unavailability of part of the nodes through the use of approximate answering techniques. Recently, there has been a significant amount of work on approximate query answering [2, 8, 11] where the main focus is to provide fast approximate answers to complex queries that can take minutes, or even hours to execute.

The technique presented in this paper - data warehouse striping - provides a flexible approach for distribution, inspired in both distributed data warehouse architecture and classical round-robin partitioning techniques. The data is partitioned in such a way that the load is uniformly distributed to all the available computers and, at the same time, the communication requirements between computers is kept to a minimum during the query computation phase.

This paper marries the concepts of distributed processing and approximate query answering to provide a fast and reliable relational data warehouse implemented with the existing computers of an organization.

3. The DWS-AQA System

The proposed technique uses the basic star schema approach to represent multidimensional data, distributing it over a set of computers that are available in the organization. This section discusses the major issues related to this topic. First, we describe the approaches used in DWS-AQA for setting up the environment and the minimal requirements that a computer must meet to be usable in DWS-AQA. Next, we discuss data loading, query distribution and result merging phases. These are very important aspects of DWS-AQA, as they support the distributed processing that lies in the kernel of the system, resulting in a very good speedup (typically DWS-AQA achieves a linear speedup of N, the number of computers in the system). The policy to manage the list of computers catalogued in DWS-AQA and to manage their inaccessibility or unavailability is also discussed. Furthermore, we show how DWS-AQA computes results to deliver fast early estimations of the final result using the partial results as they arrive from the computing nodes on the network. Additionally, to present the aggregation results we propose an exploration interface that permits users to observe the progress of their aggregation queries. Statistical confidence intervals are also shown helping the user assess the proximity of estimated result to the final result. A periodic data load strategy is proposed, providing *24x7* availability which is an important requirement in some applications areas. Finally, we point out some of the limitations of the proposed technique.

3.1. Setting up the environment

The data warehouse administrator is responsible for creating the setup in all computers that compose the DWS-AQA environment. First, s/he must catalogue the computers that will be used in DWS-AQA, inserting their address in a hot list. Second, s/he is responsible to create the same star schema in all DWS-AQA computers.

The hot list contains relevant information about the DWS-AQA environment. Basically, each computer must fulfill two major conditions in order to be used in the DWS-AQA system:

- Memory, processor, and disk should have enough capacity to support a database engine. Modern computers can easily meet this condition.
- The normal computer utilization profile should not use all the resources (memory and processor) during all the time. It is worth noting that typical users normally use only a relatively small fraction of computer resources. Furthermore, most of the time the computers are simply not being used, either because the users are not connected or because the computer is idle waiting for user keystrokes.

One important aspect is that the use of the available processing capacity should not slow down the normal activity of the computer user. In principle, this can be achieved by a correct administration of the priorities given to the database background processes.

Another important aspect is that even when the computer user agrees to share the computer resources with DWS-AQA, there are still no guarantees that the computer will be available when a query is issued. There are many reasons for the momentary unavailability of a computer: it may be disconnected, have a failure, be temporarily too busy to provide a quick answer or network problems occur. The approximate query answering technique proposed in this paper solves these problems.

3.2. Data Loading Phase

In this section we show how DWS-AQA approach distributes the warehouse data over the catalogued computers. The data distribution used here is basically the same proposed originally in [5] and is summarized here to make this paper self-contained. The data is disseminated over the available computers according to the following guidelines:

- Dimension tables are replicated in each machine (i.e., each dimension has exactly the same data in all the computers).
- The fact data is distributed to the fact tables of each computer using a strict row-by-row round-robin partitioning approach (see also Figure 1). Each computer has *1/N* of the total amount of fact rows in the star schema, with *N* being the number of computers.

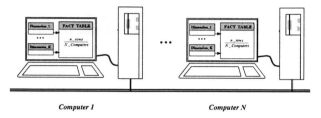

Figure 1. Data Warehouse Striping

This data partitioning for star schemas balances the workload by all computers supporting parallel query processing as well as load balancing for disks and processors. The replication of dimension tables doesn't represent a serious overhead because usually the dimensions only take less than 5% of the total required storage [18]. With this approach typical OLAP queries are executed in parallel by all the computers that constitute the DWS-AQA system.

An important aspect of the DWS technique is that it ensures a uniform distribution of fact data over all computers as this distribution is in fact a random sample method called systematic sampling [10]. The systematic sampling method has as sample basis one file or the elements list of the population, satisfying the hypothesis $M=N.n$, where M is the population size and N is a number that belongs to the natural number set (in our case represents the number of computers used by DWS-AQA system) and n is the sample size.

The procedure to apply the systematic sample method consists in choosing randomly one number k in the interval $[1,N]$, which serves as seed and the first element of the sample. The systematic sample is composed by the elements with the following numbers k, $k+N$, $k+2N$, ..., $k+(n-1)N$. If we have a population X_1, X_2, ..., X_M and if we want to choose a systematic sample of this population ($M=N.n$), we can write

X_1	X_{1+N}	X_{1+2N}	...	$X_{1+(n-1)N}$
X_2	X_{2+N}	X_{2+2N}	...	$X_{2+(n-1)N}$
...	...	...	...	...
X_N	X_{N+N}	X_{N+2N}	...	$X_{N+(n-1)N}$

Each line is a systematic sample draw with n elements, selected from every N^{th} element. In our case, each of these lines represents the fact rows in each one of the N computers of the DWS-AQA system. This means the DWS technique uses a probabilistic sample method that is not biased due to its theoretical characteristics based on probabilistic theory. Another advantage is the possibility to compute the degree of uncertainty, i.e. the error of the estimate, in the form of confidence intervals. This is only due to the fact we have uniform random samples.

In [4] we have used real data from Dow-Jones stock index to show the round-robin data partitioning technique of DWS is uniform, i.e., the data is uniformly distributed over the computers. In the next section, we will see the query modifications required to distribute the queries over all the computers.

3.3. Query Distribution

DWS-AQA is a three-tier-architecture consisting of (1) Clients, (2) Query distribution and processing layer and (3) the various computers that represent the database nodes. The three-tier architecture is shown in Figure 2. Clients issue queries to the DWS-AQA system in SQL. The query distribution and processing layer is the heart of DWS-AQA system that provides a transparent interface to the data warehouse computing nodes. It is responsible for the following processes: query rewriting, query distribution and merging of partial results. The third layer consists of the set of computers that run the database independently of each other. In a DWS-AQA system the database nodes can also acts as clients, simultaneously.

Queries are distributed through all the computers that constitute the DWS-AQA system and their parallel execution by the available computers maintains the best load balance because the number of fact rows stored in each computer is about the same.

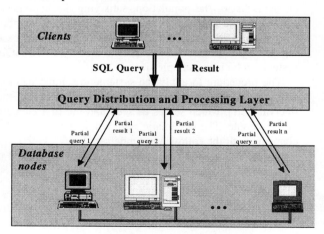

Figure 2. DWS-AQA Architecture

Most of the queries over a star schema can be transformed into N independent partial queries due to their nature (and because the fact rows are partitioned in a disjoint way: i.e., the rows stored in a computer are not replicated in the other computers). In a star schema, typical OLAP queries join and aggregate a large number of rows in the fact table and return few groups as final result. These queries use aggregation functions sum, count, average, standard deviation, and variance as operators. These are the functions that we study in our experiments.

3.4. Result merging of aggregation functions

In DWS-AQA system a query q is converted into a set of partial queries that compute partial results. These partial results are obtained independently in the different computers and sent to a coordinator computer where they are used for result merging. The result merging phase collects the partial results and computes running and final results for the user. The running results are estimations of the final result that are computed as soon as partial results arrive from each computer catalogued in DWS-AQA. These running results provide very accurate estimations even when some computers are temporarily busy or inaccessible. This section describes the merging strategy and the approach used to compute current estimations.

- **Computing SUM and COUNT functions**

If the original query contains the sum or count aggregation functions, then it is sent to all computers without modification (i.e. partial queries are exactly the same as the original query).

Now, we will see how DWS-AQA computes the approximate aggregation values when one or more computers cannot contribute to the final result. Consider the number of computers used in DWS-AQA to be $N = Nu + Na$, where Nu is the number of computers that are unavailable and Na is the number of computers that are available, contributing to compute the estimated aggregation value. The running results for the SUM and COUNT aggregation functions are basically computed as:

$$SUM_{estimated} = SUM_a + N_u \frac{SUM_a}{N_a} = SUM_a \frac{N}{N_a}$$

$$COUNT_{estimated} = COUNT_a \frac{N}{N_a}$$

where N is the number of computers used in the DWS-AQA system, SUM_a and $COUNT_a$ are the results of SUM and COUNT computed from the available computers. The attributes of the functions are not shown for simplicity. These formulas will be used in the experiments to compute the estimated value of final result.

- **Computing AVERAGE function**

Additionally, if the original query contains the aggregation function AVG, it must be modified before being sent. The modification are illustrated in this simple example:

```
select AVG(atr) ➔ select SUM(atr), COUNT(atr)
from table        from table
```

If the aggregation function to compute is average and one or more computers are unavailable the running average is simply given by

$$AVG_{estimated} = \frac{SUM_a + N_u \dfrac{SUM_a}{N_a}}{COUNT_a + N_u \dfrac{COUNT_a}{N_a}} = \frac{SUM_a}{COUNT_a}$$

where SUM_a and $COUNT_a$ represents the partial sum and count from the available computers. Intuitively, the overall estimated average is the average taken from the available nodes.

- **Computing VARIANCE and STDDEV functions**

In order to compute the variance, the original query is transformed into a sum, count and average that is sent to each database node.

As before, the queries containing STDDEV and VARIANCE aggregation functions have to be rewriting following the rules illustrated in this example:

```
select stddev(atr) ➔ select count(atr),var(atr),avg(atr)
from table              from table
select var(atr) ➔ select count(atr),var(atr),avg(atr)
from table            from table
```

The running variance and standard deviation functions are simply evaluated from the partial results of the computers that respond or

$$VARIANCE_{estimated} = VAR_a$$
$$STDDEV_{estimated} = STDDEV_a$$

The previous formulas reveal us the modifications suffered by the original query before it is sent to all computers. While queries containing the aggregation functions SUM and COUNT, didn't require any modification the others functions (AVG, STDDEV and VARIANCE) need rewriting. The query distribution and processing layer is responsible for the transformation of the original queries and the merging of all the partial results, according to the operation, to obtain the final result.

- **GROUP BY and HAVING clauses**

The final result of queries containing GROUP BY and HAVING clauses is computed from the partial results by applying a query similar to the original to the partial results. The HAVING clause can be used to specify a further restriction over the groups. This clause only exists if we have the GROUP BY clause. In that case the HAVING clause is removed from the original query and is only applied after regrouping the partial results from all DWS-AQA nodes.

- **ORDER BY clause**

The final result of queries containing ORDER BY clause is computed from the partial results by applying a query similar to the original to the partial results. The ORDER BY clause, when it exists in the original query can also be sent to the DWS-AQA nodes. This means that each computer orders its partial set and the merging phase runs a faster algorithm to find the overall order from the partially ordered sets. This option means that each computer has more processing time but the merging phase has less work. In another way, sending the original query without ORDER BY clause meaning the result is only ordered in the merging phase. This has the disadvantage of more processing at final (merging phase). In both cases the results must be ordered when we merge the partial results.

3.5. Management of computer accessibility in DWS-AQA

DWS-AQA systems have a special computer, the controller, which has special requirements. The controller computer is used for specific tasks as to coordinate the operations in this environment but also acts as one of the nodes of the system. We describe how the controller manages a dynamic list of catalogued computers that can enter or leave the system as time evolves and how it manages the accessibility and availability of the DWS-AQA computers. The major tasks of the controller are described next.

- **Management of the list of computers catalogued in DWS-AQA**

The controller computer manages the list of computers catalogued in a DWS-AQA system. It is responsible to evaluate the accessibility of each computer during the query distribution and the loading phase and to manage these phases (it verifies if a computer is accessible or not). The inaccessibility circumstances are managed differently depending if it is a query distribution or loading phase. If a computer is not accessible during query distribution, the controller simply doesn't send the query to it. If this inaccessibility is verified during the loading phase, the controller is responsible to continue trying to load the data. The controller computer keeps track of the computers that are updated and where updates are not possible at this moment.

- **Management of the inaccessibility and unavailability of DWS-AQA computers**

The controller is responsible to check the accessibility of DWS-AQA computers before sending the queries and the hot list is updated accordingly. After that, the query is only sent to those computers that are accessible and the controller waits for the partial results. In this way, when partial results are presented, the estimations (running results) are computed. When new partial results are obtained these estimations are updated, providing increasingly more accurate results. At each point, the number of computers that have already contributed to the estimations is always pointed out (as will be described in the next section). For the "lazy" computers, we propose a timeout mechanism. This timeout can be set with a waiting time double to the last query response time. The user can always stop the processing or wait for the new partial results from the computers that didn't answer yet. If the user requests to stop the progress of execution, the controller sends a message to lazy computers to stop.

3.6. Exploration interface

In a DWS-AQA environment we expect the computers to answer the queries at different speeds. It is therefore necessary to offer an exploration interface, which shows current estimations continuously as the overall result is being computed. These estimations are more accurate each time a new computer contributes with new partial results. This exploration interface (see Figure 3) shows at least the query groups, the different estimations for each aggregation function and the respective confidence interval with a given probability, together with the indication of the fraction of computers which contributed and the corresponding degree of completeness of the query.

Such interface has some similarities with the one proposed in [12], which also provided continuous feedback to the user as the result is being computed. However, while their interface is continuously estimating the results as rows are fetched from one single source, DWS-AQA uses the interface to return early answers from the computers that have completed the processing while lazy ones are still working on the query. Furthermore, the user does not need to wait for the lazy computers, as the system typically returns very accurate estimations even when only a small set of computers have already answered (as we will see in section 4.3).

DWS-AQA online aggregation interface provides running aggregation results (**RESULT** column), i.e., an estimate of the final result based on the values returned by the computers that have finished their computation. The **Interval** column gives a probabilistic estimate of the current running aggregate to the final result.

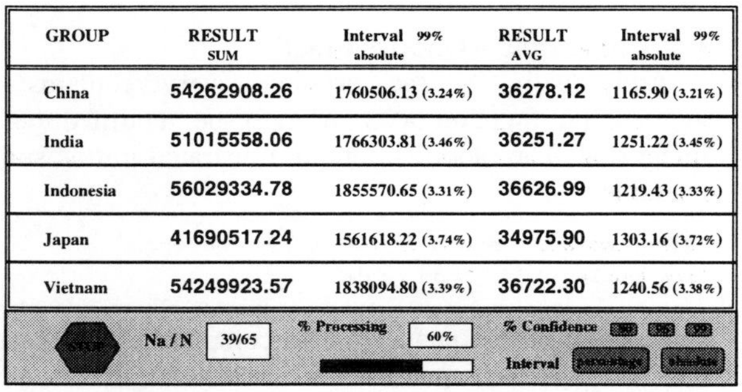

GROUP	RESULT SUM	Interval 99% absolute	RESULT AVG	Interval 99% absolute
China	54262908.26	1760506.13 (3.24%)	36278.12	1165.90 (3.21%)
India	51015558.06	1766303.81 (3.46%)	36251.27	1251.22 (3.45%)
Indonesia	56029334.78	1855570.65 (3.31%)	36626.99	1219.43 (3.33%)
Japan	41690517.24	1561618.22 (3.74%)	34975.90	1303.16 (3.72%)
Vietnam	54249923.57	1838094.80 (3.39%)	36722.30	1240.56 (3.38%)

Na / N 39/65   % Processing 60%   % Confidence   Interval

Figure 3. DWS-AQA Exploration Interface

At each time, the user knows how many computers answer (*Na*) and the total number of DWS-AQA computers (*N*). For example, according to Figure 3, the current average of India's revenue is within ±1251.22 of the exact result with 99% confidence. The interval 36251.27±1251.22 is called a running confidence interval. The size of such confidence intervals can be used as a measure of the precision of the estimator. We also give the possibility to display those intervals as a percentage, which approximately indicates the error that can be contained in the given approximate answer (these are the values shown within parenthesis in **Interval** columns). To compute confidence intervals we use formulas based in the standard central limit theorem that are based on the ones proposed in [4, 11].

3.7. Running the periodic load strategy that allows permanent availability

The controller computer runs a periodic data load strategy that allows permanent availability. Traditionally, data warehouses are refreshed periodically (for example, nightly) by extracting, transforming, cleaning and consolidating data from several data sources. During this period the data warehouse is unavailable for querying. However, there are business intelligence applications in telecommunications, electronic commerce, and other industries, that are characterized by very high data volumes and data flow rates, and that require continuous analysis and mining of the data. In the DWS-AQA environment we could provide a *24x7* availability. We propose a strategy where only one fraction of computers is updated each time and not all computers simultaneously. Two situations can be dealt with. First, if availability is not one of the main concerns in the organization, then all computers are loaded simultaneously (e.g. nightly loading without analysis). Second, if the organization requirements are *24x7* availability, then only 50% of the computers are updated each time, so that the system can still provide approximate answers during the update. This can also be done during the night where only the computers that are being refreshed are offline but this requirement is not essential because DWS-AQA system continues working normally providing approximate query answering.

The controller computer keeps the information if a computer belongs to the fraction that is answering the queries or not (a query can be answered by either the computers already updated or the ones that are waiting to be updated). In those cases where the accuracy of the query result may be very important and approximate aggregates are not the solution, a mechanism that can be employed is the use of mirrored nodes.

3.8. Limitations of DWS-AQA technique and aspects not addressed in the present work

The proposed DWS-AQA approach seems to provide a very promising contribution to the scalability and efficient processing of huge data warehouses. However, the technique has some intrinsic limitations:

- DWS-AQA is specifically targeted to data warehouses organized as star schemas. This means that this technique cannot be arbitrarily adapted to other type of databases, in particular operational databases (OLTP). DWS-AQA is suitable essentially for those data warehouses that are predominantly dominated by one or more very large fact tables;
- Typically, the dimensions of a star schema are small in size when compared with the big fact table. However, there are exceptions to this rule, in which case the space overhead of DWS-AQA becomes more significant;
- Correlated queries and queries having sub-queries which use references from outer query blocks cannot be handled directly by this approach. To overcome this problem one solution is to use query de-correlation, as proposed in literature [19]. Using these techniques it is possible to rewrite the correlated query in such a way that outer references no longer exist. One problem with the rewriting strategy is that query de-correlation is not always possible and in some cases, although possible, it may not be efficient.
- The use of the available computers in a network raises very important security problems that are not addressed in this paper. Although this is not an intrinsic limitation of the DWS-AQA technique, as the use of security techniques to assure confidentiality is an orthogonal aspect of DWS-AQA (i.e., it does not interfere with the basic mechanisms of DWS-AQA), the actual use of DWS-AQA is clearly dependent on the assurance of the adequate level of security.

We are currently working further on these issues. Particularly, the security problem is one of the issues that is intensively being investigated, with particular emphasis on the study of the impact of the different security mechanisms on the DWS-AQA performance.

4. Assessing the speedup and accuracy of DWS-AQA

In this section, we present the results of an experimental evaluation of the DWS-AQA system. Using data from TPC-H benchmark [21], we show the effectiveness of DWS-AQA in providing speedup and highly accurate answers.

The rest of this section is organized as follows. We begin by describing our experimental testbed. We then evaluate the speedup of DWS-AQA and the accuracy of the approximate query answers as more computers contribute to the final result.

4.1. Experimental testbed

We ran the experiments on data from the TPC Benchmark™ H, with Oracle 8 as the back-end DBMS. TPC-H benchmark models a realistic business data warehouse, with sales data from the past seven years. It contains a large central fact table called **Lineitem** and several much smaller dimension tables. We used a scale factor of one for generating our test data. This results in a database size of approximately 1 GB. Table 1 summarizes some of the important features of the tables of TPC-H database used in the experiments.

Table 1. Characteristics of TPC-H tables

Table name	# of columns	# of rows
Customer	8	150,000
Lineitem	16	6,001,215
Nation	4	25
Orders	9	1,500,000
Region	3	5
Supplier	7	10,000

In the experiments we apply our technique to 100 computers, which corresponds to DWS-100. The use of N computers was simulated by dividing the n_fact_rows (6,001,215) of the fact table, using DWS-AQA technique, into N partial fact tables (LINEITEM_1,..., LINEITEM_N). Each computer has n_fact_rows/N rows and the dimensions are replicated in each computer. For example, DWS-100 simulates the use of 100 computers (N=100) having 100 partial fact tables (LINEITEM_1,..., LINEITEM_100) with each one having 60,012±1 fact rows, while the dimensions are equivalent to those of a centralized data warehouse system. This simplification doesn't influence the results presented.

We are interested in typical queries that perform multiple aggregations and joins, processing a large number of rows of the fact table and returning a very small number of rows as result. We are also interested in analyzing the influence of group-by queries where the groups have different sizes. Therefore, in accordance with these criteria, we have chosen to implement query Q5 of TPC-H benchmark.

4.2. Speedup of DWS-AQA

Although this is not the main point of this paper, it is important to mention that DWS-AQA achieves an optimal speedup. We have made comprehensive experiments using 3, 5 and 10 computers with the same hardware characteristics [5]. Comparing the query execution time for a set of typical queries of a benchmark, we obtain an average speedup of 3, 5.1 and 11 using 3, 5 and 10 computers, respectively. In fact, the speedup is higher than the theoretical value, because the centralized data warehouse that was used as the reference experiment worked near the workstation memory and I/O limits. These results show that this technique can be applied to an arbitrary number of computers improving query execution speedup by almost N, the number of computers used. This is due to the fact that when we distribute the data we are working on more manageable data sets that could be more treatable in computers usually limited by memory space.

4.3. Accuracy of DWS-AQA

In this section, we consider a set of aggregate functions that are computed on the result of a complex select-join query. The query used is based on query Q5 of TPC-H benchmark that lists the revenue volume done through local suppliers. We modify it to return also the average, standard deviation and count of revenue. The query lists for each Nation in a Region the revenue volume (plus average, standard deviation and count) that resulted from Lineitem transactions in which the Customer ordering parts and the Supplier filling them were both within that Nation. The query considers only Parts ordered in a given year, displaying the Nations, and revenue volume, average, standard deviation and count ordered by nation name. The SQL statement for the query is:

```
select
    n_name,
    sum(l_extendedprice * (1 - l_discount))
as sum_revenue
    avg(l_extendedprice * (1 - l_discount))
as avg_revenue
    stddev(l_extendedprice * (1 -
l_discount)) as stddev_revenue
    count(*) as count
```

```
from
    customer, orders, lineitem, supplier,
    nation, region
where
    c_custkey = o_custkey
    and l_orderkey = o_orderkey
    and l_suppkey = s_suppkey
    and c_nationkey = s_nationkey
    and s_nationkey = n_nationkey
    and n_regionkey = r_regionkey
    and r_name = 'ASIA' and o_orderdate >=
'1994-01-01'
    and o_orderdate < ADD_MONTHS('1994-01-
01',12)
group by
    n_name
order by
    n_name;
```

This query is a 5-table join of large and small tables, where the data aggregated is reduced down to 1/5 of the Customers and Suppliers (representing one Region out of five) and 1/7 of the Lineitems (one year out of seven). The largest detail table has no direct selection applied to it. Five rows are returned constituting the revenue for each nation in the selected region:

```
N_NAME   SUM_REVENUE   AVG_REVENUE   STDDEV_REVENUE   COUNT
-------------------------------------------------------------
CHINA     53724494.26   36005.2483    21539.2708       1502
INDIA     52035512.00   36138.2886    22249.3627       1438
INDONESIA 55502041.17   36643.7337    22213.3269       1509
JAPAN     45410175.70   35227.3708    22113.7948       1288
VIETNAM   55295087.00   36755.0601    22519.8905       1506
```

In our experiments we evaluated the error obtained with this query for the SUM, AVG, STDDEV, and COUNT aggregation functions, when the number of computers that contribute to the final result is variable.

- **Error in estimated values**

When a query is sent to DWS-AQA system some of the computers could be too busy to answer or some problems in network arise. To simulate these situations we made experiments where the percentage of computers that are on-line varies from 10 to 90 percent and compute the relative error of the running results.

At each point the relative error of the running result is computed as:

$$error_{rel} = \frac{|exact\_value - estimated\_value|}{|exact\_value|} \times 100$$

The relative error obtained for Q5 query of TPC-H benchmark using DWS-100 and considering only the SUM aggregation function is shown in Figure 6 for each group (Nation). The x-axis represents the percentage of computers that are contributing to the final result.

In these experiments, the error decreases with the increment of the number of computers that are on-line (as expected). However, this error is not very large, as it does not exceed 15% with SUM aggregation function (not shown) and less than 20% with COUNT function.

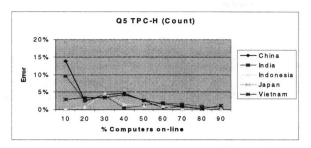

Figure 6.   Revenue Error for SUM and COUNT

These are worst case results because only 10% of the computers have contributed with values. Furthermore, these errors are obtained for the smallest group, Japan, which aggregates only 104 elements. This also explains the oscillations in the error for this group.

Figure 7 shows the revenue error for Q5 query for all groups (Nations) when we are applying AVG function.

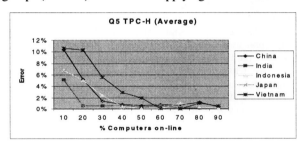

Figure 7.   Revenue Error for AVG and STDDEV

In these cases the error obtained is even small, not exceeding 11%. And if we assume that half of the computers contribute to the result we can see from the figure that the error is always less than 2%.

The experimental results empirically demonstrate that DWS-AQA can give extremely quick answers with high precision for many queries and the user is also informed of errors incurred in the estimations by means of confidence intervals. Similar results were obtained for other TPC-H queries but due to space limitations we only show a synopsis of those results. Figure 8 shows the typical results obtained for queries Q1, Q6 and Q7 of TPC-H.

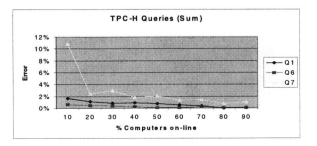

Figure 8.   Error in queries Q1, Q6, Q7 using SUM

The queries Q1 and Q6 present better results due to the large number of tuples in the aggregated groups. The average number of tuples by group in queries Q1 and Q6 is 38,854 and 114,160 respectively, while in query Q7 the group only contains 1512 tuples. Since the groups are randomly distributed over 100 computers, it means that for query Q7, the individual computers only have 15 tuples in average, which results in less accuracy. Consequently, the accuracy of approximate query answers is highly dependent on the number of "samples" consisting of tuples from each group in individual computers.

- **Confidence intervals**

The confidence intervals give valuable feedback on how reliable an answer is. In the results we show four curves: the confidence interval limits (*lower_limit* and *upper_limit* curves), the estimated value of the aggregation function (*estimated_FUNCTION* curve) and also the exact value (*exact_FUNCTION*). The confidence interval indicates that the exact value (*exact_FUNCTION* curve) lies between the values represented by the *lower_limit* and *upper_limit* curves, with probability 95% or 99% (user choice). Figure 9 shows the 99% confidence interval for the China group of query Q5 using the sum aggregation function.

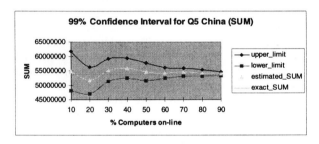

Figure 9. 99% Confidence Interval for query Q5, China group, using SUM

Figure 9 shows that the exact value is always within the limits of the confidence interval. The results also show that the magnitude of the confidence interval decreases, which means better precision, as the number of computers contributing to the running result increases. Figure 10 shows the results for the Japan group using variance aggregation function.

These experiments confirmed the effectiveness of using confidence bounds with the approximate results. The exact values (*exact_FUNCTION* curve) of the aggregation functions are always within the limits defined by the confidence interval and are very close to the estimated value (*estimated_FUNCTION* curve). Even when a large fraction of the computers didn't contribute to the results we obtain accurate approximate query answers.

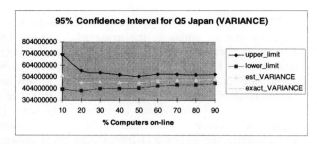

Figure 10. 95% Confidence Interval for query Q5, Japan group, using VARIANCE

In summary, using the techniques proposed in this paper, one can design a query answering system within the framework of the DWS-AQA system which not only produces accurate approximate query answers for complex join aggregates but also provides good error bounds using statistical techniques.

5. Conclusions

In this paper we proposed DWS-AQA as a technique to implement a large data warehouses using the available computers in the organizations. This approach, called data warehouse striping with approximate query answering (DWS-AQA), is based on the combination of two simple ideas: 1) uniform data striping to partition the data warehouse facts over an arbitrary number of computers, in such a way that queries can be executed in a true parallel fashion (a query is actually split into many partial queries), and 2) an approximate query answering strategy to deal with the momentary unavailability of one or more computers in the network. As the data warehouse shares computers that are also being used for other purposes, most of the times only a fraction of the computers will be able to execute the partial queries in time. However, as we show in the paper, the approximated answers estimated from partial results have a very small error for most of the plausible scenarios. Given the specific nature of the decision support activities, a small error is normally acceptable. Moreover, as the data warehouse facts are partitioned in a strict uniform way, it is possible to calculate tight confidence intervals for the approximated answers, providing the user with a measure of the accuracy of the query results. We also proposed an exploration interface to produce statistical confidence intervals for the estimated results, helping the user assessing the accuracy of the estimations. A periodic data load strategy that allows permanent data warehouse availability is also discussed. Experimental results show that the system returns fast and very accurate query results, while taking full advantage of available and inexpensive processing power in enterprise networked computers.

References

[1] Mahdi Abdelguerfi and Kam-Fai Wong. Parallel Database Techniques. IEEE Computer Society Press, 1998.

[2] S. Acharaya, P. Gibbons, V. Poosala, "Congressional Samples for Approximate Answering of Group-By Queries", ACM SIGMOD Int. Conf on Management of Data, May 2000, pp.487-498.

[3] S. Agrawal, S. Chaudhuri, V. Narasayya, "Automated Selection of Materialized Views and Indexes for SQL Databases", Proc. of the 26th International Conference on Very Large Databases, Cairo, Egypt, 2000, pp.496-505.

[4] J. Bernardino, P. Furtado, H. Madeira, "Approximate Query Answering Using Data Warehouse Striping", Journal of Intelligent Information Systems, Kluwer Academic Publishers, accepted to publication.

[5] J. Bernardino and H. Madeira, "Experimental Evaluation of a New Distributed Partitioning Technique for Data Warehouses", Proc. Int. Database Engineering & Applications Symposium, IDEAS'01, pp.312-321.

[6] S. Brobst, B. Vecchione, "Starburst Grows Bright, DB2 UDB", Database Programming & Design, 1998.

[7] J. Catozzi, S. Rabinovici, "Operating Systems Extensions for the Teradata Parallel VLDB", Proc. of the 27th Int. Conf. on Very Large Databases, Roma, Italy, 2001, pp.676-679.

[8] S. Chaudhuri, G. Das, V. Narasayya, "A Robust, Optimization-Based Approach for Approximate Answering of Aggregate Queries", ACM SIGMOD Int. Conference on Management of Data, May 2001, pp.295-306.

[9] S. Chaudhuri and V. Narasayya, "An Efficient, Cost-Driven Index Selection Tool for Microsoft SQL Server", Proc. of the 23rd VLDB Conference, Greece, 1997, pp.146-155.

[10] William G. Cochran. Sampling Techniques. Third edition, John Wiley & Sons, New York, 1977.

[11] P. J. Haas, "Large-sample and deterministic confidence intervals for online aggregation", Proc. Int. Conf. on Scientific and Statistical Database Management, 1997, pp.51-62.

[12] J. M. Hellerstein, P. J. Haas, and H.J. Wang, "Online aggregation", ACM SIGMOD Int. Conference on Management of Data, pp.171-182, May 1997.

[13] Informix Corp., "Informix Decision Support Indexing for the Enterprise Data Warehouses", White Paper, 1998.

[14] H. Lu, B. Ooi, K. Tan. Query Processing in Parallel Relational Database Systems. IEEE Computer Society, 1994.

[15] P. E. O'Neil and D. Quass, "Improved Query Performance with Variant Indexes", Proc. of ACM SIGMOD Int. Conference on Management of Data, 1997, pp.38-49.

[16] Oracle Corporation, "Star queries in Oracle 8", White paper, 1997.

[17] M. Ozsu, P. Valduriez. Principles of Distributed Database Systems. Second edition, Prentice-Hall, New Jersey, 1999.

[18] T. Pederson, C. Jensen, "Multidimensional Database Technology", IEEE Computer, December 2001, pp.40-46.

[19] J. Rao, K. A. Ross, "Reusing Invariants: A New Strategy for Correlated Queries", Proc. of ACM SIGMOD Int. Conference on Management of Data, 1998, pp.37 – 48.

[20] Red Brick Systems, Inc. "Star Schema Processing for Complex Queries", White Paper, 1998.

[21] TPC Benchmark H, Transaction Processing Council, June 1999. Available at http://www.tpc.org/.

Fast Filter-and-Refine Algorithms for Subsequence Selection

Beng Chin Ooi[1]   Hwee Hwa Pang[2]   Hao Wang[1]   Limsoon Wong[2]   Cui Yu [1]

[1]Department Computer Science
National University of Singapore
3 Science Dr 2, Singapore 117543
{ooibc,wanghao,yucui}@comp.nus.edu.sg

[2]Lab for Information Technology
21, Heng Mui Keng Terrace
Singapore 119613
{hhpang,limsoon}@lit.org.sg

Abstract

Large sequence databases, such as protein, DNA and gene sequences in biology, are becoming increasingly common. An important operation on a sequence database is approximate subsequence matching, where all subsequences that are within some distance from a given query string are retrieved. This paper proposes a filter-and-refine algorithm that enables efficient approximate subsequence matching in large DNA sequence databases. It employs a bitmap indexing structure to condense and encode each data sequence into a shorter index sequence. During query processing, the bitmap index is used to filter out most of the irrelevant subsequences, and false positives are removed in the final refinement step. Analytical and experimental studies show that the proposed strategy is capable of reducing response time substantially while incurring only a small space overhead.

1. Introduction

Large sequence databases, such as protein, DNA and gene sequences in biology, are becoming increasingly common. In such applications, users need to elicit from a sequence database those subsequences that match certain query strings. For instance, a biologist may want to retrieve all known gene sequences that contain certain segments of nucleotides.

While subsequence matching capability may be programmed into individual applications, it would be desirable for the DBMS to offer this capability so as to improve programmers' productivity and system efficiency.

While modern database systems provide facilities to store data sequences, there is a paucity of support for sequence manipulation. For example, many systems have a *text* data type for variable-length strings and support some form of keyword indexing such as signature files. In conventional database systems, there are substring matching operators such as LIKE. Alternatively, data sequences can be stored in external files where system utilities like *grep* and *fgrep* can operate on them. However, these approaches allow only exact keyword or substring matching, but not the sophisticated approximate subsequence matching required by the applications described above.

Approximate subsequence matching can be defined as an operation that takes as input an edit distance [23] $EditDist$ and a query string $*Q_1 * Q_2 * .. * Q_m*$, where $*$ is a variable length don't care (VLDC) segment, and each Q_i is a segment of at least one data element and possibly some fixed length don't care characters. As output, the operation returns all subsequences $*D_1 * D_2 * .. * D_m*$ in the database that each can be transformed into the query string by replacing at most $EditDist$ characters, after an optimal substitution for the VLDCs. With this definition, substring matching can be viewed as a special case of subsequence matching where $m = 1$ [17].

In this paper, we propose a two-step filter-and-refine query processing strategy for subsequence matching, in the context of DNA sequences in particular. We introduce *BIS*, a bitmap indexing scheme for adding approximate subsequence matching capability to database systems. The most attractive feature of the scheme is that it can speed up queries very significantly while incurring only the space overhead of a small fraction of the data size. The data structure, *BIS*, uses a hash function to encode and reduce each data sequence in a collection to a shorter index sequence. At runtime, the index sequences are used to efficiently filter out most of the subsequences that do not match a submitted query string. A very desirable characteristic of *BIS* is that the false drop rate (the number of subsequences that filter through even though they do not match the query) declines exponentially as the query length increases. Two notable objectives of *BIS* are (1) reducing the space complexity of the index, and (2) improving the performance of index processing. For the purpose of performance tuning and evaluation, a cost model of the scheme that estimates the achievable response time savings is also presented. We have implemented the processing strategy as part of a proteomic application system, and also as a stand alone system to study its efficacy.

The remainder of the paper is organized as follows. Section 2 describes a motivating example. Section 3 introduces the basic algorithm and Section 4 presents its extended form. Section 5 shows the derivation of a cost model for *BIS*, which is verified through the experiments reported in Section 6. The section also analyzes the behavior of *BIS* and studies its efficiency. A discussion of related work appears in the Section 7. Finally, Section 8 concludes the paper.

2. A Motivating Genetic Sequence Application

In this section, we shall describe an application in proteomics. The primary goal in proteomics is to discover what are the functions of proteins. An important idea in this process is the use of protein "motif". A protein motif is in essence a signature for an associated protein function. If a particular motif is detected in a protein, then the protein has some likelihood of possessing the function associated with that motif. In order to properly exploit protein motifs, three items are necessary: (a) a database of known protein motifs, (b) a tool to automatically discover protein motifs, and (c) a tool to scan protein databases for motifs obtained from (a) and (b). One of the most common type of queries asked by molecular biologists has the form "Which sequences in a protein database has the function (i.e., motif) that I am interested in?", and needs to be answered in real time.

To further motivate our work, consider the polyprotein of the denguevirus [14] which is known to have helicase activity [8]. However, the Swiss Prositescan [2, 3], the most widely used software for motif checking, reports no helicase activity for this protein in question. There are only two possible explanations. The first possibility is that the PROSITE motif collection used by Prositescan does not contain helicase motifs. The other possibility is that PROSITE does contain helicase motifs, but they are derived from organisms that are too distantly related to denguevirus.

Actually, PROSITE contains the helicase motif [GSAH].[LIVMF]{3}DE[ALIV]H[NECR]. This motif is to be read as follows: The first residue is any one of G, S, A, H; the second residue is a "don't care", i.e., a FLDC of length 1; the next three residues are any of L, I, V, M, F; the next residue must be D; the one after that must be E; the next residue is any of A, L, I, V; this is then followed by a H, and the final residue is any of N, E, C, R. The actual helicase site in denguevirus polyproteins is NLIIMDEAHF, which disagrees with that of PROSITE at the two flanking residues. This explains the failure of Prositescan to detect the helicase site in denguevirus polyproteins.

The proposed algorithm underlying a PROSITE application must support matching modulo Fixed Length Don't Care (FLDC), character classes, and edit distance, and must be able to rapidly report that denguevirus polyproteins have helicase sites with 2 mutations on the flanking residues of the PROSITE helicase motif.

Besides the PROSITE application, we have also developed several other proteomics applications, including: 1) *ScanSeq* that searches segments of sequences satisfying a given motif; 2) *Signature* that discovers conserved motifs in amino acid sequences; 3) *Duplicate* that looks for repeats in amino acid sequences; 4) *DNADuplicate* that finds tandem and inverted repeats in DNA sequences.

These applications are currently being used by biologists in their work. Taking advantage of the filter-and-refine utility that is introduced in this paper, the developers were able to quickly complete the applications to the users' requirements.

3. The Basic Algorithm

When the database is populated, each sequence is encoded into a smaller-size bitmap index. During query processing, this bitmap index is used at the filtering step to efficiently eliminate most of the subsequences that do not match a given query string. At the refinement step, each matching sequence is further checked using real data sequence to remove false positives. Figure 1 illustrates the process. The idea behind *BIS* is similar to that of signature file schemes, where compact signatures are used to filter out data objects that are irrelevant to a query. Unlike work in that area which focused on sophisticated signature extraction and storage structures for the signature files [28], however, *BIS* has a simple and efficient index generation and storage mechanism. Rather, our contribution is a scheme for using a single, compact bitmap index to quickly find subsequences that match arbitrary-length patterns in an ad-hoc querying environment.

In constructing the index, a data element is mapped via a hash function into an index element that is smaller in size. In practice, a data element could be a character, a short integer, a long integer, a float, or a double float field, while an index element could range from one bit to a few bytes. Figure 1 shows a hash function f that maps a multi-bit data element into a single index bit. By applying the same hash function to every data element in a sequence and to each sequence in the database, we produce a smaller bitmap index that can be retrieved and matched quickly during query retrieval.

When a query string is presented, the filtering step uses *BIS* to evaluate the index representation of each sequence in turn to isolate its subsequences that might satisfy the query string. Only the fraction of subsequences that "drops" through the index filter will have their data representation

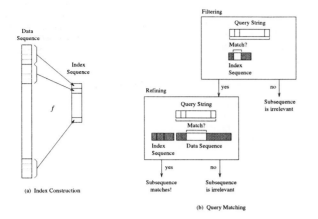

(a) Index Construction

(b) Query Matching

Figure 1. Filtering and Refining

Notation	Meaning	Default
N	Index element	
N_{bits}	Number of bits in an index element	1
D	Data element	
D_{bits}	Number of bits in a data element	8
$NumSeq$	Number of data sequences	1
$SeqLen$	Avg. number of elements per data sequence	512 million
$QLen$	Number of query elements	16

Table 1. Algorithm Parameters

checked for an actual match at the refinement step; the remaining subsequences can be disqualified immediately. By selecting the hash function judiciously, most of the irrelevant subsequences can be eliminated through the filtering step. Since the bitmap index is more compact than the database, the savings from *sequential read* of fewer data subsequences and comparing fewer data subsequences is expected to outweigh the overhead of searching the index. The notations, which will be explained as they are used, are summarized in Table 1.

3.1. BIS Index Construction

The first step in index construction is to define a hash function

$$f : D \to N$$

to map each element d in the database to an index element n. For *BIS* to be effective, N_{bits}, the number of bits that make up an index element, has to be smaller than D_{bits}, the number of bits in a data element. This means that several data

values will map to the same index value, hence several different data subsequences could be represented by the same index subsequence. Consequently, false drops may occur. If the false drop rate is too high, the overhead of examining the subsequences at the refinement step makes the whole processing strategy ineffective.

To ensure the filtering power of *BIS*, we would like the maximum number of data subsequences that can be represented by any index subsequence to be as small as possible. This happens when every index value is equally likely to occur, i.e., when N follows a uniform distribution. To derive such a hash function, we first find the frequency distribution of D by data sampling, then partition D into intervals with equal frequency, and finally assign each interval to an index value. The philosophy is somewhat similar to the bit strings in high-dimensional database indexing in [25].

To illustrate, suppose D is an unsigned char (1 byte) that is uniformly distributed between 0 and 255, and N is a single bit. If the hash function f maps data values from 0 to 171 to 0, and data values in [172, 255] to 1, the index value 0 will be 3 times as likely to occur as 1. In the worst case, this allows $\frac{3}{4} \times \frac{3}{4} = \frac{9}{16}$ of the subsequences to drop through the index filter for a 2-character query string. In contrast, if the hash function splits D into equal halves, only $\frac{1}{2} \times \frac{1}{2} = \frac{1}{4}$ of the subsequences are expected to filter through against any 2-character query string.

While the above illustration shows that N should be uniformly distributed if possible, D is *not* required to be uniformly distributed as well. Indeed, such a requirement would prove unrealistic as there are often some correlation among the elements in real-life data sequences. By analyzing the distribution of the data elements, whatever that may be, it is always possible to define a hash function f that produces a uniform index distribution during index construction. The challenge really is to make *BIS* robust against updates that shift the data distribution, and consequently the index distribution, at runtime. Indeed, our performance study indicates that the proposed strategy does not deteriorate appreciably unless N becomes highly skewed.

Having determined a hash function f, we then apply it to the elements of every sequence in the database to produce a bitmap index. The index preserves the relative position of the data elements. This property is pivotal in the runtime performance of *BIS*, as locating the data representation of those subsequences that filter through becomes straightforward. There is no need for any pointers between the index and data files, nor any computation overhead. The positional relationship also simplifies updates greatly.

Since the index construction process involves only a quick scan through the database, and possibly an earlier scan to determine the distribution of D, the process has a time complexity of O(DBSize) and requires only two I/O buffers, one for the database and one for the index. In terms of storage overhead, the index is $\frac{N_{bits}}{D_{bits}}$ the size of the database. Depending on whether D is a character, a short integer, an integer, a float or a double float, D could be 8, 16, 32, or 64 bits long. As for N, we restrict it to be a divisor or a multiple of a byte in our implementation to avoid grappling with index elements that straddle two bytes. We will show in the next section that this does not diminish the usefulness of *BIS* in practice.

Example 1. Suppose D is an unsigned character that is uniformly distributed in [0, 255], and N is 1 bit in size. We choose a hash function that maps [0, 127] to 0, and [128, 255] to 1; this hash function can be implemented very efficiently by a single comparison operation, or by extracting the leftmost bit in the binary representation of D. Given a data sequence [75 3 95 189 165 106 229 239 8 222 122 236 200 146 75 33 ...], the hash function would produce the index sequence [0 0 0 1 1 0 1 1 0 1 0 1 1 1 0 0 ...].

3.2. Filtering Step

Having introduced the index construction process, we shall explain how the filtering step uses the *BIS* index to speed up the search for subsequences that satisfy a submitted query string. We shall begin with the scenario where N is one or more bytes in size; sub-byte index elements necessitate bit manipulations that will be described shortly.

Given a query string of $QLen$ data elements, the filtering algorithm first applies the hash function f to derive the corresponding bitmap index representation. This bitmap representation of the query is then matched against each sequence in the index in turn. The filtering algorithm is designed to iterate over every sequence in the collection. In each iteration, the algorithm maintains *pos*, the position in the current sequence, and a state array $state[1..q]$. If and only if $state[i]$ = TRUE, then the last i index elements in the sequence match the first i index elements in the query string. The algorithm marches through each element in the index in turn; there is no backtracking. After reading a new index element n from the sequence, *pos* is advanced and the state array is updated as follows:

$$state[i] := \begin{cases} (query[1] = n) & \text{if } i = 1 \\ (query[i] = n) \text{ AND } state[i-1] & \text{if } i > 1 \end{cases} \quad (1)$$

where $query[i]$ is the ith index element of the query string. Thus, whenever $state[QLen]$ = TRUE, the subsequence of length $QLen$ ending at *pos* "drops" through the index filter and its data representation is tested for a match. The algorithm is given below.

```
Filter-and-Refine Subsequence Selection Algorithm

/* definition */
NumSeq = number of seq. in the database;
```

```
DSeq[i][j] = element at position j of data seq. i;
DIdx[i][j]= element at position j of data index i;
SeqLen[i] = number of elements in data seq./index i;
QSeq[i] = element at position i of query seq.;
QIdx[i] = element at position i of query index;
QLen = number of elements in query seq./index;

for i = 1 to NumSeq { /* filtering step */
  for j = 1 to QLen
    s[j] = FALSE;
  for j = 1 to SeqLen[i] {
    for k = QLen downto 2
      s[k] = ((QIdx[k] == DIdx[i][j]) AND s[k-1]);
    s[1] = (QIdx[1] == DIdx[i][j]);
    if (s[QLen] == TRUE)    /* refinement step */
      if (DSeq[i][(j-QLen+1)..j] == QSeq[1..QLen])
        output("Match at pos %d of seq. %d",j,i);
  }
}
```

Let us now focus on the case where N is less than a byte, the smallest unit that is directly addressable. Since we had restricted N_{bits} to be a divisor of a byte, the number of index elements per byte $\frac{BYTE}{N_{bits}}$ is an integer. We note that there are $\frac{BYTE}{N_{bits}}$ possible ways in which a matching index subsequence could be aligned with respect to the byte boundaries. In all but one of the alignments, the leading index elements of the subsequence only partially occupy a byte; the left side of the byte contains index elements belonging to other subsequences that must be masked out. The same is true of the trailing index elements of the subsequence, except that here the irrelevant index elements are located at the right side of the byte. To handle this situation, we need to modify the filtering sequence matching algorithm slightly.

We re-define $query[i]$ to be a byte in which the jth position from the right contains the $(i - j + 1)$th index element of the query string. *pos* is now incremented by $\frac{BYTE}{N_{bits}}$ after each new index byte. Furthermore, the state array has $QLen + \frac{BYTE}{N_{bits}} - 1$ entries, and is updated as follows:

$$state[i] := \begin{cases} (query[i] = Right(n, i)) \\ \quad \text{if } 1 \leq i \leq min(QLen, \frac{BYTE}{N_{bits}}) \\ (query[i] = Left(Right(n, i), QLen + \frac{BYTE}{N_{bits}} - i)) \\ \quad \text{if } QLen < i \leq \frac{BYTE}{N_{bits}} \\ (query[i] = n) \text{ AND } state[i - \frac{BYTE}{N_{bits}}] \\ \quad \text{if } \frac{BYTE}{N_{bits}} < i \leq QLen \\ (query[i] = Left(n, QLen + \frac{BYTE}{N_{bits}} - i)) \text{ AND} \\ \quad state[i - \frac{BYTE}{N_{bits}}] \\ \quad \text{if } max(QLen, \frac{BYTE}{N_{bits}}) < i < QLen + \frac{BYTE}{N_{bits}} \end{cases} \quad (2)$$

where $Left(n, i)$ and $Right(n, i)$ mask out the bits in n except for the i index elements from the left and right, respectively. The two functions are implemented efficiently by pre-computing a bit mask for each state entry. Whenever

246

$state[i]$ = TRUE for some $QLen \leq i < QLen + \frac{BYTE}{N_{bits}}$, and $pos + QLen > i$, the subsequence of length $QLen$ ending at position $(pos + QLen - i)$ drops through the index filter.

While the modified scheme is more complicated, it can deliver significant speed-ups. The reason is that each comparison operation matches $query[i]$ against $\frac{BYTE}{N_{bits}}$ index elements *concurrently* now, rather than only one at a time.

Now we shall prove the correctness of the algorithm.

Theorem 1. The *BIS* algorithm is correct, returning all matching subsequences and no false matches.

Proof: Two cases to consider: *Case 1.* Suppose that a subsequence a satisfies a query string q. This implies that both query strong and subsequence contain the same data representation. Therefore, $a[i] = q[i] \; \forall 1 \leq i \leq QLen$. It follows that $f(a[i]) = f(q[i])$ where f is the hash function, and that a and q have the same index representation too. Consequently, a will pass the filtering step and the subsequent refinement step.

Case 2. Suppose subsequence a does not match q. This implies $a[i] \neq q[i]$ for some $1 \leq i \leq QLen$, but $f(a[i]) = f(q[i])$. Since a drops through the index filter, its data representation will be examined. At this stage, *BIS* will discover that the ith data element is different and reject a.

We therefore conclude that the *BIS* algorithm is correct – all matching subsequences are returned, and there are no false matches. □

4. Extended Subsequence Matching

While the basic algorithm works only with query strings that comprise an arbitrary number of data elements, it can be extended easily to handle more general queries. Here, we extend it to support the following queries:

1. *Fixed length don't cares* (FLDC). Besides data elements, a query string may also include one or more FLDCs that are meant to match any data value. When updating the state array, the index elements that correspond to the FLDCs are simply masked out.

2. *Variable length don't cares* (VLDC). A VLDC separating the data elements in a query is supposed to match any string of contiguous elements in a subsequence. Unlike FLDCs, the introduction of VLDCs allows matching subsequences to be longer than the query string. In our implementation, we first extract from a query string those segments of contiguous data elements and FLDCs that are separated by the VLDCs. Next, we treat each segment as a separate query and find its set of matching subsequences. Finally, we return all combinations of subsequences in which the matching subsequence for segment i precede the matching subsequence for segment $i + 1$.

3. *Edit distance.* Instead of returning only subsequences that match a query string exactly, an application may require all subsequences that contain up to a certain number of mismatches; i.e., all subsequences that are within a certain edit distance $EditDist$ from the query. To accommodate this, we need only re-define the state array so $state[i]$ counts the total number of mismatches between the first i index elements of the query and the last i index elements in the current sequence. Whenever $state[i] \leq EditDist$ for any $i \geq QLen$, the subsequence ending at position $(pos + QLen - i)$ is deemed to have passed the filtering step.

4. *Alternative characters.* A user may need to specify a set of candidate characters for some position in the query string, rather than stating one single character or an FLDC. If all of the candidate characters hash to the same index value, the filtering step proceeds as per the single-character case; only subsequences that filter through need to be matched against the candidate set. If the candidate characters hash to different index values, they are treated as an FLDC in the filtering step, i.e., the index elements corresponding to that position are masked out when updating the state array. Since the presence of alternative characters does not require special handling in the filtering step, we shall not address it further.

5. Cost Model

To study the effectiveness and efficiency of the processing strategy, we develop a cost model. The purpose of the model is three-fold. First, when constructing an index for a sequence database, the model can provide the best setting for N_{bits}, the number of bits needed for each index element. Second, the model can help a database system to decide whether *BIS* will speed up a particular query. Third, the model can estimate the processing time if *BIS* is employed.

For reference purposes, we also present the cost of applying the Baeza-Yates and Gonnet algorithm [1] to the data sequences directly (denoted by BYG; a brief description of BYG algorithm is given in Section 7). Besides the algorithm parameters in Table 1, we shall also make use of the cost parameters in Table 2.

5.1. Cost of BYG

The BYG algorithm essentially marches through each data element in the sequence collection and compares it with the $QLen$ entries in the state array. This incurs the cost of retrieving the data element ($C_{I/O}$[1]), the cost of looping

---

[1]Obviously, we do not issue a disk I/O for each data element. Rather, data are retrieved in large blocks to reduce I/O costs. For this reason, $C_{I/O}$

Notation	Meaning
$C_{I/O}$	Avg. I/O time for fetching a data element in CPU cycles[1]. Default=75
C_{loop}	# of CPU cycles to loop through each state entry. Default=5
C_{state}	# of CPU cycles to compare data element with an entry in the query array and store the result in a state entry. Default=18
C_{string}	# of CPU cycles to match elements of two data sequences. Default=11.
C_{cache}	# of CPU cycles to cache interim results. Default=11
R_{BYG}	Response time of Baeza-Yates & Gonnet algorithm
R_{BIS}	Response time of *BIS* algorithm
$Speedup$	Response time speed-up, $= \frac{R_{BYG}}{R_{BIS}}$

Table 2. Cost Parameters

through the state array ($C_{loop} \times QLen$), and the cost of comparing the data element with $query[i]$, $1 \leq i \leq QLen$; see Formula (1). The expected cost of comparing $query[i]$ is $C_{state}/|D|^{i-1}$ where $|D|$ is the data alphabet size, as this comparison is done only if $state[i-1] = $ TRUE, i.e., all of the previous $i-1$ data elements matched. Since $|D| > 1$, the cost diminishes quickly as i increases. For simplicity, we will include only the first-order term. Therefore, the response time for matching a sequence collection is

$$R_{BYG} = NumSeq \times SeqLen \times \\ (C_{I/O} + C_{loop} \times QLen + C_{state}) \quad (3)$$

This equation suggests that the I/O cost for retrieving and the CPU cost for testing each data element is independent of the number of bytes it contains. While this is not true in practice, in an efficient implementation the costs increase only very marginally as D goes from one to several bytes. We will demonstrate in the next section that dropping D_{bits} is acceptable.

5.2. Cost of *BIS* Processing Strategy

The proposed algorithm consists of two steps: (1) searching the index representation to weed out irrelevant subsequences at the filtering step, and (2) examining the data representation of subsequences at the refinement step. If each index element N occupies one or more bytes, the filtering cost alone will match R_{BYG}. Therefore N has to be smaller than a byte for the index *BIS* to be effective.

The computation of the filtering cost is similar to that of R_{BYG}. There are altogether $NumSeq \times SeqLen \times \frac{N_{bits}}{BYTE}$ bytes in the index. In processing each byte, there is an

is obtained by dividing the time needed to fetch a block, by the number of data elements in the block. The default of 75 CPU cycles is based on a block size of 8 KBytes.

I/O cost ($C_{I/O}$), the cost of looping through the state array ($C_{loop} \times (QLen + \frac{BYTE}{N_{bits}} - 1)$), the cost of matching with $query[i]$, and the cost of recording subsequences that filter through (C_{cache}). According to Formula (2), we have to evaluate $Query[i]$ for at least $1 \leq i \leq \frac{BYTE}{N_{bits}}$. Hence, the filtering cost is

$$R_{filter} = NumSeq \times SeqLen \times \frac{N_{bits}}{BYTE} \times \\ (C_{I/O} + C_{loop} \times (QLen + \frac{BYTE}{N_{bits}} - 1) + \\ C_{state} \frac{BYTE}{N_{bits}} + C_{cache}) \quad (4)$$

Next, we consider the cost of matching the subsequences that filter through. These are expected to make up only $2^{-N_{bits} \times QLen}$ of the $NumSeq \times (SeqLen - QLen + 1)$ subsequences, as the hash function f is chosen so that N is (roughly) uniformly distributed between 0 and 1. For each of these subsequences, there is an I/O cost, the cost of looping through each element in the subsequence, and the cost of comparing with the query string. Here, we are fetching an entire subsequence all at once rather than element by element, so the I/O cost does not appreciate significantly with $QLen$. This is why the I/O cost is only $C_{I/O}$. Also, C_{string}, the cost of comparing with the query string, is lower than C_{state} because we are not updating the state array here. The refinement cost is, therefore,

$$R_{match} = \frac{NumSeq \times (SeqLen - QLen + 1)}{2^{N_{bits} \times QLen}} \times \\ (C_{I/O} + C_{loop} \times QLen + C_{string}) \quad (5)$$

and the response time of *BIS* is

$$R_{BIS} = R_{filter} + R_{match} \quad (6)$$

5.3. Extended Subsequence Matching

Besides query strings consisting of contiguous data elements, the cost models presented above can also capture the cost of the extended queries. Only a few modifications are necessary.

1. *Fixed length don't cares* (FLDC). For a query string with length $QLen$ that includes i FLDCs, the response time of the BYG algorithm remains as in Equation (3). In the case of *BIS*, the filtering cost (Equation (4)) is not affected, but the cost of checking subsequences that filter through (Equation (5)) becomes:

$$R_{match} = \frac{NumSeq \times (SeqLen - QLen + 1)}{2^{N_{bits} \times (QLen - i)}} \times \\ (C_{I/O} + C_{loop} \times (QLen - i) + C_{string}) \quad (7)$$

to account for the larger number of potentially matching subsequences.

248

Parameter	Meaning	Default
$NumSeq$	# of data seq. in the database	1
$SeqLen$	Avg. # of elements per data seq.	512 million
D_{dist}	Distribution of data element	uniform
D_{bits}	# of bits in a data element	8
N_{bits}	# of bits in an index element	1
$QLen$	# of query elements	16

Table 3. Experiment Parameters

2. *Variable length don't cares* (VLDC). As explained in Section 3.4, a query string with VLDCs is processed by combining the subsequences that match the segments separated by VLDCs. As the combination cost is relatively low, the overall cost is approximately the sum of the segment refinement costs. This applies to both R_{BYG} and R_{BIS}.

3. *Edit distance*. If all subsequences that are within an edit distance i from a query are needed, Equation (3) becomes

$$R_{BYG} = NumSeq \times SeqLen \times$$
$$(C_{I/O} + C_{loop} \times QLen + C_{state}(1 + i)) \quad (8)$$

because we now need to evaluate i more elements to disqualify an irrelevant subsequence. Similarly, Equation (4) is changed to

$$R_{filter} = NumSeq \times SeqLen \times \frac{N_{bits}}{BYTE} \times$$
$$(C_{I/O} + C_{loop} \times (QLen + \frac{BYTE}{N_{bits}} - 1) + \quad (9)$$
$$C_{state}(\frac{BYTE}{N_{bits}} + i) + C_{cache})$$

In the case of R_{match}, the fraction of subsequences that filter through increases by a factor of $\sum_{j=1}^{i} \mathbf{C}_j^{QLen}$. The reason is that there are $\mathbf{C}_j^{QLen}$ different ways in which a subsequence can differ from the query string and yet have an edit distance of j. Accordingly,

$$R_{match} = NumSeq \times (SeqLen - QLen + 1) \times$$
$$min(1, \frac{\sum_{j=1}^{i} \mathbf{C}_j^{QLen}}{2^{N_{bits} \times QLen}}) \times \quad (10)$$
$$(C_{I/O} + C_{loop} \times QLen + C_{string}(1 + i))$$

6. Experimental Study

To study the performance of the proposed strategy, we have implemented the strategy *BIS*, and Baeza-Yates and Gonnet's algorithm [1], in the C language. The experiment

platform consists of Sun UltraSparc 170 machines, each equipped with a 167 MHz CPU, 64 MB of memory, and a 2.1 GB Fast and Wide SCSI 2 hard disk. We have isolated and timed relevant portions of the implementation on this platform to obtain settings for the various cost parameters; the settings are listed in Table 2. For example, the *average* I/O time for fetching a data element, $C_{I/O}$, is set to 75 CPU cycles, or 450 nsec on a 167 MHz CPU (i.e., about 3.7 msec for each 8 KByte block).

The performance metrics that will be used to present the results are response time and speed-up, defined as R_{BYG}/R_{BIS}. For every experiment, we run 100 queries and average their results. Each query string is composed from randomly picked portions of one of the data sequences, so the query elements have the same distribution as the data elements. The parameters for the experiments are summarized in Table 3.

Apart from analytical experiments, the proposed algorithm was implemented as part of the system described in Section 2, which is being used by molecular research scientists for supporting their work.

6.1. Effect of N_{bits}

Before we construct an *BIS* index, we first need to determine a setting for N_{bits}, the number of bits per index element. We note that a smaller N_{bits} lowers filtering cost (Equation (4)) but raises R_{match} (Equation (5)). The key factor that decides whether the net effect is beneficial is the query length $QLen$. Since both R_{BYG} and R_{BIS} increase with $QLen$, we want to configure *BIS* for large $QLen$'s. With a large $QLen$, the number of subsequences that filter through is small regardless of N_{bits}. Consequently, filtering cost dominates, leading us to conclude that N_{bits} should be as small as possible, i.e., 1 bit.

To verify the above conclusion, we first build a database with $NumSeq = 1$, $SeqLen = 512$ million elements, D following a uniform distribution and $D_{bits} = 16$. Different indices are then created for $N_{bits} = 1, 2, 4$, and 8. Finally, query strings of the form $q_1 q_2 .. q_{16}$ are generated and run against each of the indices, and against the database directly.

Figures 3 and 4 plot the average response times and the speed-ups, respectively, produced by both the experiment and the cost models. The experiment results agree with the estimations from Equations (3) and (6). Moreover, the results confirm that performance worsens as N_{bits} increases. We shall therefore set N_{bits} to 1 from now on.

6.2. Effect of Query Length

Having determined the best N_{bits} setting for index construction, we now need a criterion for deciding when *BIS* will speed up query processing. Referring to Equations (3),

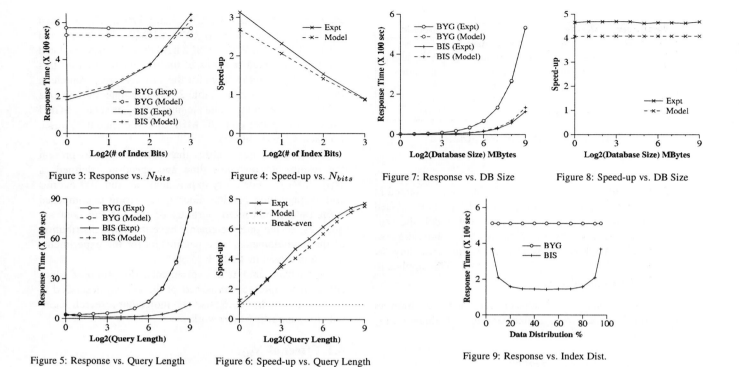

Figure 3: Response vs. N_{bits} Figure 4: Speed-up vs. N_{bits} Figure 7: Response vs. DB Size   Figure 8: Speed-up vs. DB Size

Figure 5: Response vs. Query Length   Figure 6: Speed-up vs. Query Length

Figure 9: Response vs. Index Dist.

(4) and (5), we note that $NumSeq$ and $SeqLen$ get cancelled out in Speed-up $= R_{BYG} / R_{BIS}$ when $SeqLen \gg QLen$, leaving $QLen$ as the only variable. In other words, whether BIS is beneficial depends only on the length of the query string.

In this experiment, we set D_{bits} to 8, N_{bits} to 1, and vary $QLen$. The rest of the parameter settings remain as before. The resulting response times and speed-ups are plotted in Figures 5 and 6.

While it may not be obvious in Figure 4 because the x-axis represents $log_2 QLen$ rather than $QLen$, the time taken by the BYG algorithm increases linearly with $QLen$. This agrees with Equation (3). As for BIS, its response time reduces initially as savings from fewer subsequences filtering through dominate rising filtering cost. However, eventually filtering cost prevails, and the response time of BIS embarks on a gradual uptrend. Nevertheless, overall there is a net savings over BYG. As Figure 6 shows, BIS breaks even at $QLen = 2$, and the speed-up rises roughly linearly with $log_2 QLen$. Again, the experiment results corroborate the cost models.

6.3. Effect of Data Size

In this experiment, we want to verify if the performance gain of the proposed strategy is sustainable as the database scales up. Theoretically, they should, as Speed-up $= R_{BYG}/R_{BIS}$ is independent of $NumSeq$ and $SeqLen$.

For this experiment, we fix the query length at 16, $NumSeq$ at 1, and vary $SeqLen$. We create databases with $SeqLen$ ranging from one to 512 million. The results, given in Figures 7 and 8, confirm that response time increases linearly, and that the speed-up achieved remain constant, exactly as predicted by the cost models.

6.4. Effect of Data Distribution

While gene and protein collections are fairly static, it is important for any processing strategy to be dynamic and perform well under different data distributions with different skewness. It is therefore necessary to see how BIS copes with updates that shift the data and, consequently, index distributions at runtime. This experiment is intended to profile any adverse effect that skewed index distributions might have on the performance of BIS.

Here, we build a database with $NumSeq = 1$, $SeqLen = 512$ million, D following a uniform distribution and $D_{bits} = 8$. Various skewed index distributions are generated via a family of hash functions that map $x\%$ of the data values to 0, and the rest to 1. Having done that, we then run queries with $QLen = 16$ against each of the indices and against the database directly.

Figure 9 plots the response time against the filter element distribution x. The figure shows that the performance of BIS remains stable as x swings from 20% to 80%. As the filter element distribution becomes even more skewed, however,

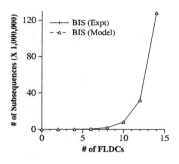

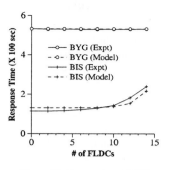

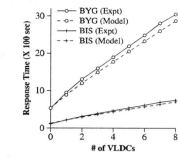

Figure 10: # Subsequences vs. FLDCs   Figure 11: Response vs. FLDCs

Figure 12: Response vs. VLDCs

BIS deteriorates rapidly, though it remains beneficial even at $x = 5\%$ and $x = 95\%$. Nevertheless, when the distribution becomes so skewed, the filter should be re-constructed with an updated hash function to restore *BIS*'s effectiveness.

6.5. Effect of Fixed Length Don't Cares Segments

In this experiment, we set $NumSeq = 1$, $SeqLen = 512$ million, $D_{bits} = 8$, $N_{bits} = 1$ (uniformly distributed) and $QLen = 16$. Moreover, we introduce FLDCs at randomly selected positions in the query strings.

As Figure 10 indicates, the average number of subsequences that pass *BIS*'s filtering step in the experiment matches the cost model's prediction almost exactly. The number increases very slowly initially as we introduce more FLDCs. Consequently, *BIS*'s response time remains almost unchanged until the number of data elements in the query strings becomes less than six, as shown in Figure 11. This is yet another confirmation that filtering cost (Equation (4)) dominates refinement cost (Equation (7)) unless there are very few data elements in the query string. Even then, *BIS* is still faster than *BYG*, which is not affected by the FLDCs.

6.6. Effect of Variable Length Don't Cares Segments

Besides FLDCs, another kind of extended subsequence matching operations involves variable length don't cares (VLDC) in the query strings. Such queries are processed by matching the component segments separately and then combining the results. Consequently, the overall response time is the sum of the individual segment's processing time. This is confirmed in Figure 12, which is obtained with the same parameter settings as in the previous experiment, except that there are no FLDCs.

6.7. Effect of Edit Distance

The third kind of extended subsequence matching operations that we have implemented is support for edit distances. Using the same parameter settings as the previous

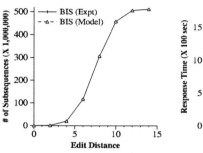

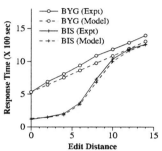

Figure 13: # Subsequences vs. Edit Dist.   Figure 14: Response vs. Edit Dist.

experiment (minus the VLDCs), we run *BIS* and *BYG* with different edit distances. The experiment results, together with the estimations from Equations (8)-(10), are given in Figures 13 and 14. The number of subsequences that filter through in the experiment (plotted in Figure 13) again matches those obtained from Equation (10). As for response time, the agreement is not as good as before – the experiment shows *BIS* outperforms *BYG* up to an edit distance of 14, whereas the cost models indicate only 10. Nevertheless, both *BIS* and the cost models are useful for edit distances that are low relative to the query length.

Experimental results show that *BIS*'s speed-up improves with $QLen$, and *BIS* remains advantageous for larger edit distances if the query string is longer. For example, at $QLen = 32$, *BIS* outperforms *BYG* even when the edit distance reaches 30.

6.8. Effect of D_{bits}

In deriving the cost models, we have omitted the impact of D_{bits} on the ground that, in an efficient implementation, both CPU and I/O costs increase only marginally as D goes from one to several bytes. To verify this, we ran several experiments to investigate the impact of D_{bits} at different $QLen$ and N_{bits} settings. Figures 15 and 16 give the response times produced by *BYG* and *BIS* in one of these experiments, where $QLen = 16$ and $N_{bits} = 1$. As the figures show, the variations introduced by higher D_{bits}'s have

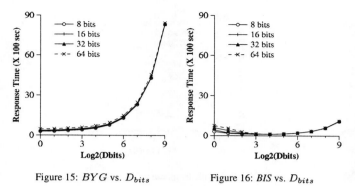

Figure 15: *BYG* vs. D_{bits} Figure 16: *BIS* vs. D_{bits}

little effect on either the efficacy of *BIS* or the accuracy of the cost models.

7 Related Work

Many algorithms have been proposed to address the problem of approximate subsequence matching. In this section, we shall discuss work related to our proposal, and highlight the differences between them.

The general approach to subsequence matching is to evaluate every sequence in response to a query, by constructing for it an automaton or a dynamic-programming table. Algorithms of such nature include the classical Knuth-Morris-Pratt (KMP) [9] and Boyer-Moore (DM) [5] algorithms, and algorithms proposed in [16, 19, 10, 1, 27]. If these algorithms are applied directly to the data sequences, the processing time may be unacceptably long, especially if the sequence database is large. However, they can be employed in conjunction with *BIS* to examine its index sequences. An earlier work related to our own was carried out by Karp and Rabin [7]. In [7], the authors presented a scheme in which each *subsequence* is mapped to an index number. Subsequently, rather than the longer, original subsequences, the index numbers are employed to search for matching subsequences. This scheme is similar to *BIS* in using a filter to weed out most of the irrelevant subsequences. However, there is a fundamental difference: Since the subsequences to consider are not defined until the query is known (as they need to have the same length), Karp and Rabin's scheme is not suitable for pre-indexing in database systems that must process ad-hoc queries. In contrast, *BIS* encodes and maps each *data element* to an index element during index construction. The processing of subsequence matching is performed dynamically at runtime, at which point the bitmap index representations are *dynamically* defined from the index that correspond to the data elements in the subsequences. Hence, *BIS* offers greater flexibility as it is not tailored to a particular query.

BYG [1] is a well-known algorithm for string matching with mismatches, which consists in representing the state of the search by a bit number and, at each step, in performing a number of bit operations. The algorithm searches a pattern in a text (without errors) by parallelizing the generation of a non-deterministic finite automation that looks for the patterns. For a search pattern of length m, and a text of length n, the automation has $m + 1$ states. The algorithm first builds a table B which for each alphabet character c stores a bit mask $B[c] = b_m..b_i$. The mask in $B[c]$ has the bit b_i in one if and only if the ith character in the pattern is equal to c. The state of the search in kept in a machine word $D = d_m..d_1$, where d_i is one whenever $P_{1..i}$ matches the end of the text read up to now (i.e. the ith state). A match is reported whenever $d_m = 1$. D is set to 1^m originally, and for each new text character T_j, D is updated using the formula $D' = ((D >> 1) \mid 10^{m-1}) \& B[T_i]))$, where $>>$ is the bitwise shift, $\mid$ is the bitwise OR, and $\&$ is the bitwise AND operation. For patterns longer than the computer word, the algorithm uses $\lceil m/w \rceil$ words (w is the length of a computer word). The algorithm achieves $O(mn/w)$ worst-case time, $O(m/w (m+|\Sigma|))$ preprocessing time, and $O(m/w |\Sigma|)$ extra space, where Σ denotes the alphabet.

An alternative approach to subsequence matching is to build a suffix tree [24, 12] index for the sequence database in advance, and to search the index rather than the actual data sequences at runtime. Solutions based on this approach include those reported in [11, 20, 22]. Suffix trees suffer from a number of performance problems.

For a sequence database consisting of l elements, each with a size of D_{bits} bits, a suffix tree index may need up to l leaf nodes and $l - 1$ internal nodes [17]. Since each node stores its corresponding starting and ending positions in a data sequence, together with a child pointer and a sibling pointer, the suffix tree could reach 32 times the database size with typical 4-byte fields. Moreover, many nodes need to be traversed for long query strings, while the presence of *don't care* segments blows up the number of branches that need to be searched, all of which lead to significant performance degradation. Finally, update is expensive as it affects both the structure, and the starting and ending positions recorded in multiple leaf nodes.

In [6], Faloutsos et al took a different approach. They proposed an algorithm that extracts the features in a window as it slides over the data sequence, thus transforming the sequence into a trail in a multi-dimensional feature space. The trail is then divided into sub-trails that are represented by their minimum bounding rectangles, and are indexed using traditional spatial access methods like the R^*-tree [4]. The algorithm is designed for sequences of continuous numbers, where the metric is the average Euclidean distance between a data element and the corresponding query element. In contrast, our algorithm targets sequences of discrete symbols, where the concern is whether a data element has the same value as the corresponding query element. For example, the subsequences ADC and AEC have different distances from ABC under Faloutsos' algorithm, whereas both are equally good/bad matches under our algorithm.

Recently, bitmap indexing has been used increasingly in other applications such as data warehouse query processing [26] and attribute based query processing [13] [15]. In [25], the VA-file (vector approximate file) which uses short bit strings to represent attribute values to index high-dimensional databases for similarity search. The performance gain due to shorter compact presentation and linear scan of the transformed vector file makes it a simple and yet one of most efficient high-dimensional indexes so far. Although the applications are different, the design philosophy is similar: they are designed to reduce index space overhead while improving query performance.

In [29, 30] Altschul et al. proposed the BLAST technique to find local similarities. BLAST, the most popular string matching tool for biologists, runs in two phases. In the first phase, all the substrings of the query of some pre-specified length (typically between 3 and 11) are searched in the database for an exact match. In the second phase, all the matches obtained in the first phase are extended in both directions until the similarity between the two substrings falls below some threshold. This technique keeps a pointer to the starting locations of all possible substrings of the pre-specified length in the database to speedup the first phase. Therefore, the space requirement of BLAST is more than the size of the database. Furthermore, BLAST does not find a similar substring to the whole query string, only similarities between the query substrings and the database substrings.

8 Conclusion

In this paper, we propose a filter-and-refine two-step processing strategy for approximate subsequence matching in large sequence databases. It employs *BIS* to map a data element to an index element that is smaller in size. The hash function is applied to every data element in a sequence and to each sequence in the database to produce an index. When a query string is presented, the filtering step evaluates the index representation of all the subsequences to isolate those that might be relevant. Only this fraction of subsequences need to have their data representation tested for a match at the refine step. Since the index is more compact than the database, doing so is expected to shorten the response time while saving on index storage space.

To evaluate performance, we have developed a cost model. The model enables us to determine the best size for an index element during *BIS* index construction. It also helps a DBMS to decide when to exploit *BIS* for query processing. Finally, the model can estimate the achievable response time savings over searching the database directly.

Extensive experiments were conducted using both synthetic and genetic sequence databases. The results of these experiments agree closely with the estimations of the cost model. More importantly, the experiments consistently confirm that *BIS* is space efficient, that it significantly reduces response time, and that it scales up with the database. For example, by constructing an index that is $\frac{1}{8}$ the size of the database, we have achieved more than 5 times speed-ups for query strings that are longer than 100 data elements.

We are currently conducting experiments and analysis using the large genomic databases, such as GenBank [31, 32] which contains approximately 1.3 billion bases, to develop the confidence in these early, but intriguing results. We also plan to improve the algorithm by compressing the bitmap index: frequent substrings in the sequences and queries can be encoded into much shorter index elements, and the filtering step can be speed up by the quick lookup of the frequent substrings in the index.

References

[1] R. Baeza-Yates, G.H. Gonnet, "A New Approach to Text Searching", *Communications of the ACM, Vol. 35, No. 10*, pp 74-82, October 1992.

[2] A. Bairoch, P. Bucher, "PROSITE: Recent Development", *Nucleic Acids Research, Vol. 22, No. 5*, pp 3583–3589, 1994.

[3] A. Bairoch, P. Bucher, K. Hofmann, "The PROSITE database, its status in 1997", *Nucleic Acids Research, Vol. 25, No. 1*, pp 217–221, January 1997.

[4] N. Beckmann, H.P. Kriegel, R. Schneider, B. Seeger, "The R^*-tree: An Efficient and Robust Access Method for Points and Rectangles", *Proc. of the ACM SIGMOD Conf.*, pp 322-331, May 1990.

[5] R.S. Boyer, J.S. Moore, "A Fast String Searching Algorithm", *Communications of the ACM, Vol. 20, No. 10*, pp 762-772, October 1977.

[6] C. Faloutsos, M. Ranganathan, Y. Manolopoulos, "Fast Subsequence Matching in Time-Series Databases", *Proc. of the ACM SIGMOD Conf.*, pp 419-429, May 1994.

[7] R.M. Karp, M.O. Rabin, "Efficient Randomized Pattern-Matching Algorithms", *IBM Journal of Research and Development, Vol. 31, No. 2*, pp 249-260, March 1987.

[8] G. Kadare and A.-L. Haenni, "Virus-encoded RNA helicases", *Journal of Virology, Vol. 71, No. 4*, pp 2583-2590, April 1997.

[9] D.E. Knuth, J.H. Morris, V.R. Pratt "Fast Pattern Matching in Strings", *SIAM Journal on Computing, Vol. 6, No. 2*, pp 323-350, June 1977.

[10] G.M. Landau, U. Vishkin, "Efficient String Matching in the Presence of Errors", *Proc. of the 26th IEEE Symp. on Foundations of Computer Science*, pp 126-136, October 1985.

[11] G.M. Landau, U. Vishkin, "Fast Parallel and Serial Approximate String Matching", *Journal of Algorithms, Vol. 10, No. 2*, pp 157-169, June 1989.

[12] E.M. McCreight, "A Space-Economical Suffix Tree Construction Algorithm", *Journal of the ACM, Vol. 23, No. 2*, pp 262-272, April 1976.

[13] P. O'Neil, D. Quass, "Improved Query Performance with Variant Indexes", *Proc. of the ACM SIGMOD Conf.*, pp 38-49, 1997.

[14] K. Osatomi, H. Sumiyoshi, "Complete Nucleotide Sequence of Dengue Type 3 Virus Genome RNA", *Virology, Vol. 176, No. 2*, pp 643-647, 1990.

[15] D. Rinfret, P. O'Neil, E. O'Neil, "Bit-Sliced Index Arithmetic", *Proc. of the ACM SIGMOD Conf.*, 2001.

[16] P.H. Sellers, "The Theory and Computation of Evolutionary Distances: Pattern Recognition", *Journal of Algorithms, Vol. 1, No. 4*, pp 359-373, December 1980.

[17] G.A. Stephen, *String Searching Algorithms*, Lecture Notes Series on Computing and Problems, World Scientific, 1994.

[18] K.S. Trivedi, *Probability and Statistics with Reliability, Queuing, and Computer Science Applications*, Prentice-Hall, Inc., pp 132, 1982.

[19] E. Ukkonen, "Finding Approximate Patterns in Strings", *Journal of Algorithms, Vol. 6, No. 1*, pp 132-137, March 1985.

[20] E. Ukkonen, D. Wood, "Approximate String Matching with Suffix Automata", *Algorithmica, Vol. 10, No. 5*, pp 353-364, November 1993.

[21] E. Ukkonen, "On-line Construction of Suffix Trees", *Algorithmica, Vol. 14, No. 3*, pp 249-260, September 1995.

[22] J.T.L. Wang, G.W. Chirn, T.G. Marr, B. Shapiro, D. Shasha, K. Zhang, "Combinatorial Pattern Discovery for Scientific Data: Some Preliminary Results", *Proc. of the ACM SIGMOD Conf.*, pp 115-125, May 1994.

[23] R.A. Wagner, M.J. Fischer, "The String-to-String Correction Problem", *Journal of the ACM, Vol. 21, No. 1*, pp 168-173, January 1974.

[24] P. Weiner, "Linear Pattern Matching Algorithms", *Proc. of the IEEE 14th Annual Symposium on Switching and Automata Theory*, pp 1-11, 1973.

[25] R. Weber and H. Schek and S. Blott, "A quantitative analysis and performance study for similarity-search methods in high-dimensional spaces". *Proc. 24th International Conference on Very Large Data Bases*, pp 194-205, 1998.

[26] M.-C. Wu, "Query optimization for selections using bitmaps", *Proc. of the ACM SIGMOD Conf.*, pp 227-238, 1999.

[27] S. Wu, U. Manber, "Fast Text Searching Allowing Errors", *Communications of the ACM, Vol. 35, No. 10*, pp 83-91, October 1992.

[28] P. Zezula, F. Rabitti, P. Tiberio, "Dynamic Partitioning of Signature Files", *ACM Trans. on Information Systems, Vol. 9, No. 4*, pp 336-369, October 1991.

[29] Altschul, S.F., Gish, W., Miller, W., Myers, E.W., Lipman, D.J., "Basic Local Alignment Search Tool", *Journal of Molecular Biology, Vol 215*, pp 403-410, 1990.

[30] Altschul, S.F., Madden, T.L., Schffer, A.A., Zhang, J., Zhang, Z., Miller, W., Lipman, D.J., "Gapped BLAST and PSI-BLAST: A New Generation of Protein Database Search Programs", *Nucleic Acids Research, Vol 25*, pp 3389-3402, 1997.

[31] Benson DA, Karsch-Mizrachi I, Lipman DJ, Ostell J, Rapp BA, Wheeler DL, "GenBank", *Nucleic Acids Research, Vol 28, No. 1*, pp 15-18, 2000.

[32] http://www.ncbi.nlm.nih.gov/Genbank/index.html

Paper Session VII

(Applications II)

Scalable QoS-Aware Disk-Scheduling

Walid G. Aref[1]*   Khaled El-Bassyouni[2]   Ibrahim Kamel[2]   Mohamed F. Mokbel[1]*

[1] Department of Computer Sciences, Purdue University, West Lafayette, IN 47907-1398

[2] Panasonic Information and Networking Technologies Laboratory. Two Research Way Princeton, NJ 08540

{aref,mokbel}@cs.purdue.edu, ibrahim@research.panasonic.com

Abstract

A new quality of service (QoS) aware disk scheduling algorithm is presented. It is applicable in environments where data requests arrive with different QoS requirements such as real-time deadline, and user priority. Previous work on disk scheduling has focused on optimizing the seek times and/or meeting the real-time deadlines. A unified framework for QoS disk scheduling is presented that scales with the number of scheduling parameters. The general idea is based on modeling the disk scheduler requests as points in the multi-dimensional space, where each of the dimensions represents one of the parameters (e.g., one dimension represents the request deadline, another represents the disk cylinder number, and a third dimension represents the priority of the request, etc.). Then the disk scheduling problem reduces to the problem of finding a linear order to traverse these multi-dimensional points. Space-filling curves are adopted to define a linear order for sorting and scheduling objects that lie in the multi-dimensional space. This generalizes the one-dimensional disk scheduling algorithms (e.g., EDF, SATF, FIFO). Several techniques are presented to show how a QoS-aware disk scheduler deals with the progressive arrival of requests over time. Simulation experiments are presented to show a comparison of the alternative techniques and to demonstrate the scalability of the proposed QoS-aware disk scheduling algorithm over other traditional approaches.

1. Introduction

Building reliable and efficient disk schedulers has always been a very challenging task. It has become even more so with today's complex systems and demanding applications. As applications grow in complexity, more requirements are imposed on disk schedulers, for example, the problem of disk scheduling in multimedia servers. In addition to maximizing the bandwidth of the disk, the disk scheduler has to take into consideration the real-time deadline constraints of the page requests, e.g., as in the case of video streaming. If clients are prioritized based on quality of service guarantees, then the disk scheduler might as well consider the priority of the requests in its disk queue. Writing a disk scheduler that handles real-time and quality of service constraints in addition to maximizing the disk bandwidth is a challenging and a hard task [2]. Similar issues arise when designing schedulers for multi-threaded CPUs, network-attached storage devices (NASDs) [9, 16], etc.

In the attempt to satisfy these concurrent and conflicting requirements, scheduler designers and algorithm developers depend mainly on heuristics to code such schedulers. It is not always clear that these schedulers are fair to all aspects of the system, or controllable in a measurable way to favor one aspect of the system over the other. The target of this paper is to revolutionize the way disk schedulers are developed. The general idea is based on modeling the disk requests as points in the multi-dimensional space where each dimension represents one of the parameters (e.g., one dimension represents the request deadline, another represents the disk cylinder number and the third dimension represents the priority of the request, etc.). Then the scheduler problem reduces to finding a linear order to traverse these multi-dimensional points.

The underlying theory is based on space-filling curves (SFCs). A space-filling curve maps the multi-dimensional space into the one-dimensional space. It acts like a thread that passes through every cell element (or pixel) in the multi-dimensional space so that every cell is visited exactly once. Thus, space-filling curves are adopted to define a linear order for sorting and scheduling objects that lie in the multi-dimensional space. For example, in a QoS-aware disk scheduler, when a request arrives to the disk queue, the request's parameters (e.g., its disk cylinder number, its real-time deadline, etc.) are passed as arguments to the space-filling curve function, which returns a one-dimensional value that represents the location of the re-

* This reasearch is supported by the National Science Foundation NSF under Grant No. IIS-0093116

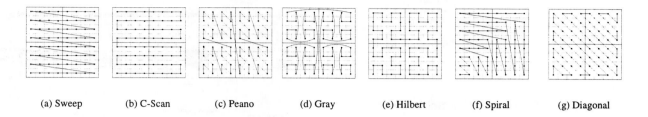

| (a) Sweep | (b) C-Scan | (c) Peano | (d) Gray | (e) Hilbert | (f) Spiral | (g) Diagonal |

Figure 1. Two-dimensional Space-Filling Curves.

quest in the disk queue. As a result, the disk queue is always sorted in the specified space-filling curve order. Using space-filling curves as the bases for multi-parameter disk scheduling has numerous advantages, including scalability (in terms of the number of scheduling parameters), ease of code development, ease of code maintenance, the ability to analyze the quality of the schedules generated, and the ability to automate the scheduler development process in a fashion similar to automatic generation of programming language compilers.

The rest of this paper is organized as follows. Section 2 discusses the related work of disk scheduling and the use of space-filling curves in different applications. In Section 3, we develop new space-filling curve based disk scheduling algorithms. Section 4 adopts the notion of *irregularity* as a measure of the quality of the scheduled order provided by a space-filling curve. Section 5 presents a comprehensive study of the developed algorithms on different space-filling curves. Finally, Section 6 concludes the paper.

2. Related Work

The problem of scheduling a set of tasks with time and resource constraints is known to be NP-complete [19]. Several heuristics have been developed to approximately optimize the scheduling problem. Traditional disk scheduling algorithms [5, 8, 12, 28] are optimized for aggregate throughput. These algorithms, including SCAN, LOOK, C-SCAN, and SATF (Shortest Access Time First), aim to minimize seek time and/or rotational latency overheads. They offer no QoS assurance other than perhaps absence of starvation. Deadline-based scheduling algorithms [1, 4, 15, 25] have built on the basic earliest deadline first (EDF) schedule of requests to ensure that deadlines are met. These algorithms, including SCAN-EDF and feasible-deadline EDF, perform restricted reorderings within the basic EDF schedule to reduce disk head movements while preserving the deadline constraints.

Like previous work on QoS-aware disk scheduling, space-filling curves explicitly recognize the existence of multiple and sometimes antagonistic service objectives in

the scheduling problem. Unlike previous work that focuses on specific problem instances, we use a more general model of mapping service requests in the multi-dimensional space into a linear order that balances between the different dimensions. Disk schedulers based on space-filling curves generalize traditional disk schedulers. For example, SATF can be modeled by the Sweep SFC (Figure 1a) by assigning the access time to the vertical dimension. Similarly, EDF is modeled by the Sweep SFC by assigning the deadline to the vertical dimension.

Space-Filling curves are first discovered by Peano [24] where he introduced a mapping from the unit interval to the unit square (Figure 1c). Hilbert [11] generalizes the idea for a mapping of the whole space (Figure 1e). Following the Peano and Hilbert curves, many space-filling curves have been proposed, e.g., see [3, 6]. In this paper, we focus on the space-filling curves shown in Figure 1, namely the Sweep, C-Scan, Peano, Hilbert, Gray, Spiral, and Diagonal SFCs. However, the developed theory and scheduling algorithms apply to other space-filling curves. Space-filling curves are used in many applications in computer science and engineering fields, e.g., spatial join [22], range queries [13], spatial access method [7], R-Tree [14], multi-dimensional indexing [18], and image processing [29]. Up to the authors' knowledge using space-filling curves as a scheduling tool is a novel application.

3. Disk-Scheduling Algorithms based on Space-Filling Curves

In the QoS-aware disk scheduler, a disk request is modeled by multiple parameters, (e.g., the disk cylinder, the real-time deadline, the priority, etc.) and represented as a point in the multi-dimensional space where each parameter corresponds to one dimension. Using a space-filling curve, the multi-dimensional disk request is converted to a one-dimensional value. Then, disk requests are inserted into a priority queue q according to their one-dimensional value with a lower value indicating a higher priority. Figure 2 gives an illustration of an SFC-based disk scheduler. To help in understanding the proposed algorithms, we present

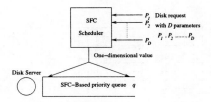

Figure 2. SFC-based Disk Scheduler

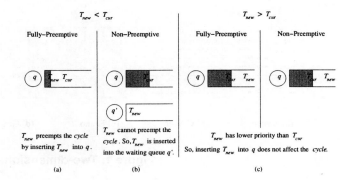

Figure 3. The Non-Preemptive and Fully-Preemptive SFC disk schedulers.

the notion of a full *cycle* in a space-filling curve.

Definition 3.1: *A full cycle in a space-filling curve with N priority levels in each dimension of a D-dimensional space is a contiguous move from the first point, say point 0, to the last point, say point N^D, passing through all the points in the space exactly once.*

A disk request T takes a position in the *cycle* according to its space-filling curve value. Disk requests are stored in the priority queue q according to their *cycle* position. The disk server walks through a *cycle* by serving all disk requests in q according to their *cycle* position. Figure 3 presents two straightforward approaches of using space-filling curves in disk-scheduling.

The Non-Preemptive SFC Disk Scheduler: In this approach, once the disk server starts to walk through a full *cycle* of a space-filling curve, the *cycle* is never preempted. A newly arrived request T_{new} is inserted in the disk queue q if and only if it will not preempt the current *cycle* (Figure 3c). If T_{new} needs to preempt the *cycle* (i.e., T_{new} has higher priority than T_{cur}), then it is inserted in a waiting queue q' (Figure 3b). The *cycle* is finished when the disk request with the lowest priority in q is served, then, all requests from q' are moved to q and a new *cycle* is generated.

The Fully-Preemptive SFC Disk Scheduler: This is the simplest approach. All requests are inserted into a single disk queue q according to their space-filling curve priority. This scheduler is fully-preemptive in the sense that any incoming request T_{new} with higher priority than T_{cur} preempts the current *cycle* and starts a new one (Figure 3a). However, when T_{new} has lower priority than T_{cur}, it is inserted in q without affecting the current *cycle* (Figure 3c).

The fully-preemptive SFC disk scheduler serves all disk requests according to their priority. Low priority requests may starve due to the continuous arrival of high priority requests. On the other hand, the non-preemptive SFC disk scheduler does not lead to starvation since it guarantees that lower priority disk requests in a certain *cycle* will be served before starting a new *cycle*. However, a priority inversion takes place where higher priority disk requests may wait for lower priority disk requests to be served. The drawbacks of the two approaches raise the motivation for having a combined disk scheduler that has the merits of both schedulers. In the following section, we present a novel disk schedul-

ing algorithm that avoids the drawbacks of these algorithms, i.e., respects the disk request priority and avoids starvation.

3.1. The Conditionally-Preemptive SFC Disk Scheduler Algorithm

As a trade-off between the fully-preemptive and the non-preemptive disk schedulers, in the conditionally-preemptive disk scheduling algorithm, a newly arrived disk request T_{new} preempts the process of walking through a full *cycle* if and only if it has significantly higher priority than the currently served disk request T_{cur}. To quantify the meaning of significantly higher priority, we define a blocking window with size w (the rounded box with thick border in Figure 4) that slides with T_{cur} in q. Then, T_{new} is considered as a priority significantly higher than T_{cur} if and only if $T_{new} < T_{cur} - w$. The window size w is a compromise between the fully-preemptive and the non-preemptive disk schedulers. Setting $w=0$ corresponds to the fully-preemptive disk scheduler, while setting w to a very large value corresponds to the non-preemptive disk scheduler. When T_{new} arrives while the scheduler is going to serve T_{cur}, then one of the following three cases takes place:

1. $T_{cur} < T_{new}$ (Figure 4a). This means that T_{new} has lower priority than T_{cur}. Hence, T_{new} is inserted into q as inserting it into q will not preempt the *cycle*.

2. $T_{cur} - w < T_{new} < T_{cur}$ (Figure 4b). This means that T_{new} lies inside the blocking window w. Although T_{new} has a priority higher than that of T_{cur}, but it is not high enough to preempt the space-filling curve *cycle*. So, T_{new} is inserted in the waiting queue q'.

3. $T_{new} < T_{cur} - w$ (Figure 4c). This means that T_{new} has a priority that is significantly higher than that of

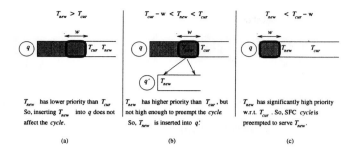

(a)   (b)   (c)

Figure 4. The Conditionally-Preemptive SFC Disk Scheduler.

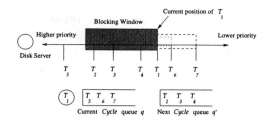

Figure 5. Example of Conditionally-Preemptive SFC Disk Scheduler.

T_{cur}. So, it is worth to preempt the space-filling curve *cycle* by inserting T_{new} in q.

There are two issues that need to be addressed; first, how to deal with the occurrence of priority inversion that result from disk requests that lie inside the blocking window w (stored in q') and have higher priority than some requests in q. Second, with any value of w less than N^D (the last point in a *cycle*), there is still a chance of starvation, where a continuous stream of very high priority requests may arrive. The next two sections propose alternative approaches for dealing with these two problems.

3.2. Minimizing Priority Inversion

The disk requests that lie in window w are stored in q'. This results in priority inversion as the blocked requests have higher priority than T_{cur}. In this section, we propose three alternatives to deal with this situation. Figure 5 gives an example that demonstrates the difference among the three proposed scheduling policies. Assume that while T_1 is being served, all the other disk requests T_2, T_3, T_4, T_5, T_6, and T_7 have arrived. Notice that T_2, T_3, and T_4 are inserted in q' since they lie inside the window w. T_6 and T_7 are inserted in q since they have lower priority than T_1. T_5 is inserted in q since it has a significantly higher priority than T_1.

Serve and Resume (SR): The space-filling curve *cycle* is preempted only by inserting the newly arriving request T_{new} of significant high priority into q. After preempting the *cycle* and serving T_{new}, the process of serving the *cycle* is resumed.

As in Figure 5, after serving T_1, following the *cycle* order would result in serving T_6. However, the *cycle* is preempted to serve T_5 (T_5 has a significantly higher priority than T_6). After serving T_5, the *cycle* is resumed to serve the disk requests in q (T_6 and T_7). Finally, the next *cycle* (waiting) queue q' is considered and is served. Hence, the final order is T_1, T_5, T_6, T_7, T_2, T_3, T_4.

Serve, Resume and Promote (SRP): SRP acts exactly as SR. In addition, before the disk starts to serve a request from q, it checks q' for any request that becomes with a significantly higher priority. If such a request is found, SRP promotes this request and inserts it in q. So, the space-filling curve *cycle* can be preempted either by a newly arrived request or by an old request that eventually becomes of significant higher priority.

In Figure 5, after serving T_1, the *cycle* is preempted to serve T_5. Then, before serving T_6, SRP detects that T_2 now lies outside the window of T_6. Hence, T_2 is served before T_6. Continuing in this way, the final order will be T_1, T_5, T_2, T_6, T_3, T_7, T_4.

Serve and Scan (SS): When the *cycle* is preempted due to the arrival of a new disk request T_{new}, all the requests in q' are scanned and served in their priority order.

In Figure 5, when the *cycle* is preempted to serve T_5, all the disk requests inside the window (next *cycle* queue q') are served before returning to the current *cycle* queue. Hence, the final order will be T_1, T_5, T_2, T_3, T_4, T_6, T_7.

3.3. Starvation Avoidance

If the window size w remains fixed, an adversary would still select disk requests in a manner that results in a starvation of other disk requests. To avoid starvation, we propose to expand the window size w during the course of executing the scheduling algorithm. As w increases, it eventually becomes large enough to prevent preemption and hence avoids starvation. In this section, we propose two policies for expanding the window size w.

Always Expand (AE): In AE, the window size w is increased by a constant factor, expansion factor e, with any preemption of the space-filling curve *cycle*. Eventually, w will be large enough to prevent any *cycle* preemption and hence, the disk scheduler works as the non-preemptive disk scheduling algorithm which avoids starvation.

Expand and Reset (ER): ER is the same as AE where we increase the window size w by a constant factor e. However, when a disk request is served and another disk request from

q is dispatched, ER resets w to its original value. The objective is to achieve a balance between the non-preemptive and the fully-preemptive schedulers. While in AE, once a scheduler becomes a non-preemptive one (due to the increase of w), it continues to work as the non-preemptive scheduler, in ER, the scheduler moves back and forth between working as the non-preemptive scheduler and as the conditionally-preemptive scheduler with different values of w.

4. The Quality of Space-Filling Curves

An optimal space-filling curve is one that sorts points in space in ascending order for all dimensions. In reality, when a space-filling curve attempts to sort the points in ascending order according to one dimension, it fails to do the same for the other dimensions. A good space-filling curve for one dimension is not necessarily good for the other dimensions. In this section, we introduce the concept of *irregularity* as a measure of goodness of space-filling curves [20]. Then, we show how the irregularity can be used as an indicator for the practical performance measures, e.g., disk utilization, priority inversion, and deadline losses.

4.1. Irregularity in Space-Filling Curves

In order to measure the scheduling quality of a space-filling curve, we introduce the concept of irregularity as a measure of goodness for the scheduling order imposed by a space-filling curve. Irregularity is measured for each dimension separately. It gives an indicator of how a space-filling curve is far from the optimal. The lower the irregularity, the better the space-filling curve is.

Definition 4.1: *For any two points, P_i and P_j, in the D-dimensional space with coordinates $(P_i.u_1, P_i.u_2, \ldots, P_i.u_D), (P_j.u_1, P_j.u_2, \ldots, P_j.u_D)$, respectively, and for a given space-filling curve, if P_i is visited before P_j, we say that an irregularity occurs between P_i and P_j in dimension k iff $P_j.u_k < P_i.u_k$.*

Figure 6 demonstrates all possible scenarios that can lead to an irregularity in the two-dimensional space, where the arrows in the curves indicate the order imposed by the underlying space-filling curve, i.e., point P_i is visited before point P_j. Formally, for a given space-filling curve in the D-dimensional space with grid size N, the number of irregularities for any dimension k is:

$$I(k, N, D) = \sum_{j=1}^{N^D} \sum_{i=1}^{j-1} f_{ij} \, , \quad f_{ij} = 1 \ iff \ P_i.u_k > P_j.u_k$$

An optimal schedule for any dimension k would have no irregularity. In contrast, the worst-case schedule for any dimension k is to sort all the requests in reverse order with respect to k.

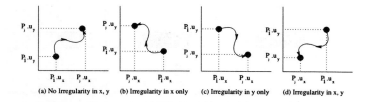

Figure 6. Irregularity in 2D space.

4.2. Irregularity as a Measure of Performance

In this section, we show that the irregularity can be used as a practical measure of performance. Three experiments have been conducted to show the effect of lower irregularity on disk utilization, priority inversion, and deadline losses. In the experiments, we assume eight priority levels with one disk request for each level. This results in 8! possible different schedules. The optimal schedule would have no irregularity while the worst-case schedule would have 28 irregularities [20].

4.2.1 Disk Utilization

In this section, we investigate the correlation between irregularity as a measure of goodness and disk utilization. We conduct the following experiment. Assume that we have a disk with eight consecutive disk cylinder zones, say C_1 to C_8. We map these consecutive cylinder zones to eight levels of priority in the irregularity frame of work. Assume that each cylinder zone contains one disk request. The objective is to serve all disk requests while minimizing seek time overhead (i.e., increasing the disk utilization). The disk head is initially located at the first cylinder C_1. The seek time between any two consecutive cylinders is T_s. Irregularity is computed based on the shortest possible seek time from the current location. For example, the best schedule is $C_1 C_2 C_3 C_4 C_5 C_6 C_7 C_8$ which results in a seek time of $7T_s$ and has zero irregularity. The worst-case schedule is $C_8 C_1 C_7 C_2 C_6 C_3 C_5 C_4$ where each time the scheduler chooses the furthest cylinder to serve, this results in 28 irregularities and a seek time of $35T_s$. Figure 7a gives the relation between irregularity and disk utilization, where for each possible number of irregularities I (varies from 0, the optimal, to 28, the worst), we compute the average seek time over all schedules that result in I irregularity. From Figure 7a, we notice that the average seek time and the irregularity in a sequence of disk request schedule are almost linearly correlated, i.e., the lower the irregularity the better the disk utilization is and vise versa. Therefore, we can deduce that irregularity can be used as a measure of goodness for disk performance. The advantage of using irregularity as a measure of goodness is that we can compute it analytically, and hence be able to analytically quantize the

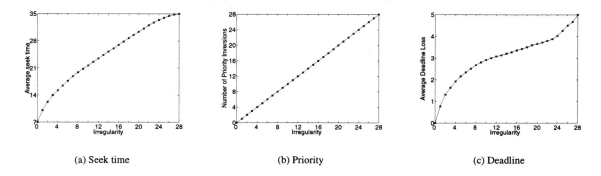

| (a) Seek time | (b) Priority | (c) Deadline |

Figure 7. Irregularity as a practical measures.

scheduling quality for a given scheduling policy.

4.2.2 Priority Inversion

Priority inversion takes place when a higher priority disk request is waiting for a lower priority disk request to be served. In this experiment, we assume that all disk requests lie in the same cylinder, so there is no seek time overhead. There are eight levels of priorities P_1 to P_8, and one disk request per priority level. When a disk request with priority P_i is served, we compute the priority inversion as the number of disk requests with priority $P_j > P_i$ that are waiting for P_i to be served. Figure 7b gives the effect of irregularity on priority inversion. As can be seen from the figure, irregularity and priority inversion are linearly correlated. The lower the irregularity, the lower the occurrence of priority inversion is and vise versa. Hence, irregularity may be used as a good performance measure that reflects the quality of a schedule generated by a given scheduler w.r.t. priority inversion.

4.2.3 Deadline Loss

In this experiment, we assume that we have eight priority levels from $P_1 = 1$ to $P_8 = 8$, and there is one disk request per priority level. Assume that each disk request needs constant service time, say a msec. Assume further that higher priority requests have more tight deadlines, so, the deadline for each request is bP_i where $b > a$. Notice that $b \leq a$ means relaxed deadlines, and hence no deadline violation would take place. We conduct this experiment in the following way: For each possible number of irregularities I (varies from 0, the optimal, to 28, the worst), we compute the average deadline losses over all schedules that result in I irregularity. Figure 7c gives the relationship between irregularity and the number of deadline losses where we set a=20 msec and b=25 msec. The same figure is obtained for any values for a, b where $b > a$. From the figure, notice that

the lower the irregularity, the lower the deadline losses, and vise versa. Also, the figure demonstrates a linear correlation between irregularity and the number of deadline losses. Hence, irregularity can be used as a measure of goodness for deadline loss performance as well. Therefore, lowering the irregularity is favorable in the case of real time applications.

5. Performance Evaluation

The SFC-based disk scheduler has three major components; the irregularity policy, the starvation policy, and the underlying space-filling curve, and two parameters; the window size w and the expansion factor e. In this section, we perform comprehensive experiments to construct an SFC-based disk scheduler by appropriately choosing its components and parameters. In Section 5.1, we perform experiments to evaluate all the proposed policies for minimizing irregularity and avoiding starvation In Section 5.2, we study the effect of each space-filling curve on the scheduler In Section 5.3, we study the effect of the initial window size w For all experiments we set the expansion factor e to be 5% of w. All experiments in this section are performed with the disk simulation model developed at Dartmouth College [17]. It simulates the Hewlett Packard 97560 disk drive [23] that is described in detail in [27]. This disk simulation model has been widely used in many projects, e.g., in the SimOS project at Stanford University [10, 26] and in the Galley project at Dartmouth College [21]. The HP 97560 disk drive contains 1962 cylinder with 19 tracks per cylinder. Each track contains 72 sectors with 512 bytes each. The revolution speed is 4002 rpm and the disk has a SCSI-II controller interface.

To reflect the irregularity of the SFC scheduler, we measure the mean irregularity over all the space dimensions. The standard deviation of request waiting time is considered as a measure of starvation, the higher the standard deviation the higher the chance that starvation may occur. For

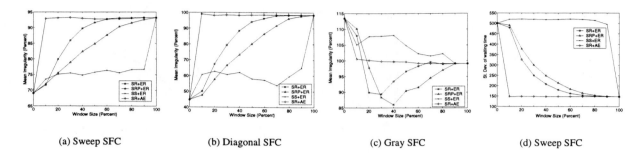

| (a) Sweep SFC | (b) Diagonal SFC | (c) Gray SFC | (d) Sweep SFC |

Figure 8. Comparison among different policies.

comparison purposes, we use the FCFS scheduler as our base point. The irregularity and the standard deviation of the waiting time are presented as a ratio to the irregularity and the standard deviation of the waiting time caused by FCFS, respectively. Recall that traditional disk schedulers, e.g., EDF and SATF can be modeled as special cases of an SFC-based disk scheduler. Hence, we do not have to compare with each one of them separately.

5.1. Selecting the Policy

In this section, we compare the proposed algorithms in Sections 3.2 and 3.3. All experiments consider disk requests with four QoS parameters that arrive exponentially with mean interarrival time 25 msec. The initial window size w is expressed as a percentage of the total points in the space. The expansion factor e is set to 5% of w. The notation "+" is used to indicate a combination of two disk scheduling policies. For example SR+AE indicates that the disk scheduler uses Policies SR (Serve and Resume) to handle irregularity and AE (Always Expand) to handle starvation. Figures 8a, 8b, and 8c give the mean irregularity for the Sweep, Diagonal, and Gray SFCs, respectively at different values for w. To simplify the graph, we only plot SR+AE as a representative of disk schedulers that use policy AE. Other disk schedulers that use the same policy (AE) give the same performance as SR+AE. At $w=0$, all the schedulers degenerate to the Fully-Preemptive SFC disk scheduler. Similarly, at $w=100$, all the schedulers degenerate to the Non-Preemptive SFC disk scheduler. Except for the case where $w=0$, the AE (Always Expand) Policy results in very high irregularity even with small window size. The reason is that w is always increasing and eventually it becomes large enough to block all incoming disk requests as in the non-preemptive scheduler.

In Figures 8a and 8b, Policy SS gives the lowest irregularity when $w > 25\%$. As w increases, more disk requests are blocked and stored in the disk queue q'. The blocked disk requests are served according to their SFC order. Thus,

respecting the SFC-order lowers the irregularity. SR+ER and SRP+ER give reasonable increase in irregularity as w increases. The Spiral and Peano SFCs exhibit similar behavior as the Sweep and Diagonal SFCs. The Diagonal SFC gives the lowest irregularity for any window size w. However, the choice of the appropriate space-filling curve does not rely only on irregularity. Other aspects that control the choice of a space-filling curve are investigated in the next section. Figure 8c represents the performance of the Gray, C-Scan, and Hilbert SFCs. Unlike the Sweep and Diagonal SFCs, in SR+ER and SRP+ER policies, increasing w from 0 to 40 results in lowering the irregularity.

Figure 8d gives the standard deviation of the waiting time for the Sweep SFC. All space-filling curves give the same curve for waiting time. SS+ER gives very high standard deviation, which indicates a high possibility of starvation. In Policy SS, disk requests that are blocked by window w are accumulated and stored in the queue q'. So serving them in one scan may result in starving lower priority requests. SR+AE works as the non-preemptive scheduler. SRP+ER and SR+ER give lower starvation as w increases.

As can be seen from the experiments, SR+ER and SRP+ER give the best scheduling performance where they result in a moderate schedule that balances between irregularity and starvation. However, Policy SR has a vital drawback, that it penalizes disk requests for their early arrival. Assume that a disk request T arrives within window w, then it is stored in q'. The service of T is postponed till all disk requests in q are served. If T was smart enough to delay itself so that it arrives when the blocking window w slides ahead so that T becomes outside w and stored in q, then it will be eligible for being served immediately. This scenario highlights the fact that T may be served better if it arrives late. This problem is dealt with in Policy SRP, that after serving each request, SRP checks the queue q' for those requests that become eligible to service and move (promote) them to q. For the rest of experiments in the following sections, we use the Policies SRP+ER in the Conditionally-Preemptive SFC disk scheduler.

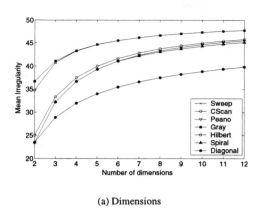 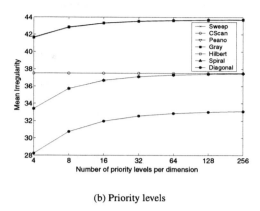

(a) Dimensions   (b) Priority levels

Figure 9. Scalability of SFC Scheduler.

5.2. Selecting the Space-Filling Curve

In this section, we perform comprehensive comparison between the seven space-filling curves in Figure 1. The objective is to determine which space-filling curve will best fit in the SFC-based disk scheduler. All experiments in this section are performed with SRP+ER policies.

5.2.1 Scalability of SFC-based Schedulers

In this section, we address the issue of scalability of SFC-based schedulers, e.g., when the number of dimensions (schedule parameters) increases or when the number of priority levels per dimension increases. The experiments in this section are performed with SRP+ER policies with $w = 50\%$, and the mean interarrival time of disk requests is 25 msec. In Figure 9a, we measure the irregularity of the SFC-based disk scheduler using different space-filling curve for up to 12 QoS parameters (scheduling dimensions) where each dimension has 16 priority levels. The Diagonal SFC gives the best performance especially with higher dimensions. The Sweep, Peano, and Spiral SFCs have almost the same performance.

Figure 9b compares the space-filing curves in the four-dimensional space, while the number of priority levels varies from 4 to 256. After 16 priority levels, all space-filling curves tend to exhibit constant behavior. The Diagonal SFC gives the best performance. The Hilbert and Gray SFCs have the worst performance with respect to irregularity. The Sweep, Peano, and Spiral SFCs have similar performance that tends to be equal to the performance of the C-Scan SFC in high priority levels. The C-Scan SFC has constant performance regardless of the number of priority levels.

From the experiments, it can be seen that the SFC-based disk scheduler scales easily and without additional coding

difficulty to higher QoS parameters. Also when using the appropriate SFC, the SFC-based scheduler can exhibit low irregularity even at higher dimensions. The time complexity for converting a point in the D-dimensional space into the one-dimensional space is $O(D)$ [20].

5.2.2 Fairness of SFC-based Schedulers

A very critical point for SFC-based disk schedulers is how to assign the QoS disk request parameters (i.e., the deadline, priority, etc.) to the dimensions of the space-filling curve. For example, the EDF disk scheduler can be modeled by the Sweep SFC when assigning the vertical dimension (Figure 1a) to the deadline parameter. Also SATF can be modeled using the Sweep or the C-Scan SFC by assigning the vertical dimension to the access time. We say that a space-filling curve is biased to dimension k if it results in low irregularity in k relative to the other dimensions. Also, we say that a space-filling curve is fair if it results in similar irregularity for all dimensions. In this section, we use the standard deviation of irregularity over all the dimensions as a measure of the fairness of space-filling curves. The experiment in this section is performed on four QoS parameters using SRP+ER policies with $w = 50\%$, and the interarrival time of disk requests is 25 msec. In Figure 10a, we measure the standard deviation of irregularity over all dimensions. A low standard deviation indicates more fairness. The Diagonal SFC is the most fair space-filling curve among the space-filling curves we consider in this study (the standard deviation is less than 10%). For a medium window size, the Spiral SFC has a very low standard deviation. The C-Scan and Sweep SFCs give the worst performance. This is because they have no irregularity in the last dimension while having high irregularity in the other dimensions.

Some applications may have only one important dimension, while the other dimensions are not with the same sig-

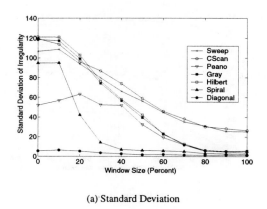

(a) Standard Deviation

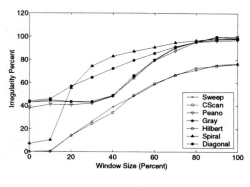

(b) Favored Dimension

Figure 10. Fairness of SFC Scheduler.

nificant importance. One example is optimizing the mechanical movements of the disk head over the cylinders. Another example is the real time requests, where in some applications the most important factor would be to meet the request deadline, and then the other parameters can be scheduled. EDF favors the deadline, while ignoring all other dimensions. CSCAN favors the cylinder dimension. SATF favors the access time dimension. For these applications, we develop the experiment given in Figure 10b. Although, we run the experiment in a four-dimensional QoS space, we plot only the most favored dimension for each space-filling curve. Figure 10b shows that the C-Scan and the Sweep SFCs are always the best for a small window size. They have no irregularity in small window sizes. This is also an interpretation of why they have very high standard deviation (Figure 10a).

5.3. Selecting the Initial Window Size

In this set of experiments, we investigate how the value of the window w can be determined. We develop a design curve for each space-filling curve that demonstrates the effect of changing w on the irregularity and starvation in the three-, four-, and five-dimensional spaces. We use the same experiment as in Section 5.1 while varying the number of dimensions from three to five. Figure 11 gives the design curves for the Peano, Hilbert, and Diagonal SFCs, respectively. The C-Scan and the Gray SFCs have similar shapes as that of the Hilbert SFC. All other SFCs have similar design curves as that of the Peano and Diagonal SFCs with different irregularity values.

Determining the value of the window size w depends on the space-filling curve. For the Peano SFC, setting w=35% results in the best trade-off between the irregularity and the standard deviation of waiting time. For the Hilbert and Di-

agonal SFCs, setting w=35%, 40%, respectively would result in the best trade-off.

6. Conclusion

In this paper, we have proposed a new scalable disk scheduling algorithm for serving requests that require QoS parameters (i.e., deadline, priority, etc.). The idea is to map the multiple QoS parameters into the one-dimensional space. Then, we use the ordering imposed by space-filling curves to serve the disk requests. We introduce the *irregularity* as a measure of quality of the space-filling curve order. We show how irregularity is linearly correlated with other measures of goodness for scheduler performance, e.g., disk utilization, deadline losses, and priority inversion. The window size tuning parameter w is introduced to tune the irregularity and starvation of an SFC-based disk scheduler. Our comprehensive simulation experiments show that using the disk-scheduling algorithm SRP+ER achieves the best performance for any space-filling curve. From the set of the discussed space-filling curves, we show the different properties that motivates the use of each space-filling curve.

References

[1] R. K. Abbot and H. Garcia-Molina. Scheduling i/o requests with deadlines: A performance evaluation. In *Proc. of the IEEE Real-Time Systems Symp., RTSS*, pages 113–125, Florida, Dec. 1990.

[2] W. G. Aref, I. Kamel, and S. Ghandeharizadeh. Disk scheduling in video editing systems. *IEEE Trans. on Knowledge and Data Engineering, TKDE*, 13(6):933–950, 2001.

[3] T. Asano, D. Ranjan, T. Roos, E. Welzl, and P. Widmayer. Space-filling curves and their use in the design of geometric data structures. *Theoretical Computer Science, TCS*, 181(1):3–15, 1997.

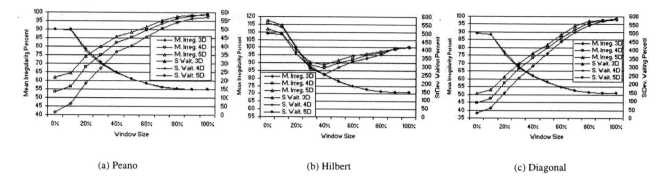

(a) Peano   (b) Hilbert   (c) Diagonal

Figure 11. Design Curves.

[4] S. Chen, J. Stankovic, J. Krouse, and D. Towsley. Performance evaluaion of two new disk scheduling algorithms for real-time systems. *Journal of Real-Time Systems*, 3:307–336, 1991.

[5] E. G. Coffman, L. Klimko, and B. Ryan. Analysis of scanning policies for reducing seek times. *SIAM Journal on Computing*, 1(3):269–279, Sept. 1972.

[6] C. Faloutsos. Multiattribute hashing using gray codes. In *Proc. of the Int. Conf. on Management of data, ACM SIGMOD*, pages 227–238, Washington D.C., May 1986.

[7] C. Faloutsos and Y. Rong. Dot: A spatial access method using fractals. In *Proc. of the Int. Conf. on Data Engineering, ICDE*, pages 152–159, Kobe, Japan, Apr. 1991.

[8] R. Geist and S. Daniel. A continuum of disk scheduling algorithms. *ACM Trans. of Computer Systems, TOCS*, 5(1):77–92, Feb. 1987.

[9] G. Gibson, D. Nagle, K. Amiri, J. Butler, F. W. Chang, H. Gobioff, C. Hardin, E. Riedel, D. Rochberg, and J. Zelenka. File server scaling with network-attached secure disks. In *In Proc. of the ACM Int. Conf. on Measurement and Modeling of Computer Systems, SIGMETRICS*, pages 272–284, Seatle, Washington, June 1997.

[10] S. A. Herrod. *Using Complete Machine Simulation to Understand Computer System Behaviour*. PhD thesis, Stanford University, Feb. 1998.

[11] D. Hilbert. Ueber stetige abbildung einer linie auf ein flashenstuck.*Mathematishe Annalen*, pages 459–460, 1891.

[12] M. Hofri. Disk scheduling: Fcfs vs sstf revisited. *Communications of the ACM, CACM*, 23(11):645–653, Nov. 1980.

[13] H. V. Jagadish. Linear clustering of objects with multiple attributes. In *Proc. of the Int. Conf. on Management of data, ACM SIGMOD*, pages 332–342, Atlantic City, NJ, June 1990.

[14] I. Kamel and C. Faloutsos. Hilbert r-tree: An improved r-tree using fractals. In *Proc. of the 20th Int. Conf. on Very Large Data Bases, VLDB*, pages 500–509, Santiago, Chile, Sept. 1994.

[15] I. Kamel, T. Niranjan, and S. Ghandeharizedah. A novel deadline driven disk scheduling algorithm for multi-priority multimedia objects. In *Int. Conf. on Data Engineering, ICDE*, pages 349–358, San Diego, CA, Mar. 2000.

[16] R. H. Katz. High performance network- and channel-attached storage. *Proceedings of IEEE*, 80(8), Aug. 1992.

[17] D. Kotz, S. Toh, and S. Radhakrishnan. A detailed simulation model of the hp97560 disk drive. Technical Report PCS-TR94-220, Department of Computer Science, Dartmouth College, 1994.

[18] J. K. Lawder and P. J. H. King. Querying multi-dimensional data indexed using the hilbert space filling curve. *SIGMOD Record*, 30(1), Mar. 2001.

[19] J. K. Lenstra, A. R. Kan, and P.Brucker. Complexity of machine scheduling problems. *Annals of Discrete Mathematics*, 1:343–362, 1977.

[20] M. F. Mokbel and W. G. Aref. Irregularity in multi-dimensional space-filling curves with applications in multimedia databases. In *Proc. of the Int. Conf. on Information and knowledge Management, CIKM*, Atlanta, GA, Nov. 2001.

[21] N. Nieuwejaar. *Galley: A New Parallel File System for Scientific Applications*. PhD thesis, Computer Science Department, Dartmouth College, 1996.

[22] J. A. Orenstein. Spatial query processing in an object-oriented database system. In *Proc. of the Int. Conf. on Management of data, ACM SIGMOD*, pages 326–336, Washington D.C., May 1986.

[23] H. Packard". *HP97556/58/60 5.25 inch SCSI Disk Drive*, technical reference manual, 2nd edition edition, June 1991.

[24] G. Peano. Sur une courbe qui remplit toute une air plaine. *Mathematishe Annalen*, 36:157–160, 1890.

[25] A. Reddy and J. C. Wyille. Disk scheduling in multimedia i/o systems. In *Proc. of the 1st ACM Multimedia*, pages 225–233, Anaheim, CA, Aug. 1993.

[26] M. Rosenblum, S. Herrod, E. Witchel, and A. Gupta. Complete computer simulation: The simos approach. In *Proc. IEEE Parallel and Distributed Technology*, 1995.

[27] C. Ruemmler and J. Wilkes. An introduction to disk drive modeling. *In Proc. IEEE Computer*, 27(3):17–28, Mar. 1994.

[28] A. Silberchatz and P. Galvin. *Operating System Conceps*. Addison-Wesley, 5th edition, 1998.

[29] L. Velho and J. Gomes. Digital halftoning with space filling curves. *Computer Graphics*, 25(4):81–90, July 1991.

Using the F2 OODBMS to Support Incremental Knowledge Acquisition

Lina Al-Jadir, Ghassan Beydoun
Department of Mathematics and Computer Science
American University of Beirut
P.O. Box 11-0236, Beirut, Lebanon
{lina.al-jadir, ghassan.beydoun}@aub.edu.lb

Abstract

Ripple Down Rules (RDR) is an incremental knowledge acquisition (KA) methodology, where a knowledge base (KB) is constructed as a collection of rules with exceptions. Nested Ripple Down Rules (NRDR) is an extension of this methodology which allows the expert to enter her/his own domain concepts and later refine these concepts hierarchically. In this paper we show similarities between incremental knowledge acquisition and database schema evolution, and propose to use the F2 object-oriented database management system (OODBMS) to implement an NRDR knowledge based system. We use the existing non-standard features of F2 and show how multiple instantiation and object migration (known as multiobjects feature in F2), and schema evolution capabilities in F2 easily accommodate all the update mechanisms required to incrementally build an NRDR KB. We illustrate our approach with a KA session.[1]

1. Introduction

Incremental knowledge acquisition (KA) is the process of building a knowledge based system (KBS) through interactions with an expert. It has been popularised with the success of the Ripple Down Rules (RDR) approach [13]. This approach has been successful in a number of applications, pathology [14], search heuristics [7], ion chromatography [19], controlling dynamic systems [22]. An RDR knowledge base (KB) is constructed as a collection of rules with exceptions. Input cases are given to the KB which outputs their descriptions. If the expert does not agree with the KB answers, s/he modifies the KB. Nested Ripple Down Rules (NRDR) [8] was conceived to further ease this incre-

mental KA process by allowing experts to introduce their own terms (concepts), and operationalise these terms while they are incomplete. A concept may be defined using other concepts and thus depends on their current definitions. A case has a description for each concept. Adding or modifying a concept may change the descriptions of past seen cases (because of concept dependencies) and cause inconsistencies that the expert has to fix.

An NRDR KBS is usually implemented as a tailored application [7] [8], written in C for example, which manipulates concepts and cases in related files. In this paper, we take another approach where we implement an NRDR KBS using an existing database system. Our starting point was to see conceptual similarities between an *incrementally built knowledge base* and a *database with evolving schema*. On one hand, a domain expert defines concepts and refines them incrementally. Thus her/his definitions change over time. This may have repercussions on past seen cases and cause inconsistencies. On the other hand, a designer defines a database schema according to an application domain, and implements the database (schema and data). Due to changes in the real world or to an incomplete schema, s/he changes the database schema over time. This may have repercussions on already stored data, and may let the database in an inconsistent state.

Many research efforts have been done in the 80's to integrate KB and database systems. Different methods of integration have been proposed, which can be categorized in three groups [11]: 1) extended KBS (KB systems are extended with data management functions associated with relational DBMS technology), 2) extended relational DBMS (RDBMS are extended with rule management functions), 3) interfacing KBS to RDBMS (the two systems are coupled). Later, integrating KB and object-oriented database systems has also been proposed [21]. Our approach has two main differences with the mentioned ones. The first is that we are dealing with incremental knowledge acquisition. The second and more important is that we did not look for

---

[1] This work was supported by a grant from the University Research Board of the American University of Beirut.

266

integrating a KB system and a database system. Our work is the result of a meeting between two areas. As said before, we found similarities between incremental knowledge acquisition and database schema evolution. We modeled then NRDR features in the F2 model and used the F2 OODBMS [1], which is a general-purpose database system, *as it was* (we did not extend it) to implement an NRDR KBS. This was possible thanks to the F2 features.

F2 is a research prototype which combines the following non-standard features: uniformity of objects [1] as in [23], multiobjects [3] as in [20] [16] [17], and schema evolution [1] [2] [3] [4] as in [6] [18] [23] [15]. Uniformity of objects allows us to extend the F2 meta-schema in order to implement NRDR concepts. Concepts are implemented as classes, and cases as objects. The multiobject mechanism supports multiple instantiation and object migration. Multiple instantiation allows us to store cases which have multiple descriptions. Object migration allows us to handle cases whose descriptions may change as a consequence of concept modification. Schema evolution is the ability to update the schema of a populated database. This allows us to add and modify concepts as needed during the incremental KA process.

Any OODBMS supporting the mentioned features can be used to implement an NRDR KBS. The advantages of doing so are the following: from a DB perspective, we add a new service to a database system. In addition to the usual functionalities (store, query, manipulate data), we show that a database system can be used to support incremental KA and hence a new application area. From a KA perspective, this suggests an economic process for building a KBS using an existing DBMS platform. Moreover, the same software can also be used to store, query, and manipulate the cases.

The paper is organised as follows: section 2 presents the NRDR methodology in the context of incremental KA. Section 3 presents F2 and highlights its features which allow us to implement an NRDR KBS. Section 4 shows an example of an NRDR incremental KA session, and describes how this session is implemented with F2. This will further expose the similarities between the two perspectives. Finally, section 5 concludes the paper.

2. Incremental KA with NRDR

In recent years of development of KBSs, it has become evident that knowledge provided by a human expert is always context dependent. Moreover experts do not normally have complete introspective access to their knowledge, they tend to give justifications of their considerations rather than a complete explanation. This led to new modern *incremental KA methodologies* which aim to incrementally re-construct experts knowledge in the context of its use. RDR [13] [12] is such a methodology which aims to improve the KA process by providing a framework for incrementally collecting knowledge from experts, for later inferring conclusions on future situations. A substantial extension of the RDR framework, Nested RDR, was introduced in [8] to allow the expert to introduce her/his own domain terms and to capture the relationships between such terms. In the rest of this section, we first describe RDR, and then NRDR.

2.1. Ripple Down Rules (RDR)

An *RDR KB* is a collection of simple rules organised in a binary tree structure. Each rule has the form "if *condition* then *conclusion*" where the condition is a boolean expression. Every rule can have two branches to other rules: a false-branch and a true-branch (also called the "exception" branch). An example RDR tree is shown in figure 1.

A *case classification* starts at the root node whose condition is always satisfied (this guarantees the KB to return an answer). Afterwards, when a rule applies (i.e. its condition is satisfied), the true branch is taken, otherwise the false branch is taken. This is repeated until a terminal node *t* is reached: if the condition of *t* is satisfied then the conclusion of *t* is returned by the KB. Otherwise, the conclusion of the parent node of *t* is returned, i.e. the conclusion of the last applied rule on the path to *t* is returned. When the expert disagrees with the conclusion returned by the KB, it is said to *fail* and requires modification.

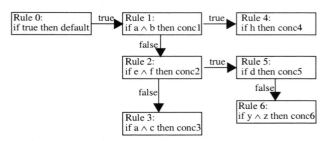

Figure 1. An RDR tree. Rules 1, 2, 3 are exceptions of rule 0, and rule 0 is their parent.

An RDR tree is *incrementally constructed* by adding new rules when the expert wants to correct a system failure. A new rule is added as a leaf node and attached as an exception of the last applied rule. Implicitly, the condition of a rule *r* conjuncts: (i) the conditions (or their negation) of the rules on the path from the root node to *r*, and (ii) the negation of conditions of the exceptions of *r*. For example, the implicit condition of rule 2 is: $\neg(a \wedge b) \wedge (e \wedge f) \wedge \neg(d) \wedge \neg(y \wedge z)$. Rules are never deleted or modified. Each rule has only a local effect. In [8], the RDR framework was substantially extended into Nested RDR. This is described in the next subsection.

2.2. Nested Ripple Down Rules (NRDR)

An *NRDR KB* is a hierarchy of concepts where each concept is represented as an RDR tree. Conclusions of concept rules have a boolean value indicating whether or not the concept is satisfied by a given case. Concepts may be defined using other concepts. When the condition of a concept rule contains expert-defined concepts, the boolean value of the condition is calculated in a backward chaining manner. An example of NRDR KB is given in figure 2: it has four concepts *A, B, C, D*. In concept *A*, the conclusions of rules are either *A* or ¬*A* (similarly for *B, C* and *D*). Note that the conclusion of a rule is always the negation of the conclusion of its parent rule (e.g. see rules A.1 and A.0, rules A.2 and A.0). Concept *A* is defined using concepts *B* and *C* (rule A.1) and *D* (rule A.2). No recursive or circular definition of concepts are allowed. The *concept hierarchy* of the NRDR example is shown in figure 3 where *A* is the highest level concept.

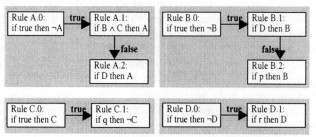

Figure 2. Each concept in an NRDR KB is represented as a separate RDR tree.

An NRDR KB is said to *fail* and requires modification if the expert disagrees with the conclusion returned by the highest level RDR tree. Given a case that requires an NRDR KB to be modified, the modification can occur in a number of places. In our previous example, a case satisfies *B*, ¬*C* and *D*, and is then classified by the KB as *A*. If the expert disagrees, s/he can add a new rule as an exception of rule A.2 in the *A* RDR tree. Alternatively, s/he can change the meaning of *D*, by adding a new rule to the *D* RDR tree. The choice of refinement depends on the expert's judgment. Localized updates in the hierarchical KB can lead to *inconsistencies*, e.g. if the expert modifies the RDR tree of a concept *D*, and *D* is used in the definition of a higher concept *A*, the expert may inadvertently cause a change in the meaning of *A*. This may cause inadvertent inconsistencies with respect to cases previously classified by *A*. Following every KB update, inconsistencies are checked by the KBS and have to be fixed by the expert. F2 is presented in the next section. We highlight its features which allow us to implement an NRDR KBS.

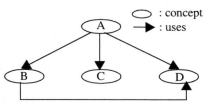

Figure 3. Concept hierarchy of the NRDR KB of fig. 2

3. F2 Object-Oriented Database Management System

In this section, we introduce the F2 model. Then we describe F2 multiobjects and schema evolution features. We discuss how they are used to implement an NRDR KBS.

3.1. F2 Model

In the F2 object-oriented model [1] an *object* o_C is an instance of *class C*. The object o_C is identified by $<id_C, id_o>$, where id_C is the class identifier and id_o is the instance identifier within *C*. Objects structure is defined by class attributes. Objects behaviour is defined by primitive methods (create, update, delete) and triggered methods (i.e. methods that are automatically executed when an event occurs).

A class, called *subclass*, can be declared as a specialization of another class called *superclass*. The class hierarchy is a forest, i.e. a set of specialization trees: a subclass has only one superclass (single inheritance), and there is not a root system-defined class. *Specialization constraints* may be defined on a subclass (and shared by other subclasses). They have the form <attribute, operator, value>. An object belongs to a subclass if and only if it satisfies the specialization constraints of the subclass (as in [5]). Specialization constraints are evaluated when creating or updating a multiobject (see section 3.2), and when creating or updating a specialization constraint (see section 3.3).

A concept rule in an NRDR KB can be viewed as a subclass in F2, and its implicit condition can be viewed as a set of specialization constraints defined on that subclass (see section 4).

3.2. Multiobjects in F2

We assume that the real-world consists of *entities* with several facets. For example, a human being may be seen as a person, an employee, a tennis player, a student, etc. An entity is implemented in the multiobject mechanism [3] by a set of objects in distinct classes of a specialization tree, $M_o = \{o_{C1}, o_{C2}, ..., o_{Cn}\}$, called *multiobject*. Each object o_{Ci} denotes a facet of the entity and carries data specific to its corresponding class Ci. All the objects of M_o have the same instance identifier. A multiobject M_o satisfies the following constraint: if o_{Ci} (where $1 \leq i \leq n$) belongs to M_o and Ci is a subclass of Cj, then there must be an object o_{Cj} which belongs to M_o (where $1 \leq j \leq n$ and $j \neq i$). In other words, if an entity possesses an object in a class C, then the entity must also possess objects for all the ancestors (direct and indirect superclasses) of C. Subclasses can be inclusive, i.e. a multiobject may contain two objects o_{Ci} and o_{Cj} where Ci and Cj are sibling classes. For example in figure 4, a person who is a student *and* a tennis player is implemented by a multiobject containing three objects: o_{Person} in *Person*, $o_{Student}$ in *Student* and $o_{TennisPlayer}$ in *TennisPlayer*. Attributes are not inherited but reached; since the name of o_{Person} is Smith, the name of $o_{Student}$ is Smith.

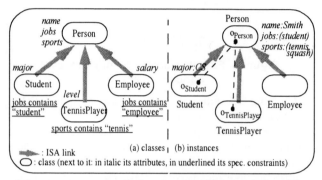

Figure 4. A multiobject representing a person who is student and tennis player

A multiobject can be created, deleted, and updated [3]. Creating a multiobject adds a set of objects (sharing the same instance identifier) to distinct classes of a specialization tree (this is referred to as multiple instantiation), according to the given attribute values and to the classes specialization constraints. Deleting a multiobject removes all its objects from their respective class. Updating a multiobject updates one of its attribute values. This may have as consequence adding and removing objects (this is referred to as object migration), since the multiobject may now (with the new attribute value) validate or invalidate specialization constraints.

A case is described by every concept in an NRDR KB, so we later view a case as a multiobject in F2 containing an object for each concept (see section 4).

3.3. Schema Evolution in F2

An important feature of F2 is the uniformity of its objects described in [1]. We consider objects of three levels: database objects (e.g. the person Smith), schema objects (e.g. the class Person), and meta-schema objects (e.g. the class CLASS). Uniformity of objects in F2 includes uniformity of representation, and uniformity of access and ma-

nipulation. It allowed us to build a set of more than 30 schema changes and to easily implement them [1]. We defined the semantics of each schema change in F2 with pre-conditions and post-actions in order to keep the database consistent when changing its schema. We implemented pre-conditions and post-actions by triggered methods. In F2 schema changes are propagated immediately [2] [4], i.e. the repercussions of a schema change are executed as soon as the schema change is performed. Another benefit of uniformity of objects is that it allows us to easily extend the meta-schema.

For later implementing an NRDR KBS using F2, we extend its meta-schema (see section 4.1) and use the following existing schema changes to add and modify concepts: create a subclass, create a specialization constraint, modify a specialization constraint, create an attribute, create an event, create a trigger (see section 4.2). The implementation of NRDR using F2 is presented and discussed in the next section.

4. Implementing an NRDR KBS using the F2 OODBMS

In this section, we first explain how each feature in an NRDR KB is represented in the F2 data model. Then we give an example of a KA session. We show how this proceeds exposing the technical details of our implementation of NRDR using F2.

4.1. Implementing NRDR using F2

A KA domain is represented in F2 as a root class D, and a case in that domain corresponds to an object in D. Each concept is represented in F2 as a subclass C of D, and class D has two corresponding boolean attributes: c_{value} and c_{expert}. For each object in D, c_{value} is the response of the KB, while c_{expert} is the answer of the expert. c_{value} is automatically set by triggered methods in F2, while c_{expert} is set by the domain expert. For an object not yet classified by the expert, c_{expert} has the null (i.e. unknown) value. In F2, a rule of an NRDR concept is represented as a subclass R of C, its implicit condition is represented as specialization constraints on R, its scope is the set of objects that belong to subclass R (note the scope of a rule in an NRDR KB is the set of cases correctly classified by it). If the condition of a rule contains another concept $C2$, the attribute $c2_{value}$ will be used in the corresponding specialization constraint.

The F2 meta-schema contains the meta-classes *CLASS*, *SubClass*, *Attribute*, *Key*, *SpecConstraint*, *Trigger*, *Event*, *Method* (see [1]). To represent an NRDR KB, we extend it once by adding three new meta-classes: *NRDRAttribute* (as subclass of *Attribute*), *NRDRConcept* and *NRDRRule* (as subclasses of *SubClass*) (see figure 5). We also add the method *UpdateKBAnswer* (object in the meta-class *Method*) that updates the boolean KB answer for a case. Note that the F2 meta-schema is accessible and easily updatable by an F2 user.

```
subclass NRDRAttribute of Attribute
when attributeType = "NRDRAttribute";

subclass NRDRConcept of SubClass
when subClassType = "NRDRConcept" (
        kbAnswer:            NRDRAttribute,
        expertAnswer :       NRDRAttribute,
        usedIn:              set-of NRDRConcept,
        defaultRule:         NRDRRule );

subclass NRDRRule of SubClass
when subClassType = "NRDRRule" (
        conclusion:          Boolean,
        right:               NRDRRule,
        left:                NRDRRule );
```

**Figure 5. Extension of F2 meta-schema in F2
Data Definition Language**

4.2. KA example with F2/NRDR

The KA task here is to build a KB to classify male models for an army scene in a Hollywood movie. The domain is a set of actors (see table 1) and the expert is an eccentric film producer. His decisions and their justifications are used to build an NRDR KB. In F2, each case is an object in the class *Person* with attributes *nb, weight, height, fat,* and *age*.

We identified three operations when building the NRDR KB: creating a new concept, creating a default rule for a concept, and creating a new rule as an exception of an existing rule. We implemented each of them by a set of F2 primitives.

n o.	weight (kg)	height (m)	body fat %	age (year)	expert comment	expert decision
1	90	1.75	40	21	too heavy	reject
2	60	1.9	3	26	too lean	reject
3	81	1.7	6	27	too heavy and too lean	accept
4	79	1.81	9.5	39	too lean	reject
5	80	1.6	9.8	25	too heavy	reject

Table 1. KA input cases. These correspond to the objects $\{p1_{Person}, p2_{Person}, p3_{Person}, p4_{Person}, p5_{Person}\}$.

The expert consults the cases. For each case, we explain: (i) the NRDR steps, and show the F2Web interface used by the expert to perform these steps, (ii) the corresponding actions done in the underlying F2 DBMS, which are not shown to the expert (like a blackbox).

Start. (i) The KB starts with the default rule *"if true then Accept"*. In the F2Web interface, the expert adds the highest level concept "Accept" for the "Person" domain and chooses a positive conclusion for its default rule (see figure 6).

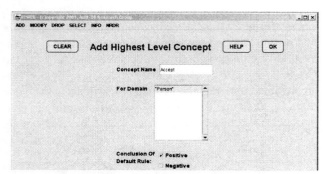

Figure 6. F2Web: adding the highest level concept Accept

(ii) Clicking OK will perform the following two initialisation steps in F2 (see figure 10.a):
1. Creating the concept "Accept": a) *Accept* is created as subclass of *Person*; as a result (post-action of this schema change) five objects are added to it. b) two boolean attributes are added to the class *Person*: *Accept* and *Accept_expert*, for which all objects of *Person* take the null value.
2. Creating a default rule "Accept0" for the concept "Accept": a) *Accept0* is created as subclass of *Accept*; five objects are consequently added to it. b) the attribute *Accept* is set to 1 for all objects of *Accept0* (since it has a positive conclusion). c) the event *(post-create Accept0)* is created, and a trigger is created to associate the method *UpdateKBAnswer* to this event. This, when an object is added to *Accept0*, will update automatically its attribute *Accept* to 1 (positive conclusion).

Case 1. (i) The expert finds case 1 too heavy and rejects it, so he enters the rule *"if TooHeavy then Reject"* (Reject is same as not Accept). He explains the concept "TooHeavy" with the rule *"if weight > 80 then TooHeavy"* (see figure 7).

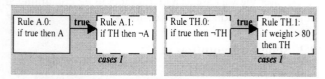

Figure 7. Evolving NRDR KB after Case 1. Added rules are dashed.

In the F2Web interface, the cases are presented to the expert. When he clicks on case 1, the KB answers for this case appear (see figure 8). When he clicks on the answer "Ac-

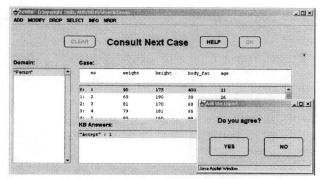

Figure 8. F2Web: consulting Case 1

cept: 1", a pop-up window appears with the question "Do you agree?". When he clicks on "NO", a new window "Add rule Accept1" opens to add a rule (see figure 9 back). The expert can either enter the rule condition or add a new concept and then enter a rule condition using this concept. He clicks on "Add Concept". A pop-up window appears where he enters the name of the new concept "TooHeavy" and the positive conclusion of its rule. Then a second window "Add rule TooHeavy1" opens (see figure 9 front). The expert enters the condition "weight > 80", gets back to the "Add rule Accept1" window and enters the condition "TooHeavy = 1". As a result, case 1 which was shown classified by rule "Accept0" will be shown classified by rule "Accept1".

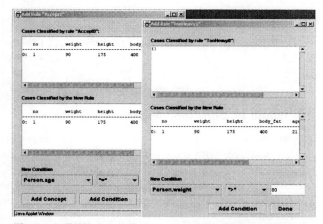

Figure 9. F2Web: adding concept TooHeavy with rule TooHeavy1, and then adding rule Accept1 which uses this concept.

(ii) In F2, this corresponds to the following steps (see figure 10.b):

3. Creating the concept "TooHeavy" (similar to step 1).

4. Creating a default rule "TooHeavy0" for the concept "TooHeavy" (similar to step 2).

5. Creating an exception rule "TooHeavy1" of the rule "TooHeavy0": a) *TooHeavy1* is created as subclass of *TooHeavy*; five objects are consequently added to it. b) on this new subclass, are added the specialization con-

straints of subclass *TooHeavy0*, and a new specialization constraint $weight > 80$ [2]. Objects $\{p2_{TooHeavy1}, p4_{TooHeavy1}, p5_{TooHeavy1}\}$ are consequently removed (post-action of these schema changes). c) the attribute *TooHeavy* is set to 1 for all objects of *TooHeavy1* (positive conclusion). d) the negation of the new specialization constraint, i.e. $weight \leq 80$, is added on subclass *TooHeavy0*. Objects $\{p1_{TooHeavy0}, p3_{TooHeavy0}\}$ are consequently removed. e) an event and a trigger are created for *TooHeavy1* as before. f) the attribute *TooHeavy_expert* of object $p1_{Person}$ (current case) is set to 1. g) inconsistencies are checked (explained later with case 5).

6. Creating an exception rule "Accept1" of the rule "Accept0" (similar to step 5).

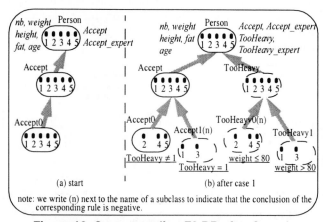

Figure 10. Corresponding F2 DB after Case 1. Added classes are dashed.

Case 2. (i) The expert finds case 2 too lean and rejects it. The KB accepts it (conclusion of rule A.0), so he enters a new rule to the highest level concept "Accept": *"if TooLean then Reject"*. This is an exception of rule A.0 (false branch of rule A.1). He explains the new concept "TooLean" with the rule *"if body fat < 7% then TooLean"*. The scope of rule A.2 is only case 2 as this does not contain previously classified cases. The current KB is shown in figure 11 (a case in the scope of a rule is underlined if the expert did not visit the case, i.e. did not give an answer, for the concept of that rule, e.g. the expert said that case 2 is too lean, he said nothing about too heavy).

(ii) In F2, the above corresponds to the following 4 steps: 1. creating the concept "TooLean", 2. creating a default rule "TooLean0" for the concept "TooLean", 3. creating an exception rule "TooLean1" of the rule "TooLean0", 4. cre-

---

[2] The first schema change here involves modifying each of the specialization constraints on *TooHeavy0* to add *TooHeavy1* to the set of subclasses on which they are defined. In this particular case, *TooHeavy0* has no specialization constraints. The second schema change is creating a new specialization constraint on *TooHeavy1*.

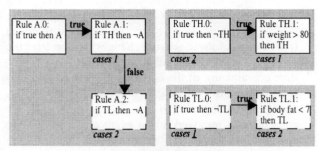

Figure 11. Evolving NRDR KB after Case 2.

ating an exception rule "Accept2" of the rule "Accept0". These 4 steps are correspondingly similar to steps 3 to 6 above. Note that subclass *Accept2* has two specialization constraints (see figure 12): the first is shared with *Accept0*, the negation of the second is added on *Accept0*. Note also that $p2_{Accept0}$ is removed from *Accept0* and $p2_{Accept2}$ is added to *Accept2*.

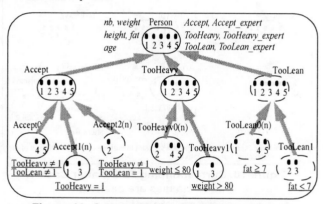

Figure 12. Corresponding F2 DB after Case 2.

Case 3. (i) The expert finds case 3 too heavy and too lean and accepts it although it is too heavy. The KB rejects it (by rule A.1), so he enters a new rule *"if TooLean then Accept"*. This is an exception rule of A.1, which implies that if a case is too heavy and too lean then it is accepted (see figure 13).

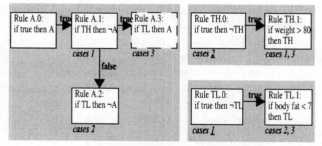

Figure 13. Evolving NRDR KB after Case 3.

In the F2Web interface, the expert clicks on the KB answers for case 3, agrees with "TooHeavy: 1" and

"TooLean: 1", and disagrees with "Accept: 0". When disagreeing, a window opens to add a new rule (see figure 14).

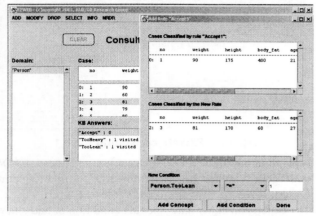

Figure 14. F2Web: adding rule Accept3.

(ii) This corresponds in F2 to creating an exception rule "Accept3" of the rule "Accept1" (similar to step 5 earlier). See figure15.

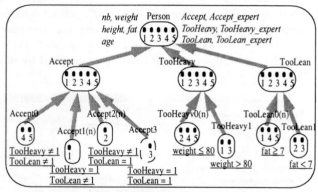

Figure 15. Corresponding F2 DB after Case 3.

Case 4. (i) The expert finds case 4 too lean and rejects it. This disagrees with the KB (by default rule A.0), so he modifies the concept "TooLean" by adding the rule *"if height > 1.8 then TooLean"* (exception of rule TL.0). The KB now agrees with the expert on the basis of rule A.2 (see figure 16).

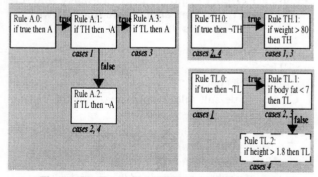

Figure 16. Evolving NRDR KB after Case 4.

(ii) This corresponds in F2 to creating an exception rule "TooLean2" of the rule "TooLean0" (similar to step 5). It is interesting to note here that the re-classification of case 4 for the concept "TooLean" leads to its re-classification for the concept "Accept" (see figure 17). Since the object $p4_{TooLean2}$ is added to *TooLean2* and its value on the attribute *TooLean* set to 1, this (see section 3.2 updating a multiobject) causes the removal of object $p4_{Accept0}$ and the addition of object $p4_{Accept2}$ with its attribute *Accept* updated to 0 (by triggered method *UpdateKBAnswer*).

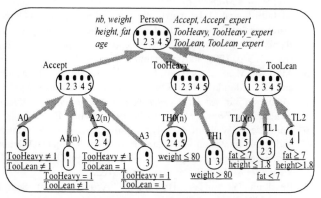

Figure 17. Corresponding F2 DB after Case 4.

Case 5. (i) The expert finds case 5 too heavy and rejects it. This again disagrees with the KB (conclusion of rule A.0), so he updates the concept "TooHeavy" by adding the rule: *"if body fat > 9% then TooHeavy"* (exception of rule TH.0). Case 5 is now rejected by the KB (by rule A.1). The newly added rule TH.2 also covers case 4 which was not visited by the expert for the "TooHeavy" concept. This case becomes now accepted by the KB (by rule A.3), it was earlier rejected by the expert. Case 4 becomes an inconsistency, which to fix, the expert needs to modify the KB. He has two options: rethink his change to the concept "TooHeavy" (e.g. using the limit of 9.7% for body fat instead of 9%), or modify the higher concept "Accept" by entering a new exception of rule A.3 (e.g. *"if age > 35 then Reject"*). See figure 18.

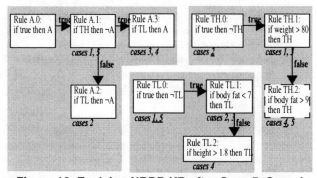

Figure 18. Evolving NRDR KB after Case 5. Case 4 which was rejected before (rule A.2) becomes now accepted (rule A.3); this is an inconsistency.

In the F2Web interface, after adding the rule "TooHeavy2", a pop-up alert window appears indicating the inconsistency to the expert, and asking him to enter another rule.

(ii) In F2, this corresponds to creating an exception rule "TooHeavy2" of the rule "TooHeavy0". Note that the subclass *TooHeavy2* contains $p4_{TooHeavy2}$ with its attribute *TooHeavy* set to 1 (see figure 19). This in turn removes $p4_{Accept2}$ and adds $p4_{Accept3}$ (its attribute *Accept* is then updated to 1 by the triggered method, while its attribute *Accept_expert* was previously set to 0). Further, any object with different values on attributes *Accept* and *Accept_expert* is an inconsistency and requires expert intervention.

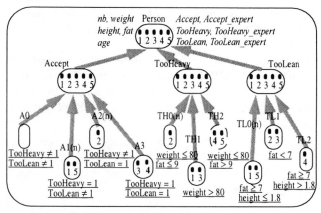

Figure 19. Corresponding F2 DB after Case 5. $p4_{Person}$ takes 0 on the attribute Accept_expert (set before), and takes now 1 on the attribute Accept; this is an inconsistency.

5. Conclusion

We showed in this paper similarities between an incrementally built knowledge base and a database with evolving schema. This led us to implement an NRDR KBS using the F2 OODBMS. Our implementation relies on F2 nonstandard features. In particular, F2 multiobject mechanism allows cases in the domain of expertise to be queried against multiple concepts simultaneously as is required in NRDR. Further, F2 schema evolution well accommodates modifying the classes representation of NRDR concepts, as far managing the migrating cases between concept rules.

From our experience we can say that a database management system, which is initially not designed for knowledge management, but which supports uniformity of objects, multiobjects and schema evolution, can be used for incremental knowledge acquisition. Consequently it can offer a new service and extend data management to involve knowledge acquisition. This is the main benefit from a DB perspective. From a KA perspective, it suggests an economic process for building a KBS using an existing DBMS platform. Moreover, the same software can also be used to store, query, and manipulate the cases.

In our F2/NRDR implementation, we did not add a single line of code to the F2 OODBMS. We extended the F2 meta-schema once in F2-DDL, and used the existing F2 primitives. We added the NRDR menu to the F2Web graphical interface developped in Java (see figure 20 right). This menu guides the expert to enter her/his rules during the incremental KA process (see section 4.2.). Moreover it allows her/him to traverse the NRDR KB (see figure 20 top) and the concept hierarchy. It also allows the expert her/himself to enter the domain (e.g. Person) with its attributes (e.g. height, weight, ...) and the cases. Using this menu does not require any knowledge of F2. Indeed the expert will build an NRDR KB without knowing that s/he is using a DBMS.

We illustrated our approach with the actors example. We plan to use F2/NRDR to build a CAD tool. Testing our approach in real life applications will allow us to see possible limitations of our F2 implementation of NRDR and to improve it.

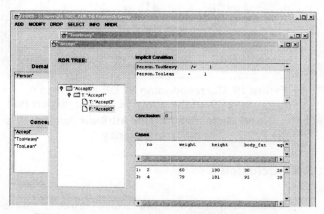

top: Clicking on concept *Accept* shows its RDR tree; clicking on rule *Accept3* shows its implicit condition, its conclusion, and cases classified by it. Each concept is viewed in a window (Accept, TooHeavy).
right: the items of the NRDR menu in the F2Web interface.

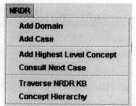
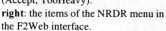

Figure 20. F2Web: traversing the NRDR KB.

Acknowledgments

The authors would like to thank Fatmé El-Moukaddem for adding the NRDR menu to the F2Web interface.

References

1. Al-Jadir L., T. Estier, G. Falquet, and M. Léonard. "Evolution Features of the F2 OODBMS". in *4th Int. Conference on Database Systems for Advanced Applications (DASFAA'95)*. 1995. Singapore: World Scientific.
2. Al-Jadir L., *Evolution-Oriented Database Systems (Ph.D. thesis)*, in *Faculty of Sciences*. 1997, University of Geneva: Geneva.
3. Al-Jadir L. and M. Léonard. "Multiobjects to Ease Schema Evolution in an OODBMS". in *17th Int. Conference on Conceptual Modeling (ER'98)*. 1998. Singapore: Springer.
4. Al-Jadir L. and M. Léonard. "Transposed Storage of an Object Database to Reduce the Cost of Schema Changes". in *Workshop of 18th Int. Conference on Conceptual Modeling (ECDM'99)*. 1999. Paris: Springer.
5. Atkinson M., F. Bancilhon, D. DeWitt, K. Dittrich, D. Maier, and S. Zdonik. "The Object-Oriented Database System Manifesto". in *1st Int. Conference on Deductive and Object-Oriented Databases (DOOD'89)*. 1989. Kyoto: Elsevier.
6. Banerjee J., W. Kim, H-J. Kim, and H.F. Korth. "Semantics and Implementation of Schema Evolution in Object-Oriented Databases". in *Int. Conference on Management Of Data (ACM SIGMOD'87)*. 1987. San Francisco: ACM.
7. Beydoun G. and A. Hoffmann. "Acquisition of Search Knowledge". in *10th European Knowledge Acquisition Workshop (EKAW'97)*. 1997. Spain: Springer.
8. Beydoun G. and A. Hoffmann. "NRDR for the Acquisition of Search Knowledge". in *10th Australian Conference on Artificial Intelligence*. 1997. Australia: Springer.
9. Beydoun G. and A. Hoffmann. "Hierarchical Incremental Knowledge Acquisition". in *12th Banff Knowledge Acquisition for Knowledge-Based Systems Workshop (KAW'99)*. 1999. Canada: SRDG publications.
10. Beydoun G. and A. Hoffmann. "Theoretical Framework of Incremental Hierarchical Knowledge Acquisition". Int. Journal of Human Computer Interactions, 2001. 54.
11. Blair A. "Methods of Integrating Knowledge-based and Database Systems". in *5th Australasian Database Conference (ADC'94)*. 1994. New Zealand: World Scientific.
12. Compton P., G. Edwards, B. Kang, L. Lazarus, R. Malor, P. Preston, and A. Srinivasan. "Ripple down rules: Turning knowledge acquisition into knowledge maintenance". Artificial Intelligence in Medicine, 1992. 4: p. 463-475.
13. Compton P. and R. Jansen. "Knowledge in Context: a strategy for expert system maintenance". in *2nd Australian Joint Artificial Intelligence Conference (AI'88)*. 1988.
14. Edwards G., P. Compton, R. Malor, A. Srinivason, and L. Lazarus. "PEIRS: a pathologist maintained expert system for interpretation of chemical pathology reports". Pathology, 1993. 25: p. 27-34.
15. Ferrandina F., T. Meyer, R. Zicari, G. Ferran, and J. Madec. "Schema and Database Evolution in the O2 Object Database System". in *21st Int. Conference on Very Large Data Bases (VLDB'95)*. 1995. Zürich: Morgan Kaufmann.
16. Kuno H.A., Y-G. Ra, and E.A. Rundensteiner. "The Object-Slicing Technique: A Flexible Object Representation and Its

Evaluation". Technical Report, CSE-TR-241-95, University of Michigan. 1995.

17. Ling T.W. and P.K. Teo. "Object Migration in ISA Hierarchies". in *4th Int. Conference on Database Systems for Advanced Applications (DASFAA'95)*. 1995. Singapore: World Scientific.

18. Penney D.J. and J. Stein. "Class Modification in the GemStone Object-Oriented DBMS". in *Conference on Object-Oriented Programming Systems, Languages and Applications (OOPSLA'87)*. 1987. Orlando.

19. Ramadan Z., M. Mulholland, D.B. Hibbert, P. Compton, P. Preston, and P.R. Haddad. "Towards an Expert System in Ion Chromatography Using Multiple Classification Ripple Down Rules (MCRDR)". in *Int. Ion Chromatography Symposium (IICS'97)*. 1997. Canada.

20. Sciore E. "Object Specialization". ACM Transactions on Information Systems, vol. 7, no 2, april 1989.

21. Sheng O.R.L. and C-P. Wei. "Object-Oriented Modeling and Design of Coupled Knowledge-base/Database Systems". in *8th Int. Conference on Data Engineering (ICDE'92)*. 1992. Tampe: IEEE.

22. Shiraz G.M. *Building Controller for Dynamic Systems (Ph.D. thesis)*, in *School of Computer Science and Engineering*. 1998, New South Wales: Sydney.

23. Tresch M. "A Framework for Schema Evolution by Meta Object Manipulation". in *3rd Int. Workshop on Foundations of Models and Languages for Data and Objects (FMLDO'91)*. 1991. Aigen.

Methodology For Creating a Sample Subset of Dynamic Taxonomy to Use in Navigating Medical Text Databases

Dennis Wollersheim, Wenny Rahayu

Dept. of Computer Science and Computer Engineering
La Trobe University, Bundoora, Victoria 3086Australia
email: {dewoller, wenny}@cs.latrobe.edu.au

Abstract

The amount of text available in electronic form is increasing, especially since the rise of the web. So too are the potential interconnections between concepts, given the advent of ontologies and other relationship based data sources. Text could be navigated using the structure from the ontologies, specifically, using dynamic taxonomies to navigate the is-a relationships.

Dynamic taxonomies are rooted index structures that dynamically prune themselves in response to zoom requests. The use of dynamic taxonomies with existing ontologies, and in the medical field, is unexplored. This paper details the process of connecting index terms from a medical text database to a taxonomy extracted from an existing medical ontology.

1. Introduction

There exist large collections of text. The number and volume of such collections are growing. Additionally, the number of computer usable interconnections between the concepts in the text are growing, due to the development of ontologies. This work explores use of ontologies for information retrieval.

An ontology is a set of concepts, linked by relationships. In this paper we use an a particular subset of ontology, a *taxonomy*. A taxonomy is a set of concepts linked by *IS-A* type relationships.

Text has been traditionally navigated through indexes, table of contents, and browsing. As the text become larger, browsing becomes problematic, and even the other methods become unmanageable; as the text size grows, so too grow the indexes.

1.1. Information retrieval by browsing

Browsing, the retrieval of information by recognition rather than recall, has many advantages. The foremost of these is that human memory is better at recognising items than remembering them without cues [1].

One way to increase recall in a text browsing environment is to increase the number of ways to gain access to a certain bit of data, in other words, to increase the number of entry points into a text. Examples of this include deepening the detail of a table of contents, or increasing the number of index entries.

The latter could be readily accomplished by marrying existing index terms with entries from a taxonomy. The problem with this strategy is that the utility of browsing as a strategy declines as the number of terms increase, unless there are subsequent ways of ordering or reducing the term set.

Sacco uses dynamic taxonomy (DT) [2] as a solution to this problem of term overload. Firstly, DT provides standard taxonomic ordering of the index term set, allowing complexity to be hidden under higher level terms. Secondly, it provides a zoom operator, which can be used to reduce the term set.

The zoom operation functions in the following manner. In response to a request to zoom in on a term, the system dynamically prunes the taxonomy, retaining only the taxonomic elements which categorise the set of text atoms which are also categorised by the zoom term. For example, figure 1 shows a sample taxonomy derived from the medical field. Figure 2 shows the pruned taxonomy after a zoom on the concept amoxycillin. In this example, if a text atom is not classified by amoxycillin, it is not included in the pruned taxonomy. More importantly, any terms in the taxonomy that do not either directly or indirectly classify the remaining text atoms are also pruned.

Original DT retrieved from a database of discrete newspaper articles. The present paper describes work based on a medical therapy encyclopaedia, retrieving small chunks of text from a continuous stream of highly interrelated content. Because of complexity and interest, much text processing work has been done in the field of medical text. There are many medical term sets. Where Sacco used a hand crafted purpose-built taxonomy, our taxonomic source

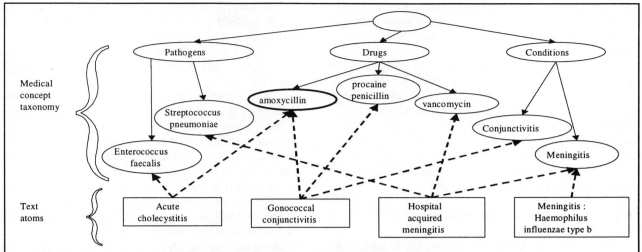

Figure 1 Example taxonomy, and subsequently classified text atoms. Solid lines shows taxonomic is-a links, dotted lines denoted classification by a taxonomic term

is extracted from a pre-existing medical ontology, the Unified Medical Language System (UMLS, 2001 version) [3,4,5].

In DT, document index terms were manually assigned. Application of UMLS to a text base would be facilitated if the connection between UMLS and the text base could be computer generated. This paper uses shallow natural language processing techniques to assign concepts from UMLS. This technique has been explored by others (for example, see [6, 7])

Browsing alone can be cumbersome, as web surfing testifies. In practice, browsing is often combined with a query. For example, when using a reference book, we often look up a primary index word, then scan sub headings. The work in this paper will be used in a system that models this synergy. It will use query to narrow selection, and browse to traverse a DT generated hierarchal semantic categorisation of results.

Similarly, in Dynacat [8, 9] medical documents are categorised using UMLS, queries are mapped to the medical

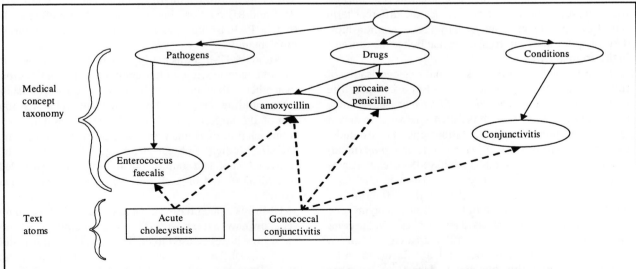

Figure 2 Remaining taxonomy after a zoom on the concept amoxycillin. Atoms that are not classified by amoxicillin are pruned; also pruned are the sections of the taxonomic tree that would be unused.

domain, and results browsed taxonomically. Importantly, Dynacat was found to be significantly more useful in satisfying user information requests than either cluster or ranking tools. Dynamic taxonomy improves on Dynacat. It is more flexible, as the taxonomy can be dynamically regenerated, in response to zoom or other queries.

The medical field is highly complex, and the amount of available information is increasing rapidly. The democratisation of information brought about by the web has impacted medicine in particular, due to its very personal nature. The audience for this particular material is expanding and becoming less professional, which bodes a demand for alternative access methods.

1.2. Existing Medical Information

The specific medical text we will use will be taken from the Dermatology edition of the Therapeutic Guidelines Limited (TGL) series of electronic medical handbooks [10]. As there are 10 such titles, and the amount of information is increasing, TGL seeks to increase information retrieval capability. The use of computer implemented guidelines has been investigated for this purpose, but more fundamental information retrieval techniques were found to be needed [11, 12]. The increased accessibility due to dynamic taxonomy will be well received.

For the taxonomy we use an extraction from the UMLS. UMLS is a project of the USA National Institute of Health, originally built in order to unify medical term sets. It consists of two main sections: the Metathesaurus, and the Semantic Network.

The Metathesaurus is an ontology of medical knowledge [13]. A key constituent of the metathesaurus is a *concept*, which serves as nexus of terms across the different term sets. Concepts are interconnected by a set of relationships, derived for the most part from those that linked the concepts in the original term sets.

The Semantic Network is a systematic categorisation of the concepts by semantic type. For example, the Metathesaurus concept *Dyshidrotic Eczema* has the semantic type *Disease or Syndrome*. It is called a network because it too has structure via a set of relationships. For example, the semantic types *Mental or Behaviour Dysfunction* (mind) and *Neoplastic Process* (body) both have IS-A relationships with the semantic type *Disease or Syndrome*.

UMLS is an amalgamation of more than 50 term sets; this breadth makes it strong in the area of synonymy, and useful for natural language based approaches. On the other hand, the term sets were generally created for human controlled indexing activities and not designed to be computer usable; this has led to less than rigorous construction.

This construction process leads to problems. UMLS has greatly varying granularity, is not rigorously defined or systematic, and is often inconsistent within and across term sets [7]. As a result, we must develop strategies to deal with specific problems that arise when extracting a taxonomy.

UMLS has 8 major relationship types and 212 subtypes. While these relationships may have been rigorously defined in the documentation of their original term sets, upon amalgamation into UMLS, all the user is left with is the relationship specifier, and the concepts that they describe. This is definition by example. Some of the relationships have a well defined intrinsic meaning (eg. IS-A, PART-OF), while others are quite nonspecific (eg. OTHER).

Strictly speaking, the relationships in a taxonomy are IS-A relationships. This means that a concept at a lower level is a more specific type of a concept at a higher level. The problem comes in that, while UMLS does contain information about IS-A relationships between concepts, they are few, comprising less than 2% of total number of relationships.

Because of the paucity of strict IS-A relationships, we choose to use less well defined but more numerous set of 'broader' type relationships, that of *parent* (PAR) and *relation-broader* (RB). These comprise a set of relationships similar to those specified by IS-A, and more importantly, make up greater than 15% of the total number of relations in UMLS.

The variety of term sets that make up UMLS mean that relationships are defined in a variety of ways. The decision to the broaden our inclusion criteria for relationships that will make up our taxonomy means that the relationships we extract are more often internally inconsistent. For example, PAR and RB relations between concepts are often cyclic (e.g. a PAR b and b PAR a); this makes taxonomy problematic!

Although UMLS was not rigorously defined, some of its constituent term sets are more comprehensive and rigorous than others. To avoid the problem of cyclical relationships when building our taxonomy, we use only relations from two of the largest term sets: SNOMED (Systematized Nomenclature of Human and Veterinary Medicine), and MESH (Medical Subject Headings). Even with this restricted set of data sources, not all problems are avoided. SNOMED in and of itself has cycles, as can be seen in figure3.

UMLS is a potentially valuable resource, but we do not yet know how to use it with DT. More generally, we do not know how it can be used to facilitate medical information retrieval. UMLS is a large dataset, containing more than 700,000 concepts, and 9,000,000 relationships. This size necessitates the creation of a sample subset of document base and connected UMLS concept-relation hierarchy.

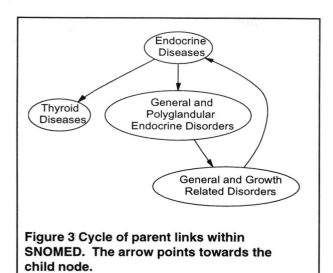

Figure 3 Cycle of parent links within SNOMED. The arrow points towards the child node.

The sample subset will be used 1) as a basis for a prototype DT medical text browser, 2) to judge the veracity of the methodology, and 3) as raw material upon which to tune the DT zoom algorithm. Lessons learned here will be used more widely in further synthesis of ontologies and text databases.

The subset was built in the following way. First, medical reference text was taken from the TGL medical therapy encyclopaedia. Noun phrases were then extracted to generate a list of potential index phrases. The phrases were normalised to create a standard form that could then be used to match against UMLS strings which had been similarly normalised. Finally, a taxonomy was grown from the SNOMED and MESH derived relations in UMLS, based on the UMLS concepts found in the previous step. Figure 4 diagrammatically describes the process.

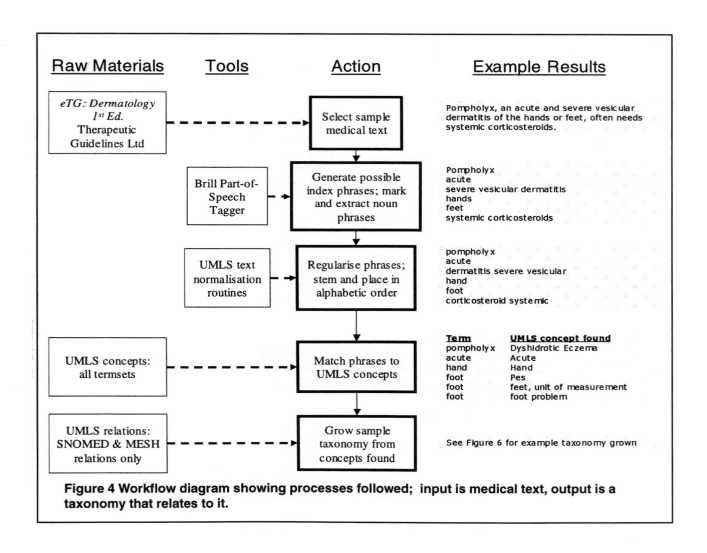

Figure 4 Workflow diagram showing processes followed; input is medical text, output is a taxonomy that relates to it.

2. Methodology for Creating a Subset Dynamic Taxonomy

A dynamic taxonomy needs a set of documents which are multiply classified by topics embedded in an taxonomy. This paper describes a methodology for the construction of such a structure. It consists of 5 steps:

1) choose subset of medical text to work with,
2) generate possible index phrases,
3) stem and order phrases,
4) match phrases to UMLS concepts, and
5) grow taxonomy from found concepts.

The choice of medical text to work with was arbitrary, but had some rationale. We chose the 6 sections covering the general topic of dermatitis from eTG: Dermatology because:

· the content is related, which will help test precision of DT, i.e. evaluate the usefulness of using DT for fine grained distinction, and

· there are many index words within each section, and as a result, the resulting taxonomy is dense.

The sections were taken from the electronic version of the book, which is more atomised than the paper book. This is because disconnection from a linear book sequence necessitates sections that can stand alone.

The text was divided into paragraphs, for later retrieval purposes. This division was done on a purely lexical level, with paragraphs being denoted as strings separated by 1 or more new line characters. An example paragraph is "Pompholyx, an acute and severe vesicular dermatitis of the hands or feet, often needs systemic corticosteroids." [10].

The next step was to find phrases in the text that could be used as index terms. This was done by first tagging the parts of speech in the text using the Brill tagger [14]. Then, possible index phrases were extracted by selecting maximum length consecutive groups of nouns and adjectives. The possible index phrases extracted from the above example include "feet", "severe vesicular dermatitis", and "systemic corticosteroids".

The resulting words were converted to a standard form using the UMLS provided dictionary assisted suffix trimmer, and then sorted into alphabetic order within the phrase. This process converts "feet" to "foot", and "systemic corticosteroids" to "corticosteroid systemic".

The normalised phrases were then matched against a similarly processed master list of phrases representing all the concepts in UMLS. Concepts with exact matches were said to exist in the original text. Other work [7] used a technique of looking for an increasingly smaller portions of the phrase until a match was found, but our more restrictive condition found an adequate number of index concepts. In the example, *pompholx* matched the concept *Dyshidrotic Eczema*, while *foot* matched 3 concepts: the feet on the human body, problems of those feet, and the unit of measurement.

At this point, we have a list of UMLS concepts relating to a set of text documents. To be used in dynamic taxonomy, these concepts need to be embedded in a taxonomy. The algorithm used to build the taxonomy is as follows. For each concept, repeatedly add any new PAR or RB link and

---

Extract all links that have as children the matched concepts, make them $level_0$ relations
level = 0;
while more_relations_to_extract
    level = level + 1
    for each concept $C_{level-1}$
        for each concept C_{level} that is a parent to $C_{level-1}$
            if C_{level} is already in the chain $C_0 .. C_{level-1}$,
                mark link $C_{level-1}..C_{level}$ as bad, to exclude it from
                    further consideration (to eliminate loops)
            else if the link $C_{level-1}..C_{level}$ has not already been extracted
                extract it
                extract concept C_{level}
        loop
    loop
loop

Figure 5 Algorithm for generating taxonomy without cycles.

related concept where the target concept is of the same semantic type as the source concept.

It is necessary to eliminate cycles during this process. The first link detected that would cause a cycle is marked as 'bad', barring it from being chosen for this path, or as part of any other path. Figure 5 shows a more formal explanation of the algorithm.

The end result of the above algorithm is a set of separate hierarchies, because not all concepts have a common ancestor. We go on to use the UMLS semantic network to provide a single consistent root. As there are no cycles in the semantic network, this extraction algorithm is simpler: for each parentless node in the forest, find its semantic type. Then, from the semantic network, follow the IS-A relationships up to the root, extracting each relations traversed. Figure 6 shows the result of this process, a hierarchy consisting of some of the ancestors of the concept *Dyshidrotic Eczema*.

Due to the level of detail in UMLS and the fact that we work with a limited sample of medical text, the resulting hierarchy is narrow and deep, often having only one child per parent. We ameliorate this by promoting grandchildren which are children of sole children, eliminating the 'only child' node. This has the advantage of making the hierarchy shallower but not wider.

3. Implementation of the Subset Creation Methodology

The following methodology has been implemented using Oracle database. First, the UMLS dataset was imported into Oracle. The Therapeutic Guidelines content, originally in HTML form, was converted to raw text. Noun phrases were extracted using a Linux based Brill tagging program, stemmed, and then matched against the UMLS master phrase

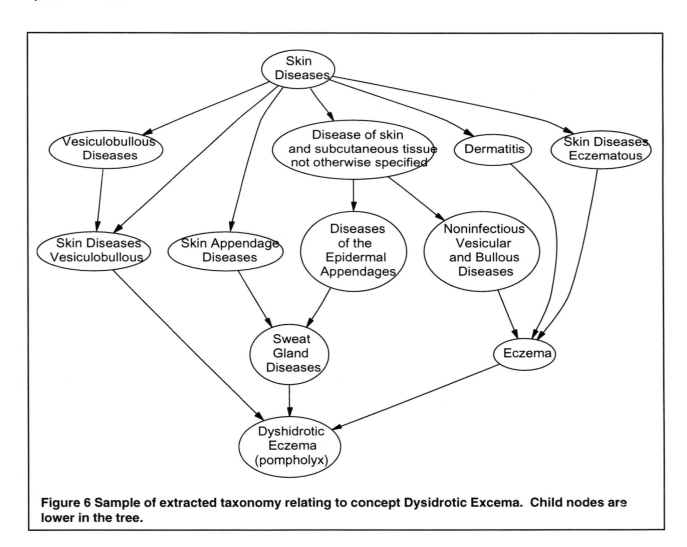

Figure 6 Sample of extracted taxonomy relating to concept Dysidrotic Excema. Child nodes are lower in the tree.

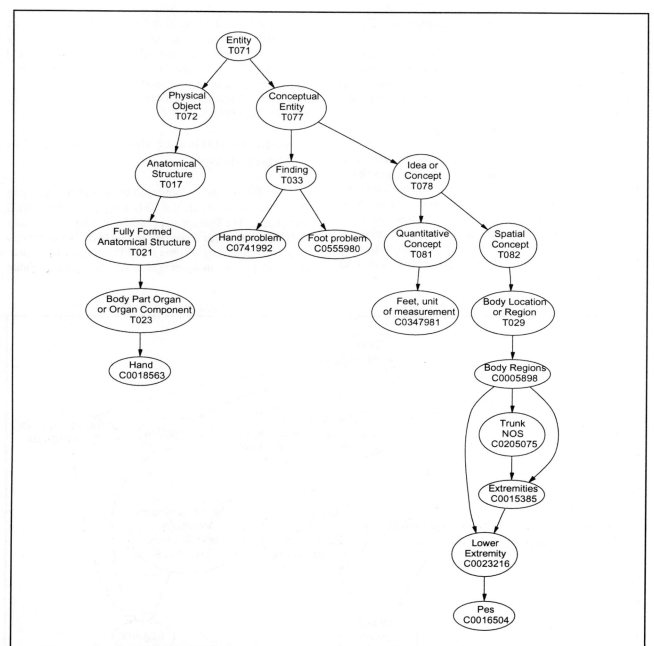

Figure 7 Partial taxonomy, consisting of parents of concepts derived from the strings in the text 'hand' and 'foot'. The C number is the concept id from the UMLS metathesaurus, the T number is the semantic node id from the semantic network.

list. From the list of matches, a taxonomy extracted from UMLS using Perl scripts and Oracle SQL queries.

This process divided up the original 6 book sections into 146 paragraphs, from which 489 unique UMLS concepts were extracted. These concepts formed the base of a hierarchy which contained 1021 distinct concepts and semantic network nodes, joined by 1328 relationships.

Figure 7 shows a subset of the extracted taxonomy. It consists of the parent nodes to the concepts that were generated due from the phrases 'hand' and 'foot'. Problems are apparent. Hand and foot are classified by UMLS editors into entirely different branches of the semantic network, defying common sense. These words are also ambiguous, having multiple senses for each.

Figure 8 shows a partially expanded treeview of the taxonomy. The level of detail retrieved by this method is

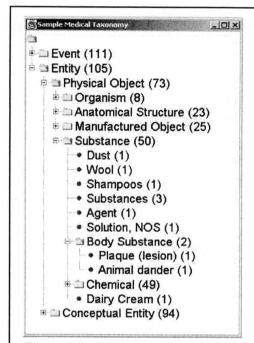

Figure 8 Sample of taxonomy grown. The number in brackets after the term is the total number of unique paragraphs classified by either this term, or by the children of this term.

apparent. This would overwhelm a real user. We must reduce the detail in some way.

During this sample generation process, errors were found. These include:

- the noun phrase extraction process had low the precision and recall, because of the specialised medical vocabulary,
- UMLS synonymy itself is a problem; words are sometimes misidentified into an incorrect context; for example, the string 'proven' is a type of anti-venom,
- even where the correct sense of the word is identified, the resulting terms sometimes would

have little meaning in an index, e.g. 'agent' or 'week', and

- there is a problem with scope. The concepts are assumed to apply at paragraph level; but some terms apply more widely. For example, in this sample, the term 'dermatitis' applies everywhere.

4. Future Work

A weakness of this work is that it is difficult to judge the dynamic taxonomy that was created, as there is no gold standard by which to judge the precision and recall of the concept generation algorithm. A candidate for such a standard would be to match the current, manually assigned index terms to UMLS concepts.

A solution to the problems with UMLS would be to use a more systematically constructed term set instead. SNOMED CT (Systematized Nomenclature of Medicine, Clinical Terms) [15], and GALEN (Generalised Architecture for Languages, Encyclopaedias and Nomenclatures in Medicine) [16] are two possibilities. While not as diverse as UMLS, they both were designed to be used in a more structured way, and as such, have the potential to be more systematically ordered.

5. Conclusion

Medicine is a complex field, as is evident from the scope of UMLS itself. The mere addition of 8 million relationships to a problem does not in and of itself make it less complex. We must also add order. Dynamic taxonomy provides a way to order a complex field.

This work shows a reasonable methodology for generating a sample subset that joins a section of text database to a taxonomy. The result will be useful for dynamic taxonomy.

6. Bibliography

[1]   E. F. Mulhall, "Experimental studies in recall and recognition", *American Journal of Psychology*, vol. 26, pp. 217-228, 1915.

[2]   G. Sacco, "Dynamic taxonomies: a model for large information bases", *IEEE Transactions on Knowledge & Data Engineering*, vol. 12, pp. 468-79, 2000.

[3]   K. E. Campbell, D. E. Oliver, K. A. Spackman, and E. H. Shortliffe, "Representing thoughts, words, and things in the UMLS", *Journal of the American Medical Informatics Association*, vol. 5, pp. 421-31, 1998.

[4] D. A. B. Lindberg, B. L. Humphreys, and A. T. McCray, "The Unified Medical Language", *System. Meth. Inform. Med.*, vol. 32, pp. 281-291, 1993.

[5] A. T. McCray, A. R. Aronson, A. C. Browne, T. C. Rindflesch, A. Razi, and S. Srinivasan, "UMLS Knowledge for Biomedical Language Processing", *Bulletin of the Medical Library Association*, vol. 81, pp. 184-194, 1993.

[6] A. R. Aronson, "Effective Mapping of Biomedical Text to the UMLS Metathesaurus: The MetaMap Program", presented at *American Medical Informatics Association Annual Symposium*, Washington DC, 2001.

[7] P. Nadkarni, R. Chen, and C. Brandt, "UMLS Concept Indexing for Production Databases: A Feasability Study", *Journal of American Medical Informatics Association*, vol. 8, pp. 80-91, 2001.

[8] W. Pratt, "Dynamic Categorization: A Method for Decreasing Information Overload", in *Medical Information Sciences*: Stanford University, 1999, pp. 171.

[9] W. Pratt and L. Fagan, "The Usefulness of Dynamically Categorizing Search Results", *Journal of American Medical Informatics Association*, vol. 7, pp. 605-617, 2000.

[10] M. Stevens, "eTG: Dermatology", 1 ed. Melbourne: Therapeutic Guidelines Ltd, 1999.

[11] D. Wollersheim, "A Review of Decision Support Formats with Respect to Therapeutic Guidelines Limited Requirements", presented at Ninth National Health Informatics Conference, Canberra, ACT, Australia, 2001.

[12] D. Wollersheim and W. Rahayu, "Implemenation of Dynamic Taxonomies for Clinical Guidelline Retrieval", presented at International Conference on Medical Informatics, Hyderabad, India, 2001.

[13] D. M. Pisanelli, A. Gangemi, and G. Steve, "An Ontological Analysis of the UMLS Metathesaurus", presented at *American Medical Informatics Association Annual Symposium*, 1998.

[14] E. Brill, "Some Advances In Rule-Based Part of Speech Tagging", *AAAI*, 1994.

[15] SNOMED, "SNOMED International: SNOMED Clinical Terms (SNOMED CT)", http://www.snomed.org/snomedct_txt.html, 2001.

[16] W. D. Solomon, C. J. Wroe, A. L. Rector, J. E. Rogers, J. L. Fistein, and P. Johnson, "A Reference Terminology for Drugs", presented at *American Medical Informatics Association Annual Symposium*, 1999.

Rules Termination Analysis Investigating the Interaction between Transactions and Triggers

Danilo Montesi *
Dip. Scienze Informazione
Università di Bologna
Mura Anteo Zamboni, 7
40127 Bologna, Italy

Elisa Bertino † Maria Bagnato ‡
Dip. Scienze Informazione
Università di Milano
Via Comelico, 39/41,
20135 Milano, Italy

Peter Dearnley
School of Information Systems
University of East Anglia
Norwich, NR4 7TJ, UK

Abstract

We introduce a new method for rule termination analysis within active databases. This method analyzes interaction between transactions and triggers, by means of Evolution Graphs introduced in [16]. In this paper triggers information and transaction updates are considered in order to study rules termination and simulate execution. First we present the algorithm for testing rule termination and then we show that several termination analysis methods are captured by our method. The proposed approach turns out to be practical and general with respect to various rules languages and thus it may be applied to many database systems.

1 Introduction

Active databases have been the focus of several researches aiming to extend the functionality of traditional (passive) databases [9, 18]. They generally use active rules to express their active behaviour. Active rules have a tripartite structure, called Event-Condition-Action (ECA). There are several commercial databases using active rules, among the others, DB2, Oracle, SQL Server and Informix. An important issue in designing a set of rules is to generate rules for which it is possible to guarantee the execution termination. In fact, rules can trigger each other infinitely. This behaviour is not acceptable, and thus many commercial systems impose severe restrictions to prevent non-terminating rules execution. For instance, DB2 [20] defines the maximum depth of cascading triggers as 16. If this limit is reached an error occurs and the execution of all rules is

* montesi@cs.unibo.it
† bertino@dsi.unimi.it
‡ bagnato@netdev.usr.dsi.unimi.it

aborted. Similarly, in Oracle and SQL Server 2000 this limit is 32 [15, 19], whereas the limit in Informix is 61 [12].

In the literature there are several static and run-time approaches for active rules termination analysis. We consider only static methods that at compile time detect potential non-terminating active rules execution. Furthermore no method uses information provided by updates used to form transactions. There are static methods using only some of the active rules properties like Starburst [3, 22], which use only the triggering property, and Chimera [4, 8], in which triggering and activation are considered but deactivation is used only in restrictive cases (a rule cannot deactivate other rules, but only itself). Methods based on Abstract Interpretation [5] or on Petri Nets [17] examine all properties. Widom and Baralis in [7] proposed the termination analysis for a different kind of rules (CA, Condition Action rules) that are a subset of ECA rules. Other theoretical approaches are not considered in this paper because their goal is different. Indeed, their aim is to deal with decidability and undecidability of rule termination addressing the problem of determining the boundary between decidability and undecidability of active rule languages [6]. Instead our aim is to propose a static analysis method that considers how user transaction information and structures can affect active rule execution termination.

The proposed method improves a techniques, introduced in [16]. This new method (refined method) considers the analysis of three relationships among rules (triggering, activation and deactivation) that can be statically checked. Furthermore the properties of updates forming transactions that trigger active rule processing are used to enrich analysis. Refined method is simple and easy to understand, but powerful and flexible enough to be used with current active database languages. This is possible because it investigates relationships among rules and transaction updates that are independent of the specific rule language. The approach is presented using an event-preserving policy and immediate rule semantics. The same approach can be easily extended for different rule semantics and policies.

The remainder of this article is structured as follows. In Section 2, an overview of our approach is shown through an example. In Section 3, we define the main concepts concerning rules, graphs and transactions. In Section 4, the improved termination analysis method using transactions is described with its algorithms. In Section 5 our analysis methods with and without transactions information are compared. In Section 6 the relationship between existing approaches and our methods is discussed.

2 Overview of our approach

Consider a transaction T and a program P formed by a set of active rules. If P has cycles, our approach considers two phases. The various components of the active rule termination analysis are depicted in Figure 1. The first phase checks whether P presents some kind of recursion by testing the termination using a method (considering only P) introduced in [16]. If this test is not sufficient for termination, then the second phase is activated. The second phase, presented in this paper, considers a transaction T in addition to P and performs a more detailed analysis.

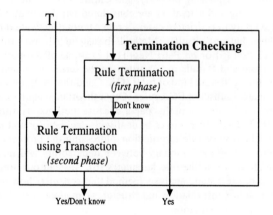

Figure 1. Components of rule termination analysis.

In this section we introduce an active program example and the consideration that guide us to our approach. We use Oracle 8.1.7 DDL [14]. The syntax to define a rule (trigger) is shown in Figure 2.

Only to simplify the example we consider as actions numerical value assignments (just 0 and 1) to the database table attributes and we just use the equality relation. To define a partial ordering on the set of defined rules, we as-

sume that r_i is executed before r_{i+1} for each i[1]. Each rule is introduced just to support the proposed approach, and so does not have any particular meaning. We consider a simple database schema with three tables: R(A, B, C, D), S(E, F, G) and Q(H, I, L, M, N). The rules are defined in Figure 3.

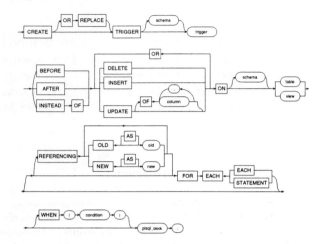

Figure 2. Oracle create trigger syntax.

In our approach we consider three relations among rules: triggering, activation, and deactivation. Informally, there is a triggering relation between two rules if one of the rule's actions has the corresponding event in the other rule. There is an activation relation, if the possible execution of the rule's actions makes the other rule's condition true. Finally, there is a deactivation relation, if the possible execution of the rule actions makes the other rule condition false. A triggered and activated rule is considered potentially executable (or eligible for execution). The formal definitions are presented in Section 3.3.

To describe the relation among active rules we discuss the example of Figure 3 using Oracle's triggers. We start with triggering relation. r_2 begins its execution when an update on attribute D of table R is executed. This update is executed with the action of r_1, thus r_1 triggers r_2. In the same way: r_2 triggers r_3; r_3 triggers r_1 and r_5; r_4 triggers r_2.

Note that the r_1 triggering induces r_2 triggering that induces r_3 triggering that induces again r_1 triggering. This situation implies a cyclical triggering. The triggering guides the rules execution; thus this is a potential non-terminating active program.

To discuss the activation relation consider the table Q updated through r_1's action. This operation sets the attribute L of Q to 0 value; the condition of r_5 verify if attribute L of

---

[1]Oracle forces a deterministic computation using a total order among rules. Our methods do not need such a restriction and thus can be applied also to DB2 that does not impose a total order among rules.

```
create trigger r_1                      create trigger r_2
after update of E on S                  after update of D on R
when (S.F = 1)                          when (Q.H = 1)
begin                                   begin
    update table Q                          update table R
        set H = 0, L = 0;                       set A = 1, C = 0;
    update table R                      end;
        set D = 1;
end;

create trigger r_3                      create trigger r_4
after update of A on R                  after update of M on Q
when (R.B = 0)                          when (Q.I = 1)
begin                                   begin
    update table S                          update table Q set N = 1;
        set E = 1, G = 0;                   update table R
end;                                            set D = 1, B = 1;
                                        end;
create trigger r_5
after update of G on S
when (Q.L = 0)
begin
    update table R set C = 1;
    update table Q set H = 1;
end;
```

Figure 3. An example with Oracle's triggers.

Q has 0 value. Thus r_1 execution sets to true the condition of r_5. Thus, there is an activation relation between r_1 and r_5. In the same way r_5 activates r_2. Finally there are deactivation relations between r_1 and r_2, and between r_4 and r_3. The update action of r_1 on table Q sets to 0 the column H; the condition of r_2 tests if column H of table Q has value 1. If r_1 is executed then, r_2's condition becomes false.

As we have said, rules execution depends on triggering relations as well as on rules condition. To test conditions we have to know the attribute value matching with values stored in the database. This is possible only at run time during real rules execution. Therefore, a static condition analysis starts monitoring deactivation and activation relations. For example, active rules r_1, r_2 and r_3 of Figure 3 form a (triggering) cycle. If the execution of one rule (or of transaction update) deactivates a rule involved in a cycle (and other rule executions do not activate the deactivated rule) then the rule execution terminates. Consider again the example of r_1, r_2 and r_3, we do not state the termination of (r_1, r_2 and r_3) rules execution since the information that we have are not sufficient: r_1 execution deactivates r_2, but r_5 execution activates r_2. Using only information about rules for Figure 3 we can state nothing. At this point we have to use other information provided by transaction submitted to the database that can involve rules execution. Consider for example the transaction composed by two updates: "T = **update** Q **set** M=0; **update** R **set** C=1;". The first update of T triggers r_4, while the second triggers no rule of the active program reported in Figure 3. With this new information we refine our analysis. Considering the updates in T, we can easily

discover that the execution starts from rule r_4. Furthermore r_4 execution deactivates r_3 and no rule activates r_3. Thus execution of r_1, r_2 and r_3 terminates. Therefore if transaction T is submitted to the system, we can state that the triggers set in Figure 3 terminates. We represent the fact that a rule may deactivate other rules by considering it in conjunction with rules triggering and activation through a new graph: the *Refined Evolution Graph* (REG). We simulate rule execution using REGs that store information about the simulated execution in abstract states (see Section 3.4).

3 Basic concepts

3.1 Active rules and programs

We consider a simple form of active rules that, however, captures a considerable portion of core languages described in the literature and implemented systems (see [18, 9]). An *active rule* has the form:

$$r_i : E \circ C \rightarrow A_1; \ldots ; A_m$$

where: r_i is a label that uniquely identifies the rule, it is used to express priority among rules (if i<j then r_i has priority over r_j); E is an event; C is a condition; and $A_1; \ldots ; A_m$ is a sequence of actions. An *action* is an operation to change the database state inserting, deleting or updating tuples. An *event* implies the fact that a corresponding insertion/deletion/update operation has been performed on a database instance. A *condition* is a set of literals defined as usual [1] that allows to define a query in SQL. We assume that conditions are always *satisfiable*, that is, they are not always false (e.g., ($A = c$ and $A \neq c$) is not satisfiable). The rule action and event are a subset of DML operations composed by constant operations. An *active program* P is a set of active rules. An *active database* is a pair (s, P) where s is a database instance and P is an active program.

The execution semantics describes the behaviour of an active program. We say that when a rule is triggered (if several rules are triggered, a selection policy must be established, usually based on priorities among rules), the system evaluates its condition. If the condition is satisfied, the rule is eliminated from the triggered rules set and its action is performed. If the condition is not satisfied, then there are different ways to proceed: the system can both leave or eliminate the rule from the triggered rules set; in the first case an *event-preserving* execution model (the worst case) is adopted, in the latter an *event-consuming* [8]. In this article we use event-preserving execution model, the proposed method can be easily extended to event-consuming model.

Finally, a *transaction* $T = U_1; \ldots ; U_n$ is an atomic sequence of operations, that means a sequence of insertions, deletions and updates, such that all of them are executed or none has to be performed [11]. Like events and actions, transaction operations are DML too, with the same constraint above described.

3.2 Transaction Execution Semantics

Transaction operations execution can trigger events that are part of one or more active rules. When a rule is triggered by a transaction update, usually rule condition evaluation and the possible actions are executed inside the transaction which has triggered the rule. Instead there are applications in which it is useful to delay condition evaluation and action execution and create a new transaction to include them. There are different ways to define the transactional relation by triggering event and condition evaluation or by condition evaluation and action execution. Using *immediate execution semantics*, action execution takes place just after the event of the rule containing the action is triggered and its condition is evaluated, all in the same transaction. Using *deferred execution semantics*, the event that triggered the rule is generated by the execution of one update, but condition evaluation is postponed at the end of original transaction when we execute rule action. While using *decoupled execution semantics*: the condition evaluation is performed in a different transaction in which we also execute rule action. In this article we use immediate semantics. However our approach can be easily extended to other semantics.

3.3 Graphs

We consider three different relations among active rules. Let r_i and r_j be two rules then r_i *triggers* r_j, if one of the r_i's actions produces the event defined in r_j; r_i *activates* r_j, if the possible execution of the r_i's actions makes r_j's condition true; r_i *deactivates* r_j, if the possible execution of the r_i's actions makes r_j's condition false. These relations can be described with three directed graphs called *Triggering Graph* (TG), *Activation Graph* (AG), and *Deactivation Graph* (DG), respectively. Nodes in those graphs represent rules, whereas arcs represent specific relations among rules. For triggering relations we use direct arrows, for activation relations the arrows are broken and deactivation relations are denoted with dashed and broken arrows (see Example 3.1).

Triggering relation was first introduced by *Widom et al.* [2]. It describes the rules mutual ability to "wake up" each other. The notion of cycle is defined starting from a TG. We define a *cycle* C in P as a subset C of P, such that the rules of C form a cycle in TG. We say that a rule is *involved in the execution by a cycle* C if the rule is activated, deactivated or triggered by the rules of C. The notion of activation relation was introduced by *Ceri et al.* in Chimera [4]. We describe it through an example. Let r_i and r_j be two active rules, and

R(A, B, C) be a database relation. Suppose that r_i's action sets the attribute A of R to 1 (i.e. A = 1) and the condition of r_j is A = 1. Then we can say that r_i activates r_j. Ceri et al. also defined a preliminary notion of deactivation. They assumed that a rule might only deactivate itself. The notion of deactivation was introduced by *Bailey et al.* [5] without the corresponding graph. This relation is the exact opposite of the activation one: let r_i and r_j be two active rules and R(A, B, C) be a database relation; if r_i's action sets the attribute A of R to 1 (i.e. A = 1) and the condition of r_j is A = 0, then we can say that r_i deactivates r_j.

To analyze how a database query can be affected by the execution of a data modification operation Widom and Baralis [7] use an algorithm that analyzes query and operation syntax. This algorithm is based on an extension of relational algebra and can be used to state activation and deactivation. It can be used also to state activation and deactivation of our active programs.

Example 3.1 Let P=$\{r_1, r_2, r_3, r_4\}$ be an active program. Suppose that r_1 triggers r_2, r_2 triggers r_3, r_3 triggers r_4, r_4 triggers r_2, r_2 activates r_3 and r_3 deactivates r_2. The corresponding graphs are shown in Figure 4. The rules $\{r_2, r_3, r_4\}$ form a cycle in P.   •

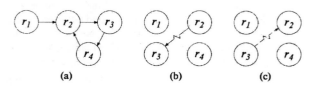

(a)   (b)   (c)

Figure 4. TG (a), AG (b) and DG (c) of the Example 3.1.

3.4 Abstract state

Now we introduce the notion of *(rule) abstract state* describing rule characteristics, such as whether the rule is triggered, activated or deactivated or relevant combinations of these relations. We do not use any abstraction device to infer our new abstract state (as in [5]), but we only want to determine a way to characterize a rule in a certain possible execution point. In this way we can establish the relevant abstract computational states with respect to termination. Let **as** be a function that for each rule describes its abstract state. Every rule r_i of an active program can be in one of the four following abstract states **as**(r_i):

- **as**$(r_i) = s_i$ denotes that r_i is triggered and activated (or eligible for execution);
- **as**$(r_i) = s_i^t$ denotes that r_i is triggered and deactivated;
- **as**$(r_i) = s_i^a$ denotes that r_i is activated and not triggered;

- $\mathbf{as}(r_i) = s_i^n$ denotes that r_i is deactivated and not triggered.

An abstract state can be changed by update execution (i.e. rule action or user update operation).

Example 3.2 Consider the active program of Example 3.1. Suppose that r_3 is triggered and activated. Its abstract state is thus s_3 and we can execute it. Furthermore, assume that the state of r_4 is s_4^n and the one of r_2 is s_2^a. The execution of r_3 triggers r_4 (thus its abstract state becomes s_4^t) and deactivates r_2 (thus its abstract state becomes s_2^n). Now suppose that we can execute the rule r_2 (thus its state is s_2). Moreover r_3 and r_4 are activated (s_3^a and s_4^a). In this way the execution of r_2 induces the state s_3, while the r_4's configuration remains unchanged (s_4^a). $\bullet$

We generalize the notion of rule abstract state to an active program. This generalization allows us to describe the situation of program's rules during static analysis. The *abstract state* of P is the set of all abstract states of the rules in P: $\mathbf{as}(P) = \bigcup_{r_i \in P} \mathbf{as}(r_i)$. The notion of active program abstract state provides at compile time an abstract snapshot of the situation of the active program.

4 Rule Termination Analysis using Transactions

Our method is organized as follows. First we create the TG of P. If there are not cycles in TG, then termination is assured based on the results of *Widom et al.* [2]. If there are cycles in TG, then it is necessary to create both the AG and DG to exploit further information contained in the active rules. Assume that $\{C_1, \ldots, C_n\}$ are the TG's cycles in P. At this point we apply method expose in [16]. If we can say nothing about the termination of P, we can consider user transactions submitted to the system and analyze the situation with this new information. Using a transaction, the termination analysis is more specific, because now we consider in our simulation only the ones triggered by transaction execution. After using the first phase of rule analysis (see Figure 1) there are two possible situations. In the first case the termination analysis of P doesn't produce any critical situations thus no further analysis is required. In the second case the termination analysis of P produces critical situations thus we can refine the analysis (second phase Figure 1) considering the scheme of the transaction involved and constructing the Refined Evolution Graph (REG). If the REG is acyclic then the execution of P for T will terminate; otherwise we cannot state if the program will terminate.

4.1 Refined Evolution Graph

We consider a transaction T and all active rules, because we don't know which rules will be involved in transaction execution. This means that the Refined Evolution Graph has to take this into account as shown below.

In order to introduce the REG it is necessary to define two subsets of the active rules set.

Definition 4.1 (Activation Rules) Let P be an active program and let C_i be a cycle in P. Let $AR_i \subseteq (P \backslash C_i)$ be a subset of P's rules that are not part of the cycle C_i, but they are involved in the rules execution from C_i rules The rules in AR_i are rules of $P \backslash C_i$ that have no action A such that the execution of A deactivates one rule of C_i. $\bullet$

Definition 4.2 (Deactivation Rules) Let P be an active program and let C_i be a cycle in P. Let $DR_i \subseteq (P \backslash C_i)$ be a subset of P's rules that are not part of the cycle C_i, but they are involved in the rules execution from C_i rules. The rules in DR_i are rules of $P \backslash C_i$ that have an action A such that the execution of A deactivates at least a rule of C_i. $\bullet$

In brief we can say that there is no arc in DG between any rule of AR_i and any rule of C_i. Instead there is at least an arc in DG between each rule of DR_i and at least a rule of C_i.

Example 4.1 With reference to the program defined in Example 3.1, we identify the cycle $C_1 = \{r_2, r_3, r_4\}$. No rules are involved in the execution by the ones in C_1, so $DR_1 = \emptyset$ and $AR_1 = \emptyset$. $\bullet$

Example 4.2 Consider P = $\{r_1, r_2, r_3, r_4, r_5\}$ and the relations among the five rules as described in Figure 5 through TG, AG and DG. The cycle is $C_1 = \{r_1, r_5\}$ and the rules involved in the execution by the cycle itself are r_2, r_3 and r_4. r_4 deactivates r_5, rule of C_1, so we insert it in DR_1; on the contrary we insert r_2 and r_3 in AR_1, because they are involved by C_1 but they do not deactivate any rule of the cycle. Thus $DR_1 = \{r_4\}$ and $AR_1 = \{r_2, r_3\}$ $\bullet$

Next definitions describe two parts that compose an REG node N, that is S and R.

Definition 4.3 (S) Let P be an active program and let C_i be a cycle of P. $S \subseteq \mathbf{as}(C_i \cup AR_i \cup DR_i)$, such that contains rules abstract states that describe each rule involved in each execution simulation step. $\bullet$

Definition 4.4 (R) Let P be an active program and let C_i be a cycle of P. $R \subseteq P$, such that the rules in R have their simulated execution postponed when more than one rule is eligible for execution. R is empty whenever there is only one rule at a time that is eligible for execution (i.e. is triggered and activated). $\bullet$

Now we define the REG which allows us to graphically visualize the cycle execution simulation analyzing interaction with transaction.

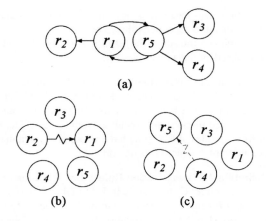

(a)

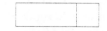

(b)   (c)

Figure 5. TG (a), AG (b) and DG (c) of the Example 4.2.

Definition 4.5 (Refined Evolution Graph) Let P be an active program and T a transaction. The *Refined Evolution Graph* (REG) is a directed labeled graph $<N, D, \varphi>$ where N is a set of nodes (at least one is empty), D is a set of arcs and φ the labeling function. Each node $N_i \in N$ is a pair: $N_i = <S, R>$ where S and R are described in Definition 4.3 and Definition 4.4. An arc from node N_i to node N_{i+1} of a REG, specifies the abstract state changes resulted from the execution of the triggered and activated rule of N_i or from the execution of one of the updates in T. Each arc is labeled through φ with the rule or the transaction update for which we simulate execution.   •

Figure 6. First REG node.

Example 4.3 If we examine AG, DG and TG of the Example 3.1, then we will have all the information concerning the relationships among rules. The initial node of all possible REG (not depending on user transactions) is empty because no update has executed yet (Figure 6). If the transaction update involved P rule's event the following nodes were filled with the abstract state of these triggered rules. Now consider the transaction $T = U_1$, where U_1 triggers r_2. Starting from the empty node and according to the TG, AG and DG of the Example 3.1, we can build the other nodes and arcs of REG. We assume that all rule's abstract state is activated before including them in the node (the worst case: all rules can be executed).

With U_1 execution simulation r_2 is triggered thus its abstract state becomes s_2 and the second node of REG is filled

Figure 7. Incremental REG drawing.

(Figure 7). The arc from the empty node new node is labeled with U_1 (update of T transaction). r_2 is triggered and activated thus eligible for execution. r_2 execution simulation triggers r_3 (so the abstract state changes from s_3^a to s_3), and activated (that does not change its abstract state). We have created third node of Figure 8 (the new arc is labeled with u_2, the update part of rule r_2 of which we simulate the execution).

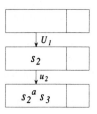

Figure 8. Incremental REG drawing.

r_3 is eligible for execution thus we can now simulate the execution of r_3. The execution of this rule deactivates r_2 and triggers r_4 (that becomes eligible for execution). At the end, the simulation of r_4 execution produces the final node with are no triggered and activated rules Figure 9).   •

If more than one rule is triggered and activated in S, then the first one (according to the definition order) will not be modified, whereas the others become only activated and added in R (with decreasing label order).

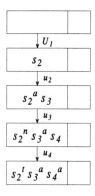

Figure 9. REG for active program cycle C of the Example 4.3

The rules are added in R in order to postpone their execution. If we proceed with the simulation we will find another case of more activated and triggered rules. Then we add into R the rules whose simulation is postponed, following a LIFO method. In this way, as discussed in the introduction we use an immediate execution model. Thus R has a stack structure (see example of Section 2). It is possible, changing this algorithm, to obtain termination analysis for the deferred rules execution model.

4.2 Algorithm to Create the Refined Evolution Graph

We now present the algorithm REFINED_CREATION to decide when a transaction T can be executed without termination problems using the REG graph.

The REFINED_CREATION (Figure 10) algorithm considers one transaction update at time and monitors the rules set to see if it is affected by update execution, that is if some rules are triggered, activated or deactivated by its execution. We consider an immediate execution semantic, so when a rule is triggered by update execution, its condition is evaluated and, if true, its action is executed, and so on. When no more rules are triggered the algorithm considers the next transaction update operation. The REFINED_CREATION algorithm stops when it finds a cycle on the REG graph (while creating it) or when it completes the transaction execution simulation.

```
Algorithm REFINED_CREATION
Input: P, T = U₁; . . . ; Uₙ, TG, AG, DG;
Output: {true, false}
begin
        S := {∅};      // Creation of the initial node
        R := ∅;
        M := S ∪ R;
        N := {M};      // Initialization of the configuration set
        for i = 1 to n
        begin
                if REFINED_BUILD(M, Uᵢ, T, N) = False
                        then return(False);
        end;
        return(True);
end.
```

Figure 10. Algorithm REFINED_CREATION

The function REFINED_BUILD (Figure 11), called by the algorithm has four inputs: M which identifies the abstract state of rules belonging to P; u_i which specifies the update of the transaction or of the rule of which the algorithm simulates execution; T the transaction with its updates and N the configuration set. A new node for the REG is generated for each function call. This new node is created by updating the rules abstract states of the previous one. To *update* S_1 *with reference to* u_i we consider each rule $r_j \in S_1$ involved

in the execution of u_i. We calculate the new configuration of r_j, $\mathbf{as}(r_j)$ in the following way:

- if u_i deactivates r_j and $\mathbf{as}(r_j) = s_j^a$, then s_j^n replaces s_j^a;
- if u_i triggers r_j and $\mathbf{as}(r_j) = s_j^a$, then s_j replaces s_j^a;
- if u_i activates r_j and $\mathbf{as}(r_j) = s_j^n$, then s_j^a replaces s_j^n;
- if u_i deactivates, activates or triggers a rule $r_j \in P$ such that $s(r_j) \notin S_1$, then we assume that $\mathbf{as}(r_j) = s_j^a$. $\mathbf{as}(r_j)$ is updated as described above and inserted in S_1;
- in the all others cases there are no configuration changes.

```
Function REFINED_BUILD
Input: M, uᵢ, T, N ;
Output: an REG node or False
begin
        Update S₁ with respect to uᵢ execution;
        if (uᵢ ∉ T) and (((∃ M₂ = M₁ such that M₂ ∈ N) and
                (M ≠ M₁)) or ((∃ S₂ = S₁) and
                (in R₁ is inserted the same rules sequence repeatedly)))
        then
        begin
                //label for the new arc from M₂ to existing node
                arc(M, M₂) := uᵢ;
                //procedure call termination
                return(false);
        end;
        arc(M, M₁) := uᵢ;      //label for the new arc from M to M₁
        N := N ∪ {M₁};
        while ((R₁ ≠ ∅) and (∄ configuration in S₁ such that sᵢ))
                MODIFY S₁;
        if (∃ configuration in S₁ which
                describes a triggered and activated rule rⱼ )
        then
        begin
                S₁ := REFINE(S₁);
                if REFINED_BUILD(M₁, uⱼ, T, N) = False
                        then return(False);
        end;
end.
```

Figure 11. Function REFINED_BUILD

If the new node has some triggered and activated configuration the REG creation is not yet complete. We can proceed to the creation of another node. Before calling again the REFINED_BUILD function we have to insert a new arc (when this arc creates a cycle the function will be terminated) and we have to check if more than one active rule is triggered and activated; to do this we run the REFINE function. When there is no triggered and activated rule in S_1 we have to check whether some rules have been postponed in R_1. In this case we delete the first rule r_j from R_1 (according to a LIFO policy) and MODIFY r_j's configuration in S_1 as follows: if $\mathbf{as}(r_j) = s_j^a$ then, s_j replaces s_j^a. If after this change there are no triggered and activated rules in S_1, we can not create a new node and the function terminates.

The function REFINE in event-preserving execution keeps the first triggered and activated rule in S_1, in order to simulate its execution in the next step and inserts in R_1 the other rules with activated and triggered configuration to postpone their execution. These rule configurations change in S_1 and they become s_i^a. When no more rules are eligible for execution then these rule configurations will be brought back in S_1 and they will be executed. If the function REFINED_BUILD finds a cycle then it returns *False*. This result is propagated to the output of the algorithm REFINED_CREATION.

4.3 Testing Termination

It is well known that if during the execution of a program the same computational state (memory contents and next instruction to execute) arises again, the same actions will be repeated again. So there will be a possible non-termination of the program. The same situation can arise in rule execution. If an abstract states set presents itself again during a computation we cannot guarantee the termination. Using REG this termination test can be implemented by checking the presence of a cycle. If the graph is acyclic we can assure the termination; otherwise we cannot say anything.

Note that each node of REG is a possible abstract state of $(C_i \cup AR_i \cup DR_i)$ rules and to postpone the execution of a rule we store it in R. We can know state the condition for rule termination.

Theorem 4.1 (Termination Test) Let P be an active program and C a cycle of P. If the REG for C are acyclic, then the C's rules execution will terminate.

Proof. All paths in the refined evolution graph are finite. Each concrete execution follows one of these paths. Hence, all concrete executions terminate. □

Example 4.4 Consider the active program in Example 3.1. We have developed the REG for T in Example 4.3 (Figure 9). REG is acyclic, so the execution terminates. •

5 Relationship between our analysis methods

In this section we proceed to compare our analysis methods through the example informally introduced in Section 2. Figure 12 denotes the TG, AG and DG of the program P $= \{r_1, r_2, r_3, r_4, r_5\}$ introduced in Figure 3.
P has only one cycle C= $\{r_1, r_2, r_3\}$. EG drawing follow the same rule of REG develop, but we do not know from which rule execution starts (we have not transaction updates). Thus we have to analyze all possible cycle execution starting from each cycle rule, see [16]. The EG are

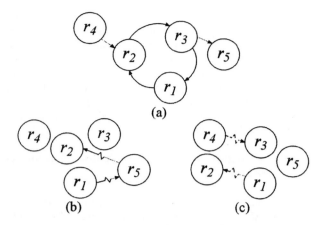

Figure 12. TG (a), AG (b) and DG (c) of above defined rules.

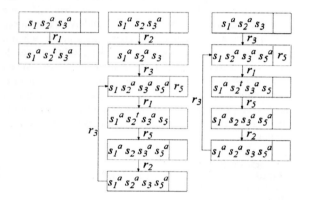

Figure 13. EG for rules in Figure 12.

shown in Figure 13: as we can see only in one EG there is no cycle, thus the defined rules execution may not terminate. Now consider the same transaction considered in Section 2: "T = **update** Q **set** M=0; **update** R **set** C=1;". The first update triggers r_4, while the second one triggers no rule of P. With this new information we can restrict termination analysis. We need only one graph (REG), starting from r_4 (see Figure 14). In REG there are no cycles, thus the rule execution terminates for transaction T.

Termination analysis based on EG construction captures more termination situations than the most practical approaches in literature as we will discuss in Section 6. This approach considers all possible triggering of a cycle on TG, introducing a transaction we know exactly from which rule we start and which ones we will not execute. This important feature restricts the analysis without losing the detecting capabilities and leads to more efficient rules analysis methods. Furthermore we create only one REG graph for every transaction submitted to the system instead of the many EG graphs which had to be created for P. Another consideration is related to the fact that updates in a transaction can manipulate data that are involved in rules checks to satisfy condition parts. This means that different situations, critical for the EG method, can terminate when some transactions are submitted to the system because transaction updates may have modified the data.

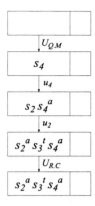

Figure 14. REG for rules in Figure 12

As you might expect the rule analysis method *general method* (GM) captures a smaller class of terminating cases than the refined analysis method using transactions *refined method* (RM).

6 Related Works

Now we apply the Starburst analysis technique introduced in [3] to the example. If there are no cycles in TG, then the rules are guaranteed to terminate. As we can see in Figure 15 (a), TG has two cycles, thus rules may not terminate their execution.

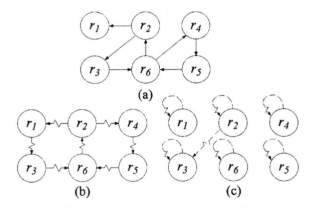

Figure 15. TG (a), AG (b) and DG of Example.

We now show the application of the static Chimera ap-

proach [4]. The technique consists of two steps. The first step of Chimera approach states that if the active rules set of a knowledge base is reduced to the empty set by the *Rule Reduction Algorithm*, then the rule set cannot exhibit a non-terminating behavior. To apply the Rule Reduction Algorithm to the given rule set we must overlap the triggering and activation graphs, and then eliminate one by one the nodes for which exists neither an incoming arc on TG nor on AG. Figure 16 shows the two overlapping graphs. TG arcs are represented by solid lines, whereas AG arcs are represented by dashed lines. As we can see, we cannot eliminate any rule: in fact each node has incoming arcs both in TG and AG. So we have an Irreducible Active Rule Set. At this point we cannot state the termination of the rule set.

The second step considers the priorities stated among the rules. From rule definitions we have that $p(r_3) < p(r_4) < p(r_1) < p(r_2) < p(r_5) < p(r_6)$[2]. To apply this new step we must consider the two cycles on TG: $C_1 = \{r_2, r_3, r_6\}$ and $C_2 = \{r_4, r_5, r_6\}$. In this step we determine whether C_1 contains an inhibited rule, that is, a rule that may not be executed due to execution of other higher priority rules. For C_1 rule r_3 is a candidate for inhibition. In fact two rules r_t and r_a exist such that $r_t \neq r_a$, and an arc exists in TG from r_t to r_3 but no arc exists in AG. Moreover, an arc exists in AG from r_a to r_3 but no arc exists in TG, as we can see in Figure 16 $r_t = r_2$ and $r_a = r_1$. Now we can define the *reaching set*[3] from r_3 to r_1 and from r_3 to r_2: $S_{\text{reach}}(r_3, r_1) = \{\{r_6, r_2, r_1\}\}$[4] and $S_{\text{reach}}(r_3, r_2) = \{\{r_6, r_2\}\}$. We now calculate the *dominant priority* $P(\text{reach}(r_3, r_1))$ and $P(\text{reach}(r_3, r_2))$, that is, the lowest priority associated with the rules in the reaching sets: $P(\text{reach}(r_3, r_1)) = p(r_1)$ and $P(\text{reach}(r_3, r_2)) = p(r_2)$. Let p_t be the lowest priority among $P(S_{\text{reach}}(r_3, r_2))$ and let p_a be the highest priority among $P(S_{\text{reach}}(r_3, r_1))$: in this case $p_t = p(r_2)$ and $p_a = p(r_1)$. The rule r_3 is inhibited if $p_a < p_t$ and $p_a < p(r_3)$: the first condition, $p(r_1) < p(r_2)$, is true but the second, $p(r_1) < p(r_3)$, is false. By applying the same analysis to rules in cycle C_2 we can see that no rule in this cycle is inhibited. Therefore, both C_1 and C_2 are not inhibited. Thus we cannot establish the termination of the given rule set.

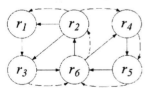

Figure 16. TG overlapping AG for rules in Figure 15.

---

[2]$p(r_i)$ indicates the priority of r_i.
[3]To understand what they are and how to create these sets see [4].
[4]This is the set which includes all the sets reach(r_3, r_1), because there can be many distinct for the same pairs of rules.

Now we use our general approach to detect the termination of the active program defined in Figure 15, using event-preserving execution semantics. We consider deactivation information by representing it in conjunction with rules triggering and activation in the Evolution Graph (EG).

The main difference between EG and REG creation is the introduction of transaction information (in REG). Thus for each cycle on TG we develop a number of EG, corresponding to the number of rules in a cycle. If all the developed EG are acyclic, then rule execution will terminate.

Considering the active program P, of Figure 15 for C_1 the EG are in Figure 17 where all EG are acyclic. Similarly for C_2, thus rules execution terminates. We have shown how Chimera and Starburst methods work. Both these approaches cannot establish anything about termination of P. Instead our general method captures this case of rule execution termination.

Figure 17. EG for rules in Figure 15.

We show an active program analysis. Using Chimera and Starburst approach nothing can be state about possible termination. Instead using our general method this case of termination is captured. Considering the result of Section 5 if the general analysis method captures more termination cases than Chimera and Starburst approach, then our refined method also assures this termination case.

References

[1] S. Abiteboul, R. Hull and V. Vianu. *Foundation of Databases*. Addison-Wesley, 1994.

[2] A. Aiken, J. M. Hellerstein and J. Widom. *Behaviour of Database Production Rules: Termination, Confluence and Observable Determinism*. ACM-SIGMOD, pp. 59-68, 1992.

[3] A. Aiken, J.M. Hellerstein, J. Widom. *Static Analysis Techniques for Predicting the Behavior of Database Production Rules*. ACM TODS, pp. 3-41, 1995.

[4] E. Baralis, S. Ceri, S. Paraboschi. *Improved Rule Analysis by Means of Triggering and Activation Graphs*. RIDS'95, Lecture Notes in Computer Science, pp. 165-181, 1995.

[5] J. Bailey, L. Crnogorac, K. Ramamohanarao, H. Sondergaard. *Abstract Interpretation of Active Rules and Its Use in Termination Analysis*. ICDT'97, Lecture Notes in Computer Science, pp. 188-202, 1997.

[6] J. Bailey, G. Dong, K. Ramamohanarao. *Decidability and Undecidability Results for the Termination Problem of Active Database rules*. PODS'98, pp. 264-273, 1998.

[7] E. Baralis, J. Widom. *An Algebraic Approach to Static Analysis of Active Database Rules.*, ACM Transactions on Database Systems, September 2000.

[8] S. Ceri, P. Fraternali, S. Paraboschi, L. Tanca. *Active Rule Management in Chimera*. in S. Ceri, J. Widom, "Active Database Systems", Morgan Kaufmann, 1996.

[9] S. Ceri, J. Widom. *Active Database Systems: Triggers and Rules for Advanced Database Processing*. Morgan-Kaufmann, 1996.

[10] W. Dietrich, A. P. Karadimce, M. K. Tschudi, S.D. Urban. *An Implementation and Evaluation of the Refined Triggering Graph Method for Active Rule Termination Analysis*. RIDS'97, Lecture Notes in Computer Science, pages 133-148, 1997.

[11] J. Gray, A. Reuter. *Transaction Processing: Concepts and Tecniques*. Morgan-Kaufmann, 1993.

[12] *Informix. Guide to SQL: Reference, February 1998.*

[13] A. P. Karadimce, S. D. Urban. *Refined Triggering Graphs: A Logic-Based Approach to Termination Analysis in an Active Object-Oriented Database*. ICDE'96, IEEE Computer Society, pp. 384-391, 1996.

[14] L. Leverenz et al. *SQL Reference, Handbook*. Oracle Corporation, 2000.

[15] L. Leverenz et al. *Oracle8 Concepts, Handbook*. Oracle Corporation, 2000.

[16] D. Montesi, M. Bagnato and C. Dallera. *Termination Analysis in Active Databases*. In Proc. IDEAS'99, IEEE Computer Society Press, Montreal, 1999.

[17] A. Mackenstock, R. Unland, D. Zimmer. *Rule Termination Analysis based on Petri Nets*. Technical Report 3/1996 of C-Lab, R&D Institute of University-GH Paderborn and Siemens Nixdorf Informationssysteme AG, 1996.

[18] N. W. Paton. *Active Rules in Database Systems*. Springer-Verlag, 1999.

[19] *SQL Server 2000: Books Online.*

[20] *IBM DB2 Universal Database SQL Reference, Appendix A - SQL Limits, 1998.*

[21] A. Siebes, L. van der Voort. *Termination and Confluence of Rule Execution*. CIKM'93, ACM Press, pp. 245-255, 1993.

[22] J. Widom. *The Starburst Rule System: Language Design, Implementation, and Applications*. IEEE Data Engineering Bulletin, pp. 15-18, 1992.

Author Index

Press Operating Committee

Chair
Mark J. Christensen
Independent Consultant

Editor-in-Chief
Mike Williams
Department of Computer Science
University of Calgary

Board Members

Roger U. Fujii, *Vice President, Logicon Technology Solutions*
Richard Thayer, *Professor Emeritus, California State University, Sacramento*
Sallie Sheppard, *Professor Emeritus, Texas A&M University*
Deborah Plummer, *Group Managing Editor, Press*

IEEE Computer Society Executive Staff
David Hennage, *Executive Director*
Angela Burgess, *Publisher*

IEEE Computer Society Publications

The world-renowned IEEE Computer Society publishes, promotes, and distributes a wide variety of authoritative computer science and engineering texts. These books are available from most retail outlets. Visit the CS Store at *http://computer.org* for a list of products.

IEEE Computer Society Proceedings

The IEEE Computer Society also produces and actively promotes the proceedings of more than 160 acclaimed international conferences each year in multimedia formats that include hard and soft-cover books, CD-ROMs, videos, and on-line publications.

For information on the IEEE Computer Society proceedings, please e-mail to csbooks@computer.org or write to Proceedings, IEEE Computer Society, P.O. Box 3014, 10662 Los Vaqueros Circle, Los Alamitos, CA 90720-1314. Telephone +1-714-821-8380. Fax +1-714-761-1784.

Additional information regarding the Computer Society, conferences and proceedings, CD-ROMs, videos, and books can also be accessed from our web site at *http://computer.org/cspress*

Revised 11 March 2002